'These intriguing surveys of marketing history cover a broad geographic, conceptual and historic range and should pique curiosities to learn more about the interlinked patterns of trade, marketing and consumption that have long shaped our world.'

—*Russell Belk, York University Distinguished Professor of Marketing*
and Kraft Foods Canada Chair in Marketing, Canada

'Brilliantly conceptualized, expertly researched, and well written, *The Routledge Companion to Marketing History* offers cutting-edge chapters on historical and international aspects of marketing theory. This important book should be required reading for scholars in marketing and consumer-related fields!'

—*Inger L. Stole, Professor of Communication,*
University of Illinois at Urbana-Champaign, USA

'Both marketing academics and students are showing an increasing interest in understanding the historical background of marketing practice and marketing thought. Brian Jones and Mark Tadajewski have done an outstanding job of preparing a volume that is truly a "companion" for advancing historical scholarship and historical understanding.'

—*Shelby D. Hunt, The Jerry S. Rawls and P.W. Horn Professor of Marketing,*
Rawls College of Business Administration, Texas Tech University, USA

'Readers will find that this valuable companion volume provides ready access to formative and definitive contributions of leading marketing history and history of marketing thought scholars, filling an existing void. Professors Jones and Tadajewski once again contribute very meaningfully to our understanding and appreciation of the neglected marketing history area.'

—*William Lazer, Professor Emeritus, Michigan State University, USA*

The Routledge Companion to Marketing History

The Routledge Companion to Marketing History is the first collection of readings that surveys the broader field of marketing history, including the key activities and practices in the marketing process.

With contributors who are leading international scholars working in marketing history, this companion provides nine country-specific histories of marketing practice as well as a broad analysis of the field, including: the histories of advertising, retailing, channels of distribution, product design and branding, pricing strategies, and consumption behaviour. While other collections have provided an overview of the history of marketing thought, this is the first of its kind to review marketing history.

The Routledge Companion to Marketing History ranges across many countries and industries, engaging in substantive detail with marketing practices as they were performed in a variety of historical periods extending back to ancient times. It is not to be missed by any historian or student of business.

D. G. Brian Jones is Professor of Marketing and Advertising at Quinnipiac University, USA.

Mark Tadajewski is Professor of Marketing at Durham University, UK.

Routledge Companions in Business, Management and Accounting

Routledge Companions in Business, Management and Accounting are prestige reference works providing an overview of a whole subject area or sub-discipline. These books survey the state of the discipline including emerging and cutting edge areas. Providing a comprehensive, up to date, definitive work of reference, Routledge Companions can be cited as an authoritative source on the subject.

A key aspect of these Routledge Companions is their international scope and relevance. Edited by an array of highly regarded scholars, these volumes also benefit from teams of contributors which reflect an international range of perspectives.

Individually, Routledge Companions in Business, Management and Accounting provide an impactful one-stop-shop resource for each theme covered. Collectively, they represent a comprehensive learning and research resource for researchers, postgraduate students and practitioners.

Published titles in this series include:

The Routledge Companion to Marketing History

Edited by D.G. Brian Jones and Mark Tadajewski

LONDON AND NEW YORK

First published 2016
by Routledge
2 Park Square, Milton Park, Abingdon, Oxon OX14 4RN

and by Routledge
711 Third Avenue, New York, NY 10017

Routledge is an imprint of the Taylor & Francis Group, an informa business

British Library Cataloguing in Publication Data
A catalogue record for this book is available from the British Library

Library of Congress Cataloging in Publication Data
The Routledge companion to marketing history / edited by D.G. Brian
Jones and Mark Tadajewski.
     pages cm. – (Routledge companions in business, management and
     accounting)
  Includes bibliographical references and index.
  1. Marketing – History. I. Jones, D. G. Brian (Donald Gordon Brian),
  1955– editor. II. Tadajewski, Mark, editor.
  HF5415.R6427 2016
  381.09–dc23   2015031325

ISBN: 978-0-415-71418-1 (hbk)
ISBN: 978-1-315-88285-7 (ebk)

Typeset in Bembo
by HWA Text and Data Managment, London

Contents

Contents

Figures

Tables

Contributors

Andrew Alexander is Professor of Retail Management, Surrey Business School, University of Surrey, UK. He has published widely on retail history and consumers' reactions to retail innovations, with a focus on large-scale retailing and most recently the supermarket. He is on the Editorial Advisory Board of the *Journal of Historical Research in Marketing*.

Fred K. Beard is the Gaylord Family Research Professor of Advertising in the Gaylord College of Journalism and Mass Communication, University of Oklahoma. He is author of *Humor in the Advertising Business: Theory, Practice, and Wit* (2007) and more than 100 sole- and co-authored articles, chapters, abstracts and conference papers. He is also a member of the Editorial Advisory Board for the *Journal of Historical Research in Marketing*.

Barry E. C. Boothman is Professor of Strategic Management, Faculty of Business Administration, University of New Brunswick, Canada. His historical research has focused upon the evolution of retailing and the development of business in Canada. He is a member of the Editorial Advisory Board for the *Journal of Historical Research in Marketing*.

Robert Crawford is Associate Professor in Public Communication in the School of Communication at the University of Technology Sydney. He is the author of *But Wait, There's More: A History of Australian Advertising 1900–2000* (2008). He is a member of the Editorial Advisory Board for the *Journal of Historical Research in Marketing*.

Karen F. A. Fox is Associate Professor Emerita of Marketing, Leavey School of Business, Santa Clara University, Santa Clara, California, USA. She has carried out research in Russia since 1995, including Fulbright grants in 1998 and 2002–3.

Ronald A. Fullerton has explored marketing history since the 1970s. His work has dealt with, among other topics, publishing history, including the development of trashy fiction for mass audiences, the development of branding in the US, John Wannamaker, the pioneering work on advertising thought by a nineteenth-century German thinker, the pioneering work on retail evolution by a twentieth-century German scholar, and the immense diversity over time of explanations for the same phenomenon – kleptomania. He is currently semi-retired, teaching one semester a year at California State University – Northridge, USA.

Zhihong Gao is Professor of Marketing at Rider University, USA. Her research interests include international marketing, cross-cultural consumer behaviour and public policy issues. Her research has been published in *Asia-Pacific Journal of Marketing & Logistics*, *Journal of Advertising*, *Journal of Consumer Policy*, *Journal of Macromarketing*, *Journal of Public Policy & Marketing*, and the *Journal of Historical Research in Marketing*.

Richard A. Hawkins is Reader in History at the University of Wolverhampton, UK where he is a member of the Centre for the History of Retailing and Distribution (CHORD). Richard is an Associate Editor for the *Journal of Historical Research in Marketing* and has been a member of the Board of Directors of the Conference on Historical Analysis and Research in Marketing (CHARM) Association since 2009. His research is principally in the area of American economic and business history.

D.G. Brian Jones is the current and founding Editor of the *Journal of Historical Research in Marketing* and co-editor of the Routledge Studies in the History of Marketing series. His research focuses on the history of marketing ideas and has been published in the *Journal of Marketing*, *Journal of the Academy of Marketing Science*, *Journal of Marketing Management*, *European Journal of Marketing*, *Journal of Macromarketing*, *Marketing Theory*, *Psychology & Marketing*, *Journal of Historical Research in Marketing*, and other publications. He is the author of (2012) *Pioneers in Marketing*, and co-editor, with Mark Tadajewski of the (2008) three-volume set of readings titled *The History of Marketing Thought*.

Ingo Köhler is interim director of the Institute for Social and Economic History at the University of Göttingen, Germany. His research focuses on the rise of marketing management, market research and corporate communication after the Second World War. Moreover, he is interested in the history of business failures and strategies of corporate crisis management. His research has been published in the *Business History Review* and he is co-editor of the volume *Pleitiers und Bankrotteure. Geschichte des ökonomischen Scheiterns vom 18. bis 20. Jahrhundert (Flops and Breakdowns: The History of Business Failures from the 18th to the 20th Century)* (2012).

Erik Kloppenborg Madsen is an Associate Professor at the Department of Management, Aarhus University, Denmark. His research interests are in business ethics, CSR, sustainable consumption and history of marketing thought.

Jan Logemann teaches history at the Institute for Social and Economic History at the University of Göttingen, Germany. His research focuses on comparative history and transnational transfers in marketing and mass consumption in Europe and the United States. He is the author of *Trams or Tailfins: Public and Private Prosperity in Postwar West Germany and the United States* (2012) and of the edited volume *The Development of Consumer Credit in Global Perspective* (2012). He is a member of the Editorial Advisory Board for the *Journal of Historical Research in Marketing*.

Delphin A. Muise is Emeritus Professor of History, Carleton University, Canada. He has researched widely on the social and economic history of pre-Confederation Nova Scotia and Atlantic Canada.

Leighann C. Neilson is Associate Professor of Marketing at the Sprott School of Business, Carleton University, Canada. Her research interests include Canadian marketing and tourism history. She is a member of the Editorial Advisory Board for the *Journal of Historical Research in Marketing*.

Ross D. Petty is a prolific marketing law author in both marketing and law journals and his work has been recognized for excellence by both disciplines. He is also the author of two books: *Advertising Law: Its Impact of Business and Public Policy* (1992) and the forthcoming *Branding Law: A Guide to Legal Issues in Brand Management* (2016). Before becoming an academic, Professor Petty practised with the Federal Trade Commission. He is also a member of the Editorial Advisory Board for the *Journal of Historical Research in Marketing*.

Thomas L. Powers is Professor of Marketing in the Collat School of Business at the University of Alabama at Birmingham, USA. He received his PhD in Marketing and Transportation Administration from Michigan State University, and has been a Fulbright Scholar. Prior to his academic career he was a marketing manager with Ford Motor Company. He is a member of the Editorial Advisory Board for the *Journal of Historical Research in Marketing*.

Andrew D. Pressey is a Reader in Marketing at the University of Birmingham, UK, and has published in a variety of journals including *Journal of Public Policy and Marketing*, *Industrial Marketing Management*, *European Journal of Marketing*, *Technological Forecasting and Social Change*, and *Psychology and Marketing*, among others. He is a member of the Editorial Advisory Board for the *Journal of Historical Research in Marketing*.

Stefan Schwarzkopf studied modern history and the history of science at the University of Jena, Germany and did his PhD at Birkbeck College in London. He teaches marketing and economic sociology at Copenhagen Business School, Denmark. His research focuses on economic ideologies in the twentieth century and the (theo)politics of markets. Stefan is an Associate Editor of the *Journal of Historical Research in Marketing*.

Stanley Shapiro is Emeritus Professor of Marketing at Simon Fraser University in Canada. He serves as an Associate Editor for the *Journal of Historical Research in Marketing*.

Eric H. Shaw is Professor Emeritus of Marketing at Florida Atlantic University, USA. He teaches PhD seminars in his major research interests: the history of marketing thought and the development of marketing theory. He has published numerous articles, book chapters and monographs; and he serves on a number of editorial review boards. He is an Associate Editor for the *Journal of Historical Research in Marketing*.

Hari Sreekumar is an Assistant Professor of Marketing at the Indian Institute of Management Tiruchirappalli, India. His research interests are in the area of consumer culture theory and Indian marketing history.

Mark Tadajewski is Professor of Marketing at Durham University, UK. He is the Co-Editor of the *Journal of Marketing Management*, an Associate Editor of the *Journal of Historical Research in Marketing*, the Co-Editor of the Routledge Studies in Critical Marketing monograph series, Co-Editor of the Routledge Studies in the History of Marketing, and author of numerous books and articles. He also serves on the Editorial and Policy Boards of the *Journal of Macromarketing*, the Editorial Board of *Marketing Theory*, the Board of Directors of the Conference on Historical Analysis and Research in Marketing (CHARM), and on the Academy of Marketing Research Committee.

Robert D. Tamilia retired as Honorary Professor of Marketing, School of Business, University of Quebec at Montreal, Canada. His research interests are in the areas of channels, retail history, marketing thought and its role in marketing education. He currently serves on the editorial review boards of numerous academic journals including the *Journal of Historical Research in Marketing* and has received several awards of academic excellence for his teaching and research.

Yumiko Toda is Associate Professor of Marketing at Nihon University, College of Commerce, Tokyo, Japan. Her primary research interests include the development of marketing theory and the history of marketing practices in Japan, the United States and the United Kingdom. Her recent work on practices of knowledge transfer between Japanese and British retailers was published in 2014 under the title of 'British Retailer and its Influence on the Development of Private Brand Strategy at Daiei Inc., in Japan' in *Distribution Studies, the Journal of Japan Society for Distribution Sciences (JSDS)*.

Diana Twede is a Professor in the School of Packaging at Michigan State University, USA. Her research deals with the relationship between packaging, marketing and logistics over history, with a special emphasis in the history of shipping containers.

Rohit Varman is a Professor of Marketing at Deakin University, Australia. His research interests are broadly in the fields of critical marketing and consumer culture. He has published his research in some of the top international management journals that include *Journal of Consumer Research*, *Journal of Retailing* and *Organization Science*. He serves on the editorial boards of *Journal of Macromarketing*, *Consumption, Markets, and Culture* and *Journal of Historical Research in Marketing*.

Terrence H. Witkowski is Professor of Marketing and Director of the International Business Program at California State University, Long Beach, USA. Educated at Northwestern (BA), UCLA (MS), and UC Berkeley (PhD), he has published over 120 journal articles, book chapters, conference papers and abstracts, book reviews, and other works. His research focuses on marketing and consumer history with additional research in international marketing. He serves on the Editorial Advisory Board for the *Journal of Historical Research in Marketing*.

Preface

One of the editors of this Companion collection teaches an undergraduate course in marketing history and the assigned reading in that course is Strasser's (1989) *Satisfaction Guaranteed: The Making of the American Mass Market*, arguably the only book-length survey of marketing history and, at that, one which has a fairly narrow chronological focus on the late nineteenth and early twentieth century, as well as an obviously narrow geographic focus. Since 1989 there has been a dramatic growth of research in marketing history but to survey the field one must search a wide range of periodic literature. That was a driving force behind the writing of this Companion volume. We wanted to assemble the first survey of marketing history written by some of the leading scholars in the field.

Marketing students and scholars alike need to know their history if they are to avoid reinventing theoretical, conceptual, methodological and substantive wheels. Whereas until relatively recently such a view was a marginal one, it is increasingly accepted that a knowledge of marketing history and the history of marketing thought is relevant for all levels of teaching and scholarship. This renewed interest in our disciplinary history is reflected in the fact that undergraduate, postgraduate and research students are all being exposed to the history of the subject, with major scholars calling for further engagement on this front.

Broadly speaking, most marketing historians recognize two overlapping, but relatively distinct, general fields within historical research in marketing – 'marketing history' and the 'history of marketing thought'. Marketing history includes, but is not limited to, the histories of consumption, market segmentation, market research, product branding, packaging, advertising and promotion, retailing, channels of distribution, pricing strategies, selling and sales management, macromarketing and marketing regulation – all studied from the perspective of companies, industries, or even whole economies. The history of marketing thought examines marketing ideas, concepts, theories, and schools of marketing thought including the lives and times of marketing thinkers.

That literature exists in bits and pieces scattered across numerous different periodicals and a handful of books, few of which have attempted to survey the field. In the history of marketing thought, the standard text literally for decades was Bartels's (1962, 1977, 1988) *The Development of Marketing Thought* which provided an encyclopedic survey of the marketing textbook literature. The first readings collection in this subfield, with the misleadingly simple title *Marketing*, was published in 1993 by Hollander and Rassuli and is long out of print. A more recent such collection was published in 2008, a three-volume collection titled *The History of Marketing Thought* edited by Tadajewski and Jones. Until now, there was no comparable survey collection of readings (or Companion) covering marketing history.

This Companion volume fills a gap in the literature by gathering together in one collection a set of readings that surveys the field of marketing history. A unique feature of this collection are nine chapters that focus on country-specific marketing histories.

Acknowledgements

Robert Crawford's Chapter 16 in this volume was supported by the Australian Research Council's *Discovery Projects* funding scheme – DP120100777.

Karen Fox's Chapter 24 in this volume benefited from assistance of the librarians and consultants of the Russian National Library, St Petersburg; the Library of Congress; the Hagley Museum and Library, Wilmington, Delaware; Orradre Library, Santa Clara University; and Stanford University Libraries. Special thanks go to Irina Skorobogatykh, Chair of the Marketing Department, and Olga Saginova, Head of the Entrepreneurship and Logistics Department, Plekhanov Russian University of Economics, Moscow; and to Professor Jane Curry, Santa Clara University.

The history of marketing practice

Mark Tadajewski and D.G. Brian Jones

Over the past 30 years, interest in the history of marketing has grown substantially. There have been many major contributions that have sought to highlight the origins of key concepts, theories, ideas, scholarly biographies and schools of thought (e.g. Jones, 2012; Jones and Tadajewski, 2011; Shaw and Jones, 2005; Tadajewski and Jones, 2008; see also the *Journal of Historical Research in Marketing* special issue on the evolution of key concepts, 2012). This body of scholarship cuts to the heart of marketing theory, often in a deeply critical fashion, arguing against current received wisdom regarding the emergence of the marketing concept, relationship marketing, market research, market segmentation, and self-service retailing to name just a few of the areas that have been contested by marketing historians (e.g. Cochoy, 2016; Fullerton, forthcoming).

We are, in short, a discipline that has moved on considerably from the days when Fullerton (1987, 1988) could argue that marketing was ahistorical. We are now rich with historical reflection. Whether this permeates mainstream marketing research and study is, however, questionable and it does seem as if marketing scholars are wilfully ignorant of their historical antecedents (Jones and Richardson, 2007). The same can be said of other disciplines, of course, and there are many reasons for this. These include the turn towards the behavioural sciences of the 1950s and 1960s which marginalized historical study (Tadajewski and Jones, 2014); the desperate desire of scholars to make claims of originality through the neglect of their historical forebears (Tadajewski and Saren, 2009); limited academic attention spans that consider only literature produced in the last ten years to be worthy of merit, as well as possibly more understandable pressures to 'publish or perish' which encourage turning out 'quick and dirty' research. Historical research scarcely falls into the latter category and thus slips off the academic radars of those under pressure to perform in the various research assessment exercises that dominate our intellectual landscape.

Certainly, the idea that marketing history (i.e. the study of the history of marketing practice) and knowledge of the history of marketing thought (i.e. studying the conceptual and theoretical basis of many of our key ideas and traditions) should merit our attention is easy to justify. By not knowing our history we are probably going to repeat mistakes that our predecessors tackled and overcame (Jones and Shaw, 2002). Clearly, not knowing our history does have (dys)functional benefits. It enables the repackaging of ideas that have long been practised. It helps us cast our predecessors as working in intellectual and practical dark ages before the wisdom of the marketing concept lit their lives with the beacon of customer-centricity (Jones and Richardson, 2007).

If we were being charitable, we might say that this is a function of a lack of exploration of the history of marketing practice (Strasser, 1989). That is, the history of the actual activities of marketers, advertisers, retailers, wholesalers, market researchers and so forth in the marketplace, rather than just theoretical ruminations on what they should do. Rarely have scholars sought to focus their energies on the history of marketing practice as an object of attention in its own right, unravelling what has been done by practitioners from the origins of marketing in the ancient and medieval world all the way through to the present day. This was the task we set ourselves as editors. But we wanted to go beyond a contribution to the history of marketing practice. The history of marketing literature is still overwhelmingly dominated by US voices in terms of the companies being studied and the location that forms the historical, social, political, economic and technological backdrop for the mass of literature currently available. There have, naturally enough, been exceptions to this statement and some of this material has been of extremely high quality (e.g. Fullerton, 1988, 1990). Generally speaking, though, we wanted to look beyond the borders of the United States to examine other countries' experiences of the development of marketing practice. We hope that this volume makes a first movement in that direction, but we are acutely aware that more research needs to be done.

Our first chapter is provided by one of the most active contributors to the history of marketing practice as well as thought. Eric Shaw is uniquely positioned to write about ancient and medieval marketing practice by virtue of his distinctive record of publications on this topic. Specifically, Shaw argues that we need to look back to the origins of humanity and explore the use of bartering by Neanderthal man. Subsequently he turns his attention to surveying the role of marketing in antiquity, notably ancient Greece. There were various reasons for the emergence of markets, he suggests. One of the most important was the development and use of coinage. With exchangeable currency people no longer had to engage in long (bartering) negotiations about what items they were going to exchange and whether their value was commensurate.

Charting the history of the move from bartering to marketing, Shaw offers us close readings of philosophical tracts, biblical accounts and a wealth of business history and economics writings. As he illuminates, the development of marketing was contingent on a variety of factors including the division of labour as well as retailers operating in specific locations. From the medieval period, he outlines the growth of trade fairs, the development and usage of new financial methods for enabling transactions, and the power of the guilds. Marketing practice, for Shaw, has a history that spans at least 40,000 years.

Terry Witkowski telescopes us slightly closer to the present, moving us from Europe to the United States in the seventeenth century. Witkowski's chapter represents an impressive attempt to document a vast range of scholarship dealing with the history of consumption. In doing so, he encourages us to think differently about a number of areas, most notably with respect to the impact of gender on consumption habits, particularly shopping. This is an important historical review for those interested in consumer behaviour as well as those aligned with Consumer Culture Theory inasmuch as it engages with topics like the meanings associated with consumption, how consumption practice has historically been stratified by gender (and not necessarily in the way we would anticipate), and consumer reactions to consumption that historicize recent debates around anti-consumption, consumer resistance and regulatory control.

What is interesting about Witkowski's chapter, like several other contributions to this volume (e.g. Tamilia, Chapter 10; Gao, Chapter 19; Sreekumar and Varman, Chapter 21), is that it underscores that globalization is not necessarily the recent phenomenon that we would ordinarily assume. Some consumers of the seventeenth century were able to access global flows of products, often sourcing desirable items produced by British colonies for their households. This was particularly the case with the wealthy. Complementing this focus on global consumption flows, Witkowski examines the growth of retailing in the US, the rise of credit and the sexual segmentation of household labour. In the eighteenth century, for example, women were not necessarily most closely involved with retail purchases. Men might be more frequent buyers because they were able to access credit with provincial retailers.

But lest we think that those living in the eighteenth century were experiencing a consumerist dream, Witkowski does underscore that for many their possessions were quite modest. This underwent some degree of change in the nineteenth century with the growth of interest in outfitting the home in a manner consistent with the cultural valorization of gentility, accelerating further with the rise of the debates around the 'leisure class' (Veblen, 1899/1912) and the normative structuring of consumption (e.g. Tadajewski, 2013a). Importantly, the growth of consumption spurred a reaction: the growth in anti-consumption discourse which can be traced from the mid to late eighteenth century, spiking in the early twentieth century, and gaining ground today (Higgins and Tadajewski, 2002). Consumption and politics are not separate spheres of life, Witkowski points out. They implicate and imbricate.

Taking up the marketing practice gauntlet in the late nineteenth century, Stefan Schwarzkopf engages with a key conduit in the development, extension and proliferation of marketing practice, namely the market research industry. This industry became especially vital with the growth of the national market in the United States. What this basically meant in practical terms was that the producer and consumer were frequently far distant from each other. It was no longer the case that a manufacturer sold only to those in a fairly local area and could by dint of cultural socialization understand what the market would or would not clear. Some mechanism needed to be used to provide producers and retailers with the 'voice of the customer' and into this breach strode the market research industry (Tadajewski, 2009a).

Schwarzkopf points out that we should not consider market and consumer research the invention of American pioneers. The narrative is much more complicated than this. Many scholars have argued that the Second World War, the rise of Nazism and the Transatlantic movements (in both directions) of scholars and practitioners helped foster new concepts of the consumer as well as new methodological tools with which to probe their consciousness (e.g. Tadajewski, 2006). Less well known is the narrative that Schwarzkopf bases his discussion upon when he tracks the origins of market research within the broader orbit of the social sciences, especially more activist streams of social research that sought to engage with the problems accompanying industrialization such as poverty and social dislocation. Some of these engagements provided fertile ground for the development of survey methods and sampling techniques which found their way into United Kingdom-based market research during the first half of the twentieth century. Similar themes thread through the development of the industry on the US side of the Atlantic.

Illuminating the early history of market research, Schwarzkopf discusses the roles of a number of prominent applied psychologists who were notable contributors to early debates about advertising attraction, effectiveness and efficiency, plying their trade within scholarly circles, seeking funding from industry, and keen to articulate how they could contribute to managerial, profit-driven agendas. He underscores the important contributions made by

3

advertising agencies in studying the consumer marketplace, the pioneering efforts of Charles Coolidge Parlin (see also Ward, 2009, 2010) in explicating the markets for a huge range of offerings and industries, as well as the novel methodological strategies employed by Parlin and his team.

Some of the narrative threads that follow will be familiar to those with a keen interest in the history of market research, especially the prominent position accorded to academic entrepreneurs like Paul Lazarsfeld (e.g. Fullerton, 1990), highly successful practitioners like Herta Herzog and Ernest Dichter (e.g. Tadajewski, 2006), as well as the role played by Social Research Incorporated in advancing our knowledge of brands, consumer-brand relations, symbolism (e.g. Levy, 2003, 2012), and ideas related to the extended self that would be picked up by influential consumer researchers (see Ladik *et al.*, 2015). For those interested in non-US-based contributions to marketing research practice, Schwarzkopf delves deeply into the history of German marketing research.

Usefully, he explores the emergence and application of a number of frequently invoked methodological tools used within industry, including panels, focus groups, market simulations, then turning his analytic attention to the role of key actors within the research service sector as a whole. Importantly, he articulates future directions for historical research, stressing that too much scholarship to date has paid attention to the market research industry itself, without exploring consumer reactions to industry initiatives. The danger of this is that such narratives often appear quite deterministic, stressing marketer power without factoring in consumer agency to resist marketer interventions – as Witkowski's chapter highlights very clearly, the consumer is not a passive target for marketing activities.

Our next contribution can be read as a response to a narrative that features all too prominently in marketing textbooks and journal articles on segmentation, namely that it was only truly appreciated in 1956 when a paper on the topic appeared in the flagship marketing outlet, the *Journal of Marketing* (Smith, 1956). This, clearly, is a seriously misleading argument which neglects to register the acuity of marketing practitioners who have – for a very considerable time – appreciated the need to segment the market and differentiate their offerings accordingly if they were to produce goods likely to satisfy the ultimate consumer.

There are many ways, Ronald Fullerton asserts, that the 1956 'origin' narrative can be deflated. We could turn to the fact that there were books dealing with the topic of segmentation in the 1920s. Alternatively, we could look closely at industry practice. The eighteenth century, for instance, reveals that British industrialists appreciated that the needs of their audience were often markedly different, most obviously in terms of income. Selling products at different price points simply made good business sense and was practised by many clothing producers and retailers. Josiah Wedgwood, likewise, was attentive to the need to target market his offerings, paying attention to the influence of the gentry as conduits for fashion and patronage. He was absolutely aware that different national markets had divergent ideas about what was desirable, fashionable and cutting edge. This required product modification in line with consumer sensibilities. As if this were not enough evidence to persuade us that marketing practitioners were engaged in market segmentation, Fullerton provides illustrations from a number of different industrial contexts – gun production, fountain pen manufacture, bicycle production and, in most detail, the book publishing trade – to firmly consign to the trash can of history the idea that segmentation is only a twentieth-century phenomenon.

Branding, roughly speaking, is concerned with the linkage of a name, sign, identifying mark or symbol with a product offering. It serves as a shortcut for consumers, enabling them to identify the products and services that have satisfied in the past, easily and quickly.

For brand owners, it helps them cultivate a stream of revenue that is associated with their specific product. They do this by crafting a constellation of meanings around an item that are valued by the customer. Diving into this topic, Ross Petty provides a highly innovative and timely contribution to debates dealing with brand identity, the legal protections available to brand owners, and a historical overview of the development of branding back to antiquity. It thus complements Eric Shaw's chapter in terms of providing the interested reader with appropriate citations to studies which engage with the development of branding many thousands of years ago.

Antiquity is not, however, Petty's focus. His interest is directed to the development of trademark, branding and brand protection from the 1500s onwards, ending in the middle of the twentieth century, but even so offering valuable guidance about contemporary research to take the narrative through to the present day. We should note that he is attentive to the conceptual evolution of these terms, illuminating the conceptual dynamics from trademark to brand over the course of his contribution. This is worthy of consideration in its own right.

Petty's scholarship is first rate. He excavates the contents and themes of court cases dealing with trademark infringement, moving on to the nineteenth century and the steady growth in the use of imagery and naming to identify products as well as the court system to contest trademark infringement. Impressively, his chapter ranges across the world, engaging with trademark law and protection in the US as well as Europe. In a close reading of the history of branding, he reviews the constitution of brand names, how they were selected, what influenced their production, and engages with key exemplars to flesh out his narrative.

The next chapter inspects an underexplored area in marketing history, the history of packaging. Of all the scholarship currently available on this topic, the majority has been written by Diana Twede, the author of the chapter. Once again, historical scholarship points us towards the earliest origins of humanity, noting that our far distant relatives used a variety of natural materials to protect their food sources and valuable items. More recently, the history of packaging has been greatly stimulated by changes in technology, the growth of global trade, and the need for easily transportable, secure, safe and affordable product protection.

Twede pays attention to the important technologies that have enabled the refinement of packaging science, noting that while the skills and resources to make many different types of packages have a long lineage, it was only fairly recently, with the onset of the industrial revolution, that we had the machinery to mass-produce bottles, cans, jars and so on. Mechanization drove the greater use of packaging and played a major role in fostering the expansion of the national and eventually global market for many product offerings. Indeed, as she points out, the functional utility of packaging was itself highly useful as a symbolic marketing tactic, enabling producers and retailers to stress that products were created under sanitary conditions, untouched by human hands. This, of course, was highly useful in an industrializing context riven with pollution, dirty factories and frequent critiques of the unsanitary conditions of factory production that would culminate (at least initially) in Upton Sinclair's (1906) condemnation of industrialization, dehumanization and plea for socialism, *The Jungle*.

But the history of packaging is even more complex, linked with the growth of self-service retailing, the advances stimulated by the Second World War in terms of packaging technology and logistics, and the growth in both university-level instruction in packaging management as well as professional groups. Developments continue to be made in this area, reflecting the need for packaging technology to change with the times, especially as public and governmental concern over packaging disposal, waste and environmental harm achieve critical mass.

Barry Boothman offers us a wealth of information about the development of retailing in the United States and Canada. This is a truly exceptional overview of the history of retailing which offers considerable inspiration. Boothman's emphasis is the mid nineteenth century to the present day and he articulates a number of key influences and turning points that enable us to make sense of an intricate history (Hollander *et al.*, 2005). These concern the growth of financial support for retailers which transformed the nature of competition in this sector, leading to the influence of large-scale retailers over small. Furthermore, the professionalization of management teaching and training offered large corporations the skills and know-how to more efficiently and effectively manage their distribution activities, providing a source of competitive advantage that smaller companies often lacked.

Boothman charts the development of North American retailing from the early nineteenth century to early twenty-first. The emergence of retailing was a concomitant of the shift from the self-sufficient lifestyle that many within the American context led at that time, but which radically changed with the growth of industry and the extensive migration from countryside to towns and cities. Boothman provides a large amount of detail about the various social, cultural and material factors that helped direct the growth of retailing. Like Fullerton, he identifies that retailers were often aware that they needed to segment their market, catering to specific groups of consumers and their nuanced needs for product replenishment and service provision.

As marketing historians questioning the notion of a production era have pointed out, profit was a guiding criterion for many practitioners during the timeframe that Boothman explores (Jones and Richardson, 2007; Tadajewski, 2008, 2009b, 2015a, 2015b). However, Boothman highlights the lack of knowledge of some retailers who violated their need for profit in the pursuit of a quick sale. The historical narrative around the pursuit of profit is thereby rendered that bit more complicated, although he does stress that attempts to professionalize business practice were implemented during this time. Best practice, however, does not always confer benefits on all concerned.

The development of retailing wrought a number of changes that some would contest like deskilling, the use of sweatshop labour, and the cultivation of consumer desire (Ewen, 1976). Retailers had to find ways to respond to criticism and legitimate what they were doing. One way to do so was to invoke a discourse of service, frequently service not merely to the consumer, but to society (e.g. Tadajewski, 2011). They achieved this by delivering high-quality products to the market at a reasonable cost. In fleshing out his narrative, Boothman takes the reader on a journey through the emergence and growth of new methods of retail competition and consolidation, the declines faced by department stores between the wars, the rise of cut-priced, discount store chains, big-box retailers and explosion of online retailing.

Andrew Alexander charts the development of British retail history. As he rightly points out, interest in this subject is booming, with various popular programmes and books pushing the department store to centre stage (e.g. *Mr Selfridge*). A profusion of company-specific studies over the past ten years has illuminated the dynamics of the retailing environment. Alexander provides a brief engagement with pre-1850 retailing trends, but devotes the majority of his attention to the post-1850 period, tracing the emergence of large retailers, the continued prevalence of itinerant sellers, the growth of mail order, the rise of supply chain management, the importance of the fashion market and the internationalization of the retailing industry. As we might expect, the pre-1850 period was marked by less sophistication in practice and retailers were often small operators. This was to change over the nineteenth century, when store size expanded, design and layout changes improved store atmospherics, and marketing and advertising know-how developed.

Like Boothman, Alexander challenges received wisdom regarding retail practice. Large-scale department stores are often depicted as conservative in orientation, slow to modify their practices in line with economic, social and cultural change. For Alexander, this is not accurate. Store owners were aware of the importance of branding to differentiate their business, with advertising playing a major role in supporting the cultivation of a distinct brand image in the eyes of the consuming public. But Alexander does not simply focus on the more colourful practices of the department stores, he pays due attention to another highly important section of the retailing community in the UK, namely the co-operative movement. He provides a potted survey of the development of co-operative practices, subsequently exploring the limited literature on mail order retailing.

Robert Tamilia, in the next chapter, makes a highly important point right at the start of his exploration of the history of channels of distribution, namely that many scholars focus on the idea that marketing is concerned with demand stimulation, that is, with the creation of markets or the widening of extant markets. What they devote considerably less attention to is the fact that this is only part of marketing practice; equally important is the series of activities involved in actually getting the product to the consumer: distribution, supply chain management and logistical support.

Tamilia's chapter is extremely detailed and complexly argued, so we can only gesture to some of the themes that constitute this tapestry of academic labour. As he points out, the availability of a distribution network, with its attendant intermediaries enabling the movement of goods from producers to consumers, was key in enabling the development of the mass, national market in the United States. Initially, he takes the reader through a conceptual introduction to channels, linking this with an account of the functions of the middleman, to provide a shared vocabulary for the study that follows. Middlemen have, despite the criticism they have faced, performed vital roles in the movement of goods throughout the economy for a very long time. They have been active forces in leading to the global trade in goods and services – an international trade that Tamilia avers far antedates ahistorical references to contemporary globalization – and which he genealogically positions as dynamic in the thirteenth century, accelerating markedly in the seventeenth century, and continuing to the present day.

In a fascinating account, Tamilia notes how, historically speaking, being a merchant was not necessarily considered a desirable role. Their skills in terms of reading and writing did provide an element of status and in some countries it was often viewed as far more positive for an individual to pursue a career as wholesaler than retailer. The former had credibility and cachet; the latter was viewed as a position beneath those aspiring to climb the social ladder.

He details how supply chains have been managed and enabled by certain groups throughout history. This has been achieved via the use of various legal mechanisms, through the activities of the guilds, via the active coordination of distribution activities at fairs or courtesy of the movement of itinerant salespeople across the US using the developing rail and road networks. Naturally enough, the emergence of new retailing systems like self-service, superstore outlets and the technological systems that rendered complex distribution processes manageable have been essential components in the development, extension and refinement of distribution over the last century. Accompanying structural changes to the distribution system have been shifts in power relations and legal challenges to existing business practice.

In medieval times, for example, merchants frequented fairs, sold their wares to the public, and their ability to do so was managed in quite sophisticated terms. People sometimes travelled long distances to reach fair locations. These might be short, medium or longer term events, with the infrastructure necessary to sustain the participants varying accordingly. Attendees' security was guaranteed for a price, they were provided with horses and men for transporting goods, catering supply and cooking implements were furnished, with money changing and transaction supports of various kinds lubricating the distribution of goods.

What is especially useful about Tamilia's chapter is that he not only provides a substantial level of historical information about all the various distribution channels he discusses, he frequently links his exemplars to contemporary examples to reinforce the idea that our distribution structure today often has precursors we only dimly appreciate. Medieval trade fairs, as a case in point, are refracted in our megamalls. Agricultural trade fairs are transformed into popular farmers markets. He also takes aim at core arguments relating to the idea that the customer is king, arguing that this was not original to Charles Coolidge Parlin in 1914 as many claim. Rather, for its origin, we need to look to the work of Charles Gide, specifically an argument he made in 1889 on the reign of the consumer which provides the intellectual foundation for the elevation of the consumer in marketing discourse. In fact, we find even earlier support for the belief in the sovereignty of consumers in Daniel Defoe's (1727) *The Complete English Tradesman* (Tadajewski, 2015a).

The history of advertising and sales promotion has been subject to perhaps more research than many other facets of marketing practice. And Fred Beard provides one of the most comprehensive reviews of this area available. He moves far beyond the majority of the literature by tracing advertising practice back to ancient times, signalling the use of multiple forms of advertising (e.g. signs, town criers) across multiple cultural locations (e.g. China, Egypt, Greece). What Beard shows in compelling detail is that marketing, advertising and sales promotion, as well as the distinctions between advertising as information and advertising as persuasion, are historically longstanding.

Obviously, whilst there are family resemblances between earlier and contemporary practices, there are also clear differences, reflecting the nature of innovation in printing, labelling and role of symbolism in product differentiation. Advertising and sales promotion were, as we might expect, greatly advanced by the availability of suitable vehicles for their dissemination. Beard points out that adverts and posters were pasted in public, occasionally even on the side of church buildings. This incurred a degree of public criticism and attempts were made to limit their presence – this is a recurring theme throughout the history of advertising practice, becoming notable in the late nineteenth century (Nevett, 1981), a problem in the early twentieth century in the UK, France, Germany and elsewhere (Leach, 1994), and whose outlawing is a source of public and civic pride in the twenty-first century in places like São Paulo (www.newdream.org/resources/sao-paolo-ad-ban).

It was the establishment of newspapers and regular periodicals that helped advertising achieve its potential, even if editors themselves or the state tried to curtail the prevalence of advertising through selective inclusion policies or taxation. Accompanying the rise of advertising was the growth in various forms of sales promotion ranging from lotteries to price reductions. What is interesting about the history of advertising is that, while many people actively undertook these activities, there remained an undercurrent of scepticism about their effectiveness. This continued into the nineteenth and twentieth centuries when the sophistication of both advertising and sales promotion continued to increase and the clamour for studies that could identify whether a given communication would be successful or not intensified. Scaffolding this was the rise of the advertising agency, their use of research and ability to offer a range of creative activities all under one roof. In equal measure, the saturation of the market for public attention demanded the use of ever more inventive campaigns designed to attract public notice and promotion campaigns that hinged on cultivating emotional responses in viewers, not their ability for reasoned decision-making.

In unravelling this narrative, Beard's account chimes with other chapters in this volume that remind us that the dissemination of marketing techniques, tools and know-how was not a simple process of Americanization, that is, of the transfer of skills from the US to other countries desperate for the insights of their American cousins. The process reflected a pattern of transatlantic cross-fertilization. Indeed, the process is more complicated than we allow here, with countries in Asia producing their own forms of marketing communication that were consistent with cultural values.

The next chapter by Thomas Powers is a highly useful companion to Beard's contribution. Powers suggests that selling is a practice that reaches back many centuries, running the gauntlet from the door-to-door salespeople found in Phoenician times through to professional sales management. Selling and sales promotion were a natural concomitant of the establishment of central marketplaces and fixed retailing locations, where numerous vendors touting similar offerings would congregate. Sales promotion of some type was essential in this context if a retailer wanted to attract patrons to their store. As Powers underlines, coinage assisted exchange, with additional services like delivery, packaging and competitive pricing lubricating the marketing process.

Accompanying the gradual emergence and dissemination of fixed location retailing was the specialization of marketing roles. Different tradespeople cultivated their skills in certain areas, harvesting or manufacturing items that could be sold in the local, national and international communities. Importantly, selling activities were not just the preserve of men, women were active in certain spheres, engaged in jobs that were attributed distinctly feminized inflections. Powers's narrative ties in with those provided by Shaw and Tamilia, when he traces the gradual social acceptability of the role of the merchant, linking this with the rise of Islamic traders in the fifth century, as well as by discussing the function of selling at travelling fairs in the medieval period (roughly the fifth to eleventh centuries).

Transformations in salesmanship were not only influenced by transportation. Processes of professionalization exerted a powerful force on the axiology – the values – of salesmanship itself. No longer was the salesperson, a wise-cracking, hard-drinking, cigar-smoking, individual; they had to be a professional, keeping up-to-date with the latest sales knowledge, adopting best practice in order to cultivate customer relations (Cochoy, 2016; Tadajewski, 2011, 2012). The salesperson became a mirror of society, reflecting advances in knowledge, as well as being the butt of public commentary which did not position the profession in an especially good light. Sinclair Lewis's fiction, most conspicuously, *Babbitt*, highlights this most vividly and this criticism of sales activities was marked during the Great Depression.

Despite this, the Great Depression provided an opportunity for sales education. Contrary to the promotional activities of proponents of Service Dominant Logic (e.g. Vargo and Lusch, 2004), the early twentieth century was not characterized by a focus on goods, far from it (Vargo and Morgan, 2005). As Powers and others have illuminated, goods were purchased for the services they provided, and the discourse of the time reflected this notion (Tadajewski, 2011). Similarly, and contrary to those who maintain that marketing was going through a sales-oriented period between the 1930s and 1950s (Keith, 1960), some marketing practitioners at this time did not think that every sale was a good sale (Tadajewski, 2009a, 2009b, 2011; Tadajewski and Saren, 2009). Rather, it was long-term profit that drove practitioner interest (see Boothman's chapter herein). This was reflected in the elimination of unprofitable customers, territory and products.

Concluding his narrative in the post-Second World War period, Powers points out how many of our central concepts, theories and ideas continued to be refined in managerial practice, with some more dubious activities like the pursuit of hard-selling continuing to coexist alongside more enlightened business policies (see also Fullerton, 1988; Tadajewski, 2015b). Notably, the communications revolution, changing firm relationships and the prominence of retailers have all served to drive the economy in new and innovative ways. But these are ways that often have precursors that are not sufficiently recognized within the non-historical literature, Powers submits.

Many of the chapters in this volume gesture to the idea that marketing has an impact on society and that society through laws, regulations, social criticism and consumer boycotts attempts to impact upon marketing. Central to the domain of macromarketing is the logic that the marketing system is part of a wider social system and exists as a provisioning technology, serving to provide people with the goods and services they need, want and desire or can be made to desire. This means that the study of marketing from a macro perspective often challenges managerial ways of looking at marketing practice. It does not necessarily shy away from providing a more critical evaluation of whether marketing achieves the objectives it sets itself, although this literature rarely contests the idea that the present capitalist system is the best means of meeting provisioning requirements (Tadajewski, 2013b).

However we view macromarketing and its relationship with political economy, it seems clear that exploring the development of marketing from a wider perspective indicates the extent to which marketing is affected by political, economic, technological, ethical and cultural change. Stanley Shapiro illuminates this point well in a contribution that is better positioned as an example of how scholars might go about writing a macromarketing history, rather than being a macromarketing history in its own right. He does so by investigating the case of England in the eighteenth century, exploring a number of key themes associated with macromarketing which are used as prisms to interrogate the contribution of marketing to economic and social development. These include a focus on issues relating to the generation of a standard of living, quality of life, distributive justice, marketplace regulation and the politics of distribution among others.

Tackling the issue of marketplace regulation in more detail, the chapter by Ross Petty reflects the ruminations of one of marketing's finest legal minds. As anyone who has read a marketing textbook can testify, the extent to which marketing practice is connected to national or international legal systems is woefully inadequate. Scholars prefer to stress the value of relationship formation, rather than acknowledge that it is very easy for such relationships to result in anti-competitive, collusive activities that harm marketplace efficiency and the ultimate consumer (Tadajewski, 2010).

Petty's chapter is a highly impressive survey of US antitrust law which has had serious implications for marketing managers historically and continues to exert force today. Once again, we are returned to ancient times and the critiques of monopoly that featured in the Bible, subsequently telescoping forward to the US context c.1773. He summarizes the influence of UK common law on the US (and other countries), sketching the contours and concepts that later informed major antitrust court cases. As expected given the context, the Sherman Antitrust law figures prominently, with Petty identifying how companies strove to manage their operations, cementing their control over the marketplace at the same time. This deeply concerned the wider public and spurred lawmakers into some degree of action, as evidenced by the entanglement of numerous states with the 'trusts' in legal action. But, as Petty makes clear, putting the Sherman Act on the legal books was neither an easy process nor uncontested. Nor was it used to a dramatic extent in terms of successful convictions in the first 15 years or so of its operation. It was only in 1905 that antitrust efforts were really pursued with a degree of vigour, with the state firmly flexing its muscles vis-à-vis large, powerful corporate actors. This is not to say that these actions were widely praised. There were ongoing concerns that trusts and corporations were managing to negotiate the Sherman Act. This led to a variety of revisions and extensions to the original Act through the enactment of sister proposals like the Clayton Act, with some reversals of policy provided to reflect perceived economic exigencies.

Petty comprehensively lists the expansion of antitrust activity from 1939 to 1978 in a table that functions as a counterpoint to any uncritical espousal of the idea that this period was framed by a 'marketing revolution' and placing the consumer at the centre of corporate activity (Keith, 1960). The picture is far less positive in light of this reading of antitrust activity and underscores that self-regulation has clear limits, both historically and today.

Andrew Pressey's chapter is a mirror of Petty's in that it engages with the field of competition law in Europe, rather than the US. Once more it encourages us to appreciate that there are limits to the marketing concept, with companies pursuing their own self-interest in conjunction with amenable competitors, rather than meeting, satisfying and creating delighted customers. The idealized image of marketing practice that our textbooks promote is thus firmly undermined.

Pressey begins with the legal environment in Rome, which set limits on prices for many essential products. The penalties for violating the law were extremely strict, with death hovering over those who thought to bypass price ceilings. We move with rapidity to the medieval period, the rise of the guilds and their rigid controls over production, distribution and sales. One result of the guild system was that it limited the number of people involved in the production of particular items, effectively generating a monopoly-like situation. This led to price rises. Criticism of the system led to legal challenges and changes by the fourteenth century.

These were not the only rules on the English legislative book at the time. There were various measures designed to stop individuals and groups from cornering the market, that is, to prevent engrossing and forestalling, which was apparently a feature of the local markets and town fairs that have been remarked upon in other chapters (see also Tadajewski, 2015a). Many of these laws and controls were early attempts to control monopoly power which gathered steam in the late nineteenth century. It might be here that we would expect to see some measure of US antitrust legislative influence. This was not the case, Pressey argues, proposing instead that the legal community in Austria was far more influential with respect to the development of the European legal system.

This situation changed between the World Wars when Germany assumed a more prominent position on competition law. This was a testing period for economic thinking and legal action, with internationally influential cartels helping to structure the marketplaces in a number of European contexts. Their contribution, moreover, was not condemned. It was seen as a potential antidote to the cut-throat competition that was affecting countries around the world. Where the US ceded some space for companies and trade associations to share marketplace research and data in order to assist managerial decision-making (Tadajewski, 2009c), political leaders in Europe felt that the way to defeat an excess of competition was through constructive cooperation and industry collaboration.

While we asserted above that current marketing textbooks pay little attention to the legal ramifications of marketing practice, historically marketing scholars *have* scrutinized the legal environment. As Pressey points out, from its earliest published issues the *Journal of Marketing* often featured articles and commentaries on the effects of new legislation on practice. This predominantly concerned an interest in American law, not international law. Perhaps, at best, we can say that such a focus was a result of more companies pursuing success in the national rather than international market – a fairly reasonable assumption until the mid-1950s. Even so, the post-war world experienced dramatic changes in international trade and this led to the development of a European trading bloc with a formalized legislative system that was, in terms of competition law, shared.

Fleshing out this account, Pressey draws on numerous examples of violations of competition law that effectively resulted in decreased marketplace competitiveness and efficiency. What is depressingly clear is the frequency with which marketing practitioners figure in violations of competition law and Pressey highlights detailed evidence that serves to question the idea that marketers are solely concerned with acting in the interests of their customers; the contemporary cases that he cites offer a profoundly different story.

Chapter 16 brings us to the first of our country specific contributions. Robert Crawford begins by referencing what appears to be the earliest mention of marketing in an Australian newspaper. This was not a positive notice, but a reflection of concern about the creeping effects of commercialization on religious holidays. Crawford focuses on the eighteenth century as his starting point, registering that Australia was for a long period oriented around the development and sale of primary products. This curtailed the role of marketing and salesmanship in the economy. This is not to suggest that marketing practice was not present, far from it. By the late eighteenth century, retailing was a very embryonic feature of this English colony which still had serious difficulties satisfying the basic needs of its population. As resources were identified, as appropriate support was made available from England, the marketing infrastructure started its long period of development.

Central marketplaces were established and successful. Fairly rapidly, there were importers and retailers ready to advertise their offerings, with stores catering to various tastes plying their trade (some successfully, others less so), although the typical shop was rather small, with limited ranges of products. Throughout the nineteenth century, improvements in distribution mirrored transportation developments. The rise of the department store was not welcomed wholeheartedly, however. There were concerns about the effects of these large establishments on smaller traders. In spite of this, the additional conveniences these outlets offered, and the levels of service that could be provided, helped to expand the marketplace, extending the availability of products and services to those living beyond urban locations, so that by 1901 it was possible to refer to a national market in Australia.

Over the course of the twentieth century, the patterns that were present in the retail trade, namely the rise of the department store and its commitment to service, were supported by larger expenditures on advertising and various forms of marketing promotions. Service industries, such as advertising agencies, grew in profile, their services tailored to the needs of their clients, as well as keyed to respond to public criticism of their role. They achieved the latter via the public relations conduits provided by professional groups such as the Association of Australian National Advertisers, as well as courtesy of the efforts of the agencies themselves. This became more pressing in the Great Depression which triggered a wave of interest in establishing what contribution advertising offered to business, how it was possible to determine return-on-investment, and how, in short, marketing practices could be made more efficient.

Operating in this breach were advertising agencies with an established pedigree for marketing research like J. Walter Thompson. Interestingly, the Australian context serves as another test bed for underlining the point that not all the pioneers of marketing were men. Rather, female pioneers have made impressive contributions to marketing practice (e.g.

Zuckerman and Carsky, 1990). This is no better demonstrated than by a recent special issue in the *Journal of Historical Research in Marketing* which traces their contributions to a variety of industries as well as within the university walls (e.g. Davis, 2013; Graham, 2013; Jones, 2013; Parsons, 2013; Scanlon, 2013; Tadajewski, 2013a; Tadajewski and Maclaran, 2013; Zuckerman, 2013). As Crawford explains, the first market research firm in Australia was founded by Sylvia Ashby in 1936. No doubt, similar examples will continue to be unearthed now that scholars are sensitized to this facet of marketing practice.

The Australian experience with marketing continued to be positive in view of the recognition that competition for the attention of the consumer and their pocketbook was rapidly increasing, with marketing and consumer research providing the tools to meet such challenges. This was supported by developments in sales and marketing education from the 1930s onwards, from industry groups and university providers alike. It was during the 1960s that marketing education in Australia really began a growth period, with the founding of the first professorial chair, the enrolment of undergraduates and their employment by industry. The slowdown in economic growth in the 1970s merely served to remind industry that marketing deserved significant attention whether the economy was booming or in decline, something that practitioners all too frequently ignore at their peril.

Moving from a colony to the centre of the empire, our next chapter focuses on marketing in Britain. Richard Hawkins literally traverses the entire history of the country, shifting from the experiences of the Roman Empire to the rise of the internet and e-commerce. Hawkins's study complements a number of other contributions to this collection, providing insight into medieval marketing and the growth of trade fairs, the emergence of fixed shops, the growth of printing and newspapers as well as their influence on the production of advertising materials. Like Fullerton, albeit in a different national environment, Hawkins sees the publishing trade operating at the forefront of marketing practice, especially between the fifteenth and seventeenth centuries.

It is during the eighteenth century that Hawkins argues we see the most sustained growth in the development of marketing practice. In various industries, it was being appreciated that production did not create demand, demand had to be fostered. This was achieved by way of the promotional vehicles already mentioned, combined with the provision of credit, and by improving trust in retailing establishments through the use of fixed prices.

Later, in the nineteenth and early twentieth centuries, the rise of the department store, the legal status granted to trademarks and brands, the growth of mail-order retailing and technological changes such as the invention of the telegraph, telephone and various forms of travel, all enabled the expansion of the market. These processes were further facilitated by the extension of access to instalment purchasing, the promotional opportunities provided by the cinema, not just in terms of actual product marketing, but with respect to selling a consumerist lifestyle. Marketing's influence, whilst not welcomed to the extent that we see in America, was nonetheless apparent over the rest of the twentieth century and it continues to reflect and refract political, economic, social, cultural and technological changes that will undoubtedly ensure that it remains a vital force in British business practice for the foreseeable future.

Chapter 18 takes us across the Atlantic once again, this time to Canada. The Canadian marketing history literature is underdeveloped. To deal with this issue, Leighann Neilson and Delfin Muise have delved into business and economic history, bringing back pearls of insight that shed light on the complex marketing problems facing operators in this vast country since the fifteenth century. They distinguish three periods in Canadian history. The first is oriented around the initial settlement of the country. This was not a period of great marketing advances, but restricted to the exploitation of the natural resources of the country – natural resources like fish and fur that were in high demand around the world as a function of religious admonishments regarding meat consumption and for clothing. Those working on the ships, for example, were natural targets for rapacious employers who could sell them goods via company owned stores, often leading employees to spend more money than they earned because of the high charges levelled for consumption offerings like alcohol. This period ran from the end of the fifteenth century until the middle of the seventeenth century.

Settlement efforts were replaced between the seventeenth and nineteenth centuries by more advanced marketing efforts and the rise of international trade via the Hudson's Bay Company (see also Tamilia, Chapter 10). This period was defined by greater levels of competition for the fur products and cod that were highly prized Canadian exports. The income derived from these sales enabled those selling the fur – notably the indigenous population – to negotiate preferential terms with settlers wanting to export their goods, exchanging them for high-value European items.

As Neilson and Muise register, these traders were not naïve, exchanging their offerings for beads, shiny objects and alcohol. They were far more sophisticated, often playing various interest groups off against each other in order to secure the best deal. They also note that the Hudson's Bay Company was fairly marketing oriented. They provided the Indian population with goods that met their requirements (e.g. blankets, tobacco, guns, knives) in order to try to secure access to the best beaver fur. They attempted to understand the cultural proclivities of the Indians, what motivated them to trade, what would enable the Company to secure the level and quality of stock that it required. They trained young men in their language and customs, which eased the exchange process. Moreover, the Company was well aware of the need to manage its supply chain, produce a plurality of product offerings to deal with potential changes in demand, and engage in regular new product development. In short, the international trading efforts of the Hudson's Bay Company exhibit ideas now associated with the marketing concept, customer centricity and exploratory market research.

The final period examined by Neilson and Muise concludes in the late nineteenth century, with an increase in economic protectionism. They review the activities of the coal industry, the prominent roles played by merchants throughout the history of pre-Confederation Canada, and gesture to the advanced nature of some of the practices being adopted by merchants to cement their trade positions. Their chapter adds further weight to the literature that charts the existence of relationship marketing themes well before the 1970s, that is, the point when contemporary scholars writing about this topic generally suppose practitioners discovered the importance of fostering long-term relations with their customer base. As Neilson and Muise underline, the cultivation of trust was key to business longevity, enabled access to credit and business hiring policies reflected the need to ensure that only people were employed who could be trusted (i.e. often extended family members).

From Canada we cross the world to China. Zhihong Gao begins with a summary of the nature of marketing practice before the mid-point of the nineteenth century. Prior to this juncture, income distribution was extremely uneven, with some members of Chinese society able to consume in conspicuous, luxurious ways while the mass of the population toiled at subsistence levels. There was, he writes, a fairly well established marketing system in place, with markets present across the country in important locations.

We really see modern marketing take off after 1842. This period was punctuated by advances in transportation, the emergence of newspapers, greater levels of expenditure on advertising, an emerging professional middle class and growth in international trade (albeit trade at disadvantageous terms for the Chinese). Industrialization was fairly slow, Gao explains, but China was a target for many companies seeking to enter its market in order to tap the vast potential purchasers for their offerings.

By 1911, the country was increasingly segmented on two fronts: the urban dwellers versus those remaining in the countryside. Income distribution between these groups was unequal, favouring the former at the expense of the latter. This is not to suggest that those living in the cities were enjoying lifestyles resembling cosmopolitan elites. Far from it. Poverty and limited access to material resources was a feature of daily life for many. Income was typically skewed towards the consumption of food, with only a limited proportion available for disposable expenditure. For those privileged to possess the requisite income levels, it was possible for them to actively participate in global consumer goods flows.

Within the country, local producers and retailers engaged in progressive marketing practices, segmenting their markets, identifying the requirements of their customers, competing with Western imports through the provision of goods that were commensurate or better quality. Those offering their products to lower income groups were equally sensitive to their needs, splitting packages from multi-pack offerings to single items, so that those in financially straitened circumstances could afford them.

The middle of the twentieth century witnessed major transformations of the country, with the embrace of Communism leading to significant reorientations in government policy towards the expansion of the industrial infrastructure, with concomitant less emphasis on food production and consumer goods. This had dramatic effects on the population, with those living in the cities experiencing many benefits in terms of consumption options that were simply not available to rural populations. The focus on heavy industry, in addition, meant that certain groups working in those industries being promoted by the state were paid better and had access to more salubrious working conditions.

Gao considers propaganda efforts to be synonymous with marketing and highlights how the Communist government was an active marketing force, selling its political ideology to the population by denouncing capitalist values (i.e. materialism). The post-1950 period did not see great advances in distribution. If anything the distribution system suffered as a result of nationalization policies, state planning and overall inefficiency in terms of new product development, supply chain management and consumer access to desired goods. Until 1978 and the reopening of the Chinese economy, then, the marketing system left a great deal to be desired and on the basis of Gao's interpretation of the expansion of access to consumer goods, better services and rising affluence, the global economy does seem to deliver – at least on the surface. As Gao concludes, the provision of and access to consumer goods is only a small part of a full life. Many facets of life cannot be satisfied through the mediation of the marketplace.

Previously, many scholars have argued that Germany has been an unusual context in which to explore marketing practice given that it has not been held in esteem, was not considered important or essential by corporate executives, and more generally a laggard behind the American uptake of the marketing concept, consumer orientation and related ideas. This representation is challenged by Ingo Köhler and Jan Logemann. To begin with, their focus is the nineteenth century and they articulate the reasons for the 'productivist bias' of German industry. In this case, marketing and consumption were extraneous to the real activity of production. As is usual given its public prominence, advertising was singled out for criticism and referenced as a blot on the natural landscape and cityscape respectively.

The productivist bias did not mark the whole of industry. As Fullerton (forthcoming) has elucidated with respect to the German book publishing trade, German producers, distributors and retailers were aware of the relevance of marketing. They were interested in demand stimulation and market creation. Producers and retailers sought to expand their markets. They did so by the provision of branded goods, credit and by offering mail-order services. Not all of these practices were welcomed. As mentioned above, the German environment was critical of marketing and encouraging people to consume beyond their financial resources did not pass without comment.

Between the two World Wars, Köhler and Logemann remark that German industry continued many of the practices already enumerated. There were, even so, a number of important changes to the structure of the German economy that modified the marketplace. The rise of cartels in many industries was one marked feature – as Pressey also documents in his chapter – and there was an interest in and pursuit of professionalization in marketing practice as indicated by the expansion of the advertising business, the attention given to market research, and the interest in psychology and its application to business.

Clearly, the 'election' of the Nazi government had wide ramifications for industry and marketing in particular. Its political ideology and symbolism were appropriated by advertising and branding professionals, much to the annoyance of the Party hierarchy who disliked the Führer's image plastered on pork products (Ellis *et al.*, 2011). Jewish members of the marketing and advertising communities found themselves marginalized by the problematic ideological values of the period. But, as is obvious from the well-known application of propaganda and public relations by the Nazi government, they were quick to use knowledge of marketing to attempt to control consumer behaviour, discouraging consumption to reflect wartime scarcity.

In the period after World War II there was growth in marketing, advertising and market research. Having said this, we should appreciate that there were differences between the policies undertaken in West Germany versus the Communist-controlled East. Köhler and Logemann devote attention to West Germany and contest the idea that what we see during the 1950s, 1960s and 1970s was a process of the Americanization of German marketing by virtue of the export of American models, theories, concepts and practices via advertising agencies and consultancy organizations. This is not to deny any American influence. This had already impacted on the industry prior to the cataclysmic conflict in the mid-century. Rather, Köhler and Logemann stress that there was an important 'indigenous tradition' that continued to influence the marketing and advertising activities of many firms. By the 1970s, for reasons informed by the changing international economic situation, increasing competition and an informed and sophisticated consumer, marketing processes became much more integrated with (international) customer satisfaction through the provision of high-quality products as the ultimate aim of many firms.

Chapter 21 studies the nature of marketing in India. Hari Sreekumar and Rohit Varman illuminate the extremely rich history of this nation beginning with the emergence of marketing in ancient and medieval India. At this point in its history, India was largely rural, with markets placed mainly in trading areas near the coast or important rivers. Being rural did not mean that market-based exchange was unsophisticated. Traders brought a range of items to the country, with itinerant merchants distributing the products far and wide. Within the towns, the marketing system was frequently well developed, with specific traders clustered in certain quarters. There were guilds which helped develop local, national and international trade because they undertook various functions of the middleman including risk management and financing. Sreekumar and Varman also acknowledge that merchants were able to raise their social profile by donating to religious orders, thereby securing a degree of legitimacy that was often lacking for this class.

The growth of markets, accompanied by the greater use of credit instruments and interpersonal networks, while highly useful as vehicles for provisioning, is frequently accompanied by the extension of dark-side activities as well: the less desirable practices of robbery, manipulation and violence. And although many people in India had access to relatively limited levels of income, conspicuous consumption was sometimes notable. Kings and traders demonstrated a willingness to spend freely, exchanging gifts with visitors, laying on fantastic feasts, furnishing their houses with luxurious fashions.

By the seventeenth century, India was undergoing its first exposure to colonialism. Sreekumar and Varman unpack the effects of colonial interventions on the marketplace, stressing the ongoing impact of Indian business people who possessed knowledge that the colonists simply did not have which left the latter open to manipulation. This said, the power dynamics in this case were extremely problematic in many respects. The East India Company comes in for severe and justifiable criticism given its willingness to take advantage of the marketplace in times of food shortages and crises.

Chronicling the developing marketing system, Sreekumar and Varman note the impact of colonialism in terms of fostering a market for advertising in the late eighteenth century. Moving forward rapidly, we can say that 1947 marked a turning point in Indian history, with the rejection of colonial rule. In this environment, marketing was not necessarily a state priority, they were more concerned with welfare and health indicators which were poor. The 1980s, however, witnessed a neoliberal turn in the economic policies of India, the promotion of the business community, the continued rise of the advertising profession, the greater dissemination of media vehicles like television, and steadily climbing levels of consumption. Sreekumar and Varman conclude on a cautious note that this acceptance of consumerism is not welcomed wholeheartedly in India given the dramatically unequal access to resources that persists.

Our next contribution is by Yumiko Toda who negotiates the channel structure of Japanese marketing. This account starts in the mid-nineteenth century and scrutinizes the position assumed by wholesalers in Japan as part of the government's interest in creating a strong position in export markets. We should register that the designation 'wholesaler' is complicated and Toda unpacks the various ways in which this term can be understood, as well as the diverse levels of specialism that define Japanese marketing channels.

What will strike the reader as very unusual is the extent to which the Japanese market was structured around the wholesaler – companies simply did not market directly to the consumer, even in business-to-business markets where this has traditionally been normal practice. Gradually, efforts were made to bypass the traditional channel structure, and this had concomitant effects on the use of brand names as well as the cultivation of brand images and symbolism intended to appeal to the ultimate customer. This was mainly a function of the promotion of marketing after World War II, when the American experience was studied by practitioners and scholars who travelled to the United States courtesy of funding made available via the American-led programme for economic reconstruction, the Marshall Plan. As a function of this exposure, the consumer received more attention from Japanese manufacturers, wholesalers and retailers.

This had major implications for the Japanese economy after the 1960s which underwent substantial levels of growth. The importation of Western consumer goods was popular, with clothing in high demand. Manufacturers were very important and often had substantial power in dictating retailing activities in terms of the products made available to providers. The exemplar here is Matsushita which controlled distribution, pricing (frequently) and formed long-term relationships with retailers. Over time, the power dynamic did shift towards the retailers, especially after 1990, who cultivated their own brand identities, own label products and reaffirmed their position through the control of customer data.

Chapter 23 excavates the history of marketing in Scandinavia, specifically dealing with the advertising community, marketing research providers, and retailing. Erik Madsen asserts that there has been very little research conducted in this area. He engages with the idea of Americanization and questions the impact of American practices upon those in Scandinavia. He also offers a cautious affirmative, stating that American ideas were welcomed in recognition of their utility.

Madsen points out the application of scientific management, the rise of advertising and underscores important contrasts to conventional practice in the United States. For example, in Denmark, window advertising received a substantial portion of advertising expenditure. The second industry he allocates attention to, market research, was slower to emerge. Madsen indicates that it was a post-1920s activity (see also Schwarzkopf, this volume) and suggests that it developed out of advertising practice. The final industry examined is the retail trade. He unpicks the main developments, the importance of department stores, the penetration of self-service and the appreciation of customers for this innovation.

The final chapter is an excellent study of Russian marketing practice. Alongside scholars like Marshall Goldman, Karen Fox has pioneered the study of marketing in the former Soviet Union. On face value this country seems far removed from a receptive environment for marketing or capitalist business practices. This would not be quite accurate. Various Soviet politicians have appreciated – grudgingly admittedly – the importance of the market, the skills and resources of business people, and used their knowledge and skills on occasion.

Fox's chapter is extremely wide-ranging, giving the reader a thorough exposure to the history of this country from the twelfth century through to 2015. As the reader will anticipate, marketing has often been very carefully controlled, with the state devoting its energies to rapidly developing heavy industry to the detriment of the consumer and their desire for satisfactory goods and services at reasonable prices. This has been compounded by the strict guidelines issued by the state regarding economic policy, guidance that heliographically directed the energies of those operating Russian factories, leading to an internal productivist focus, which was more concerned with meeting quantitative production demands, irrespective of whether the goods provided met the needs of the population. The latter, if they were lucky, had access to consumer goods via influential contacts, or were willing to wait in line for substantial periods, negotiating an often excessively bureaucratic retailing system, to receive the items they wanted.

Soviet political leaders did dedicate some reflection to the task of making marketing practices commensurate with their value system. On their reading, advertising was a means to help inform the consumer, not persuade. It was to guide the rational consumer, and rather usefully reaffirm Communist values through the promotion of state-sanctioned imagery, cultural products, non-materialistic consumption habits and anti-American beliefs (Tadajewski, 2009d). Fox provides a very close reading of all the above themes, engages with the relevant academic literature that was often based on first-hand knowledge of the Soviet marketing system, and charts the impact of various marketing institutions and practices within this political-economic context.

Conclusion

In this chapter we have introduced the contents of the collection. The material ranges across many industries, contexts and engages in substantive detail with marketing practices as they were performed in a variety of historical periods extending back to ancient times. This enables us to add flesh and colour to the extensive literature on the historical mobilization of marketing theory and concepts that have received the majority of attention from scholars within our discipline. We would emphasize that this is only the start of this project. Much more work needs to be done, especially with respect to the production of country-specific studies of marketing practice. The cases published here provide the interested scholar with a variety of ways in which these can be undertaken, how they can be used to contest the theoretical and historical assumptions present in the literature, thereby generating scholarship that is likely to pass the originality and contribution benchmarks employed by our most rigorous intellectual outlets. We look forward to reading it all.

References

Cochoy, F. (2016) *On the Origins of Self Service*, Routledge, London.

Davis, J.F. (2013) 'Beyond "Caste-Typing"? Caroline Robinson Jones, Advertising Pioneer and Trailblazer', *Journal of Historical Research in Marketing*, 5/3, 308–33.

Ellis, N., Fitchett, J., Higgins, M., Jack, G., Lim, M., Saren, M., and Tadajewski, M. (2011) *Marketing: A Critical Textbook,* Sage, London.

Ewen, S. (1976) *Captains of Consciousness: Advertising and the Social Roots of the Consumer Culture*, McGraw Hill, New York.

Fullerton, R.A. (1987) 'The poverty of ahistorical analysis: Present weakness and future cure in U.S. marketing thought', in F. Fuat, N. Dholakia and R. Bagozzi, R. (eds), *Philosophical and Radical Thought in Marketing*, Lexington Books, Lexington, CT, pp. 97–117.

Fullerton, R.A. (1988) 'How modern is modern marketing? Marketing's evolution and the myth of the "production era"', *Journal of Marketing*, 52 (Jan.), 108–25.

Fullerton, R.A. (1990) 'The art of marketing research: Selections from Paul F. Lazarsfeld's *Shoe Buying in Zurich* (1933)', *Journal of the Academy of Marketing Science*, 18/4, 319–27.

Fullerton, R.A. (forthcoming) *The Development of the German Book Markets, 1815–1890*, Routledge, New York.

Graham, L.D. (2013) 'Lillian Gilbreth's psychologically enriched scientific management of women consumers', *Journal of Historical Research in Marketing*, 5/3, 351–69.

Higgins, M., and Tadajewski, M. (2002) 'Anti-corporate protest as consumer spectacle', *Management Decision*, 40/4, 363–71.

Hollander, S.C., Rassuli, K.M., Jones, D.G.B., and Dix, L.F. (2005) 'Periodization in marketing history', *Journal of Macromarketing*, 25/1, 32–41.

Jones, D.G.B. (2012) *Pioneers in Marketing: A Collection of Biographical Essays*, Routledge, New York.

Jones, D.G.B. (2013) 'Pauline Arnold (1894–1974): Pioneer in Market Research', *Journal of Historical Research in Marketing*, 5/3, 291–307.

Jones, D.G.B., and Richardson, A.J. (2007) 'The myth of the marketing revolution', *Journal of Macromarketing*, 27/1, 15–24.

Jones, D.G.B., and Shaw, E.H. (2002) 'A history of marketing thought', in B. Weitz and R. Wensley (eds), *Handbook of Marketing*, Sage, London, pp. 39–65.

Jones, D.G.B., and Tadajewski, M. (2011) 'Percival White (1887–1970): Marketing engineer', *Marketing Theory*, 11/4, 455–78.

Keith, R.J. (1960) 'The marketing revolution', *Journal of Marketing*, 24/3, 35–8.

Ladik, D., Carrillat, F., and Tadajewski, M. (2015) 'Belk's (1988) *Possessions and the Extended Self* revisited', *Journal of Historical Research in Marketing*, 7/2, 184–207.

Leach, W.R. (1994) *Land of Desire: Merchants, Power and the Rise of a New American Culture*, Vintage, New York.

Levy, S.J. (2003) 'Roots of marketing and consumer research at the University of Chicago', *Consumption Markets and Culture*, 6/2, 99–110.

Levy, S.J. (2012) 'Marketing management and marketing research', *Journal of Marketing Management*, 28/1–2, 8–13.

Nevett, T. (1981) 'The Scapa Society: The first organized reaction against advertising', *Media, Culture and Society*, 3/2, 179–87.

Parsons, E. (2013) 'Pioneering consumer economist: Elizabeth Ellis Hoyt (1893–1890)', *Journal of Historical Research in Marketing*, 5/3, 334–50.

Scanlon, J. (2013) '"A dozen ideas to the minute": Advertising women, advertising to women', *Journal of Historical Research in Marketing*, 5/3, 273–90.

Shaw, E.H., and Jones, D.G.B. (2005) 'A history of schools of marketing thought', *Marketing Theory*, 5/3, 239–81.

Sinclair, U. (1906) *The Jungle*, William Heinemann, London.

Smith, W. (1956) 'Product differentiation and market segmentation as alternative marketing strategies', *Journal of Marketing*, 21/1, 3–8.

Strasser, S. (1989) *Satisfaction Guaranteed: The Making of the American Mass Market*, Pantheon, New York.

Tadajewski, M. (2006) 'Remembering motivation research: Toward an alternative genealogy of interpretive consumer research', *Marketing Theory*, 6/4, 429–66.

Tadajewski, M. (2008) 'Relationship marketing at Wanamaker's in the nineteenth and early twentieth centuries', *Journal of Macromarketing*, 28/2, 169–82.

Tadajewski, M. (2009a) 'Eventalizing the marketing concept', *Journal of Marketing Management*, 25/1–2, 191–217.

Tadajewski, M. (2009b) 'The foundations of relationship marketing: Reciprocity and trade relations', *Marketing Theory*, 9/1, 9–38.

Tadajewski, M. (2009c) 'Competition, cooperation and open price associations: Relationship marketing and Arthur Jerome Eddy (1859–1920)', *Journal of Historical Research in Marketing*, 1/1, 122–43.

Tadajewski, M. (2009d) 'Quaker travels, fellow traveler? Wroe Alderson's visit to Russia during the Cold War', *Journal of Macromarketing*, 29/3, 303–24.

Tadajewski, M. (2010) 'Reading "the marketing revolution" through the prism of the FBI', *Journal of Marketing Management*, 26/1–2, 90–107.

Tadajewski, M. (2011) 'Correspondence sales education in the early twentieth century: The case of the Sheldon School (1902–39)', *Business History*, 53/7, 1130–51.

Tadajewski, M. (2012) 'Character analysis and racism in marketing theory and practice', *Marketing Theory*, 12/4, 485–508.

Tadajewski, M. (2013a) 'Helen Woodward and Hazel Kyrk: Economic radicalism, consumption symbolism and female contributions to marketing theory and practice', *Journal of Historical Research in Marketing*, 5/3, 485–412.

Tadajewski, M. (2013b) 'What is critical marketing studies? Reading macro, social and critical marketing studies', in R. Varey and M. Pirson (eds), *Humanistic Marketing*, Palgrave Macmillan, Basingstoke, pp. 39–52.

Tadajewski, M. (2015a) 'The complete english tradesman: Business relations, trust, and honesty or let's rethink the history of relationship marketing', *Journal of Historical Research in Marketing*, 7/3, 407–22.

Tadajewski, M. (2015b) 'Charting relationship marketing practice: It really didn't emerge in the 1970s', *Journal of Historical Research in Marketing*, 7/4, 486–508.

Tadajewski, M., and Jones, D.G.B. (eds) (2008) *The History of Marketing Thought*, 3 vols, Sage Publications, London.

Tadajewski, M., and Jones, D.G.B. (2014) 'Historical research in marketing theory and practice: A review essay', *Journal of Marketing Management*, 30/11–12, 1239–91.

Tadajewski, M., and Maclaran, P. (2013) 'Remembering female contributors to marketing theory, thought and practice', *Journal of Historical Research in Marketing*, 5/3, 260–72.

Tadajewski, M., and Saren, M. (2009) 'Rethinking the emergence of relationship marketing', *Journal of Macromarketing*, 29/2, 93–206.

Vargo, S.L., and Lusch, R.F. (2004) 'Evolving to a new dominant logic for marketing', *Journal of Marketing*, 68 (Jan.), 1–17.

Vargo, S.L., and Morgan, F.W. (2005) 'Services in society and academic thought: An historical analysis', *Journal of Macromarketing*, 25/1, 42–53.

Veblen, T. (1899/1912) *The Theory of the Leisure Class*, Macmillan, New York.

Ward, D. (2009) 'Capitalism, early market research, and the creation of the American consumer', *Journal of Historical Research in Marketing*, 1/2, 200–23.

Ward, D. (2010) *A New Brand of Business: Charles Coolidge Parlin, Curtis Publishing Company and the Origins of Market Research, 1911–1930*, Temple University Press, Philadelphia, PA.

Zuckerman, M.E. (2013) 'Martha van Rensselaer and the Delineator's Homemaking Department', *Journal of Historical Research in Marketing*, 5/3, 370–84.

Zuckerman, M.E., and Carsky, M.L. (1990) 'Contribution of women to US marketing thought: The consumers' perspective', *Journal of the Academy of Marketing Science*, 18/4, 313–18.

2

Ancient and medieval marketing

Eric H. Shaw

Introduction

The genesis of trade is long lost in the mists of time, but the origins of modern marketing may be found in antiquity. The study of ancient and medieval marketing is important because the most critical developments in trading occurred during these times. First the invention of trading by barter, goods exchanged for goods, provided a competitive advantage that impacted the evolution of early modern man. Later the transformation from bartering to marketing, with goods exchanged for money, along with innovative developments in sedentary retailing, promotional branding, competitive pricing and commercial advertising impacts civilization to the present day. Moreover, the same ancient and medieval criticisms of deceptive trade practices, high prices, adulterated foods, false weights, defective goods as well as both excessive and intrusive advertising, along with the resulting calls for better laws to regulate marketing practices, are still with us today.

Compared to the earliest silent trade and later transitory or occasional markets based on barter exchange, the greatest innovation in the long history of trading, from the prehistoric Stone Age to modern times, was undoubtedly the concurrent development of (1) central markets (2) sedentary retailers and most importantly (3) coined money. These three ingredients coalesced to produce the earliest marketing systems composed of markets, marketers and marketing. First, central markets matched a seller's supply with a buyer's demand based on a competitively bargained price. Second, sedentary retailing stands, stalls and shops allowed customers to buy in small quantities, reduced travel, search and negotiation costs, and provided ready outlets for suppliers to generate bulk transactions. Third, the invention of coined money served as a convenient medium of exchange, means of payment, unit of account and store of value (Shaw 1995, 12). Relative to bartering, requiring trading partners with a double concurrence of wants, central markets with sedentary retailers using coined money combined to routinize transactions with such incredible efficiency it produced a revolution in retail marketing that rapidly spread across the civilized world.

This new and improved trading practice – now called marketing – despite producing massive gains in economic efficiency was largely taken for granted (Mulvihill, 1983) and seldom commented upon other than by a few early Greek and Roman philosophers (Shaw, 1995), except for criticism of its practitioners and practices throughout the millennia (Cassels, 1936; Kelley, 1956; Steiner, 1976), until the turn of the twentieth century when marketing was first studied as an academic discipline (Bartels, 1962). The purpose of this chapter is to explore what trade customs and rituals existed before the retailing revolution, and what, why, how, where, when and by whom marketing practices developed in ancient and medieval times to ultimately produce the marketing system that evolved into the present. The remainder of this chapter explores ancient trading practices: from bartering, with a brief note on the impact of money, through a surprisingly brief transition period, to the retail revolution in marketing practice. Then three developments during the medieval period are examined: travelling marketplaces called trade fairs, new media of exchange and of payment involving credit instruments and an anti- or non-marketing practice followed by medieval guilds. Finally, the conclusions that can be drawn from this study of ancient and medieval marketing are stated.

Ancient trading practices

What might be regarded as ancient history in the Western world, say seventh century BCE, roughly the time money and retail markets were evolving around the Mediterranean Sea, particularly in Lydia and surrounding Greek colonies, would be considered less ancient in the East, where the early civilizations of Egypt, Mesopotamia, China and India go back some 2,000 years earlier to developments in writing. Although some authors use the term 'archaic' or 'classical' to describe this time period, for convenience the term 'ancient' will be used here to describe the period roughly from the origins of the alphabet and the earliest written accounts of recorded trade, c.2700 BCE to the Fall of Rome in 476 CE, which also marks the beginning of the medieval period, also known as the Middle Ages. Events prior to the ancient period are described here as prehistoric.

Bartering: a primitive form of trading

It is so advantageous to trade things in which you have a surplus for things in which you are deficient that necessity required the invention of such a process. And it happened very early in human development. The main impediment to trade in prehistoric, as well as ancient, times was that the strong usually plundered the weak and without knowing the other party's intentions it was never clear to primitive people whether a friendly trade might turn into a deadly raid.

The story of trading begins in prehistory, long before the alphabet. Spectrographic evidence of an obsidian trade, an easily flaked volcanic rock used to make sharp Neolithic (New Stone Age, c.8000 BCE) tools, such as sharpened hand axes, have been found in many places around Mediterranean Sea distant from their volcanic sources (Dixon et al., 1968). Perhaps the only substantiated type of retail marketing practice that evolved from Neolithic times to the present was the itinerant tradesman (also known as peddler, packman or chapman). These forerunners of travelling salesmen roamed from village to village bartering polished stone axes in exchange for salt or other goods (Dixon, 1975).

Archeological evidence of rudimentary bartering, such as the silent trade between nomadic extended families and tribes of up to 50 people, probably stretches back into the Upper Palaeolithic period roughly 40,000 years ago, long before the dawn of civilization (Weiner, 1973). Such evidence of early trading is important because it represents a competitive advantage in the search for food and resources. It is argued (e.g. Harari, 2015; Horan *et al.*, 2005, 1) that specialization and trade led to the 'rise of early modern humans [formerly called Cro Magnon, preferred term *Homo Sapiens*] and the fall of Neanderthals' (*Homo Neanderthalensis*) for whom the lack of a 'division of labor and subsequent trading' placed them at a severe competitive disadvantage and ultimately extinction. According to Horan *et al.* (2005)

> Evidence also suggests travelling bands of early modern humans interacted with each other and that inter-group trading emerged. Early modern humans, the Aurignations and especially the Gravettians, imported many raw materials over long ranges, and their innovations were widely dispersed (Tattersall and Schwartz, 2000; Blades, 2001; Kuhn and Stiner, 1998; Gamble, 1999). Indeed, 'widespread evidence of long-distance trade in stone, ivory, and fossil and marine shells attest to the social and cognitive complexity of Aurignations to a much greater extent than in either the Mousterian [Neanderthals] or the Chatelperronian [Neanderthals]' (Tattersall *et al.* 1988, 64, brackets in original). Such exchanges of goods and ideas helped early humans to develop 'supergroup social mechanisms' (Sahlins, 1959). The long-range interchange between different groups both kept 'culture going' (Shreeve, 1995; Gee, 1996) and generated new 'cultural explosions' (Pfeiffer, 1982; Mithen, 1998). These intra- and inter-group interactions could enable early humans to 'increase their non-subsistence activities such as art, while simultaneously out-competing Neanderthals on their joint hunting grounds'.
>
> *(Horan* et al.*, 2005, 6)*

The significance of specialization and trade are not just a Stone Age advantage, as will be repeatedly witnessed in the historical record of ancient and medieval times.

The silent trade (also depot trade, dumb trade or trade-at-a-distance) probably represents the earliest form of trading between groups. The intent is to avoid direct contact, and possible plunder or worse, by exchanging goods without direct face-to-face communication between the traders. A sampling from numerous historical accounts of the silent trade, at approximately 900–1,000 year intervals, from ancient to early and late medieval times, show a consistent pattern of trading relationships between different peoples without a shared language or at different stages of technological development. Herodotus (c.450 BCE; known as the 'Father of History') provides the earliest written description of the 'Silent Trade' in his book *The Histories*. A retired Greek merchant turned historian, Herodotus, wrote about the Persian-Greek wars and digressed frequently to describe the strange customs he found in his travels across North Africa, Egypt and Persia. One foreign custom he described was the silent trade in knives and cloth for gold in northwest Africa.

> The Carthaginians tell us that they trade with a race of men who live in a part of Libya beyond the Pillars of Hercules [the straits between Gibraltar and Ceuta that connected the Mediterranean Sea to the Atlantic Ocean on the northwest coast of Africa, around Senegal]. On reaching this country they unload their goods [typically textiles and metal products such as knives and hatchets], arrange them tidily along the beach, and then, returning to their boats raise a smoke. Seeing the smoke, the natives come down to the beach, place on the ground a certain quantity of gold in exchange for the goods, and go off again to a distance. The Carthaginians then come ashore and take a look at the gold; and if they think it represents a fair price for the wares, they collect it and go away; if, on the other hand, it seems too little, they go back aboard and wait, and the natives come

and add to the gold until they are satisfied. There is perfect honesty of both sides; the Carthaginians never touch the gold until it equals in value what they have offered for sale, and the natives never touch the goods until the gold has been taken away.

(Herodotus, Histories, *197)*

One may question the 'perfect honesty of both sides'. However, if the trust between parties was broken then this mutually beneficial trading relationship would come to an abrupt halt. Thus, maintaining trust to ensure stable relationships was fundamental to trade since its origin, as evidenced in such historical accounts.

About a thousand years later, early in the medieval age, Cosmas the Monk (c.545 CE), also known as Cosmas Indicopleustes (i.e. 'Cosmas, the Indian navigator'), described the 'Silent Trade' in his book *Topographia Christiana.* Cosmas was a retired Alexandrian merchant turned monk, best known for his 'Flat Earth Theory', who travelled extensively to India, Sri Lanka and Ethiopia, and described the barter of beef, salt and iron for gold near the Ethiopian headwaters of the Blue Nile River in East Africa.

Now, year by year the King of the Axumites sends men of his own to Sas to acquire gold. And many others bound on the same speculation accompany them on this expedition, so there shall be more than five hundred in the party. They take with them beeves [sic], and pieces of salt and iron. And when they get near the country they make a halt at a certain place, and take a quantity of thorns with which they make a great hedge, within which they establish themselves, and there they slaughter the oxen and cut them up, and put the meat, and the pieces of salt, and the iron on the top of the hedge. So the natives then approach with gold nuggets, like peas, which they call Tancharan, and each of them deposits one or two of these upon the joints of meat or the salt or the iron as he pleases, and then stands aloof. Then the owner of the beef etc. comes up, and if he is satisfied he takes the gold, whilst the other party comes and removes the flesh, or pieces of salt or iron. But if the trader is not satisfied he leave the gold where it is, and when the native comes up and see that his gold has not been taken, he either adds to the quantity or takes up his gold and goes away.

(Cosmas the Monk, Topographia Christiana, *218–19)*

It bears repeating, maintaining stable relationships is a cornerstone of trade. Nine hundred years later, at the end of the medieval age, Alvise Da Cadamosto (1455), chief navigator in the service of Prince Henry 'the Navigator' of Portugal, in his *Diary* described the silent trade in salt for gold between Moroccan traders and the natives of Mali and Timbuktu.

Azanaghi merchants, carry salt from the Moroccan border to Timbuktu and Mali [in Guinea]. Having reached these waters [Gambia River] with the salt, they proceed in this fashion: all those who have salt pile it in rows, each marking his own. Having made these piles, the whole caravan retires half a day's journey. Then there comes another race of blacks who do not wish to be seen or to speak. They arrive in large boats, from which it appears that they come from islands, and disembark. Seeing the salt, they place a large quantity of gold opposite each pile, and then turn back, leaving salt and gold. When they have gone, the Negros who own the salt return: if they are satisfied with the quantity of gold, they leave the salt and retire with the gold. Then the blacks of the gold return, and remove those piles which are without gold. By the other piles of salt they place more gold, if it pleases them, or else they leave the salt.

In this way, by long and ancient custom, they carry on their trade without seeing or speaking with each other.

(Crone, 1937/2010)

Because the silent trade continues to serve its ancient purpose, of maintaining ongoing trading relationships without direct contact between stronger and weaker peoples, this form of barter still exists in primitive cultures and is intermittently found even in more modern times. For example, in the 1970s, the Tasaday tribe, of about 25 people, was 'discovered' in the Philippine rainforest of Mindanao. They were cave-dwelling food gatherers who used only crude stone and wood tools. Although living a virtually isolated existence, anthropological research confirmed that there had been occasional contact and probably some form of silent trade during their history (Nance, 1975).

In China, the earliest extant recorded documents relating to business date from the twenty-eighth century BCE to describe early specialization and barter. There was a clear division of labour; Lee (1983, 156) cites Shang Yang recorded around 2737 BCE:

people near the sea would do fishing, people near the mountain would plant trees, and people near land would do farming. … People could specialize in what they do better, and use the surplus of their produce to exchange for goods they did not produce. [It is also noted that farmers and villagers set up meeting places in the country for trade.] When it is noon time [on a certain day] people from everywhere would bring various kinds of goods … for [barter] exchange. All would get what they want and return home.

(Lee, 1983, 156)

But bartering is economically inefficient. The problem is the double coincidence of wants. Both parties must have the exact products or services the other wants and in equivalent qualities and/or quantities. Even a bartering system, such as a meeting place, with opportunities for multiple barter exchanges that overcomes the double coincidence of wants issue is still inefficient. The opportunity cost for spending a day travelling to and from the meeting place is a day lost from farming, fishing or making crafts, along with the cumbersome process of trading equivalent values of goods absent a convenient medium of exchange. With the growth of cities the resulting increase in specialization must have made trading by barter ever more cumbersome and a more efficient exchange mechanism necessary. Again, because invention is the child of necessity, inefficient bartering was about to be displaced by more efficient marketing. This does not suggest that barter could ever disappear; bartering will always coexist alongside or in place of marketing, as observing small children playing with toys will confirm. The point is that trading goods for goods is far less efficient compared to trading goods for money.

The impact of money

A critical prerequisite for marketing is money that serves as a medium of exchange. Money had long been available as a unit of account providing a means to equilibrate different products and services. For example, if oil serves as a unit of account, then eight ounces of oil might equal two bushels of wheat, three pairs of sandals, two haircuts, four rabbits, half an ox, or three glasses of wine; and therefore, one bushel of wheat would be equal in value to one haircut or two rabbits. There is a problem with equivalencies however; wine comes in different qualities, rabbits may be large or small, fresh or spoiling, and trying to divide up the ox expresses some of the difficulties in dealing with equivalences.

An early example of money as a medium of exchange and means of payment occurs in the book of Genesis.

> And there passed by a caravan of Midianite merchantmen came from Gilead [a mountainous region east of the Jordon River], carrying laudanum, balm and myrrh on their way to carry it down to Egypt. And they [his brothers] drew and lifted up Joseph out of the pit, and sold Joseph to the Ishmaelites [a neighbouring tribe travelling with the Midianites] for twenty shekels [about 10 ounces or 300 grams] of silver.
>
> *(Genesis 38: 27)*

The shekel was originally a unit of weight used for payment in silver. Standard coins gradually replaced these standard units of weight. But standardizing coinage was also a laborious process. Each city had its own weights, measures and coinage, and currency was not always accepted from one city to the next. There were a few ancient exceptions, particularly the 'Owls' of Athens; the silver coin stamped with the owl of Athena, which was widely accepted all along the Mediterranean and inland because Athens astutely avoided debasing its currency by reducing the silver content – as almost every other commercial city of the time had done. Thus, the Athenian 'owls' and later Roman 'denarius' were widely accepted and generally recognized as a reserve currency around the Mediterranean in ancient times, much like the Provins 'denier' across medieval Europe, and the United States 'dollar' throughout the modern world.

Simply, bartering involves product or service x exchanged for product or service y, which requires a double coincidence of product or service desires. Marketing involves product or service x exchanged for $M = money$, which serves as a middleman that, in turn, can be exchanged for any other product or service $a, b, c \ldots z$; or held for a future date. Although currency may lose value through debasement or inflation, the process is generally much slower than goods spoiling or deteriorating. Money, as Hume (1752) points out, 'is not the wheels of trade, it is the oil which renders the motion of the wheels more smooth and easy' (cited in Shaw 1995, 12–13). But this is a massive understatement; with the invention and diffusion of coined money the transition from bartering to marketing exchange in the ancient world occurs with amazing rapidity as the nature of trading undergoes a revolution of biblical proportions.

Transition from bartering to marketing

The transition from carrying out trade by bartering to a marketing system consisting of central markets, sedentary retailing and convenient coined money may be framed in bold relief by two historical accounts of trading in Jerusalem at different points in time during the Old and New Testaments of the Bible. A note on dating, the Christian calendar starts at year 1, the inaccurately estimated year of the conception or birth of Christ, BCE (Before Common Era), Jesus died in roughly 30 CE (Common Era).

Grossman (1983) described business practices in the Old Testament of the Bible. One section is titled: 'The Market: Jerusalem', but contrary to the title, Grossman does not discuss the market or marketing in the city because there was no marketplace, and absent retailers and a convenient medium of exchange no marketers or marketing. As with almost all ancient civilizations, prior to central markets, retailers and coined money, most of the citizens' daily needs were supplied by the King as wage payments in kind for required public services, such as constructing buildings and roads or military service (an exchange mechanism called redistribution), with bartering primarily for non-essential items. What is discussed in this section is the foreign trade of Jerusalem, which also was mainly bartering.

Foreign trade was primarily King's or treaty trade. Although King Solomon was described as 'one of history's greatest marketers' (Grossman 1983, 136), this form of trade is one king's commission merchant dealing with another king's commission merchant rather than independent merchants engaging in trade entirely on their own account.

> Solomon sent his agent to Hiram the King of Tyre … in building his great Temple, Solomon traded 20,000 kors of crushed wheat, 20,000 kors of barley, 20,000 baths of wine, and 20,000 baths of oil … in exchange for cedar, cypress, and algum timber from Lebanon (2 Chronicles 2: 3–10).
>
> *(Grossman, 1983, 136)*

Although some merchants did engage in trading on their own account it involved slaves and luxury goods for the wealthy, and was not a provisioning mechanism for the citizenry. During this time, the domestic trade in Jerusalem and other large cities of the world is conducted by bartering not by marketing. But this is soon to change.

In contrast to the barter based economy described in the Old Testament, c.970 BCE, Mulvihill (1983) observes that in the New Testament, some 1,000 years later, c.30 CE markets, marketing and marketers have grown so ubiquitous in Jerusalem they are now taken for granted.

> The early routinization of markets for [local or even foreign goods] … did not impress those supplied. Things appear in the market and are exchanged for other goods or money with relatively little fanfare so that no one extols the marketers, but only mentions them when the system fails … or when the marketers appear to be doing improper acts.
>
> *(Mulvihill, 1983, 141)*

By this time (c.30 CE), retailers and money markets have spread from Greece into every nook and cranny of the civilized world. Compared to the lack of a marketplace in the Old Testament, the market provides the setting for many stories and parables of Jesus in the New Testament. One of the most well-known stories involves market transactions, marketing and marketers. As Mulvihill (1983, 142) cites scripture: 'And Jesus entered the temple [of King Solomon] and drove out all those who sold and bought, and he overturned the tables of the money changers and the seats of those [retailers] who sold pigeons [for sacrifice] (Matthew 21: 12–13).'

Here we witness the rapidly moving transition from barter-based trade to market-based trade. These two historical accounts, occurring in the same place but at different times, point toward the genesis of the great transformation from bartering by traders to marketing systems consisting of sedentary retailers selling in central markets to buyers using convenient-to-carry money between the seventh and fifth centuries BCE (Shaw, 1983), discussed next.

Marketing: an advanced form of trading

The historical roots of marketing are identified by Herodotus who writes: 'The Lydians [seventh century] were the first people we know of to use a gold and silver coinage and to introduce the retail trade' (Shaw, 1995, 12). Even in ancient times, the great thinkers of the day discerned that coined money distinguished bartering from marketing based on differing motivations for trading. Aristotle (c.384–322 BCE) explains: 'When the use of coin had once been discovered, out of the barter of necessary articles arose the art of money-making, namely the retail trade ... as men learned ... by what exchanges the greatest profit might be made' (cited in Shaw, 1995, 12).

Because barter did not offer the store of value provided by money, barter involved mostly the exchange of necessities between parties. Money represents not just a medium of exchange and means of payment but also a unit of account and store of value (Shaw, 1995). 'Whatever a person saves from his revenue he adds to his capital', as Adam Smith (1776/1937, 321) observed, and capital accumulation for individuals and nations furnishes the 'path to wealth'. Societies with a small population built on altruism in a bartering system evolve into a social system with a large population built on the 'invisible hand' of self-interest in a marketing system.

As populations grew, cities became larger and specialization in the crafts increased. For example undifferentiated smiths started specializing as silversmiths, coppersmiths or blacksmiths, so too specialization in exchange increased. And increasing specialization produced increasing efficiency, according to Xenophon in the fourth century BCE.

> In a small town the same man makes couches, doors, ploughs and tables, and often he even builds houses, and still he is thankful if only he can find enough work to support himself. And it is impossible for a man of many trades to do all of them well. In large cities, however, because many people make demands on each trade, one trade alone is enough to support a man, and often less than one; for instance one man makes shoes for men, another for women, there are places even where one man earns a living just by mending shoes, another by cutting them out, another just by sewing the uppers together, while there is another who performs none of these operations but assembles the parts. Of course, he who pursues a very specialized task will do it best.
>
> *(Cited in Finley 1981, 58)*

According to Smith (1776/1937, 13), this division of labour arises from the propensity in human nature 'to truck, barter and exchange'. But even if not a human propensity, a division of labour arises because it is more efficient than self-producing all of one's desires. As the division of labour increases, so does the necessity for exchange specialists because it too is more efficient. Undifferentiated traders bartering started specializing into various types of retailers selling and buying. In the Athenian market, the Agora, during the fifth century, there were dozens of different types of very small retailers, *metaboleus,* in contrast to the regular retailers, the *kapelos,* of whom there were well over a hundred, such as different retail specialists in bread, knives, sandals, and different retailing specialties for new and old clothes, a half-dozen types of fresh fish and an equal number for salted fish (Heichelheim, 1968).

Plato explained the logic of marketing in terms of opportunity costs.

> It is inefficient if a farmer or artisan brings some of his produce to a market at a time when no one is there who wants to exchange with him. Is he to sit here idle, when he might be at work? ... No! There are people who have seen an opening here for their services ... retailers ... they have to stay where they are in the marketplace and take goods for money from those who want to sell, and money for goods from those who want to buy.
>
> *(Cited in Shaw 1983, 147)*

The most cosmopolitan market of its time in the ancient world, and one of the earliest, was the Agora in Athens from the sixth century BCE. According to all accounts (e.g. Glotz, 1926) the Agora was a crowded, bustling and noisy place.

> All who have something to sell, slaves with cloth they have just made, craftsmen from the Cerameicos, Melite or Scambonidae, peasants who left their village before daybreak, Megarians driving their pigs, fishermen from Lake Copais, pass in every direction. Through alleys planted with trees they reach the places assigned to different goods, separated by movable barriers. One after another, at the hours fixed by the regulations, the different markets open; there are markets for vegetables, fruit, cheese, fish, meat and sausages, poultry and game, wine, wood, pottery, ironmongery, and old articles. There is even a corner for books. Every merchant has his place, which he reserves by paying a fee; in the shade of an awning or an umbrella he sets out his goods on trestles, near his cart and his resting beasts. Shoppers walk about; traders call to them, porters and messengers offer their services.
>
> *(Glotz, 1926, 270)*

There were products of every description, meat, fish, fowl, wheat, bread, cakes, vegetables, fruits, wine, oil, flowers, textiles, shoes, slaves, crafts and money lenders. Price was negotiated between retailers and customers, with sellers eager to undercut the competition. Peddlers walked among the shops, and some of the earliest advertisements were market vendors in Athens crying their wares in the Agora. Crying (a cross between talking and singing) was an early form of advertising; and a forerunner of the town criers of medieval times. One early written advertisement, which was undoubtedly cried in the marketplace, was found on the preserved walls of Pompey in 79 CE.

> For eyes that are shining, for cheeks like the dawn,
> for beauty that lasts until girlhood is gone.
> For prices in reason the woman who knows,
> will buy her cosmetics at Aescalyptos.
>
> *(Maiuri, 1957, 86)*

The Athenian Agora of 2,500 years ago probably resembled the hustle and bustle of an American, European or Asian flea market of today.

Also noting the emergence of money-based trade in Greece during this period, Nevett and Nevett (1987, 1) argue that 'there is sufficient evidence, particularly from archeology, to indicate that traders were indeed involved in marketing practices'. They also state some of the conditions leading to the shift in trade from bartering to marketing, 'stimulated by the growth in population, the rise of the polis (city), the setting up of colonies and the emergence of coinage in the sixth and seventh centuries [BCE]'. Establishing colonies all along the Mediterranean was important because they not only provided outlets for exporting surplus Athenian merchandise (and excess population) but also provided transshipping points to the European, Asian and African interiors (Durant, 1939).

This transition from bartering to marketing is also demonstrated in Dixon's work. Starting with Homeric times (c.800–700 BCE) times, Dixon (1995, 74) writes: 'The Odyssey mentions Phoenician merchants who exchanged trinkets for local products but this trade took the form of barter and values were expressed in numbers of oxen.' But over the next two centuries: 'As trade expanded, barter began to be replaced by a money economy'; and

31

Dixon (1995, 75) comments that it was 'not until the end of the fifth century that silver and bronze coins became widely available to serve as the small change needed for retail trade'. This coinage system was described by Durant (1939, 274): 'The smallest Athenian coins are of copper; eight of these make an obol – a coin of ... bronze ... Six obols [a handful] make a [silver] drachma'; four drachmas equalled a tetradrachma, and so on. The Athenian owl was a 4 drachma coin.

A vivid description of the Agora was provided by Dixon (1995, 79): 'It was a large open space, about 200 meters east and west and about 250 meters north and south.' In the marketplace, 'Sellers were grouped by product category, such as fish, meat perfume, flour, incense, cheese, honey, wine, oil, and slaves' (p. 240). Around the periphery, the Agora was crowded with craft shops. Dixon (1995, 79) cites Lysias (a fourth-century orator) about the importance of retail location: 'For each of you is in the habit of paying a call at a perfumer's, a barber's, a cobbler's shop, and so forth; in most cases it is to the tradesmen who have their establishments nearest the Agora.' The closer the shop was to the market, the better the traffic flow.

The Agora was open all day 'from early in the morning' (Dixon, 1995, 81 citing the playwright Aristophanes, 409 BCE), until it 'closed in the evening' Prices were supposed to be fixed but haggling over prices was more common as shown in this description by Athenaeus in the second century BCE.

> If you ask, 'How much are you offering for these two mullets;'
> [Seller] replies, 'ten obols.'
> [Buyer] 'Too steep! Will you take eight?'
> [Seller] 'Yes, if you buy the one next to it.'
> [Buyer] 'My good man, take my offer and stop joking.'
> [Seller] 'At that price? Run along!'
>
> *(Athenaeus 6.24)*

The Agora was mostly for men socializing and servants who did the household shopping; respectable women seldom ventured into the market to buy on their own account (Dixon, 1995, 82). Several dialogues in Plato have Socrates and his students strolling through the market and asking sellers or buyers various philosophical questions about living a good life. For example, the Greek biographer Diogenes Laertius (third century CE) reports how Socrates revealed Xenophon knew more about the market than his virtue.

> They say that Socrates met him in a narrow lane, and put his stick across it and prevented Xenophon from passing by, asking him where all kinds of necessary things were sold. And when Xenophon had answered Socrates, he asked him again where men were made good and virtuous. And as Xenophon did not know, Socrates said, 'Follow me, then, and learn.' And from this time forth, Xenophon became a follower of Socrates.
>
> *(Diogenes Laertius 2.1)*

Money markets created increasing returns to scale. As marketing increases, its growth becomes self-reinforcing. 'Transactions become more commonplace and frequent, causing a chain reaction ... additional division of labor and greater economies of scale, more stable networks of trading relationships, greater marketing efficiencies and lower costs ... luxuries evolve into necessities, leading to a further increase of trade ... in a cycle that self-generates' (Shaw, 1995, 13). As with most cultural diffusion of innovation, early market innovations, particularly marketplaces for selling and buying along with sedentary retailers using small coinage as a medium of exchange, rapidly spread to other Greek city-states. For example, in Delos, a small island in the Aegean Sea, third century BCE,

> The streets are lined with shops, most of them quite small; on their fronts are the signs and symbols which advertise their wares; inside, the walls are full of niches. From the objects found on the spot we identify pottery merchants, ironmongers, sellers of household articles, the ivory-turner, and the sculptor. Near the harbor the shops are grouped according to their special line. ... The nearer we come to the markets the more shops and little windowless workshops there are. Here is a meeting-place of streets – the Small Market. On all sides we see the bakers' shops. The marble tables with the water channels along them are the butchers' and fishmongers' stalls. Further on is the square of the Great Market; there is a large altar in the middle, and the four sides are lined with spacious arcades, with rows of shops inside.
>
> *(Glotz, 1926, 262–3)*

After starting and flourishing around the Mediterranean Sea, markets, marketing and marketers swiftly spread along ancient trade routes into India and China, as well as the rest of the civilized world.

In a case study of India, from the sixth to third centuries BCE, Darian (1985, 16) described the transformation from 'the slowly changing, self-sufficient rural economy ... to a dynamic expanding market economy relying heavily on [urban retail] trade'. This transformation is attributed to technology, particularly the 'widespread adoption of iron tools in agriculture' (p. 15), and 'the resulting gains in productivity generated an economic surplus which could support a larger non-agricultural workforce'. The division of labour led to increased market exchange, which in turn resulted in 'a new economic infrastructure ... which included a merchant class, roads, distribution centers, and a fluid medium of exchange. These developments greatly expanded the level of marketing activity and gave rise to a wealthy merchant class' (p. 15).

Similarly, Kaufman (1987) describes the impact of early marketing on social change in China during the Han Dynasty (206 BCE–220 CE), the period when China transitioned from feudalism into a market-based economy. Just prior to the Han, the Ch'in Dynasty from which the name China is derived, conquered the warring feudal states, and was the first dynasty to unify and consolidate China into an empire. The Ch'in instituted a central government with standardized writing, laws, currency, weights and measures, and was perhaps best known for initiating and building most of the Great Wall.

Several developments led to the growth of a marketing system in China. First, according to Kaufman (1987, 58), '[was the] abolition of the feudal land system and the introduction of private ownership of land adopted in the fourth century B.C.' This in turn 'affected the merchant's place in society, as tradesmen took over some government positions' (because wholesale merchants were smart, mobile, wealthy and influential) (Kaufman, 1987, 58). During this transition, Kaufman notes, there were considerable differences in the treatment of merchants (which included both large-scale travelling wholesalers and small local shopkeepers) from the 'Former' Han period (206 BCE–8 CE), when they were held in high esteem, after the brief interregnum under the Wang Mang Dynasty (9–23 CE), to the 'Later' Han Dynasty (24–220), when they were held in disrepute.

The Chinese commonly believed that traditional 'agrarian occupations were ... of greater importance than trade, but the distribution of material comforts [i.e. wealth] reflected just the opposite' (Kaufman, 1987, 58). Further, wholesalers and retailers were accused of unsavoury marketing practices, Kaufman (1987, 58, citing Swann, parentheses in original) wrote: 'As to the travelling and resident merchants, the big ones hoard goods and get one hundred percent profit, while the small ones … sit in a row (at the market) and do retailing … always selling their goods at double [their value].' To restore 'society's proper order' the government imposed sumptuary laws, 'tradespeople were not to wear silk or ride in carriages' (p. 58) and merchants were heavily taxed. Ultimately, Kaufman (1987, 63) concludes, 'that marketing evolves in order to support society's needs, and in particular, to enable man's natural inclination to specialize'.

Medieval marketing practices

The medieval period covers the 1,000-year interval from the Fall of Rome in 476 CE to the Fall of Constantinople (the Eastern Roman/Byzantine Empire) in 1453. Few marketing developments established during ancient times carried over to the first half of medieval period known as the Dark Ages, from the fifth to eleventh centuries. During this period, with the sack of Rome, marauding warlords took what they wanted; law and order collapsed and there was no reliable currency, so industry and trade deteriorated to near nothing. Europe returned to self-sufficient agriculture and herding as it had before Greek and Roman times a thousand years earlier. What little trade occurred was again conducted by barter (although markets and marketing still flourished in the Eastern Empire, particularly in Constantinople). From the beginning of the Dark Ages, disease and warfare halved the population of Europe over the next few centuries. Some rays of light began to emerge with Charlemagne's (768–814) 46-year reign. After uniting most of Western Europe and creating some semblance of stability, Charlemagne was crowned Holy Roman Emperor in 800; but the Vikings began their raiding parties in 793, plunging Europe back into darkness.

By about 1000, Europe emerged from a mini Ice Age improving agricultural production and increasing population. Starting in 1095 two hundred years of intermittent Crusades began. Moving troops to and from the holy lands required fixing the old Roman roads that had fallen into disrepair, which also provided an improved means of moving merchandise by two-wheeled carts and four-wheeled wagons. Armies needed provisioning, revitalizing trade and markets to supply the troops. Returning crusaders brought back luxury goods from the East not seen since Roman times and restored knowledge lost since Greek times.

Law and order brought stability and stability brought back industry and trade throughout Europe. Villages typically held a market day once a week, bringing country folk together to trade food for crafts. Peddlers carrying backpacks filled with merchandise were a common sight walking the newly repaired roadways to country farms and rural hamlets trading their wares. Coinage was re-established in larger cities. During the period from the eleventh to fifteenth centuries, there were several significant marketing innovations: (1) travelling wholesale markets known as trade fairs (2) new more efficient media of exchange and means of payment to routinize market transactions, such as promissory notes and bills of exchange, and (3) guilds, whose members practised an extreme form of what may appear as 'non-marketing' (i.e. a non-competitive pre-determined marketing mix).

Trade fairs

Medieval trade fairs developed in the late eleventh century, reached their peak in the twelfth and thirteenth centuries, and began declining by the fourteenth. The earliest trade fairs were at first maritime events where local and foreign merchants could meet at the ports of Venice or Genoa on an annual basis (Adelson, 1962). Fairs soon spread inland from towns in Italy, then France, next northward to Flanders, Bruges and Cologne, then to England.

In England the best known fairs were immortalized in stage play and song. Bartholomew Fair was established in 1133 by grant of King Henry I, son of William the Conqueror, and commemorated in Ben Jonson's 1614 play: *Bartholomew Fayre: a Comedie*. Scarborough Faire was chartered in Yorkshire in 1253 by King Henry III, and memorialized in a ballad dated to 1670 (possibly earlier), and more recently revised by folk singers Simon and Garfunkel in 1972. Safety of life, security of goods and stability of trading relationships were so important for the maintenance of these fairs, and trade in general, that protection of merchants and merchandise was enshrined as law in 1215.

> Let all merchants have safety and security to go out from England and to come to England, and to stay and to move about through England by land as well as by sea, for purchasing and selling without all unjust tolls, according to the ancient and proper customs, except in time of war ...
>
> (Magna Carta, *chapter 41*)

The trade fairs were essentially travelling marketplaces, primarily for wholesaling, with occasional retail purchases, that lasted a number of weeks and were often tied to religious festivals. The fairs hosted large gatherings of merchants who travelled long distances, overland and across seas, to sell their home-bought goods and buy foreign goods, usually for final sales in their home markets. For example, Italian merchants sold luxury goods from Byzantium, Africa and the Orient, such as silk, fine jewellery, swords and metalwork, eyeglasses, olive oil, sugar, cinnamon, pepper, frankincense, myrrh, and other herbs and spices to merchants from Northern Europe. Northern merchants sold French Champagne, Bordeaux, and Burgundy wines, among others, Flemish cloth and textiles, English tin, wool, goose quills and sheepskins to make parchment for writing, German silver, honey and wax, Scandinavian amber, furs, leather and hides to Italian merchants. There was even occasional retail trade as some of the great aristocrats of the country would send their stewards to the fairs to buy luxury goods, such as silks and furs, and stock up on a year's supply of wines, weapons, cloth, sugar, salt, pepper and other staples.

At their height, during the twelfth and thirteenth centuries, the most successful were the Fairs of Champagne, a province northeast of Paris, which was organized into a circuit of six consecutive fairs lasting from six- to eight-week intervals spaced throughout the year. These fairs were held outside the towns of Lagny (January–February), Bar-sur-Aube (March–April), Provins (May–June and September–October), and Troyes (July–August and November–December); along with a few minor ones that were held during the gaps between the major fairs.

The church suspended usury laws for transactions at the fair because credit was crucial for successful trade. Merchants rented booths. Money-changers, who operated as bankers, handled the conversions of various coinages brought to the fair, issued transfer orders, and provided letters of credit. Marshals or wardens served as 'Guards of the Fair', kept order, witnessed and enforced contracts, and heard and settled disputes. The Count of Champagne made a tidy profit from the fair. Revenue sources included renting booths to merchants, a commission from the money-changers' profits, collecting fines for misdemeanours committed at the fair, and sales taxes for the goods brought to the fair. There were expenses, such as setting up tents for conducting business, providing shelter and provisions, as well as payments for the protection of merchants travelling to and from the fair.

Also critical were the Count of Champagne's efforts to maintain a sound silver coinage (the Provins and Troyes deniers were commonly accepted all over Europe) to serve as a reserve currency for denominating other coinages. At the end of the fair the money changers or bankers would operate a clearinghouse to settle loans, debits and credits. These bankers often provided merchants with several new instruments of credit. Ultimately, these credit instruments were a contributing cause to the decline of trade fairs. Permanent trade cities were growing, with stable credit houses reducing the necessity of bankers and large merchants risking life and limb travelling to and from trade fairs. And the risks of travel were escalating. Nothing inhibits trade more than death and destruction and the calamitous fourteenth century was plagued by contagious disease and continuous warfare. Undoubtedly, the major causes of the demise of trade in general and the fairs in particular were the social and economic upheaval resulting from the bubonic plague (1347–1400) throughout Europe, and the Hundred Years War (1337–1450) between England and France, along with numerous conflicts and fighting between Venice and Milan, Germany and Poland, Austria and Switzerland, among many others, during the fourteenth and fifteenth centuries (Grun, 1991). Fortunately for them, during these tough times, money changers and bankers did not have to travel to fairs when they could sit in their counting houses dealing with merchants and each other at a distance through the innovative new instruments of credit.

Credit instruments

During the twelfth and thirteenth centuries new media of exchange (e.g. promissory notes and bills of exchange) were developed as a more convenient means of payment for products and services. Like the invention of coinage, the invention of credit instruments created greater efficiency in routinizing market transaction. A promissory note was a written promise for one banker or merchant to pay another at a different place and at a future time. This was becoming a necessity because the English pound, for example, was a silver coin weighing one pound. Thus, with the inconvenience of travelling with pounds and pounds of coins, banking and credit instruments became increasingly popular first among the nobles and then among the merchants. For example, even before signing the *Magna Carta,* King John of England (1166–1216) sent his envoys to Rome with letters of credit requesting bankers or merchants to lend the bearer a sum of money or pay the equivalent amount in goods with promise of repayment plus commission at the Royal Exchequer in London (Bishop, 1968).

Bills of exchange were also used as a convenience by travelling nobles and lords, and later merchants, particularly at trade fairs, to avoid carrying a large quantity of coins for payment in foreign lands. The bill was a written note from one person to another to pay a specified sum of money to a designated person at a future date. This practice was first handled by the military orders, such as the Knights Templars and Knights Hospitaller, in the twelfth century but by the thirteenth century merchants were conducting the business (Bernstein, 2008). These credit instruments could be transferred to a third party, with the final holder of the instrument receiving payment.

With bills of exchange, the sellers of merchandise could obtain immediate payment from a banker at a fair or in a trading city by presenting a bill of exchange signed by the merchant buying goods who usually kept assets with money lenders/bankers at numerous trade fairs or in a number of large cities. The banker would purchase the bill at a discount from its full amount because payment was due at a future date; the purchasing merchant's account would be debited when the bill became due and the seller credited or paid in cash. Bills could also be drawn directly on the banks themselves. After the seller received payment, the bill of exchange continued to function as a credit instrument until its maturity, independent of the original transaction. Promissory notes and bills of exchange are the forerunner of more modern credit instruments, including: mail transfers, bank cheques, money orders, credit and debit cards, and digital wallets.

Guilds

While new financing methods to more efficiently routinize market transactions were making great strides, during the period, marketing-mix activities were taking a giant step backwards with the development of medieval guilds. The guilds appear to have grown out of religious brotherhoods (Bishop, 1968) into men who shared a similar occupation, such as butchers, bakers or candlestick makers. There were also smiths of every type, goldsmith, coppersmith and locksmiths, pin makers, knife makers and harness makers; in foods, bread makers, cake makers and meat-pie makers; in textiles, weavers, dyers and fullers; and in larger French cities, such as Paris and Toulouse, practising one of the few occupations open to women, the prostitutes had their own guild (Painter, 1951).

The purpose of the guild was to protect the economic welfare of its members. Each guild had a monopoly of its product or service in a particular town. Generally, members of a guild had their shops in the same locale, usually on the same street or confined to a particular section of town, thereby negating any locational advantage. Guilds rules restricted competition, regulated work hours and wages for labourers (e.g. apprentices and journeymen), standardized methods of production, set quality levels for products, established fixed prices with no allowance for negotiation, and prohibited any form of advertising, aggressive salesmanship or self-promotion. By standardizing product, price, promotion and location, the guilds eliminated any basis for differentiating one seller's marketing mix from another's. With a standardized marketing mix buyers are paired with sellers on a random basis, because one marketing mix looks just like any and every other. This medieval approach to marketing provides an extreme contrast with the differentiated marketing mixes of today that match buyers with sellers based on each party's preferences. This forces a retailer to satisfy customers – better than competitors – on some dimension of the marketing mix or face bankruptcy.

Guilds reached their height during the early thirteenth century in France and a half century later in England. They began losing their pre-eminence because they could not preserve the status quo in the face of increasing technological change. Innovators worked outside of towns, in which the guilds held jurisdiction, usually in the countryside under the protection of a noble. Much of the wool industry in England during the fourteenth century developed in the countryside to avoid the guilds. In the Netherlands during the fifteenth century, fearing innovation would render them obsolete, textile workers threw their wooden shoes, called 'sabots', into the gears of textile looms jamming the cogs that turned the wheels (hence the practice of sabotage). By the end of the medieval period guilds were in decline.

With the Fall of Christian Constantinople to Muslim forces in 1453, trade with the Far East for silks, spices and other luxury goods was cut off. To replace the now Islamic controlled overland trade routes to India, Cathay (China) and Spice Islands of the Far East, the loss of Byzantium launched the Age of Discovery in Western Europe. Vasco de Gama of Portugal sailed south along the African coast around the Cape of Good Hope, where the Atlantic meets the Indian Ocean, then northeast to arrive and establish a trading post at Calicut India in 1498. Cristopher Columbus sailed west from Spain's Canary Islands to reach Hispaniola, and other Caribbean Islands in 1492, which he mistakenly believed to be the Indies (hence 'new world' natives were called Indians). Soon after these discoveries, the Dutch and English began their oceanic forays of raiding (the weak) and trading (with the strong). With the coming of the Renaissance marketing began its resurgence.

Conclusion

For some 40,000 years, prior to the retail revolution in marketing practice, during the sixth century BCE, the major form of trade was barter, the exchange of goods for goods, particularly the silent trade. Barter was critical to the evolution of early modern man and appears to have provided the competitive advantage that lead to the rise of *Homo Sapiens* and the demise of *Homo Neanderthalis*. As nomadic peoples settled into villages, and with growing populations in larger cities requiring greater specialization, trade by bartering became ever more cumbersome.

To overcome the inefficiencies of bartering, the concomitant innovations of central markets, sedentary retailers, and particularly a fluid medium of exchange produced the retail revolution in trade, goods exchanged for money – now called marketing. The practice of marketing originated in the ancient world, probably in Athens during the sixth and fifth centuries BCE. The critical factor was a standardized convenient-to-carry coinage – the Athenian 'owl' – the medium of exchange that was generally accepted and commonly recognized all over the known world of the time. Athens had a large population and was a crossroads for sea lanes in the Mediterranean and Aegean Seas. There were Greek colonies in Europe, Asia and Africa that served as markets as well as transshipment points to the interior of the continents. Greek, particularly Athenian, retailing included such modern marketing practices as recognizing the value of high-traffic retail locations, promotional branding, competitive pricing and commercial advertising. A cornerstone of ancient trade practice was establishing trust and maintaining stable trading relationships. Because they routinized transactions with such incredible efficiency, marketing systems, consisting of central markets with sedentary retailing using a medium of exchange, rapidly spread across the civilized world to ultimately produce the marketing systems of the present.

The practice of marketing has remained basically the same since its inception – sellers offering competitive marketing mixes to buyers having varying preferences to create market transactions. What has changed over time is various marketing techniques, such as physical distribution and advertising, which have improved dramatically with changes in technology. For example, some of the changes in land and sea transportation involved moving freight by pack animals, such as mules and camels, ox or donkey-drawn two-wheeled carts, horse-drawn four-wheeled wagons and small cargo ships during ancient and medieval times to more advanced trucks, pipelines, freight trains, large container ships, and cargo in planes of modern times. In advertising media, as well, technological change abounds, from ancient cries in the marketplace along with graffiti on walls and medieval town criers along with handwritten broadsides to technologically improved printed posters, fliers, mail-order catalogues, newspapers and magazines along with broadcast radio and television; and since the turn of the twentieth century, internet and mobile marketing, with same-day or next-day delivery. Similarly, there have been technological innovations in the medium of exchange from seashells and oxen, to weights of precious metals (e.g., silver, gold), to coined money made of metals equal to their weights, to paper money backed by precious metals, to fiat paper money (with no metal backing), promissory notes and bills of exchange of ancient and medieval world to travellers and bank cheques, credit and debit cards to digital wallets of today.

A French proverb says: 'The more things change, the more they stay the same'. Technology has driven many changes in marketing practices, since ancient and medieval times, but the fundamental purpose of marketing – sellers and buyers creating stable market relationships – remains the same.

References

Athenaeus (1962) *Deipmosophistae,* in C.B. Gulick (tr.), *Athenaeus: The Deipsonophists,* Heinemann, London.

Bartels, R. (1962) *The Development of Marketing Thought,* Richard D. Irwin, Homewood, IL.

Bernstein, W.J. (2008) *A Splendid Exchange: How Trade Shaped the World,* Grove Press, New York.

Bishop, M. (1968) *The Middle Ages,* Houghton Mifflin Co., Boston, MA.

Cassels, J.M. (1936) 'The significance of early economic thought on marketing', *Journal of Marketing,* 1/4, 29–33.

Crone, G.R. (1937/2010) *The Voyages of Cadamosto and Other Documents on Western Africa in the Second Half of the Fifteenth Century,* Hakluyt Society, London.

Darian, J.C. (1985) 'Marketing and economic development: A case study from classical India', *Journal of Macromarketing,* 5/1, 14–26.

Diogenes Laertius (1853) *The lives and opinions of eminent philosophers,* tr. C.D. Yonge. Available online: http://classicpersuasion.org/pw/diogenes/dlxenophon.htm

Dixon, D.F. (1975) 'Notes on the origins of marketing', unpublished working paper, Temple University, Philadelphia, PA. Cited in Shaw, E.H. (2011) 'Reflections on the Dixon Seminar', *Journal of Historical Research in Marketing,* 3/1 131–43.

Dixon, D.F. (1995) 'Retailing in classical Athens: Gleanings from contemporary literature and art', *Journal of Macromarketing,* 15/1, 74–85.

Dixon, J.E., Cann, J.R. and Renfrew, C. (1968) 'Obsidian and the origins of trade', *Scientific American,* 218/3, 38–46.

Durant, W. (1939) *The Life of Greece,* Simon & Schuster, New York.

Finley, M.I. (1981) *Early Greece: The Bronze and Archaic Ages,* Norton Press, New York.

Glotz, G. (1926) *Ancient Greece at Work,* Barnes & Noble, New York.

Grun, B. (1991) *The Timetables of History,* Simon & Schuster, New York.

Grossman, L. (1983) 'Business in the Bible: Marketing', in S.C. Hollander and R. Savitt (eds), *First North American Workshop on Historical Research in Marketing,* Department of Marketing and Transportation, East Lansing, MI, pp. 136–40.

Harari, Y.N. (2015) *Sapiens: A Brief History of Mankind,* Penguin-Random House, London.

Heichelheim, F.M. (1968) *An Ancient Economic History,* vol. 2, Simon & Schuster, New York.

Horan, R.D., Bulte, E., and J.F. Shogren, J.F. (2005) 'How trade saved humanity from biological exclusion: An economic theory of Neanderthal extinction', *Journal of Economic Behavior and Organization,* 58/1, 1–29.

Hume, D. (1752/1970) 'Of money', in E. Rotwein (ed.) *Writings on Economics,* University of Wisconsin, Madison, WI, 33–46.

Kaufman, C.J. (1987) 'Evaluation of marketing in a society: The Han Dynasty of Ancient China', *Journal of Macromarketing,* 7/2, 52–64.

Kelley, W.T. (1956) 'The development of early thought in marketing', *Journal of Marketing,* 20/3, 62–7.

Leakey, R., and Lewin, R. (1981) *Making of Mankind,* Penguin, New York.

Lichtheim, M. (1976) *Ancient Egyptian Literature,* vol. 2, *The New Kingdom,* University of California Press, Berkeley, CA.

Lee, Kam-Hon (1983) 'A study note on businessman's image in China', in S.C. Hollander and R. Savitt (eds), *First North American Workshop on Historical Research in Marketing,* Michigan State University, East Lansing, MI, pp. 152–9.

Maiuri, A. (1957) *Pompeii,* tr. V. Priestley, Rome: Instituto Poligrafico Dello Stato.

Minowa, Y. (2007) 'The Roman games and consumption rituals', in B.J. Branchik (ed.), *Marketing at the Center*, Quinnipiac University, Hamden, CT, pp. 279–81

Mulvihill, D.F. (1983) 'Marketers in the New Testament', in S.C. Hollander and R. Savitt (eds), *First North American Workshop on Historical Research in Marketing*, Michigan State University, East Lansing, MI, pp. 141–5.

Nance, J. (1975) *The Gentle Tasaday: A Stone Age People in the Philippine Rain Forest*, Harcourt Brace Jovanovich, New York.

Nevett, T., and Nevitt, L. (1987) 'The origins of marketing: Evidence from classical and early Hellenistic Greece', in T. Nevett and S.C. Hollander (eds), *Marketing in Three Eras*, vol. 3, Michigan State University, East Lansing, MI, pp. 3–12.

Painter, Sidney (1967) *A History of the Middle Ages*, Alfred A. Knopf, New York.

Shaw, E.H. (1983) 'Plato and the socio-economic foundations of marketing: An historical analysis in the development of macro-marketing thought', in S.C. Hollander and R. Savitt (eds), *First North American Workshop on Historical Research in Marketing*, Michigan State University, East Lansing, MI, pp. 146–51.

Shaw, E.H. (1995) 'The first dialogue on macromarketing', *Journal of Macromarketing*, 15/1, 7–20.

Smith, A. (1776/1937) *An Inquiry into the Nature and Causes of the Wealth of Nations*, reprinted, Modern Library, New York.

Stead, M. (1986) *Egyptian Life*, British Museum Press, London.

Steiner, R.L. (1976) 'The prejudice against marketing', *Journal of Marketing*, 40/3, 2–42.

Tawney, R.H. (1926) *Religion and the Rise of Capitalism*, Harcourt, Brace & Co., New York.

Weiner, J.S. (1973) *The Natural History of Man*, Anchor Books, New York.

3

A history of consumption
in the United States

Terrence H. Witkowski

Introduction

The history of consumption is a potentially vast field, global in scope and arguably extending back to the earliest human civilizations. The reference list alone for such a history might exceed the length of this chapter. Thus, the present discussion is restricted to the consumption history of the United States, the world's foremost consumerist nation, from its first English settlements in the early seventeenth century until the present. The focus is upon the experiences of Europeans and to a lesser extent Africans who came to North America, rather than on the consumption history of indigenous people. This still constitutes a very broad and complex subject area, but one that is more manageable in terms of time span, people, places and cultures covered.

The reporting of past events – including the individuals, groups and societies involved and their various discourses about consumption – can be arranged chronologically, topically, geographically or in some combination of the three (Witkowski and Jones, 2006). Finding an appropriate periodization scheme for writing a history of American consumption is challenging. Ideally, significant external events and relevant consumption turning points should be used (Hollander *et al.*, 2005). For example, the American home front economy during World War II, with its full employment, high wages, rationing and price controls, was a much different environment for consumers than the subsequent years of post-war prosperity and burgeoning mass consumption. So, the end of the war in 1945 would mark a logical division. However, other milestone dates in American political history, such as the signing of the Declaration of Independence in 1776 or the end of the Civil War in 1865, have much less relevance for consumption. Thus, for reasons of convenience and readability rather than being historically event-driven, the periodization scheme used in this brief chapter will just consist of four broadly defined, and somewhat arbitrary eras. It will begin with the colonial and early federal (national) years, and then proceeds through the nineteenth century, the twentieth century to 1945, and, lastly, the post-war period to the present.

This history is informed by analytical concepts from consumer culture theory (CCT), a now major subdiscipline of consumer research. CCT emphasizes the hedonic, aesthetic and ritualistic dimensions of consumption, consumer identity projects and marketplace cultures. The field acknowledges the contribution of research on consumption history (Arnould and Thompson, 2005). The present narrative follows three cultural threads that wind through American consumption history: (1) the assigning of meaning to possessions and consumption, (2) the gendering of consumption thought and behaviour, and (3) the delivery of anti-consumption rhetoric and consumer resistance and regulation. Possessions have multiple meaning. Through consumption the meaning in objects participates in cultural reproduction (Slater, 1997). Gendered aspects of American consumption history include the allocation of household purchasing roles and influence, the cult of domesticity, and criticism of female materialism, among other topics and practices. Anti-consumption rhetoric includes religiously motivated and philosophical critiques of consumerism and, in practice, takes the form of environmentally virtuous behaviour, politically motivated boycotts of goods, and government policies of control and austerity. These cultural threads will be surveyed in each of the four broad eras. The present chapter format dictates that this history will be a mere overview of the topic. Gaps in the narrative appear during time periods where little historical research has been conducted.

The terms 'consumer history' and 'consumption history' are deployed more or less interchangeably. Consumers here are considered people (i.e. end-users), not companies, and their consumption entails acquisition, use and disposal activities. In modern economies, acquisition largely results from shopping and buyer behaviour in a commercial marketplace. However, people can also consume goods and services from sources outside the market including nature (e.g. hunting, fishing, gathering), unpaid work (e.g. domestic activities, self-production), and public provisioning (e.g. food stamps, subsidized water and sanitation services). Consumption history is more than what consumers do; it is also about what people think, feel and say about consumption. Such intellectual history will also be addressed herein.

This account of American consumption history and some of its cultural themes is largely based on secondary works including books, chapters and journal articles in American social history, as well as historical research published in the fields of marketing and consumer behaviour. It also has been informed by a small literature on consumption historiography. Historiography refers to the principles, theories and methodologies of historical writing, although it also has a second meaning as a body of literature. Contributions to consumption historiography include Fullerton (1987), Pollay (1987), Lavin and Archdeacon (1989), Smith and Lux (1993), Witkowski (1994), Elliott and Davies (2006), and Witkowski and Jones (2006). In 2011, the *Journal of Historical Research in Marketing* featured a special issue on 'historical methods and historical research in marketing' and several of its articles are very relevant to researching and writing consumer culture history (Davies, 2011; Fullerton, 2011; Pollay, 2011).

Colonial and early federal consumption

The Europeans who settled North America in the seventeenth century undoubtedly depended less on the market for goods and services than do Americans four centuries later. Still, even the earliest settlers were never totally separated from global trade and the consumption opportunities it provided. The amount of labour and skill required for complete self-sufficiency was enormous. For many goods, households performed just a step or two in the production process and then relied on craftsmen and women for the remainder. Take the production of cloth. Probate inventories indicate that only 49 per cent of households surveyed in Massachusetts in 1774 owned spinning wheels, and this percentage may have been inflated by the patriotic spinning fad brought on by the non-importation movement (Shammas, 1982a, 1982b). Fewer than 6 per cent owned the other equipment necessary for cloth production. Southern plantations, because of their large scale and pool of slave labour, were more self-sufficient than northern farms. Nevertheless, households everywhere in the colonies needed to obtain some things from other parties through barter, credit arrangements and specie in various forms.

Locally produced items accounted for the majority of market purchases, but 27.5 per cent of expenditures in the 1760s were for items produced in other British colonies, especially the Caribbean, or in England (Shammas, 1982a). Foodstuffs, primarily wine, rum, salt, tea and molasses, as well as woollen, linen and cotton cloth and garments, were the most important categories of imported merchandise. Colonial consumers also purchased imported household items, including looking glasses, brass candlesticks, glassware and ceramics, and personal items such as silver and brass buttons and buckles. Firearms have been a noteworthy consumer good throughout American history. In the colonial period, most guns were brought from England or assembled locally from parts made abroad. An analysis of several sets of probate records from different colonies recorded between 1638 and 1790 showed that 50–73 per cent of male estates, and 6–38 per cent of female estates included firearms (Lindgren and Heather, 2002). One of the authors' databases (from 1774) had more estates containing guns (54 per cent) than Bibles (25 per cent).

Retail institutions emerged gradually and by the 1760s consisted of itinerant peddlers, rural general stores, more specialized city shops, and auction sales of new and estate goods. In the coastal cities of Boston, New York, Philadelphia, Baltimore and Charleston, merchants advertised the arrival of new shipments and, when augmented through word of mouth, this market information was undoubtedly widely known among the relatively small urban populations. Surviving letters and diaries show that married couples engaged in comparison shopping (Bridenbaugh, 1950), and that upper-class males, like George Washington, ordered items from their London agents on behalf of their families (Detweiler, 1982). The relative influence of men versus women in consumer decision processes is difficult to determine. Some wives bartered independently with neighbouring females and storekeepers, trading the eggs, butter and spun linen they produced, and cooking, washing and midwife services they offered (Ulrich, 1990). Being legally part of their husbands' household, however, women's influence ultimately rested on their persuasive abilities. At all social levels, husbands usually established credit accounts with local shopkeepers (Ulrich, 1982). Men took shopping trips by themselves or with their wives; infrequently did women venture out on their own. Women made only 8 per cent of all purchases at the Simpson-Baird store in Prince George's County, Maryland, in 1769 (Kulikoff, 1986) and an analysis of the John W. Hunt Daybook, Lexington, Kentucky, July–September 1796, indicates that just 15 per cent of all visits were made by women (Perkins, 1991). Although some wives had their own store accounts, as did some single, widowed and divorced women, and while in some families wives did nearly all the shopping, such households were a minority. In the eighteenth century, America's purchasing agent was a man.

With an abundance of land for the taking and ample natural resources to exploit, colonial living standards were among the highest in the world outside of Great Britain. True, most people of the times lived in cramped, poorly heated and insufficiently lighted quarters without indoor plumbing, but by the 1700s a typical middle-class family

> owned earthenware, bed and table linen, knives, forks, and a Bible. A family with income above the median might possess a few fancy clothes, a watch, china plates, fine furniture,

some silver items, and other small amenities. The wealthy might possess fine clothes and furniture, exquisite china and silverware, nonreligious books, a man's wig, artwork, a carriage, and a large volume of luxury goods (Perkins, 1988, 228).

Slaves, indentured servants and poor whites had very few possessions aside from the tattered clothing on their backs, a few eating utensils, and perhaps a bed, table and a couple of chairs.

(Witkowski, 1989)

The meaning of possessions changed in the middle of the eighteenth century. As colonial society became richer and more established, an urge for gentility emerged. Colonists began building larger and more stylish homes and gardens, purchasing better quality furniture, using higher quality eating utensils, improving their manners by reading courtesy books, and, in general, becoming more refined (Breen, 2004; Bushman, 1992). Imports of luxury goods from the mother country increased and some colonists began to amass large debts with British middlemen (Henretta, 1973). The upper classes were among the first to adopt these newer values and behaviours; but, as documented in surviving probate records (Carr and Walsh, 1980), even people of more middling circumstances began to acquire small luxuries such as silver spoons.

Slowly rising consumerism did not go unchallenged. Colonial Americans voiced anti-consumption rhetoric and organized significant consumer resistance. Drawing from a Western Judaeo-Christian tradition sceptical of excess in acquisition, Puritans and Quakers favoured productive work for the benefit of society and frowned upon consuming more than necessity required (Shi, 1985). But whereas the Quaker critique was utilitarian and not an attack on consumption per se, Puritans were driven by a spiritual principle asserting that the love of consuming was an evil (Dröge *et al.*, 1993; Schudson, 1991). To forestall impious materialism, the Massachusetts and Pennsylvania colonies enacted sumptuary laws in the seventeenth century (Hollander, 1984), and New England ministers preached jeremiads against worldliness well into the eighteenth century. Between 1732 and 1757 in his *Poor Richard's Almanack*, the very secular Benjamin Franklin preached frugality as a moral virtue with sayings like 'Beware of little expenses; a small leak will sink a great ship' (Witkowski, 2010, 239).

American consumption practices and the concomitant meanings of possessions became highly politicized in the decade before the Revolutionary War. Three times in the 1760s and 1770s, colonists organized mass boycotts of British goods in order to put economic pressure on English manufacturers who would then force Parliament to rescind objectionable taxes. Benjamin Franklin, John Adams and many other patriots urged their fellows to forego imported 'superfluities' and, instead, to be thrifty and to produce their own goods. Such views were aired at town meetings and widely disseminated via letters reprinted in colonial newspapers. Colonial consumers responded by substituting homespun apparel for imported ribbons, laces, velvets and silks and by swearing off foreign liquors and imported teas (Witkowski, 1989). This 'nonimportation movement' was successful in that many onerous taxes, such as the Stamp Act of 1765 and most of the Townshend Duties of 1767, were repealed, but it took six years of fighting to finally settle the political dispute with Great Britain. In effect, an anti-consumption movement abetted the American Revolution (Breen, 1988, 2004; Witkowski, 1989).

American women participated actively in the non-importation movement and thus became associated with virtuous consumption. Indeed, by the 1790s, in the early federal (i.e. national) period, a 'republican-mother' ideal gained traction. Proponents believed that female virtue could be harnessed to build the new, democratic nation (Evans, 1989; Norton, 1980). On the other hand, some commentators held more critical views about women and consumption. A letter from 1787, published in a Philadelphia magazine called *American Museum*, described how female influence could override a farmer's better judgement:

> When his second daughter prepared her trousseau, his wife insisted that the girl be furnished with store-bought goods – a calico gown, stoneware tea cups, pewter spoons, and so forth. Although the farmer protested that homespun was good enough, he gave his wife the money. Upon the marriage of the next daughter, his wife again demanded money and this time she bought silk and china. From that point on, no money could be saved because all of the profits went for market luxuries.
>
> *(Cited in Shammas, 1982a, 248)*

Intended as both social and gender criticism, this letter suggests that some women placed a higher priority on household luxuries than did their menfolk, and were notably earlier adopters of the more prestigious, store-bought items. They were, in other words, developing a propensity to consume characteristic of modern consumerist culture (Slater, 1997; Witkowski, 1999). Chastising women for frivolous spending continued to be a standard part of the critical repertoire until the late twentieth century (Stearns, 2001).

Consumption in the nineteenth century

From 1800 until the Civil War (1861–5), the US economy grew in most years and material conditions gradually improved for many but far from all Americans. The nation continued to be predominantly rural and the majority of its people had only limited purchasing opportunities. Consumer goods were usually made and consumed locally, although as physical distribution systems evolved (e.g. canals, railroads), these largely generic products travelled longer distances to market (Porter and Livesay, 1971). Newly arrived immigrants and pioneers moving west usually had relatively few possessions, and African Americans, most of whom where enslaved, had even fewer goods. But some men amassed great fortunes and urban centres, above all New York City, became sites for the most fashionable consumption (Milbank, 2000; Peck, 2000). Although distribution was still spotty and advertising remained primitive, a few bold retailers, like New York's A.T. Stewart, experimented with more opulent and larger scale merchandising formats in the 1840s that would soon evolve into full-fledged department stores (Benson, 1986; Resseguie, 1964).

After the Civil War, urbanization, industrialization and technological and managerial innovations (see e.g. Chandler, 1977; Porter and Livesay, 1971) greatly transformed the country within just a few decades. Some areas of the defeated South languished and grinding poverty faced freed African Americans and many arrivals from Europe. In much of the US, however, living standards rose as incomes grew and the world of goods expanded through product innovation, mass production and new forms of distribution such as department and chain stores and direct mail (Boorstin, 1973; Leach, 1984). Montgomery Ward and Sears Roebuck catalogues brought an enormous assortment of goods to rural Americans who did not have easy access to city department and specialty stores, but who could accept packages, especially after the advent, in the 1890s, of free rural postal delivery. Advertising of the time embodied a happy optimism and flamboyance (Laird, 1998; Lears, 1994) and promotional schemes became increasingly aggressive. In the 1870s, chain stores like the Great Atlantic & Pacific Tea Company began giving away premiums such as ceramics, glassware, cutlery and kitchen gadgets (Blaszczyk, 2000). Thus, the marketing infrastructure and worldview necessary for a modern consumer culture became increasingly manifest by the end of the century.

Possessions continued to be associated with gentility and other positive values. Books and reading, for example, became 'invariably associated with that most powerful of nineteenth-century ideas, improvement' (Bushman, 1992, 285). Possessions also acquired further meanings. In his computer-assisted analysis of diaries, letters and other documents from the 1847–69 Mormon migration, Belk (1992) identified five types of meanings – sacred, material, personal, familial and communal – that the pioneers instilled in their possessions. Among the sacred meanings was the purifying act of sacrifice where small luxuries would be left behind to facilitate the move. Material meanings were expressed when migrants retained possessions for survival and sometimes picked up items other migrants had left behind. Many objects, such as guns and woodworking tools for men and sewing machines for women, embodied the personal meanings of competence, transformation and domesticity. Familial meanings were articulated through the preservation and transportation of heirlooms and wedding dresses. Communal meanings were expressed in caring for others through sharing possessions. Other nineteenth-century Americans undoubtedly bestowed similar and probably many additional meanings onto their consumer goods.

Middle-class women were becoming increasingly active as their households' purchasing agents and mavens of domesticity (Witkowski, 1999, 2004). As discussed above, men dominated family purchasing decisions in the colonial and early federal period, but in the nineteenth century trends began to favour female agency. Some middle-class single women could support themselves teaching, while their working-class counterparts could find jobs in New England textile mills or as servants. By 1850, 15–30 per cent of urban American households supported at least one live-in domestic (O'Leary, 1996). Married women generated income by taking in boarders or laundry (Bose, 1987). Further, as the nineteenth century progressed, more and more American women (primarily native-born whites) became literate, an important skill for reading ads and otherwise negotiating the marketplace (Cott, 1977). Thus, by the 1850–70 period a definite shift towards greater female agency in shopping, buying and consumption had begun.

This trend has been documented by Belk (1992, 357) who found that, although men created more of the surviving documents than women, 'the greatest number of deep possession attachments and meanings are found among women … This has been interpreted here in terms of women's desires for attachment and continuity and men's views of the journey as a challenge and a separation.' An engraving in *Gleason's Pictorial* (December 1854), titled 'Interior View of John P. Jewett & Co.'s New and Spacious Bookstore', shows well-dressed, presumably educated women out shopping for books (Burke, 2001, fig. 48). Still more visual evidence has been found in several oil paintings depicting vigorous female characters in domestic genre scenes. These images of women showing initiative as consumers were consistent with their gaining access to public places, forming associations and collectively demanding their political rights (Witkowski, 2004). In the latter part of the nineteenth century, retailers increasingly defined shopping as a feminine activity and transformed crockery emporiums, tea stores and five-and-tens into appropriate public spaces for women and girls. Department stores, in particular, were deliberately feminized for the enjoyment of women shoppers (Benson, 1986) and by the 1890s relatively few men frequented them. The tangible products they sold were also becoming increasingly gendered. F.W. Woolworth, for example, urged its suppliers to create goods with 'lady lure' (Blaszczyk, 2000).

Several forms of anti-consumption rhetoric challenged expanding consumerism in the nineteenth century. On the religious front of the 1820s and 1830s, revivalist Lyman Beecher advocated a conservative, moralistic, even Puritan 'Christian simplicity'. Reverend Beecher worried about materialism undermining the established social order (Shi, 1985), whereas other ministers simply repeated the old accusation that 'the parade of luxury' undermined the 'more durable riches than those this world can offer' (Stearns, 2001, 52). Harris (1981) contends that during the mid-century period, criticism of consumerism began shifting from a moralistic disapproval of the upper classes buying luxuries to a concern about working-class consumers unable to restrain themselves from purchasing the increasingly alluring array of goods presented in stores.

Different voices stressed a frugal domesticity. In his essays, books, and architecture, Andrew Jackson Downing (1842, 1850) advocated utilitarian cottages and farmhouses for the people and unostentatious, moderate homes for country gentlemen. Magazines, such as *Godey's Lady's Book* (founded in 1837), instructed middle-class women on how to tastefully furnish and manage their houses (Shi, 1985). Lydia Marie Child's popular manual for homemakers, *The American Frugal Housewife*, first published in 1828, and with 12 editions by 1833, was 'dedicated to those who are not ashamed of economy' (Child, 1833). Along with her advice for frugally performing the various domestic arts, Mrs Child railed against consumerism, especially 'the rage for traveling, and for public amusements' (p. 99). Catharine Beecher, the daughter of preacher Lyman Beecher, echoed these sentiments in her books, *A Treatise on Domestic Economy* (1841) and *The Domestic Receipt Book* (1846).

In their lectures and writings, philosophers Ralph Waldo Emerson and Henry David Thoreau endorsed a more spontaneous, liberating and romantic 'transcendental simplicity' (Shi, 1985). Emerson, who himself lived comfortably and genteelly, saw frugality as a means to a higher end: 'Economy is a high, humane office, a sacrament, when its aim is grand; when it is the prudence of simple tastes, when it is practiced for freedom, or love, or devotion' (cited in Shi, 1985, 133). Thoreau's sojourn at Walden Pond in 1845–7 taught him to value self-sufficiency in raising food, making clothes and building shelter and furniture. High thinking was preferable to high living: 'Most of the luxuries, and many of the so called comforts of life, are not only not indispensable, but positive hindrances to the elevation of mankind. With respect to luxuries and comforts, the wisest have ever lived a more simple and meager life than the poor' (Thoreau, 1971, 14). The audience for this supposedly uplifting philosophy may have been limited. Thoreau was not an especially frequent or popular public lecturer and it took him eight years to sell the 2,000 copies of *Walden* printed in 1854.

Authors Mark Twain and Charles Dudley Warner published a social satire in 1873 that gave the post-Civil War decades their lasting soubriquet: the Gilded Age. Although the buyer behaviour of the middle and lower classes continued to come under scrutiny (Horowitz, 1985), leading intellectuals, such as William Dean Howells, editor of the *Atlantic Monthly*, E.L. Godkin, editor of *The Nation*, Charles Eliot Norton, editor of the *North American Review*, and the philosopher William James, declared much more disgust with the crass materialism of the newly rich (Cashman, 1993; Shi, 1985). At the end of the century, Thorstein Veblen became American plutocracy's greatest critic. In his *Theory of the Leisure Class*, Veblen (1899) wrote a scholarly, but highly influential frugality sermon combining wry social criticism with new insights from economics and cultural anthropology. He contended that consumption became grossly conspicuous in order to create invidious distinctions and to mark status. Women were transformed historically from domestic labourers to household consumers and those men who could afford the show paraded their finely attired females in public as gaudy signs of their commercial or professional success. The more visible idleness these wives and daughters enjoyed, the greater their symbolic value. Images of well-dressed women at leisure appeared in a number of works by American painters around the turn of the century. This social pose irritated Veblen who had a high regard for productive work. In *The Decoration of Houses*, Edith Wharton and Ogden Codman, Jr. (1897) argued for a simple aesthetic with less cluttered domestic spaces. As her later novels would testify, Wharton (who came from old money) was a keen observer of the social ambitions of parvenus.

Consumption in the twentieth century to 1945

Despite frequent, albeit relatively mild recessions during the first three decades of the twentieth century, the US economy generally trended upward. American consumers were presented an outpouring of increasingly affordable yet transformative new products, above all the automobile, but also newly electrified household appliances (refrigerators, vacuum cleaners), as well as telephones, radios, Victrola brand phonographs for RCA Victor records, and Kodak 'Brownie' cameras to name a few. The pace of change in US consumer culture seemed to accelerate in the 1920s as 'modernization' became equated with consumerism. 'This is the age of real estate, consumer credits and cars: modern appliances, bought by modern methods, placed in a modern household' (Slater, 1997, 13).

Then, the stock market crashed in October 1929 and soon the Great Depression of the 1930s posed a serious challenge to previously established mass consumption patterns and consumerist mindsets (Ewen, 1976; Marchand, 1985). With wages down and unemployment rates averaging 17.9 per cent between 1930 and 1940, many people were forced to greatly lower their material expectations and to scrimp wherever they could (Hill *et al.*, 1997). The advertising industry discussed the threat posed by frugality in its trade publications, where writers complained about hoarders, a 'buyer's strike' and 'consumer constipation'. The gloomiest prophets worried about an impending collapse in the consumption ethic (Marchand, 1985). Cross (2000) believes that these fears of consumerism's collapse were overblown. Yes, lack of income frustrated many buying plans, but people still clung to their old habits and dreams as long as they could. Movie-goers flocked to see the opulent movie musicals of Busby Berkeley and Fred Astaire, and many films of the era seemed fixated on the lifestyles of the very rich where tuxedos and top hats seemed to be everyday attire.

Although the 1930s saw increases in the percentage of US households with inside flush toilets and electric lighting and appliances, many families still lacked a modern consumer infrastructure. In 1940, 33 per cent of all Americans still cooked with wood or coal and another 33 per cent had no inside running water. Moreover, 67 per cent lacked central heating, 47 per cent did without indoor bathing equipment, and 48 per cent had no refrigerator (Green, 1992). In 1942, 58 per cent of all US families owned at least one automobile (55 per cent urban, 69 per cent farm), a percentage about the same as in 1930 (60 per cent) and more than double the 1920 figure of 26 per cent (Lebergott, 1993). The 1930s did see continual development of mass audiences for radio, the movies and slickly promoted professional sports whose stars were lionized by the mass media (Green, 1992).

By the 1920s, sophisticated magazine advertising campaigns were finding new meanings for products. In his *Advertising the American Dream*, Marchand (1985) provides an exceptionally thorough account of this meaning creation process. Ads in the late 1920s and early 1930s frequently told stories through stock social tableaux explained by copious amounts of body copy. Brands of toothpaste, shaving creams and razors starred in the 'parable of the first impression' where they facilitated the crucially important outward appearances of consumers. Other parables included 'the democracy of goods' where everyone could enjoy the pleasure, convenience and benefits of consumption, 'civilization redeemed' where brands ensured healthy living, and 'the captivated child' where products played an instructive role in child guidance (Marchand, 1985). Presumably, this advertiser-driven meaning creation resonated with consumers.

Other product meanings emerged less from product advertising campaigns and more from consumption communities. For example, Witkowski (1988) discusses how the colonial revival movement reinterpreted early American (i.e. colonial and federal) artefacts, reproductions, and architecture. The roots of this movement go back to exhibits at Civil War charity fund-raisers, but enthusiasm for the colonial really hit its fullest stride during the first four decades of the twentieth century. Native-born WASPs (White Anglo-Saxon Protestants) purchased and displayed period antiques for status presentation and ethnic identification. They praised and even appropriated early American life in order to assert their social standing and cultural hegemony and to set themselves apart psychologically (Stillinger, 1980). Early American décor also conveyed nostalgia for authenticity, became a form of tradition making, and suggested at least a partial rejection of modernity. Proponents of neocolonialism had a specific domestic vision: 'Colonial meant cozy – a cozy home with a big kitchen, a broad chimneypiece, and ancestral relics strewn about in quaint profusion' (Marling, 1988, 34). In the 1920s and 1930s, photographs of colonial interiors depicting authentically costumed women socializing or doing household chores were extremely popular as wedding gifts (Witkowski, 1998). Finally, the taste for colonial revival objects and designs spoke of aesthetic conservatism among American consumers.

For middle-class households, spending and consumption were increasingly and perhaps even decidedly a female domain in the first part of the twentieth century (Witkowski, 2004). Women had won the right to vote in 1920 with the ratification of the 19th Amendment to the Constitution and they now could 'vote' with their family's dollars as well (see Schwarzkopf, 2011). Major magazines targeted women with ads for fast-moving packaged goods including Palmolive and Ivory soaps, Listerine, and Fleischmann's Yeast (Atwan et al., 1979; Marchand, 1985). New household technologies (indoor plumbing, gas, electric) and labour-saving devices (refrigerators, vacuum cleaners, wringer washers) aimed to reduce women's household work, albeit with mixed success (Cowan, 1985). Tobacco companies pursued the female segment with new brands and appeals, the most notorious being the 'Reach for a Lucky Instead of a Sweet' campaign of the late 1920s (Beard and Klyueva, 2010; Witkowski, 1991). Greeting cards were especially popular among women. Originating commercially in the nineteenth century, after 1900 even more types of cards with more emphasis on printed sentiments became available. Between 1913 and 1928 industry sales surged from $10 million to $60 million annually (Schmidt, 1991).

The thread of anti-consumption was picked up during World War I when popular writer Stuart Chase became convinced that reducing luxuries was 'not only a personal necessity but a patriotic duty to eliminate waste and extravagance' (cited in Horowitz, 1985, 112). Chase went on to write *The Tragedy of Waste* (1925) and, with F. J. Schlink, *Your Money's Worth* (1927). These books promoted restrained and informed buying rather than renouncing or resisting consumption altogether. Chase and Schlink also founded the advocacy group, Consumer's Research in 1929, which was the precursor organization to Consumer's Union and its publication, *Consumer's Report*. A slightly different form of anti-consumption advocacy, in the tradition of Benjamin Franklin, received new impetus with the founding of the National Thrift Movement in 1916. Crusading leaders wrote popular books and magazine articles, gave talks to civic and youth groups, and formed local Thrift Committees across the country. The movement published *National Thrift News*, sponsored a national thrift week, and organized public service ad campaigns. The American Federation of Labor passed a resolution at its 1919 convention in support of the Thrift Movement (Wolfe, 1920). In January 1920, the entire contents of the *Annals of the American Academy of Political and Social Sciences* were devoted to 'the new American thrift'.

Anti-consumption social policy took draconian turns in the 1920s and 1930s. The eighteenth Amendment to the US Constitution, for example, banned the sale of alcoholic beverages. Enforced by the Volstead Act, Prohibition (1920–33) represented a straight-laced, religious and frequently nativist breed of anti-consumption sentiment in American history. State 'blue laws' had been around since the seventeenth century. They prohibited not just the sale of alcohol on Sundays, but also the sale of less morally justified items, such as housewares. These laws privileged the political theology of conservative Protestants over that of Catholics and other religions. Other laws attempted to hobble the competitiveness of successful chain stores through legislation (Hollander and Omura, 1989). Chains stores, especially in the food and pharmacy fields, were a disruptive institutional force that benefited consumers in terms of lower prices and good assortments, but sometimes brought abuses and naturally created many enemies among hard-pressed small businesses. About half the states, mostly in the South and West, passed anti-chain tax legislation. Thanks to the lobbying of retail druggists, many states also instituted resale price controls – known at the time as 'fair trade' – that put floors under prices (Hollander and Omura, 1989; Palamountain, 1955).

By 1941, better business conditions, helped by a rapid increase in military spending, were once again creating a buoyant economy that finally put money in consumers' pockets. The problem was how to spend it. After Pearl Harbor, the war effort necessitated a redirection of raw materials and production, which quickly led to shortages of a number of consumer goods (appliances, automobiles and tyres, gasoline, some foods) and services (housing, medical). In order to mobilize the home front, the US government launched publicity campaigns that advocated being thrifty with goods and services, conserving gasoline and tyres, recycling scrap metals and other materials, growing and storing food at home, obeying price and ration controls, and buying war bonds. The Office of War Information coordinated the efforts of several federal agencies and conveyed these messages through the press, posters, radio and motion pictures. Schools, libraries, companies and volunteer groups helped this effort by disseminating posters and other messages (Witkowski, 2003). Thus, frugality received official sanction during World War II.

Consumption since 1945

A deep reservoir of consumer demand drove the immediate post-war economy. New families and new 'baby boom' babies needed provisioning and businesses quickly retooled from war production to consumer goods. This demand was funded by personal savings from the war years, encouraged by generous credit terms, and given an additional promotional boost from the new medium of television. Business, labour and government leaders agreed that future prosperity depended upon unrelenting mass consumption and this consensus firmly established once and for all the great American propensity for buying and having things. In effect, purchasing was transformed into a civic responsibility – good consumers became good citizens (Cohen, 2003). Large numbers of Americans dropped the ethos of Great Depression retrenchment and World War II home front frugality and re-embraced what Cross (2000), Ewen (1976), Twitchell (1999), and many other observers have contended is the deepest and most durable ideology of twentieth-century America: consumerism.

The material well-being of American consumers was not something to be taken lightly, as post-war politicians generally recognized. In the 1960s during the Vietnam War, President Johnson did not ask the public to sacrifice financially because he believed the nation could simultaneously afford to fight communism in Southeast Asia and build a 'Great Society' at home. After the terrible events of 11 September 2001, the Bush administration actually asked people to continue spending as usual in order to help revive an already sluggish economy. In contrast, President Carter's earnest, cardigan-clad appeals for plain living, energy conservation and lowered expectations did not help him much at the ballot box in 1980. Voters had had enough of oil shortages and stagflation and, instead, opted for Ronald Reagan's politics of early-morning optimism. In the 1980s, and again after 2001, lower taxes, private spending, and record federal budget deficits would fuel economic growth until the bubble burst in 2008 with the onset of the 'Great Recession', whose consequences for consumption still remain profound at this writing.

Any discussion of relatively recent consumption history risks making premature assessments about the past, but it seems that two trends within American consumer culture during the post-war era are particularly noteworthy. The first trend has been the growth of consumer individualism. More and more Americans have chosen to live alone, drive their own cars, watch their own TVs, tablets and smart phones, and eat their meals at the times most convenient for their hectic schedules (Cross, 2000; Putnam, 2001). In his influential book, *Bowling Alone*, Robert Putnam (2001) lamented the loss of social connections and capital caused by consumer individualism. The ideology behind such individualism has been quite influential in shaping social policy. Americans have long favoured putting primacy on what they are told is their consumer sovereignty (Schwarzkopf, 2011), rather than on community needs and collective consumption (Galbraith, 1958). However, the rise of consumer individualism may be slowing and possibly reversing in the new millennium. Young people seem to have less interest in owning their own automobiles (*The Economist*, 2012) and new services, whereby people can rent cars by the hour or day, may encourage a countertrend. Belk (2010) contends that consumer researchers have neglected the study of alternative sharing phenomena, a bias potentially making individual-centred consumption in the US appear more prevalent than it really has been.

The second trend dates to about 1980 when disparities in income and in wealth in the United States began growing more pronounced. The 1980s launched an era of accelerating globalization and ascendant neoliberal politics, with both forces apparently fuelling the rise in inequality. This was in stark contrast to the decreasing levels of inequality that started during the Great Depression and New Deal of the 1930s and stayed moderate through both Democrat and Republican administrations until the presidency of Ronald Reagan. Greater inequality in income and wealth has exaggerated differences among classes of consumers where a small minority patronizes luxury boutiques and a much larger group shops at Walmart and Dollar General stores. Consumer spending drives about 70 per cent of the US economy and the relatively slow recovery from the Great Recession since 2009 has been attributed to weak demand among the bottom 95 per cent. Incomes are too low and, unlike previously, can no longer be propped up by working longer hours, finding jobs for spouses or taking on more household debt (see e.g. Cynamon *et al.*, 2014).

As McCracken (1988) theorized, the symbolic meanings of possessions in the post-war period continued to evolve in tandem with larger shifts in the culturally constituted world. In the 1950s and 1960s Americans quickly became smitten by suburbia and by mass-market luxuries, a consumption style, attitude and aesthetic (e.g. mid-century modern, 'googie' and space age architecture, interior décor and product design) that Hine (1986) has dubbed

'Populuxe'. In the famous 1959 'kitchen debate' in Moscow between Soviet Premier Nikita Khrushchev and US Vice President Richard M. Nixon, 'Nixon seemed to be making a stand for American values right in the setting that was most meaningful to Americans, in the heart of the suburban house – the modern push-button kitchen' (Hine, 1986, 130). The cultural resonance of modernity and futurism as product meanings waned after the Kennedy assassination and with the ramping up of civil rights demonstrations and, ominously, the war in Vietnam.

In the 1970s, consumer goods took on political identities that reflected right vs left cleavages opened in the 1960s. Firearms, an ever-popular American consumer durable, became politicized in 1977 at the annual National Rifle Association convention in Cincinnati, when gun rights activists ousted the incumbent leadership, who had stressed the interests of hunters and target shooters, and installed new executives strongly opposed to gun control laws and willing to fight for pro-gun rights. In 1980, for the first time ever, the NRA endorsed a presidential candidate, Ronald Reagan. By the 1990s an anti-government, absolutist fringe favouring the abolition of all gun controls had emerged in the militia movement (Burbick, 2006; Winkler, 2011). Interestingly, gun rights advocates have portrayed their politics as a consumer civil rights issue and have equated gun purchasing with freedom from government.

Political meanings have also been assigned to different types of motor vehicles. At the start of the new millennium, sport utility vehicles, and especially General Motors' Hummer brand, became political lightning rods (Neil, 2008; Witkowski, 2010). Forces from the left disapproved of their sheer excess – their size makes them visually prominent and a nuisance to other drivers – and deplored their poor fuel economy and environmental consequences. Forces on the right scoffed at the claims of the critics and, in turn, hurled insults at hybrids and subsidized electric cars as being gimmicks of the Obama administration. By 2012, however, with the introduction of more new electric models, and after *Motor Trend* awarded the Chevrolet Volt its 'Car of the Year', right-wing pundits appeared to be backing off. Nevertheless, Democrats are more prone to purchase small, fuel-efficient vehicles, whereas Republicans favour gas-guzzling SUVs and pick-up trucks (Strategic Vision, 2012).

Technology further accelerated the attribution of political meaning in 2014 when a company called Spend Consciously introduced an app fittingly named 'BuyPartisan'. This software enabled consumers to determine whether the source of any given product leaned Democrat or Republican. While shopping users could scan a barcode with their smart phone camera, or search by individual company name or specific product, and the programme would report the ideological leanings of the company as measured by the political donations of boards of directors, chief executive offices, employees, and political action committees (*The Economist*, 2014; Nicks, 2014).

With the rise of the feminist movement in the 1960s, the accepted gendering of household consumption roles became problematic. The dominant cultural ideal – repeated endlessly in consumer magazines and portrayed memorably in situation comedies such as *Leave It to Beaver* (1957–63) – envisioned women as competent yet unpaid, stay-at-home 'consumption managers' dependent upon a male breadwinner's income (Galbraith, 1973). Betty Friedan's highly influential book, *The Feminine Mystique* (1963), challenged this orthodoxy and helped spark a new wave of feminism. Friedan described how many women felt relegated to just being housewives, living their lives through their children, and having this role definition imposed by others. The feminist movement fought to establish new norms legitimating careers and outside work for women and new thinking about a wide range of power relationships between men and women. One expression (and commercial cooptation) of this cultural shift was the highly successful advertising campaign for Charlie brand perfume launched by Revlon in February 1973. Charlie ads featured model Shelley Hack as a liberated woman, striding confidently through New York wearing a chic Ralph Lauren pantsuit (Bird *et al.*, 2011). Like the working women who comprised the target audience, Charlie had the wherewithal to buy her own fragrances and did not have to wait for a man's gift. More broadly, the incomes of newly working women could enhance their economic power within the household unit, a trend that may have accelerated in the 1970s when more and more women entered the labour force to help their families maintain living standards threatened by stagnating male incomes (US Census Bureau, 2015).

The marketing literature published studies of family purchasing roles since the 1950s. Using data collected by the University of Michigan Survey Research Center, Sharp and Mott (1956) and Wolgast (1958) focused upon decision-making patterns for different purchase categories according to whether they were more husband dominant, wife dominant, or shared equally. Husbands had greater say about buying automobiles, but wives had more influence about food spending, money and bills, and household furnishings. Decisions in other categories, such as choices of vacations and housing, were more likely to be shared. The emerging field of consumer research incorporated this interest in household decision-making and its gendered balance of power. In the very first issue of the *Journal of Consumer Research*, Ferber and Lee (1974) investigated the relative influence of husbands and wives on family purchasing behaviour. The authors conceptualized the role of the 'family financial officer (FFO)', the person or persons who, like Galbraith's 'consumption manager', paid bills, kept track of expenditures and decided on how to spend discretionary funds. In their very middle American sample drawn from the small cities of Decatur and Peoria, Illinois, they found that the FFO role was filled by wives about a third of time, by both spouses jointly about a third of time, and by husbands about one quarter of the time. These patterns have remained relatively stable for half of century with, perhaps, long-term trends in consumption balance of power favouring women (see e.g. Pew Research, 2008).

Anti-consumption thought and practice can be found throughout much of the post-war period (Witkowski, 2010). Writers of the 1950s identified and criticized the excesses of post-war consumer culture. In *The Affluent Society*, for example, John Kenneth Galbraith (1958) complained about the manipulation of demand by business, and the over-emphasis on private consumption to the detriment of the quality of public services. In *The Waste Makers*, a popular muckraking journalist, Vance Packard (1960), took on seductive packaging, planned obsolescence and the throwaway psychology of the masses. Some 'beat' poets and artists in the 1950s kept their distance from consumer culture (Shi, 1985) and a decade or so later, hippies and other highly committed adopters of the late 1960s counterculture practised alternatives to consumerism via experiments in communal living and through studied rejection of their parents' suburban values (Reich, 1970; Roszak, 1969). The first Earth Day, celebrated 21 March 1970, marked the emergence of an environmental movement in the US that reasserted the need for a conservation ethos in order to protect the planet from pollution and other afflictions (Fritsch, 1974). During the 1970s, evidence of a 'voluntary simplicity movement' emerged (Leonard-Barton, 1981) and soon numerous newspaper and magazine articles, book-length anti-consumption guides, and a modest selection of scholarly analyses instructed readers about the meaning and practice of varying degrees of voluntary simplicity (see e.g. Dominguez and Robin, 1992; Elgin, 1993; Etzioni, 1998; Schor, 1998; St James, 1996). Somewhat ironically, the movement has been faulted for its focus on personal lifestyle choices (i.e. consumer individualism) and lack of collective action to reform larger political processes (Maniates, 2002).

Conclusion

This chapter has provided a mere thumbnail sketch of the history of consumption in the United States. It does not do justice to the potential richness of the topic, but does offer a theoretically informed introduction. The narrative has followed three phenomena studied in the field of consumer culture theory – the meaning of possessions, the gender of consumption and opposition to consumption – through different time periods and has showed examples of continuity, and instances of change. The meanings of possessions have been constantly in flux over time, while the history of the gender of consumption appears more purposeful: largely male in the colonial era, it became increasingly feminized in the second half of the nineteenth century through the early twentieth centuries. Although some of the specifics have changed, anti-consumption thought has shown broad continuities in motives (religious, philosophical, political) and in its behavioural expressions (boycotts, voluntary simplicity).

These threads are important, but constitute just a small part of a larger fabric of American consumption history. Since the seventeenth century, Americans have made repeated efforts to 'protect' consumers from themselves by regulating alcohol, drugs, gambling, prostitution and other perceived vices (Hollander, 1984). In the twentieth century, the consumer movement has protected, through education, litigation and regulation, the rights of buyers from infringements by companies and governments (Herrmann and Mayer, 1997). Critiques of advertising, branding and other so-called evils perpetrated on American buyers by the marketing mixes of corporations have been a cottage industry for quite some time (see e.g. Klein, 1999; Packard, 1957). Other strands include the civil rights movement in the 1950s and 1960s where gaining equal access for African Americans to stores, restaurants, housing and other sites of consumption was a major issue. Different American subcultures – racial, ethnic, religious, sexual orientation and age-based – have had their own consumption histories. These and many additional themes in the history of US consumption should also be explored.

References

Arnould, E.J., and Thompson, C.J. (2005) 'Consumer culture theory (CCT): Twenty years of research', *Journal of Consumer Research*, 31 (Mar.), 868-882.

Atwan, R., McQuade, D., and Wright, J.W. (1979) *Edsels, Luckies, and Frigidaires: Advertising the American Way*, Dell Publishing Co., Inc., New York.

Beard, F. and Klyueva, A. (2010) 'George Washington Hill and the "Reach for a Lucky ... " campaign', *Journal of Historical Research in Marketing*, 2/2, 148–65.

Belk, R.W. (1992) 'Moving possessions: An analysis based on personal documents from the 1847–1869 Mormon migration', *Journal of Consumer Research*, 19 (Dec.), 339–61.

Belk, R.W. (1994) 'Battling worldliness in the New Zion: Mercantilism versus homespun in nineteenth-century Utah', *Journal of Macromarketing* (14 June), 9–22.

Belk, R.W. (2010) 'Sharing', *Journal of Consumer Research*, 36 (Feb.), 715–34.

Belk, R.W., and Pollay, R.W. (1985a) 'Images of ourselves: The good life in twentieth century advertising', *Journal of Consumer Research* (11 Mar.), 887–97.

Benson, S.P. (1986) *Counter Cultures: Saleswomen, Managers, and Customers in American Department Stores, 1890–1940*. University of Illinois Press, Urbana, IL.

Bird, D., Caldwell, H., and DeFanti, M. (2011) 'A fragrance to empower women: The history of "Charlie"', in L.C. Neilson (ed.), *Marketing History: Voyaging to the New World: Proceedings of the 15th Biennial Conference on Historical Analysis and Research in Marketing*, Quinnipiac University, Hamden, CT, pp. 217–19.

Blaszczyk, R.L. (2000) *Imagining Consumers: Design and Innovation from Wedgwood to Corning*, Johns Hopkins University Press, Baltimore, MD.

Boorstin, D.J. (1973) *The Americans: The Democratic Experience*, Random House, New York.

Bose, C.E. (1987) 'Dual spheres', in B.B. Hess and M.M. Ferree (eds), *Analyzing Gender: A Handbook of Social Science Research*, SAGE Publications, Newbury Park, CA, pp. 267–85.

Breen, T.H. (1988) '"Baubles of Britain": The American and consumer revolutions of the eighteenth century', *Past and Present*, 119 (May), 73–105.

Breen, T.H. (2004) *The Marketplace of Revolution: How Consumer Politics Shaped American Independence*, Oxford University Press, New York.

Bridenbaugh, C. (1950) *The Colonial Craftsman*, New York University Press, New York.

Burbick, J. (2006) *Gun Show Nation: Gun Culture and American Democracy*, New Press, New York.

Burke, P. (2001) *Eyewitnessing: The Uses of Images as Historical Evidence*, Cornell University Press, Ithaca, NY.

Bushman, R.L. (1992) *The Refinement of America: Persons, Houses, Cities*, Alfred A. Knopf, New York.

Carr, L.G., and Walsh, L.S. (1980) 'Inventories and the analysis of wealth and consumption patterns in St. Mary's County, Maryland, 1658–1777', *Historical Methods*, 13 (Spring), 81–104.

Cashman, S.D. (1993) *America in the Gilded Age: From the Death of Lincoln to the Rise of Theodore Roosevelt* (3rd edn), New York University Press, New York.

Chandler, A.D. Jr. (1977) *The Visible Hand: The Managerial Revolution in American Business*, Belknap Press of Harvard University Press, Cambridge, MA.

Child, L.M. (1833) *The American Frugal Housewife*, Carter, Hendee, & Co., Boston (reprinted by Applewood Books, Bedford, MA, n.d.).

Cohen, L. (2003) *A Consumers' Republic: The Politics of Mass Consumption in Postwar America*, Knopf, New York.

Cott, N.F. (1977) *The Bonds of Womanhood: 'Women's Sphere' in New England, 1780–1835*, Yale University Press, New Haven, CT.

Cowan, R.S. (1985) *More Work for Mother: The Ironies of Household Technology from the Open Hearth to the Microwave*, Basic Books, New York.

Cross, G. (2000) *An All-Consuming Century: Why Commercialism Won in Modern America*, Columbia University Press, New York.

Cynamon, B.Z., Fazzari, S., and Setterfield, M. (eds) (2014) *After the Great Recession: The Struggle for Economic Recovery and Growth*, Cambridge University Press, New York.

Davies, A. (2011) 'Voices passed', *Journal of Historical Research in Marketing*, 3/4, 469–85.

Detweiler, S. G. (1982) *George Washington's Chinaware*, Abrams, New York.

Dominguez, J., and Robin, V. (1992) *Your Money or your Life*, Viking, New York.

Downing, A.J. (1842 [1981]) *Victorian Cottage Residences*, Dover Publications, Mineola, NY.

Downing, A.J. (1850 [1968]) *The Architecture of Country Houses*, Da Capo Press, New York.

Dröge, C., Calantone, R., Agrawal, M., and Mackoy, R. (1993) 'The consumption culture and its critiques: A framework for analysis', *Journal of Macromarketing*, 13/2, 32–45.

Elgin, D. (1993) *Voluntary Simplicity*, Morrow, New York.

Elliott, R., and Davies, A. (2006) 'Using oral history in consumer research', in R. Belk (ed.), *Handbook of Qualitative Research Methods in Marketing*, Edward Elgar Publishing, Cheltenham, 244–54.

Etzioni, A. (1998) 'Voluntary simplicity: Characterization, selection psychological implications, and society consequences', *Journal of Economic Psychology*, 19, 619–43.

Evans, S.M. (1989) *Born for Liberty: A History of Women in America*, Free Press, New York.

Ewen, S. (1976) *Captains of Consciousness: Advertising and the Social Roots of the Consumer Culture*, McGraw-Hill Book Co., New York.

Ferber, R., and Lee, L.C. (1974) 'Husband-wife influence in family purchasing behavior', *Journal of Consumer Research* (1 June), 43–50.

Friedan, B. (1963) *The Feminine Mystique*, W.W. Norton & Co., New York.

Fritsch, A.J. (1974) *The Contrasumers: A Citizen's Guide to Resource Conservation*, Praeger Publishers, New York.

Fullerton, R.A. (1987) 'Historicism: What it is, and what it means for consumer research', in M. Wallendorf and P. Anderson (eds), *Advances in Consumer Research,* 14, Association for Consumer Research, Provo, UT, 431–4.

Fullerton, R.A. (2011) 'Historical methodology: The perspective of a professionally trained historian turned marketer', *Journal of Historical Research in Marketing,* 3/4, 436–48.

Galbraith, J.K. (1958) *The Affluent Society,* Mentor Books, New York.

Galbraith, J.K. (1973) *Economics and the Public Purpose,* Houghton Mifflin, Boston, MA.

Gordon, J., and McArthur, J. (1985) 'American women and domestic consumption, 1800–1920', *Journal of American Culture,* 8 (Fall), 35–46.

Green, H. (1992) *The Uncertainty of Everyday Life, 1915–1945,* HarperCollins Publishers, Inc., New York.

Harris, N. (1981) 'The drama of consumer desire', in O. Mayr and R.C. Post (eds), *Yankee Enterprise: The Rise of the American System of Manufactures,* Smithsonian Institution Press, Washington, DC, pp. 189–216.

Henretta, J.A. (1973) *The Evolution of American Society, 1700–1815: An Interdisciplinary Analysis,* D.C. Heath, Lexington, MA.

Herrmann, R.O., and Mayer, R.N. (1997) 'U.S. consumer movement: History and dynamics', in S. Brobeck (ed.), *Encyclopedia of the Consumer Movement,* ABC-CLIO, Santa Barbara, CA, pp. 584–601.

Hill, R.P., Hirschman, E.C. and Bauman, J.F. (1997), 'Consumer survival during the Great Depression: Reports from the field', *Journal of Macromarketing,* 17/1, 107–127.

Hine, T. (1986) *Populuxe,* Alfred A. Knopf, New York.

Hollander, S.C. (1984) 'Sumptuary legislation: Demarketing by edict', *Journal of Macromarketing,* 4/1, 4–16.

Hollander, S.C., and Omura, G.S. (1989) 'Chain store developments and their political, strategic, and social interdependencies', *Journal of Retailing,* 65 (Fall), 299–325.

Hollander, S.C., Rassuli, K.M., Jones, D.G.B., and Dix, L.F. (2005) 'Periodization in marketing history', *Journal of Macromarketing* (25 June), 32–41.

Horowitz, D. (1985) *The Morality of Spending: Attitudes toward the Consumer Society in America, 1875–1940,* Johns Hopkins University Press, Baltimore, MD, and London.

Klein, N. (1999) *No Logo: Taking Aim at the Brand Bullies,* Picador USA, New York.

Kulikoff, A. (1986) *Tobacco and Slaves: The Development of Southern Cultures in the Chesapeake, 1680–1800,* University of North Carolina Press, Chapel Hill, NC.

Laird, P.W. (1998) *Advertising Progress: American Business and the Rise of Consumer Marketing,* Johns Hopkins University Press, Baltimore, MD.

Lavin, M., and Archdeacon, T.J. (1989) 'The relevance of historical method for marketing research', in E.C. Hirschman (ed.), *Interpretive Consumer Research,* Association for Consumer Research, Provo, UT, pp. 60–8.

Leach, W.R. (1984) 'Transformations in a culture of consumption: Women and department stores, 1890–1925', *Journal of American History,* 71 (Sept.), 319–42.

Lears, J. (1994) *Fables of Abundance: A Cultural History of Advertising in America,* Basic Books, New York.

Lebergott, S. (1993) *Pursuing Happiness: American Consumers in the Twentieth Century,* Princeton University Press, Princeton, NJ.

Leonard-Barton, D. (1981) 'Voluntary simplicity lifestyles and energy conservation', *Journal of Consumer Research* (8 Dec.), 243–52.

Lindgren, J., and Heather, J.L. (2002) 'Counting guns in early America', *William and Mary Law Review,* 43/5, 1777–1842.

McCracken, G. (1988) *Culture and Consumption: New Approaches to the Symbolic Character of Consumer Goods and Attitudes,* Indiana University Press, Bloomington, IN.

Maniates, M. (2002) 'In search of consumptive resistance: The voluntary simplicity movement', in T. Princen, M. Maniates and K. Conca (eds), *Confronting Consumption,* MIT Press, Cambridge, MA, 199–235.

Marchand, R. (1985) *Advertising the American Dream: Making Way for Modernity 1920–1940*, University of California Press, Berkeley, CA.

Marling, K.A. (1988) *George Washington Slept Here: Colonial Revivals and American Culture, 1876–1986*, Harvard University Press, Cambridge, MA.

Milbank, C.R. (2000) '"Ahead of the world": New York City fashion', in C.H. Voorsanger and J.K. Howat (eds), *Art and the Empire City: New York, 1825–1861*, Metropolitan Museum of Art, New York, pp. 243–57.

Neil, D. (2008) 'Hummer: Requiem for a heavyweight?', *Los Angeles Times* (7 June), C1, C2.

Nicks, D. (2014) 'Meet the app that helps you put your money where your mouth is', *Time* (23 Sept.). Available online: http://time.com/3418502/shopping-beer-buypartisan-politics (accessed Oct. 2014).

Norton, M.B. (1980) *Liberty's Daughters: The Revolutionary Experience of American Women, 1750–1800*, Little, Brown & Co., Boston, MA.

O'Leary, E.L. (1996) *At Beck and Call: The Representation of Domestic Servants in Nineteenth-Century American Painting*, Smithsonian Institution Press, Washington, DC.

Packard, V. (1957) *The Hidden Persuaders*, David McKay, New York.

Packard, V. (1960) *The Waste Makers*, Pocket Books, New York.

Palamountain, J.C., Jr. (1955) *The Politics of Distribution*, Harvard University Press, Cambridge, MA.

Peck, A. (2000) 'The products of empire: Shopping for home decorations in New York City', in C.H. Voorsanger and J.K. Howat (eds), *Art and the Empire City: New York, 1825–1861*, Metropolitan Museum of Art, New York, pp. 259–85.

Perkins, E.A. (1991) 'The consumer frontier: Household consumption in early Kentucky', *Journal of American History*, 78 (Sept.), 486–510.

Perkins, E.J. (1988) *The Economy of Colonial America*, Columbia University Press, New York.

Pew Research (2008) 'Women call the shots at home: Public mixed on gender roles in jobs', Pew Research Social and Demographic Trends (25 Sept.). Available online: http://www.pewsocialtrends.org/2008/09/25/women-call-the-shots-at-home-public-mixed-on-gender-roles-in-jobs (accessed Jan. 2015).

Pollay, R.W. (1987) 'Insights into consumer behavior from historical studies of advertising', in M. Wallendorf and P. Anderson (eds), *Advances in Consumer Research*, vol. 14, Association for Consumer Research, Provo, UT, pp. 447–50.

Pollay, R.W. (2011) 'Biographic and bibliographic recollections re: collections and contributions', *Journal of Historical Research in Marketing*, 3/4, 507–27.

Porter, G., and Livesay, H.C. (1971) *Merchants and Manufacturers: Studies in the Changing Structure of Nineteenth-Century Marketing*, Johns Hopkins Press, Baltimore, MD.

Potter, D.M. (1954) *People of Plenty: Economic Abundance and the American Character*, University of Chicago Press, Chicago, IL.

Putnam, R.D. (2001) *Bowling Alone: The Collapse and Revival of American Community*, New York: Touchstone.

Reich, C. (1970) *The Greening of America*, Random House, New York.

Resseguie, H.E. (1964) 'A.T. Stewart's marble palace: The cradle of the department store', *New York Historical Society Quarterly*, 48 (Apr.), 131–62.

Roszak, T. (1969) *The Making of a Counter Culture: Reflections on the Technocratic Society and its Youthful Opposition*, Doubleday, Inc., Garden City, NY.

Schudson, M. (1991) 'Delectable materialism: Were the critics of consumer culture wrong all along?' *The American Prospect*, 5 (Spring), 26–35.

Schmidt, L.E. (1991) 'The commercialization of the calendar: American holidays and the culture of consumption, 1870–1930', *Journal of American History*, 78 (Dec.), 887–916.

Schor, J.B. (1998) *The Overspent American: Upscaling, Downshifting, and the New Consumer*, Basic Books, New York.

Schwarzkopf, S. (2011) 'The consumer as "voter", "judge", and "jury": Historical origins and political consequences of a marketing myth', *Journal of Macromarketing*, 31/1, 8–18.

Shammas, C. (1982a) 'How self-sufficient was early America?', *Journal of Interdisciplinary History,* 13 (Autumn), 247–72.

Shammas, C. (1982b) 'Consumer behavior in colonial America', *Social Science History,* 6 (Winter), 67–86.

Sharp, H., and Mott, P. (1956) 'Consumer decisions in the metropolitan family', *Journal of Marketing* (23 Oct.), 149–56.

Shi, D.E. (1985) *The Simple Life: Plain Living and High Thinking in American Culture*, Oxford University Press, Oxford.

Slater, D. (1997) *Consumer Culture and Modernity*, Polity Press, Cambridge, UK.

Smith, R.A., and Lux, D.S. (1993) 'Historical method in consumer research: Developing causal explanations of change', *Journal of Consumer Research*, 19/4, 595–610.

Stearns, P.N. (2001) *Consumerism in World History: The Global Transformation of Desire*, Routledge, London and New York.

Stillinger, E. (1980) *The Antiquers*, Alfred A. Knopf, New York.

St James, E. (1996) *Living the Simple Life: A Guide to Scaling Down and Enjoying More*, Hyperion, New York.

Strategic Vision (2012) 'Democrat vs. Republican: Who's buying what car?' Available online: www.strategicvision.com/press_release.php?pr=42 (accessed Sept. 2014).

The Economist (2012) 'The future of driving: Seeing the back of the car' (22 Sept.). Available online: www.economist.com/node/21563280 (accessed Oct. 2014).

The Economist (2014) 'BuyPartisan: Voting with your wallet' (13 Sept.), 38.

Thoreau, H.D. (1971) *Walden*, Princeton University Press, Princeton, NJ.

Twitchell, J.B. (1999) *Lead us into Temptation: The Triumph of American Materialism*, Columbia University Press, New York.

Ulrich, L.T. (1982) *Good Wives: Image and Reality in the Lives of Women in Northern New England, 1650–1750*, Alfred A. Knopf, New York.

Ulrich, L.T. (1990) *A Midwife's Tale: The Life of Martha Ballard, Based on her Diary, 1785–1812*, Vintage, New York.

US Census Bureau (2015) 'Historical income tables: People'. Available online: www.census.gov/hhes/www/income/data/historical/people (accessed Jan. 2015).

Veblen, T. (1899/reprint 1953) *Theory of the Leisure Class*, New American Library, New York.

Wharton, E., and Codman, O. Jr. (1897/reprint 1997) *The Decoration of Houses*. W.W. Norton, New York.

Winkler, A. (2011) *Gun Fight: The Battle over the Right to Bear Arms in America*, W.W. Norton & Co., New York.

Witkowski, T.H. (1989) 'Colonial consumers in revolt: Buyer values and behavior during the nonimportation movement, 1764–1776', *Journal of Consumer Research* (16 Sept.), 216–26.

Witkowski, T.H. (1991) 'Promise them anything: A cultural history of cigarette advertising health claims', *Journal of Current Issues and Research in Advertising*, 13/2, 393–409.

Witkowski, T.H. (1994) 'Data sources for American consumption history: An introduction, analysis, and application', in J. Sheth and R.A. Fullerton (eds), *Research in Marketing: Explorations in the History of Marketing*, supplement 6, JAI Press, Inc., Greenwich, CT, pp. 167–82.

Witkowski, T.H. (1998) 'The early American style: A history of marketing and consumer values', *Psychology and Marketing* (15 Mar.), 125–43.

Witkowski, T.H. (1999) 'The early development of family purchasing roles in America, 1750–1840', *Journal of Macromarketing* (19 Dec.), 104–14.

Witkowski, T.H. (2003) 'World War II poster campaigns: Preaching frugality to American consumers', *Journal of Advertising*, 32 (Spring), 69–82.

Witkowski, T.H. (2004) 'Re-gendering consumer agency in mid-nineteenth-century America: A visual understanding', *Consumption, Markets, and Culture* (7 Sept.), 261–83.

Witkowski, T.H. (2010) 'A brief history of frugality discourses in the United States', *Consumption, Markets and Culture* (13 Sept.), 235–58.

Witkowski, T.H. and Jones, D.G.B. (2006) 'Qualitative historical research in marketing', in R.W. Belk (ed.), *Handbook of Qualitative Research Methods in Marketing*, Edward Elgar Publishing, Cheltenham, pp. 70–82.

Wolfe, F.E. (1920) 'Organized labor's attitude toward the national thrift movement', *Annals of the American Academy of Political and Social Science*, 87, *The New American Thrift*, 50–1.

Wolgast, E.G. (1958) 'Do husbands or wives make the purchasing decisions?', *Journal of Marketing* (23 Oct.), 151–8.

4

In search of the consumer

The history of market research from 1890 to 1960

Stefan Schwarzkopf

What is and to what end do we study the history of market research?

Although market research is an integral part of modern marketing management, its history has been much less studied than, for example, the history of advertising, branding and retailing. In order to understand the emergence of a consumer-oriented capitalism over the last two centuries, the role of market research is a key factor to be studied. Market research consists of a number of activities, including survey research on consumer expenditure patterns; retail and sales research; consumer (behaviour) research; media and audience research for printed media, radio, television and cinema; product research for new product development; and finally advertising research, for example in the form of copy testing and advertising tracking studies. In many definitions of market research, opinion polling is also included since research for political marketing uses similar methods to those developed for product marketing. Market research comprises much more than just general survey research on the structure and size of market demand for a particular commodity (Phillips, 2007; Stewart, 2010, 80).

Marketing and business historians have often connected the development of market research to the rise of a managerial marketing and consumer-orientation during the early twentieth century. From this viewpoint, market research helps companies underpin their marketing strategies with information about market demand and the competitive situation. This information about competitor products and consumer demand is seen as potentially elusive since it resides outside the boundaries of the firm; and the firm that successfully internalizes this information is then understood to be marketing- and consumer-oriented:

> The marketing-oriented company aims to discover consumer wishes, which are depicted as 'external' to the firm, and does so through market research, psychological understanding, and product development systems. To achieve its goal, it ends the segregation of business functions and integrates them in a manner best able to satisfy

consumer desires. For the marketing-oriented company, it is the consideration of 'external' exigencies that generates success.

(Fitzgerald, 2007, 398; similar in Bakker, 2003)

Although this conceptualization of market research essentially repeats a positivist stance, which assumes that consumer preferences are objectively 'out there', it certainly characterized the way early market and consumer researchers understood their own role (Ward, 2009). This chapter will trace the origins of market research in Europe and North America back to its nineteenth century origins and outline its development up until the mid-twentieth century. In doing so, this chapter takes a critical rather than a positivist stance on market research and its historical development. This chapter is therefore not written in terms of the rise of market research as a 'success story', but also tries to embed market research within wider debates surrounding the politics of market capitalism and consumer society.

Market research and its origins in the social sciences

The scientific methods that allowed market and consumer research to emerge were not developed by entrepreneurs or managers of commercial enterprises, but instead by social survey researchers interested in problems of unemployment, poverty, household expenditure and public health. Key market and consumer research techniques, like the questionnaire survey, household sampling techniques and the focused interview, were first refined by social researchers studying the effects of urbanization, mass unemployment and war on modern social life, consumer expenditure and media usage.

Because of the early exposure of British society to the negative side-effects of industrialization and mass urbanization from the 1840s onwards, the story of social research methods ultimately begins in Britain. It was British philanthropists, statisticians, social scientists and industrialist such as Henry Mayhew, Charles Booth, Beatrice and Sidney Webb, Seebohm Rowntree and Arthur Bowley who pioneered the development of methods for conducting social surveys and the analysis of statistical data (Bulmer, 1985; Bulmer *et al.*, 1991; Converse, 1987, 11–24; Englander and O'Day, 1995; Jones, 1949; Schwarzkopf, 2011a). A key figure in the translation of survey research methods from poverty studies to the field of commercial market research was the London School of Economics Professor in Economic Statistics, Arthur Lyon Bowley, whose earlier work focused on the statistical analysis of household incomes and poverty levels (Abrams, 1951, 19–52; Bowley, 1915; Bowley and Bennett-Hurst, 1915; Dale and Kotz, 2011). Bowley's later work on the development and refinement of sampling techniques, especially the sampling of households, laid the foundations for commercial market research and opinion polling after the First World War (Converse, 1987, 41–3; Germain, 1993). During the late 1920s and 1930s, Bowley edited various market research studies as part of the London and Cambridge Economic Service (LCES), which he co-founded, and he became the first President of the Market Research Society in 1946. The heads of Britain's first market research organizations were virtually all pupils of Bowley (Abrams, 1951, 55; Blythe, 2005, 50; Henry, 1971).

This historical logic of social survey research methods being pioneered by social reformers and then subsequently adopted and reshaped by market researchers repeated itself in many other markets, with the notable exception of France, where the mining engineer and statistician Frédéric Le Play conducted data-intensive social surveys from the 1840s onwards, yet without inspiring commercial applications of the methods that he developed (Converse, 1987, 19; Porter, 2011). In the United States, the social research of Charles Booth, the Webbs and Seebohm Rowntree spawned a whole generation of activist-researchers who 'made of the American survey a more sprawling affair of community participation than their predecessors had done in England' (Converse, 1987, 23). Among these were the survey of a Chicago slum (Hull House) in 1895, W. E. B. DuBois's study of the 'Philadelphia Negro' in 1896 and Paul Kellogg's Pittsburgh Survey from 1907 (Converse, 1987, 22–39; Lissak, 1989). One of the many young researchers inspired by the social reformist climate of the era was Robert Staughton Lynd, who conducted field surveys on the working conditions at a Rockefeller oil-camp in Wyoming. In 1923, the Rockefellers installed him as Director of 'Small City Studies' at the Rockefeller-funded Institute of Social and Religious Studies. In this function, Lynd went to a small town called Muncie, in Indiana, to conduct fieldwork for the classic *Middletown* study, which appeared in 1929 (Igo, 2007, 23–102; Lynd and Lynd, 1929).

Although Lynd was highly critical of the marketing industry, he became a key player who facilitated many crossovers between academic social research and commercial market research. His 1929 *Middletown* study became an inspiration for the research group around Paul Felix Lazarsfeld in Vienna, who in 1933 studied the effects of long-term mass unemployment in Marienthal, a working-class suburb of Vienna. This so-called *Marienthal* study, in turn, was used by Lynd in his 1937 follow-up study *Middletown in Transition*. Lynd became a mentor for Lazarsfeld and arranged for him to come to Columbia University as a visiting scholar on a Rockefeller Grant. Lynd was also instrumental in installing Lazarsfeld as Director of the Rockefeller-financed Princeton Radio Research Project, which in turn provided the springboard for many aspiring researchers like Herta Herzog, Ernest Dichter and Hans Zeisel. Lazarsfeld became a key figure in connecting applied social research and market research through his Columbia University-based Bureau of Applied Social Research (BASR), which conducted market research for the Ford Motor Corporation, Chrysler, CBS, General Mills (Betty Crocker), *Life* magazine and advertising agencies like BBDO (Barton, 1984; Converse, 1987, 267–304; Fleck, 1998; Hyman, 1991, 218–19; Jahoda *et al.*, 1933; Lynd and Lynd, 1937).

Lazarsfeld's research group was linked to the University of Vienna, where he taught statistical research methods. The methods he developed to study social effects, attitudes and behaviours were applied by the group to conduct research into marketing-related problems of tea, coffee and milk brands, and buying behaviour of consumers in Germany, Austria and Switzerland (Fullerton, 1990, 1994). In 1932, Lazarsfeld's group analysed 36,000 questionnaires that the Austrian radio corporation RAVAG had gathered from listeners and in which they reported on their listening behaviour (Desmond, 1996). The research design developed in this extensive survey was then further developed as Lazarsfeld joined forces with Frank Stanton of CBS, Robert Merton, and various German immigrant sociologists like Theodor W. Adorno and Max Horkheimer at the Radio Research Project, which began in 1937 (Converse, 1987, 133–52; Lazarsfeld, 1969).

The story of Lazarsfeld's influence on the development of market and consumer research techniques is far from unique, as can be studied in the history of advertising research. The beginnings of this part of the market research industry can be found in the advertising recognition and memory studies conducted between 1895 and 1897 by Harlow Gale, Professor of Psychology at Minnesota University, and between 1901 and 1904 by Walter Dill Scott, Psychology Professor at Northwestern University (Coolsen, 1947; Kreshel, 1993). Others, like Harry Dexter Kitson and Harry Levi Hollingworth, both of Columbia University, followed this type of research that focused on trying to measure statistically what kind of advertisements were recognized and understood better than others, worked better in terms of attracting attention, and were memorized better than others (Kitson, 1921). Some

American academic psychologists and business professors left their university posts behind altogether and brought their expertise to bear in a commercial context. Among them was Ralph Starr Butler, who left the University of Wisconsin in 1917 to first work as director of commercial research at US Rubber and then as director of advertising at General Foods (Wood, 1961). Famously, the founder of behaviourism, John Broadus Watson, left Johns Hopkins University in 1920 to work for the J. Walter Thompson (JWT) advertising agency (Kreshel, 1990). Paul Terry Cherington left Harvard Business School in 1922 to join JWT as research director (Thorp, 1943). Daniel Starch set up his research company Daniel Starch and Staff in 1923, while still working as Professor at Harvard Business School. In 1926, he left Harvard to concentrate on this commercial work, and developed the first commercially viable advertising readership tests, the so-called Starch Test. This test procedure involved the interviewing of several hundred readers of popular magazines and allowed the measuring, on a continuous basis, of the number of people who had read a particular advertisement (at least in parts) and were able to remember its content and the brand it advertised (Maloney, 1994; Starch, 1966, 7–15).

From 1948, the former Journalism and Advertising Professor at Northwestern University and Columbia University, George Horace Gallup, began offering his own version of advertising readership research services through Gallup and Robinson, Inc. Another researcher who left academia for market research in the United States was Louis D. H. Weld, who held a chair in Business Administration at Yale University before becoming research director at the McCann Erickson advertising agency in 1926, a post he held until 1946 (Assael, 1978; Cowan, 1960). Yet others, like Paul Nystrom and Frederick Stephan, made significant contributions to market research from their positions within academia. Nystrom was a Professor at Columbia University and created many of the conceptual tools that enabled retail and sales research, such as the idea of product category-specific channels of distribution (Nystrom, 1915). In 1931, Stephan took over directorship of the Pittsburgh-based Bureau of Social Research, and later became Professor of Social Statistics at Princeton University. From here, he exerted a strong influence that helped bring novel statistical techniques into the market research and opinion polling industry (Stephan, 1948, 1957).

After World War II, the University of Chicago created a number of academic talents who influenced the further development of consumer research. In 1946, together with anthropologist Burleigh Gardner and clinical psychologist William Henry, the sociologist William Lloyd Warner set up the research consultancy Social Research Incorporated (SRI), which worked on consumption motives for soap, beer, cigarette and car companies. Famously, while working at SRI, Burleigh Gardner and Sidney Levy developed a new type of anthropological approach to the study of the symbolism of brands (Gardner and Levy, 1955; Kassarjian and Goodstein, 2010; Kassarjian, 1994; Levy, 2006).

The influence of academia on the making of the market research industry is by no means a uniquely American story. In Germany, too, university-based research groups turned into successful commercial research companies in their own right. The oldest German market research company, the Gesellschaft für Konsumforschung (Gfk; 'Society for Consumption Research') developed in 1934 out of an academic department based at the Handelshochschule Nürnberg (Nuremberg Business School), where Wilhelm Vershofen and his research associates began in 1926 to study sales and distribution-related problems of consumer goods like hosiery, cigarettes, soap, drugs and toiletries. In 1936, the GfK conducted Germany's first brand recognition study on the cross-logo of the pharmaceutical company Bayer, and from 1937 onwards it began to publish figures on consumer purchasing power in various German cities and regions (Bergler, 1960; Schäfer, 1940; Vershofen, 1940). Meanwhile, at the University of Cologne, Rudolf Seyffert had set up an Advertising Research Institute in 1922 and an Institute of Retail Research in 1928, both of which produced a number of graduates who then continued to work in the market research industry (Seyffert, 1929, 1932, 1939). There was an equally strong impact of academic psychologists on the development of advertising research through the work of Edmund Lysinski at Mannheim University and Walther Moede at the Technical University in Berlin. In the mid-1920s, Moede and Lysinsky used tachistoscopes and other physiological instruments for their advertising research (Regnery, 2003).

A key issue that explains the importance of social researchers and trained academics on the making of market research is the resistance shown by many marketing practitioners towards the concept of sampling. Taken for granted today, this practice often required surprisingly elaborate explanations and justification. Because of their suspicion of small sample sizes, early marketing practitioners relied on quota sampling and the method of stabilization: in the course of a research project, new samples were added until the new samples did not any longer significantly change the distribution and means of the results that had been gathered up to that point. Naturally, this method did lead to unnecessarily large sample sizes. American, British and continental European market researchers before the 1940s agreed that a reliable consumer survey would have to be based on at least 10,000 responses (Germain, 1993, 444; Stewart, 2010, 77–81). When Arnold Plant, a business professor at the LSE, conducted the first survey on radio listening in the United Kingdom in early 1936, some BBC executives doubted the results because the survey had been based on a sample of 'only 20,000' (Anon., 1936). From the 1940s onwards, researchers with statistical training from universities, like Alfred Politz and Samuel Stouffer, introduced probability sampling into market research and opinion polling, a method that European statisticians Arthur Bowley, Ronald Fisher and Anders Kiær had developed decades earlier. As late as 1947, the United Nations Statistical Commission established a Sub-commission on Statistical Sampling, and it was not before the early 1950s that a theory of probability sampling had been completed (Bethlehem, 2009, 16; Fisher, 1925; Lockley, 1974, 13–15; Williams, 1950).

Market research and marketing planning

While social scientists in Europe and America struggled to develop more sophisticated sampling techniques and data analysis methods, marketing practitioners often relied on more intuitive and descriptive methods which, combined with business experience, created market research *practices* that can be traced back to the late nineteenth century. The first instance of a company creating research data in order to advise a client on business strategy is said to have taken place in 1879, when the Philadelphia-based advertising agency of N.W. Ayer wired state officials and publishers throughout the country for information about grain production in order to assist their client Nichols-Shepard Company, a manufacturer of agricultural equipment. The market survey that Ayer came up with broke down the production of grains by county and state, and based on that survey the agency proposed an advertising plan (Hower, 1939, 88–90). This survey in effect hailed the beginning of research-based advertising and media planning, ultimately a function of market research.

Using quantitative data in order to make marketing communications campaigns more efficient became a standard practice from 1890. In that year Ralph Tilton, advertising manager for *The Century Dictionary and Encyclopedia*, developed the method of 'keying' advertisements, which allowed advertising agents to print a unique code into a coupon as part of an advertisement that was placed in a particular publication at a particular time. The coupon invited consumers to request a free sample of a product, a brochure or a promotional gift. Not only were those coupons collected to build up a register of consumers that were potentially interested in the product, the code on the coupon also allowed analysis of which advertising design (message) and which publication (medium) drew most responses. The idea of measuring return on investment (ROI) through market research was born. Especially retailers now began to measure how much money they had to spend through what medium, and for how long, in order to increase the number of visitors to a retail site by a particular number (Calkins and Holden, 1905, 268).

Early market researchers of the progressive era had different ways of creating data about consumption patterns. In 1902, George B. Waldron, working for John Lee Mahin's advertising agency in Chicago, used tax registers, city directories and census data to show advertisers the proportion of educated versus illiterate inhabitants in different districts; the earning capacity of different classes of occupations of people working for the railroad companies; the number and distribution of foreign farmers, especially Germans, and the publications they read, and so forth (Calkins and Holden, 1905, 302–305; Coolsen, 1947, 81–2). At about the same time, publishing houses that tried to attract advertisers to their periodicals also began to collect statistical data on their subscribers. Of course, sample selection and the wording of questionnaires used in this research were biased so as to present their subscribers as well-to-do folks susceptible to print advertising.

Yet this kind of research was also innovative in many ways. For example, the idea of the 'representative sample' was clearly at work when *McClure's Magazine* made a complete list of its subscribers in Cleveland, Ohio, and classified them by social class (leisure class, professional class, working class) and further by occupation in order to show to potential advertisers the magazine's readership. In 1904, the advertising managers for the Butterick Publishing Company in New York, Thomas Balmer, went a step further and inserted a detailed questionnaire into each issue of the company's magazines in order to find out what advertised goods were bought by readers, how many of these goods they used were recognized as advertised brands, how many readers bought these brands because they had seen them advertised, and what type of goods readers were generally interested in. The questionnaire focused on 16 broad product categories (foods, furniture, toilet articles, wearing apparel, etc.), under the heading of which specific product types were listed (e.g. wearing apparel: gloves, boots and shoes, men's shirts, ready-made suits, etc.). For each product type, in turn, there was a list of brands. Readers were asked what brand of product they bought, why they had selected this brand, if they would buy it again and why. Possible answers for the crucial question as to why they had bought a brand included the reason that they had seen it advertised, because the brand was considered the best in its class, the product was durable, or because it had been recommended by sales staff. Over 5,000 completed questionnaires, which contained the names of thousands of brands, were received by Balmer's research staff, who then tabulated the results (Calkins and Holden, 1905, 296–7). Less focused on generating quantifiable data, but equally innovative, was the idea developed by the advertising manager of *Ladies' World* to photograph the homes of subscribers in selected towns in order to give advertisers a sense of the 'character of the homes' they would reach through that periodical (Calkins and Holden, 1905, 291). The *Ladies' World* thus acted as a distant precursor to the ensemble of methods today known as visual ethnography and videography in market and consumer research.

1911 – a service sector is established

The development of these and other research practices was encouraged by retailers and manufacturers who wanted to know what audiences they were reaching through what medium. The scarcity of information about 'which half' of their money advertisers were wasting, in turn, stimulated further interest among marketing practitioners to provide such information. In 1911, the former advertising copywriter and editor of the trade journal *Printers' Ink*, J. George Frederick, set up the Business Bourse on Fifth Avenue in New York as the world's first independent market research company. His wife, Christine Frederick, conducted the research for the seminal *Selling Mrs. Consumer* under the auspices of the Business Bourse, a book that became a path-breaking account of the role of market research in understanding women's consumption practices (Frederick, 1929, 89–101). In many ways, the year 1911 was a seminal year in the establishment of market research services. In that year, the advertising manager of Kellogg's, R.O. Eastman, began systematic readership research and later set up his own firm, the Eastman Research Bureau, which worked for clients such as *Cosmopolitan*, *Christian Herald*, and General Electric. The same year saw the establishment of the Bureau of Business Research at Harvard Business School, which under Paul Cherington conducted numerous retail and distribution research studies and published a regular bulletin (Lockley, 1950; Swanson, 1914). In June 1911, Charles Coolidge Parlin set up the Commercial Research Division at the Curtis Publishing Company in Philadelphia, publisher of *Country Gentleman*, *Ladies' Home Journal*, and *Saturday Evening Post*, among many other titles.

The arrival of Parlin at Curtis Publishing brought market research to a new level. Whereas before 1911, advertising agencies and publishing houses would conduct occasional research surveys, the Commercial Research Division was the first market and consumer research department created on a permanent basis. Together with a number of research assistants, Parlin conducted large-scale studies of the marketing structure of entire industries, including agricultural equipment, textiles, foods and automobiles (Ward, 2010). The aim of these surveys was once again to use them as tools to sell the pages of Curtis periodicals to advertisers and increase their advertising spending. What these advertisers wanted from Parlin's research department was a structural and quantitative overview of patterns of consumption, broken down by income, class and occupation, but also by geography and season. To this end, Parlin collected data on the volumes of sales of department stores in the country's 100 largest cities. These data gave advertisers an overview of how cities compared in terms of the 'climate of consumption' which these locations offered. Published in 1913 as *Encyclopedia of Cities*, this survey provided the first national mapping of consumptions patterns (Parlin and Youker, 1913).

Advertisers also needed qualitative insight into the different sections of the American mass market. To this end, Parlin took a dozen field workers to the small Kansas town of Sabetha in 1920, in order to study homes, shops and farms, and record the influence that new merchandising, distribution, advertising and branding techniques had on a typical community in the Mid-West. In this research, Parlin's staff used questionnaires with open end-type questions, and also cameras to document visual evidence on the lifestyles of people and the character of Sabetha's main shopping district (Ward, 2010, 99–103). Parlin's influence on the making of market research cannot be overestimated. It was Parlin personally who inspired many companies to create market research departments, such as the US Rubber Company in 1915 under Paul H. Nystrom, and the food-processing company Swift & Company in 1917 under Louis D. H. Weld (Lockley, 1950, 735). In 1943, Parlin's successor Donald M. Hobart turned the Curtis Research Division into an independent market research company, known as National Analysts (Wood, 1962).

At the time of Parlin's Sabetha survey, the first market research manuals and textbooks appeared, which provided practitioners and university students alike with a grounding in different research techniques, including both primary and secondary, and quantitative and qualitative research methods (American Marketing Association, 1937; Bartels, 1962, 106–19; Brown, 1937; Duncan, 1919; Frederick, 1918; Reilly, 1929; Shaw, 1916; White, 1921, 1927, 143–63, 1931). The inter-war era was also a crucial period for the expansion of market research activities from surveys for consumer durables, textiles and agricultural machinery, which had dominated research between 1905 and 1915, to surveys for fast-moving consumer goods and media surveys (readership and audience research). Methodological milestones which allowed this expansion to take place were the development of the panel technique, the focus group interview, the consumer taste test, the simulated shopping environment and test marketing techniques.

Panels

During the early 1930s, the panel technique emerged in two forms: retail panels and consumer panels. While the former is an observational form of market *survey*, the latter relies on consumer *interviews*. The first retail panel, A.C. Nielsen's Food and Drug Index, was developed in 1933. Nielsen managed to sign up a representative sample of retailers who allowed research workers to take a census of their stock every other month. The Index gave Nielsen's clients a reliable picture of the impact that product and price promotion strategies had on the sales of their products. What's more, manufacturers were for the first time given a figure that estimated the share that their product had in total sales of all products in that category ('market share'). Part of this innovation was also that Nielsen separated the national market into sub-sections, so-called Nielsen Areas, which allowed manufacturers to compare the impact a radio commercial or print campaign had on sales in that particular region with sales figures in areas where the commercials did not run.. Nielsen introduced the retail index and the Nielsen Area system to Britain in 1939 and West Germany in 1954 (Schröter, 2004, 324).

Retail panels have to be differentiated from consumer and household panels, which began to be used at about the same time. In 1934, Pauline Arnold conducted a national diary study for NBC, which recruited 3,042 housewives to keep a diary of radio listening and other household activities for one week (Beville, 1988, 29). In 1935, General Foods and the publisher of *Woman's Home Companion* began to form groups of consumers and readers, who would repeatedly be asked to test products, or fill in questionnaires about what features of the *Companion* they liked and disliked. The key difference to previous consumer surveys was that this group of respondents, the consumer panel, was *continuous* and only a part of it rotated after some months. The *Companion* reader panel consisted of 1,500 women, and the General Foods consumer panel quickly grew to 2,000 (Lazarsfeld and Fiske, 1938; Sellers, 1942). In 1937, this type of panel research was introduced to the British Broadcasting Corporation (BBC) by Robert Silvey. The first survey was of a small experimental type: 350 respondents were asked to complete questionnaires about each play or feature programme they had heard over the course of four months. During 1938 and 1939, Silvey began instituting much larger panels using the diary method, which eventually helped analyse the opinions and behaviours of millions of listeners. The BBC panel studies and face-to-face interviews with listeners and, from 1948, television viewers, constitute the first and largest continuous audience research programme in the world (Schwarzkopf, 2014; Silvey, 1944).

Paul Lazarsfeld introduced the continuous panel technique to radio research in 1938, recognizing that the repeated interviews of the same listeners allowed to measure attitude changes over time and relate people's opinions of programmes to their personal characteristics. In 1940, CBS extended the panel survey of radio listeners to consumer choices for household products. Using so-called 'pantry checks', CBS interviewers visited the homes of selected housewives over a period of several weeks and recorded what consumer brands appeared and disappeared. These changes were then linked to the advertising that housewives had read or heard on the radio. Through this shift in research focus the consumer panel became a household panel. In 1942, Samuel Barton's Industrial Surveys Inc. began a National Consumer Panel consisting of 2,500 households who reported on their purchases of foods, pharmaceuticals and cosmetics in weekly purchase diaries. Through this panel, long-term tracking studies of consumer brand loyalty were possible for the first time (Converse, 1987, 92; Fleiss, 1940; Lazarsfeld and Fiske, 1938; Schwarzkopf, 2011b; Sudman and Ferber, 1979, 7–8; Womer, 1944).

In the same year, A.C. Nielsen rolled out the Nielsen Radio Index (NRI), which allowed industrial subscribers to follow the radio listening behaviour of initially 800 families in the Eastern United States. Families on the NRI panel filled in weekly diaries and their radios were fitted with an Audimeter, which mechanically recorded which radio wave lengths the radio was tuned in, and for how long. As the size of the NRI panel increased and eventually covered over 90 per cent of American radio homes, Nielsen repeated what CBS had done a few years earlier and combined the radio panel with a household consumer panel in 1946. Nielsen researchers who visited the homes of panel members to collect diaries and Audimeter tapes now also checked household pantries and recorded which brands they found (Beville, 1988, 20–2, 34–8; Buzzard, 2012, 13–30; Nielsen, 1946). The J. Walter Thompson advertising agency also developed a household panel during the 1940s, both in the United States and in the United Kingdom, in order to track people's brand-switching behaviour for their major advertising clients, especially Unilever. In 1948, Attwood Statistics in London set up a panel of 2,000 British households (Wadsworth, 1952). By the 1950s, both the consumer and the household panel had become standard techniques and large research companies and advertising agencies often ran their own panels. At that stage, the idea of cross-national household panels emerged in Europe, where in 1960 the German research company GfK and their French counterpart Taylor Nelson Sofres (TNS) set up the first panel that spanned national boundaries. Other companies followed suit, among them Attwood Statistics, which created a European consumer panel comprising some 16,000 households (Behrens, 1966, 176).

Focus groups

The origins of the panel technique are closely bound up with the desire of market researchers to delve deeper into the reasons why specific people formed a particular attitude towards a product. Researchers like Lazarsfeld therefore began to move the field away from merely recording the aggregates of consumer decisions and instead investigate reasons for attitude formation that preceded consumers' choices (Lazarsfeld, 1935, 1937). At the Office of Radio Research, Paul Lazarsfeld, Robert Merton, Herta Herzog and Marjorie Fiske developed a procedure which allowed them first to measure and then interpret audience reactions to radio shows and movies. While listening to a broadcast or watching a film clip, research subjects were given an electro-mechanical device on which they could turn a dial either left or right and thus express whether they liked or disliked what they heard or saw. The combined reactions of the audience members were then recorded as a graph. This Lazarsfeld-Stanton Program Analyzer allowed gauging whether an audience, in general, liked or disliked a programme (Levy, 1982). Afterwards, the subjects would be taken into a different room, where researchers engaged them in a more conversational interview that focused on people's attitudes and opinions, for example with regards to social and political issues that had cropped up in a radio programme or a propaganda movie (Herzog, 1944). The Program Analyzer device and the focus group interview technique were adapted by George Gallup's Audience Research Institute (ARI) and by Leo Handel's Motion Picture Research Bureau (MPRB), which from 1940 and 1942, respectively, researched film audience reactions for Hollywood studios (Fiske and Handel, 1946; Handel, 1950; Ohmer, 2006).

Although sociologists like Karl Mannheim and Emory Bogardus, and psychotherapists like Jacob Moreno had used group settings to research attitude formation and change during the 1920s and 1930s, it was only from around 1940 that these so-called 'focus groups' were used more regularly, first in communications research and then in market research, too (Merton, 1987; Merton and Kendal, 1946; Morrison, 1998, 121–46; Stewart et al., 2007, 1–16). The research practices in the group around Merton and Lazarsfeld were inspired by the social-psychological methods of attitude research. By contrast, psychotherapeutic influences, especially those inspired by Sigmund Freud and Jacob Moreno, influenced the way depth interviews with individual consumers and focused sessions with consumer groups developed in motivation research from the 1950s onwards (Dichter, 1947, 1960; Fullerton, 2013; Schwarzkopf and Gries, 2010).

Market simulation

Typical for market research from the 1930s onwards was the creation of simulated, virtual environments which blurred the distinction between 'social reality' and the researcher's representation of this reality (Bogart, 1957, 137–8). Consumer taste tests in controlled laboratory environments, such as those conducted at General Foods for Jell-O and Certo, and by Rowntree's for chocolates in the United Kingdom during the inter-war years, enabled market researchers to change the ingredients of new products and test them on juries of consumers (Fitzgerald, 1995, 301–44; Sellers, 1942). These methods were also used during the Second World War in order to design functional foods for troops abroad (Ehrenberg and Shewan, 1960; Pangborn, 1964).

After the war, American and British researchers began to create simulated shopping environments in the form of experimental supermarkets, where the impact of changes in pricing and packing could be tested. Mark Abrams's Research Services ran such a supermarket in central London (Pessemier, 1959). Film camera technology was used for the first time in order to observe consumers at the point of purchase (Alberts, 1955). On a greater scale, research organizations began to develop the method of test marketing. In this procedure, a new product would be launched in selected towns or regions of a larger national market, a test market, in order to gauge the reaction of consumers to a new product. Lazarsfeld's BASR conducted such test marketing for the Ford Edsel in 1957 and 1958 (Wallace, 1961). During the 1970s, the idea emerged of fixing the location of such test markets, for example by choosing a city with a socio-demographic make-up which resembles that of the wider national market. In the United States, Albany, New York, and Columbus, Ohio, have traditionally served that role. In Germany, the research company GfK runs a very elaborate continuous field-experiment on the impact of promotion and pricing on product choices in the little town of Hassloch. In that town, several thousand households and virtually all retailers are linked up to a 'Behaviour Scan' system that records purchases, cable television carries advertising for new products that are only available in local shops, and print media that people receive through subscription carry different advertisements, too (Wildner, 2007, 208–9).

Advertising agencies

Another factor that shaped the market research industry during the mid-twentieth century is the multiplication of institutional actors promoting market research services. Among these actors were advertising agencies. Even before 1911, agencies like N.W. Ayer and Lord & Thomas in Chicago ran Research and Information Departments (Maloney, 1994, 14–15). Under the direction of Albert B. Blankenship, Ayer's advertising research department developed a particular strength in copy testing (Blankenship, 1946). In 1916, J. Walter Thompson set up a research department which quickly became an important hub for market and consumer research in the United States. Here, Paul Cherington would develop the 'ABCD' typology of households, the first socio-demographic market segmentation tool (Cherington, 1924; Converse, 1987, 93). In 1933, the London subsidiary of JWT created the British Market Research Bureau (BMBR), which played a similarly important role for the development of market research in post-war Europe. JWT ran studio kitchens in New York and London, where for research purposes housewives could be observed trying out the products that the agency advertised (Schwarzkopf, 2009). Amongst JWT's most important clients were Unilever and Rowntree, which in some product categories directly competed with Procter & Gamble and General Foods. This competition was passed on to the companies' advertising agencies: Compton worked for P&G, and Benton & Bowles did research for General Foods. All three agencies therefore became early innovators in the field of market and advertising research (Lipstein, 1986; Maloney, 1994, 24–5, 30–2).

Another important player in this game was the McCann Erickson agency under Marion Harper. McCann's research department was first led by Louis Weld and in 1943 it employed Herta Herzog and Hans Zeisel, with Zeisel becoming Research Director after the war; Leo Bogart became its Associate Director. In 1959, the agency formed a research subsidiary MarPlan, headed by Herzog, which was represented in New York and in all major European markets (Maloney, 1994, 29–30; Perse, 1996, 207). Equally influential was Young & Rubicam, where George Gallup set up a research department in 1932. In the same year, the first European advertising agency to set up a research unit was the London Press Exchange (LPE); the unit was led by Mark Alexander Abrams from 1934. After the war, Abrams returned to the LPE and formed a research subsidiary, Research Services (Schwarzkopf, 2011a).

Research companies

In an increasingly competitive market, these agency subsidiaries had to compete with independent research companies. After George Frederick's Business Bourse and Eastman's Research Bureau followed Percival White's research organization in 1923 (Jones, 2012, 70–93). The first independent research companies in Europe were the London Research & Information Bureau, set up by Henry George Lyall in 1922, and Sales Research Services in 1928 (Blythe, 2005, 13). Back in the United States, Arthur C. Nielsen started his firm in 1923 and provided clients with information on the market share of major food, toiletries and drug brands (Honomichl, 1984, 103–7). Also in 1923, Daniel Starch formed his research consultancy Daniel Starch and Staff. In 1926, Archibald Crossley formed Crossley Inc., a research firm which from 1930 would provide the first national radio audience measurement service, known as Cooperative Analysis of Broadcasting, and Pauline Arnold formed Arnold Research Services in St Louis (Beville, 1988, 4–7; Jones, 2013). In 1933, Elmo Roper and the former JWT man Paul Cherington formed Cherington, Wood and Roper. Later, he set up his own firm, Elmo Roper, Inc. (Igo, 2008, 115). A year later, in 1934, Percival White's organization merged with Pauline Arnold's to become the Market Research Corporation of America (Jones and Tadajewski, 2011). That same year, Claude E. Hooper left the Starch organization and, with a colleague, set up Clark-Hooper Inc., which ran a syndicated radio audience measurement service in 16 American cities. The so-called 'Hooper Ratings' relied on the polling methods developed by George Gallup, who set up his Institute of Public Opinion in 1935 (Chappell and Hooper, 1944, 1–9; Igo, 2008, 114–18). In 1937, two British researchers Charles Madge and Tom Harrison set up Mass Observation, a group that from the beginning had the critical input of leading anthropologists like Bronisław Malinowski, and which in 1949 became a commercial market research company (Hinton, 2013; Hubble, 2006). Much of what today is known as lifestyle research and as consumer ethnography emerged with the observational practices of Mass Observation (Sudman and Ferber, 1979, 7). In 1943, Alfred Politz launched his research firm, the same year that Charles Parlin's former research department at Curtis Publishing became National Analysts. In 1946 Ernest Dichter formed his Institute for Motivational Research, which in 1956 became Ernest Dichter Associates International. In 1948, Gallup moved into the field of commercial market research by setting up Gallup & Robinson, a firm that specialized on advertising research (Field, 1961; Hardy, 1990, 1–14; Schwarzkopf, 2007).

In-house research departments

The in-house research departments of large manufacturers, retailers and media organizations played an important role, too. Their story began with Charles Coolidge Parlin at Curtis Publishing, continued with Louis Weld at the meat producer Swift & Company, Paul Smelser at Procter & Gamble's market research department from 1925 (Swasy, 1993, 75–82), and carried on with Henry Grady Weaver, who in 1932 became Head of the Customer Research Department at General Motors. Weaver is credited with having applied the survey questionnaire to the problem of finding out consumer preferences for different functional elements and design features in new car models (Clarke, 1996; McGraw, 2000, 49–52). Other pioneering researchers employed directly by companies were Frank Stanton from 1935 at CBS and Robert J. Silvey from 1936 at the BBC (Silvey, 1974, 85–6). After the war, General Electric brought in Herbert Krugman from MarPlan as Head of Corporate Public Relations. In this capacity, Krugman conducted the first experiments with EEGs while consumers were watching GE television commercials (Krugman, 1971). In the United Kingdom, Unilever had conducted consumer and market research on a regular basis since 1926, and its in-house research department became an independent subsidiary, Research International, in 1962 (Wilson, 1968, 92–3).

University departments

Lastly, the psychology, sociology and economics departments of American universities continuously transgressed the borders between academic and commercial research in marketing. One of the earliest academics who realized this opportunity was Columbia psychology professor James McKeen Cattell, who in 1921 set up the Psychological

Corporation, a company that 'rented out' academics to solve problems of industry, such as conducting personnel tests. In 1930, Yale psychologist Henry Charles Link added the Market Surveys Division to the Psychological Corporation, which from 1932 ran continuous surveys on consumers' brand purchase behaviours and their knowledge of advertising slogans, known as the quarterly 'Psychological Brand Barometer' (Converse, 1987, 107–9). In 1941, Chicago University set up the National Opinion Research Center. Three years later, Lazarsfeld's Office of Radio Research became the Bureau of Applied Social Research, which continued to conduct commercial market research until the late 1960s (Converse, 1987, 267–304). In 1946, George Katona, Rensis Likert and other academics formed the Survey Research Center at the University of Michigan, where Katona began the Consumer Sentiment Index (Wärneryd, 1982). During the 1950s and 1960s, Social Research Incorporated (SRI), a commercial spin-off of Chicago University's sociology department, conducted qualitative research into consumers' understandings of brands. Using the same acronym, the Stanford Research Institute in California (SRI) began to research consumer lifestyles during the 1970s; research that would ultimately lead to the development of the Values, Attitudes and Lifestyles methodology of psychographic market segmentation (Mitchell, 1983).

International exchange and professionalization

As a practice, market research before 1960 always combined quantitative with qualitative methods: 'nose-counting' statistical analysis always sat side-by-side with participant observation known from cultural anthropology. What's more, practical innovations did not always emerge in the United States, as is often assumed. Psychodynamic modelling of consumer behaviour arrived in the United States via Jewish immigrants like Paul Lazarsfeld, Herta Herzog and Ernest Dichter. These Austrian researchers, but also their German counterparts around Wilhelm Vershofen in Nuremberg, developed a form of market research that moved beyond the simplistic 'yes-no', 'like-dislike' binary codes on which American market research practice still relied at that time (Conrad, 2004).

It was because of the forced expulsion of many European social researchers that these innovations reached the American marketing scene. In this story, émigré Jewish researchers played a prominent role. They included economic psychologists like George Katona, originally from Hungary, and consumer psychologists like Louis Cheskin. Cheskin was born in the Ukraine in 1907, from where his parents fled famine and civil war to the United States in 1921. In 1945, Cheskin set up the Color Research Institute in Chicago which provided insights into consumers' psychological reactions to packaging and company logos for clients like Philip Morris and McDonald's. In the year that Cheskin's family left for the United States, another Jewish market researcher was born in the Ukraine, Leo Bogart. In New York, Bogart was to become a leading advertising and media researcher, who worked for McCann Erickson and the Newspaper Advertising Bureau (Bogart, 2003). Alfred Politz, albeit not of Jewish origin, followed a similar path. He was born in Berlin in 1902 and in 1937 fled the Nazis to New York, where he first worked for Elmo Roper before setting up his own research outfit (Hardy, 1990, 1–14).

The influence of Europeans on the making of American market research cannot be overestimated. Freudian and Adlerian psychoanalysis entered American research practices through Paul Lazarsfeld, whose mother was an Adlerian analyst, Herta Herzog and Ernest Dichter. American motivation researchers of the 1950s, like Pierre Martineau, then further developed these essentially European methods (Martin, 1991; Packard, 1957, 27–53). Market research today is a hybridization of a social-investigative 'spirit', which came from Europe in the form of talent, challenging ideas and methodological innovations, and the 'iron cage' of bureaucratic and commercially successful research organizations, which were first created in Philadelphia, New York and Chicago. Market research practices continue to develop because this spirit never fully left its cage. Transatlantic exchange and commercialization processes allowed research spirit and organizational discipline to form a more perfect union. During the 1930s, American research companies formed subsidiaries in Europe: Gallup set up a subsidiary in London in 1937, and A.C. Nielsen opened a London office in 1939. These commercial moves extended a fragile but pre-existing union since the practices they represent already existed in Europe by the late 1930s. From the 1970s onwards, European companies like TNS, Ipsos and GfK reversed the direction of transatlantic expansion by taking over American firms. Today, the top ten global research firms include both American firms like Nielsen and IMS, as well as European firms, which cluster in company groups such Kantar, Ipsos S.A. and GfK SE.

   The professionalization and institutionalization of market research need to be understood within this framework of transatlantic exchange processes (Schwarzkopf, 2013). These processes led to the establishment of specialized academic and trade journals, such as *Der Markt der Fertigware,* the publication series of the German GfK (1929); *Market Research,* published since 1932 by the Market Research Corporation of America; *Public Opinion Quarterly* and *Journal of Marketing,* the two foremost American academic journals, were both founded in 1937; and *Sondage,* a French journal of public opinion research started in 1939. In Canada, many early market research studies appeared in the *Quarterly Review of Commerce,* which began in 1933 (Robinson, 1999, 19). Coinciding with the end of the Second World War, professional and academic organizations in market and opinion research sprang up all over the world. The first of them had already been set up in New York in 1926 as the Market Research Council, under its first President, Percival White (White *et al.*, 1957). Twenty years later in London, the Market Research Society (MRS) was set up. Today, it is the world's largest professional organization for market researchers, and it began publishing *Commentary,* the predecessor of the *International Journal of Market Research,* in 1959. In 1947 followed the American Association of Public Opinion Research (AAPOR) and the World Association of Public Opinion Research (WAPOR), which publishes the *International Journal of Public Opinion Research* since 1989. In 1948, the European Society of Market and Opinion Research (ESOMAR) was set up (Schwarzkopf, 2012a).

A new historical research agenda

The history of market research as laid out so far might give readers the conventional impression of a social science-infused business activity developed mostly by white, male researchers for companies operating within the familiar context of liberal market democracies. Readers might even walk away with the idea that market research falls firmly within the framework of a managerial paradigm that sees firms as the active party and consumers as the passive counterpart, who are relegated to a position of offering responses to research endeavours. Most of the existing secondary literature about the history of market research does indeed seem to follow a slant that privileges this male, managerial, market-mainstream perspective. The recent shift towards more critical perspectives in marketing and business history, however, has also brought in a new set of historiographical and theoretical approaches which are bound to challenge long-cherished Western, managerialist assumptions (Schwarzkopf, 2015; Scranton and Fridenson, 2013; Tadajewski, 2012).

   Research into the history of market research is already moving away from the model of studying single firms, industries or brands within the confines of a single market. Such case studies too often reinforce cause–effect narratives and are thus susceptible to the fallacy of retrospective rationalizations of managerial action instead of highlighting the contingency of managerial decision-making, and the fortuitous and inconsistent nature of managerial and organizational strategy-making. At least as interesting as the uses of market research information for corporate strategy are the circumstances that lead managers and their research partners to *misuse* such information in order to protect realms of authority and other symbolic resources within firms. In the same vein, the recent hype surrounding the challenge of 'Big Data' might encourage marketing historians to better understand reasons that might lead researchers to *over*-supply their clients with data.

An equally fruitful path for historians of market research is to move outside the familiar Western European and North American context. We know very little for example about market and consumer research practices as they developed in colonial and post-colonial contexts. There is some evidence that Unilever's in-house advertising agency Lintas researched the uses of soap amongst housewives in India as early as 1937 (Tandon, 1971, 15–22). Even earlier, British and American consuls in Africa, Asia and South America provided market data to firms interested in selling to these markets (Department of Commerce, 1919; Nicholas, 1984). It would be interesting to know more about the extent to which market researchers had to adapt their data gathering and interpretation methods to accommodate socio-cultural contexts that defied Western models of the rational individual or the suburban, nuclear family as central buying unit (Miracle, 2014).

The same goes for histories of market research that move beyond the boundaries of capitalist markets. Contrary to popular assumptions, market and consumer research was used widely in Communist Eastern Europe. In East Germany, there existed during the 1960s and 1970s an Institute of Youth Research and a separate Institute of Market Research with its own research publication. In General Tito's Yugoslavia, a Marketing Research Association and a similar bureau existed that carried out advertising and product research. In socialist Bulgaria, market and consumer research was used to develop new cigarette brands. In the Soviet Union, research was conducted on the preferences amongst bilingual audiences in various Soviet Republics for movies in either Russian or their local language. Across Eastern Europe, market research aimed at increasing the functionality of household products was surprisingly common (Hilgenberg, 1979; Neuburger, 2012; Patterson, 2003; Welsh, 1981).

We also know very little about what consumers themselves and civil society at large made of their enrolment in market research. In most market research histories that are available so far, the voice of the manager and the researcher is heard clearly, yet not necessarily that of the consumer. In order to avoid firm- and sender-centric accounts, future historians should concentrate more on bringing back the perspective of consumers themselves on their own surveillance by market researchers. With regard to this, the files of Lazarsfeld's Radio Research Project held at Columbia University Archives, and the extensive collections of the BBC Audience Research Department in Caversham near Reading, UK, provide fascinating insights into how radio listeners used the research encounter in order to provide often challenging feedback to CBS and the BBC. During the early days of both research units, open-ended questionnaires were used which allowed consumers to express freely what they felt about the radio programmes they listened to. Over time, the methodological strictures that managers imposed on the interview process tightened. The development of the Likert Scale, the Lazarsfeld-Stanton Program Analyzer, and the Nielsen Radio Index service are among the many processes which made market and consumer research more rigorous, but also 'disciplined' and 'framed' what consumers were able to say (Likert, 1932; Schwarzkopf, 2011c, 2014).

Critical inquiries into market research history might also give more space to concepts of technology, gender and knowledge. It is surprising, for example, that we still do not have a historical account of the influence of computerization on the development of market and consumer research, although it is clear that lifestyle research and psychographics were only possible because of advances in multivariate data analysis and structural equation modelling, which in turn relied on a new kind of computer technology which did not become available before at least the late 1950s (Hanson, 1957; Stewart, 2010, 84). Electromechanical tabulating and accounting machines of the type produced by Hollerith, Powers-Samas and IBM had been used by market researchers since at least the 1920s. In 1948, A.C. Nielsen ordered two Univac computers to help with the statistical processing of market and consumer research data; however, the first computer, an IBM 650, was not installed at A.C. Nielsen before 1954 (Beville, 1988, 35; Stern, 1982). In 1951, the British food retailer Lyon's produced the world's first computer dedicated to business purposes, the 'LEO I', which from 1953 was used by British market research companies to conduct market and advertising research (Gosden, 1960; Land, 2000). The arrival of hand-held data gathering devices, laptops with modems and video/teletext technology from the 1970s and 1980s onwards hailed an era of mobile, real-time and interconnected data gathering in market research. The full implications of these technological changes on the very nature of the knowledge about consumers have yet to be analysed.

In parallel to the breath-taking technological changes in market research, there were also social changes in the professional structure of the industry, especially those brought about by the arrival of more female social science graduates. Market research had always known women in leading business positions. Australia's first independent market research company was set up in 1936 by Sylvia Rose Ashby, who created much of the initial demand for market research services in that country before the era of post-war affluence (Goot, 1993). In the United States, Pauline Arnold was a pioneer in the development of telephone surveys, in-home interview methods and radio audience research methods (Arnold, 1947; Jones, 2013). Also in the US worked Herta Herzog, who for many years headed McCann Erickson's international market research unit MarPlan (Perse, 1996). Coming from the United States to London in 1951, American clinical psychologist Elizabeth Nelson first worked as market research manager for the advertising agency Benton & Bowles, then moved to Mass Observation, and in 1965 co-founded Taylor Nelson Sofres (TNS), today the third largest market research company in the world (Kleinman, 2000). However, historiography has to move beyond an individual focus on 'great industry leaders' and instead ask whether female market researchers coming from sociology and psychology departments changed the nature of data gathering and knowledge creation during the post-war years more fundamentally than hitherto acknowledged (Tadajewski and Maclaran, 2013; Zuckerman and Carsky, 1990).

Finally, the market research and opinion polling industry is not a neutral industrial service sector, but in itself part of power formations which include state and political ideology. Early market and consumer researchers became entangled in issues of political surveillance and even dictatorship. It is widely known, for example, that during the 1950s famous market and opinion researchers like Ernest Dichter, Samuel Stouffer and Paul Lazarsfeld were spied upon by the FBI for suspected Communist sympathies (Hyman, 1991, 86–7; Keen, 1999, 6, 159–67; Tadajewski, 2013). At the same time, on the other side of the Atlantic, the German market research and opinion polling industry was being remade by former supporters of the Nazi regime. The early West German research industry was dominated by three companies, the GfK in Nuremberg, Elisabeth Noelle-Neumann's Institute for Demoscopy in Allensbach (IfD) and the Emnid Institute in Bielefeld. Although the GfK had initially been set up by economic liberals like Wilhelm Vershofen and future chancellor Ludwig Erhard, the research outfit was led by Wilhelm Mann, who became President of the GfK in 1935. Not only was Mann a member of the NSDAP and leader of a mounted paramilitary unit within the 'Brownshirt' movement, he was also a Director of IG Farben, the company that produced the Zyklon-B gas used to kill millions in concentration camps. In this position, he knew of the 'medical' experiments conducted by the Auschwitz-doctor Joseph Mengele, and he supported them financially as well as steering industry funding to the GfK during the war years. He remained President of the GfK until 1955 (Jeffreys, 2009, 275–7; Wiesen, 2011, 160–6). Elisabeth Noelle-Neumann, co-founder in 1947 of the IfD Allensbach, wrote her doctoral thesis in 1940 on American practices of opinion research under the auspices of and with direct financial support from Joseph Goebbels's Ministry of Propaganda, and during the Second World War continued to do research and journalistic work for the security apparatus and propaganda outlets like *Das Reich* (Splichal, 2015). Emnid was founded in 1945 by Georg von Stackelberg, who during the war worked as journalist in an army propaganda section and produced numerous articles and books, amongst others on the exploits of the 'Legion Condor', a *Luftwaffe* unit that bombed the civilian population of Guernica during the Spanish Civil War, and on the Panzer divisions that overran Poland on the outbreak of the war (Meyen, 2010).

These and many other under-researched perspectives on the history of market research range from issues of managerial unreason and failure, the involvement and 'disciplining' of consumers, post-colonialism and globalization, gender and technology, all the way to political ideology and even organized mass murder. Doubtlessly, therefore, the historiography of market research is still in its infancy and promises to develop into an intellectually productive field in its own right.

References

Abrams, M. (1951) *Social Surveys and Social Action*, Heinemann, London.

Alberts, N. (1955) 'Location vs. brand-preference in supermarket milk purchases', MSc Thesis, Purdue University.

American Marketing Association (1937) *The Technique of Marketing Research*, McGraw Hill, New York.

Anon. (1936) Memo 18 March, R44/23/2 Publicity Department, Audience Research, File 2 (1934–1936) BBC Written Archives Centre, Caversham Park, Reading, UK.

Arnold, P. (1947) 'Woman's role in market research', *Journal of Marketing*, 12/1, 87–91.

Assael, H. (ed.) (1978) *A Pioneer in Marketing, L. D. H. Weld: Collected Works, 1916–1941*, Arno Press, New York.

Bakker, G. (2003) 'Building knowledge about the consumer: The emergence of market research in the motion picture industry', *Business History*, 45/1, 101–27.

Bartels, R. (1962) *The Development of Marketing Thought*, Richard Irwin, Homewood, IL.

Barton, J. (1984) *Guide to the Bureau of Applied Social Research*, Clearwater Publishing, New York.

Behrens, K.C. (1966) *Demoskopische Marktforschung*, Verlag Gabler, Wiesbaden.

Bergler, G. (1960) *Die Entwicklung der Verbrauchsforschung in Deutschland und die Gesellschaft für Konsumforschung bis zum Jahre 1945*, Lassleben Verlag, Kallmünz.

Bethlehem, J. (2009) *The Rise of Survey Sampling*, Discussion Paper/09015, Statistics Netherlands, The Hague.

Beville, H.M. (1988) *Audience Ratings: Radio, Television, Cable*, Lawrence Erlbaum, Hillsdale, NJ.

Blankenship, A.B. (ed.) (1946) *How to Conduct Consumer and Opinion Research*, Harper Bros., New York.

Blythe, I. (2005) *The Making of an Industry: The Market Research Society, 1946–1986. A History of Growing Achievement*, Market Research Society, London.

Bogart, L. (1957) 'Opinion research and marketing', *Public Opinion Quarterly*, 21/1, 129–140.

Bogart, L. (2003) *Finding Out: Personal Adventures in Social Research. Discovering what People Think, Say and Do*, Ivan R. Dee, Chicago.

Bowley, A.L. (1915) *The Nature and Purpose of the Measurement of Social Phenomena*, P. S. King & Sons, London.

Bowley, A.L., and Bennett-Hurst, A.R. (1915) *Livelihood and Poverty: A Study in the Economic Conditions of Working-Class Households in Northampton, Warrington, Stanley and Reading*, G. Bell, London.

Brown, L.O. (1937) *Market Research and Analysis*, Ronald Press, New York.

Bulmer, M. (ed.) (1985) *Essays on the History of British Sociological Research*, Cambridge University Press, Cambridge.

Bulmer, M., Bales, K., and Sklar, K.K. (eds) (1991) *The Social Survey in Historical Perspective, 1880–1940*, Cambridge University Press, Cambridge.

Buzzard, K. (2012) *Tracking the Audience: The Ratings Industry from Analog to Digital*, Routledge, New York.

Calkins, E.E., and Holden, R. (1905) *Modern Advertising*, Appleton & Co., New York.

Chappell, M., and Hooper, C. (1944) *Radio Audience Measurement*, Stephen Daye, New York.

Cherington, P.T. (1924) 'Statistics in market research', *Annals of the American Academy of Political and Social Science*, 115, 130–5.

Clarke, S. (1996). 'Consumers, information, and marketing efficiency at General Motors, 1921–1940', *Business and Economic History*, 25/1, 186–95.

Conrad, C. (2004) 'Observer les consommateurs: Études de marché et histoire de la consommation en Allemagne, des années 1930 aux années 1960', *Le Movement Sociale*, 206, 17–39.

Converse, J. (1987) *Survey Research in the United States: Roots and Emergence, 1890–1960*, University of California Press, Berkeley, CA.

Coolsen, F. (1947) 'Pioneers in the development of advertising', *Journal of Marketing*, 12/1, 80–6.

Cowan, D. (1960) 'A pioneer in marketing: Louis D. H. Weld', *Journal of Marketing*, 25/2, 63–6.

Dale, A., and Kotz, S. (2011) *Arthur L Bowley: A Pioneer in Modern Statistics and Economics*, World Scientific Publishing, Singapore.

Department of Commerce (1919) *Selling in Foreign Markets*, Miscellaneous Series, 81, Department of Commerce, Washington, DC.

Desmond, M. (1996) *Paul Lazarsfeld's Wiener RAVAG Studie 1932: Der Beginn der modernen Rundfunkforschung*, Guthmann-Peterson, Vienna and Mülheim/Ruhr.

Dichter, E. (1947) *The Psychology of Everyday Living*, Barnes & Noble, New York.

Dichter, E. (1960) *The Strategy of Desire*, Doubleday, New York.

Duncan, C.S. (1919) *Commercial Research: an Outline of Working Principles*, Macmillan, New York.

Ehrenberg, A., and Shewan, J. (1960) 'The development of a taste panel technique – a review', *Occupational Psychology*, 34/4, 241–8.

Englander, D., and O'Day, R. (1995) *Retrieved Riches: Social Investigation in Britain, 1840–1914*, Ashgate, Aldershot.

Field, M. (1961) 'In memoriam: Claude E. Robinson', *Public Opinion Quarterly*, 25/4, 669–70.

Fisher, R. (1925) *Statistical Methods for Research Workers*, Macmillan, New York.

Fiske, M., and Handel, L. (1946) 'Motion picture research: content and audience analysis', *Journal of Marketing*, 11/2, 129–34.

Fitzgerald, R. (1995) *Rowntree and the Marketing Revolution, 1862–1969*, Cambridge University Press, Cambridge.

Fitzgerald, R. (2007) 'Marketing and Distribution', in G. Jones and J. Zeitlin (eds), *The Oxford Handbook of Business History*, Oxford University Press, Oxford, pp. 396–419.

Fleck, C. (1998) 'The choice between market research and sociography, or: What happened to Lazarsfeld in the United States?', in J. Lautman and B. P. Lécuyer (eds), *Paul Lazarsfeld (1901–1976): La sociologie de Vienne à New York*, Editions L'Harmattan, Paris, pp. 83–119.

Fleiss, M. (1940) 'The panel as an aid in measuring effects of advertising', *Journal of Applied Psychology*, 24/6, 685–95.

Frederick, C. (1929) *Selling Mrs. Consumer*, Business Bourse, New York.

Frederick, G. (1918) *Business Research and Statistics*, Appleton, New York.

Fullerton, R. (1990) 'The art of marketing research: Selections from Paul F. Lazarsfeld's *Shoe Buying in Zurich* (1933)', *Journal of the Academy of Marketing Science*, 18/4, 319–27.

Fullerton, R. (1994) 'Tea and the Viennese: A pioneering episode in the analysis of consumer behaviour', *Advances in Consumer Research*, 21, 418–21.

Fullerton, R. (2013) 'The birth of consumer behavior: Motivation research in the 1940s and 1950s', *Journal of Historical Research in Marketing*, 5/2, 212–22.

Gardner, B.B., and Levy, S.J. (1955) 'The product and the brand', *Harvard Business Review*, 33/2, 33–9.

Germain, R. (1993) 'The adoption of statistical methods in market research, 1915–1937', in S. Hollander and K. Rassuli (eds), *Marketing*, Edward Elgar, Cheltenham, vol. 1, pp. 435–48.

Goot, M. (1993) 'Sylvia Rose Ashby', in J. Ritchie (ed.), *Australian Dictionary of Biography*, vol. 13, Melbourne University Press, Carlton, Victoria, pp. 77–78.

Gosden, J.A. (1960) 'Market research applications on LEO', *Computer Journal*, 3/3, 142–3.

Handel, L. (1950) *Hollywood Looks at its Audiences*, University of Illinois Press, Urbana, IL.

Hanson, R. (1957) 'The machine revolution in the processing of data', *Public Opinion Quarterly*, 21/3, 410–13.

Hardy, H.S. (ed.) (1990) *The Politz Papers: Science and Truth in Marketing Research*, American Marketing Association, Chicago, IL.

Henry, H. (1971) 'Some observations on the Market Research Society of Great Britain', in H. Henry (ed.), *Perspectives in Management, Marketing and Research*, Crosby Lockwood, London, pp. 347–62.

Herzog, H. (1944) 'What do we really know about day-time serial listeners', in P.F. Lazarsfeld and F. Stanton (eds), *Radio Research 1942–43*, Duell, Sloane & Pearce, New York, 3–33.

Hilgenberg, D. (1979) *Bedarfs- und Marktforschung in der DDR: Anspruch und Wirklichkeit*, Verlag Wissenschaft und Politik, Cologne.

Hinton, J. (2013) *The Mass Observers: A History*, Oxford University Press, Oxford.

Honomichl, J. (1984) *Marketing/Research People: their Behind-the-Scenes Stories*, Crain Books, Chicago, IL.

Hower, R.M. (1939) *History of an Advertising Agency: N. W. Ayer & Son at Work, 1869–1939*, Harvard University Press, Cambridge, MA.

Hubble, N. (2006) *Mass-Observation and Everyday Life: Culture, History, Theory*, Palgrave Macmillan, Basingstoke.

Hyman, H.H. (1991) *Taking Society's Measure: A Personal History of Survey Research*, Russell Sage, New York.

Igo, S. (2008) *The Averaged American: Surveys, Citizens and the Making of a Mass Public*, Harvard University Press, Cambridge, MA.

Jahoda, M., Lazarsfeld, P.F., and Zeisel, H. (1933) *Die Arbeitslosen von Marienthal: Ein soziographischer Versuch über die Wirkungen langandauernder Arbeitslosigkeit*, Hirzel, Leipzig.

Jeffreys, D. (2009) *Hell's Cartell: IG Farben and the Making of Hitler's War Machine*, Bloomsbury, London.

Jones, D.C. (1949) *Social Surveys*, Hutchinson's University Library, London.

Jones, D.G.B. (2012) *Pioneers in Marketing: A Selection of Biographical Essays*, Routledge, London.

Jones, D.G.B. (2013) 'Pauline Arnold (1894–1974): Pioneer in market research', *Journal of Historical Research in Marketing*, 5/3, 291–307.

Jones, D.G.B., and Tadajewski, M. (2011) 'Percival White: Marketing engineer (1887–1970)', *Marketing Theory*, 11/4, 455–78.

Kassarjian, H. (1994) 'Scholarly traditions and European roots of American consumer research', in G. Laurent, G.L. Lilien and B. Pras (eds), *Research Traditions in Marketing*, Kluwer, Boston, MA, pp. 265–82.

Kassarjian, H., and Goodstein, R. (2010) 'The emergence of consumer research', in P. Maclaran, M. Saren, B. Stern, and M. Tadajewski (eds), *The SAGE Handbook of Marketing Theory*, Sage, London, pp. 59–73.

Keen, M.F. (1999) *Stalking the Sociological Imagination: J. Edgar Hoover's FBI Surveillance of American Sociology*, Greenwood Publishers, Westport, CT.

Kitson, H.D. (1921) *The Mind of the Buyer: A Psychology of Selling*, Macmillan, New York.

Kleinman, P. (2000) 'Interview with Liz Nelson: Where research goes wrong', *Market Research News*, 3 (Sept.). Available online: www.mrnews.com/sample1.html

Kreshel, P. (1990) 'John B. Watson at J. Walter Thompson: The legitimation of "science" in advertising', *Journal of Advertising*, 19/2, 49–59.

Kreshel, P. (1993) 'Advertising research in the pre-depression years: A cultural history', *Journal of Current Issues and Research in Advertising*, 15/1, 59–75.

Krugman, H. (1971) 'Brain wave measures of media involvement', *Journal of Advertising Research*, 11/1, 3–9.

Land, F.F. (2000) 'The first business computer: A case study in user-driven automation', *IEEE Annals of the History of Computing*, 22/3, 16–26.

Lazarsfeld, P.F. (1935) 'The art of asking WHY in marketing research', *National Marketing Review*, 1/1, 26–38.

Lazarsfeld, P.F. (1937) 'The use of detailed interviews in market research', *Journal of Marketing*, 2/1, 3–8.

Lazarsfeld, P.F. (1969) 'An episode in the history of social research: A memoir', in D. Fleming and B. Bailyn (eds), *The Intellectual Migration: Europe and America, 1930–1960*, Harvard University Press, Cambridge, MA, 270–337.

Lazarsfeld, P.F., and Fiske, M. (1938) 'The "panel" as a new tool for measuring opinion', *Public Opinion Quarterly*, 2/4, 596–612.

Levy, M. (1982) 'The Lazarsfeld-Stanton Program Analyzer: An historical note', *Journal of Communication*, 32/4, 30–8.

Levy, S. (2006) 'History of qualitative research methods in marketing', in R. Belk (ed.), *Handbook of Qualitative Methods in Consumer Research*, Edward Elgar, Cheltenham, pp. 3–16.

Likert, R. (1932) 'A technique for the measurement of attitudes', *Archives of Psychology*, 22/140, 1–55.

Lipstein, B. (1986) 'An historical retrospective of copy research', *Journal of Advertising Research*, 24/6, 11–14.

Lissak, R.S. (1989) *Pluralism and Progressivism: Hull House and the New Immigrants, 1890–1919*, University of Chicago Press, Chicago, IL.

Lockley, L.C. (1974) 'History and development of market research', in R. Ferber (ed.), *Handbook of Marketing Research*, McGraw Hill, New York, pp. 3–15.

Lockley, L.C. (1950) 'Notes on the history of marketing research', *Journal of Marketing*, 14/5, 733–6.

Lynd, R.S., and Lynd, H.M. (1929) *Middletown: A Study in Modern American Culture*, Harcourt Brace, New York.

Lynd, R.S., and Lynd, H.M. (1937) *Middletown in Transition: A Study in Cultural Conflicts*, Harcourt Brace, New York.

McGraw, T. (2000) *American Business, 1920–2000: How it Worked*, Harlan Davidson, Wheeling, IL.

Maloney, J. (1994) 'The first 90 years of advertising research', in E.M. Clark, T.C. Brock and D.W. Stewart (eds), *Attention, Attitude, and Affect in Response to Advertising*, Lawrence Erlbaum, Hillsdale, NJ, pp. 13–54.

Mark, D. (ed.) (1996) *Paul Lazarsfeld: Wiener RAVAG Studie 1932. Der Beginn der modernen Rundfunkforschung*, Guthmann-Peterson, Vienna.

Martin, D. (1991) *The Advertising Legacy of Pierre Martineau*, American Advertising Federation, New York.

Merton, R. (1987) 'The focussed interview and focus groups: Continuities and discontinuities', *Public Opinion Quarterly*, 51/4, 550–66.

Merton, R., and Kendal, P. (1946) 'The focused interview', *American Journal of Sociology*, 51/6, 541–57.

Meyen, M. (2010) 'Karl-Georg Kurt Gustav Graf von Stackelberg', in *Neue Deutsche Biographie (NDB)*, vol. 24, Duncker & Humblot, Berlin, p. 781.

Miracle, G. (2014) 'International advertising research: A historical review', in H. Cheng (ed.), *The Handbook of International Advertising Research*, Wiley-Blackwell, Malden, MA, pp. 3–31.

Mitchell, A. (1983) *Nine American Lifestyles: Who we are and Where we're Going*, Macmillan, New York.

Morrison, D. (1998) *The Search for a Method: Focus Groups and the Development of Mass Communication*, University of Luton Press, Luton.

Neuburger, M. (2012) 'The taste of smoke: Bulgartabak and the manufacturing of cigarettes and satisfaction', in M. Neuburger and P. Bren (eds), *Communism Unwrapped: Consumption in Cold War Eastern Europe*, Oxford University Press, New York, pp. 91–115.

Nicholas, S.J. (1984) 'The overseas marketing performance of British industry, 1870–1914', *Economic History Review*, 37/4, 489–506.

Nielsen, A.C. (1946) *How you can Get the Ideal Radio Research Service*, A.C. Nielsen Co., Chicago, IL.

Nystrom, P.H. (1915) *The Economics of Retailing*, Ronald Press, New York.

Ohmer, S. (2006) *George Gallup in Hollywood*, Columbia University Press, New York.

Packard, V. (1957) *The Hidden Persuaders*, McKay Co., New York.

Pangborn, R. (1964) 'Sensory evaluation of food: A look backward and forward', *Food Technology*, 18/9, 1309–13.

Parlin, C.C., and Youker, H.S. (1913) *Encyclopedia of Cities*, Curtis Publishing Co., Philadelphia, PA.

Patterson, P.H. (2003) 'Truth half told: Finding the perfect pitch for advertising and marketing in socialist Yugoslavia, 1950–1991', *Enterprise and Society*, 4/2, 179–225.

Perse, E. (1996) 'Herta Herzog', in N. Signorielli (ed.), *Women in Communication: A Biographical Sourcebook*, Greenwood Publishers, Westport, CT, pp. 202–11.

Pessemier, E.A. (1959) 'A new way to determine buying decisions', *Journal of Marketing*, 24/2, 41–6.

Phillips, A. (2007) 'What is market research', in M. van Hamersveld and C. de Bont (eds), *The Market Research Handbook* (5th edn), Wiley, Chichester, pp. 37–60.

Porter, T. (2011) 'Reforming vision: The engineer Le Play learns to observe society sagely', in L. Daston and E. Lunbeck (eds), *Histories of Scientific Observation*, University of Chicago Press, Chicago, IL, pp. 281–302.

Regnery, C. (2003) *Die Deutsche Werbeforschung, 1900–1945*, Monsenstein & Vannerdat, Münster.

Reilly, W.J. (1929) *Marketing Investigations*, Ronald Press, New York.

Robinson, D. (1999) *The Measure for Democracy: Polling, Market Research and Public Life, 1930–1945*, Toronto University Press, Toronto.

Schäfer, E. (1940) *Grundlagen der Marktforschung, Marktuntersuchung und Marktbeobachtung*, Krische Verlag, Nürnberg.

Schröter, H. (2004) 'Zur Geschichte der Marktforschung in Europa im 20. Jahrhundert', in R. Walter (ed.), *Geschichte des Konsums*, Franz Steiner, Stuttgart, pp. 320–41.

Schwarzkopf, S. (2007) '"Culture" and the limits of innovation in marketing research: Ernest Dichter, motivation studies and psychoanalytic consumer research in Great Britain, 1950–1970', *Management and Organizational History*, 2/3, 219–36.

Schwarzkopf, S. (2009) 'Discovering the consumer: Market research, product innovation and the creation of brand loyalty in Britain and the United States in the interwar years', *Journal of Macromarketing*, 29/1, 8–20.

Schwarzkopf, S. (2011a) 'A radical past? The political history of market research in Great Britain, 1900–1950', in K. Brückweh (ed.), *The Voice of the Citizen Consumer: A History of Market Research, Consumer Movements, and the Political Public Sphere*. Oxford University Press, Oxford, pp. 29–50.

Schwarzkopf, S. (2011b) 'The consumer as "voter", "judge" and "jury": Historical origins and political consequences of a marketing myth', *Journal of Macromarketing*, 31/1, 8–18.

Schwarzkopf, S. (2011c) 'The statisticalization of the consumer in British market research, *c.*1920–1960: Profiling a good society', in T. Crook and G. O'Hara (eds), *Statistics and the Public Sphere: Numbers and the People in Modern Britain, c.1800–2000*, Routledge, London, pp. 144–62.

Schwarzkopf, S. (2012a) 'Managing the unmanageable: The professionalisation of market and consumer research in postwar Europe', in R. Jessen and L. Langer (eds), *Transformations of Retailing in Europe after 1945*, Ashgate, Aldershot, pp. 163–78.

Schwarzkopf, S. (2013) 'From Fordist to creative economies: The de-Americanization of European advertising cultures since the 1960s', *European Review of History*, 20/5, pp. 859–79.

Schwarzkopf, S. (2014) 'The politics of enjoyment: competing television audience measurement systems in Britain, 1950–1980', in J. Bourdon and C. Méadel (eds), *Television Audiences Across the World: Deconstructing the Ratings Machine*, Palgrave, London, pp. 33–52.

Schwarzkopf, S. (2015) 'Marketing history from below: Towards a paradigm shift in marketing historical research', *Journal of Historical Research in Marketing*, 7/3, 1–15.

Schwarzkopf, S., and Gries, R. (eds) (2010) *Ernest Dichter and Motivation Research: New Perspectives on the Making of Post-War Consumer Culture*, Palgrave Macmillan, London.

Scranton, P., and Fridenson, P. (2013) *Reimagining Business History*, Johns Hopkins University Press, Baltimore, MD.

Sellers, M. (1942) 'Pre-testing of products by consumer juries', *Journal of Marketing*, 6/4, 76–80.

Seyffert, R. (1929) *Allgemeine Werbelehre*, Poeschel, Stuttgart.

Seyffert, R. (1932) *Handbuch des Einzelhandels*, Poeschel, Stuttgart.

Seyffert, R. (1939) *Das Kölner Einzelhandelsinstitut 1928–1938: Bericht über 10 Jahre Forschung und Lehre*, Poeschel, Stuttgart.

Shaw, A.W. (1916) *An Approach to Business Problems*, Harvard University Press, Cambridge, MA.

Silvey, R. (1944) 'Methods of listener research employed by the British Broadcasting Corporation', *Journal of the Royal Statistical Society*, 107/3–4, 190–230.

Silvey, R. (1974) *Who's Listening? The Story of BBC Audience Research*, Allen & Unwin, London.

Splichal, S. (2015) 'Legacy of Elisabeth Noelle-Neumann: The spiral of silence and other controversies', *European Journal of Communications*, 30/3, 353–63.

Starch, D. (1966) *Measuring Advertising Readership and Results*, McGraw Hill, New York.

Stephan, F. (1948) 'History of the uses of modern sampling procedures', *Journal of the American Statistical Association*, 43/241, 12–39.

Stephan, F. (1957) 'Advances in survey methods and measurement techniques', *Public Opinion Quarterly*, 21/1, 79–90.

Stern, N. (1982) 'The Eckert-Mauchly computers: Conceptual triumphs, commercial tribulations', *Technology and Culture*, 23/4, 569–82.

Stewart, D. (2010) 'The evolution of market research', in P. Maclaran, M. Saren, B. Stern and M. Tadajewski (eds), *The SAGE Handbook of Marketing Theory*, Sage, London, 74–88.

Stewart, D., Shamdasani, P., and Rook, D. (2007) *Focus Groups: Theory and Practice*, Sage, Thousand Oaks, CA.

Sudman, S., and Ferber, R. (1979) *Consumer Panels*, American Marketing Association, Chicago, IL.

Swanson, A.E. (1914) 'The Harvard Bureau of Business Research', *Journal of Political Economy*, 22/9, 896–900.

Swasy, A. (1993) *Soap Opera: The Inside Story of Procter & Gamble*, Times Books, New York.

Tadajewski, M. (2012) 'History and critical marketing studies', *Journal of Historical Research in Marketing*, 4/3, 440–52.

Tadajewski, M. (2013) 'Promoting the consumer society: Ernest Dichter, the Cold War and FBI', *Journal of Historical Research in Marketing*, 5/2, 192–211.

Tadajewski, M., and Maclaran, P. (2013) 'Remembering female contributors to marketing', Special Issue of *Journal of Historical Research in Marketing*, 3/3, 260–412.

Tandon, P. (1971) *Beyond Punjab, 1937–1960*, Chatto & Windus, London.

Thorp, W.L. (1943) 'Paul T. Cherington, 1876–1943', *Journal of the American Statistical Association*, 38/224, 471–2.

Vershofen, W. (1940) *Handbuch der Verbrauchsforschung*, 2 vols, Heymann, Berlin.

Wadsworth, R. (1952) 'The experience of a user of a consumer panel', *Journal of the Royal Statistical Society*, C1/3, 169–78.

Wallace, D. (1961) 'Background and objectives of the Edsel panel study', Paul F. Lazarsfeld Papers, Box 6, Subject File BASR, Columbia University Archives.

Ward, D.B. (2009) 'Capitalism, early market research, and the creation of the American consumer', *Journal of Historical Research in Marketing*, 1/2, 200–23.

Ward, D.B. (2010) *A New Brand of Business: Charles Coolidge Parlin, Curtis Publishing Company, and the Origins of Market Research*, Temple University Press, Philadelphia, PA.

Wärneryd, K.E. (1982) 'The life and work of George Katona', *Journal of Economic Psychology*, 2/1, 1–31.

Welsh, W. (ed.) (1981) *Survey Research and Public Attitudes in Eastern Europe and the Soviet Union*, Pergamon Press, Elmsford, NY.

White, P. (1921) *Market Analysis: Its Principles and Methods*, McGraw Hill, New York.

White, P. (1927) *Scientific Marketing Management: Its Principles and Methods*, Harper Bros., New York.

White, P. (1931) *Marketing Research Technique*, Harper Bros., New York.

White, P., Blankenship, A.B., West, D.E., and Richmond, H.A. (1957) *The Market Research Council, 1927–1957*, Market Research Council, New York.

Wiesen, S.J. (2011) *Creating the Nazi Marketplace: Commerce and Consumption in the Third Reich*, Cambridge University Press, New York.

Wildner, R. (2007) 'Launch and monitoring of in-market performance', in M. van Hamersveld and C. de Bont (eds), *The Market Research Handbook* (5th edn), Wiley, Chichester, pp. 199–216.

Williams, R. (1950) 'Probability sampling in the field: A case history', *Public Opinion Quarterly*, 14/2, 316–30.

Wilson, C. (1968) *Unilever, 1945–1965: Challenge and Response in the Postwar Industrial Revolution*, Cassell, London.

Womer, S. (1944) 'Some applications of the continuous consumer panel', *Journal of Marketing*, 9/2, 132–6.

Wood, J.P. (1961) 'Ralph Starr Butler', *Journal of Marketing*, 25/4, 69–71.

Wood, J.P. (1962) 'Donald M. Hobart', *Journal of Marketing*, 26/1, 79–80.

Zuckerman, M.E., and Carsky, M.L. (1990) 'Contribution of women to US marketing thought: The consumers' perspective, 1900–1940', *Journal of the Academy of Marketing Science*, 18/4, 313–18.

5

Segmentation in practice

An historical overview of the eighteenth and nineteenth centuries

Ronald A. Fullerton

Introduction

Segmentation is the very essence of marketing – giving people what they want. A popular definition of segmentation is that it is 'the act of dividing a market into distinct and meaningful groups of buyers who might merit separate products or marketing mixes' (Kotler, 1980, 294). Why do these buyers merit separate product mixes? Because they have different *preferences*, they do not all want the same offering and they do not necessarily want what is currently on the market. The academic, theoretical, literature on segmentation dates to the twentieth century, first to the German Kliemann (1928) and then to the better known work by the American Wendell Smith (1956). These authors, especially Smith, were among the first to use the term 'segmentation'.

But the practice of segmentation is *much* older, just as the practice of aggressive marketing that aims to please is far, far older (Fullerton, 1988): the practice of segmentation long antedates formal thought about it. Wind (1980) finds that segmentation thought 'really just' codifies and improves 'things that smart marketers had been doing intuitively for a long time'. This chapter gives examples of what smart marketers had been doing about segmentation, looking at the history of practice in Britain, Germany and the United States from the eighteenth to the early twentieth centuries.

Myriad examples will be given, starting with an extended analysis of the publishing industry in Britain, Germany and the United States. This will be followed by a series of other examples from silverware, clothing fashions, buttons and miscellaneous metal goods, bicycles, fountain pens, ceramics and pottery, and weapons manufacture. Except for silverware all of these businesses were long characterized by some form of 'mass' production, usually through amassing a great deal of hand labour – at the same time as their owners were offering differing products for different preferences. Markets were segmented by preferences based on age, race, gender, occupation, religion, region, occasion, income, tastes and social class. The markets chosen are only a part of a much larger universe; it is actually harder to find examples of producing one size (and colour) for all, than it is to find examples of segmentation being practised.

When individual hand production was the rule, before the expansion of mass production in the later eighteenth century, it would have been very easy to customize products according to individual buyer tastes. Anyone who has seen European museum collections of early modern weapons (from 1517 onwards) will have seen how carefully designed these were for the buyer's taste, with elaborate engravings and inlays. Of course those fancy weapons were far too expensive for most people who had little if any discretionary money, which leads us to the conclusion that high costs did constrain the variety and number of product offerings as well as their sales. It was the desire to drive down costs and hence widen markets that led to the aggressive development of mass production. But, as we shall see, mass production, even in its early stages, did not preclude producing differing products for different preferences.

Why focus on the eighteenth and nineteenth centuries? There are two reasons for my choice. With few exceptions, previous writers on the history of segmentation have concentrated on the late nineteenth and the twentieth centuries. Even if one accepts the idiotic and discredited logic of the 'Production-Sales-Marketing eras model' (see Jones and Richardson, 2007, for a detailed critique) that marketing fully began in 1950, 66 years ago, modern marketing abounds in segmentation. Also, there are a multitude of good examples of segmentation being practised across Western Europe and in the United States during the eighteenth and nineteenth centuries.

Previous writing on the history of segmentation

Several writers have dealt with one aspect or another of the history of segmentation (e.g. Banham, 2012; Branchik, 2002, 2007, 2010; Fullerton, 2012; Hollander and Germain, 1992; Quickendon and Kover, 2007; Petty, 1995; Powers and Steward, 2010; Tedlow, 1990, 1997; Tedlow and Jones, 1993). Four discuss the eighteenth century (Banham, 2012; Fullerton, 2012; Quickenden and Kover, 2007; Witkowski, 1985) and two (Fullerton, 2012; Henning and Witkowski, 2013) discuss much of the nineteenth century. Three of these publications have been books, covering a wider topical swath than most of the articles (Hollander and Germain, 1992; Tedlow, 1990; Tedlow and Jones, 1993).

Tedlow's (1990) book-length study focuses upon the United States after about 1880. The bulk of it consists of excellent paired case studies, e.g. General Motors and Ford, framed by a disappointing attempt to generalize about US segmentation history. Tedlow's framework posits three historical phases: (1) fragmentation of the US market prior to about 1880, with geographic segmentation enforced by inadequate transportation and institutional development; (2) unification of the whole US market and the development of mass marketing centred on individual products – e.g. Henry Ford's insistence on the Model T painted black; and (3) segmentation, which began at different times for different companies and markets. As we shall see below, the first two generalizations have numerous exceptions: there were national markets for some products well before 1880, and large-scale production was often coupled with production of many versions of products for different segments. Before 1840 transportation was pathetic compared to what came later with the railroads – yet there had been transportation of goods long distances since antiquity, water-borne transportation by sea and by river being widely used.

The chapters in the 1993 book edited by Tedlow and Geoffrey Jones cover Great Britain and other countries as well as the United States, trying to assess the generalizability of Tedlow's historical framework. Tedlow's US periodization is show to have exceptions overseas, e.g. Scotch whisky. The charming 1992 book by Hollander and Germain deals with US companies appealing to 'youth' segmentation. Such segmentation is found to have been increasingly widespread as the twentieth century went on, well before Pepsi Cola emphasized in the 1960s that it was the choice of youth and youthful-feeling people. The studies by Banham, Fullerton, Quickendon and Kover, and Witkowski will be dealt with in the text of the chapter. Those by Branchik and Powers and Steward, deal exclusively with the twentieth century and thus are beyond the scope of this chapter.

The use of segmentation in the book trade

The major example of this chapter concerns the book trade in Western Europe and America, which has actively practised different forms of segmentation for centuries. The history is extremely rich, and I attempt but an overview. Although often associated with high culture, far from the gritty hustle and bustle of more prosaic industries like beer brewing and shipbuilding, the book trade was one of the pioneer businesses of the Western world and has remained vibrant down to the present day. Long before the industrial revolution of the eighteenth century, bookmen had developed complex regional, national and international distribution networks; the most successful book people had always shown responsiveness to market demand (Febvre and Martin, 1976, ch. 4). No early trade made greater use of advertising, and even during most of the nineteenth century only patent medicine advertising rivalled the volume of that for books.

The key to understanding the book trade as a business is to recognize the central role of publishers, not only in promoting and distributing, but also in creating books (Fullerton, 1975, 131, 237–42; Fullerton, 1977, 1979; Sarkowski, 1976, 73–4, 86). Most books – especially popular ones – came into being because a publisher had an idea and commissioned others to develop it into a book. Books which did not originate with a publisher were only accepted if they meshed with the publisher's ideas. A substantial element of the publisher's thinking had to do with market demand. German publishers especially were fond of saying that they published quality books with no thought of demand. No doubt some did. But they were businessmen and to stay in business some of their ideas had to reflect market demand which was sometimes, but hardly exclusively, for works of high quality. Long before the nineteenth century, publishers had known that market demand displayed heterogeneity – different people had different preferences.

Among publishers in the eighteenth and early nineteenth centuries it was common practice to have copies of popular works printed on two to five different grades of paper (the top grade was usually vellum), with a noticeable price differential between the grades. The printing plates, which had to be laboriously assembled by hand, remained the same. More expensive paper versions might have separate pages of illustrations, ranging from elegant and expensive copperplates to cruder but cheaper woodcuts.

In Germany, for example, a 20-volume edition of the literary giant Johann Wolfgang von Goethe's works was available in the early nineteenth century on four grades of paper, the vellum (parchment) costing twice as much as the lowest-priced 'ordinary' cotton rag paper (*Monatsbericht*, 1816, 8–11). The set could be purchased either on subscription or by cash in advance at a saving of 27 to 33 per cent (depending on edition) – an indication of what today would be considered using deal-proneness and price sensitivity as segmentation variables. The most expensive editions made up less than 10 per cent of most printings. Elegant and costly, they were intended for the wealthy builders of imposing mansion, castle, court and cloister libraries who had been a major segment for centuries.

In the United States, the late eighteenth-century American publisher Thomas offered a variety of sizes of the Bible: duodecimo for schools and private reading, quarto for reading aloud to families, folio for the pulpit. The British publisher Brown exported to America a 'New York' edition of the Bible that was sold in sections by subscription ($0.25 per part) and specifically targeted at working families. Its sales were substantial (Gross and Kelley, 2010, 83).

The American publisher Mathew Carey in the years after 1811 began issuing a wide variety of versions of the Bible, ranging in cost from $3.50 to $12.50. He used three sets of standing type (which didn't have to be taken apart after printing) to issue both duodecimo and quarto Bibles in a variety of paper grades from coarse to superfine. He offered quarto-sized Bibles in a variety of bindings from plain calf to red morocco gilt; and a variety of contents with or without plates, maps, Apocrypha, and concordance (Gross and Kelley, 2010, 97–8).

Banham's (2012) article on occasional publishers in the UK between 1771 and 1844 asserts that 'Segmentation was used to target specific market segments both by price point, location, and special interest, in some cases repackaging the same product in order to promote it to a different audience' (p. 535). The Gyles and Giles Blaine Company, when they published for open markets, tended to publish pamphlets rather than books – because they were cheaper and easier to print, and could be priced to sell to a broad market, especially publications dealing with news about political and religious issues, and graphic court proceedings. For 'The London Stage', a series of books of plays, they offered books in parts or as a whole – at different price levels.

The children's book segment was large and it kept growing. German parents, like their counterparts in England (McKendrick *et al.*, 1982, ch. 7), believed that nothing could do more to further their children's social standing than exposure to reading matter. Meeting the opportunity, publishers produced a considerable volume of children's material, much of it with the heavy doses of didactic and moral messages parents liked. One German bookshop selected 200 children's titles to push in 1820; there were many other titles as well. Employing considerable amounts of cooperative advertising with booksellers, publishers advertised children's works heavily during late autumn as Christmas gifts, thus using occasion and season as segmentation variables along with the demographic and socio-economic ones. In other words, they were practising multi-variable segmentation.

Gift books for adults for the Christmas season had been introduced in France and Germany sometime during the eighteenth century. In the 1820s United States publishers, following those of Britain, introduced them to the New World. They employed fancy bindings – morocco leathers stamped in gold, often with gilt edges and decorated paper end sheets. Examples include annual anthologies of verse and short prose with engraved illustrations (Gross and Kelley, 2010, 117).

Publishers' actions in Germany reveal that they saw distinct segments within the overall children's book category – a Catholic segment, a Protestant segment and an emerging girls' segment (*Backfischliteratur*) which itself had religious sub-segments (Fullerton, 1975, 66–7; Grenz, 1981). Another growing segment was made up of middle-class women, among whom both literacy and the range of socially acceptable reading matter had been increasing. In the nineteenth century a family having servants was the mark of having entered the middle classes; this, combined with taboos against respectable women working, meant that middle-class women had (whether they wanted it or not) a great deal of time for reading. Many of the books which publishers produced for this segment were intended to be gifts, another instance of combined demographic and occasion-based segmentation. These included religious works, cookbooks and annual illustrated 'almanacs' of poetry and prose.

Women were voracious readers of novels and romances, which were usually written to formulas known to appeal to them. Few individuals purchased novels, however, even as gifts

– they were considered too expensive and ephemeral to belong in home libraries. The market for novels in Germany consisted mainly of fee or 'circulating' libraries (*Leihbibliotheken*) where one paid a fee to borrow a book, just as in Britain (Altick, 1957). Fee libraries were also a major market for popular works of non-fiction. Publishers were well aware of fee libraries and their needs – some ran their own libraries. Many catered to this segment. Starting about 1821, for example, German publishers followed the British example and began issuing novels in three-volume editions intended for circulating libraries, which charged on a per-volume rather than a per-title basis.

Scholars, lawyers, doctors, clergy, Freemasons and teachers were each important segments for the book trade. In Germany they often formed reading societies to pool their resources, since the books they needed were costly. Growing state school systems were another major segment for publishers. On balance, segmentation rather than aggregation characterized the approach of most bookmen. The only books intended for a broad general market were popular devotional works (e.g. Thomas à Kempis's *Imitation of Christ*) and the Bible, which were purchased by all except the very poorest. Yet here too, as we have seen, there was segmentation as publishers issued editions of these works in different sizes, degrees of elegance and price.

The segmentation policies in use earlier in the nineteenth century were based on observation and practical business sense; there is no evidence of formal market research. Research would have been less useful than it is today since the trade and its markets were small. Most publishers retailed books. Thus they gained the first-hand experience of consumers which their present-day counterparts, isolated in large bureaucracies, must experience vicariously through market research. As the nineteenth century went on, and markets grew dramatically, astute publishers saw the need for more formal and systematic market planning. Formal planning was common in the larger firms by the 1890s. One of its stated goals was to identify 'gaps' (*Luecke*) in the market – promising new products or segments (Luetge, 1928, 129). The market was studied by personal observation and by questioning – which were perceptive and thorough in some cases – and by examining the ever-growing array of trade literature – newspapers (from 1810), directories, and manuals. There were trenchant published market analyses as early as the 1820s, although they did not develop the formal concept of segmentation. Survey research to identify buyers by profession and geography was used from the 1880s, but not widely. Though crude by current standards, such planning methods were the genesis of those used today.

More book publishers became entrepreneurial and aggressive. Increasingly, segmentation strategies were devised and used to open up new areas of the book market. Some failed, more were successful. As the book market expanded, for example, there was increasing use of true mass production techniques such as high-speed steam-driven presses, bringing down the cost of books and further enlarging market as more price-sensitive segments could be reached (Altick, 1957; Fullerton, 1975).

The use of segmentation was manifest in three important long-term trends: (1) the growth of specialization and conscious market planning; (2) the development of new types of publication; and (3) the establishment of new forms of retail distribution to reach new buyers.

Specialization and planning

By the 1850s, publishers were tending to specialize, hoping thereby to get to know their markets well in the face of increased competition. Some specialized by subject area, others by type of book, for example, the ostentatious 'display editions' (*Prachtausgabe*) popular in the 1870s with the newly rich in Germany, whose numbers grew dramatically in the economic boom years following German unification. Many small publishers who produced a variety of books actually specialized in a geographical sense since they focused their marketing efforts upon their local areas. In the larger cities bookstores, too, came to specialize during the century, as did other retail book institutions.

Reaching new segments

Throughout the nineteenth century, ambitious and creative publishers reached new groups and strengthened their appeal to existing segments with innovative and market-oriented works. The German publishing firm of B.F. Voigt developed a whole new market segment with its series of handbooks for artisans. A category of books just for adolescent girls (*Backfischliteratur*) began to be published in Germany about 1850 (Grenz, 1981). The important gift book market was expanded into several new segments. By the 1880s there were three distinct price segments and several taste segments. With the enormous success of selling weekly instalments of Charles Dickens's *Pickwick Papers* beginning in 1836, the market for fiction in this form really took off in Britain, breaking the near-monopoly of circulation libraries. Instalments were affordable for far more people than the traditional three-volume work aimed for circulating libraries had been (Altick, 1957, 279). From the 1860s, Germany's publishers consciously opened up new segments of price-sensitive middle-class book buyers by issuing more and more inexpensive (i.e. 1 mark or less) books; in 1885, 42.5 per cent of all titles were inexpensive, compared with 33.3 per cent in 1875. This market was further segmented by content. When the copyright on the German-language literary classics of the late eighteenth and early nineteenth centuries expired in 1867, ten publishers were ready with series. Nearly every one of these was aimed at a different segment. In the 1870s and 1880s, German publisher-entrepreneurs opened up the newly urbanized working masses as a market for regular purchases of light fiction by creating exciting reading material, promotional methods and a distribution system especially for this group. Similar markets had been opened up in Britain, France and the US earlier (Fullerton, 1977, 1979).

Long before the nineteenth century, British and German publishers had produced very inexpensive material for the barely (if that) literate masses – pictures, calendars, broadsides, ballads, chapbooks dealing with gory murders, well-attended executions, marriages and deaths in royal families. This segment of the market continued to be served in the nineteenth century. A German news flier of the mid-nineteenth century, for example, had a crude woodcut cover and contained three stories: (1) the 'gruesome' murder of five people in the village of Ober-Uilingen; (2) a robbery and murder in the village of Schussenried; and (3) a 'horrible' murder in the region of Bochum near Berlin (Hebsacker, 1968, 129). When wanting more material, these publishers made up stories, too. In 1828 the British publisher, James Catnach, reportedly sold 1,166,000 copies of 'The Last Dying Speech and Confession' of a famous murderer. In 1837, he supposedly sold 1,650,000 copies of a piece on the then-famous murder team of James Greenacre and Hannah Brown. The market for such material was quite distinct from middle- and upper-class buyers. It was made up of factory hands, manual labourers and domestic servants (Altick, 1957, 287–92).

Around 1830 British publishers began cultivating common readers with a new format – cheap series of books (Altick, 1957, 274), the publication occurring at weekly or fortnightly intervals. The famous (and notorious) 'Penny Dreadfuls' followed this pattern and were enormously successful for decades. They were similar to the Bibliothèque Bleu in France, the Dime Novels in the United States and 'Colporteur Novels' in Germany (Fullerton, 1977). All promised the reader non-stop thrilling and usually violent action. It is almost impossible to tell which country first developed these serials, although it was most likely either France or Britain.

New retail outlets to reach new segments

It was symptomatic of the more assertive marketing orientation as the century went on that many publishers designed explicit retail strategies to reach, or to better reach, target segments. Most of these strategies involved either supplementing or bypassing conventional bookstores. Publishers in Germany, for example, knew that lower- and even many middle-class people would never enter a bookstore. They found them intimidating. They also knew that even people who did not find them intimidating would buy more if reached through more direct methods. Bookstores' selling methods were simply too passive for ambitious publishers, who developed an arsenal of more proactive and wide-reaching retail outlets; these included direct mail, several types of direct personal selling, government officials, binders, used-book dealers, merchants and innkeepers, discount book stores (Modernes Antiquariat), department stores and even the American innovation of book vending machines (Steinen, 1912). Travelling book salesmen, wrote a Berlin bookman in 1859, were able 'to cultivate ... fields which have been completely neglected by the retail book shops and thus open up new, very significant markets' (quoted in Fullerton, 1975, 257, see also 140–55). The adventure pamphlet series that were enormously popular with working class people and children of all classes after 1880, for example, were distributed through peddlers, news kiosks, cigar and stationery stores, and railway station book stalls, never through conventional book stores (Fullerton, 1979).

On the other hand, many publishers came to realize that the bookstores served some important heavy buyer groups better than any other method of retailing. These groups included university students and faculty and wealthy and cultivated people who appreciated the bookstores' refined atmosphere and service – any book published in Germany could be examined on approval. Measures to protect the stores were enacted by the powerful national trade association (*Boersenverein*) in 1888.

Other examples of segmentation in practice

Eighteenth-century Britain: pioneering aggressive marketing

Britain in the eighteenth century became the world's first 'consumer society', that is, a society with large numbers of relatively wealthy people who aspired, and were allowed, to consume ever more things and experiences (McKendrick *et al.*, 1982). There were no legal sumptuary prohibitions on aping the upper classes (McKendrick *et al.*, 1982, 20). Broad sections of the population had rising incomes and, to a great extent, accepted what we would call modern consumer attitudes. Among businesspeople there was increasingly a 'new commercial approach which deliberately and consciously aimed at controlling the market, sustaining consumer interest, and creating new demand' (McKendrick *et al.*, 1982, 31). When, for example, cheap calico and muslins began to flood in from India, English clothing producers saw an opportunity – they realized that they could open up vast new markets for clothing by producing lower priced fashions for those of lower income, who came to aggressively imitate as fashions trickled down the social classes (McKendrick *et al.*, 1982, 14). There was an ever-increasing pace of fashion change in especially women's clothing, eventually down to a change every year. After about 1770, producers of clothing worked with printers in producing literature to foster sales, creating ladies almanacs and pocket books filled with new fashion prints to stimulate demand. These publications aimed at a segment composed of the many 'ordinary young gentlewomen, not the extravagant few' (McKendrick *et al.*, 1982, 51). While clothing was produced by hand – the sewing machine was decades in the future – producers hired many people to do the cutting and sewing. The term 'manufacturer' comes from such amassing of men (labourers) which was used in several industries. Hundreds of people might be employed in one place.

An enormous number of different products were produced by some industries in eighteenth-century England, especially as the century went on. Manufacturers manipulated markets by following fashion trends and offering a wide range of products for individual market segments. Taking as an example the 'brass' producers of Birmingham, we find them producing a great number of different products for different tastes. For example, Mathew Boulton's 1778 pattern books had 1,470 designs of cut steel buttons, buckles, watch guards, sword hilts, and so on. A Boulton correspondence of 1772 lists for offer the following.

> Men and Women's Steel, pinchbeck, and Gilt Watch Chains – Steel pinchbeck Gilt and Teutenague, and Silver Buttons – platina, Sterling Gilt and plated Steel, Bath Metal and filigree plated Buttons on Box and on Box Moulds – gilt, Silver, plated Shagreen Tortise plain and inlaid with Silver and Gold in 4 Colours, Snuff Boxes, Instrument Cases, toothpick Cases – gilt, glass and steel Trinkets, Silver filligree Boxes, Needle Books, etc., etc.
>
> *(McKendrick et al., 1982, 71)*

Birmingham brass producers issued pattern cards and pattern books in different European languages – French, Italian and Dutch – and for the American market. National tastes were accommodated, e.g. there were elaborate rococo designs for the Dutch market when English tastes had become much more restrained (McKendrick *et al.*, 1982, 68).

Josiah Wedgwood

To marketing historians the best known and most celebrated eighteenth-century English producer was Josiah Wedgwood, famous for his clay and ceramic pieces. Ronald Savitt, who spent several months researching the Wedgwood archives, told me that there was almost no facet of present-day marketing that had not been anticipated by Wedgwood. There wasn't anything he could have learned from current marketing thought (Savitt, 1988). Wedgwood adapted products to suit market segments as following illustrates:

- doing expressive nudity on vases designed for the English aristocracy, but draping the nudes on works intended for the more prudish middle-class market;
- issuing different clay heads for different national markets – popes for Italy and Spain, saints for South America, Mohammed for Turkey;
- making 'green and gold ware' for hot climates, whose inhabitants did not like the pale and minimally coloured potteries favoured in northern Europe;
- producing a special range of exotic potteries for Turkey, cheap goods and seconds for America, cups in the Saxon fashion for Germany, small cups for Venice and rococo goods for France long after they had passed out of fashion in England.

(McKendrick et al., 1982, 113, 132)

To reach new markets, especially among the working classes and outside of London, Wedgwood used newer methods of distribution – a new class of itinerant salesmen and provincial shopkeepers. Provincial shops were open all year unlike the older annual fairs. 'Manchester Men' sold not to individuals but to individual shops (McKendrick et al., 1982, 86–9).

Silver manufacturing in the eighteenth century

Finally, all manufacturing by silver producers in eighteenth-century Britain and the American colonies, was done on a small scale and by hand until the very end of the century. Small producers sold mostly from their shops. They would meet individual needs by adding a buyer's initials, coat of arms, or other personal touches for a small fee. More successful producers made almost anything a client required, the ultimate in segmentation. Going beyond appealing to individual tastes, there were four basic segments in the market: (1) churches and civic groups, a relatively small market; (2) royalty and aristocrats (in England) buying for personal use, official entertainment and gifts; (3) (the largest and especially in America most lucrative) rich citizens, about 5 per cent of society; producers had be alert to fashion style shifts; and (4) middle- and some working-class people (Witkowski, 1985). Quickendon and Kover (2007) find that the claims of Briton Matthew Boulton that efficient production enabled him to sell silverware to the middle classes were exaggerated. Most of his production went to the upper classes. But this was true even in the United States. The manufacturers appealed to different taste segments in the upper classes.

Segmentation in the nineteenth century

The heavy use of many forms of segmentation by numerous businesses continued during the nineteenth century. Three of these businesses are considered here.

American firearms manufacture

Henning and Witkowski's (2013) article on the Remington Arms Company in the nineteenth century demonstrates very clearly that the firm understood segmentation. To Remington, the overall market consisted of civilian and military segments, each of which had quite different needs. Furthermore, Remington recognized that civilian markets actually consisted of two different civilian segments: (1) a rural and farm market interested in hunting and target shooting; and (2) an urban segment more interested in self-defence.

Fountain pens

The fountain pen, invented by Waterman during the second half of the century, quickly became a large market. The pen could be carried in pocket or purse, freeing the writer from having to be near an ink bottle. Fountain pen firms quickly segmented the overall market, sensing different preferences among different people. The Parker Pen Company's 1898 catalogue showed 40 different pens, ranging in price from $1.50 to $20.00, the latter probably directed at gift givers. The catalogue declared that the firm's largest and fattest pen was ideal for doctors, who were assumed to have big egos and a big need to impress people (Lawrence, 1977).

Bicycles in Western Europe and the United States

The bicycle industry had enormous growth during the final decades of the nineteenth century in England, France, Germany, and the United States. Sales peaked during the 1890s, yet it was not until 1913 that sales of automobiles exceeded those of bicycles in the United States which had by far the fastest growing automobile market in the world. The industry made active use of segmentation from the 1870s. According to Petty (1995, 42), 'bicycles were marketed to various discrete segments defined by usage, price, gender, and image/ life style ... Even with the dominance of the safety bicycle [vs the high wheeler] by 1890, different models were marketed to different segments, such as racers, tourists, women, and tandemists (sic)'.

Conclusion

The practice of segmentation clearly preceded formal thought about it; it was also considerably more advanced and subtle than the thought which did appear in trade literature and in academic dissertations (e.g. Steinen 1912). In such sources there is at most the vague notion that the market had more than one component, with social class the most often mentioned variable (e.g. Sarkowski 1976, 235, 238; Steinen 1912, 11–21).

This review of segmentation practice in several industries during the eighteenth and nineteenth centuries should dispel any doubts that segmentation was practised long ago. The practices of publishers, clothing manufacturers, brassware producers, silver merchants, bicycle manufacturers, gun manufacturers, pen manufacturers and, of course, many other businesses shows the purposeful use of most of the segmentation variables cited in current discussions (age, sex, occupation, education level, religion, geography, social class, income, shopping preference, benefit expectations, deal-proneness, price sensitivity, and lifestyle). Multi-variable strategies were often used. Underlying many strategies were astute and rational, if unexpressed, analyses by people who understood and responded to demand heterogeneity.

References

Altick, Richard (1957) *The English Common Reader: A Social History of the Mass Reading Public 1800– 1900*, University of Chicago Press, Chicago, IL.

Banham, Rob (2012) 'Occasional publishers: Producing and marketing books in England, 1771– 1844', *Journal of Historical Research in Marketing*, 4/3, 408–39.

Branchik, Blaine (2002) 'Out in the market: A history of the gay market segment in the United States', *Journal of Macromarketing*, 22, 86–97.

Branchik, Blaine (2007) 'Pansies to parents: Gay male images in American print advertising', *Journal of Macromarketing*, 27, 38–50.

Branchik, Blaine (2010) 'Silver dollars: The development of the elderly market segment', *Journal of Historical Research in Marketing*, 2/2, 174–97.

Febvre, Lucien, and Martin, Henri-Jean (1976) *The Coming of the Book: The Impact of Printing 1450– 1800*, tr. D. Gerard, NLB, London.

Fullerton, Ronald A. (1975) '*The Development of the German Book Markets, 1815-1888,*' unpublished Ph.D. Dissertation, History Department, University of Wisconsin-Madison, Madison, WI.

Fullerton, Ronald A. (1977) 'Creating a mass book market in Germany: The story of the "Colporteur Novel" 1870–1890', *Journal of Social History*, 10, 265–83.

Fullerton, Ronald A. (1979) 'Towards a commercial popular culture in Germany: The development of pamphlet fiction 1871–1914', *Journal of Social History*, 12, 489–511.

Fullerton, Ronald A. (1988) 'How modern is "modern" marketing? Marketing's evolution and the myth of the "production era"', *Journal of Marketing*, 52 (Jan.), 108–25.

Fullerton, Ronald A. (2012) 'The historical development of segmentation: The example of the German book trade, 1800–1928', *Journal of Historical Research in Marketing*, 4/1, 56–67.

Grenz, Dagmar (1981) *Maedchenliteratur*, Stuttgart: J.B. Metzlersche Verlagsbuchhandlung.

Gross, Robert A., and Kelley, Mary (eds) (2010) *A History of the Book in America*, vol. 2, *An Extensive Republic: Print, Culture, and Society in the New Nation, 1790–1840,* University of North Carolina, Chapel Hill, NC.

Hebsacker, Joachim U., ed. (1968) *Rueckblick fuer die Zukunft*, Ensslin: Reutlingen.

Henning, Robert A., and Witkowski, Terrance (2013) 'The advertising of E. Remington & Sons: The creation of an iconic brand, 1854–1888,' *Journal of Historical Research in Marketing*, 5/4, 418–48.

Hollander, Stanley C., and Germain, Richard (1992) *Was there a Pepsi Generation Before Pepsi Discovered it? Youth-Based Segmentation in Marketing*, NTC, Lincolnwood, IL.

Jones, D.G. Brian, and Richardson, Alan J. (2007) 'The Myth of the Marketing Revolution', *Journal of Macromarketing*, 27/1, 15–24.

Kliemann, Horst (1928) *Wie und wo erfasse ich Kaeuferschichten*, Poeschel, Stuttgart.

Kotler, Philip (1980) *Marketing Management* (5th edn), Englewood Cliffs, NJ: Prentice Hall.

Lawrence, Cliff (1977) *Fountain Pens*, Collector Books, Pudacah.

Luetge, Friedrich (1928) *Das Verlagshaus Gustav Fischer in Jena*, Fischer, Jena.

McKendrick, Neil, Brewer, John, and Plumb, J.H. (1982) *The Birth of a Consumer Society: The Commercialization of Eighteenth-Century England*, Indiana University Press, Bloomington, IN.

Monatsbericht fuer Teutschland, zum Behufe aller Ankuendigungen, Anzeigen und Notizen des teutschen Buch- und Kunsthandeis (1810–30) Published in Weimar.

Petty, Ross (1995) 'Peddling the bicycle into the 1890s', *Journal of Macromarketing*, 15/1, 32–46.

Powers, Thomas L., and Steward, J.L. (2010) 'Alfred P. Sloan's 1921 repositioning strategy', *Journal of Historical Research in Marketing* 2,/4, 426–42.

Quickenden, Kenneth, and Kover, A.J. (2007) 'Did Boulton sell silver plate to the middle class?', *Journal of Macromarketing*, 27, 51–64.

Sarkowski, Heinz (1976) *Das Bibliographisches Institut: Verlagsgeschichte und Bibliographie 1826–1976*, Bibliographisches Institut, Mannheim.

Savit, Ronald (1988) personal conversation with the author.

Smith, W.R. (1956) 'Product differentiation and marketing segmentation as alternative marketing strategies', *Journal of Marketing*, 21, 3–8.

Steinen, Helmut von (1912) *Das moderne Buch*, published Ph.D. dissertation, Steinen, Heidelberg.

Tedlow, Richard (1990) *New and Improved: The Story of Mass Marketing in America*, Basic Books, New York.

Tedlow, Richard (1997) 'The beginning of mass marketing in America: George Eastman and photography as a case study', *Journal of Macromarketing*, 17/2, 67–81.

Tedlow, Richard, and Jones, G. (eds) (1993) *The Rise and Fall of Mass Marketing*, Routledge, London.

Wind, Yoram (1980) 'Going to market: New twists for some old tricks', *Wharton Magazine*.

Witkowski, Terrence H. (1985) 'Marketing silver in the eighteenth century', in Stanley C. Hollander and Terrence Nevett (eds), *Second Workshop on Historical Research in Marketing*, Michigan State University, Lansing, MI, 200–9.

6

A history of brand identity protection and brand marketing

Ross D. Petty

Introduction

The practice of branding dates back to ancient times and has served a number of purposes over the years including accounting for goods in large shipments and identifying product source for guild authorization and quality control (e.g. Richardson, 2008; Moore and Reid, 2008, 421). Wengrow (2008) argues that symbolic branding occurred in the fifth and fourth centuries BCE in Mesopotamia through the use of seals and standardized packaging. From about the tenth century CE onwards, the sale of goods differentiated by brand, by names of producers, sellers, product attributes or other symbols became commonplace in China (Hamilton and Lai, 1989; Eckhardt and Bengtsson, 2009). The long history of product branding begs the question of when did brand-oriented marketing begin? In other words, when did brand identity (and brand personality) become a focal point of marketing efforts?

This chapter presumes that a prerequisite of brand marketing is the development of brand names or markings that can be protected from unauthorized imitation (Wilkins, 1992). Indeed Duguid (2009, 3–4) notes: 'The history of modern brands is to a significant degree dependent on the history of trademarks.' Without such brand identity protection, imitators would offer products of varying quality levels and consumers would come to mistrust brand identifiers, thereby decreasing incentives for marketers to invest in brand quality and brand promotion. For example, medieval guild regulations served this purpose of controlling unauthorized imitation by other guild members but guilds had to seek legal protection to prevent imitation by those outside the guild (Schechter, 1925).

Guilds discouraged the individual promotion of particular members' products, seeking instead to use guild marks for quality control to maintain a reputation for high-quality goods for the guild itself. Schechter (1925, 78) concludes that medieval guild marks were liabilities to users who were forced to use them as a method of policing quality rather than as a method to promote their individual brands. Such marks were not the basis for modern brand marketing.

This chapter discusses the replacement of industry-specific guild regulations with laws of broad applicability across industries such as court-created protection against passing off and later trademark infringement as well as governmental registration systems for copyrights, design patents and trademarks. This discussion is presented in broad roughly half-century periods in marketing history based on the prior literature, historical developments and inductive reasoning (Hollander *et al.*, 2005). This analysis asks two questions. First, were abstract brand identifiers being used and legally protected from unauthorized imitation? Second, was brand identity a central focus of promotion efforts to create an abstract brand personality that was at least somewhat distinct from the goods using the brand?

Defining brand marketing

Merely developing brand names, symbols and other brand identifiers that are reasonably secure from unauthorized imitation does not by itself prove that products were marketed using those identifiers nor guarantee that brand-centric marketing will develop. Initially, brand identifiers typically were small, barely noticeable marks. Such small marks would be less useful as a focus of marketing promotion than more prominent marks. Therefore, historians must search not only for branded goods but also examine the 'noticeability' of brand identifiers and promotional efforts for brand focus. Brand marketing would prominently identify the brand as the primary means of differentiating the branded products from competing offerings (Petty, 2013, 210–11).

Some commentators suggest determining the existence of brand marketing is a simple yes or no question. Ultimately, the question is whether the signs that are used as brand identifiers become symbols with the specific connotation of identifying the brand (Bastos and Levy, 2012, 349). This is consistent with the International Trademark Association's definition of a brand as a trademark that 'has acquired significance over and above its functional use by a company to distinguish its goods or services from those of other traders' (cited in Davis and Maniatis, 2010, 120). In the historical research context, determining when one brand has 'become a symbol rather than a mere sign' or 'acquired significance' beyond distinguishing product source presents a challenge.

In contrast, Berthon *et al.* (2003) suggest a more complex formulation of the question. They offer the concept of a brand space that has two dimensions: the enacted-functional dimension where brand promotion varies from promoting the meaning of the brand to promoting the functionality of the branded products and the abstract-reified dimension where at one extreme brand identity is more independent of the branded products in contrast to situations where the brand is closely identified with particular product(s). They use these two dimensions to suggest four specific quadrants in brand space from the function-reified quadrant that is most closely tied to the product to the enacted-abstract quadrant where the brand is the least tied to particular products and product functionality and is the most abstract. Thus, for them the issue of whether brand identity/personality is being promoted compared to a description of the branded products is a question of degree. Their analysis suggests that brand marketing certainly occurs when brand personality is promoted more heavily than product performance or attributes, but also when brand identity is emphasized when discussing product performance or attributes.

One important set of historical evidence related to brand marketing, then, is the types of words and signs used as brand identifiers. The use of descriptive brand identifiers such as company or founder names or words descriptive of the product performance or attributes seem less likely to develop brand value or personality outside of the product itself than the use of more creative and abstract brand identifiers. Yet the use of company founder names was common practice in the 1800s. Sivulka (1998, 37) lists 19 'New Brand Names' in a table of examples and only the last, Budweiser – the most recent (1876) name in the table – was not a name referring to the company founder. Similarly in *The Branding of America,* Hambleton (1987) collects 60 brand names derived from product innovators' names.

In contrast, Room (1998, 16–18) suggests that non-descriptive categories of brand names in use by the 1890s include: status names (e.g. Crown Pianos, Victor Bicycles); good association names (e.g. Quaker Oats, Sunlight Soap); and artificial names (e.g. Kodak, Uneeda Biscuit). Mercer (2010, 17) tends to agree, suggesting that brand names must be developed specifically for the product, often as a coined or made-up word or an existing word out of context, rather than the adoption of a company or family name or name that is merely descriptive of the product. This distinction is consistent with early US trademark law that disallowed exclusive use for descriptive identifiers such as the manufacturer's name or a descriptive name of the goods such as New York City flour (Petty, 2011, 87–90). Such descriptive names also did not qualify for UK trademark registration (Mercer, 2010).

It is probably easier to discover abstract brand identifiers than to determine how the brands so identified were promoted. For example, Eckhardt and Bengtsson (2009, 6–7) suggest that White Rabbit sewing needles were sold in tenth-century China. The 'white rabbit' name appears to have a contemporary cultural meaning of good luck that was particularly significant for women – the primary purchasers of sewing needles. The needles' paper wrapping portrayed a white rabbit crushing herbs with a pestle and advised customers to look for the stone white rabbit in front of the maker's shop. It seems clear that this marketer was using the white rabbit sign as a brand identifier, but it is not clear that the brand had any personality beyond the functional attributes touted on the packaging such as being made from high-quality steel and being easy to use. Advising customers to look for the stone rabbit in front of the shop could be locational directions or assurance of the correct brand. Without more evidence, it is difficult to determine whether the seller was seeking to promote the brand personality such as providing good luck to the user.

Given the modern conceptualization of the brand and brand marketing, it is clear today that the promotion of personal, company or descriptive names as a means of selling the branded product may qualify as brand marketing. Therefore, seeking only abstract brand identifiers may underestimate the amount of brand marketing that is occurring. For example, McKendrick *et al.* (1982, 124) note that Wedgwood writes to his then partner Thomas Bentley in 1773 that it was 'absolutely necessary' that they mark their goods and that they 'advertise the mark'. If subsequent advertising (and other promotion) focused on the brand identity evidenced by the Wedgwood & Bentley circular mark, this would appear to be brand marketing even though the brand identifier consists of personal names written within a circle. Alternatively, Wedgwood could have been insisting that the mark be advertised only to educate consumers to avoid counterfeits. This still would be promotion of the brand identifier but not the development of an abstract brand personality at least beyond genuineness. In addition, Wedgwood obtained a sort of celebrity status so it is difficult to distinguish promotion of what today would be called his 'personal brand' as a well-known business person from promotion of the brand in order to sell china. Therefore for each historical period discussed below, relevant evidence is presented regarding the evolution of brand marketing without attempting to determine a definitive start of brand marketing.

Pre-nineteenth century

While McKendrick *et al.* (1982) have produced a marvellous study of commercialization in eighteenth-century England, Schechter (1925) goes back further to examine the product marking practices of British medieval guilds. As noted above, the guilds policed the use of authorized marks, carefully seeking to condemn both counterfeit products and authorized products that were defective or otherwise not of the high level of quality the guild expected. While such marks were not promoted to users to become assets to the mark owners, Richardson (2008) argues that town/guild names did function as collective brand identifiers in medieval Europe and did provide consumers with reputational information about the quality of goods. Thus guild identifiers served as a rough equivalent to collective and certification trademarks today (Duguid, 2012).

From the 1500s through the 1700s, marks in the English cloth and cutlery industries evolved from quality control guild marks to marks used to promote the products of individual merchants –what Schechter (1925, 122) describes as changing from 'liability' to 'asset' marks. The earliest court cases brought by individual merchants against counterfeiters also occurred during this period. *Southern v. How* (1618) is generally recognized as the first court case to discuss the fraudulent counterfeiting of a merchant's mark, but Schechter (1925, 8–10) argues the actual discussion in that decision was a judge's recollection of an earlier decision. The earlier decision involving unauthorized use of a cloth maker's mark may be *Sandforth's Case* decided in 1584. Stolte (1997, 509) argues that this court decision demonstrates that Britain judicially recognized a common law right against trademark infringement at that time. Court decisions during that time were rendered in Latin and not widely reported, which explains why this particular decision was only rediscovered recently.

Schechter (1925, 10) asserts that, after *Southern v. How* in 1618, the next court decision was *Blanchard v. Hill* (1742). This decision denied injunctive relief for trademark infringement that was in part based on an old and no longer valid law that gave the plaintiff in that case the exclusive right to use the words 'Great Mogul' stamped on his cards. Enjoining the use of the same name on cards by another would have appeared to have supported the repealed law and provided the seller with an undesirable monopoly. Despite this outcome, later court decisions would sometimes recognize this as the beginning of judicial trademark enforcement (Schechter, 1925, 136–8).

Thus while marks were used on products throughout this time, there was not much judicial activity in enforcing exclusive rights until more modern times. Lack of judicial enforcement does not mean counterfeiting was not condemned. Schechter (1925, 119) notes that in the early 1700s, one London cutler ran newspaper ads describing his particular guild mark and urging customers to avoid counterfeits. Marks had by this time become clear assets that were sometimes sold or inherited, but without promotion of the value of the genuine mark/brand in the newspaper notices or elsewhere, it is not clear that brand marketing was commonly practised during this period even as marks/brands gained a reputation for quality through use of the products and word of mouth. Again, Wedgwood is the classic example (Koehn, 2001, 11–42).

Early nineteenth century

For the most part, guild laws continued to protect marks during this period in the UK. By the 1875 Trademark Registration Act, many guild industries claimed their marks had been in use for 50 to over 100 years (Higgins, 2012, 266–7). British court decisions also began to develop more consistency in protecting trademarks from unauthorized imitation. After the 1824 UK decision that found liability for the intentional counterfeiting of marks, an 1839 Chancery court decided that intent to deceive need not be proven to obtain injunctive relief (Bently, 2008, 6–7). English marks in some industries tended to be quite similar to each other. This suggests they were used administratively to track wares rather than as brand markings for consumer recognition. This similarity among marks would create trademark registration problems once registration started (Higgins, 2012, 279–82).

In contrast to the UK, France abolished trade guilds in 1791, but within a decade a resurgence in counterfeiting caused the government to enact specialty laws to protect jewellery, plates and cutlery from counterfeit marks. France also enacted a general prohibition of counterfeiting manufactured goods or marks in 1802–3. In 1824, this prohibition was expanded to protect names and places of manufacturers from imitation (Duguid, 2009, 24).

For the US (and Europe) in the early nineteenth century, Laird (1998, 17) argues that consumers selected items for purchase based on inspection and merchant reputations. Thus she appears to place merchant names (to which reputation attaches) in a different category from brand names. Yet even if merchant names were not true abstract brand names, they were sufficiently important to merchants at this time that merchants sought ways to prevent unauthorized imitation. US courts began to consider trade name cases in the early 1800s (Petty, 2011, 87–8). By the 1840s, some US court decisions began discussing trademarks by name. These early cases did not always condemn passing off or trademark infringements. The plaintiff marketer obtained relief only in about 60 per cent of reported federal court decisions before 1870 (Petty, 2012, 136–7). Duguid (2009, 11–13) indicates that trademark-related court decisions in the 1850s were reported upon and followed internationally.

The growth of trademark court decisions in the UK and US has led most historians to examine trademark cases and registrations, but not look for other forms of brand identity protection. In the US, Petty (2012, 2011) examines two predecessors to trademark registration: the registration of labels under copyright law and the registration of labels, bottles and packages as US design patents. Indeed, some goods such as cotton had brand identifier registration systems dating back to colonial times, although those were probably for product quality tracking and perhaps taxation rather than brand marketing purposes (the marks were small and discreet) (Petty, 2012, 121).

Registering product labels as copyrights in local federal courts started at least by the late 1830s (Petty, 2012, 132–5). Attempts to register product labels as books, engravings or prints suggest that marketers did seek exclusivity for their product labels. Bently (2008, 6) argues that in Britain firms also tried to register labels as copyrights or designs. Many of these labels contained a pictorial element either of the product or a person or other sign.

Unfortunately, it is difficult to tell the extent to which such symbols were promoted to possibly create a brand identity. Some of the symbols were clearly descriptive, showing the product in use (Petty, 2012, 134). Others may have been simple stock woodcut images with visual appeal. However, patent medicines often used symbols of reassurance such as angels, doctors and grandmothers, symbols of power or symbols of exotic origin (Laird, 1998, 16–18). The systematic examination of copyright records in the US and other countries could provide important information regarding this early period of brand identity protection and possible brand marketing if some images appear related to brand personality.

Latter half of the nineteenth century

US marketing historians agree that, after the American Civil War, improvements in transportation, communication and production/packaging technology allowed US marketers to begin to develop national brands (e.g. Strasser, 1989; Tedlow, 1990). This led to additional demands for brand identity protection and is a watershed period for brand identity protection, if not brand-centric marketing.

One outlet for the demand for brand identity protection in the US became the design patent. Patents on ornamental (rather than functional) designs were first authorized in 1842, but when courts began denying copyright protection to merely descriptive labels starting in 1848, marketers became worried. They still continued to seek copyright registrations but starting in 1855, they also sought to register labels and bottle designs as design patents (Petty, 2012, 139). Such 'Trade Mark Designs' could include a bottle or other unique packaging as well as labels, so long as the name was not in 'ordinary type'. Unlike copyrights that were registered in local federal courts, design patents were registered in the Patent and Trademark Office, so that when trademark registration was authorized in 1870, the Office stopped accepting trademark design patent registrations. From 1861 to 1870, the number of trademark design patent registrations consistently exceeded trademark court cases (Petty, 2012, 140).

Duguid (2013) points out that US federal trademark registration in 1870 was preceded by state registration schemes starting with California in 1863. Contrary to the story that national industrialization stimulated the demand for trademark registration in the US, California and other early registration states were primarily agricultural. Of the 151 marks registered in California during the first decade of registration. 83 per cent were from small companies in the medicine, food, drink, alcohol, tobacco and cosmetic industries (Duguid, 2013, 588–90). State registrations laws were preceded by anti-counterfeiting (for stamps, labels, wrappers and eventually trademarks) statutes, beginning with New York in 1845 and other eastern states in the next five years (Petty, 2012, 137–8).

Patent medicines are often credited with accounting for roughly half of all advertising after the American Civil War and were the largest group of advertisers by 1870 when the first federal trademark registration statute was enacted (Laird, 1998; Sivulka, 1998). This industry led the 'packaging revolution' to replace bulk-packed merchandise marketed to retailers with consumer-packaged products with labelling designed to attract the attention of consumers (Sivulka, 1998, 48). Patent medicines were the second largest industry registrants of trademark design patents, with 32 between 1855 and 1870, exceeded only by the personal care/clothing industry with 42 (Petty, 2012, 142).

However, by the end of 1870, 121 marks were registered federally and medicines were only the third most common category: 21 registrations were for tobacco or snuff; 10 for whisky or liquor; nine for medicines; six for soaps and other cleaners; five for fertilizers; four for brooms, dry and other types of goods, and white lead; three for metal and metal tubing, bitters, burning fluids, various foods, and various powders. Even items like steam governors, sewing machines, wagon axles and wheels and watches received trademarks in this first year (Commissioner of Patents, 1870, 260–1).

Courts also were active during this period. Most importantly, the US Supreme Court declared the national trademark registration statute of 1870 to be unconstitutional in 1879 after some 8,000 marks had been registered. A new statute was enacted in 1881 but it only authorized registration of marks used in foreign commerce (Petty, 2011, 89). US courts also developed the judicial distinction between descriptive trade names (e.g. marketer's name or location) that received weaker judicial protection based on proving intentional fraud from technical trademarks (e.g. made-up words) that were treated more like property. The unauthorized use of a technical trademark was condemned without any showing of intent to deceive or defraud (Bone, 2006, 564–6). Furthermore, not all made up terms were protected. In 1879, the US Supreme Court affirmed that the use of three letters – 'A.C.A.' as a quality indicator was not a trademark indicating the company of origin of the goods. Therefore, the same letters would be available to use as a quality indicator by rival manufacturers (*Manufacturing Co. v. Trainer*, 1880).

Other countries also struggled with the question of what types of words and devices could be protected as trademarks (Higgins, 2012, 271–4). In Britain, the 1862 Merchandise Mark Act defined trademark to include words and names but only provided for criminal sanctions for intentional use of another's mark to defraud (Bently, 2008, 9–10). The 1875 Trademark Act was the first in Britain to provide for registration of trademarks, but permitted registration of individual or firm names only if they were presented in a distinctive manner, such as an individual's signature. This act reversed the broad definition in the 1862 Act, by excluding mere words even if they were invented or fanciful in the industry context or were otherwise non-descriptive of the products they identified. Like US courts, British courts struggled to determine which words in the context of a specific industry were too descriptive to merit protecting them as a trademark belonging to only one firm (Bently, 2008, 22–3, 27).

In contrast, in 1824 France expanded its law to protect names and places of manufacturers from imitation (Duguid *et al.*, 2010, 24). Similarly, the Germanic countries of Germany, Austria and the Netherlands excluded words commonly used in an industry as well as marks consisting or mere letters, words or numbers or the arms of states or countries (Bently, 2008, 26). Britain struggled with geographic marks that indicated the place of manufacture since its guild history was based on geography (Bently, 2008, 30–1). Eventually the 1888 Act allowed registration of 'invented words' that did not describe the character, quality or geographic origin of the goods. Soon after, Denmark, Switzerland, the Netherlands, Germany, Sweden and Japan all allowed word trademarks that were not descriptive. Switzerland set up separate protection for geographic indicators (Bently, 2008, 40). In 1905, Britain also allowed geographic indicators to be registered as certification marks (Higgins, 2008, 60).

Not only did countries develop similar concepts of trademarks during this time, but they also developed national trademark registration systems. France initially started judicial registration in 1803 as a precursor to bringing an enforcement action, but it didn't develop a centralized registration system until 1857. By that time Spain had started its programme in 1850 (Duguid, 2009, 24; Saiz and Perez, 2012). The Spanish system recognized trademarks as property rights but would only grant them to companies, domestic or foreign, with a location in Spain. While some portion of these foreign trademarks were registered only to protect them against imitation in Spain, Saiz and Perez (2012, 256–7) assert that other marks were registered in order to enable brand marketing in distant cities, department stores, international exhibitions and to facilitate magazine advertising.

France followed Spain's lead when it enacted an effective system of national registration of trademarks to create property rights in 1857. Registration would be available also to foreign firms with an establishment in France or foreign firms whose home country provided reciprocal protection for trademarks of French firms. At the time, the only country with which France enjoyed such a bilateral trade agreement was Russia. But within the next ten years, a dozen countries including the UK signed similar agreements with France and the US followed suit in 1869 (Duguid, 2009).

Portugal started trademark registration in 1883 but within the first two years nearly two-thirds of the registrations were from foreign firms. This figure dropped to 13 per cent by 1905 (Duguid *et al.*, 2010, 26). Ultimately, global firms found their relatively famous trademarks were frequently imitated by local firms in any given country (e.g. Higgins, 2008, 46; Petty, 2012, 136). Indeed, some countries such as Japan and some in Latin America set up registration systems on a first to file system so that local firms could control famous foreign trademarks if they registered before the foreign firm (da Silva Lopes and Casson, 2012, 300, 304–5).

To address the usurpation of internationally known trademarks, brand marketers first encouraged their home counties to sign bilateral agreements with their largest foreign markets. These bilateral agreements led to the Paris Convention for the Protection of Industrial Property of 1883 that established the general principle of reciprocity of intellectual property rights so that foreign firms from signatory countries were treated the same as domestic firms in signatory countries. They could register their trademarks in foreign countries just like domestic firms in those countries (Higgins, 2012, 273–4). The 1891 Treaty of Madrid established 'one stop' registration for signatory countries, allowing firms to register in their home country and include an international registration that was then forwarded to designated other signatory countries (da Silva Lopes and Casson, 2012, 295).

The industries that first adopted brand identity protection in other countries were pretty similar to those first movers in the US. As noted above, US trademark registrations in this period covered not just pharmaceuticals and tobacco but also liquors, food (Lonier, 2010), textiles and many other products including durables like metal goods (Higgins, 2012, 266). UK tobacco firms also were some of the first to use abstract brand names starting in 1860s (Mercer, 2010, 19).

Duguid *et al*. (2010) compared trademark registrations by industry in France, the US and UK. For example, in 1890, France registered about 65 per cent trademarks for nondurable consumer products compared with 55 per cent for the US and 43 per cent for the UK. In 1870 and 1880, tobacco captured about 20 per cent of registrations in the US, plummeting to 3 per cent in 1890. In the UK, tobacco accounted for only about 5–7 per cent of registrations during the same period, with an even smaller proportion of registrations in France. Medicine accounted for about 15 per cent of US registrations in 1870–1900. France had the same proportion in 1900 but prior to that and in the UK for the entire period for medicine registrations the range was 3–8 percent. Beverages were the leading category of French registrations, ranging from 15 to 28 per cent but only accounted for 6 to 12 per cent of registrations in the UK and US during the same time periods. In Spain, one area, Catalonia, had almost half the trademark registrations led by textile companies and then the chemical industry and food, beverages and tobacco. The (cigarette) paper-making industry also was an early leader in trademark registrations (Saiz and Perez, 2012).

The latter half of the nineteenth century is generally recognized as the period when brand marketing, enabled by the development of trademark law, began. While certain industries such as medicines, tobacco and alcohol took the lead in brand marketing, by the turn of the century, the practice appears widespread. One unexplored question is the number of marketers using abstract brand identifiers known in US law as technical trademarks versus the number of marketers using more descriptive trade names of the company, its founder or location. As noted in the earlier conceptual definition discussion, it is not clear whether firms using descriptive trade names were focusing their advertising on the brand itself or merely identifying important attributes in their advertising of particular products.

However, the use of people's names often included their image or at least an image of someone. The Quaker Oats man appeared on oatmeal and it outsold the same product being sold as the FS brand. Similarly, when Lydia Pinkham finally agreed to let her image appear as a trademark on the label of her 'Vegetable Compound', sales 'boomed' (Laird, 1998, 177, 252). Unlike Wedgwood, neither of these two symbols sought personal celebrity status so their images present an image and some personality for their brands.

Figure 6.1   Lydia Pinkham Label, source: 1904 pamphlet

Figure 6.2   Quaker Oats Man, source: 1905 packaging

Early twentieth century

If the later 1800s saw the popularization of brand marketing, the early 1900s saw its formalization. Strasser (1989, 118) notes that character image trademarks like the Campbell Kids experienced a 'population explosion' around 1900. Of course some characters, if not most such as the Underwood Devil, had been used before being registered as a trademark. The 1905 registration of the devil claims it was first used in commerce in 1868.

This use of more abstract marks such as characters instead of trade names that described the firm founder or its location was encouraged in the US by the 1905 trademark statute that recognized the judicially developed distinction between descriptive trade names (protected by unfair competition law) and associative, imaginative or artificial technical trademarks that could now be registered if used in interstate commerce for more than ten years. This distinction between strong national technical trademark registration and weaker protection for trade name passing off was important for the history of brand marketing because it encouraged businesses to switch from the traditional practice of identifying products solely by company or personal names and instead to adopt suggestive, fanciful or artificial names as well as logos, symbols and even characters (Petty, 2011). The development and use of technical trademarks satisfies the more conservative definition of brand marketing – the development of abstract rather than descriptive brand identifiers.

Similarly, in the UK, the concepts of 'fancy words' and later 'invented words' had been considered in trademark law in the latter 1800s, but precise definition eluded the legal system until its 1905 Act clarified that only words making direct reference to the quality or character of the goods could not be registered (Mercer 2010, 25). That would appear to allow suggestive brand names as well as fanciful names (e.g. Apple computer) and fabricated words that have no meaning beyond brand identification.

Marketers and others recognized the additional value of technical trademarks over descriptive trade names during this period of trademark law and brand marketing development (Petty, 2011). Acheson (1917, 9) asserted 'There is no more valuable and permanent property, if insured by continued publicity, than the trade mark of a staple commodity which has been well standardized by years of consistent advertising.' Royal brand baking powder's goodwill in 1905 was valued at $5 million – a million dollars per letter (Pope, 1983, 69). In less than a decade Coca-Cola and Nabisco for its Uneeda brand were claiming similar valuations for their trademarks (Strasser, 1989, 47). Thus, the concept of what today would be called brand equity became recognized during this period.

This excitement about technical trademarks led to the first known discussions of brand marketing using the term 'trademark advertising'. Perhaps the earliest discussion appears in a 1903 booklet titled 'The Value of Advertised Trademarks' by Ben B. Hampton Co., Advertising Agents, that appears to be a reprint of material run in the trade journal, *Printers' Ink*. This work quotes from a graduation speech given by famous industrialist Andrew Carnegie: 'If you can sell a hat for one dollar you can sell it for two dollars if you stamp it with your name and make the public feel that your name stands for something' (Ben B. Hampton Co., 1903, 6). While Carnegie clearly understands the modern concept of brand marketing that a unique and protected name allows the marketer to promote what it 'stands for', it is not clear whether he is thinking of 'your name' as a personal name or a name selected to brand your product.

Another candidate for the earliest discussion of 'trademark advertising' is the J. Walter Thompson (JWT) advertisement published sometime in the mid-1900s. This advertisement explains the value of 'trademark advertising' – if a firm advertises its technical trademark directly to consumers, they will request the brand by name from retailers. The advertiser will no longer be dependent on jobbers or retailers for brand promotion because the brand is now meaningful to consumers (Schwarzkopf, 2010, 174; Petty, 2011, 91). Direct-to-consumer advertising was not a new concept, but by tying advertising to the trademark, JWT was promoting brand marketing where the brand, rather than the marketer (in the past typically retailers), developed a direct relationship with its consumers. The English advertising agency of Spottiswoode, Dixon & Hunting, Ltd published a similar ad in the June 1907 issue of *The Strand Magazine,* touting the antiquity of the trademark idea and its value in modern trade when it is advertised. In 1908, one advertising man estimated that '[a]t least fifty percent of advertising being done today is for the purpose of creating property in trademarks' (Pope, 1983, 69).

Petty (2011, 91–3) identifies several articles, pamphlets and books that discuss the value of trademark advertising during the early 1900s. Stern (2006, 217) claims 'brand' entered the marketing lexicon in 1922 as part of the compound 'brand name' but Bastos and Levy (2012, 353) suggest that the term brand was in common usage at least by 1920. They provide an example of a quote from P. T. Cherington (1920, 150): 'the appeal to the buy … by brand has become so general as to be in many lines of merchandise the characteristic rather than the exception method of sale'. Later in the same chapter on 'Sales under Brand,' Cherington (1920, 153) notes 'The most common device for accomplishing this [appeal to the large mass of final consumers] is the use of a trade-mark or other means of identification.'

The evolution from 'trademark advertising' to 'brand marketing' can be illustrated by looking at Cherington's earlier books. In *Advertising as a Business Force,* Cherington (1913, 331) does not yet offer a chapter on 'Sales under Brand' but instead in a chapter on 'Trade-Mark Problems' he notes: 'The trade-mark has become one of the elements of almost every successful appeal to the consumer.' He goes on to describe the trademark as a 'commercial signature for its exploiter'. In a nod to the notion of trademark advertising, he notes that the trademark has no intrinsic value but only produces business value if it is consistently advertising:

> The trade-mark, however, is only an emblem. It actually produces no business nor has it in itself any creative power. The value lies wholly in the action it inspires, its ability to suggest by continued appearance … Powerful, persistent publicity tends to invest an article with more value in the purchaser's mind who unconsciously associates it with merit and becomes predisposed in its favor.
>
> *(Cherington, 1913, 332)*

Thus, in this 1913 book, Cherington recognized the importance of the trademark advertising concept. In his second book *The Advertising Book 1916,* he offers a chapter on 'Trademarks and Brands' and presents numerous examples of the benefits of trademark advertising. He summarizes these arguments by quoting from a trade journal series of advertisements that concludes: 'Trademarks and national advertising are the two greatest public servants in business to-day. Their whole tendency is to raise qualities and standardize them, while reducing prices and stabilizing them' (Cherington, 1916, 496). Thus, he still emphasizes trademark advertising but now ties it to brands and broadens the benefits from just sales to other consumer benefits. Four years later he announces the commonality of brand promotion enabled by protectable trademarks (Cherington, 1920).

Other general advertising books were published in the second decade of the twentieth century including one published in the UK that may have been the first to use the word brand (Petty, 2011, 92):

> The manufacturer advertises his brand direct to the public and thus liberates himself from entire dependence on the wholesaler's and retailer's goodwill…[T]hese intermediaries can no longer afford not to stock what the ultimate consumer is asking by name as a consequence of the manufacture's advertising. Important features in the successful marketing of a proprietary article are a distinguishing name and mark, and, if practicable, a distinctive package or wrapping, so that substitution is difficult.
>
> *(Goodall, 1914, 5, 48, cited in Petty, 2011)*

Three years later a US book, *Marketing Methods,* by Ralph Starr Butler (1917, 140–56) also used the term brand repeatedly in chapter 10 'The Retailer and National Advertising', although the term was not deemed sufficiently important to be included in the chapter title.

Not all books followed this pattern. Duncan (1921, 394–9) contains a rather confusing discussion of the difference between trade names and trademarks, which he says may overlap, after which he offers some basic requirements for the latter and touts the value of their good will. Thus, it would seem that by the mid-1910s, the concept of trademark advertising, itself only about ten years old, was being refined toward brand marketing and by the 1920s, trademarks were recognized as enabling brand marketing so that the brand rather than the trademark became the important marketing concept.

Behavioural research conducted during this time period also helped establish the intrinsic value of well-known brands (Petty, 2011, 93). In addition, advertising agencies like JWT were conducting research on why consumers bought particular brands and how they used them so that they could recommend both advertising copy and brand line extensions to reinforce and expand consumer behaviour. Their advertising copy moved trademarks from decoration alone to brands with social meanings for consumers and personalities that lived in advertising and the minds of consumers. Thus advertising agencies such as N.W. Ayer included registering new trademarks and promoting the brand identity as services offered during this time (Schwarzkopf, 2010, 170–6).

Because of their widespread use and growing trademark law enforcement, the period of 1915–9 has been called the 'Golden Age' of manufacturer brands on consumer products. It was also the period where marketers began to develop the concept of brand managers (Low and Fullerton, 1994, 177). Stole (2006, 20) notes: 'By the 1920s, advertising had gone from being a peripheral business activity to a dominant force in US life.' As Cherington (1920) noted, advertising was predominantly brand-based at this time. Additionally, trademark law expanded to cover descriptive names that had acquired secondary meaning and trademark law shifted from unfair competition and passing off to the protection of property rights of brand owners (Petty, 2011).

So, brand marketers argued that the legal system needed to protect their efforts to invest in these trademarks through advertising expenditures that created brand meaning. Indeed advertisers at least in the US sought to have advertising expenditures treated as capital expenditures rather than short-term business expenses for accounting and tax purposes. In addition, US courts looked beyond the amount of time a trademark had been in use to explicitly examine advertising expenditures to determine whether a descriptive mark had developed secondary meaning (Bartholomew, 2008). Furthermore, Frank Schechter (1927), in a still famous *Harvard Law Review* article, argued that the old legal concept of a trademark as a mere identification of source was obsolete. Rather he argued that, while the use of the same mark would indicate products from the same source, consumers may not know and may not even care the specific identity of the source. They may only know they like the brand. He further stated:

> Today the trademark is not merely the symbol of good will but often the most effective agent for the creation of good will…The mark actually *sells* the goods. And, self-evidently, the more distinctive the mark, the more effective is its selling power.
>
> *(Schechter, 1927, 819; emphasis in the original)*

Schechter (1927, 825) argued that in cases of trademark use on non-competing products, while there is no trade diversion from the trademark owner, there would be 'a gradual whittling away or dispersion of the identity and hold upon the public mind of the mark'. He argued that protection against such trademark dilution should be provided for truly unique (arbitrary, coined or fanciful) marks, but not for descriptive marks. Trademark dilution as a method of brand protection would not become popular until the twenty-first century (Petty, 2011, 96).

The Great Depression

When Schecter's article was proposing expanding trademark law for the benefit of brand marketers, brand marketing, despite its entrenchment, also faced criticism. In 1929, Chase and Schlink first published *Your Money's Worth: A Study in the Waste of Consumer's Dollars*. This book was heralded as the *Uncle Tom's Cabin* of the consumer movement. Within ten years, it had sold an estimated 100,000 copies (Stole, 2006, 23, 174). Chase and Schlink (1929, 166) quote an advertisement by a famous advertising agency: 'The final purpose of advertising is not to prove the comparative superiority of the article in competition. The object of advertising is to *take it out of competition*, that it will no longer be compared but will be accepted by the buyer' (emphasis in the original). Economists also joined in the discussion of brand marketing. Both Chamberlain (1933) and Robinson (1933) argued that competition among differentiated products was imperfect because such products enjoyed some level of monopoly power over their specific brand. However, brand monopoly power was limited by competition from other brands so the system was not as harmful as a complete monopoly.

These attacks influenced some courts to narrow trademark protection for non-competing goods and to find more marks descriptive (without secondary meaning) or generic (McClure, 1979, 331). Indeed, courts were unsympathetic to firms whose patent monopoly had expired and who then sought a trademark monopoly in the product name. Nabisco was denied a trademark for 'shredded wheat' and DuPont was denied a trademark for 'cellophane' (Petty, 2011, 95–6).

While brands were being criticized for high prices enabled by brand differentiation, the Great Depression caused many consumers to be more price sensitive. Editorials in *Advertising Age* (1932, 1934) argued that brands protected consumers from shoddy products by offering consistently high quality and for this reason consumer did (and should) trust brand advertising as a reliable guide to quality. Brand marketers also spent legal resources attempting to limit price competition first by defending their attempts at resale price maintenance in the courts (requiring retailers to sell at a fixed price set by the brand owner) and later by seeking federal antitrust exemption (passed in 1937) for state 'Fair Trade' laws that legalized resale price maintenance (Strasser, 1989, 269–85).

Despite the depression and criticism of brand marketing, its practice continued to develop during the 1930s. JWT continued using market research to develop branding strategies for Lever Brothers and Kraft (Mercer, 2010, 33). It went beyond brand identification and promotion to include research to understand a brand's existing 'personality' and to use research to track attempts to change that personality. This focus development on emotional connections between consumers and brands enabled JWT to successfully rejuvenate the Lux brand during this time and would set the stage for much greater emphasis on brand personality in the 1950s (Schwarzkopf, 2010, 180–8). Similarly, the London firm of William Crawford was talking about 'product personality' and the 'advertising idea'. The firm applied Dale Carnegie's concept of 'winning friends and influencing people' to advertised brands (Schwarzkopf, 2009).

Thus it seems clear that the practice of modern brand marketing became popular in the later 1800s, but the literature discussing the concept of brand marketing started in the early 1900s. Indeed by the 1930s, the concept of brand marketing was being further developed by marketing experts and attorney Schechter (1927) but also criticized both by consumer groups and economists (Petty, 2011, 96).

Later half of the twentieth century

In 1946 when the current trademark statute was enacted, only some 300,000 trademarks had been nationally registered. Among other things, the 1946 Lanham Act boosted brand marketing by permitting trademark licensing to other firms that would make products related to those of the trademark holder (Petty, 2011, 96). However, the new statute still did not allow the sale of trademarks without the sale of the underlying business. Otherwise, consumers would be deceived into believing that the continued use of the trademark indicated the continued production of goods by the original trademark user that would not be the case if just the trademark could be sold (Rewoldt, 1948).

The statute also expanded the sorts of marketing devices that could be used as trademarks by first explicitly including service marks and certification marks (Phelps, 1949). Later trademark office and judicial interpretations allowed registration of sensory marks such as sounds, slogans and non-functional product colours and designs. Given this expansion of trademark law and use, it is not surprising that the brand manager form of organization became popular during this period (Low and Fullerton, 1994, 181).

This liberalization of US trademark law also ultimately coincided with the dramatic increase in the brand marketing literature. Moor (2007, 3) suggests that the modern brand literature started in 1990 with Aaker and Keller's seminal article on brand extensions. Not only does Moor (2007) neglect the early trademark advertising literature of the beginning of the century, but she also overlooks important mid-century works. In 1942, Wolfe published the first *Journal of Marketing* article to explicitly discuss brands. This was followed by Gardner and Levy's (1955) classic article discussing the difference between the product and the brand in the *Harvard Business Review* and Cunningham's (1956) article on brand loyalty in the same publication. Schwarzkopf (2010, 188) asserts that the article by Gardner and Levy (1955) was the inspiration for adman David Ogilvy's emphasis on brand image and brand personality, but Ogilvy also was influenced by Claude Hopkins's 1923 book, *Scientific Advertising* (Schwarzkopf, 2009).

The Gardiner and Levy (1955) article created a 'sensation in the business world' (Bastos and Levy 2012, 355–6). Academic work continued with Cunningham's (1956) article on brand loyalty and Tucker's (1964) early research on the same concept. Bastos and Levy (2012) further note that the *Oxford English Dictionary* disdainfully recognized 'brand image' in 1959. Petty (2011, 86) summarizes the post-World War II brand marketing literature from Morein (1975) through Ries and Trout (1981).

Conclusion

The traditional US-centric brand marketing story couples innovation in products and production processes with the development of national distribution by railroad and national advertising in newspapers and magazines to spur the modern development of brand marketing. The desire for brand marketing led to demands to protect unique product names, insignia, packaging and labels from imitation and to the development of the modern concept of trademarks as protectable identifiers of product source. Manufacturers developed brands to wrestle control of distribution away from wholesalers and distributors.

However, this story ignores other roots of the development of brand marketing. Duguid's (2003) study of the alcohol industry suggests that branding in that industry developed not by large mass distributed products but rather from a struggle among the small firms in the value chain to determine which firm could earn the largest share of profit. The registration of labels with local US courts for copyright protection also suggests that small local firms were seeking brand identity protection as early as the 1830s.

This chapter summary attempts to paint a broader picture of the development of brand marketing. While evidence of small relatively inconspicuous trade or guild marks date back to ancient times, it seems unlikely such modest marks served as the focus of marketing for those products. However, we can't rule out the possibility that Chinese sewing needles sold under the 'white rabbit' name may have been promoted under that name as having a particular cultural meaning. If that turns out to be true then brand marketing may predate modern times. The literature does suggest that ancient and medieval buyers often came to understand and appreciate the small trade and guild marks as they sought out high-quality goods. By the 1700s, firms were promoting their marks to buyers as a way of avoiding being deceived by counterfeit goods.

During the nineteenth century, trademark law developed extensively to support the development of brand marketing. However, legal enforcement was not the only tactic used by early brand marketers to limit unauthorized imitation. Often they also would try to develop good local relationships to provide business intelligence and settle disputes about imitation rather than rely on expensive formal litigation (da Silva Lopes and Casson, 2012). An alternative for small entrepreneurial firms that would struggle to afford litigation might be acquisition by large firms that could professionally manage the brands (da Silva Lopes and Casson 2007).

The crucial concept of developing a unique brand identity with advertising promoting the brand to develop brand personality and connect with consumers seems to have emerged in the 1800s. Without further research, we can't tell whether the registration of product labels as copyrighted prints in the early 1800s was simply another technique to avoid imitation or at some point the label identity became the focus of brand advertising. While additional research on labels and advertising in the first half of the 1800s would seem to be warranted, the period of the early 1900s seems reasonably well established as a time where brand marketing became the dominant marketing practice complete with its own literature and the development of the brand manager system of management.

References

Acheson, A. (1917) *Trade-Mark Advertising as an Investment,* Evening Post, New York.

Advertising Age (1932) 'Advertised brands as a protection to the consumer', 3/31, 4.

Advertising Age (1934) 'Consumers have faith in advertising', 5/3, p. 4.

Bartholomew, M. (2008) 'Advertising and the transformation of trademark law', *New Mexico Law Review*, 38/1, 1–48.

Bastos, W., and Levy, S.J. (2012) 'A history of the concept of branding: Practice and theory', *Journal of Historical Research in Marketing*, 14/3, 347–68.

Ben B. Hampton Co. (1903) *The Value of Advertised Trademarks,* Ben B. Hampton Co., New York.

Bently, L. (2008) 'The making of modern trade mark law: The construction of the legal concept of trademark', in L. Bently, J. Davis and J.C. Ginsburg (eds), *Trademarks and Brands: An Interdisciplinary Critique,* Cambridge University Press, Cambridge, 3–41.

Berthon, P., Holbrook, M.B., and Hulbert, J.M. (2003) 'Understanding and managing the brand space', *MIT Sloan Management Review.* 44/2, 49–54.

Bone, R. G. (2006) 'Hunting goodwill: A history of the concept of goodwill in trademark law', *Boston University Law Review*, 86/3, 547–622.

Butler, R.S. (1917) *Marketing Methods,* Alexander Hamilton Institute, New York.

Chamberlain, E.H. (1933) *A Theory of Monopolistic Competition,* Harvard University Press, Cambridge, MA.

Chase, S., and Schlink, F.J. (1929) *Your Money's Worth: A Study in the Waste of the Consumer's Dollar,* Macmillan Co., New York.

Cherington, P.T. (1913) *Advertising as a Business Force,* Doubleday, Page & Co., New York.

Cherington, P.T. (1916) *The Advertising Book 1916,* Doubleday, Page & Co, New York.

Cherington, P.T. (1920) *The Elements of Marketing,* Macmillan Co., New York.

Commissioner of Patents (1870) *Annual Report of the Commissioner of Patents,* Government Printing Office, Washington, DC.

Cunningham, R. M. (1956) 'Brand loyalty – What, where how much?', *Harvard Business Review,* 34/1, 116–28.

da Silva Lopes, T., and Casson, M. (2007) 'Entrepreneurship and the development of global brands', *Business History Review,* 81/4, 651–80.

da Silva Lopes, T., and Casson, M. (2012) 'Imitation, brand protection and globalization of British business', *Business History Review,* 86/2, 287–310.

Davis, J., and Maniatis, S. (2010) 'Trademarks, brands, and competition', in T da Silva Lopes and P. Duguid (eds), *Trademarks, Brands, and Competitiveness,* Routledge, New York, 119–37.

Duncan, C.S. (1921) *Marketing: Its Problems and Methods,* D. Appleton & Co., New York.

Duguid, P. (2003) 'Developing the brand: The case of alcohol', *Enterprise and Society,* 4 /3, 405–41.

Duguid, P. (2009) 'French connections: The international propagation of trademarks in the nineteenth century', *Enterprise and Society,* 10/1, 3–37.

Duguid, P. (2012) 'A case of prejudice? The uncertain development of collective and certification marks', *Business History Review,* 86/2, 311–33.

Duguid, P. (2013) 'California marketing and collective amnesia', *University of California Davis Law Review,* 47/2, 581–600.

Duguid, P., da Silva Lopes, T., and Mercer, J. (2010) 'Reading registrations: An overview of 100 years of trademark registrations in France, the United Kingdom and the United States', in T. da Silva Lopes and P. Duguid (eds), *Trademarks, Brands, and Competitiveness,* Routledge, New York, 9–30.

Eckhardt, G.M., and Bengtsson, A. (2009) 'A brief history of branding in China', *Journal of Macromarketing,* 30/3, 210–21.

Gardner, B.B., and Levy, S.J. (1955) 'The product and the brand', *Harvard Business Review,* 33/2, 33–9.

Hamilton, G.G., and Lai, C. (1989) 'Consumerism without capitalism: Consumption and brand names in late imperial China', in H.J. Rutz and B. S. Orlove (eds), *The Social Economy of Consumption,* University Press of America, Lanham, MD, pp. 253–79.

Hambleton, R. (1987) *The Branding of America,* Yankee Books, Dublin.

Higgins, D. M. (2008) 'The making of modern trade mark law: The UK, 1860–1914. A business history perspective', in L. Bently, J. Davis, and J.C. Ginsburg (eds), *Trademarks and Brands: An Interdisciplinary Critique,* Cambridge University Press, Cambridge, 42–61.

Higgins, D.M. (2012) 'Forgotten heroes and forgotten issues: Business and trademark history during the nineteenth century', *Business History Review,* 86/2, 261–85.

Hollander, S.C., Rassuli, K.M., Jones, D.G.B., and Dix, L.F. (2005) 'Periodization in marketing history', *Journal of Macromarketing,* 25/1, 32–41.

Hopkins, C.C. (1923) *Scientific Advertising,* Lord & Thomas, New York.

Koehn, N.F. (2001) *Brand New: How Entrepreneurs Earned Consumers' Trust from Wedgwood to Dell,* Harvard University Press, Boston, MA.

Laird, P.W. (1998) *Advertising Progress: American Business and the Rise of Consumer Marketing,* Johns Hopkins University Press, Baltimore, MD.

Lonier, T. (2010) 'Alchemy in Eden: Entrepreneurialism, branding and food marketing in the United States, 1880–1920', *Enterprise and Society*, 11/4, 695–708.

Low, G.S., and Fullerton, R.A. (1994) 'Brands, brand management, and the brand manager system: A critical-historical evaluation', *Journal of Marketing Research*, 31/2, 173–90.

McClure, D.M. (1979) 'Trademarks and unfair competition: A critical history of legal thought', *The Trademark Reporter*, 69/4, 305–56.

McKendrick, N. Brewer, J., and Plumb, J.H. (1982) *The Birth of a Consumer Society: The Commercialization of Eighteenth-Century England*, Indiana University Press, Bloomington, IN.

Manufacturing Co. v. Trainer (1880) 101 U.S. 51.

Mercer, J. (2010) 'A mark of distinction: Branding and trade mark law in the UK from the 1860s', *Business History*, 52/1, 17–42.

Moor, L. (2007) *The Rise of Brands*, Berg, Oxford.

Moore, K., and Reid S. (2008) 'The birth of brand: 4000 years of branding', *Business History*, 50/4, 419–32.

Morein, J.A. (1975) 'Shift from brand to product line marketing', *Harvard Business Review*, 53/5, 56–64.

Petty, R.D. (2011) 'The co-development of trademark law and the concept of brand marketing in the US before 1946', *Journal of Macromarketing*, 31/1, 85–99.

Petty, R.D. (2012) 'From label to trademark: The legal origins of the concept of brand identity in nineteenth century America', *Journal of Historical Research in Marketing*, 4/1, 129–53.

Petty, R.D. (2013) 'Towards a modern history of brand marketing: Where are we now?', *Varieties, Alternatives, and Deviations in Marketing History, Proceedings of the 16th Biennial Conference in Historical Analysis and Research in Marketing*, Copenhagen, Denmark, pp. 210–20.

Phelps, D.M. (1949) 'Certification marks under the Lanham Act', *Journal of Marketing*, 13/4, 498–505.

Pope, D. (1983) *The Making of Modern Advertising*, Basic Books, New York.

Rewoldt, S.H. (1948) 'Assignment of trade-marks', *Journal of Marketing*, 12/4, 483–7.

Richardson, G. (2008) 'Brand names before the industrial revolution', *National Bureau of Economic Research*, 13930, available online: www.nber.org/papers/w13930 (accessed Oct. 2012).

Ries, A., and Trout, J. (1981) *Positioning: The Battle for your Mind*, McGraw Hill, New York.

Robinson, J. (1933) *The Economics of Imperfect Competition*, Macmillan & Co., New York.

Room, A. (1998) 'The history of branding', in S. Hart and J. Murphy (eds), *Brands: The New Wealth Creators*, New York University Press, New York, pp. 13–23.

Saiz, P., and Perez, P.F. (2012) 'Catalonian trademarks and the development of marketing knowledge in Spain, 1850–1946', *Business History Review*, 86/2, 239–60.

Schechter, F.I. (1925) *The Historical Foundation of the Law Relating to Trade-Marks*, Columbia University Press, New York.

Schechter, F.I. (1927) 'The rational basis of trademark protection', *Harvard Law Review*, 40/6, 813–33.

Schwarzkopf, S. (2009) 'What was advertising? The invention, rise, demise, and disappearance of advertising concepts in nineteenth- and twentieth-century Europe and America', *Business and Economic History Online*, 7, www.thebhc.org/publications/BEHonline/2009/schwarzkopf. pdf (accessed Mar. 2013).

Schwarzkopf, S. (2010) 'Turning trademarks into brands: How advertising agencies practiced and conceptualized branding, 1890-1930', in T. da Silva Lopes and P. Duguid (eds), *Trademarks, Brands, and Competitiveness*, Routledge, New York, pp. 165–93.

Sivulka, J. (1998) *Soap, Sex, and Cigarettes: A Cultural History of Advertising*, Wadsworth Publishing Co., Belmont, CA.

Stern, B.B. (2006) 'What does brand mean? Historical-analysis method and construct definition', *Journal of the Academy of Marketing Science*, 23/2, 216–23.

Stole, Inger L. (2006) *Advertising on Trial: Consumer Activism and Corporate Public Relations in the 1930s*, University of Illinois Press, Urbana, IL.

Stolte, K.M. (1997) 'How early did Anglo-American trademark law begin? An answer to Schechter's conundrum', *Fordham Intellectual Property, Media and Entertainment Law Journal*, 8/2, 505–47.

Strasser, S. (1989) *Satisfaction Guaranteed: The Making of the American Mass Market*, Pantheon Books, New York.

Tedlow, R.S. (1990) *New and Improved: The Story of Mass Marketing in America*, Basic Books, New York.

Tucker, W.T. (1964) 'The development of brand loyalty', *Journal of Marketing Research*, 1/3, 32–5.

Wengrow, D. (2008) 'Prehistories of commodity branding', *Current Anthropology*, 49 /1, 7–34.

Wilkins, M. (1992) 'The neglected intangible asset: The influence of the trade mark on the rise of the modern corporation', *Business History*, 34/1, 66–95.

Wolfe, H.D. (1942) 'Techniques of appraising brand preference and brand consciousness by consumer interviewing', *Journal of Marketing*, 6/4, 81–7.

7

History of packaging

Diana Twede

Introduction

For as long as humans have been hunting, gathering and trading, we have used packages for collecting, storing and shipping. The earliest primitive packages were made from leaves, skins and gourds. Early basket-weaving technology developed to craft packages made from grasses and other natural fibres, especially for dry and harvested food.

For longer distance shipping of liquids like wine and oil, sturdy shipping containers were developed. Clay amphorae were used throughout the Mediterranean by ancient Egyptians, Greeks and Romans (see Figure 7.1). Amphorae led to the use of wooden barrels/casks in Northern Europe and its colonies, where wood was a more plentiful natural resource than

Figure 7.1   Ancient commercial amphorae. Used by permission, American School of Classical Studies at Athens, Agora Evacuations, photo by Alison Frantz, Grace, 1961

clay. Wooden crates and shipping sacks rode in on the industrial revolution with its boxcars, sawmills and textile mills.

This long history of such shipping containers reveals functional similarities to today's corrugated boxes, pallets and ocean containers. Amphorae, barrels, crates and sacks were made from plentiful natural resources like mud, bushes and trees, and exploited contemporaneous technologies, like pottery-making, woodwork and weaving. They were economical to make. Their shapes were efficient to handle and fit the geometry of the transportation modes. They were produced to meet standards administered by guilds and/or government (see Twede, 2002, 2005, 2015, for shipping container history reviews).

But it was not until the late 1800s that packaging moved beyond simple bulk shipping containers to household-sized packs designed to appeal directly to consumers. This chapter explores the twentieth-century progression of packaging technology and the professionalization of the field. It shows how consumer packaging was developed to satisfy the growing demands of modern marketing and logistical systems.

1800–1890: emerging consumer packaging technologies

The technology to make glass and sheet metal was advanced enough at the beginning of the 1800s to be used for housewares and refillable household packages like jars, canisters and bandboxes. But production was slow and manual. The cost of producing such packages was prohibitive for them to be used in routine transactions, and the marketing value had yet to be established. Nineteenth-century technology developments in glass blowing, papermaking and canning led to the first consumer sales-unit packages in the mid-1800s.

Wine bottles that could withstand shipping were first developed in 1709, even though glassmaking was an ancient art (developed by Phoenicians and Egyptians). The first successful American bottle factory was built in 1739 to supply rum distillers, and by 1820 the US glass bottle industry was supplying a growing demand for alcohol, patent medicines, perfumes and cosmetics. Heavy reusable bottles were developed for carbonated beverages. But throughout the 1800s, production was still a labour-intensive, mouth-blown process. Although production was organized in factories, the basic process was unchanged from its ancient origins (Diamond, 1953).

Wraps and paperboard cartons were enabled by the invention of the papermaking machine and lithographic printing in 1798. The invention of pulp made from straw and wood, later in the 1800s, ushered in the 'age of paper', including the production of low-cost disposable paper and paperboard products and packages (Hunter, 1947). This too was a labour-intensive manual process of sheet-fed printing, guillotine cutting and gluing.

Canning was invented by Nicholas Appert in 1809 (in France) and extended to tinplate cans in 1810 (by Peter Durand and commercialized by Bryan Donkin who also built the first papermaking machines in the UK). By 1820, canned food began to be sold in the UK and the US, followed by a century of developments to control the heat-treatment process. But the cans were made in yet another manual process of cutting and soldering the tinplated steel. It was not until the end of the 1800s, after Pasteur discovered the role of microbiology in food preservation, that the role of sterilization was understood, leading to better control of heat processing which accelerated the demand for canned food (Prescott and Underwood, 1897).

By the late 1800s, branded paper wraps and bags, bottled and canned food slowly began to replace the practice of the shopkeeper parcelling purchases. Although the earliest cartons, cans and bottles were made in Europe, the US came to dominate in the packaging technology progress of the 1800s (Davis, 1967).

Figure 7.2   Norton's automated can-making line, source: *American Machinist*, 1883

1890–1920: packaged and branded

The technology to mechanically form cans, bottles and cartons was developed in the US after the Civil War, between 1880 and 1910. This mechanization was key to the mass production that would be required by the emerging strategy of nationwide distribution and mass-marketing.

Whereas consumer product marketing had begun as a geographically limited, low-volume, high-margin business, the 1880s marked a 'profound paradigm shift'. The US had become more unified by its political stability, railroad and telegraph networks. This infrastructure enabled the concept of a new nationwide mass market, 'the democratization of consumption … a distinctively American contribution to the world' (Tedlow, 1996, p. xxiii). Many brands that benefited from early adoption – Nabisco, Quaker Oats, Campbell Soup, Heinz and Coca-Cola – sustain the advantage today, over 100 years later (Tedlow, 1996, pp. xxiii, 346).

Standardized packages were interchangeable parts for the continuous-process systems that were invented 'almost simultaneously' for making everything from processed food to soft drinks (Hounshell, 1984). During the period 1880–1910 the processes for making tinplate cans, glass bottles and paperboard cartons were mechanized by Edwin Norton, Michael Owens and Robert Gair. Package converting was an early application of mass production, and Norton's can-making line (Figure 7.2) was credited with inspiring Henry Ford's assembly line process (Twede, 2012).

Manufacturers who chose to invest in consumer packaging 'found themselves literally making a new kind of product'. Their factories required mechanized filling into mechanically made packages. Packaging provided distinctive marketing benefits, extended shelf-life and gave the producer greater control over product quality. Ads featured the sanitary nature of packaged products; even bar soap was sold as 'untouched by human hands'. Labelled packages 'showed where they came from and who is responsible for their condition and character' (Strasser, 1989, 32).

Packages could be branded, and 'what the manufacturer could name, he could advertise' (Tedlow, 1996, 14). The number of magazine advertisements (for packaged goods) that featured

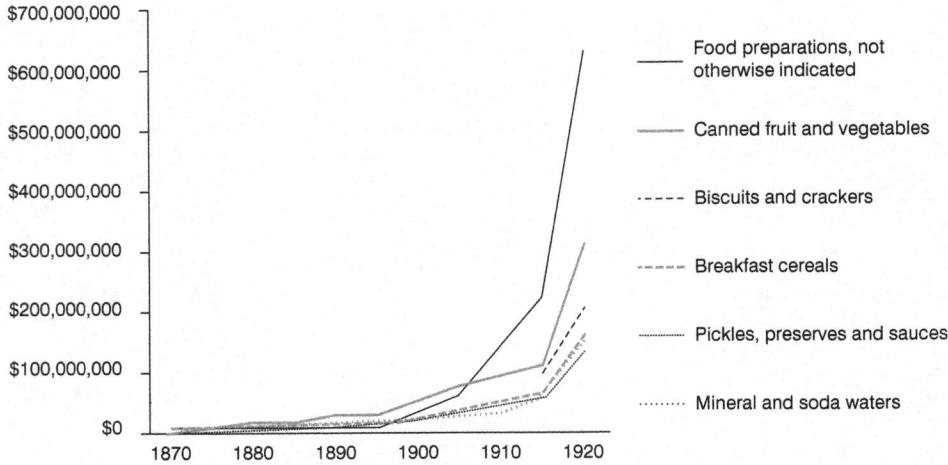

Figure 7.3   Growth in the value of six categories of packaged food and beverages

the package rose from 39 per cent in 1900 to 75 per cent in 1920 (Franken and Larrabee, 1928). Packaging was key to changing the paradigm of consumption to favour national brands:

> Packages enabled the creation of a new consumer culture with new domestic habits and activities involving packages. Americans everywhere and of all classes began to eat, drink, clean with, wear, and sit on products made in factories. Toothpaste, corn flakes, chewing gum, safety razors and cameras – things nobody ever made at home or in small crafts shops – provided the material basis for new habits and the physical expression of a genuine break from earlier times.
>
> *(Strasser, 1989, 6)*

The emerging and later dominant US agricultural engineering industry developed new systems for food harvesting and processing, as well as package filling, weighing and closing. The best thing since sliced bread was the machine to automatically wrap it, introduced in 1911. By the time of the first supermarket in 1920, annual sales of packaged foods and beverages had increased by 60-fold over 1880 levels, 80 per cent of which occurred after 1910 (Figure 7.3, Twede, 2012)

At the same time, paper technology also gave birth to the corrugated box in 1894 as a substitute for wooden shipping containers. Although railroads first resisted the new shipping container, by 1914 an alliance was formed between the corrugated fiberboard industry, the railroads and the US Interstate Commerce Commission to develop standard properties and 'rules' for acceptable use. Widespread adoption followed for the cheap corrugated regular slotted container (Figure 7.4) which could be mechanically produced from roll-stock containerboard and easily erected, filled and shipped. Cheap, lightweight corrugated boxes, shipped in 'boxcars', *were* mass distribution (Bettendorf, 1946).

Packages became a strategic advantage for brands like Uneeda Biscuit, sometimes touted as the 'first consumer package' introduced in 1897 (Twede, 1997). Moreover, they were a strategic advantage for the packaging suppliers. For example, the primary Uneeda package manufacturer, Robert Gair Co., became one of the most successful suppliers of paperboard cartons and corrugated boxes in the US (Figure 7.5).

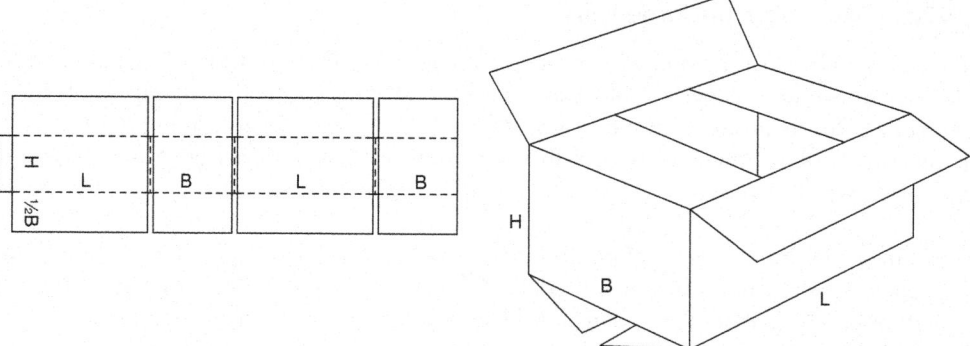

Figure 7.4 Regular slotted corrugated fiberboard shipping container, adapted with permission of FEFCO

Making folding boxes
for the leaders in every industry

INTO every American home these packages find their way! They deliver their contents—biscuits, coffee, tea, cereals, dates, foodstuffs—clean, fresh, untouched on the long journey from manufacturer to consumer.

Billions of these products are sold yearly because their quality is high and *unvarying* —because people know that these products will be delivered in perfect condition.

Once the product leaves the manufacturer, *the protection of its quality depends upon its package.*

The package is, therefore, of great merchandising importance. It should be planned and manufactured specifically to carry the particular product most economically, most securely, with greatest advertising effect.

The packages illustrated above, packages for hundreds of other famous products, are made by the Robert Gair Company.

Each had its packaging problem which we solved—by an ingenious device to lock the contents in its carton, a new design of a character suited to the high quality of the merchandise, a special ink to assure uniformity of color, or a guarantee of adequate resources to keep pace with large scale production.

Packages for a billion dollars' worth of goods

This ability to meet all demands for highest quality or greatest quantity is characteristic of Robert Gair Company's four departments —Folding boxes, Labels, Shipping cases, Window display advertising.

Because the greatest merchandisers of the country recognize this ability, more than a billion dollars' worth of merchandise was carried last year in folding boxes, in shipping cases, and under labels made by Robert Gair Company.

We control the whole process of manufacture from wood-pulp to finished product. We operate our own paper mills, make our own inks and glues, maintain our own art, engraving, printing, lithographing departments. Our chemistry department regulates and improves our processes and tests finished products. We operate the largest plant of its kind in the world.

With its facilities we are prepared to offer a complete service for packaging and displaying your product—folding boxes, labels, shipping cases, window display advertising—giving unity to your packages from factory to consumer.

Our Timber display container gives your goods prominence on the retailer's counter

We serve the greatest packagers merchandisers of the country. Among our clients are:

National Biscuit Company
American Sugar Refining Co.
Hansen & Son
Kirkman & Son
Johnson & Johnson
Colgate & Company
Hecker-Jones-Jewell Milling Company
Royal Baking Powder Co.
Beare & Black
Palmolive Company
American Chicle Company
Andrew Jergens Company
Armour Bros.
N. K. Fairbank Company
Hayler's
Robt. H. Ingersoll & Bro.
Beech-Nut Packing Co.
Eclixo Storage Battery Co.
Charles B. Knox Gelatine Co.
Julius Kayser & Company

ROBERT GAIR COMPANY
BROOKLYN

Folding boxes   *Shipping cases*
Labels   *Window display advertising*

The group of Gair buildings with docks on the East River

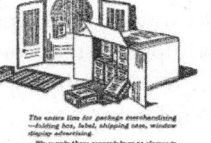

The entire line for package merchandising —folding box, label, shipping case, window display advertising.
We supply these separately or as elements of a carefully organized merchandising unit.

Figure 7.5 Robert Gair advertisement, source: *New York Times*, February 1920

1920–1940s: 'The package sells'

Packaging enabled the brand owner to advertise and sell directly to the consumer, bypassing the traditional shopkeeper's control over product offerings with the message, 'ask for it by name'. But its greatest advantage was the package itself as advertisement. In 1928, the pioneering book by Franken and Larrabee demonstrated how the package had changed the buying habits of a nation:

> The American of day before yesterday asked for a pound of crackers. Today his grandson demands a box of Uneedas…The consumer used to buy anonymous goods in bulk. His grandchildren demand the products by name and get them in packages… sealed, the weights are marked, and the quality is guaranteed by the manufacturer's name. Every field of retailing has been affected to a greater or less extent…, changed the very appearance of stores…, revolutionized window display. It has brought about surprising economies for both the manufacturer and the consumer, and it has given to the consumer great gifts in the way of convenience. It has opened new markets and completely changed the character of old outlets.
>
> *(Franken and Larrabee, 1928, 1)*

They go on to show how 'each and every part of the modern package' can be made to stimulate sales, including chapters on materials, shape, size, colour and design from physical and psychological points of view. They praise the ability of the package to promote in the store and consumers' homes. They show how scientific methods can be applied to selecting the best package and product name, including consumer testing, sample selection and statistical evaluation of the results. Despite noting that 'commodities' were still sold in bulk at the time (e.g. 5 per cent of sugar, 3 per cent of flour, 25 per cent of tea, 46 per cent of butter and 60 per cent of bread), they foresee that 'the future will see every industry which can possibly use the package doing so' (Franken and Larrabee, 1928, 275).

Branded packages led to the rise of self-service retail stores in the 1930s, when it was found that 'the housewife sold herself far more than the best clerk' (Zimmerman, 1955, 52). Retailers were able to cut labour costs and exploit a low-price, high-volume, nationally advertised strategy. Marketing strategies of segmentation and differentiation led to stock-keeping unit (SKU) proliferation in which the package became the primary differentiating feature.

As consumer product goods (CPG) manufacturers grew and consolidated, so did the surrounding industry. By the late 1920s, an identifiable 'packaging supply industry' began to emerge, deriving from the previous material-based industries that made glass bottles, metal cans and paperboard cartons.

The first industry-wide trade journal and encyclopedia, *Modern Packaging*, premiered in 1927. From the beginning (initial issue shown in Figure 7.6) the subjects ranged from cost to value, from standardization to technology to colour trends, all sponsored by advertisements for packaging and machinery suppliers.

Family-owned package-converting businesses gradually consolidated into publicly held national suppliers that competed at the same time as they cooperated with one another to grow the overall industry. There was a rich history of consolidation and antitrust collusion within and between container industries in the twentieth century. The trusts formed (like the tin can trust) were broken up into corporations (like American Can and National Can) and trade associations (like the Fibre Box and Can Manufacturers' Associations) grew to provide leadership in technology, markets and politics. For example, the can producers strongly

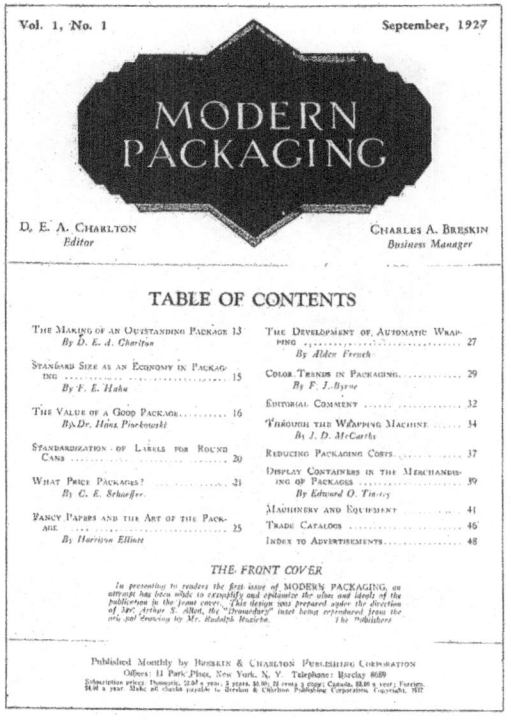

Figure 7.6 Table of contents for *Modern Packaging*, 1927, used with permission of *Packaging Digest* which acquired *Modern Packaging*

influenced the development of food science programmes in universities and emerging food safety regulations like the Federal Food, Drug and Cosmetic Act in 1938, which aimed to prevent product adulteration. In 1933 the Packaging Machinery Manufacturers Institute was organized to promote mechanized packaging processes.

This was also a period of new materials, improved graphics and opportunities to improve packaging protection. Victorian design was replaced by simpler brand messaging. Colour printing became more widespread after the development of the four-colour halftone process (Opie, 1987).

Sparkly new flexible materials like cellophane, aluminum foil and, later, plastic film were introduced with the promise of increasing sales (Figure 7.7). Film wraps also improved water- and oxygen-barrier protection for food packaging. Cellophane's barrier property was used during World War II to make 'gas tents' for US soldiers, and after the war's disruption, its use skyrocketed. Kraft paper, with its long, strong fibres, was introduced in the 1930s to replace paper reinforced with jute.

World War II provided opportunities to improve food preservation as well as improve the efficiency of logistics. The need to produce troop rations stimulated growth in the canning (C-rations) and tobacco industries, and the consumption of both became more mainstream in US homes after the war (Risch, 2009). Pallets and forklifts, which enabled the logistics necessary to supply the war on two fronts, later came to dominate civilian handling too (LeBlanc and Richardson, 2003).

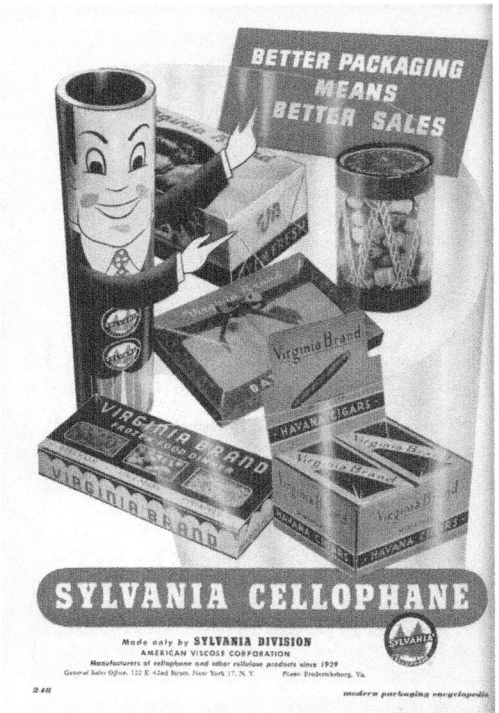

Figure 7.7 Cellophane brings sparkle to packaging, source: *Modern Packaging Encyclopedia*, 1948, p. 248. Used with permission from *Packaging Digest*

1950–1970: growth of packaging management

By the 1950s, packaging was developing to be a discipline and profession of its own. Almost as a defence against the growing power of packaging suppliers, the profession of packaging developed in consumer goods companies to provide expertise for comparing packaging material alternatives and managing the packaging function. Professional divisions were developed within trade organizations, like the American Management Association (AMA) and Institute of Food Technology (IFT). Two professional organizations were developed, the Packaging Institute and Society of Packaging and Handling Engineers (SPHE), which later morphed into the current Institute of Packaging Professionals (IoPP).

Packaging education (aside from a few canning courses at agricultural colleges) began at Michigan State College (later named Michigan State University, MSU) in 1952, to be followed by other universities such as Rochester Institute of Technology, University of Wisconsin (Stout), Rutgers and Clemson. MSU developed an education model that focuses on evaluating and choosing packaging materials (metal, glass, paper and plastic), container types and filling machinery, as well as managing the packaging development process (Twede and Goff, 1999).

The American Management Association published a series of management briefings on subjects like 'package design and its management' (AMA, 1965), 'tomorrow's realities' (AMA, 1969), 'vital packaging management' (Lansdale, 1978), and 'corporate identity and product recognition' (Selame *et al.*, 1982). The professional organizations, SPHE and IoPP, likewise developed education/certification programmes for packaging professionals who have university degrees from other educational backgrounds. Textbooks and handbooks of packaging management, design and engineering were introduced (e.g. Jones, 1950; Paine, 1963; Hanlon, 1971; Milgrom and Brody, 1974; and later Griffin, *et al.*, 1985).

Scholarship emerged in product protection areas like distribution dynamics and food shelf-life. As the protective nature of packaging became better understood, standards were developed for testing and comparison. The research was extended to the shelf-life of other fast-moving consumer goods and the fragility of multi-component electric and mechanical goods. Although fragility assessment began as a means to predict the properties of package cushioning, it led to product design factors that reduce fragility and the need for cushioning, factors that would become increasingly critical for the new electronics industry.

'There is only one thing certain about the future of packaging: there will definitely be plenty of change' (Brody, 1969, 8). It is interesting to note how many of the 'Tomorrow's Realities' envisioned almost 50 years ago in AMA's briefing proved to be correct predictions. Food packaging predictions included the growth of single-serve meal and snack packages (and decline of family togetherness), the use of packaging to signal market segmentation, cook-in packages and pre-packed meat and vegetables. Retail chain growth did increase the demand for palletized shipping and in-store displays. Ocean containerization did move from port-to-port delivery to origin/destination shipping and handling. And the use of plastic bottles was to grow rapidly, although the plastic of future bottles was not PVC, as expected, but PET because of toxicity concerns (AMA, 1969).

In the 1960s, packaging material developments began to enable new supply chains. Plastic became inexpensive enough to be used for packaging applications, and as an infinitely formable material (Barthes, 1957), plastic bottles, coatings and films became widespread substitutes for older materials. The use of paperboard cartons coated with wax, later plastic, enabled supermarket milk distribution, replacing reusable glass bottles and household delivery. New food packaging systems were developed along with concerns about their safety (Sacharow and Griffin, 1973). Preserved and frozen food, like TV dinners, were followed by flexible plastic packaging of food (Brody, 1970), which prompted better barrier properties for plastic film. Flexographic printing, first introduced for simple printing on paper bags and corrugated boxes, was adapted to flexible plastic. The widespread adoption of palletization accelerated mass shipping.

The growing consumption of packaged products changed the way that people lived. Housewives learned to cook with packaged ingredients, as producers like General Mills and Pillsbury promoted cooking with Betty Crocker and the Dough Boy. Bottled soft drinks and beer became commonplace. Refrigerated and frozen foods (along with ubiquitous refrigerators and automobiles) increased the length of time between shopping trips and increased the amount purchased on each trip. And the growing promotion of packaged health and beauty products extended peoples' lives and increased the number of times per week that they bathed (Strasser, 1989).

But packages also conceal food, and in 1966 the government protected consumers by regulating packaging. The US Fair Packaging and Labeling Act established terms of labelling a product's identity, ingredients, producer and net contents. The US government's previous food packaging regulation had begun in 1906 with the Meat Inspection Act, in response to the unhealthy sanitation and working conditions in the meat packing industry reported in *The Jungle* (Sinclair, 1906) and the Federal Food, Drug and Cosmetic Act in 1938, which aimed to prevent product adulteration. Later, in the 1990s, FDA regulation was extended to include nutrition and drug facts.

During 1960–80, other countries began to embrace the US mass-marketing model. For example, *The Silent Salesman* provides a 1961 British perspective on the trend:

> In Great Britain there are still many shop assistants. They can sell for you. It's their job. Make it worthwhile and they may give your goods an extra push. All very nice. But they are dying out. Newer distribution methods are taking over. Self-service moves in quickly not only in food, but in hardware, clothing, cosmetics, stationery, almost every area of consumer merchandise. Die-hards may slow the momentum of change. But they won't stop it. The future is clear. In the United States, for example, the job of selling to the consumer has swung largely to the package. TIME magazine reckons that if the U.S. were to go back to traditional ways of shopping, it would find itself short of one and a half million shop assistants.
>
> *(Pilditch, 1961, 2–3)*

1980–2020: increasing functionality and technology of packaging

After the 1980s, materials grew increasingly tailored for specific uses, and a packaging research community began to develop. Packaging suppliers like Dow, Dupont, American Can, Riegel, Continental Can, Owens-Illinois and Tetrapak were joined by research institutes and university scholars. The International Association of Packaging Research Institutes, formed in 1973, led to the field's first international research journal, *Packaging Technology and Science* in 1988, justified by the need for packaging science to emerge from being 'partially buried in scientific journals related principally to disciplines on the margin of the subject' (Paine, 1988).

Much of the new research focused on advancements to improve the quality (and quantity) of processed food. The military and space programmes developed retorted pouched foods. Microwave cooking prompted developments in materials to conduct or deflect heat to improve crispness and/or deliver a hot meal with a cold side dish. Aseptic packaging, which began in Europe in 1950s and was commercialized by TetraPak in the 1960s, was finally adopted in the US in 1981, producing fresher processed food and beverages (Robertson, 2013). Research in the barrier properties of plastics led to tailored polymer blends and coatings to increase the shelf-life of processed food. Vacuum packing and modified atmosphere gas flush systems were developed in the 1990s to lengthen the shelf-life of fresh meat and produce (Brody, 1994). After 2000, research turned to antimicrobial films (Joerger, 2007).

As a result, high-quality ('fresh-like'), convenient packaged food has grown to dominate Western consumption, saving time for busy households, transforming the real cooking of 'whole foods' to a cultural hobby rather than a necessity. The consumption of bottled drinks is taken for granted, even in a state like Michigan that is surrounded by fresh water. Most meals today are simply reheated by microwave. This represents a significant opportunity for business to develop relationships with consumers (Bastos and Levy, 2012), considering the fact that we eat and drink several times a day.

As marketing research has increasingly focused on consumers, packaging has proved its value as a legitimate marketing variable (although some marketing scholars persist in maintaining it as an 'illegitimate' variable, packaging even has its own 'P', a fact practically overlooked by earlier (McCarthy, 1960) marketing mix theories. The recognition that packaging influences consumer choice in stores and their consumption behaviour has led researchers to develop scientific methods to 'evaluate the degree to which a product's personality, claims and benefits are communicated through the structure and graphics of the

Figure 7.8   QR Code

package' (Stern, 1981, p. v). By the 1990s, point-of-purchase (POP) promotion outperformed other (increasingly fragmented) media, leading the corrugated board industry to advance their technology to be able to print colourful POP display designs. Government-mandated nutrition and 'drug fact' labelling was established to help consumers understand the quality and characteristics of food and drug products. From focus groups to ergonomics to safety to ethnographics, packaging research moved closer to consumers (Azzi *et al.*, 2012).

Packaging technology has also improved the ability to better serve segmentation and supply chain strategies. Shorter production runs and faster set-up times enabled SKU proliferation to serve ever-smaller, customized target markets. Packaging technology that successfully extended food shelf-life also extended supply chain efficiency.

Since the late twentieth century, packaging technology has also advanced to meet new needs. Threats of package tampering and counterfeiting led to packaging security improvements. Concerns about food safety and the migration of 'indirect additives' into food led to research and regulation of food-contact surfaces. In an increasingly electronic world, the availability of sensors and electronics is leading to 'smart' and 'intelligent' packaging that communicates with devices to report product and shelf-life details. Printed QR codes (Figure 7.8) can take the device-enabled consumer directly to the producer's website, to expand the available information and deepen the consumer's relationship to the brand.

Likewise, shipping container developments profoundly changed the nature of physical distribution by the end of the twentieth century, making supply chains shorter, cheaper and more diverse. Much like corrugated boxes (in the 1920s) and pallets (in the 1960s) improved efficiency, intermodal containerization (Figure 7.9) enabled long-distance supply chains and the 'Walmart' phenomenon to exploit cheap labour overseas (Levinson, 2006). Automatic

Figure 7.9   Intermodal containerization dramatically reduced the cost of long-distance supply chains; used with permission from Maersk

identification like barcodes streamlined data entry for logistics information systems, reducing the need for inventory buffers. Fulfilment packaging solutions that minimize the cost of order picking and home delivery have contributed to the growth of online marketing.

For packaging suppliers, the late twentieth century was a period of incremental developments, consolidation and increasing dominance of plastics. The glass bottle and aluminum can industries shrank as the use of plastic bottles grew exponentially, serving a growing demand for bottled water, soft drinks and other liquid products. Plastic coatings improved the ability of paperboard to contain liquids. Glass coatings improved the barrier properties of plastic bottles. The canned food industry developed thinner, safer plastic-lined cans with easy-open ends. The increase in electronic products stimulated research into product fragility and enabled the engineering of plastic foam cushioning. Most importantly, flexible plastic packages have been developed to substitute for almost every other packaging material, as their functionality and the quality of flexographic printing improved.

Throughout the twentieth century, other countries have 'caught up' with (and sometimes bypassed) US packaging technology. The consumer demand for packaged products grows along with a developing economy. Packaging plays a critical role in the economic development of a country's internal trade and exports, and many governments support packaging education and technical development. Countries undergoing economic development today are less likely to develop a packaging industry based on glass, metal and paper, due to the large capital and natural resource investment required. Instead, they are quickly developing flexible packaging solutions that minimize the use of resources and exploit current plastics technology. From a global perspective, the current prevalence of American rigid packaging is an artefact of our history.

Resistance to the 'throw-away' culture

Garbage is a subplot of the packaging story. Unlike products that only begin their useful life when they are purchased, packaging has nearly completed its useful life when it reaches the consumer. Once the product is used, the package is no longer necessary.

The 1950s–1960s practically celebrated the luxury of the 'throw-away culture, consumerism and style obsolescence' (Whiteley, 1987). But the 1970–1980s marked a dawn of environmental consciousness, in which packaging waste was an easy target (Darney and Franklin, 1969; Milgrom and Brody, 1974).

In response, governments and industry mobilized to increase recycling in the 1980s. New symbology was developed (Figure 7.10) and the various types of materials were identified for separation to increase their secondary value. The 1990 German legislation that taxes packaging producers to pay for municipal recycling was adopted by other European

Figure 7.10 Universal symbol shows recyclability or recycled content

countries. Packaging producers became more involved in waste management by designing for recycling, as well as facilitating collection and reprocessing (Selke, 1990; Stilwell *et al.*, 1991).

By 2010, sustainability was the new wave of environmentalism. In response to retailer demand, brand owners added packaging life cycle analysis to their brand image tools. As a result, packaging is increasingly designed to minimize environmental impacts. For example, the sustainable movement has led to developments in bio-based and biodegradable polymers (Mohanty *et al.*, 2002).

Conclusion

Packaging continually evolves to serve supply and demand, reflecting supply changes in materials and technology, and demand changes from supply chains, consumers and cultures. During the twentieth century, the field developed to satisfy the growing demands of marketing by increasing sales and reducing logistics cost.

What makes consumer packaging unique in the marketing mix is that, like the product itself, packaging has the most intimate relationship to consumers. It performs in our homes. We give it power to reflect our personality and to enhance our lifestyle. We let it make dinner for our family and lunch for our kids. It delivers the product and brand symbolism that are at the core of marketing.

The consumer packaging history of the twentieth century has been enabled by concurrent developments in the shipping containers that deliver the goods. What makes shipping containers unique in supply chain management history in that they have always served to integrate and extend logistical systems. Twentieth-century corrugated boxes, reusable packaging, wooden pallets and ocean containerization have increasingly streamlined physical transfer and extended export geography. Similarly, automatic identification has streamlined the timely sharing of logistics information.

The history of packaging is a story of adaptation, which provides a clear indication for its future. Packaging will continue to evolve to meet the needs of future markets and value chains. It can be expected to take advantage of future technology and sources of material supply with an ever-smaller environmental footprint.

References

AMA (1965) *Package Design and its Management; Meeting the Design Requirements of Modern Packaging*, American Management Association Packaging Division, New York.

AMA (1969) *Planning for Tomorrow's Packaging Realities*, American Management Association Packaging Division, New York.

American Machinist (1883) 'Norton's automatic can-making machinery', *American Machinist*, 6 (14 July), 1–2.

Azzi, A., Battini, D., Persona, A., and Sgarbossa, F. (2012) 'Packaging design: General framework and research agenda', *Packaging Technology and Science*, 25/1, 435–56.

Barthes, R. (1957) *Mythologies*, París: Seuil, English tr. by A. Lavers, Hill & Wang, New York, 1972.

Bastos, W., and Levy, S.J. (2012) 'A history of the concept of branding: Practice and theory', *Journal of Historical Research in Marketing*, 4/3, 347–68.

Bettendorf, H.J. (1946) *Paperboard and Paperboard Containers: A History*, Board Products Publishing, Chicago, IL.

Brody, A.L. (1969) 'Increased profits through better packaging', in AMA, *Planning for Tomorrow's Packaging Realities*, American Management Association Packaging Division, New York, pp. 7–17.

Brody, A.L (1970) *Flexible Packaging of Foods*, CRC Press, Cleveland, OH.

Brody, A.L (ed.) (1994) *Modified Atmosphere Food Packaging*, Institute of Packaging Professionals, Herndon, VA.

Darnay, A., and Franklin W.E. (1969) *The Role of Packaging in Solid Waste Management 1966 to 1976*, US Bureau of Solid Waste Management, Rockville, MD.

Davis, A. (1967) *Package and Print: The Development of Container and Label Design*, Faber, London.

Diamond, F. (1953) *The Story of Glass*, Harcourt, New York.

Franken, R.B., and Larrabee, C.B. (1928) *Packages that Sell,* Harper & Brothers, New York.

Grace, Virginia (1961) *Amphoras and the Ancient Wine Trade,* American School of Classical Studies at Athens, Princeton, NJ.

Griffin, R.C., Sacharow, S., and Brody, A. (1985) *Principles of Package Development*, AVI, Westport, CT.

Hanlon, J.F. (1971) *Handbook of Package Engineering*, McGraw-Hill, New York.

Hounshell, D.A. (1984) *From the American System to Mass Production, 1800–1932: The Development of Manufacturing Technology in the United States,* Johns Hopkins University Press, Baltimore, MD.

Hunter, D. (1947) *Papermaking: The History and Technique of an Ancient Craft,* Alfred A. Knopf, New York.

Joerger, R. (2007) 'Antimicrobial films for food applications: A quantitative analysis of their effectiveness', *Packaging Technology and Science*, 20/4, 231–73.

Jones, H. (1950) *Planned Packaging*, Allen & Unwin, London.

Lansdale, D.B. (1978) *The Vital Signs of Effective Packaging Management*, AMA Management Briefing, AMACOM, New York.

LeBlanc, R., and Richardson, S. (2003) *Pallets: A North American Perspective,* PACTS Management, Cobourg, Ontario.

Levinson, M. (2006) *The Box: How the Shipping Container Made the World Smaller and the World Economy Bigger,* Princeton University Press, Princeton, NJ.

McCarthy, E. J. (1960) *Basic Marketing: A Managerial Approach*, Irwin, Homewood, IL.

Milgrom, J., and Brody, A. (1974) *Packaging in Perspective: Report to the Ad Hoc Committee on Packaging*, Arthur D. Little, Cambridge, MA.

Modern Packaging (1927) *Modern Packaging*, 1/1, Breskin & Charlton Publishing Co., New York.

Modern Packaging Encyclopedia (1948) McGraw Hill, New York, p. 44 shows 'Red letter dates of packaging history'.

Mohanty, A.K., Mistra, M., and Drzal, L.T. (2002) 'Sustainable bio-composites from renewable resources: Opportunities and challenges in the green materials world', *Journal of Polymers and the Environment,* 10/112, 19–26.

Opie, R. (1987) *The Art of the Label: Designs of the Times,* Chartwell, Secaucus, NJ.

Paine, F.A. (1963) *Fundamentals of Packaging*, Blackie, London.

Paine, F.A (1988) 'Editorial', *Packaging Technology and Science*, 1, 1.

Pilditch, J. (1961) *The Silent Salesman; How to Develop Packaging that Sells,* Business Publications Ltd., London.

Prescott, S.C., and Underwood, W.L. (1897) 'Contributions to our knowledge of micro-organisms and sterilizing processes in the canning industries', *Science*, 6/152, 800–2.

Reuter, H. (1988) *Aseptic Packaging of Food*, tr. C. Moeckli, Behr's Verlag, Hamburg.

Risch, S.J. (2009) Food packaging history and innovations, *Journal of Agricultural and Food Chemistry*, 57, 8089–92.

Robertson, G. (2013) *Food Packaging: Principles and Practice,* CRC Press, Boca Raton, FL.

Sacharow, S., and Griffin, R.C. (1973) *Basic Guide to Plastics in Packaging*, Cahners Books, Boston, MA.

Selame, E., Selame, J., and Kolligan, G.S. (1982) *Packaging Power: Corporate Identity and Product Recognition*, AMA Management Briefing, AMACOM, New York.

Selke, S.E.M. (1990) *Packaging and the Environment: Alternatives, Trends, and Solutions*, Technomic, Lancaster, PA.

Sinclair, U. (1906) *The Jungle*, Doubleday/Jungle Publishing Co., New York.

Stern, W. (ed.) (1981) *Handbook of Package Design Research*, Wiley & Sons, New York.

Stilwell, E.J., Canty R.C., Kopf, P.W., and Montrone A.M. (1991) *Packaging for the Environment*, AMACON division of American Management Association, New York.

Strasser, S. (1989) *Satisfaction Guaranteed: The Making of the American Mass Market*, Pantheon Books, New York.

Tedlow, R.S. (1996) *New and Improved: The Story of Mass Marketing in America*, Harvard Business School Press, Boston, MA.

Twede, D. (1997) 'Uneeda biscuit: The first consumer package?', *Journal of Macromarketing*, 17 (Fall), 82–7.

Twede, D. (2002) 'Commercial amphoras: The earliest consumer packages?', *Journal of Macromarketing*, 22/1, 98–108.

Twede, D. (2005) 'The cask age: The technology and history of wooden barrels', *Packaging Technology and Science*, 18/5, 253–64.

Twede, D. (2012) 'The birth of modern packaging: Cartons, cans and bottles', *Journal of Historical Research in Marketing*, 4/2, 245–72.

Twede, D., and Goff, J. (1999) 'The history of packaging thought: The first university packaging curriculum', in P. Cunningham and D. Bussiere (eds), *Marketing History: The Total Package: Proceedings of the 9th Conference on Historical Analysis and Research in Marketing (CHARM)*, Michigan State University, East Lansing, MI, pp. 123–47.

Twede, D., Selke, S.E.M., Kamdem, D.P., and Shires, D. (2015) 'Introduction and historical background', in *Cartons, Crates and Corrugated Board*, Lancaster, PA, DesTech, pp. 1–69.

Whiteley, N. (1987) 'Towards a throw-away culture: Consumerism, "style obsolescence", and cultural theory in the 1950s and 1960s', *Oxford Art Journal*, 10/2, 3–27.

Zimmerman, M.M. (1955) *The Super Market: A Revolution in Distribution*, McGraw-Hill, New York.

8

Distributive orders

The evolution of North American retailing

Barry E.C. Boothman

We must distinguish between innovators…who to achieve their purposes can force the issue and those who must use persuasion. In the second case, they always come to grief, having achieved nothing; when, however, they depend on their own resources and can force the issue, then they are seldom endangered. That is why all armed prophets have conquered, and unarmed prophets have come to grief…

Niccolo Machiavelli

New types of retail institutions are often established by highly aggressive, cost-conscious entrepreneurs who make every penny count and who have no interest in unprofitable frills. But…these men may relax their vigilance and control over costs as they acquire age and wealth. Their successors may be less competent. Either the innovators or their successors may be unwilling, or unable, to adjust to changing conditions.

Stanley C. Hollander

As the Christmas holidays approached one year during the 1990s, an outlet in Toronto's Maclean-Hunter complex posted a window sign declaring, 'We have survived another year in retail.' By the next spring the store was gone, a failure that reflected not only the experiences of many retailers but the past of the shopping complex. Constructed during the late 1920s as the gorgeous art deco flagship of Eaton's, Canada's largest department store chain, the building deteriorated across several generations and was sold off for redevelopment, while Eaton's attempted to hold on to a declining status that later led to bankruptcy. Histories of retailers understandably have emphasized the roles of entrepreneurial founders and the dynamics of store development but the demise of these companies underscored basic issues associated with the evolution of retailing: shifts in the drivers of strategic rivalry, difficulties in sustaining competitive capabilities, problems with consumer behaviour or loyalty.

The organization of contemporary distribution in North America is a product of several reconfigurations that have unfolded across the past 150 years. In particular, it has been bound up with institutional transformations associated with the development of managerial capitalism, which were explored by Alfred D. Chandler (1977). Traditional business firms controlled by proprietors, partners or families still comprise a major component of retailing. The companies are small, handle single product lines, operate in one geographic area and usually are short-lived. However, since the late nineteenth-century large enterprises have dominated many aspects of distribution. These firms internalize different business functions, handle multiple goods and services, and conduct economic transactions that are coordinated by salaried managers versus external market mechanisms. The formation of managerial hierarchies as the key mode of business organization constituted 'a source of permanence, power, and continued growth', which enabled enterprises to become very big with strong competitive positions for lengthy periods (Chandler, 1977, 8).

With few exceptions, such as the fine study by Richard Tedlow (1990), research proceeding from a managerial capitalism perspective has concentrated on industrial enterprise because it has been perceived as *the* crucial phenomenon. The historical organization of distributive activities in North America remains underexplored and the available studies are fragmented and selective in coverage. Nothing approaching a synthesis can be found. Most of the academic research relates to events in the United States and comparisons with other countries remain few. Within the marketing literature, numerous generalizations about cyclical, conflict or adaptive patterns of retail change have been advanced. Most are not supported by systemic evidence derived from an analysis of historical developments (Brown, 1987). Geographers and sociologists have conducted locational and cultural analyses of retailing but to date these works have not been utilized well by marketing researchers. Popular or journalistic accounts remain a major component of the available studies. These focus upon the success/early emergence of firms or their later travails and descent into oblivion, but often the authors do not provide references or have relied just upon press reports or interviews.

This chapter seeks to redress this deficiency by providing an overview of retailing in North America from the mid-nineteenth century to the present day. The organization or order of distribution activities was transformed by alterations in economic drivers; social conditions; shopping practices and geographic locations; and the relationships among manufacturers, wholesalers and retailers. The combination of these issues tended to generate distinctive *gestalts* during particular eras. Subsequent time periods became more complex as new configurations altered, or were layered upon, established practices. Of necessity, this chapter sketches a portrait in broad strokes. Any scheme of periodicity entails generalizations and simplifications since trends can be traced into earlier or later times. This chapter also cannot capture the variations that unfolded within alternate sub-sectors or across geographic regions. Nonetheless, it endeavours to survey experiences in two neighbouring countries. Developments in Canada typically followed those in the United States but while moving in parallel directions the markets sometimes varied in competitive practices or the acceptance of innovations.

The evolution of modern retailing, it is argued, conformed to the tenets of the managerial capitalism thesis but an analysis requires a more sophisticated approach than most authors have presented. To a greater degree than has been acknowledged, corporate development was characterized by instability and difficulties in retaining competitive positions. The chapter unfolds with four chronological sections. Attention first is given to conditions during the nineteenth century. The emergence of big retailers, particularly department and chain stores, then is appraised. The third section considers developments during the mid-twentieth century, with the spread of consumer culture and shopping centres. The final section examines the turnover and instability that has unfolded since 1980.

The advent of North American retailing

Retailing emerged in the United States between 1830 and 1860, and in Canada from 1860 to 1910. Previously, self-sufficient family farms were the primary economic units, with towns and villages comprising less than 5 per cent of the population during the colonial era in each country. The movement and distribution of goods was haphazard, with uncertain communications, because transportation was limited to foot and water and was dependent upon weather. There was no 'national market' in either country, rather a variety of separate and small areas. General merchants tended to dominate local economies. They bought and sold numerous goods and carried out functions like wholesaling, exporting, importing, transportation or supplying credit. The merchants relied upon personal associations to develop networks of business connections and were well acquainted with buyers and sellers alike. Population and economic growth, however, slowly propelled individuals to specialize in different aspects of distribution and rely more upon impersonal commercial relations, which were coordinated through market transactions and physical shipments (Porter and Livesay, 1971, 7–36; Chandler, 1977, 15–36).

The construction of interregional railroad and telegraph systems after 1850 contributed to a growing concentration of social activity in urban areas. The proportion of the American population living in towns and villages rose from 15.3 per cent by 1850, to 25.7 per cent in 1870 and 45.6 per cent by 1910 (US Bureau of the Census, 1975, 11–12). The United States expanded more rapidly and was transformed more completely than any other Atlantic economy during this period. Canada's growth rate also surpassed most other economies and therefore a similar pattern occurred. Urban residents constituted a fifth of the Canadian population in 1871 but increased to 45 per cent by 1911 (Urquhart and Buckley, 1983, A67–9). The dynamics of consumption consequently were altered. Demographic concentration and constraints on urban living space eviscerated the possibility of self-sufficiency for many people, thereby compelling individuals to purchase basic goods from local sellers. As had occurred previously in Europe, emergent urban culture also fostered norms about the need to buy goods that were in 'fashion' and thereby demonstrate social status (Barth, 1980).

A mix of general merchants, peddlers and public markets had serviced towns and villages, but after mid-century specialized retailers met a growing demand for basic and supplementary goods. Information about such activities was not collected by government agencies until the 1920s but the available data are suggestive about (although they also likely underestimate) the degree of expansion. Retail trade in the US increased from $500 million during 1869 to $2.8 billion by 1909, while retail employment expanded from 716,000 to 3,177,000 (US Bureau of the Census, 1975, 839–40). Wholesale and retail trade in Canada expanded from C$21.2 million to C$204.4 million and the contribution to GNP rose from 5.9 to 10.4 per cent. Between 1871 and 1910 the number of Canadian retailers rose from 25,000 to 80,000 (Urquhart, 1986, 42; Monod, 1996, 23).

Retailing in urban areas was segmented into 'upper-end' goods and 'lower-end' goods. Higher-priced or 'shopping' goods such as jewellery, furniture or home hardware (which were purchased infrequently and entailed comparison shopping) were located on streets in central (predominantly non-residential) business districts, particularly those with high traffic. Convenience goods like food and personal needs were bought frequently and with limited selection. Those stores therefore tended to locate near residential areas. Wholesalers were positioned close to port or transport facilities. Over time, as urban centres grew in size and density, not only did central business cores expand but in new districts spatial clusters of retail establishments emerged that provided alternate types of goods. Complete ranges of retail outlets prevailed in stable moderate income areas, while poorer areas lacked the income to support a broad variety of retailers and were serviced by dispersed 'corner shops'. Where shopping was conducted by overworked pedestrians on tight budgets of time and money, ease of access and cheap goods available from lower rent and non-central stores was essential, a phenomenon that propelled a replication of convenience stores and concentrations of shopping goods outlets in new districts. Major waves of immigration in the late nineteenth century further diversified metropolitan areas into ethnic sub-sections, particularly in the United States (Schnore, 1975; Conzen and Conzen, 1979; Domosh, 1996).

Channel organization was composed of isolated and autonomous units. The pace of business by modern standards was slow and intermittent. Clients shopped on a daily basis since they lacked storage space or refrigeration at home. Most retailers sold staples or generic products whose traits were understood by buyers and sellers. The shops often carried out artisan production or preparation of goods for sale (butchers, bakers, druggists, shoemakers). Day-to-day store operations were labour-intensive because certain activities (like the handling of meat products) required specialized skills and because goods had to be packaged for consumers (Barger, 1955; Mayo, 1994). Advertising, if conducted at all, took the form of listing available goods and their origins, without reference to price (Porter and Livesay, 1971). Working without reliable national currencies (or sometimes even the availability of coinage in different locales) until the closing decades of the nineteenth century, retailers were compelled to extend credit or to accept payment in truck, a situation that frequently led to cash flow difficulties. Accounts often were paid at a customer's convenience, and thus many store owners offered enticements (like Christmas 'bonuses' of goods or favourable arrangements) to retain clients. Transactions leading to the exchange of goods could be lengthy and difficult. All issues, including price, were subject to interpersonal negotiation and contingent upon a person's credit, social status or perceived honesty. Indeed, entering a shop was widely considered as a commitment to purchase, a process then embarked upon if both sides felt confident that a successful outcome could be reached (Monod, 1996).

Barriers to entry were low. Premises easily could be rented (especially outside core business districts) and external credit secured from wholesalers or other firms. As one commentator noted, individuals could convert 'their front parlours into stores, knocking out some street facing wall to accommodate the larger window that retailing demanded. ... For many more struggling retailers, "business" consisted of even less: the back of a truck or wagon, a push cart, or ... a peddler's pack' (Monod, 1996, 30–1). Small retailers fought for stable shares of the modest trade available in a locale. Most were marginal outlets, their owners frequently had little experience or skills in store and stock management. Despite slim operating margins, the temptation to slash prices below costs to gain sales was strong. It appears likely that few firms lasted as long as ten years in most product classes. A life-long 'career' in retail was rare.

These activities altered between 1850 and 1900 as greater proportions of agricultural, manufacturing and resource output entered social distribution. Railway networks linked geographic markets, generating a need for wholesale middlemen to manage the movement of goods. The available evidence suggests their activities grew at a faster pace than retailing until the closing decade of the nineteenth century (Barger, 1955, 20–8). Wholesaling became separate from importing and specialization propelled the formation of full-service wholesalers. These enterprises typically were based in major cities, had developed considerable financial resources, and with greater business volume sought discounts on bulk purchases from producers. Agents or 'drummers' sold dry goods and other manufactured products to local wholesalers or retailers. By the 1880s wholesaling in both countries often became a bottleneck dominated by a small number of firms with substantial resources and trade connections. Extension of credit and the ability to reap purchase discounts enabled the enterprises to exercise market power over small retailers. In addition, the wholesalers tried to establish exclusive relationships with suppliers or manufacturers by agreeing to control retail prices. The Dominion Wholesale Grocers' Guild in Canada, for example, regulated trade practices and constructed price-fixing arrangements with processors that covered tobacco, baking power, starch, pickles and other goods. It set the prices under which goods were resold to retailers and compliant manufacturers then refused to supply any price-cutting wholesaler or retailer (Beckman and Engle, 1949; Bliss, 1974).

Retailers, while accepting this mode of market organization, made numerous efforts to limit 'the waste of competition' and stabilize economic conditions. The firms negotiated voluntary agreements (or failing that, demanded legislation) to control shop hours or constrain the types of goods various retailers could sell. Many attempts were made to cut off sources of competition, including the 'guerrilla trade' of sellers who were not based in local communities – farmers, peddlers and the like – through licensing. Drives were made to regulate store hours, blacklist delinquent clients, restrict wholesalers to wholesaling, control credit practices and regularize bankruptcy practices. Few of these efforts met with much success in either country. Small retailers therefore attempted to professionalize the trade, to 'adopt correct methods'. This was reflected in the formation of retailer associations during the late 1880s. Through the associations and trade press, information was disseminated about how to manage stores, develop accounting capabilities and utilize display as a marketing tool (Walden, 1989; Tedlow, 1990; Laird, 1998).

Economic growth and further railway construction incrementally transformed retailing. Linkage of different geographic areas expanded access to markets and allowed factories to increase output, with cheaper prices through volume production. Wholesale houses were utilized as agents because individual stores remained too small to permit economies of scale among channel intermediaries. However, this arrangement had two problems. The new technologies of electricity and petroleum allowed expansions of output that exceeded demand but a manufacturer had no guarantees that a wholesaler would push its products rather than those of competitors. The producer also was dependent upon the agent for information about markets and customer perspectives. Accordingly, by the 1890s manufacturers in both countries increasingly elected to bypass wholesalers with their own sales forces, building direct links with retailers. Branding and advertising were utilized as tools to ensure people would demand their products (Friedman, 2004, 88–96; Strasser, 1989; Laird, 1998).

These developments had several implications. First, the transition to prepackaged and branded products unleashed retailing's potential. The range of retail activities expanded to many items from a comparatively select group of goods like dry goods, furniture, groceries, china or glassware. Staples remained important sales items but retailers preferred premanufactured and packaged goods because they could be sold at premium prices and meet customer aspirations for superior quality (Strasser, 1989; Laird, 1998). Second, the change began a process of 'de-skilling' retail operations that would unfold to the present day, a movement away from in-shop artisan production or sophisticated expertise. Third, relationships altered as responsibility for packaging, stocking, evaluating and pricing goods moved from retailers to wholesalers and manufacturers. Manufacturers did not just define products and their traits but also sought to control pricing and sale conditions. To a significant degree, retailers thus lost personal responsibility for the individuality of the goods they sold. Fourth, branding altered the balance of power in distribution away from wholesalers by enabling manufacturers to develop relationships with end users through advertising about which products to buy, thereby permitting more stable and predictable sales.

Mass distribution

Retail organization expanded rapidly and was separated into two solitudes between the closing decades of the nineteenth-century and the Second World War. American national income originating in retail activities grew from $1.3 billion in 1899 to $5.9 billion in 1919 and $9.3 billion by 1929 (US Bureau of the Census, 1975, 839). The annual volume of wholesale business across the period nearly quadrupled. Nonetheless, by 1929 one half of American retail stores accounted for just 8.6 per cent of business, with average annual revenues less than $5,000; 75 per cent of all stores earned less than $30,000 per year and represented only 25 per cent of sales. A quarter of total business was conducted by 1 per cent of stores, with average sales of $300,000 yearly. Corporate enterprises represented 15.8 per cent of retail outlets and garnered 48.2 per cent of sales. Proprietorships still constituted 84 per cent of stores but accounted for 51.4 per cent of sales (US Bureau of the Census, 1933, 15, 21). Canadian data suggests a similar direction to development. GDP income generated by retail trade increased by seven times between 1900 and 1930 (Urquhart, 1986, 13–15; Urquhart and Buckley, 1983, F56–75). By legal form, corporate enterprise accounted for 48 per cent of 1930 sales and partnerships or proprietorships accounted for 51.3 per cent; 56 per cent of stores earned less than C$10,000 per year; 25 per cent of retail outlets accounted for 78.2 per cent of annual sales; 7.5 percent for 54.5 per cent of sales; and the top 1 percent, for 28.5 per cent (Dominion Bureau of Statistics, 1931, 38, 73). Co-operative associations, although promoted as an alternative organizational form, accounted for less than 1 per cent of sales in North America.

The forces behind this structural transformation accelerated after the turn of the century. National railway networks enhanced delivery speeds and cut shipping costs, enabling manufacturers and retailers to exploit larger markets. Concurrently, the ability of people to travel was enhanced, allowing them to visit cities and come into contact with new trends and consumer goods. The novel technologies of electricity and petroleum facilitated the creation of new products, allowed rapid increases in manufacturing output, and triggered significant drops in product costs and prices. These developments convinced many business people that 'a crisis of distribution' was imminent – mass over-production with warehouses of unsold goods. Concurrently, industrialization facilitated urbanization and growth in personal income. Business leaders and analysts therefore promoted the need for a 'democratization of goods', i.e. an elaboration of distribution techniques making goods more accessible. As part of this ideology, 'service', not merely sales, was portrayed as the key function of retailing. Clients were not 'customers' who had personalized relationships with retail craftspeople but 'consumers' who bought factory-made standardized goods and a goal was to link those products with buyer desires (Leach, 1993, 15–38). Several new types of retailers emerged, following the notions of large size and professional management utilized by manufacturers. The companies were portrayed by their founders as fulfilling a social mission, a stance that was not mere boilerplate but reflected a belief in the need to match mass production with mass distribution.

Numerous firms had tapped new markets via catalogue sales as railroad systems were extended. Between the 1890s and the 1920s several enterprises developed distribution networks through warehouse centres linked to the transportation systems. Some 'supply companies' (Sears Roebuck, Montgomery Ward, Spiegel) avoided capital investment in fixed-store outlets, but many firms like Eaton's of Canada and Hammacher Schlemmer developed mail order facilities along with their existing stores. The companies targeted consumers in rural areas or small towns by offering an array of goods hitherto unavailable from local firms. Sears and Eaton's, in particular, gained dominant positions with broad product ranges and then developed manufacturing facilities to ensure security of supply. They garnered lower transaction costs by circumventing wholesalers and dealing directly with manufacturers. Buyers were enticed by incredibly low prices along with unprecedented 'money back if not satisfied' guarantees and low shipping costs. Volume purchase discounts conferred price advantages, while the elaboration of managerial structures to coordinate activities enabled the firms to achieve unprecedented economies of scale and scope. Organizational systems exploited the latest technological innovations to handle mail, record consumer orders and then process purchases expeditiously with minimal labour (Emmet and Jeuck, 1950; Chandler, 1977; Santink, 1989).

The second type of mass distributor, department stores, arose in the United States prior to 1870 and in Canada after 1880. These enterprises specialized in the display, promotion and sale of goods in centralized urban locations. The firms typically started either as adjuncts of wholesale businesses or as small retailers specializing in products like dry goods or clothing. As enterprises like Eaton's in Toronto, Macy's in New York, Marshall Field in Chicago and Wanamaker's in Philadelphia added new lines of merchandise, the combination of larger purchases and the diversification of product lines enabled the companies to gain discounts from manufacturers and to reduce dependence upon sales of specific goods. Small to medium-size stores operated in most cities but it took until the early twentieth century for the biggest firms to gain dominant positions in local or regional distribution.

Diversification of merchandise allowed department stores to offer one-stop shopping without cutting selection or making the buying experience awkward. The largest enterprises eventually dwarfed independent firms with huge display areas. Accounting, advertising and administration were centralized managerial functions. Stock was segmented into separate quasi-independent departments, each with specialized buyer and sales personnel, a practice that facilitated comparative evaluation of personnel and use of numerical criteria for judging performance (Pasdermadjian, 1954, 11; Hower, 1943, 199–200).

Merchandise was laid out carefully. Impulse buying, for example, was encouraged by displays of luxury or other goods that individuals had to pass while they travelled to areas with basic or staple goods. Most firms utilized promotions and periodic sales, which allowed them to minimize seasonal slumps and to trigger buyer frenzies (Santink, 1989; Leach, 1993). Numerous stores established manufacturing operations or created buying offices abroad to ensure supply of popular products. In their initial development, the retailers tended to make gains by price-cutting tactics. Their strategies stressed low profit margins and quick turnover. As business expanded, the firms attempted to bypass wholesalers and buy directly from producers. They then demanded not just purchase discounts but extracted advertising allowances, rebates, special premiums and transport concessions.

Department stores facilitated cultural alterations in shopping practices and exchange relationships. Central location, store size and product range ensured that their primary clients represented the emergent urban affluent. The earliest firms catered to middle- and upper-class consumers by specializing in the purchase, purchasing, display and sale of quality goods. Some firms like Macy's and Eaton's stressed sales to upper-working-class citizens but their operations always promoted the desire to rise to the standards of 'social betters' (Hower, 1943; Santink, 1989). Over time, department stores were inclined to push fashionable and 'up-market' goods that provided higher profits and to relegate cheap products to basement or annex areas. Rural and small urban retailers continued to provide credit to secure customers but department stores altered the terms of trade by setting fixed-price policies and selling goods on a cash-only basis. Rather than a process of negotiation with a retailer, purchasing was depersonalized, with the customer expected to buy based upon the willingness to accept a pre-stipulated worth. Fixed prices also allowed the use of cheap unskilled labour, whereas negotiation required staff with considerable expertise. Mass distribution from the beginning thus was predicated upon low wages as a tool of competitiveness (Chaney, 1983; Leach, 1993).

Department store executives invariably stereotyped shopping as 'women's work'. Individuals in urban occupations had limited time for making goods like food or clothing but received cash wages, which facilitated purchases of necessities and other goods. The purchase of household requirements constituted one of women's primary responsibilities. Shopping also represented for many an escape from domesticity and their purchases became means of demonstrating identity or status. Department stores were promoted as safe zones for unchaperoned women, with free entry and unlimited browsing policies. Operating expenses consequently were raised as the firms undertook investments for amenities like restaurants, nurseries, postal stations, music concerts, first aid facilities and reading rooms. However, despite the expectations of store managers, over time customers' power expanded as they exploited their ability to decline purchases or to shop elsewhere (Benson, 1988; Halttunen, 1989; Wright, 1992).

Department stores hence did not become mass distributors simply by utilizing economic drivers as Chandler (1977) has implied. Mass manufacturing entailed long product runs with standardized goods, protected by capital barriers and proprietary technology that allowed firms to recoup investment costs. Mass distributors never built capital resources and assets to anywhere near the levels of giant manufacturers and they had a key vulnerability: dependence upon consumer behaviour for new sales. Shoppers often showed little loyalty. The retailers had to anticipate shifts in fashion or fad and supply new goods to meet perceived consumer desires. Diffusion of information about their choices or sales techniques could not be restricted. Competitors imitated, often quickly, making strategic advantages ephemeral.

The retail influence of department stores peaked during the early inter-war period. The 17 largest department stores in the United States accounted for 34 per cent of total department store sales during 1930. The top three Canadian retailers accounted for 70 per cent. At its height in 1930, Eaton's was the third largest Canadian employer, one of the biggest retailers (measured by revenues) in the world, and it accounted for approximately 10 per cent of all retail revenues in Canada (Belisle, 2011). Nonetheless, the status of department stores weakened during the 1920s. Executives of the firms were very conservative. Having made large investments in downtown locations, they were reluctant to create outlets elsewhere. The competitive status of department stores was dependent upon public transport systems and the geographically compact character of North American cities. However, population growth triggered urban sprawl, while a growing affordability of automobiles enabled customers to shop around or utilize less centralized locations (McNair and May, 1963). Moreover, as department stores encountered competition from other mass distributors, there was a tendency to 'trade up' by catering to higher income classes and raising mark-ups (Pasdermadjian, 1954, 63–5).

The third type of enterprise, multi-location or 'chain' retailing, radically extended the transition towards mass distribution. The first firm originated around 1859 but a proliferation unfolded after the turn of the century. Their scope varied from local operations to province/ state, region or national. By one estimate, there were 700 American companies controlling 4,500 stores in 1900, 5,200 companies with 21,500 stores in 1914, and 20,000 with 119,600 by 1928 (Federal Trade Commission, 1932, 66–7). A 1929 survey mapped 7,061 chains with four or more stores, comprising 159,638 outlets and accounting for 22.2 per cent of American retail activity, up from 4 per cent a decade earlier. If smaller firms were included, the estimate rose to 212,620 stores, accounting for more than 30 per cent of annual sales (US

Bureau of the Census, 1933, 28–30). Multi-store retailing was very limited in Canada before 1920, but 506 chains operated with 8,557 outlets by 1930 and accounted for 18.3 per cent of total business (Dominion Bureau of Statistics, 1931, p. xxx).

Whereas department stores brought people inward to their facilities, chain networks extended outward to potential customers. The key targets were women and the lower middle class. Outlets were less successful in garnering trade from the poor, workers or groups with strong ethnic identities, who preferred the personalized service and credit available from traditional retailers (Deutsch, 2010: Cohen, 2003). Attractive displays, bright lighting, cleanliness and advertising were used to entice customers. Corporate officers created outlets not just in central business areas but also in high traffic zones or near residential subdivisions. The networks were extended to small towns and rural communities, areas where mass distribution had been perceived as impractical. Growth frequently was financed through issues of common and preferred equity that were popular among investors and brokers.

Chain store retailing expanded with stunning speed in almost all sub-sectors of merchandising but the penetration varied widely. Networks of grocery stores, which accounted for 31.7 per cent of American sales by 1929, were the most conspicuous phenomenon. A&P ran 15,700 outlets, more than any other retailer until the twenty-first century. In Canada, multi-unit companies like Dominion Stores and Loblaw gained control of 30 per cent of annual grocery business (Boothman, 2009). Chains accounted for 82.9 per cent of the sales of variety stores by 1929, 26 per cent of apparel stores and 38 per cent of filling stations. Efforts to develop networks tended to be less successful in sub-sectors like hardware or eating places where high turnover rates could not be sustained, large inventories had to be retained, or wholesalers still controlled proprietary technology.

Chain retailers carried out extensive experimentation in operating practices, administrative arrangements and consumer management but by the early 1920s the key principles were well understood (Hayward and White, 1922). Most firms worked with several assumptions about the exchange relationship; customers bought principally on price and were willing to shop around. Outlets hence did not attempt to offer the range of goods or high-quality merchandise available from department stores. Rather, they stressed the distribution of standardized products with dependable quality for low prices. The size of individual stores was small, not much different from comparable independent retailers. Outlets in a network had uniform formats, employed unskilled low-cost personnel, and operated whenever possible from rented premises. Speed of merchandise turnover rather than profit margins was stressed but corporate policies ruthlessly enforced earnings quotas. Credit and delivery services were abandoned, while most stores operated on a cash-and-carry basis with no negotiation (Hollander and Omura, 1989).

A central office controlled decision-making about openings or closings, store layout, accounting and advertising. Major networks created sophisticated real estate departments, which assessed locations for rent and traffic levels. Volume buying enabled the offices to demand discounts from producers, control the specifications and quality of merchandise and distribute goods manufactured by suppliers as their own brands. Many chains sought to eliminate the wholesale mark-up altogether by internalizing the function and receiving goods directly at their warehouses. This practice further propelled distribution away from the collusion and dominance that full-service wholesalers had exercised (see also Cheasley, 1930; Lebhar, 1952).

Early chains and the largest systems encountered considerable resistance from manufacturers. Some producers preferred the existing practices and refused to sell to multi-unit networks. Many chains introduced private-label products but found processors reluctant

139

to supply merchandise, fearful that it could cut into their advertised brands. Consequently, numerous multi-unit retailers integrated backwards, owning or controlling manufacturing and agricultural operations. Some discovered various products could be sold more cheaply from company-owned plants and with superior quality control compared to reliance upon other suppliers. Internalization of manufacturing, or the threat of doing so, also could be used to demand discounts and other concessions from producers. The combination of mass purchasing with vertical integration thus gave chains the ability to undercut independent stores by wide margins. Whether they did varied: grocery and drug stores commonly slashed prices whereas 'five and dime' enterprises like S.S. Kresge and F.W. Woolworth rarely would.

Many contemporaries believed, as an article of faith, that the economies realized by mass distributors were similar in degree to those garnered by mass manufactures. Alfred Chandler similarly claimed they 'increased the productivity and reduced the costs of the distribution of consumer goods in the United States' (1977, 237). Given the policies for fast turnover, average sales per outlet of retail chains were much higher than for independent stores. However, the actual gains during this period were more limited. The companies tried to shift functions like packaging to producers but they incurred new costs like after-sales service, trial and return schemes, product testing, real estate assessment and advertising. While bypassing wholesalers, the firms concurrently increased administrative overheads with internalized purchasing activities. Chain stores enhanced customer experiences with initiatives like air conditioning, careful display of goods or cleanliness, but these hardly lowered costs. The advantages for the networks came from policies stipulating low profit margins but rapid stock turnover and from tight cost controls over individual outlets. Indeed, only two innovations, cash registers and self-service, decisively improved labour productivity in retailing across the first half of the twentieth century (Barger, 1955, 37–41). Chain operations have been characterized as self-service-oriented but this issue can be overstated. Goods were kept behind counters in most stores and the buying process still entailed intermediation by employees. 'Self-help' did not spread until the late 1920s when the labour savings became apparent. The exceptions were 'groceteria' food stores or restaurants, which allowed clients to handle and choose many goods, although often only in certain departments. Most retailers were slow to change from personalized selling and were concerned about thievery, so adoption occurred incrementally across the following two decades. Productivity in retailing hence grew slowly, far less than in agriculture or manufacturing (Barger, 1955).

The expansion of the networks terrified independent storeowners and cut into the sales of department stores and mail order companies. Montgomery Ward and Sears Roebuck, for instance, were forced to counter with their own retail outlets. The emergent ascendancy of the chains, however, ground to a stop in 1929 and across the following two decades their status (aggregate and in most sub-sectors) remained static or declined. This development was derived from several issues. First, the Great Depression and then wartime restrictions affected the availability of investment capital, thereby limiting firms to slow growth and reliance upon internal funds. Second, in attempting to build positions, many chain retailers became over-extended, with excess capacity and networks of small economically marginal shops. Rapid growth also generated personnel problems, notably a shortage of middle- and senior-level managers who could coordinate operations and maintain cost controls. Third, while the firms were launched as price cutters, within a few years many traded up, not only expanding inventories but enhancing quality and price until their offerings began to converge with those from department stores. Some companies set up separate operations offering more luxurious goods. Five and dime retailer S.S. Kresge, for example, created a distinctive group of department stores. Thus, within a few years, the scale of price advantages could be eroded. Many initiatives relied upon external financing, making the payment of dividends and bond interest paramount goals. Especially in the 1930s, to avoid default, this created pressure for chains to ensure earnings were maintained, even if prices were increased (Boothman, 2009).

The growth of the chains triggered a dialectical process that restricted their expansion. The companies represented monopsonistic purchasers. A countervailing movement of integration and acquisitions unfolded among manufacturers that sought to achieve further efficiencies and to reassert greater control in distribution. Determined to slow the erosion of their influence, wholesalers organized independent shops into voluntary chains. These networks provided uniform brand identity (with standardized signs and advertising) to their members and gained from centralized warehouses and volume purchases. Stores belonging to the voluntary chains never reached the average sales levels enjoyed by their corporate counterparts but did close part of the earnings gap. To offset the loss of business to department and chain stores, smaller enterprises increasingly adopted their innovations – particularly the physical attributes of store operations and 'service' as a key *raison d'être*. In addition, extensive lobbying led to the passage of 'fair trade acts' by many American states aimed at restricting chain retailers by legitimating retail price maintenance where manufacturers stipulated final sale prices. These statutes, along with the passage of federal legislation in the US, constrained the discounts available to mass distributors. Finally, consumer behaviour developed a cast from the rigours of the Great Depression. Buyers treated price as *the* paramount issue, a perspective that became an entrenched norm among subsequent generations (Cross, 2000, 76; Jacobs, 2005).

Observers and industry participants were aware of the practices necessary to extend mass distribution but economic conditions complicated the transition. Not only did consumer demand decline during the Great Depression, customers shifted towards inexpensive staples and bought in small lots – patterns that favoured traditional retailers who offered credit and delivery services. This behaviour continued until the late 1940s because wartime rationing restricted the allocation of goods, forcing customers to travel store to store for their purchases.

Consumption and size

The era from the Second World War to 1980 was characterized by a rapid spread of consumption culture as distribution, rather than production, increasingly drove economic growth. American retail trade collapsed from $48.5 billion to $32.8 billion between 1929 and 1938 but it then kept rising: $75.8 billion by 1945, $140.2 billion during 1950 and $310 billion by 1967. Although inflation subsequently impacted sales data, by 1980 trade nominally amounted to $952 billion, (US Bureau of the Census, 1983, 802). Canadian retail sales followed a similar pattern from C$2.5 billion during 1938 to C$9.6 billion by 1950, then C$24.2 billion in 1967, and in C$103 billion by 1981 (Urquhart and Buckley, 1983, V1–24).

After decades of deprivation from economic depression and rationing, Canadians and Americans believed the post-war era should allow the realization of long-delayed dreams: the creation of happy family units; the possession of goods formerly deemed luxuries, including household appliances and televisions; personal fulfilment including the pursuit of leisure activities. The two post-war decades were characterized by sustained economic growth and rising incomes, which made the fulfilment of those expectations realistic. A proliferation of novel financial mechanisms (including the introduction of credit cards) enhanced buying capabilities. Moreover, the new medium of television provided a powerful tool for spreading a consumption-oriented culture, with advertisements emphasizing branded goods and portraying idealized images of individuals achieving happiness through their purchases.

Large enterprises became dominant forces in servicing this demand, although small firms fared well in some forms of distribution. The number of small stores in the United States declined dramatically between 1939 and 1967, both overall and in sub-sectors like food, hardware and drug stores. The number of single-unit retailers shrank, especially among department stores, clothing or apparel, and groceries (US Bureau of the Census, 1975, 141, 843–5). Corporate retailers, versus proprietorships or partnerships, expanded from 47.1 per cent of total sales in 1939 to 67.4 per cent by 1967. The number of establishments controlled by multi-unit enterprises nearly doubled, while their share of overall sales grew from 21.7 per cent to 39.8 per cent (US Bureau of the Census, 1975, 841, 843, 846). Higher levels of oligopoly characterized distribution, although the trend towards concentration varied among different sub-sectors due to the rapid expansion of retailing and the emergence of new firms. For example, the eight biggest American retailers rose from 12 per cent of total annual sales in 1960 to 28 per cent by 1967 and 36.6 per cent by 1980 (Nowakhtar, 1987, 117–18). Canadian data are fragmentary but indicate similar trends. Total retail sales octupled between 1939 and 1967. Proprietorships and proprietorships declined from 55.4 per cent to 30.7 per cent of yearly sales, while corporate organizations rose from 40.7 per cent to 64.4 percent. The number of outlets of chain firms doubled, while the firms' share of retail activity rose from 16.7 per cent to 24.9 per cent (Urquhart and Buckley 1983, V314–19).

A dual phenomenon unfolded in both countries: the physical size of stores expanded significantly and the share of sales accounted for by the largest stores grew by an even faster pace. This development unfolded across most sub-sectors (Moyer and Snyder, 1967, 89–97) although it was most obvious in food retailing. During the 1930s independent firms such as Big Bear and King Kullen imitated the strategies of chain sellers (with low margins and high volume turnover) but gained stronger economies by expanding store size five to ten times. These 'supermarkets' sold groceries and other products at prices well below those of other firms. Positioned in urban outskirts or warehouse districts, they benefited from low rents and access via automobiles. The outlets relied upon self-service and catered to consumer demand for nationally advertised brands. Based upon growing ownership of automobiles and refrigerators, it was assumed that shopping practices would change from a daily to a once-a-week task carried out at a single marketplace (Markin, 1968; Mayo, 1994). Chains initially dismissed the supermarkets as 'cheapies' but launched similar initiatives within a few years when it became clear that the outlets could achieve higher sales and profits. For most, this took the form of a two-step cycle: closing or updating outlets and constructing bigger stores. The development cycle became repetitious as even more mammoth outlets replaced larger stores. Cheapies disappeared as companies expanded inventories, added services and traded up for less price conscious consumers (Deutsch, 2010; Boothman, 2011). Growth initially was carried out from internal resources or debt and equity issues but by the mid-1950s companies employed acquisition or merger to jump in size and gain control over wholesale or warehousing activities (Appel, 1972).

Retailers characterized this trend as a benevolent contribution to public welfare, a perspective sketched with messianic fervour that went beyond mere self-interest. The new stores were portrayed as designed for more efficient handling of merchandise, offering a broader range of goods, and capable of achieving stronger economies of scale and scope with savings that could be passed on to consumers. Incremental cost improvements certainly occurred, along with increases in sales per outlet, but gains were partially offset by new expenses. In addition, the novelty of big stores quickly became commonplace and retailers found they had to make further investments to remain competitive with fickle consumers through updates of facilities or adding more product lines (Boothman, 2011).

Similarly a transition unfolded towards the homogenization of store operations as retailers catered to consumer desires for 'modern service'. Not only did self-service (along with the shopping cart) become ubiquitous but innovations developed by chain retailers became (regardless of firm size) normal aspects of selling: convenient displays for impulse buying, loss leaders, selective aisle organization and careful location of goods within stores to enhance overall sales. This trend was evident in manuals or textbooks, which increasingly made few distinctions between management practices for independent and corporate retailers (see Brand, 1963; Davidson *et al.*, 1966). Store architecture shifted into regularized product-placement formats among department stores (Longstreth, 2010), supermarkets (Mayo, 1994; Longstreth, 1999), gas stations (Jakle and Sculle, 1994), and diners or fast food outlets (Langdon, 1986; Hurley, 1997; Jakle and Sculle, 1999).

Retail activities also relocated away from city cores. Between 1945 and 1970 a significant proportion of Americans and Canadians moved to low-density suburban areas located in the hinterland between cities and rural zones. Low interest rates, government assistance for mortgage lending, low unemployment and rising incomes combined to permit unprecedented opportunities for home ownership. Young adults favoured the new communities because they permitted an escape from congested industrial zones and facilitated an emergent child-centred orientation among families (Cohen, 2003, 194–256). Subdivisions were popularized as the latest innovation in scientific social engineering. This framework facilitated a self-conscious modernism among residents, reflected in a desire to possess appliances and other goods, as well as tolerance of homogenization and impersonal service delivery. Moreover, the communities relied upon motor vehicle transportation.

Strip malls geared to servicing local neighbourhoods had been a feature of many cities for decades. During the 1950s retailers met the needs of suburbanites for a merger of consumption and community with the construction of regional shopping centers. These complexes reversed the logic of city core retailers (which relied upon nodes in public transport systems) by ensuring access by private automobile transport and by locating near highways or major thoroughfares. The construction of shopping centres entailed heavy investments and lengthy payback periods, so a successful project depended upon negotiations with 'anchor tenants' (typically supermarkets or department stores) about rents and locations, and then the selection of other retailers. Developers targeted retail chains as preferred participants since they had purchasing power, brand identity and greater efficiency. Moreover, chain retailers were focused upon white middle-class customers who formed the bulk of early movers to suburban areas. Within each mall, firms sought to negotiate terms or locations that could constrain competitors within their retail sub-groups. Local retailers often were forced into chain or franchise relationships in order to survive. The restriction of direct rivalry produced predictable profits for both developers and retailers. Developers also sought to ensure spatial monopolies by lobbying government officials to exclude the creation of alternative centres nearby. Taken together, regional shopping centres replicated the roles and spatial distribution of central urban retailers but with greater perceived safety for customers and much less duplication. Proponents suggested they represented 'modern-day downtowns' that avoided the 'ugliness' and 'anarchy' of selling in central city areas (Sternlieb, 1962, 32; Vernon, 1959, 66–7; Cohen, 1996, 1056–61).

A variety of geographically decentralized retail areas consequently emerged, ranging from simple strip malls with a few outlets to gigantic complexes with hundreds of stores and several anchors. There were 4,500 shopping centres accounting for 14 per cent of retail sales in the US by 1960 and 15 years later 16,400 malls accounted for 33 per cent. The social impact extended beyond a narrow definition of retailing. Suburban shopping centres offered a range of civic and entertainment activities, fundamentally reconfiguring public space. Shopping centres also utilized part-time personnel, often relying upon suburban housewives willing to accept flexible labour conditions. However, they emphasized nuclear families as consumer units and thereby gave stress to male purchasers as the primary income-earners. Credit cards and other forms of consumer lending became the legal tender of mall purchasing. This development strengthened male oversight of purchases (since their names and credit ratings conditioned access for wives or children) until the passage of equal credit legislation during the 1970s (Cohen, 2003, 257–89; Scharoun, 2012).

Contractual relationships also became more varied across the post-war era. During the emergence of mass distribution, department stores and chains utilized vertical integration since it ensured supply for their strategies based the sale of a narrow range of high volume goods. With the increase in size of retailer outlets, wider selections of products were stocked, decreasing the need for unified relational contracting. As a result, later entrants employed vertical integration selectively, while firms like Sears and Eaton's sold off manufacturing operations and utilized contract supply and multiple sourcing. An exception from this pattern was wholesaling as retailers fortified their internal purchasing functions or purchased independent wholesale and warehousing activities.

Organizational systems similarly became more complex as the use of franchising escalated in the United States and Canada. Earlier in the century firms like Rexall Drug had employed this form of quasi-integration as a means of network construction. During the inter-war period petroleum companies minimized their risk exposure by converting company-owned gasoline stations into franchise operations. The construction of modern highways, which enhanced mobility and the use of automobiles, was a key stimulant to this development. A veritable 'road culture' of enterprises emerged to service travellers and busy commuters: Holiday Inn, Sheraton, A&W, McDonald's, Burger King, Wendy's, KFC, Dunkin' Donuts, Tim Horton's, Midas, 7-Eleven, Dairy Queen, Orange Julius. The companies normally employed business format franchising, a variation upon the techniques employed by chain retailers. An outlet's franchisee received a defined business scheme and brand identity in exchange for fees paid to a central office. The franchisor centralized strategic decision-making, buying and enforced policies specifying territorial domains and ensuring network uniformity. This approach soon spread into other forms of retailing. Less than 100 American companies employed franchising during 1950 but by 1970 almost a third of retail trade was conducted by 396,300 franchised outlets (Dicke, 1992).

During the immediate post-war years in the United States, discount stores (Zayres, Arlans, Gibson's and Two Guys) were created to meet demand for less expensive goods like television sets and household appliances. The companies replicated the supermarket concept with warehouse outlets in suburban locations and policies geared to minimizing overhead costs (McNair and May, 1976, 46). The look of the stores altered during the 1950s as discounters assumed a department-store-like appearance by adding household goods, apparel and other products. The appeal of the stores was facilitated by rising inflation levels during the following decade and consumers increasingly showed little loyalty to older organizations. Nonetheless, the range and quantities of goods sold by the firms remained limited because 'fair trade' laws in many states permitted manufacturers to restrict sales if retailers did not sell at their 'suggested list prices'. As the state statutes were repealed or ruled unconstitutional, an influx into the discount sector occurred. Many entrants were inexperienced and underfinanced but in 1962 four firms were established that later dominated the sector: Kmart, Woolco, Wal-Mart and Target. The first three were new operations by 'five and dime' retailers S. S. Kresge, F. W. Woodworth, and Walton's. The companies established large facilities with standardized layouts in or near shopping centres and sold a mix of hard and soft goods. During the 1970s they expanded into regional or national chains, reinforcing competitive positions by acquiring other companies.

Despite the social acceptance of a consumption-oriented culture, public disparagement of mass distribution became widespread during the 1960s and 1970s. Price inflation increased across the two decades. This development first triggered scepticism about claims that retailers would maintain low prices and then was manifested by vociferous protests and boycotts of stores that were perceived as gouging consumers. Demand escalated for 'no-frills' or warehouse stores that offered cheaper goods but with few shopping amenities, a trend that facilitated the growth of the discount department store sector.

Cumulatively, the different changes reconfigured North American retailing. Traditional department stores retained a steady share of overall sales but the status of individual firms was more problematic. Independent department stores, locally managed and family controlled, slowly moved towards extinction. The companies were located in central city areas with sub-optimal size and inadequate capital. Some corporate stores prospered though diversification into suburban locations and other services (JC Penney, Sears) or through merger into financial holding enterprises (Allied Department Stores, Federated Department Stores) that built regional chain clusters around what had been downtown department stores (McNair and May, 1976). Others (Simpson's, Eaton's, Montgomery Ward) weakened from competition by discounters or specialty retailers. Variety stores were undercut by discount department stores and a later generation of cost-conscious 'dollar stores'.

Retailing in Canada remained domestically owned despite the presence of various American chains like F.W. Woolworth and S.S. Kresge. Canadian firms tended to be entrepreneur or family-controlled for much longer periods than in the United States. Geared toward servicing local or regional areas, the companies often were managed very conservatively. They were less inclined to undertake aggressive price-based competition and, although well aware of retail innovations, could be quite slow in making changes. This pattern shifted in several sub-sectors across the post-war generation. Safeway and A&P expanded in food retailing, while American firms elaborated franchise systems in restaurants, automobile-related services, and motels. Several Canadian chains emerged in counterpoise like Harvey's, Tim Horton's, and Canadian Tire. The most prominent foreign entry was by Sears via a joint venture with Simpson's during the 1950s whereby the American firm developed shopping centre locations in medium-sized towns and suburban areas, while its Canadian partner managed downtown or shopping mall stores in the biggest cities. Simpson-Sears forced the other two leading department stores, Eaton's and Hudson's Bay, to play catch-up, with less success (McQueen, 1998). Nonetheless, most American retailers remained uninterested in the smaller Canadian market or perceived entry problematic because of trade barriers or cultural variations.

A final tectonic shift during this era was a growing emphasis by retailers upon market segmentation. Mass marketing during the first half of the century tended to stress homogeneity of supply and demand, with the distribution of standardized products. Efforts to shift away from this orientation can be traced into 1930s as firms tried to increase sales by servicing segments like women's clothing (Srigley, 2007) or teenagers (Rollwagen, 2012). During the post-war decade the dominant notions (especially among retail chains) remained that consumer markets were unified and the appropriate orientation was towards the supply of goods aimed at middle-class citizens or aspirants. Several factors altered this perspective.

First, retailers came under sustained challenge by the late 1950s in sustaining sales due to a recession and an anticipated saturation of markets for goods like cars and household appliances. Second, marketing analysts discerned that markets could be split into discrete elements. The earliest initiatives often were focused upon teenagers but as personal standards of living rose blue-collar workers were targeted as a group with extensive purchase power but distinctive tastes and interests. Across the 1960s, retailers focused upon 'lifestyle' segmentation among buyers, based upon stage of life, social status, gender or race. Third, as a medium television facilitated the ability to utilize 'spot commercials' or 'narrowcast' advertising to specific groups who watched particular types of programmes. These developments occurred as the size of mass markets in North America exceeded the levels necessary to achieve scale economies and as industrial production techniques became more flexible, thereby allowing smaller product runs to meet diverse demand from consumer groups.

Concentration and fragmentation

The era from 1980 to 2015 was characterized by a never-ending struggle as retailing was restructured in critical ways. Annual data fluctuated between periods of prosperity and recession and were impacted by inflation, but American retail sales expanded from $960 billion in 1980 to $4.9 trillion by 2012. Canada retail trade grew from C$84.4 billion during 1980 to C$485.8 billion in 2012. Wholesale and retail employment in the United States went through periods of boom and bust but started at 20.8 million in the US in 1980 and was 21 million in 2012 (US Bureau of the Census, 2012; Industry Canada, 2013, 2). Despite the long-term pattern of overall growth, many well-known enterprises deteriorated, were taken over or went bankrupt, while significant turnover and instability unfolded among smaller firms. More than 75 per cent of the top 50 retailers in Canada and the United States during 1980 no longer were among those groups or existed three decades later. But even among new firms there was considerable competitive volatility.

Sharp increases in levels of market concentration unfolded in overall retailing and various sub-sectors. The leading retailers grew faster than other firms and the share accounted for by the eight largest American firms rose from 9.3 per cent to 17.8 per cent just between 1980 and 2003 (Xu, 2007, 52, 55). During the mid-1980s the top 50 American companies accounted for 20 per cent of all retail sales. This share rose to 26 per cent in 1997 (Sieling et al., 2001) and about 32 per cent by 2014 (author's estimate). However, trends varied by sub-sector, with little change, for example, in concentration levels among department and specialty store companies. However, a sharp concentration of business unfolded among discount department stores and by the early 1990s in the US the top three chains accounted for 75 per cent of sales. Canadian data suggest a similar phenomenon occurred. By 2011, the top 30 retailers accounted for 66 per cent of non-automotive retail sales. The three largest companies (Weston Group, Wal-Mart and Empire) had 3,148 outlets and accounted for 24 per cent. In five of nine retail sub-sectors, four firms conducted more than 55 per cent of annual sales (Industry Canada, 2013, 11–12).

Most of the growth in the number of stores and employment came from firms that operated multiple outlets. The chain store share increased to nearly two-thirds of retail employment. 71 per cent of American consumer dollars were spent at chain stores in 2007, more than double the share of 50 years earlier (Jarmin et al., 2009, 240). In Canada, chains accounted for 31 per cent of retail sales in 1980 and 48 per cent by 2011 (Industry Canada, 2013, 13). Stand-alone firms still typified retailing in areas like motor vehicles and convenience stores but those types of companies were reduced to small shares of sales in food, clothing, sporting goods, electronics, hardware, and health or personal care (Dinlersoz, 2004, 209). The revenue share of chains in excess of 100 stores more than tripled between 1977 and 2007. Market concentration weakened the influence of manufacturers over distribution channels in favour of the big chains (Grant, 1987; Jarmin *et al.*, 2009). Moreover, department stores became an endangered species. Major firms like Eaton's and Montgomery Ward went bankrupt, many others including Sears and JC Penney struggled just to survive.

These developments were derived from a set of complementary issues. Just as distributors previously seized upon organizational concepts from mass production, so companies during this period exploited information technology (IT) to build competitive positions. The introduction of bar-code technology readers halved labour costs of processing shipments (Vance and Scott, 1994). Radio Frequency Identification facilitated tracking shipments. Computers and software allowed chains to move away from time-consuming inventory schemes and to link stores, distribution centres and suppliers. Some of the biggest enterprises developed satellite systems for tracking and coordinating developments. And, of course, sophisticated software enabled the firms to analyse purchase patterns with greater detail and predictability than previously considered possible. The innovations enhanced the ability to operate larger stores and to elaborate 'buyer-driven' supply chains. Various retailers were able to act as 'channel captains' within supply chains, which shifted from 'supply push' to 'demand pull' in character. Firms developed 'lean retailing': integrated logistics that connected reordering to real-time electronic point-of-sales, thereby reducing inventory holdings and capital tied up in those holdings (Abernathy *et al.*, 2000).

Observers, often with heliographic zeal, pointed to Wal-Mart or Amazon as exemplars but the reality was more complex. In some cases (such as optical scanners and product codes) the 'new' technology had been around for decades but what mattered was the willingness and ability to exploit it. Virtually all gains in retail productivity were related to net entry, that is, new and more productive companies either displaced older firms or compelled survivors to undertake superior efforts (Foster *et al.*, 2006). Moreover, big retailers accounted for most investments in IT and gained from them disproportionately vis-à-vis small firms. In part, this was a chicken and egg cycle; enterprise size facilitated the ability to undertake IT investments but the investments, in turn, reinforced capabilities and growth. Still, entrants appear to have been more inclined towards the exploitation of IT innovations than older retailers (Doms *et al.*, 2004; Basker, 2007).

The elaboration of network strategies and economies of density became crucial aspects of chain activities. Firms in the transport sectors had discovered the ability to realize economies through an agglomeration of different activities in specific locations with shared costs in distribution, training and advertising. Chain retailers previously tended to pursue decentralized expansion strategies, jumping from a starting location to other urban centres and subsequently filling in the spaces between. During the late twentieth century, some chose to develop from a central geographic area and build networks from the inside-out, placing new outlets near where they already had store density. There was a potential for cannibalizing sales but the gains included shared knowledge and an amplification of economies at the store and chain levels (Holmes, 2011). Wal-Mart was the best-known practitioner of the approach but other retailers soon attempted to agglomerate activities within their networks (Jia, 2008).

Moreover, by 2015 the stores people shopped in were radically different than those of 50 years earlier. Not only were they more likely to shop at chain retailers but the average size of stores more than doubled. This pattern occurred even among single outlet retailers. During the 1980s firms like Costco, Home Depot and Wal-Mart extended the supermarket concept with the construction of 'big box' or warehouse outlets that were several times larger than

147

the prevailing norms. Located in accessible locations and promoted through advertising, the outlets did not need malls, expensive anchor tenants or pedestrian traffic to attract customers. Not only did the big box concept spread into forms of retailing that had been the province of small enterprises, it shifted influence away from shopping centre developers to the retailers (Graff, 1998). Often, the innovation took the form of 'power centres' comprised of one or more big boxes around which smaller stores were clustered. There were few amenities and minimal links among the outlets. Consumers increasingly focused upon a big box as a 'destination store' rather than going to an older shopping centre. Over time, the gigantic sites squeezed out not just smaller firms in downtown or suburban areas but cut into the business of shopping centres. In one sense, therefore, market concentration propelled homogeneity of market offerings with fewer (but very big) retailers supplying similar or identical goods (Basker *et al.*, 2012; Scharoun, 2012; Schinder, 2012).

However, these changes stimulated the creation of new consumption sites that enabled producers and consumers to engage in a broader range of exchange relationships. By the early 1990s the significance of shopping centres weakened due to demographic shifts, periods of recession and the creation of gigantic stores. Developers generated alternate types of facilities through the assembly of stores into strategic locations that might attract suburban and urban consumers (Lowrey, 1997; Marston and Modarres, 2002). 'Commercial gentrification' entailed the upscale redevelopment of shopping areas towards prosperous residents, often with the introduction of national chains into downtown areas. 'Lifestyle centres' that mixed housing, entertainment and restaurants were built as part of larger projects or constructed on the sites of demolished shopping areas. 'Outlet malls' consisted of stores controlled by manufacturers for the supply of their branded goods and purported to provide low-cost alternatives to chain stores. 'Festival marketplaces' clustered food, entertainment and specialty retailers as a means of revitalizing downtown areas but many did not meet expectations and incurred serious financial losses. Ironically, as mergers or bankruptcy decreased the presence of older retailers in major malls, big box retailers moved into many even though they had initially avoided them. Cumulatively, these changes fragmented shopping experiences from the homogeneity of the mid-twentieth century but cemented the market presence of large chain retailers.

These trends were complicated by increases in the levels of competition. Across the three decades a diversification of product mix unfolded that blurred traditional sub-segments. Grocery stores introduced general merchandise and goods previously available only in discount and specialty stores, as they attempted to become one-stop shopping outlets. Discount stores like Wal-Mart and Target moved into food sales and traded up in quality or fashion, supplying goods previously available in department stores. By expanding the breadth of product lines, discount stores became direct competitors with supermarkets (and food stores more discount store-like). Category 'superstores' provided offered assortments of goods not always part of their standard product lines, either to broaden customer appeal or as part of sales promotions. Drug stores added convenience products and competed with discount stores. 'Category killers' (big boxes with limited product ranges like Best Buy or Toys 'R' Us), off-price stores, mail order retailers moved into rivalry with specialty retailers. Although it still has not been accurately mapped, specialty stores themselves frequently de-specialized (Leszczyc *et al.*, 2000; Basker *et al.*, 2012).

Market fragmentation also was propelled by demographic alterations in both countries. Retailing during the mid-twentieth century had been conditioned by the significance of young (predominantly white) nuclear families in suburbs, as well as by popular mythology that this was an optimal status. But by the early twenty-first century, social conditions fragmented into an array of segments, sub-segments and micro-segments that retailers could service. Extensive immigration brought a wider array of ethnic nationalities into the social mix of each country, with associated variations in cultural preferences and tastes. Life-long marriages and stable nuclear families became minority social institutions, whereas they had been the norm 50 years earlier. Equal rights legislation and court rulings impacted patterns of racial and female mobility within society, as well as transformed gender relationships and notions of what constituted 'a family'. In addition, by 2015 the largest demographic group became the old – the young of the post-war generations.

An expansion of international retailing further reshaped competitive rivalry. During the 1990s foreign brand franchises set up outlets in the United States, which were aimed at upper-income goods and located in shopping malls or major urban centres. The internationalization of retailing was most noticeable in Canada where foreign-controlled firms had represented less than 3 per cent of retail sales during the early 1980s. This share rose to 30 per cent by 2002 and was expected to exceed 45 per cent by 2015. In 2011, 53 per cent (or 66) of the top 124 leading retail organizations in Canada were foreign owned and operated. The companies accounted for approximately 40 per cent of total leading retail corporations' sales. American based or controlled retailers accounted for 95 per cent of retail sales by foreign companies (Industry Canada, 2013, 12–13). A critical factor behind this development was the adoption of the FTA/NAFTA, which eliminated tariffs between Canada and the United States and eased restrictions on services, personnel movement and service contracts between the two countries. In addition, by the 1990s numerous American firms approached saturation in their domestic market and perceived Canada as culturally similar with consumers familiar with business offerings south of the border through tourism or media exposure.

The American infusion into Canada particularly entailed retailers that utilized big box stores and sophisticated inventory management to operate as low-cost suppliers: Wal-Mart, Best Buy, Home Depot, Costco and most recently Target. They escalated price-based competition and propelled emphases upon service and links to manufacturers in corporate operations. Entry into the apparently 'similar' market often proved troublesome. Even Wal-Mart had a difficult launch, while Target experienced a multi-billion dollar fiasco and then withdrew. But the long-term impact was devastating, particularly for many of the family-controlled enterprises that had long characterized Canadian retailing. Some, like Canadian Tire and George Weston, successfully repositioned their strategies. Others like Eaton's responded poorly and fell into bankruptcy or were taken over. In counterpoise, Canadian retailers rarely experienced the same success when they expanded into the American market, although a handful prospered.

To cope with fragmented consumer markets, large retailers utilized multiple distribution channels, providing alternate mechanisms for purchases of products and services (Venkatesan et al., 2007; Wind and Mahajan 2002). The introduction of e-commerce triggered further complexity towards the close of the period covered by this chapter. By 2012, more than 80 per cent of Americans and Canadians were regular users of the internet or smart phones. The so-called 'Echo Boomers' constituted the first generation with access to computers and mobile devices throughout their education. E-commerce experienced an average growth of 20 per cent per annum after 2001. Online retailing amounted to a $365 billion business in North America by 2012 but the share of the total retail sales still was only 5.7 per cent. The ultimate consequences of this mode have not yet become evident but exchange relationships already have been impacted in key ways. It provided consumers with new capabilities: research in detail, transact with quasi-anonymity (just a name and credit card account), purchase from companies previously inaccessible and expect price matches from physical retailers with those of online vendors. Retailers analogously secured cross-channel information about consumers and their preferences, which could be utilized for product design, pricing and inventory management in physical stores. Thus, e-commerce bound markets closer together but also fragmented them into more channels and shopping experiences.

With the growing popularity of e-commerce, physical retailers tried to enhance in-store shopping by stressing social interaction, immediate gratification from purchases and the ability to sense and feel (Lueg et al., 2006; Konus et al., 2008). While major firms established an online presence, the effectiveness of such operations as part of multi-channel strategies remains mixed. Some constructed online platforms to build brand identity and online communities. Other companies moved beyond online catalogues and email lists to create 'spoke and hub' schemes (online order and store pickup) or in-store computer kiosks where consumers could browse products or order out-of-stock items. Still, by 2015 e-commerce had spurred structural changes such as a decrease or outright displacement of some retail categories like music and book stores.

There are indications that big box retailing may have passed its peak, just a generation after its emergence. By 2012 nearly 35 per cent of empty retail area in the United States was big box space. Analysts initially attributed this issue to the 2008 recession, the construction of excess facilities or the abandonment of existing outlets for even bigger superstores (Schinder, 2012, 474–5) but the causes extended further. First, as noted above, traditional sub-segment boundaries were blurred. Other firms learned either to imitate the operations of the big box companies or to match their prices. The result was an erosion of advantages and distinctiveness even for firms like Wal-Mart. Second, consumers shifted away from single-trip shopping and if they had price-comparison technology sought deals. Third, firms selling specialty goods encountered 'showrooming', where shoppers examined items in a store but purchased from online rivals for lower prices. Some enterprises therefore began to shift to smaller outlets (with decreased inventories or display models) that stressed customer service and product expertise. These actions portended further alterations in North American retailing but certainly did not herald the 'death' of big box companies as some observers claimed.

Conclusions

What observations might we draw from the patterns that have unfolded? First, the historical evidence supports the managerial capitalism thesis. Overall, there has been a trend across time towards market concentration in major categories of retailing, that is, a greater share of sales by large-scale retailers. In the popular literature, this development has sometimes been called 'the Wal-Mart factor'. However, that is putting the cart before the horse. The trend has unfolded for more than a century and Wal-Mart's actions are just part of the most recent iteration, not something unprecedented. Very much, this trend unfolded as a series of punctuated waves, each with distinctive drivers. Small firms obviously survived and prospered in niches or by supplying customized services but over time large firms gained superior positions by exploiting economies and professional management techniques.

A second issue relates to the issue of competitive stability versus turnover. Chandler's (1977) thesis posits that once large firms emerged they secured 'permanence, power, and continued growth'. They could entrench long-term advantages, retain stable shares of economic activities and reinforce competitive status with oligopolistic conduct. The historical reality in retailing is more muddled. Certainly firms like Sears, Eaton's or Wal-Mart held leading positions for long periods in their sub-sectors. However, this should not be overstated. In both Canada and the United States the evidence shows patterns of high turnover and change. Although it goes beyond the scope of this chapter, historical analysis of individual companies or sub-sectors would make this issue clearer. Case analysis or company biographies will highlight the strategic problems firms encountered and the insecurity and competitive turbulence perceived by executives even in periods of 'stability'.

A final issue critically shaped the previous two; retailing always has been as much culturally as economically driven. Retailers obviously have attempted to attract consumers and to mould their desires but consumers are not passive participants in exchange relationships. Their choices are voluntary. Over time, their expectations about what to buy, when, how and where alter. This matter lies beneath the strategic and spatial transformations that have occurred. Indeed, the organization of retailing might be conceptualized not just as a longitudinal series of changes, as outlined in this chapter, but also a layering of different formats. Some enterprises still function very much like the traditional companies of the nineteenth century. Others adhere to the gestalts of later periods. The historical background thus frames the organization of distribution in North America and the strategic development of contemporary firms that will face new challenges and complexities. Perhaps they, unlike that store in the Maclean-Hunter building, will manage to 'survive another year in retail'.

References

Abernathy, F.H., Dunlop, J.T., Hammond, J.H., and Weil, D. (2000) 'Retailing and supply chains in the information age', *Technology in Society*, 22/1, 5–31.

Appel, D. (1972) 'The supermarket: Early development of an institutional innovation', *Journal of Retailing*, 48/1, 39–53.

Barger, H. (1955) *Distribution's Place in the American Economy since 1869*, Princeton University Press, Princeton, NJ.

Barth, G. (1980) *City People: The Rise of Modern City Culture in Nineteenth-Century America*, Oxford University Press, New York.

Basker, E. (2007) 'The causes and consequences of Wal-Mart's growth', *Journal of Economic Perspectives*, 21/3, 177–89.

Basker, E., Klimek, S., and Van, P.H. (2012) 'Supersize it: The growth of retail chains and the rise of the "big box" store', *Journal of Economics and Management Strategy*, 21/3, 541–82.

Beckman, T.N., and Engle, N.H. (1949) *Wholesaling: Principles and Problems*, Ronald Press, New York.

Belisle, D. (2011) *Retail Nation: Department Stores and the Making of Modern Canada*, UBC Press, Vancouver, BC.

Benson, S.P. (1988) *Counter-Cultures: Saleswomen, Managers, and Customers in American Department Stores, 1890–1940*, University of Illinois Press, Chicago, IL.

Bliss, J.W.M. (1974) *A Living Profit: Studies in the Social History of Canadian Business 1883– 1911*, McClelland & Stewart, Toronto, ON.

Boothman, B.E.C. (2009) 'A more definite system: The emergence of retail food chains in Canada, 1919–1945', *Journal of Macromarketing*, 29/1, 21–36.

Boothman, B.E.C. (2011) 'Mammoth market: The transformation of food retailing in Canada, 1946–1965', *Journal of Historical Research in Marketing*, 3/3, 279–301.

Brand, E.A. (1963) *Modern Supermarket Operation*, Fairchild, New York.

Brown, S. (1987) 'Institutional change in retailing: A review and synthesis', *European Journal of Marketing*, 21/6, 5–36.

Chandler, A.D. (1977) *The Visible Hand: The Managerial Revolution in American Business*, Harvard University Press, Cambridge, MA.

Chaney, D. (1983) 'The department store as cultural form', *Theory, Culture, Society*, 1/3, 22–31.

Cheasley, C.H. (1930) *The Chain Store Movement in Canada*, McGill University Economic Studies, 17, Packet-Times Press, Orillia, ON.

Cohen, L. (1996) 'From town center to shopping center: The reconfiguration of community marketplaces in postwar America', *American Historical Review*, 101/4, 1050–81.

Cohen, L. (2003) *A Consumers' Republic: The Politics of Mass Consumption in Postwar America*, Vintage, New York.

Conzen, M.P., and Conzen, K.N. (1979) 'Geographic structure in nineteenth-century urban retailing: Milwaukee, 1836–90', *Journal of Historical Geography*, 5/1, 45–66.

Cross, G. (2000) *An All-Consuming Century: Why Commercialism Won in Modern America*, Columbia University Press, New York.

Davidson, W.R., Doody, A.F., and Brown, P.L. (1966) *Retailing Management*, Ronald Press, New York.

Deutsch, T. (2010) *Building a Housewife's Paradise: Gender, Politics, and American Grocery Stores in the Twentieth-Century*, University of North Carolina Press, Chapel Hill, NC.

Dicke, T.S. (1992) *Franchising in America: The Development of a Business Method, 1840–1980*, University of North Carolina Press, Chapel Hill, NC.

Dinlersoz, E.N. (2004) 'Firm organization and the structure of retail markets', *Journal of Economics and Management Strategy*, 13/2, 207–40.

Dominion Bureau of Statistics (1931) *Census of Merchandising and Service Establishments*, King's Printer, Ottawa, ON.

Domosh, M. (1996) *Invented Cities: The Creation of Landscape in Nineteenth-Century Boston and New York*, Yale University Press, New Haven, CT.

Doms, M.E., Jarmin, R.S., and Klimek, S.D. (2004) 'Information technology investment and firm performance in U.S. retail trade', *Economics of Innovation and New Technology*, 13/7, 595–613.

Emmet, B., and Jeuck, J.E. (1950) *Catalogues and Counters: A History of Sears Roebuck and Company*, University of Chicago Press, Chicago, IL.

Federal Trade Commission (1932) *Chain Stores: Chain-Store Leaders and Loss Leaders*, Government Printing Office, Washington, DC.

Foster, L., Haltiwanger, J., and Krizan, C. J. (2006) 'Market selection, reallocation, and restructuring in the U.S. retail trade sector in the 1990s', *Review of Economics and Statistics*, 88/4, 748–58.

Friedman, W.A. (2004) *Birth of a Salesman: The Transformation of Selling in America*, Harvard University Press, Cambridge, MA.

Ghosh, A., and McLafferty, S. (1991) 'The shopping center: A restructuring of post-war retailing', *Journal of Retailing*, 7/3, 253–67.

Gillette, H. (1985) 'The evolution of the planned shopping center in suburb and city', *American Planning Association Journal*, 51/4, 449–60.

Graff, T.O. (1998) 'The locations of Wal-Mart and Kmart super centers: Contrasting corporate strategies', *Professional Geographer*, 50/1, 46–57.

Grant, R.M. (1987) 'Manufacturer–retailer relations: The shifting balance of power', in G. Johnson (ed.), *Business Strategy and Retailing*, Wiley, London, pp. 43–58.

Halttunen, K. (1989) 'From parlor to living room: Domestic space, interior decoration, and the culture of personality', in S.J. Bronner (ed.), *Consuming Visions: Accumulation and the Display of Goods in America, 1880–1920*, Norton, New York, pp. 157–90.

Hayward, W.S., and White, P. (1922) *Chain Stores: Their Management and Operation*, McGraw-Hill, New York.

Hollander, S.C., and Omura, G.S. (1989) 'Chain store developments and their political, strategic, and social interdependencies', *Journal of Retailing*, 65/3, 299–325.

Holmes, T.J. (2011) 'The diffusion of Wal-Mart and economies of density', *Econometrica*, 79/1, 253–302.

Hower, R.M. (1943) *History of Macy's of New York, 1858–1919*, Harvard University Press, Cambridge, MA.

Hurley, A. (1997) 'From hash house to family restaurant: The transformation of the diner and post-World War II consumer culture', *Journal of American History*, 83/4, 1282–1308.

Industry Canada (2013) *Canada's Changing Retail Market*, Office of Consumer Affairs, Ottawa, ON.

Jackson, P., and Holbrook. B. (1995) 'Multiple meanings: Shopping and the cultural politics of identity', *Environment and Planning*, 27/12, 1913–30.

Jakle, J.A., and Sculle, K.A. (1994) *The Gas Station in America*, Johns Hopkins University Press, Baltimore, MD.

Jakle, J.A., and Sculle, K.A. (1999) *Fast Food: Roadside Restaurants in the Automobile Age*, Johns Hopkins University Press, Baltimore, MD.

Jacobs, M. (2005) *Pocketbook Politics: Economic Citizenship in Twentieth-Century America*, Princeton University Press, Princeton, NJ.

Jarmin, R.S. Klimek, S.D., and Miranda, J. (2009) 'The role of retail chains: National, regional and industry results', in T. Dunne, J.B. Jensen and M.J. Roberts (ed.), *Producer Dynamics: New Evidence from Micro Data*, National Bureau of Economic Research, University of Chicago Press, Chicago, IL, pp. 237–62.

Jia, P. (2008) 'What happens when Wal-Mart comes to town: An empirical analysis of the discount retail industry', *Econometrica*, 76/6, 1263–1316.

Katz, D.R. (1987) *The Big Store: Inside the Crisis and Revolution at Sears*, Viking, New York.

Konus, U., Verhoef, P.C., and Neslin, S.A. (2008) 'Multichannel shopper segments and their covariates', *Journal of Retailing*, 84/4, 398–413.

Laird, P.W. (1998) *Advertising Progress: American Business and the Rise of Consumer Marketing*, Johns Hopkins University Press, Baltimore, MD.

Langdon, P. (1986) *Orange Roofs, Golden Arches: The Architecture of American Chain Restaurants*, Knopf, New York.

Leach, W. (1993) *Land of Desire: Merchants, Power, and the Rise of a New American Culture*, Pantheon, New York.

Lebhar, G.M. (1952) *Chain Stores in America, 1859–1950*, Chain Store Publishing, New York.

Leszczyc, P.P., Sinha, A., and Timmermans, H.J.P. (2000) 'Consumer store choice dynamics: An analysis of the competitive market structure for grocery stores', *Journal of Retailing*, 76/3, 323–45.

Longstreth, R, (1999) *The Drive-in, the Supermarket, and the Transformation of Commercial Space in Los Angeles, 1914–1941*, MIT Press, Cambridge, MA.

Longstreth, R. (2010) *The American Department Store Transformed, 1920–1960*, Yale University Press, New Haven, CT.

Lowrey, J. (1997) 'The life cycle of shopping centers', *Business Horizons*, 40/1, 77–86.

Lueg, J.E., Ponder, N., Beatty, S.E., and Capella, M.L, (2006) 'Teenagers' use of alternative shopping channels: A consumer socialization perspective', *Journal of Retailing*, 82/2, 137–53.

McNair, M.P., and May, E.G. (1963) *The American Department Store 1920–1960: A Performance Analysis Based on the Harvard Reports*, Harvard University, Graduate School of Business, Cambridge, MA.

McNair, M.P. and May, E.G. (1976) *The Evolution of Retail Institutions in the United States*, Harvard Marketing Science Institute, Cambridge, MA.

McQueen, R. (1998) *The Eaton's: The Rise and Fall of Canada's Royal Family*, Stoddart, Toronto, ON.

Markin, R.J. (1968) *The Supermarket: An Analysis of Growth, Development, and Change*, Washington State University Press, Pullman, WA.

Marston, S.A., and Modarres, A. (2002) 'Flexible retailing: GAP Inc. and the multiple spaces of shopping in the United States', *Tidjscrift voor Economische en Sociale Geografie*, 93/1, 83–99.

Mayo, J.M. (1994) *The American Grocery Store: The Business Evolution of an Architectural Space*, Greenwood Press, Westport, CT.

Monod, D. (1996) *Store Wars: Shopkeepers and the Culture of Mass Marketing, 1890–1930*, University of Toronto Press, Toronto, ON.

Moyer, M.S., and Snyder, G. (1967) *Trends in Canadian Marketing*, Dominion Bureau of Statistics, Ottawa, ON.

Nowakhtar, S. (1985) 'Structure of the general merchandise retail market: An empirical analysis of the seller concentration (1959–1983)', unpublished PhD thesis, Purdue University, West Lafayette, IN.

Parr, J. (1999) *Domestic Goods: The Material, the Moral, and the Economic in the Postwar Years*, University of Toronto Press, Toronto, ON.

Pasadermadjian, H. (1954) *The Department Store: Its Origins, Evolution, and Economics*, Newman, London.

Porter, G., and Livesay, H.C. (1971) *Merchants and Manufacturers: Studies in the Changing Structure of Nineteenth-Century Marketing*, Johns Hopkins University Press, Baltimore, MD.

Rollwagen, K.E. (2012) '"The market that just grew up": How Eaton's fashioned the teenaged consumer in mid-twentieth century Canada', unpublished PhD dissertation, University of Ottawa.

Santink, J. (1989) *Timothy Eaton and the Rise of his Department Stores*, University of Toronto Press, Toronto, ON.

Scharoun, L, (2012) *America at the Mall: The Cultural Role of a Retail Utopia*, McFarland, Jefferson, NC.

Schinder, S. (2012) 'The future of abandoned big box stores: legal solutions to the legacies of poor planning decisions', *University of Colorado Law Review*, 83/2, 471–548.

Schnore, L.F. (ed.) (1975) *The New Urban History*, Princeton University Press, Princeton, NJ.

Sieling, M., Friedman, B., and Dumas, M. (2001) 'Labor productivity in the retail trade industry, 1987–99', *Monthly Labor Review*, 124/12, 3–12.

Srigley, K. (2007) 'Clothing stories: Consumption, identity, and desire in depression–era Toronto', *Journal of Women's History*, 19/1, 82–104.

Sternlieb, G. (1962) *The Future of the Downtown Department Store*, Harvard University Press, Cambridge, MA.

Strasser, S. (1989) *Satisfaction Guaranteed: The Making of the American Mass Market*, Smithsonian Institution Press, Washington, DC.

Tedlow, R.S. (1990) *New and Improved: The Story of Mass Marketing in America*, Basic, New York.

Urquhart, M.C. (1986) 'New estimates of gross national product, Canada, 1870–1976: Some implications for Canadian development', in S.L. Engerman and R.E. Gallman (ed.), *Long-Term Factors in American Economic Growth*, University of Chicago Press, Chicago, IL, pp. 9–94.

Urquhart, M.C., and Buckley, K.A.H. (1983) *Historical Statistics of Canada* (2nd edn), Macmillan, Toronto, ON.

US Bureau of the Census (1933) *Census of Retail Distribution, 1929*, Government Printing Office, Washington, DC.

US Bureau of the Census (1975) *Historical Statistics of the United States*, Government Printing Office, Washington, DC.

US Bureau of the Census (1983) *Statistical Abstract of the United States*, Government Printing Office, Washington, DC.

US Bureau of the Census (2012) *Annual Retail Trade Survey Historical Data*, available online: www.census.gov/retail/arts/historic_releases.html.

Vance, S.S., and Scott, R.V. (1994) *Wal-Mart: A History of Sam Walton's Retail Phenomenon*, Twayne, New York.

Venkatesan, R., Kumar, V., and Ravishanker, N. (2007) 'The impact of customer-firm interactions on customer channel adoption duration', *Journal of Marketing*, 71/2, 114–32.

Vernon, R. (1959) *The Changing Economic Function of the Central City*, Committee for Economic Development, New York.

Walden, K. (1989) 'Speaking modern: Language, culture, and hegemony in grocery window displays, 1887–1920', *Canadian Historical Review*, 70/3, 285–310.

Wind, Y., and Mahajan, V. (2002) 'Convergence marketing', *Journal of Interactive Marketing*, 16/2, 64–79.

Wood, S. (2008) 'Reinterpreting the great U.S. department store bankruptcies of the 1980s: A catalyst to strategic structural change', *Journal of Management History*, 14/4, 404–23.

Worthy, J.C. (1984) *Shaping an American Institution: Robert E. Wood and Sears Roebuck*, New American Library, New York.

Wright, C.J. (1992) 'The most prominent rendezvous of the feminine toronto: Eaton's College Street and the organization of shopping in Toronto: 1920–1950', unpublished PhD thesis, University of Toronto.

Xu, W. (2007) 'The market structure of the U.S. retail industry: 1984–2003', unpublished Ph.D. thesis, Purdue University, West Lafayette, IN.

9

The study of British retail history
Progress and agenda[1]

Andrew Alexander

Introduction

The importance and indeed attraction of the history of retailing is illustrated by the current interest shown by the mass media, with, for example, a number of TV series portraying aspects of retailing and shopping in bygone periods. Alongside period dramas like ITV's *Mr Selfridge*, based on the life of Harry Gordon Selfridge and his London department store in the early twentieth century, factual histories such as the BBC's series on the lives and work of *Shopgirls*, presented by historian Pamela Cox, with accompanying book (Cox and Hobley, 2014), provide the interested viewer with insights into the history of the retail sector and those who worked in it.

Researchers interested in the history of retailing can gain further insight from new business histories of some of the country's larger and well-known retailing businesses. Examples include those of Tesco (Ryle, 2013), The Co-operative Group (Wilson *et al.*, 2013), and shoe manufacturer and retailer Clarks (Palmer, 2013). New research is also helping us to develop our understanding of far less well known firms. For example, Tyler's (2014) study of the development of the multiple (chain store) corn merchant Sanders Bros., the store network of which grew to 263 stores by 1937, and of its demise in the first half of the 1950s, helps in part to address the longstanding criticism of survivor bias in the study of business history (Jones, 2008). Similarly, studies such as Heal's (2014) history of Sir Ambrose Heal – a designer, manufacturer and retailer of furniture – point to an increased interest in a wider variety of trades among academics concerned with the history of the retail sector, a theme returned to later in this chapter. This greater academic interest is also reflected in the volumes of a specialist book series on the history of retailing and consumption published by Ashgate, by the journals the *Journal of Historical Research in Marketing* (first published by Emerald in 2009) and the *History of Retailing and Consumption* (first published by Taylor & Francis in 2015), and by the CHORD conference series organised by the University of Wolverhampton.

Many of the business histories mentioned above draw upon archival sources, and the custodians of a number of archives related to the retail industry are seeking to enhance accessibility to their collections. In the case of Marks and Spencer, for example, the archive was opened to the public following its relocation to the University of Leeds. The digitization of sources and the publication of online catalogues are also improving accessibility. The catalogue of the archive of grocery retailer J. Sainsbury became available online in 2014, following the earlier digitization and uploading to the internet of the company's in-house magazine. Of course many retailers, including Britain's largest, Tesco, have no comparable business archives. However, in the case of Tesco, a collection of oral histories commissioned by the firm is now available to the public as part of the British Library's Sound Archive, and offers useful material for both business and social historians alike.

Given the level of activity and interest in the history of retailing at present, the invitation to write a chapter reviewing current progress and debates in British retail history in the modern period seems timely. Previous reviews of work in the field exist, of course (e.g. Shaw, 1992; Alexander and Akehurst, 1999; Benson and Ugolini, 2003; Tadajewski and Jones, 2014), and it is widely accepted that academic study of the history of retailing is now no longer as 'under-valued and under-explored' as was argued with some justification in a review of the field towards the end of the last millennium (Alexander and Akehurst, 1999, 1). A quick overview of the more recent literature on retail history reveals that the kaleidoscope of perspectives and approaches remarked upon in a previous review remains (Shaw, 1992). Indeed the disciplines contributing to the debate now extend beyond those such as economics, history, business and management studies and geography, all widely mentioned in past reviews of the field, to include contributions from disciplinary and subject areas such as English, cultural studies and design studies. The inherently multidisciplinary nature of the field continues to create opportunities for new debate and for the reassessment of existing arguments, as well as the incorporation of new methodologies. Nonetheless, there remains a concern that insufficient truly interdisciplinary studies will result in a failure to exploit potential synergies between approaches.

This chapter focuses in particular upon some of the more recent research on retailing history in the modern era, and predominantly after 1850. Even within this remit it is necessarily selective; for example, it does not consider the history of retail banking (see Newton, 2009, for a discussion of this sector in the twentieth century). In terms of developing an understanding of geographical context, this chapter is best read alongside others in the volume, including Barry Boothman's work on North American retail history (Chapter 8) and the contributions on country-specific marketing histories, especially Chapter 17 on British marketing history. That said, this does not mean that the chapter is narrow in terms of the debates encountered. First, whilst the focus is largely on studies of the history of retailing in the period after 1850, a period that witnessed the rapid growth of large-scale retailers such as the multiple and department store firms, the chapter begins with a brief consideration of recent research into the history of retailing in the period before 1850, and particularly that focused on retailing during the long eighteenth century. This is a vibrant area of research, and is important to our understanding of the degree of both continuity and change between retailing in this period and that which provides the main focus of this chapter. Second, the study of the retail sector, including but not only in relation to historical analysis, has benefited from a surge of interest in the theme of consumption among academics across a range of disciplines, opening up new lines of enquiry and also new and sometimes competing interpretations of how we should frame the study of retail history. Third, an analysis of British retail history must also include a consideration of the influence of the processes of internationalization upon the sector, a theme considered in more detail later in the chapter.

Early modern and modern retailing: continuities and changes

A now established theme within the literature is that earlier studies of the retail industry often inadequately reflected and addressed the extent and modern characteristics of the retail system in the period before 1850. That shop-based retailing, including that of petty retailers, had developed to a far greater extent and in a wider diversity of trades in eighteenth-century England than had previously been acknowledged was demonstrated by Mui and Mui (1989). They highlighted regional variations in the level of shop development and argued that the practices of these retailers were more innovative than hitherto acknowledged. More recent studies have sought to provide further detail and explanation as to the development of fixed-shop retailing at both the inter-urban and intra-urban scale (see e.g. Stobart and Hann, 2004; Stobart, 2014; Walsh, 2014).

Turning to the debate on the characteristics of retail practice, Cox's (2000) study of retailing in the period before 1820 provides considerable evidence to challenge the perception of retailing at this time as being somewhat primitive. Exploring retailing in the eighteenth century, she identifies increasing adoption of practices previously more associated with later periods; available sources suggest that many shops were increasing in size and in the sophistication of their interior design and layout, with glazed shop windows becoming more common (Cox and Walsh, 2000; see also Edwards, 2005; Riello, 2006). These changes at once reflected and encouraged new practices of retail salesmanship. Retailers often relied upon handbills and trade cards to promote their shops, although it seems that an increasing volume of printed newspaper advertising, particularly of branded goods, had the effect of encouraging fixed price and cash sales in some areas of trade, another practice hitherto more commonly associated with retailing in later historical periods (Cox and Walsh, 2000; Walsh, 2000).

The interest in exploring the intersections between consumption and retailing defines many of the recent studies of retailing in the period before 1850. Consequently, most display a broader remit than typical business or marketing histories. They can provide valuable insight into the development of the retail sector for, as Cowan (2012, 252) observes,

> it has become increasingly clear to historians and social theorists that the places where consumption took place, or where consumer desires were stimulated, and the social milieux in which consumers were located are just as important to understand as the actual acts of consumption.

Riello's (2006) analysis of the retailing and consumption of footwear in the eighteenth century is perhaps characteristic of this approach. Exploring the theme of consumers' attitudes and behaviours, and related arguments on the existence of a marketing concept in the late eighteenth and early nineteenth century, he suggests: '[t]he history of retailing is no longer the historical analysis of practices, shops, or products. It appears, instead, as the historical investigation of the rationality and strategic actions that influenced consumers, producers, and retailers' (Riello, 2006, 91, 92). His study illustrates how the retailing of footwear began to be transformed long before its mechanized mass production, with the emergence in London from the mid-1730s of new 'shoe warehouses' selling to consumers. The latter traded alongside more traditional outlets that retained the link between production and distribution and still dominated the marketplace, adapting to meet the challenge of the increased competition (Riello, 2006). The early decades of the nineteenth century witnessed a marked rise in the number of shoe shops, and at the top end of the market craft skills and knowledge were used to establish retailer identity in the market, part of what

Riello terms 'the invention of tradition' (p. 103). Turning to the grocery trade, Stobart's (2013) study *Sugar and Spice* seeks to provide an integrated analysis of the grocery trade in England, from merchant to consumer via retailer, in the period from the middle of the seventeenth to the early nineteenth century. He shows how the increased trade in imported goods like sugar, tobacco, tea and coffee had a significant effect in strengthening the retail sector. Stobart argues that the growth in the trade of these goods provided an important complement to grocers' established stock, although it did not necessitate or bring about a fundamental transformation of the sector as has previously been suggested (Stobart, 2013, 64). Again, we see debates on notions of continuity and change, with new retailing practices underpinned by established virtues of trust, service, reputation and respectability (Stobart, 2013).

Some studies of the early modern period seek to explain the significance of the changes in the retail sector that they identify to our understanding of the longer term development of the retail industry. For example, Stobart and Hann (2004) argue that the eighteenth century acts as a bridge between the traditional and the modern in retailing. Mitchell (2014), studying a range of retailing types, including itinerant, fixed shop and market trading, argues that the evolution of retailing was more fragmented and fractured in the century and a half before 1850 than some of the literature suggests. Identifying what he considers to be evidence of some radical changes in retailing in the decades after the 1820s, he suggests that the middle decades of the nineteenth century should be reinstated as a key watershed in the history of retailing: 'This is not because earlier retailing was in any way primitive', but it was 'essentially structured to meet the needs of a commercial rather than an industrial society' (p. 11). Mitchell (2014) adopts some of the language of retail innovation and change that is perhaps more commonplace among studies of more recent periods of retail history, an approach which offers at least the potential for more truly comparative analyses.

The development of British retailing since 1850

Large-scale and small-scale retailing

As has been widely commented upon, Jefferys's (1954) *Retail Trading in Britain 1850–1950* has had a significant impact upon the subsequent study of the history of retailing, and helps to explain much of the focus on large-scale institutional types such as the multiple, co-operative and department store retailer.

Historical analysis of each of these has enjoyed something of an uplift since the mid-1990s, again stimulated in part by the greater interest in the subject of consumption. The department store, like the co-operative movement discussed below, has been subject to particularly wide-ranging thematic attention. As Crossick and Jaumain (1999, 35) observe, in many ways the department store represents a means to explore cultural and social, as well as economic, change in Europe, noting that at times one may feel that one 'is learning more about the place of the department store in contemporary discourse than about what went on in the department store itself'. The breadth of approaches can be seen, for example, by contrasting Lancaster's (1995) historical survey of the British department store, with its focus on the business and social history of this type of retail institution, with Rappaport's (2000) study of the place of the department store in the creation of Victorian London's West End as a shopping centre that involved a 'reinterpretation of public life, the economy and consumption, and class and gender ideology' (Rappaport, 2000, 7).

Recent work by Scott and Walker (2012) provides new perspectives on what went on in the inter-war department store with regard to issues of retail management. In a comparative analysis of US and British department stores, they utilize contemporary survey data to reveal how British retailers were quick to embrace the 'retail managerial revolution' and enjoyed high returns on their investments to improve management systems and processes. In a related study they examine the importance of advertising and promotion to the prosperity of many British department store retailers seeking to establish their store brands in the minds of consumers in a bid to stave off increased domestic competition from the multiples (Scott and Walker, 2010). Advertising spending, they argue, was most significant among those department stores located in the centre of larger towns and cities and reliant on drawing trade from an extensive catchment area, whilst the promotional activities of suburban stores and those in market towns were more focused upon display and hence were more like those of their multiple retailer competitors (Scott and Walker, 2010, 1125).

Multiple retailers, defined by Jefferys (1954) as firms, other than department stores and co-operative societies, with ten or more retail establishments, have also been subject to more recent historical analyses, including economic-historical and more cultural interpretations (Morelli, 1998; Winship, 2000). Some studies prioritize a geographical perspective, building upon earlier work which sought to identify the effects of new retail institutional types like the multiples on the changing patterns of retailing in the Victorian city (see e.g. Shaw and Wild, 1979). For example, Alexander et al. (2003) used sector and firm-level data to illustrate regional variations in the development of multiple retailing in England in the grocery and provisions and variety store trades, in the period between 1890 and 1939. They conclude that marked regional variations existed in the development of the store estates of multiples in these trades, with consequent spatial variations in both the economic and social impacts resulting from this transformation of retailing. A related study (Alexander et al., 1999) focuses on evidence from the inter-war period to further understanding of the disruptive competition of the multiples in various retail trades, and of its impacts on independent retailers in particular. It explores the notion of competition in three inter-related dimensions: locational competition, the enlargement and improvement of store space, and the use of advertising and promotion to establish the store brand in consumers' perception or 'mind-space'. Subsequent research has explored aspects of the use of multiple retailing techniques by firms selling a range of consumer goods and services, including its use by public houses (Mutch, 2006), and chain cafés and restaurants (Shaw et al., 2006). It also focuses on the effects on shopping of multiple retailers' marketing practices, an example of such research being Walsh's assessment of the activities of F.W. Woolworth in Northern Ireland and the Irish Republic (Walsh, 2014).

Turning to co-operative retailing, the Rochdale Equitable Pioneers Society, established in 1844 in the northern English mill town of Rochdale in Lancashire, provided a blueprint for subsequent consumer co-operative societies (see Wilson et al., 2013). The co-operative business model remained distinct from that of its competitors, representing a member-owned model based upon voluntary and democratic notions. Allied to this is its structure of local and regional societies with independent identities, supported by central co-operative bodies. In part this helps to explain the commercial opportunities for the movement, but also some of the challenges that it has encountered in much of its more recent history. The tensions between local societies and central bodies, and between the central bodies themselves, have on occasion proved an impediment to change. Just how much of an impediment is made clear in Wilson et al.'s (2013) substantial new business history of the Co-operative Group, published to mark its 150th anniversary. Their analysis shows how tensions and rivalries served to derail several major initiatives designed to adapt and reform co-operative commercial activities in the face of growing competition (see also Black, 2009, on the Cooperative Independent Commission). In the final chapters of their study, Wilson *et al.* (2013) consider evidence of what has subsequently transpired to be a rather short-lived renaissance in the commercial fortunes of the group after 1997. By way of explanation, they point towards revitalized leadership, an aggressive strategy to merge previously separate and often underperforming parts of the business, new organizational initiatives in the retail supply chain and elsewhere, and new marketing activities based on notions of ethical trading. More generally, co-operative principles mean that the movement has been the focus of attention for historical research into the interconnections between retailing practices and matters of consumer protection (e.g. Robertson, 2009), and of wider debates in consumerism.

Co-operative societies' share of the retail market is estimated to have reached as much as 7 per cent by 1900, and to have risen to 9 per cent by 1920 (Jefferys, 1954). Yet national market share figures mask clear regional variations. As Purvis (1999) revealed in his historical-geographical analysis of co-operative development, early success in growing membership in industrial and mining centres, and some smaller and medium-sized urban centres, contrasted with the situation in larger cities like Manchester and Birmingham. Only by the 1920s did the movement become more firmly established in London, thanks to a process of amalgamation that spawned a few larger societies (Purvis, 1999). By 1950 the co-operative accounted for as much as 12 per cent of total retail sales (Jefferys, 1954), but its zenith would soon pass; its market share had fallen back to 10.8 per cent by 1961 (Wilson *et al.*, 2013) and several decades of decline were to follow, with market share declining to 4 per cent by 1994 (Walton, 2009). Membership also suffered a general decline from the late 1960s. In a recent volume of essays on the co-operative movement, Walton argues that the resulting spate of society amalgamations, their new strategies of retail development including large out-of-centre superstores, together with the abandonment of the dividend, damaged co-operative societies' identity and broke the often hard-earned link between societies and the localities that had spawned them (Walton, 2009, 23, 24).

The movement suffered a decline in market share in both food retailing and non-food trades, despite being at the forefront of radical innovations including self-service grocery retailing in the immediate post-war years (Alexander, 2008; Shaw and Alexander, 2008). With regard to the non-food trades, Gurney (2012) highlights the challenges that a growing mass consumer culture in inter-war Britain posed to the co-operative movement. He observes that, in categories such as furniture and furnishings, radios, gramophones and vacuum cleaners, categories that he sees as being at the vanguard of the new consumer culture of inter-war Britain, co-operative retailing performed with ominous weakness compared to its department store and multiple retailer rivals (Gurney, 2012, 912). In part, this reflected business and commercial weaknesses, which persisted despite some progressive attempts to improve the design and hence desirability of its durable goods, and to enhance the salesmanship connected to them (Whitworth, 2009). As Gurney (2005, 963) argues, the post-war co-operative movement also endured deep divisions among activists concerning the economy and the culture of co-operation which would impact upon its ability to recruit new consumers.

In contrast to the renewed interest in the study of the department store, multiples and co-operatives, the historical development of British mail order retailing received little in the way of new and detailed attention from academics before the work of Coopey, O'Connell and Porter (see Coopey *et al.*, 2005). They illustrate how mail order retailers operated largely on the basis of credit provision, and how they were organized through a system of often spare-time neighbourhood-based agents, at least until enhanced computerization led to the 'depersonalization' of this form of selling. Consequently, they argue that 'retailers in this sector were not driven solely by the logic of scale and scope but by the need to mould their operations onto the contours of working class life' (Coopey et al., 2005, 232). They characterize the period between 1950 and 1980 as the heyday of traditional mail order retailing, offering an increasing array of consumer goods to the sections of the working class that were enjoying greater affluence following the post-war austerity. The percentage of total UK retail sales by value accounted for by mail order retailing is estimated to have risen from less than 1 per cent in 1950 to 5.3 per cent (and 9.2 per cent of total non-food retail sales) by 1979 (Coopey et al., 2005). Turning to more recent times, Coopey (2012) suggests that the rise of internet retailing has left the mail order companies struggling to adapt, although rationalization through mergers and mail order firms' own online strategies have led to some signs of reinvigoration.

Despite the growth of large-scale retailing organizations described above, smaller scale retailing, whether from fixed shops or otherwise, remained a significant component of the retail landscape after 1850 and accounted for about two-thirds of total retail sales in 1939 (Jefferys, 1954). Independent fixed-shop retailing was itself a very varied activity, encompassing the many 'small shops' as well as the more substantial, high-end outlets in urban centres, and also the village shop – a retail form that has received much-needed consideration of late (see Bailey, 2015). As Winstanley (1983) observes, modification and adaptation meant that the survival of the private shopkeeper might well have surprised Edwardian commentators. Such adaptations reflected concerns over the mass of small 'family shops' serving the growing if irregular working-class market, as well those over large-scale retail institutions such as the multiples, co-operatives and department stores (Winstanley, 1983; Hosgood, 1989).

Itinerant trading also remained an important part of the retailing mix, with data suggesting an increase in the number of traders per capita over the second half of the nineteenth century (see Benson and Ugolini, 2010). Similarly, markets were still significant in the retailing of food, and they represented an integral feature of many rapidly growing industrial centres, providing a wider range of typically low-cost commodities than is often recognized (Hodson, 1998). Exchange beyond the shop, though, was more diverse than this and could extend beyond the retail sector itself, as illustrated by contributions to a special issue of the *Journal of Historical Research in Marketing* in 2010. Richmond (2010) explores the development of the church jumble sale, noting how they were quickly integrated into the budgeting strategies of some poorer consumers. Charitable enterprises of this sort represented one less formal channel for sale and exchange; another quite different one existed for the illicit trading of goods (Toplis, 2010).

Changing relations and the altering balance of power between different types of retailers, and between them and other members of the supply chain, can be identified throughout the period, in debates over the politics of shopkeeping. Retailer associations emerged in a bid to protect the perceived interests of differing classes of retailer from the effects of horizontal competition (see e.g. Hosgood, 1992), and there were occasional attempts to pass legislation. Analysis of the case of the failed Balfour Bill of 1937, a bill that was intended to limit the effects on independent retailers of competition from heavily capitalized large-scale retail businesses in inter-war Britain, reveals how fracturing among the ranks of the independent retailers could often weaken their position. Consequently the state saw no significant movement in favour of regulation (Shaw et al., 2000).

The situation was rather different in relation to vertical competition between the retailer and the manufacturers. Debates surrounding the effects of Resale Price Maintenance (RPM), which extended across a widening array of goods in the first part of the twentieth century, and of its abolition in 1964, provide a critical insight into the changing relationships between suppliers, wholesalers and retailers. Mercer (2014), for example, provides a new and detailed evaluation of its impact across a range of retail trades in the middle years of the twentieth century. She argues that the operation of individual RPM in the period between 1956 and 1964 in itself did not subdue competition in the retail trades to the extent that was sometimes claimed. Its abolition intensified earlier trends: 'Multiples could promote their own brands, brands that marginalized minor manufacturer brands, and squeezed all suppliers through manipulating brands and through pressure for buyer discounts, a process accentuated by physical expansion' (Mercer, 2014, 159). Bailey (2011) explores debates on retailer power and RPM in his case study of the relationships between confectionery goods manufacturer Cadbury and its retailer and wholesaler clients in the period leading up to and immediately following the abolition of RPM. He reveals how the balance of power in the confectionery supply chain shifted to the multiples and particularly to supermarket retailers during the 1960s, identifying this as a process that was already under way before RPM's abolition. Wholesalers and smaller independent retailers consequently found themselves in a less favourable position.

A focus on a widening range of retailers and their supply chains

Recent scholarship on the history of retailing illustrates an increasing concern with understanding the development of retailing across a breadth of retail trades. This section begins with an assessment of some of the latest research on two of the main consumer goods groups, food and clothing, which are estimated to have accounted for more than 58 per cent and 19 per cent of total retail sales respectively by 1900, and which still combined to account for 59 per cent of total retail sales some 50 years later – the difference being the result of a fall in the share of food as a proportion of total retail sales (Jefferys, 1954). This section then turns to examining studies that contribute to our understanding of the history of retailing in a number of other commodity groups, reflecting a trend in a literature that now encompasses trades as varied as the retailing of medicines (Anderson, 2006) and that of domestic furnishings (Edwards, 2005). The discussion not only highlights the diversity of retail activity in the modern period, but also underpins the preceding discussion by revealing how differing types of businesses have competed and occasionally collaborated in order to win a share of changing consumer markets.

Food and clothing

That the grocery trade remains an important focus of attention in studies of retail history is understandable given both the scale of the market, and that of some of the leading firms within the trade. Analyses of the grocery trade highlight varying aspects of the structural change in the market, particularly the growth in importance of the multiple retailers. Some of this has taken on a geographical dimension, as in the aforementioned studies of multiple retailing in which the grocery trades represent a significant focus. Economic historians have also explored this structural change. Morelli (1998), for example, has sought to qualify a perspective that ties the increasingly oligopolistic market conditions of 1970s Britain, in which a small number of multiples enjoyed a rapid growth in their share of food sales, to the incremental evolutionary development of the firms themselves. He points to the years between 1958 and 1964 as being of fundamental importance as the grocery multiples sought to redefine their competitive environment against the backdrop of complex changes in the market, including the breakdown of RPM in food retailing, and conflicts over the changing balance of price and non-price competition (Morelli, 1998).

More recently there has also been a focus within the academic literature on detailing the development of critical innovations within the grocery trade, with particular attention having been given to the development of self-service retailing and the related supermarket format trading in the post-war decades (e.g. Bowlby, 2000; Shaw *et al.*, 2004). Studies consider issues of management and decision-making control in the operating of such formats (Alexander, 2015) and explore consumers' reactions to the changing retail landscape (Usherwood, 2000; Alexander *et al.*, 2008; Bailey *et al.*, 2010), including some deleterious outcomes for retailers, such as shoplifting (Nell *et al.*, 2011). The significance of these innovations can also be identified in developments in the wider retail grocery supply chain that reflect a changing balance of power between retailers and their suppliers in favour of the former. Godley and Williams (2009), for example, reveal how Sainsbury's sought to instigate and control collaborative relationships in the British poultry industry during the 1950s and 1960s, becoming a driving force behind the transformation of intensive rearing methods and of factory processing of poultry in Britain. They argue that this influence was vital to Sainsbury's as it enabled them to control the standardization of poultry products that was necessary as the firm transformed its retail estate from counter to self-service stores. More widely, they suggest that the learning derived from this experience of extending their influence along the supply chain would be an important element underpinning the firm's success during the 1980s (Godley and Williams, 2009). The growing power of retailers in the supply chain can also be seen in relation to the often overlooked wholesaling sector, and the work of Quinn and Sparks (2007) provides much-needed insight into the historical development of that sector through an international comparison of the situation in Britain and Ireland from the 1930s onwards.

Retailing in the clothing trades has also remained a significant focus of study, both in terms of recent business histories (e.g. Worth, 2007, on Marks and Spencer), and wider analyses of trends in retailing and consumption, including those of the menswear (Ugolini, 2007) and childrenswear trades (Rose, 2010). Ugolini's (2007) analysis of menswear retailers, and particularly independent tailors, in the period 1880–1939 provides insight into the strategies and tactics they adopted as they sought to cope with the challenges of rapidly changing market conditions brought about both by wartime conditions, and by increasing competition between different types of menswear retailers during the inter-war decades. In particular she explores the effect of the rise of the multiple concerns, and the impacts on the independents of very successful businesses like Burtons, which focused on the sale of made-to-measure factory-produced suits. Ugolini also examines the image of the retailers in the eyes of their patrons, trade press commentators and other interested observers, and explores how some portrayed the practices of the independent bespoke tailor as anachronistic in comparison to those of the multiples. The trade press stressed the importance of menswear retailers adopting modern practices of advertising, window display and other merchandising, and salesmanship, and of highlighting the individuality of their store and the personal service offered (Ugolini, 2007). However, as Ugolini observes, the larger multiples with their financial muscle were themselves prioritising improvements in shop display, advertising and salesmanship among other practices.

Honeyman's (2000) analysis of the Leeds clothing industry provides further insight into the growth of many of these larger multiples, the city's vertically integrated firms being responsible for the manufacture and retailing of over 60 per cent of all suits sold in Britain for several decades from the 1930s onwards. She also charts the challenges they faced in post-war Britain, with its markedly changed demand for men's fashion, arguing that these same firms were typically too reluctant to switch away from manufacturing and instead concentrate more on retailing, despite clear market signals that they should do so. Multiple retailers were also to play a more significant role in the distribution of women's and girl's clothing during the inter-war period and thereafter. In the hosiery and knitwear segment of the trade, in which the influence of multiple retailing practices became more quickly established, some manufacturers vertically integrated into retailing and others established what would evolve into large-scale and long-term contracts for sales direct to retail, such as that, for example, between Corah & Son of Leicester and Marks and Spencer (Chapman, 2002).

Consumer durables and other household goods

The growth in consumption of a widening range of consumer durables towards the end of the nineteenth century, and particularly during the first half of the twentieth century, and the stimulus that this provided to the retailing of such goods, has been the subject of another body of research that contributes to our understanding. Godley's (2006) analysis of the British retailing operation of the US firm Singer in the period 1850–1920 explores the development of a direct sales operation to target the family market, with canvassers working out of retail stores and operating door to door, demonstrating the sewing machines and collecting orders and weekly payments in people's homes. Subsequently the roles of canvasser and collector were separated to enable a check to be placed on the quality of accounts being opened. Godley shows how the success of the system was reflected both in a tripling of UK sales between 1875 and 1884, and the rapid expansion of the supporting network of retail outlets, which numbered some 303 by 1885. A further revised canvasser-collector system was introduced during the 1880s in order to better control costs, with branch managers supervising the transactions (Godley, 2006).

Scott (2008) reveals a generally similar approach to the retailing of electric vacuum cleaners in the 1930s – part of his wider project to explore the retailing and consumption of consumer goods in early twentieth-century Britain. He explores methods for the recruitment, training, management and daily activities of door-to-door salesmen in US manufacturer Hoover's British operation, which by 1939 was claimed to represent the UK's largest salaried outside sales force. Hoover developed relationships with established retailers, including major department store retailers such as Selfridges and Harrods. This enabled the promotion of the Hoover product, reduced the firm's distribution costs, and passed the management of hire purchase (HP) agreements on to these retailers (Scott, 2008). Yet Scott argues that, ultimately, the firm's sales management failed to develop an incentive system to reconcile the twin objectives of motivating salesmen to maximize sales whilst limiting any damaging opportunistic behaviour, leading to consumer resistance and, he suggests, resulting in long-term damage to the image of door-to-door selling in the minds of many consumers (Scott, 2008, 787).

Furniture represented a highly prioritized consumer good for working-class and lower-middle-class consumers alike during the inter-war years, and the extension of the market among lower-income groups saw the rapid growth of the sector (Scott, 2009). Department stores, and particularly the new multiple operations, which catered more to the demand from the growing working-class market, were significant players in the market, with the co-operative becoming more involved in the retailing of furniture from the 1930s (Edwards, 2005). Scott (2009) analyses the innovative marketing formula of multiples in that part of the trade that was typically reliant upon offering HP agreements to working-class customers, and the national advertising campaigns seeking to legitimize the use of HP for buying furniture and showcasing the lifestyle benefits of such purchases. He concludes, 'the HP furniture multiples enabled many households to realize a higher standard of material comfort and display, if at a substantial cost' (Scott, 2009, 826).

The importance of symbolic meaning and consumer lifestyle aspirations are also identified in Carnevali and Newton's (2013) study of a less widely diffused good, the piano. They argue that improvements in production, and increased competition among both manufacturers and specialized musical instrument retailers, resulted in greater choice and lower prices in the retail market, at least from the 1860s onwards. From the 1890s, department store retailers such as Harrods, Whiteleys, and later Selfridges, began to transform the retailing of both new and second-hand pianos, being joined subsequently by the Co-operative Wholesale Society (Carnevali and Newton, 2013). Carnevali and Newton illustrate how manufacturers and retailers alike used the symbolic meaning of the piano to promote the product, and sought to use notions of brand value in an attempt to tap into many middle-class consumers' concerns over social status.

Retailing and the creative industries

Studies of the retailing of the products and services of the creative industries, as well as the impact of industries such as advertising (see Beard, Chapter 11) and product and packaging design (Whitworth, 2009; Trunk, 2011) on the retail sector itself, represent important areas of more recent exploration within the stream of historical analysis. As Friedman and Jones (2011) observe, these industries are not represented in the business history literature to the extent that their importance warrants. Two examples of recent work are considered here, related to the couture and music entertainment industries, which are illustrative of a wider concern with understanding the relationships between the creative industries and the retail sector.

Whilst much of the interest in the history of fashion surrounds its cultural meaning, recent work also reveals the potential to explore the clothing fashion industry from a business and economic history perspective, despite the challenges involved in studying empirically a trade that has evidently left behind comparatively few documentary sources (Giertz-Mårtenson, 2012). This body of work includes a 2012 special issue of *Business History*, the editors of which stress that 'the fashion business depends on more than the creative genius of a designer-couturier. It instead draws sustenance from a complex institutional network' (Polese and Blaszczyk, 2012, 8). Font's (2012) study of international couture in the period 1880–1920 highlights the connectivity in the network between designers and retailers. She explores the business activities of Parisian couture houses, which at the time were establishing international branches and courting alliances with British and American department store retailers.

Turning to the retailing of a quite different output of the creative industries, Tennent's (2013) analysis of the changing distribution of music between 1950 and 1976 reveals how the big four UK-based record manufacturers, EMI, Decca, Pye and Phillips, each developed their wholesale distribution activities in the later 1950s and 1960s. In this way, he argues, they enhanced their control of the supply chain through exclusive distribution and the imposition of stricter ordering terms for retailers as the threat of the abolition of RPM in the trade increased. The retail sector they supplied was itself changing, with specialist record stores becoming more important throughout the 1950s and 1960s, the selling of records having previously been frequently undertaken through electrical shops (Tennent, 2013). Tennent explains how, in the later 1960s, firms like Pye and EMI integrated further into retailing, first by acquiring record shops, which in the case of EMI would lead to the establishment of the nationwide chain of HMV outlets, and then by overseeing the display and stocking of full-price records in supermarkets and stores such as Woolworths.

The internationalization of retailing

Even a cursory reflection on the discussion in the preceding sections reveals that the historical development of retailing in Britain, at least since the last decades of the nineteenth century, has taken place within a context of the growing internationalization of retailing. Such internationalization encompasses both foreign direct investment such as that by Hoover and Woolworth, and also the transfer and adaptation of innovations observed in other retail markets, such as, for example, the principles of self-service retailing and supermarket format trading from North America (de Grazia, 2005). Consequently, it is important to consider the character, extent, influences and directions of such internationalization, and also how the literature on the internationalization of retailing illustrates attempts to develop theoretical debate within the subject of retail history.

In relation to the British market, Fletcher and Godley's (2000) study of foreign direct investment (FDI) in retailing during the period 1850–1962 reveals that it grew through the twentieth century. They identify that this investment occurred in three broad waves that each display some temporal concentration, comprising first luxury retail FDI, particularly before 1900, then consumer durables particularly in the latter decades of the nineteenth and first decades of the twentieth centuries, and thirdly consumer non-durables, which represented a more significant component of activity in the subsequent decades. Importantly, their analysis of the firms investing in British retailing reveals that early waves of FDI were dominated not by retailers, as has typically been the case in more recent phases of the internationalization of the retailing industry of course, but more so by foreign manufacturers (Fletcher and Godley, 2000; Godley, 2003). As discussed above, this provided opportunities for existing retailers to work with these incoming firms, such as was the case for the department stores in the durable consumer goods trades. Fletcher and Godley argue that, with the exception of a half-dozen firms, it was not until the 1950s that foreign investment was undertaken by a large number of firms that can be identified as being principally retailers (Fletcher and Godley, 2000, 58).

Similarly, British firms were involved in overseas retailing ventures, as described by Alexander (2011) in his assessment of the characteristics of such activities during the first half of the twentieth century. Again, what is notable is the overseas investment in retailing by businesses whose primary focus often lay beyond the retail sector. Such businesses included trading companies like Booker Brothers, McConnell and Company and the United Africa Company, which were principally engaged in trading in primary products in colonial markets (Alexander, 2011, 535; Godley and Hang, 2012). The activities of such trading companies, and their responses to the changes leading up to and following decolonization, have been the focus of research highlighting the need to understand the rich interconnection between the economic, cultural and political spheres if we are to fully comprehend the evolution of the retailing enterprises that these companies established (e.g. Decker, 2007; Murillo, 2011).

The importance of analyses of the historical development of international retailing lies not only in their empirical contribution to our understanding of the extent and characteristics of firms' activities, but also in the fact that they highlight the need for, and potential of, theoretical debate to enhance our understanding of the processes at hand. Attempts to situate and explain the phenomena of internationalization in relation to theoretical propositions, typically drawn from business management, has led to useful debate (see e.g. Godley and

Hang, 2012; Alexander, 2013) and prompted new empirical case-study research in the search for verification (see e.g. Doherty and Alexander, 2014).

Conclusion

The history of British retailing represents a vibrant research area, and one that has received a significant stimulus over the past 20 years from the surge in interest in matters related to consumption across many disciplinary areas. Arguably, the impact of this has been felt most strongly in relation to studies of retailing in the period before 1850, with the consequence that we now have far more insight into earlier retailing systems than was hitherto the case. Other recent research offers much-needed insight into the retailing of a wider range of consumer durable goods and the outputs of the creative industries. The retailing of such goods has previously been comparatively overlooked, despite their social and economic significance. Alongside this, the increased attention given to the changing relationships between retailers, manufacturers and wholesalers informs our understanding of retailers' increasing importance in the supply chain.

The wide range of disciplines contributing to our understanding of British retail history suggests that there will continue to be a diversity of both approaches applied and emerging research topics. From my own disciplinary perspective, I suggest four topic areas that are perhaps particularly worthy of further attention. First, whilst there have been welcome contributions more recently exploring the wider supply chain, there clearly remains scope for further enquiry into historical trends and their implications for the retail sector. One example of a topic for study in this context concerns the new organizational forms such as wholesaler voluntary groups and retailer buying groups that emerged in the grocery trade in the later 1950s. Second, more recently the issue of retail work has begun to attract more of the attention that it deserves (see e.g. the programme of the Annual CHORD Conference, 2014). Structural changes to the retail sector and the evolving commercial strategies of retail organizations such as those discussed in this chapter have had significant implications for the nature of retail work. Consequently, there is an opportunity to more fully synthesize contemporary debates on the evolving nature of retail work (see e.g. Bozkurt and Grugulis, 2011) with historical analyses of change in the sector (Alexander, 2015; Purvis, 2015). The third topic area particularly worthy of further study, the impact of developments in information technology on retailing practices, is more wide-ranging in scope, with its potential to fundamentally alter both the nature of retail work, and retailers' supply chain relations, both downstream with wholesalers and producers and upstream with consumers, including through internet retailing (Cortada, 2003). Finally, although some areas of research advance theoretical arguments in their contribution to retail history, perhaps most notably that concerned with the history of the internationalization of retailing, there remains a clear need, and indeed considerable opportunity, for more such theoretically informed debate.

Note

1 Most of the material considered in this chapter relates to the retail history of Britain but some sources consider retailing in the UK.

References

Alexander, A. (2008) 'Format development and retail change: Supermarket retailing and the London Co-operative Society', *Business History*, 50/4, 489–508.

Alexander, A. (2015) 'Decision-making authority in British supermarket chains', *Business History*, 57/4, 614–37.

Alexander, A., Benson, J., and Shaw, G. (1999) 'Action and reaction: Competition and the multiple retailer in 1930s Britain', *International Review of Retail, Distribution and Consumer Research*, 9/3, 245–59.

Alexander, A., Phillips, S., and Shaw, G. (2008) 'Retail innovation and shopping practices: Consumers' reactions to self-service retailing', *Environment and Planning A*, 40/9, 2204–21.

Alexander, A., Shaw, G., and Hodson, D. (2003) 'Regional variations in the development of multiple retailing in England, 1890–1939', in J. Benson and L. Ugolini (eds), *A Nation of Shopkeepers. Five Centuries of British Retailing*, I.B. Tauris & Co., London, pp. 127–54.

Alexander, N. (2011) 'British overseas retailing, 1900–60: International firm characteristics, market selections and entry modes', *Business History*, 53/4, 530–56.

Alexander, N. (2013) 'Retailing in international markets, 1900–2010: A response to Godley and Hang's "Globalisation and the evolution of international retailing: a comment on Alexander's 'British overseas retailing, 1900–1960'"', *Business History*, 55/2, 302–12.

Alexander, N., and Akehurst, G. (1999) 'Introduction: The emergence of modern retailing, 1750–1950', in N. Alexander and G. Akehurst (eds), *The Emergence of Modern Retailing 1750–1950*, Frank Cass, London, 1–15.

Anderson, S. (2006) 'From "bespoke" to "off-the-peg": Community pharmacists and the retailing and medicines in Great Britain 1900–1970', in L. Hill Curth (ed.), *From Physick to Pharmacology. Five Hundred Years of British Drug Retailing*, Ashgate, Aldershot, pp. 105–42.

Bailey, A.R. (2011) 'Regulating the supermarket in 1960s Britain: Exploring the changing relationship of food manufacturers and retailers through the Cadbury archive', *Business Archives*, 103 (Nov.), 1–24.

Bailey, A.R., Shaw, G., Alexander, A., and Nell, D. (2010) 'Consumer behaviour and the life course: Shopper reactions to self-service grocery shops and supermarkets in England c. 1947–75', *Environment and Planning A*, 42/6, 1496–1512.

Bailey, L.A. (2015) 'Squire, shopkeeper and staple food: The reciprocal relationship between the country house and the village shop in the late Georgian period', *History of Retailing and Consumption*, 1/1, 8–27.

Benson, J., and Ugolini, L. (2003) 'Introduction: Historians and the nation of shopkeepers', in J. Benson and L. Ugolini (eds), *A Nation of Shopkeepers: Five Centuries of British Retailing*, I.B. Tauris & Co., London, pp. 1–24.

Benson, J., and Ugolini, L. (2010) 'Beyond the shop: Problems and possibilities', *Journal of Historical Research in Marketing*, 2/3, 256–69.

Black, L. (2009) '"Trying to sell a parcel of politics with a parcel of groceries": The Co-operative Independent Commission (CIC) and consumerism in post-war Britain', in L. Black. and N. Robertson (eds), *Consumerism and the Co-operative Movement in Modern British History: Taking Stock*, Manchester University Press, Manchester, pp. 33–50.

Bowlby, R. (2000) *Carried Away: The Invention of Modern Shopping*, Faber & Faber, London.

Bozkurt, Ö., and Grugulis, I. (2011) 'Why retail work demands a closer look', in I. Grugulis and Ö. Bozkurt (eds), *Retail Work*, Palgrave Macmillan, Basingstoke, pp. 1–21.

Carnevali, F., and Newton, L. (2013) 'Pianos for the people: The manufacture, marketing and sale of pianos as consumer durables, 1850–1914', *Enterprise and Society*, 14/1, 37–70.

Chapman, S.D. (2002) *Hosiery and Knitwear: Four Centuries of Small-Scale Industry in Britain, c.1589–2000*, Oxford University Press, Oxford.

CHORD Conference Programme (2014) Retail Work: Historical Perspectives, 11 Sept., University of Wolverhampton, available online: www.wlv.ac.uk/research/research-institutes-and-centres/

centre-for-historical-research/centre-for-the-history-of-retailing-and-distribut/conferences-workshops--past-events/chord-conference-retail-work---historical-perspe (accessed June 2015).

Coopey, R. (2012) 'Mail order retailing in Britain since 1945: Credit, community and technology', in R. Jessen and L. Langer (eds), *Transformations of Retailing in Europe After 1945,* Ashgate, Aldershot, pp. 115–26.

Coopey, R., O'Connell, S., and Porter, D. (2005) *Mail Order Retailing in Britain: A Business and Social History,* Oxford University Press, Oxford.

Cortada, J.W. (2003) *Digital Hand: How Computers Changed the Work of American Manufacturing, Transportation, and Retail Industries,* Oxford University Press, Oxford.

Cowan, B. (2012) 'Public spaces, knowledge and sociability', in F. Trentmann (ed.), *The Oxford Handbook of the History of Consumption,* Oxford University Press, Oxford, pp. 251–66.

Cox, N. (2000) *The Complete Tradesman: A Study of Retailing, 1550–1820,* Ashgate, Aldershot.

Cox, N., and Walsh, C. (2000) '"Their shops are Dens, the buyer is their prey": Shop design and sale techniques', in N. Cox, *The Complete Tradesman: A Study of Retailing, 1550–1820,* Ashgate, Aldershot, pp. 76–115.

Cox, P., and Hobley, A. (2014) *Shopgirls: The True Story of Life behind the Counter,* Hutchinson, London.

Crossick, G., and Jaumain, S. (1999) 'The world of the department store: Distribution, culture and social change', in G. Crossick and S. Jaumain (eds), *Cathedrals of Consumption: The European Department Store 1850–1939,* Ashgate, Aldershot, pp,. 1–45.

Decker, S. (2007) 'Corporate legitimacy and advertising: British companies and the rhetoric of development in West Africa, 1950–1970', *Business History Review,* 81/1, 59–86.

de Grazia, V. (2005) *Irresistible Empire: America's Advance through Twentieth-Century Europe,* Belknap Press of Harvard University Press, London.

Doherty, A.M., and Alexander, N. (2014) 'Liberty in Paris: International retailing, 1889–1932', *Business History,* 57/4 485–511.

Edwards, C. (2005) *Turning Houses into Homes: A History of the Retailing and Consumption of Domestic Furnishings,* Ashgate, Aldershot.

Fletcher, S.R., and Godley, A. (2000) 'Foreign direct investment in British retailing, 1850–1962', *Business History,* 42/2, 43–62.

Font, L.M. (2012) 'International couture: The opportunities and challenges of expansion, 1880–1920', *Business History,* 54/1, 30–47.

Friedman, W.A., and Jones, G. (2011) 'Creative industries in history', *Business History Review,* 85, 237–44.

Giertz-Mårtenson, I. (2012) 'H&M – documenting the story of one of the world's largest fashion retailers', *Business History,* 54/1, 108–15.

Godley, A. (2003) 'Foreign multinationals and innovation in British retailing, 1850–1962', *Business History,* 45/1, 80–100.

Godley, A. (2006) 'Selling the sewing machine around the world: Singer's international marketing strategies, 1850–1920', *Enterprise and Society,* 7/2, 266–314.

Godley, A., and Hang, H. (2012) 'Globalisation and the evolution of international retailing: A comment on Alexander's "British overseas retailing, 1900–1960"', *Business History,* 54/4, 529–41.

Godley, A.C., and Williams, B. (2009) 'The chicken, the factory farm and the supermarket: The emergence of the modern poultry industry in Britain', in W. Belasco and R. Horowitz (eds), *Food Chains: From Farmyard to Shopping Cart,* University of Pennsylvania Press, Philadelphia, pp. 47–61.

Gurney, P. (2005) 'The battle of the consumer in postwar Britain', *Journal of Modern History,* 77/4, 956–87.

Gurney, P.J. (2012) 'Co-operation and the "new consumerism" in interwar England', *Business History,* 54/6, 905–24.

Heal, O.S. (2014) *Sir Ambrose Heal and the Heal Cabinet Factory 1897–1939,* Oblong Creative, Wetherby.

Hodson, D. (1998) '"The municipal store": Adaptation and development in the retail markets of nineteenth-century urban Lancashire', *Business History,* 40/4, 94–114.

Honeyman, K. (2000) *Well Suited: A History of the Leeds Clothing Industry, 1850–1990,* Oxford University Press, Oxford.

Hosgood, C.P. (1989) 'The "Pigmies of Commerce" and the working-class community: small Shopkeepers in England, 1870–1914', *Journal of Social History,* 22/3, 439–60.

Hosgood, C.P. (1992) 'A "Brave and Daring Folk"? Shopkeepers and trade associational life in Victorian and Edwardian England', *Journal of Social History,* 26/2, 285–308.

Jefferys, J.B. (1954) *Retail Trading in Britain 1850–1950,* Cambridge University Press, Cambridge.

Jones, G. (2008) 'Business archives and overcoming survivor bias', *Business Archives,* 97 (Nov.), 7–12.

Lancaster, B. (1995) *The Department Store: A Social History,* Leicester University Press, London.

Mercer, H. (2014) 'Retailer–supplier relationships before and after the Resale Prices Act, 1964: A turning point in British economic history?', *Enterprise and Society,* 15/1, 132–65.

Mitchell, I. (2014) *Tradition and Innovation in English Retailing, 1700 to 1850: Narratives of Consumption,* Ashgate, Aldershot.

Morelli, C. (1998) 'Constructing a balance between price and non-price competition in British multiple food retailing 1954–64', *Business History,* 40/2, 45–61.

Mui, H-C., and Mui, L.H. (1989) *Shops and Shopkeeping in Eighteenth Century England,* Routledge, London.

Murillo, B. (2011) '"The devil we know": Gold Coast consumers, local employees, and the United Africa Company, 1940–1960', *Enterprise and Society,* 12/2, 317–55.

Mutch, A. (2006) 'Public houses as multiple retailing: Peter Walker & Son, 1846–1914', *Business History,* 48/1, 1–19.

Nell, D., Phillips, S., Alexander, A., and Shaw, G. (2011) 'Helping yourself: Self-service grocery retailing and shoplifting in Britain, c.1950–1975', *Journal of Cultural and Social History,* 8/3, 371–91.

Newton, L. (2009) 'British retail banking in the twentieth century: Decline and renaissance in industrial lending', in R. Coopey and P. Lyth (eds), *Business in Britain in the Twentieth Century,* Oxford University Press, Oxford, pp. 189–224.

Palmer, M. (2013) *Clarks: Made to Last. The Story of Britain's Best-Known Shoe Firm,* Profile Books, London.

Polese, F., and Blaszczyk, R.L. (2012) 'Fashion forward: The business history of fashion', *Business History,* 54/1, 6–9.

Purvis, M. (1999) 'Crossing urban deserts: Consumers, competitors and the protracted birth of metropolitan co-operative retailing', *International Review of Retail, Distribution and Consumer Research,* 9/3, 225–43.

Purvis, M. (2015) 'Direction and discretion: The roles of centre and branch in the interwar management of Marks and Spencer', *History of Retailing and Consumption,* 1/1, 63–81.

Quinn, J., and Sparks, L. (2007) 'The evolution of grocery wholesaling and grocery wholesalers in Ireland and Britain since the 1930s', *International Review of Retail, Distribution and Consumer Research,* 17/4, 391–412.

Rappaport, E.D. (2000) *Shopping for Pleasure: Women in the Making of London's West End,* Princeton University Press, Princeton, NJ.

Richmond, V. (2010) 'Rubbish or riches? Buying from church jumble sales in late-Victorian England', *Journal of Historical Research in Marketing,* 2/3, 327–41.

Riello, G. (2006) *A Foot in the Past: Consumers, Producers and Footwear in the Long Eighteenth Century,* Oxford University Press, Oxford.

Robertson, N. (2009) '"Co-operation: the hope of the consumer"? The co-operative movement and consumer protection, 1914–60', in L. Black and N. Robertson (eds), *Consumerism and the Co-operative Movement in Modern British History: Taking Stock,* Manchester University Press, Manchester, pp. 222–39.

Rose, C. (2010) *Making, Selling and Wearing Boys' Clothes in Late-Victorian England,* Ashgate, Aldershot.

Ryle, S. (2013) *The Making of Tesco: A Story of British Shopping,* Bantam Press, London.

Scott, P. (2008) 'Managing door-to-door sales of vacuum cleaners in interwar Britain', *Business History Review,* 82/4, 761–88.

Scott, P. (2009) 'Mr Drage, Mr Everyman, and the creation of a mass market for domestic furniture in interwar Britain', *Economic History Review,* 62/4, 802–27.

Scott, P., and Walker, J. (2010) 'Advertising, promotion, and the competitive advantage of interwar British department stores', *Economic History Review,* 63/4, 1105–28.

Scott, P., and Walker, J. (2012) 'The British "failure" that never was? The Anglo-American "productivity gap" in large-scale interwar retailing – evidence from the department store sector', *Economic History Review,* 65/1, 277–303.

Shaw, G. (1992) 'The study of retail development', in J. Benson and G. Shaw (eds), *The Evolution of Retail Systems c1800–1914,* Leicester University Press, Leicester, pp. 1–14.

Shaw, G., and Alexander, A. (2008) 'British co-operative societies as retail innovators: Interpreting the early stages of the self-service revolution', *Business History,* 50/1, 62–78.

Shaw, G., Alexander, A., Benson, J., and Hodson, D. (2000) 'The evolving culture of retailer regulation and the failure of the Balfour Bill in interwar Britain', *Environment and Planning A,* 32/11, 1977–90.

Shaw, G., and Wild, M.T. (1979) 'Retail patterns in the Victorian city', *Transactions of the Institute of British Geographers,* 4, 278–91.

Shaw, G., Curth, L., and Alexander, A. (2004) 'Selling self-service and the supermarket: The Americanisation of food retailing in Britain, 1945–60', *Business History,* 46/4, 568–82.

Shaw, G., Hill Curth, L., and Alexander, A. (2006) 'Creating new spaces of food consumption: The rise of mass catering and the activities of the Aerated Bread Company', in J. Benson and L. Ugolini (eds), *Cultures of Selling: Perspectives on Consumption and Society since 1700,* Ashgate, Aldershot, pp. 81–100.

Stobart, J. (2013) *Sugar and Spice: Grocers and Groceries in Provincial England, 1650– 1830,* Oxford University Press, Oxford.

Stobart, J. (2014) 'The shopping streets of provincial England, 1650–1840', in J. H. Furnée and C. Lesger (eds), *The Landscape of Consumption. Shopping Streets and Cultures in Western Europe, 1600–1900,* Palgrave Macmillan, Basingstoke, pp. 16–36.

Stobart, J., and Hann, A. (2004) 'Retailing revolution in the eighteenth century? Evidence from North-West England', *Business History,* 46/2, 171–94.

Tadajewski, M., and Jones, D.G. (2014) 'Historical research in marketing theory and practice: A review essay', *Journal of Marketing Management,* 30/11–12, 1239–91.

Tennent, K.D. (2013) 'A distribution revolution: changes in music distribution in the UK 1950–76', *Business History,* 55/3, 327–47.

Toplis, A. (2010) 'The illicit trade in clothing, Worcestershire and Herefordshire, 1800–1850', *Journal of Historical Research in Marketing,* 2/3, 314–26.

Trunk, J. (2011) *Own Label: Sainsbury's Design Studio 1962–1977,* FUEL, London.

Tyler, N. (2014) *Sanders Bros: The Rise and Fall of a British Grocery Giant,* History Press, London.

Ugolini, L. (2007) *Men and Menswear: Sartorial Consumption in Britain 1880–1939,* Ashgate, Aldershot.

Usherwood, B. (2000) '"Mrs Housewife and her grocer": The advent of self-service food shopping in Britain', in M. Andrews and M.M. Talbot (eds), *All the World and her Husband,* Cassell, London, pp. 113–30.

Walsh, B. (2014) 'Chain store retailing in Ireland: A case study of F.W. Woolworth & Co. Ltd, 1914– 2008', *Journal of Historical Research in Marketing,* 6/1, 98–115.

Walsh, C. (2000) 'The advertising and marketing of consumer goods in eighteenth-century London', in C. Wischermann and E. Shore (eds), *Advertising and the European City: Historical Perspectives,* Ashgate, Aldershot, 79–95.

Walsh, C. (2014) 'Stalls, bulks, shops and long-term change in seventeenth- and eighteenth-century England', in J. H. Furnée and C. Lesger (eds), *The Landscape of Consumption: Shopping Streets and Cultures in Western Europe, 1600–1900,* Palgrave Macmillan, Basingstoke, pp. 37–56.

Walton, J.K. (2009) 'The post war decline of the British retail co-operative movement: Nature, causes and consequences', in J. Black and N. Robertson (eds), *Consumerism and the Co-operative Movement in Modern British History: Taking Stock,* Manchester University Press, Manchester, pp. 13–32.

Whitworth, L. (2009) 'Promoting product quality: The Co-op and the Council of Industrial Design', in L. Black and N. Robertson (eds), *Consumerism and the Co-operative Movement in Modern British History: Taking Stock,* Manchester University Press, Manchester, pp. 174–96.

Wilson, J., Webster, A., and Vorberg-Rugh, R. (2013) *Building Co-operation: A Business History of the Co-operative Group, 1963–2013,* Oxford University Press, Oxford.

Winship, J. (2000) 'New disciplines for women and the rise of the chain store in the 1930s', in M. Andrews and M.M. Talbot (eds), *All the World and her Husband*, Cassell, London, pp. 23–45.

Winstanley, M. (1983) *The Shopkeeper's World 1830–1914,* Manchester University Press, Manchester.

Worth, R. (2007) *Fashion for the People: A History of Clothing at Marks & Spencer,* Berg, Oxford.

10

History of channels of distribution

Robert D. Tamilia

Introduction

The economic development of countries, such as the USA or Canada, has been well documented by economic and business historians. They have focused their attention on particular industries or sectors of the economy (e.g. fur, wheat, lumber, cars). They have explored how the history of technology has transformed the economy into a mass market. However, no matter how extensive the manufacturing sector or how technologically advanced the products are, if these products cannot be distributed to markets where demand exists, all will be for naught. The history of channels of distribution is intimately tied to the economic development and growth of any country. It is, in particular, no easy task to isolate the economic and technological contributions of channel members from those made by manufacturing.

The transformation of the US economy or any economy, from a local or regional, to a mass national one could not have taken place had it not been for the establishment of a complex distribution network made up of manufacturers, wholesalers, retailers and transportation channel specialists, all of whom collectively enabled goods to flow to consumers. From the late nineteenth century, manufacturers began to brand their products, which required them not only to assume more marketing responsibilities but also to have a direct interest in the soundness of the middlemen involved in product distribution. Innovative vertical distributive alternatives also emerged at about the same time, alternatives such as department stores, mail order houses, chain stores and supermarkets. When combined with the rise of manufacturers in the economy, they drastically changed established methods of marketing and distributing both goods and services. New retail and wholesale formats had a profound impact on the economy of the twentieth century and transformed the way that consumers purchased goods and services.

Channels of distribution

The concept of 'channels of distribution' has been an elusive one to grasp because it is linked with what channel members do and what distributive functions they perform. Given the intangible nature of such functions, their importance has not been easy to grasp, even in

173

academic marketing. Moreover, the channel of distribution is intimately linked with the marketing process itself, a process that only became better understood in the early part of the twentieth century with the establishment of marketing as a discipline worthy of study in its own right.

All channels of distribution are both economic and political entities. They all have a historical origin which reflects the social and economic structure of a country, a region or a market. They have been structured, moulded and organized over time to reflect the legal, cultural and social values of the participants and their environment. Channel participants (involved in buying and selling from one level to the next) have established economic, political and social relationships based on cooperation, trust and power, relationships which influence the way they do business with each other.

Over the years, numerous explanations and interpretations of the meaning of channels of distribution have been proposed (Beckman and Davidson, 1967). Davidson (1961, 85) said that the 'term is part of the working vocabulary of every business executive, yet many would be hard pressed to define its meaning precisely'. According to McCammon and Little (1965, 322) 'channels are among the most complicated phenomena encountered in an advanced economy'. Also, channel members do not always think of themselves of being part of a broader economic organization made up of members other than those they deal with on a regular basis, such as their immediate suppliers and customers. There is, finally, a tendency to define a channel from a manufacturer's perspective, thus oversimplifying the number of interfirm alignments which exists beyond the first stage of distribution.

Not only have various conceptual definitions of channels been proposed but so also have types of channels of distribution, such as reverse channels, second-hand channels, underground channels, recycling channels and commercial channels, among others. The commercial channel captures the interdependent links which exist among manufacturers, wholesalers and retailers at various levels of distribution (Stern and El-Ansary, 1977, 11). Channel members organize themselves and create an infrastructure (interorganization) to better serve the consumer. But that consumer is not involved and is largely unaware of the manner by which channel members select and organize themselves, cooperate and deal with each other using numerous business-to-business (B2B) interorganizational network agreements and marketing programmes designed to manage, control and reward members. The philosophy of the commercial channel is that 'marketing proposes while the consumer disposes'. The impact of distribution channels on consumers reflects the fact that marketing is a far more formative process than an adaptive one (Beckman and Davidson, 1967). In the long run but not necessarily in the short run, the acceptance of new or modified channel arrangements among members depends on the consumer. The nature of channel arrangements is determined from the 'bottom up' rather than from the 'top down', supporting what Tosdal (1957) and others have argued that any economy is organized from the bottom up.

Some proposed channel definitions pertinent to this chapter:

- a loose coalition of business firms which have banded together for purpose of trade;
- the *route* taken by the product as it moves from points of production to points of consumption;
- the route taken by the *title* to goods and services as they move through various agencies toward buyers or consumers.

The distribution channel has been a tough concept to define, understand and study, even more so from a historical perspective. Dixon (1982) was the first author in academic marketing to trace the historical origin of the term. Surprisingly, he found it in a seventeenth-century business handbook written by Jacques Savary (1675), millennia after the essence of marketing as buying and selling had been documented (Tamilia, 2011). Dixon (1982) credits Savary as being the first to suggest an Aldersonian view of a channel as an organized behaviour system, as stated above in the first definition.

Shaw (1916) presented a list of five functions performed by middleman which were an integral part of the marketing process per se. Later, Beckman and Davidson (1967, 422) defined a marketing function as being a 'distinctive economic activity which is inherent in the marketing process, pervades it throughout and … tends to become specialized'. Thus, the work done by channel members is essentially indistinguishable from the work done within the marketing process.

Shaw (1916) also made another contribution fundamental towards an understanding of distribution channels. He postulated that the marketing process was made up of two separate but synergistically linked phases, demand creation and physical supply. Shaw (1916) went as far as to suggest these two distribution tasks needed to be harmonized in order to achieve a balance.

> Failure to coordinate any one of these activities with its group-fellows and also with those in the other group, or undue emphasis or outlay put upon any one of these activities, is certain to upset the equilibrium of forces which means efficient distribution (p. 101) … The physical distribution of the goods is a problem distinct from the creation of demand … Not a few costly failures in distribution campaigns have been due to such a lack of coordination between demand creation and physical supply. (p. 110)

Shaw's two-pronged view of the marketing process as involving both demand creation and physical supply corresponds to two fundamental types of distribution channels, one referred to as the sales or transactional channel, the other as the supply or logistics channel. The two are quite different in terms of the channel functions they perform. These two types of specialized but interdependent channels must be harmoniously coordinated among channel members if marketing is to satisfy its basic mission not only of stimulating demand (getting sales) but also of meeting demand (satisfying sales). Satisfying sales corresponds to the physical distribution of the product, as the second definition stated above suggests. It is the physical route taken by the product on its way to customers. Getting or obtaining a sale is the realization of a sale when the legal exchange of the good is transferred from seller to buyer, that is, when the buyer assumes title or ownership, as stated in the third definition above.

Ordinarily, the product's physical route follows the same path as does the title but that is not always the case. A given product may never move physically while its title may change hands numerous times. A product may move across the nation and back within a distribution network without ever changing legal ownership. Physical possession and ownership are not identical in marketing. It is likely that given the organizational structure of pre-nineteenth-century distribution channels, that product and title would have followed similar paths to market. However, the technological advances of the last century, and especially those of the last 20 years, have contributed to the growing separation between the sales channel and the supply channel.

In essence, the sales channel promotes and sells the product while the logistics channel moves, stores and services it. If the two channels are not working in tandem, both customers and the firm will be affected, either because of excess inventory of products or stock outs.

Viewing demand stimulation as the essence of mainstream marketing management presents a truncated view of the marketing process and ignores the existence of these two very different types of distribution channels. Demand stimulation activities may make customers aware of the product and may even entice them to the store, but it would be all for naught if the brand is not stocked or is unavailable in the style, colour, size and price wanted by customers.

Channels of distribution in history

The practice of marketing (as buying and selling) has been around since man recognized the benefits of exchange. That need to trade soon led to a need for traders, merchants or middlemen to facilitate business transactions, even when the producer assumed some, if not all, the distributive tasks of a middleman. Thus, marketing and middlemen have coexisted since man first recognized he could not satisfy his needs for goods and services by being totally self-sufficient. In fact, economic development and growth is highly dependent on the quality of the distribution structure which exists in any market or in any country. The more sophisticated the interorganizational arrangement among channel members and the more complex the distributive services they perform, the higher the level of market specialization and distributive efficiencies. This leads to lower prices and a greater assortment and increased availability of goods at both the retail and wholesale levels.

One of the driving forces behind economic development is the important role played by middlemen in any emerging market economy. Economies of scale can be realized through better use of both domestic and international distribution channels in which merchants perform an important cost saving role. Channel members are able to increase the efficiency of market exchanges, a fact which leads to a decline in transaction costs. Such merchants, acting as intermediary (i.e. wholesalers), help lower search costs by bringing together potential suppliers with potential customers. This results in reduced negotiation, bargaining and contract enforcement costs, and all cost components of any market transaction. Such merchants are also instrumental in establishing the required complex channel links with other economic partners which tend to lower the overall cost of doing business. The increased market efficiency they bring to trade contributes to national economic development.

The published research of economic and business historians is indeed extensive. However, they have not generally well documented either the marketing activities of merchants or the relationships between channel members. Fortunately, there are important exceptions to this rule. For example, Lopez and Raymond (1955) painstakingly traced medieval trade practices beginning with the commercial revolution using archival sources written in medieval Latin and Greek, old French, Italian, German, Spanish and other languages, all translated into English for their book. The most complete set of archival material known is the 150,000 documents of the fourteenth-century Florentine merchant, Francesco Datini, of Prado (Origo, 1957). Datini was a wholesale merchant in wool, silk, religious art, spices, weaponry, and even iron. He established an import-export business with branches in Pisa, Genoa, Barcelona and Majorca, all managed by relatives. He was a hard-working and shrewd merchant, always keen to make trade deals, personifying all the signs of a true modern-day entrepreneur. Datini amassed a vast fortune and was a forerunner of the modern CEO in charge of a multinational company.

Closer to home, the development of both French and British North Americas in the seventeenth and eighteenth centuries would not have taken place at such a high rate had it not been for the importation of goods both needed by new settlers and desired as well by the indigenous population. Goods imported to the newly discovered continents did not all come from England but from numerous other countries and colonies (e.g. West Indies, France, Holland, Spain, Portugal, Italy). It was the beginning of the fur trade in North America which eventually led the colonies to export many local goods, ranging from timber, fish and wheat. All of this both internal and external trade required the trading services of middlemen, some of whom were native North Americans.

International trade flourished from the thirteenth century, greatly facilitated by the founding of the Hanseatic League and the Merchant Adventurers of London (Carus-Wilson, 1967). From the thirteenth to the sixteenth centuries, a group of English merchants, referred to as merchant staplers, were given monopoly rights for the exportation of English wool. As English manufacturing grew in importance beyond the seventeenth century, merchant staplers fell on hard times because wool exports lessened in importance relative to other exports. International trade increased even more with the creation in the seventeenth century of the Hudson's Bay Company in British North America and of the East India Company. Multinational trade and commerce is a long-known phenomenon and channel members made such trade possible almost since man first sought goods that could not be obtained locally.

One of the first French handbooks on business practices was *Le Parfait Négociant* by Jacques Savary published in 1675, with many subsequent editions by his sons. This handbook written for business practitioners of the time was popular for at least 100 years, and it was translated into many languages, but not English. It reflected the French mercantile economic philosophy of the time, that is, a good maritime wholesale merchant was one who exported goods in order to bring in much needed currency money (precious metals) into the country. It was a practical business handbook to help a merchant succeed in business. Savary had been such a successful French merchant. After his retirement, he was commissioned by Colbert, France's Minister of Finance under Louis XIV, to help revise the laws, methods and procedures pertaining to trade, notably international trade. One of Colbert`s state-sanctioned economic objectives was to encourage French merchants to get more involved in trade, if only to be more competitive in international commerce and to thwart the then more successful English merchants. What is ironic is that Colbert had a 'strong dislike for businessmen and the business community' (Finkelstein and Thimm, 1973, 21). However, being a good mercantilist, he still wanted France to be a world-class leader in the production of high-quality, high-priced fashion goods in the hope that they would bring in more revenues and enrich the King's coffers.

Savary's book emphasized that the best trader was in fact one involved in wholesaling and not retailing because that would involve international trade. A retail merchant in France had a low-status occupation, considered to be a member of the working class or *la petite bourgeoisie*. In fact, it was actually forbidden by French law for a noble to engage in retailing under *la loi de dérogeance,* a law enacted in the fourteenth century and ended only after the French Revolution in the eighteenth century (Lévy-Bruhl, 1933). If caught doing business in retail, the aristocrat would lose his title and privileges associated with the status and be obligated to pay taxes. Savary in his book made a strong case in favour of the nobility engaging in commerce, perhaps because his own sixteenth-century family ancestors had lost their noble status after engaging in commerce. Savary wanted his work to rebrand the profession of merchant as being useful and honourable, with there being nothing illegitimate in seeking profit.

Savary also provided practical information designed to help a merchant succeed in the international world of business. He outlined the requisites needed to be a 'good' wholesaler, such as honesty, having arithmetic knowledge and skills such as being able to negotiate.

177

His book was a factual one, spelling out on how to write bills of exchange or promissory notes in many countries and how to obtain credit terms. It provided detailed information on weights and measures which varied across regions and countries as well as on currency differences. Savary believed that such information was necessary for merchants considering the soundness of proposed business transactions.

Channel member marketing practices in medieval times

The role played by the rise of a merchant class, roughly from the eleventh century to the eighteenth century, is well discussed in the literature but not in the marketing literature. This new breed of commercial businessmen disrupted the feudal political system and diminished the power of the reigning monarchs and nobles who controlled the lives of people under the heavy influence of church doctrine. That doctrine condemned the pursuit of profits, the charging of interest, reflecting the church's suspicion of the contribution of merchants to the welfare of any society other than their own. In fact, the medieval idea of charging a *just price* for goods and paying labour its *just wage* was based on the church's religious focus on seeking justice and fairness for all (De Roover, 1958). The prices charged on commodities were based largely on the cost of labour, with goods being produced one at a time. But this medieval era of the just price and just wage did not take into consideration fluctuating demand and supply conditions, or advances in production methods and technology resulting in economies of scale reflecting lowered labour inputs. It did not consider the business risk assumed by merchants who purchased goods from guilds and others for resale, never certain if they would realize a gain and unsure if the goods would reach their destination rather than being stolen, damaged or lost at sea.

Many other commercial tasks were assumed by such merchants who in return needed to sell goods for more than what they paid. They sought buyers, often during fairs, delivered the goods, and extended credit, often waiting long periods of time before they got paid. The idea of the just wage is still with us with minimum hourly wage laws, and some still feel a guaranteed living wage for all is needed. Ironically, theological and philosophical texts written by church members contributed to the gradual acceptance of merchants and business in society, among other factors.

Powerful medieval guilds imposed many restrictions both on manufacturing and on selling either at retail or wholesale. These regulations dictated who could make what, who could buy from whom and who could sell to whom, all this in order to protect the existing apprenticeship system. This was France's way of establishing roles and positions in this pre-industrial, pre-market capitalistic society. The myriad of rules and regulations imposed on commerce along with sumptuary laws severely restricted both production and distributive activities. Franklin (1894, 33) reported that, in the seventeenth century, Parisian retailers were prohibited by law from selling any products they had made themselves. Rather, these retailers (called mercers) were only allowed to sell products made by others. However, they were permitted to add some value to products (by packaging) in order to make them look more appealing to customers (*enjoliver*).

Vidal and Duru (1911) trace the history of the corporation of mercers, a corporation which laid the foundation for both retailing and wholesaling in Paris from the fourteenth century to the late eighteenth century. The authors discuss the numerous edicts of the guild system. Guilds in pre-nineteenth-century France were the forerunners of trade unions. The various edicts supported a fixed price system and put severe restrictions on both foreign and domestic itinerant sellers. The guild system, by greatly limiting the number of tasks a worker could perform, insulated artisans from competition. Guilds developed hundreds of such worker categories. Thus, a retailer by law could not encroach on the work being performed by certain craftsmen. This division of labour was mandated by law rather than by market factors. The authors also discuss the *Six Corps*, a powerful group of Parisian merchants who protected their members from competition and whose elected members, because of their financial support of the monarchy, were close to the King. The history of the distributive trades, whether in France or any other country, is one in which transformative changes occur very slowly in order to maintain the status quo and protect influential players.

Success criteria of medieval channel members

Most of the commercial documents studied by historians deal with accounting ledgers, notarial documents, and with weights and measures which varied across regions as did the type and value of coinage. Davis (1960) argues that knowledge of basic arithmetic was necessary for merchants to succeed, given the absence of standardized weights and measures, variable interest rates, credit terms which varied across regions and countries and transportation charges which varied even more. This was an era where paper money was non-existent, replaced mainly by coins, bills of exchange, promissory notes and letters of credit. Knowledge of arithmetic was also a must-have skill for a merchant due to the development of double-entry bookkeeping in the fourteenth century as 'an absolute necessity for accurate calculations of business operations in the division of the accounts into two parts' (Berlow, 1971, 22). The art of reading and writing, a skill few others possessed in the Middle Ages apart from ecclesiastics and nobles, enhanced the economic status of merchants. Along with knowledge of arithmetic and perhaps the ability some had to speak or understand other languages, this made them ideally suited for trade and commerce. Mulvihill (1987, 29–30) provides a list of personality traits that Middle Eastern merchants of the fourteenth century needed to succeed, compiled by a philosopher of the period, a list which still makes sense today:

> a merchant must concern himself with buying and selling, earning money and making a profit and this requires cunning, willingness to enter into disputes, cleverness, constant quarreling and great persistence. These are qualities detrimental to and destructive of virtuousness and manliness. It is unavoidable that there should be cheating, tampering with the merchandise which may ruin it.

Of course, these same qualities could also work against buyers because 'merchants who are not affected by those character qualities have noble souls and are magnanimous but they are very rare in this world' (Mulvihill, 1987, 30).

Sometimes certain commodities high in demand (spices) were used as a substitute for payment. The value of coinage fluctuated depending on the purity of the precious metal in coins (gold, silver). The quality of the goods was also hard to evaluate given the lack of grading and quality control standards. Prior to the eighteenth century, almost every country and even regions within a country differed in such matters. No wonder merchants possessing knowledge and expertise in such areas were successful. They greatly facilitated trade which otherwise would not have taken place or would have been much more difficult to complete in a timely manner. The contributions of such merchants to the marketing process are obvious. We can now better understand why they emerged in pre-industrialized society and why they dominated trade until the industrial revolution changed the economy at the beginning of the nineteenth century.

The establishment and acceptance of product standards is a long and tedious process, one requiring buyers, sellers, industry trade groups, consumer groups, and government agencies to work together to establish grading and quality standards (Carver, 1917). In pre-eighteenth-century commerce, production was small-scale and standardized production methods did not exist. Most goods were made in small batches, often one at a time, varying greatly in both product and performance. Interchangeable parts only became a reality in late nineteenth century. Such production realities made merchants all the more important in trade because of their keen ability to evaluate the physical and aesthetic qualities of commodities (by colour, appearance, touch, taste, odour) and to select supply sources which provided what buyers were willing to pay. It was an age where producers and retailers were small scale, while merchants, qua wholesalers, were the channel captains. Wholesalers continued to occupy that pivotal role until mass production emerged near the end of the nineteenth century and manufacturers were able to bypass them and deal more directly with their customers.

The functional school of marketing thought provides a classification scheme of marketing functions such as those proposed by Beckman and Davidson (1967), including exchange, logistics and various facilitating functions. These facilitating functions, which include commodity grading and standardization, are of particular interest here. These marketing functions were not well developed in pre-eighteenth-century trade. Astute merchants were able to fill the knowledge gap by providing their expertise which not only facilitated trade but encouraged it as well. Standardization and grading of products were not just a pre-eighteenth-century concern but a post-eighteenth-century one as well. For example, soon after the First World War began, the US government implemented a standardization and simplification programme designed to eliminate waste in commercial and industrial practices, a programme which continued for many years and resulted in

> enormous savings of manpower and materials in over 250 industries by reducing the number of styles, varieties, sizes, and colors … by standardizing sizes, lengths, widths and weights…colors of typewriter ribbons shrank from 150 to 5; buggy wheels were reduced from 232 sizes and varieties to 4; plows from 326 to 76 sizes and styles; automobile tires from 287 types to 9; steel pens reduced from 132 to 30 styles.
>
> *(Cochrane, 1966, 177–8)*

Standardization and grading make sales easier to realize (sales by samples, sales by inspection and sales by written description). A seller can obtain a premium price for goods achieving higher quality standards (eggs, wines, meats). Futures trading could not exist were it not for standardization. Sales by brand names can only be achieved by offering a product of continuously similar value (quality and quantity). Moreover, standardization and grading reduce marketing costs (storage and transportation) and force sellers to sort and price goods before deciding which ones to bring to market.

Fairs and channel marketing practices

The academic marketing literature has had very little to say about ancient marketing practices. Freidman (1984, 194) acknowledged that 'it is not easy to find information concerning marketing practices of, say, 2,000 years ago'. Yet 'many of the laws and regulations which govern the modern marketplace had their Talmudic equivalents' (Freidman, 1984, 202). He cited numerous marketing practices, some of which will be covered in this chapter. Notwithstanding the available information found in the Talmud and similar sources, the richest source of information on ancient marketing practices is provided by historians. They tell us trade flourished in the ancient civilizations of Egypt, Babylonia, Greece, Persia and Rome, among others. Phoenicia, a maritime trading civilization, occupied the western coastline of the Mediterranean from around 1500 BCE trading goods (through imports and exports) to the east with Greeks and others. No wonder the Phoenicians were called a nation of wholesalers in ancient times (Khalaf, 2015). Elisseeff (2000) presents the history of the silk trade in ancient times when precious finished silk fabrics from China were exported along the famous Silk Road to the Roman Empire, a practice which continued to the nineteenth century. Dixon, Cann and Renfrew (1968) found numerous articles in archeological sites that could only have been imported from far distant places, and similar findings at other sites were reported by Ericson and Earle (1982).

Verlinden (1963) discusses the existence of trade and fairs in the ports of Merovingian Gaul and Visigothic Spain during the pre-medieval period. Trade during the medieval period (roughly from the tenth to the fourteenth century) marked the beginning of what some historians called the commercial revolution. This was the golden age of fairs held periodically in Champagne, Lyon, Flanders and numerous other European countries, including England and Italy (Huvelin, 1897; Moore, 1985). Not only were fairs in antiquity and during the medieval period a key driver for international trade, they were also responsible for the internal distribution of goods within regions and countries. Huvelin (1897), a lawyer by trade, was the first to trace the history of such fairs. Huvelin's seminal text is more than just a description of fairs. Fairs represent the first organized periodic meeting places of buyers and sellers in history. I would include the agora, as Huvelin did, as an ancient periodic marketplace in Greek times. It served many purposes, one of which was a periodic marketplace where merchants kept stalls to sell their goods.

Fairs reflect the history of small commerce which began in local markets and evolved over time into international trade. Huvelin (1897) discusses methods of buying and selling in fairs, their organization, the commodities traded, how prices were set, when and where fairs were held, as well as the municipal and religious regulations which governed the behaviour and responsibilities of fair participants. According to Verlinden (1963, 127), 'the town magistrature and the local ecclesiastic dignitaries also exercised a certain authority over the merchants and their transactions'. Moreover, Verlinden adds that aristocrats, including kings, derived considerable revenues from fairs. The sources of that revenue included taxes on residences and stalls of merchants, entry and exit road or bridge tolls, levies on sales and purchases, charges for using weights and measures. Roads and bridges en route to fairs had to be well maintained, thus the need to charge tolls. Some toll booths also offered warehousing services for merchants who wanted to bring only a portion of their goods to the fair or were afraid to travel certain roads known for harbouring thieves.

Market fair regulations also specified when and how payments were to be made and in what currency. Both the quality and quantity of goods traded were also regulated with dispute mechanisms controlled by fair organizers and others having a final say over contested transactions. Eventually, these regulations, along with others, morphed into rules and laws that prescribed the legal obligations of trade participants with jurisprudence. The history of such enforcement procedures date back thousands of years, according to Freidman (1984, 200), who wrote,

> In Talmudic times, market commissioners were appointed to superintend businessmen using weights and measures. The Talmud also made reference to non-Jewish, government-appointed inspectors of weights and measures. This institution was,

apparently, very successful. It has carried over into modern times, and scales are inspected regularly even today.

Given the periodic nature of fairs, some of which lasted a few days and others many weeks, while still others took place yearly (Ligt, 1988), it became difficult for travelling merchants to take unsold goods from fair to fair. They did not always want to travel long distances to various fairs because that could be time consuming, and even dangerous, given the existence of bad roads with thieves always around to steal the merchandise. And when merchants travelled, they rarely travelled alone on their way to the next fair or to the next port. They were accompanied by a team who aided in the packing and physical transport of goods and who were responsible for bringing goods back to their original owners. These freight travellers, also referred to as wagoners or muleteers, 'offered their services to transport goods to and from the fair sites and meet up with the merchants' (Berlow, 1971, 18). Of course, the assortment and quantity of goods offered for sale was quite limited, given the transportation modes available, especially when horses were used. Huvelin even stated that merchants appointed representatives, called factors (i.e. selling or commission agents), who had the power to trade and negotiate on their behalf. These middlemen did not take ownership of the goods and they represented a type of wholesaler that still exists today, now known as agents and brokers or functional middlemen (Beckman and Davidson, 1967).

Transportation (logistical) services seemed to have been well organized at such fairs. A merchant could buy or sell horses depending on his needs. Courier services were also available 'to facilitate communications between the fair sites and the home base of operations' (Berlow, 1971, 21). However, some messengers did not only act as mailmen. They carried with them in a leather bag various credit papers, promissory notes, letters of exchange which detailed settlement of accounts from fair to fair, the recovery of unpaid debts, paybacks of sums owed, and even notices of payment. These messengers informed merchants at fairs what they owed and what was due to them. They also acted as money changers, converting sums in the appropriate currency desired by merchants. They assumed financial tasks but were not involved in the actual buying and selling of goods. These messengers were first employed by Italians but the practice was eventually adopted by others. Mitchell (2007, 545) reported that some 'wholesale traders used fairs more as a place to take orders or receive orders previously made and to settle accounts rather than to display their goods'. Some fairs, especially located near ports, trade routes or urban centres, became major financial centres in which wholesaling thrived. The factors or financial intermediaries that emerged in nineteenth-century America were also known as financial agents, buying manufacturers' account receivables and providing other types of financial services (Livesay and Porter, 1972).

Ligt (1988) provides a useful description of ancient fairs, distinguishing between periodic fairs that were held with a short cycle (day or week, like the agora) serving the market needs of locals versus those multifunction fairs held over many weeks or months, referred to as *panegyreis*. These fairs were international in scope and attracted merchants and participants over much wider geographical areas than local fairs. Such fairs combined trade with other social activities, such as religious celebrations or some political events. It was a time of the year when local people would meet foreign sellers who did not speak the same language. It was also a time when crafts not produced locally or exotic goods were offered for sale. Fairs offered a golden opportunity for merchants to gather business intelligence, meet and share trade experience with other merchants, and obtain knowledge about products. It was a time when a merchant's credibility and reputation were tested. Fairs were busy places of conducting business, such as taking orders, delivering ordered goods, collecting past debts, collecting rents and as Mitchell

(2007) says, even of hiring of labour such as messengers or transportation services. Fairs involved a mixture of retailing with mostly wholesaling activities.

Moore (1985) provides vivid examples of retailing and wholesaling activities in medieval English fairs of the twelfth to the fourteenth centuries. She discusses how some entrepreneurs provided lodging and sold cooked foods, while others rented cooking paraphernalia for fairgoers who cooked their own food. A multitude of bakers and pastry makers sold their goods to the public and live animals were also sold. Beer was a must during such fairs and strict rules were imposed as to who should make and sell it. Ligt (1988) adds that entertainment was present to create a festive mood with gambling and prostitution, along with jugglers, acrobats, athletic events, even theatrical performances to further amuse the people. Fairs provided a nice break from the routine that generated handsome revenues for shopkeepers, innkeepers, fair organizers and many others.

Mitchell (2007) stated that the number of fairs in England and Wales increased in the eighteenth century, with 3,200 fairs spread over to 1,500 different places in 1786, even though fairs were generally in decline elsewhere. Fairs have not entirely disappeared but have evolved over time. Long-cycle fairs serving multiple social functions are similar to world fairs which began with the 1851 London Crystal Palace Exhibition. World fairs are still with us and are regulated by the Paris-based Bureau International des Expositions. Mega malls, such as West Edmonton Mall or Mall of America, are modern examples of multifunction ancient fairs which combine retail shopping with leisure and entertainment which attract millions of tourists each year.

Annual agricultural fairs held in many cities are also a modern version of such ancient fairs. Short-cycle market fairs are better known today as street fairs, farmers' markets or municipal markets. More goods are sold at retail than at wholesale, although large wholesale produce market centres still exist in some major cities. The assortment of goods is now limited to mostly farm goods and other food items. Verlinden (1963) and Mitchell (2007) mention the wide assortment of goods sold at fairs ranging from tools to wool, cotton, wax, live farm animals, and so forth, goods not sold in today's farmers' or municipal markets. However, the selling of agricultural products seems to have been common to all fairs, as is still the case today. Some farmers' markets are still periodic and many are housed in permanent fixed locations. Over a hundred years ago, King (1913) advocated the expansion of farmers' markets as a means to reduce food costs to consumers. He said 'the twentieth century need is to encourage near-by farmers to sell at home' (p. 102). His comment of encouraging consumers to buy food from local farmers to save money reminds us of today's locavore movement. Such a social movement has a history and it is not a twenty-first-century initiative.

Merchants travelling to fairs have been credited with being largely responsible for the beginning of modern commerce and capitalism. These European merchants were involved in trade then known 'as the most perilous of all medieval occupations' (Finkelstein and Thimm, 1973, 8). They defied the prevailing church doctrine related to Christian values of humility and sacrifice by engaging in commerce which brought them wealth and comfort. However, material prosperity jeopardized their entry to the Kingdom of God and the only way to salvation was to dispose of such wealth by charity before death, preferably to the church, of course!

The history of fairs remains a fascinating topic, one largely unexplored in academic marketing. The study of fairs cannot be separated from the study of buying and selling practices in small markets, which expanded to regional and international trade. Fairs also provide an intimate look at the nature and types of business links which were established between channel members participating in fairs.

Travelling merchants and distribution

Market fairs slowly declined in importance for many reasons. It became increasingly expensive for buyers and sellers to meet periodically in some geographical region to carry on business. Other less costly and more efficient methods of doing business developed which reduced the need for face to face contacts. As travelling merchants assumed more business and marketing tasks as they went from fair to fair, port to port, often travelling long distances, either by land or water or both, they needed to be better organized. Porter (1980, 396) called them the all-purpose merchants:

> In order to carry out that basic sorting task, those engaged in marketing often had to play many other roles, including those of financier, advertiser, insurer, freight agent, warehouser, information gatherer, and risk taker. Their key position as multipurpose interconnectors between other economic units made them the most powerful persons in the economy. It also placed them among the most influential elements in the social and political systems.

These were not the itinerant peddlers (penny capitalists) who travelled rural areas selling their wares to rural customers, although some were known to attend fairs. Eventually, the all-purpose merchant did not need to travel to faraway places to buy and sell goods. Sufficient demand in one location enabled the establishment of a permanent place of business. Such merchants worked behind the scenes, building an organization and even facilities (a warehouse). They sought suppliers, matching them with buyers using their network of contacts often made up initially of family members and relatives acting as sales coordinators gathering market intelligence. It was an age before the birth of the modern corporation and only those who had close familial relations could be trusted. Those who were not family members were nevertheless well known among relatives. The information merchants received enabled them to know more about suppliers, potential buyers, assess risk, secure credit and loans, arrange payments and schedule appropriate times to transport goods. They also authorized other channel members to act on their behalf as agents. As markets expanded, some of these all-purpose merchants branched out into more specialized business functions such as financiers, exchangers, merchant bankers, maritime transporters, insurance brokers and so forth, all specialized business activities in line with an emerging capitalistic economy.

Chatelain (1971) documented the commercial life of French travelling merchants in the nineteenth century who travelled in rural areas in search of customers, becoming the source from which rural peasants acquired many of their goods. A 1798 French law gave them the right to exercise their trade but the politics of distribution meant that they were also discriminated against, harassed and even chased out of town by local shop owners because such outsiders were allegedly taking business away. In fact, the fear of outside merchants competing with local ones dates back millennia, according to Freidman (1984). Approximately 2,400 years ago,

> Ezra the Scribe allowed these peddlers to peddle from town to town; local retailers were not permitted to prevent them from doing business. This pro consumer regulation was enacted to ensure that women would have no problem acquiring their toiletries, and would thus not become repulsive to their husbands.

(Freidman 1984, 196)

Freidman (1984, 196) added that the Talmud reveals 'on market day, those outsiders were given permission to sell only in the marketplace, but not to peddle door-to-door'. And when travelling salesmen working for merchant wholesalers, either as agents or as traveling salesmen, grew both in importance and numbers after the second half of the nineteenth century, many city and state anti-drummer (anti-peddler) laws and regulations were passed to limit their presence and activities (Hollander, 1964). Local merchants feared they would take business away from them and jeopardize established distribution channels, the very same argument levied against travelling merchants centuries before.

Spufford (1984) reported that chapmen played an important role in supplying clothing and small luxuries (window curtains) to rural England in the seventeenth century. Some chapmen were in fact women and some even had a small shop. Their operating costs were low and they often were not welcome in communities where retailers had fixed shops. Some sold ready to wear clothes, such as handkerchiefs, coats, even shirts, while others sold groceries, spices and other goods. Those who had a horse offered a wider assortment of goods. The chapmen's wealth, what was sold and where, and who were their suppliers are all well described in this text.

The marketing practices of American travelling merchants were basically a refinement of the marketing and financial skills developed by colonial merchants (Porter and Livesay, 1971). Atherton (1949, 135) provided a glimpse of a marketing practice of travelling merchants in the 1840s. They delivered handbills to homes, even handing them to servants who were presumably illiterates. They were not just order-takers during their travels but they also tried to drum up business, hence the name 'drummer'. In the absence of advertising media, it made sense to hand-deliver such handbills, a marketing practice that is still with us with advertising flyers either inserted in newspapers, home delivered each week or stuffed in mailboxes. Drummers worked for jobbers (also known as merchant wholesalers or wholesale distributors) as independent selling agents (as travelling merchants) or were employed by them (as sales representatives), with some perhaps even assuming both distributive roles. Those merchants who grew in size and financial strength extended credit to small entrepreneurial manufacturers, farmers or small retailers, serving as bankers. They distributed unbranded and undifferentiated products to a diverse set of small market segments. They lacked knowledge of more distant markets and had a large number of small customers scattered all over their trading areas.

Before the 1850s, poor road conditions severely limited the quantity and assortment of goods travelling merchants could bring with them. Maritime transportation was the main transportation mode until better roads became a reality. But transportation by sail was slow and often unreliable due to its dependence on wind conditions. Steam navigation greatly improved this transportation mode. But it was rail and the telegraph that revolutionized trade in both Europe and North America from around the mid-nineteenth century. Rail made many more markets accessible and also made all year shipment of goods a possibility, unlike the case with maritime transport which was not possible during the winter months. Moreover, access to navigable water sources was limited and required the building of ports and sometimes expensive canals and waterways. Rail was much faster and reliable for both buyers and sellers. It also reduced the cost of doing business, given that there was a lesser need to stockpile costly quantities of finished and semi-finished goods, materials and supplies over long periods in order to avoid stock outs. Improvements in transportation and communications were instrumental in helping manufacturers assume channel leadership late in the nineteenth century.

It is no coincidence that the business careers of some of the world's greatest merchant princes began in New York City. Albion (1939, p. v) referred to the nineteenth-century

New York seaport as the world's greatest and busiest seaport ever, 'the economic activity of the whole world passed in review along the wharves'. The presence of large numbers of entrepreneurs, such as manufacturers, jobbers, selling agents, commission merchants, auction houses, importers and exporters, all seeking fame and fortune, both necessitated and facilitated higher levels of organizational integration among channel members. Products arriving at the New York seaport were coming from faraway places and needed to be distributed not only across a vast and expanding domestic market but to other countries as well.

Interorganizational channel networks

Dixon (1982) made no mention of pre-nineteenth-century channel members establishing networks, distribution alliances, partnerships or contractual agreements among themselves. Perhaps such arrangements existed at the time of the Hanseatic League and the East India Company, or even earlier among the Phoenicians, the Greeks, and others. However, unearthing information on the specifics of such arrangements (exactly what they did, how they were managed, the nature of the arrangement, etc.) will be no easy task. But the fact such networks almost certainly existed suggests that the benefits of specialization in distribution was known long before Adam Smith argued in the eighteenth century for a division of labour in manufacturing that would increase productivity.

Berlow (1971, 12), states that 'very few records of the formation of partnerships for the purpose of doing business' exist. Merchants may have established such partnerships locally with silent partners or family members. In some regions, only a familial partner could claim a share upon the death of a partner, an unrelated partner would have no such claim. However, Berlow was not discussing channel relationships among members but rather investment partnerships. Trade partners were venture capitalists seeking a return on their invested capital. They had little or nothing to do with the establishment of vertical relationships among channel members designed to move products more efficiently along the distribution chain.

The entrepreneurial travelling merchants that existed in America during colonial times and the nineteenth century were also present in Europe during the medieval period and even in antiquity. They assumed two distinct distributive roles, serving either as merchants or selling agents. Middlemen who assumed title to the goods they resold were known simply as 'merchants', a rather generic term which could also designate a business person. Middlemen who did not own the goods they resold were known then under various names such as commission agents, factors, sales or selling agents, warehousemen or bagmen. Thus, the use of agents means an interorganizational arrangement among channel members existed, at least in medieval times. Agency contract distribution means that agents are responsible for selling products which they do not own, and are paid on commission when goods are sold, which took up to a year. The agency method of distribution is one in which the agent acts as the marketing representative of merchant-suppliers. The medieval agency method of distribution focused mostly on the sales channel, that is, on the financial and legal aspects of the transaction of immediate concern to buyers and sellers. Both parties were preoccupied with establishing terms of trade through negotiations, terms based on information available or accessible at the time. Obviously, agents sought favourable terms of trade on behalf of the merchants they had the legal right to represent. Such agents were also involved in supply channel tasks such as setting delivery dates, making transportation arrangements, seeking insurance, etc. It was only in the twentieth century that such agents became sales specialists for their suppliers, requiring more sophisticated marketing planning and merchandising skills.

The agency method of distribution allows for the supplier to be a jobber or a manufacturer. It is likely that some jobbers assumed both distributive roles, depending on the type and quantity of goods sold, when and where the transaction took place and the terms of trade (payment, delivery dates). In other words, as jobbers, they resold some goods they owned, while for other goods they did not own, they served as selling agents in order to offer buyers a complementary assortment of goods. However, the extent to which dual distribution previously existed is uncertain, given the difficulty of assessing its usage among merchants, a measurement issue which is still present today.

A jobber may not own all the goods they sell and agents may also sell some goods they own. Similarly, manufacturers may sell goods they do not make but still own (purchased from others), thus acting as jobbers for such goods. As an economy becomes more complex so do distribution methods. Activities of manufacturing, wholesaling and retailing become blurred. In any case, these distribution methods, even dual distribution, are still with us. Demand stimulation activities such as mass advertising, branding and packaging, and visual merchandising did not exist much before the mid to late nineteenth century. The marketing effort of nineteenth-century jobbers was more business to business and not directed at consumers. They were skilled in face-to-face selling with business owners but not very skilled in merchandising practices. They did not get involved much in store displays or provide other merchandising practices for their small retailers and other customers, although they did finance their inventories. They knew the local markets they served and were often order-takers, preoccupied with their warehouse operations (supply channel), despite having well-trained drummers to get sales.

Chandler (1977, 215), stated that by 1870, nearly all travelling merchants in the US had become wholesale merchants (jobbers). This is true to some extent but it only applied to certain lines of trade dominated by large manufacturers. For Chandler, the interorganizational channel arrangement was either to distribute directly to final customers via vertical integration by using the manufacturer's sales force or distribute indirectly through independent jobbers. Chandler did not consider the contractual agency method of distribution involving independent agents nor did he consider dual distribution that is distributing both directly and through independent wholesale distributors.

The agency method of distribution was still being used in the nineteenth century and even beyond, irrespective of what Chandler says, because the use of agents was particularly attractive to small manufacturers and start-ups who could not afford their own sales organization. Even large manufacturers may find agents useful in untapped or unknown (foreign) markets. Selling costs are almost zero until sales are made. The selling agent acted like the marketing department of his suppliers without that supplier having to staff, plan, monitor and control the agent's activities, thus avoiding overheads. Large manufacturers preferred to deal with merchant middlemen rather than selling agents because they were paid quickly rather than waiting six months or more for payment until the product was sold. The money could then be invested in company operations. But it did not preclude them from using other methods of distribution in certain markets or lines of trade, as alternative channels of distribution. Even today, the contractual agency method of distribution has not disappeared, with selling agents, commission merchants, food brokers, and manufacturers' agents still handling large volumes of trade. Small manufacturers still exist and it makes good business sense for them to use selling agents rather than establishing their own costly sales force.

The department store was one of the first types of business to vertically integrate into wholesaling and manufacturing, this done long before vertical integration became more prevalent among manufacturers. Department store owners recognized the need to stimulate demand through mass advertising, frequent price deals and special sales events, actions which increased their volume of business. Department store owners were also always on the lookout for new and exclusive products made domestically or abroad because they understood consumers' shopping habits of unplanned purchases and their penchant for newness and novelties.

By the 1860s, A.T. Stewart had up to nine manufacturing plants located just in Europe. Among American importers of European dry goods, Stewart also had the most extensive foreign buying organization. Later, other large-scale retailers, such as Macy's, Marshall Field, Wanamaker and Eaton's of Canada, also backward integrated into wholesaling and manufacturing. They established foreign buying offices and entered into the manufacturing of the goods sold at retail in their stores which they also sold to wholesalers and other retailers as well (Tamilia and Reid, 2007). The buying offices were in fact wholesale organizations, most were wholly owned by department stores, while others were selling agents working under contract, but all members of the department store's channels of distribution. By 1845, A.T. Stewart became the largest and most important importer in the entire USA. He also had a wholesale division, separate from his retail one established before the 1860s, and he was not alone in this regard. His first store, the 1846 Marble Palace, was transformed into a wholesale establishment after his huge second store opened in 1862. As a result, he became a major wholesale supplier of a vast quantity and assortment of goods to other US Mid-Western wholesalers and retailers. In fact, A.T. Stewart was Marshall Field's mentor, with the latter labelled as the A.T. Stewart of the American West.

History of channel captains

Jobbers in the nineteenth century handled a wide variety of goods for numerous manufacturers often selling competing products (dry goods, rubber, jewellery, hardware, footwear). In the nineteenth century, according to Porter and Livesay (1971) and repeated by others, most manufactured goods (consumer and industrial) were distributed by the nation's network of independent merchant wholesalers, but they fail to mention the existence of agency distribution. They opened up markets not by mass advertising but with their travelling salesmen who 'crisscrossed America on trains and rode horses and stagecoaches into remote places to drum up business' (Strasser, 1989, 61). As a result, they became the channel captain of the period, especially as regard to the distribution of consumer goods. These jobbers successfully hired, trained and managed large numbers of travelling sales representatives (drummers) who covered vast territories across the US, searching for new business, taking orders and providing business intelligence back to headquarters. They reported on changing local market conditions and provided information on the credit worthiness of local buyers. More importantly, wholesalers' travelling salesmen offered personalized services to local merchants by showing them samples of goods they had brought with them or by catalogues, without such merchants needing to travel to Chicago or New York.

From the late nineteenth century onwards, producers began to dominate consumer-based distribution channels. They soon became de facto channel captains when they began to aggressively promote their brands direct to consumers, bypassing established wholesalers whose merchandising skills had not progressed. Demand pull marketing practices popularized by the department store and other mass retailers were copied and improved upon by consumer goods producers. Manufacturers also aimed their merchandising skills at omnipresent small corner grocery stores.

Strasser (1989) spent years researching trade publications studying how US consumer goods manufacturers, with their newly developed post-1880s mass-production methods, developed the new marketing practices mass production required. She described the change over from wholesaler-dominated channels in which 'wholesalers controlled marketing in both of its senses: they did the physical work of distribution and they took responsibility for product promotion' (p. 19), to a manufacturer-dominated one, at least as far as fast-moving consumer goods were concerned. In other words, both the sales and supply channels were controlled by wholesalers until consumer goods manufacturers took over control of the sales channels and left wholesalers responsible only for the physical distribution of products.

Porter and Livesay (1971) attribute the rise of the manufacturer as the dominant agent of distribution in the US to improved means of transportation and communications which facilitated contacts with distant customers. Their growing financial strength undermined the role of the wholesaler as financier. The emergence of financial intermediaries further eroded their place in distribution (Livesay and Porter, 1972). The growing complexities of products (powered by electricity) required more technical expertise to sell, install and service them, skills that the wholesalers of the time did not have.

Consumer goods manufacturers reorganized the wholesale distribution channel by first branding their products and then stimulating consumer demand. They used various marketing pull efforts, such as coupons, mass media advertising campaigns, visually appealing product packaging, stamps, premiums, in store product demonstrations, product displays, retail banners, and even publishing cookbooks and offering cooking lessons, and so forth. Of course, such consumer pull marketing efforts would not have been successful if channel push marketing efforts aimed at small food retailers had not been orchestrated at the same time. Manufacturers deployed their own sales representatives in competition with those of established suppliers (jobbers). They obtained the cooperation and trust of small retailers who believed that such new in store merchandising practices would increase traffic and sales. Consumer demand pull by manufacturers gave rise to a paradigmatic shift in consumer goods distribution in the US, a shift that took place in other countries decades later.

Consumer goods manufacturers were selling mass-produced and fast-consumed convenience goods that had not previously been marketed on a grand scale, such as toothpaste, chewing gum, safety razors, soap and cereals. These consumer goods were branded by manufacturers and offered an alternative to consumers accustomed to homemade and unbranded products sold in barrels, in bulk, or wrapped in paper or put in paper bags in small grocery stores. Additionally, these consumer goods manufacturers obtained the confidence of small food stores whose owners allowed them to do far more in store merchandising efforts, more than their regular suppliers (jobbers) had previously done.

The transition to mass distribution was not a smooth one and caused 'fundamental systemic conflicts' (Strasser, 1989, 20) between established merchant wholesalers, mass merchandisers (department stores) and mass consumer goods producers. Many mass retailers were already vertically integrated and some were more powerful than the largest manufacturers. In fact, some manufacturers' entire output was sold exclusively to a single mass retailer.

Strasser (1989) describes in detail the formidable 1912 Procter and Gamble (P&G) marketing plan for Crisco, a new solid vegetable shortening, a breakthrough in scientific discovery, it was argued, that every household in the nation should have. The elaborate marketing plan aimed first at every small grocer in the United States, each one, a month before the national advertising campaign, being urged to stock up on the product. P&G also enlisted the support of grocers urging them to write letters to customers enclosing promotional material. She did not say if participating grocers were compensated for their direct mail campaign. Her book focuses more on how large manufacturers developed business-to-consumer merchandising methods than on business-to-business efforts aimed only at grocers or other small retailers. Some of the same pull marketing effort directed at consumers, such as coupons, premiums and samples, was also aimed at grocers and even store clerks, but very few, if any, of these merchandising programmes were developed exclusively for grocers.

Transformative changes in distribution

McCammon and Bates (1965) argued that during the post-Second World War period, the distribution structure in the US underwent transformative changes that were as profound in their impact and as pervasive in their influence as those that occurred during the commercial revolution or even in the industrial revolution. This post-Second World War distribution revolution was the result of many factors which drastically changed marketing practices in distribution channels and even altered the economy's overall distribution structure.

Discount retailers first appeared in the early 1950s selling branded major appliances and electronic goods at below suggested manufacturers' prices. Manufacturers' brand names and product reputation were by then firmly established in consumers' minds. A resale price maintenance (RPM) policy also influenced the prices set by conventional retailers but not those of discounters. Instead, discounters sold the very same products at much lower prices than those found at more traditional retail outlets. Discounters adapted the supermarket method of distribution of low mark-ups and high inventory turnover rates, a mass merchandising policy, and expanded it to other lines of goods such as furniture, clothing, hardware, office supplies, building materials, and sporting goods. The rise of self service in the 1950s and 1960s also had a major impact on distribution methods and channel relationships. Discounting helped create new types of distributors with names reflecting new mass merchandising retail formats such as hypermarkets, warehouse clubs, power retailers, offprice retailers, mass merchandisers, category killers, big box stores, home renovation centers, superstores or supercentres. The lowly cash and carry wholesalers of the 1930s morphed into international mass merchandise distributors, such as Home Depot and Costco. They also began to promote aggressively their own private brands (Kenmore, Craftsman, President's Choice, Hunt Club, Great Value, generic/no name brands). The battle of the brands and the fight for shelf space among mass merchandisers and manufacturers was on.

The mass merchandising movement allowed distributors to make unprecedented changes both in the size of their stores and their operational methods with the 'application of warehouse operating principles at the retail level' (Stern and El-Ansary, 1977, 49). Revolutionary changes were also made in the way products were retailed, wholesaled and warehoused. The introduction of the computer and the UPC changed ways that products were transported, stocked, packaged, packed, labelled, ticketed, handled, ordered and displayed. The computer gave mass distributors more market power over producers with computer assisted ordering (CAO), point of sales tools (POS), RFID, category management, shelf space management and self-serve checkouts. All of this allowed for a greater product assortment, better customer value and one-stop shopping.

Larger warehouse-type stores again made distributors channel captains, a position they had lost to manufacturers almost a century before. It's no surprise that the world's largest corporation is a distributor (Wal-Mart). As the size of stores increased, so did the assortment of goods. Retailers like to add unrelated assortments of products and services to their existing product mix, a policy known as scrambled merchandising, as a means to increase volume and profits and, of course, consumer shopping convenience (one-stop shopping). Rack jobbers, also called service merchandisers, handling these additional lines soon became indispensable wholesale suppliers to mass food merchandisers and others. Large retailers cannot manage all store items. They prefer to subcontract (outsource) the distribution responsibility of some goods for many reasons (seasonal, lack of knowledge, freshness, etc.) to rack jobbers. These specialized wholesalers are currently paid on consignment and assume full responsibility for stocking, pricing, displaying and managing such goods in specified store locations.

Some marketing programmes among channel members

Marketing programmes among channel members existed long before the distribution revolution of the 1960s. They have been in place ever since manufacturers became channel captains. All marketing programmes, distribution programmes and other management aids contribute towards a greater level of interdependence among members. Such marketing programmes are used in the channel to better coordinate and control the sale of products and services. They are also a means to select, motivate, reward, evaluate, control and even eliminate non-performing channel members. They motivate and reward members and establish a lasting supplier–distributor bond by increasing switching costs. Greater support, cooperation and trust among channel members are required if distribution objectives are to be attained. Unfortunately, many channel marketing programmes are, for competitive reasons, kept confidential. However, sometimes trade journals may provide a glimpse of such programmes, following a corporate press release. The ones discussed by McCammon and Bates (1965), McCammon (1970) or Stern and El-Ansary (1977) are now obsolete but still historically informative. However, not much is said by these authors about their market impact, why they were developed in the first place, and what kinds of agreement preceded them.

Notwithstanding the marketing support small grocers and others received from manufacturers in the early part of the twentieth century, more elaborate channel to channel merchandising programmes, incentive programmes, financial reward programmes and other marketing agreements likely emerged later in the century. Jones (1905) revealed some surprising and unexpected marketing practices that showed the extent to which manufacturers were assuming an increased range of mercantile functions that 'have a direct interest in the soundness and profitableness of those businesses engaged in distributing their products' (p. 14). He then elaborated on four marketing programmes by which manufacturers had been able both to profitably regulate retail prices and to control the distribution of their products. These marketing plans were exclusive agency, price contracts, rebate plan and serial numbering plan. The price contract is an agreement regulating the selling prices of all channel members involved in the distribution process. The rebate plan is a contractual arrangement whereby a manufacturer sells to a dealer at a certain open price, along with the usual rebates for cash. The dealer is not bound to sell at a given price. At the end of a given period, the dealer provides an affidavit that the goods were not sold at less than the mentioned price; thereupon the manufacturer offers him an extra discount. The serial numbering plan is more elaborate than the others. Suffice it to say that only authorized wholesalers could handle the goods, and they were under contract to sell only to those retailers approved by the manufacturer. It was a plan that enabled the manufacturer to track product movement and to know the inventory levels of various channel members.

Finally, exclusive agency means one dealer under contract is the only one allowed to sell the goods in each market. It was a plan used by many manufacturers pre-twentieth century. In fact, the agency method of distribution discussed earlier also qualifies as such a network arrangement. Exclusive agency limits competition which is exactly what dealers want. In return, the manufacturer gives 'an extra cash discount to dealers who handle no rival goods' (Jones, 1905, 14). Manufacturers are thus able to control both the retail prices at which their goods are sold and the profit margins dealers receive. The US Industrial Commission (1901) reported that an exclusive agency contract (exclusive distribution) was a marketing practice being used by manufacturers such as Eastman Kodak. The Kodak plan offered a trade discount of 15 per cent. But under exclusivity, the dealer received an additional 12 per cent discount. Moreover, Eastman Kodak restricted distribution of its full line of products to those dealers with whom it had an exclusive agreement.

Rubinow (1905) presents a solid review of the premium craze that was very popular in the late nineteenth and early part of the twentieth century, particularly in the eastern part of the US. Manufacturers were using premiums or free prizes given to consumers for buying that manufacturer's brand, in an age where consumer branding by large manufacturers was on the rise. This marketing practice of stimulating demand direct to consumers weakened the influence of both wholesalers and retailers. Its aim was to promote brand loyalty. Rubinow (1905) estimated that 300 grocery items such as tobacco, coffee, tea, and cereal were sold with a premium. Small retailers thought that such supplier merchandising practices would increase store traffic. They did, but while premiums yielded higher profit margins for manufacturers they often failed 'to furnish the small dealer with the means for even a modest existence' (Rubinow, 1905, 586). He argued that the prices paid for branded products associated with premiums were 'considerably higher than the prices for similar commodities anywhere in the country' (p. 574). In reality, consumers wrongly perceived the premium as giving them something for nothing.

The original focus of consumer premiums was fast-moving consumer goods sold in small food shops. However, their popularity soon caught the attention of department stores and their premiums became more generous than those offered by manufacturers. Interestingly, some of these premiums were offered exclusively to channel members. Trade-oriented premiums may have been one of the first types of incentives offered to retailers. Interestingly, Hubbard's (1909) biography of A.T. Stewart, the man now recognized as being the founding father of the department store, revealed that Stewart used premiums when he opened his small dry goods store in New York City in 1823. In his first sale, 'a lady bought scallops and lace for $2, and he gave her free sundry yards of braid, a card of buttons and a paper of hooks and eyes' (Hubbard, 1909, 342).

Hood and Yamey (1957) discussed the history of the retail store cooperative movement in the UK. Initially, retail store co-operatives did not carry stocks of all merchandise for groceries made up the bulk of their sales. Such co-ops were essentially buying groups organized to pool their members' buying power to get better price concessions from suppliers (group buying). They may have also established their own warehouses. With greater bargaining power, the main goal of a retail store co-operative was to pass cost savings to consumer-members, thus lowering their food prices. There were over 80 such retail organizations in existence between 1868 and 1890. These retail store co-ops accepted cash only, products had marked prices, the consumer had to pay extra for delivery, wrote his own invoice using a price list. The consumer needed to have the invoice accepted and, with receipt in hand, then had to stand in line and wait while the goods were being assembled. Retail store co-ops in the UK, as elsewhere, were not usually efficiently managed even if consumers saved a few dollars. They were not professionally managed retail organizations, given that consumers were largely responsible for managing them. Retail store co-ops were more successful in the UK and Europe than in the US where the movement never really caught on. The first retail store co-op in the US appeared in New England between 1847 and 1859 and by 1896, New England membership totalled about 19,000. By then, British cooperative societies had a membership in the millions (Cummings, 1897).

On the other hand, Brown *et al.* (1970) report that the first retailer-sponsored co-operative in the US was established before the advent of voluntary groups, probably around the 1860s or about the same time retail store co-operatives were first established in Europe. A retailer-sponsored co-op is one in which the wholesale-supplier is owned by retail members. Wholesaler-sponsored voluntary groups came later and were first established in the US in the mid-1910s. A voluntary group is one in which numerous retailers contractually agree to purchase a large portion of their supplies from the sponsoring wholesaler. They are still buying groups and organized to get very favourable terms of trade from suppliers, benefits which are passed on to retail members. These members are not the ultimate consumer but rather member-retailers, part of an interorganizational channel arrangement and a special type of channel of distribution known as a vertical marketing system (McCammon and Bates, 1965; McCammon, 1970). Over time, voluntary groups became managerially more sophisticated than retailer co-ops and offered many more managerial and marketing services to their retail members. Both types of contractual channel arrangements are vertical marketing systems in which merchandising programming to members is the norm.

It is interesting to note that Gide (1924, 1929), an economist and one of France's most vocal supporters of retail store co-operatives, stated during the 1889 Paris Exposition that it was now time for the consumer to be king ('le règne du consommateur'), decades before Charles C. Parlin, the founding father of marketing research, uttered these same words. Gide (1929, 18) also said 'I spend, therefore I am!' ('je dépense, donc je suis'), a Cartesian slogan which shows once again that consumer orientation was not an exclusive post-Second World War preoccupation. The business model of retail store co-operatives proved to be uneconomical and unmanageable and few still exist. But wholesaler-sponsored voluntary groups and retailer-sponsored co-operative groups are still involved not only in the grocery trade (IGA) but as well in the distribution of many other product categories (hardware, building supplies). Voluntary groups appear better able than retailer sponsored co-ops to compete very favourably with corporate chains. Voluntary groups are now more national and international in scope than retailer-sponsored co-operative groups. Today, both groups operate more like corporate chains because many of their stores are under corporate ownership.

Franchising is a special type of distributive channel arrangement in which a parent company (franchisor) grants the right to a franchisee (individual or a small company) under contract to do business according to a prescribed format over a certain period of time in a specified territory. Some believe that voluntary groups, retailer-sponsored co-operative groups and franchising systems are all similar because they operate under a common logo banner. However, their business models are quite dissimilar. There is no standard franchising arrangement but rather many different types of franchise systems. Some involve marketing and licensing arrangements between manufacturer-retailer, wholesaler-retailer, manufacturer-wholesaler, and service-sponsor-retailer. The issues covered in such contractual distribution agreements may include numerous legal clauses dealing with tying agreements, territorial rights, termination clauses, royalty fees, rental fees, sales of new products, licensing fees, various promotional fees and dual distribution, all issues that are beyond the scope of this chapter (Stern and El-Ansary, 1977; Stern and Eovaldi, 1984). Franchising, as an organized channel network among members, has a long history. From the late nineteenth century on, manufacturer-dealer franchising has been the principal method of selling automobiles but not before wholesalers were first tried. Ford appointed franchised dealers to sell the Model T Ford in the early 1900s. The oil companies followed suit with franchised gas stations. Benjamin Franklin has been credited as being the first commercial franchisor in North America, this in the eighteenth century (www://franchises. about.com). However, little is known about the nature of network arrangement he might have had with his franchisees.

The distribution of the sewing machine presents a unique view of channel choice development. The sewing machine is a nineteenth-century innovation for which no single inventor can claim credit. There were thousands of patents granted over a 50-year period that began from the late 1830s. The sewing machine became the first to be manufactured with interchangeable parts, making servicing much easier. It was the first complex product with a standardized technology to be mass marketed, unlike the manufactured goods which were custom made before mass-production techniques were developed later in the nineteenth century. The sewing machine sold quite well in many countries, with marketing and distribution playing a large role in its success (Jack, 1957). The machines were sold both to individuals and to clothing manufacturers. As early as 1856, the Singer Company was the first in the US to introduce an instalment plan (deferred payments) for a sewing machine, a marketing practice which greatly expanded consumer demand. Self-employed rural customers could even rent the machine for one dollar per week. Rural farm women not only sewed clothing items, they also sewed sheets, quilts, curtains, feed sacks, gloves, shirts and other articles for sale in country stores. The sewing machine encouraged department stores to vertically integrate into the manufacturing of ready-made clothes. They hired thousands of women who worked in the upstairs floors of department stores or in buildings adjacent to the flagship store. These ready to wear clothes then sold in the department store, via mail order catalogues or to other distributors.

Jack (1957) and Godley (2007) provide a short history of distribution methods by the Singer Company. It first granted territorial rights to independent selling agents under a franchise agency system. Commission agents were also hired to work in branch stores selling the machines on consignment and were paid primarily on commission. The company then opened wholly owned and fancier stores, and unlike branch stores, were staffed by knowledgeable people, who could service and repair machines and could even offer credit to customers. Eventually, as sales grew and the company's financial strength improved, such company owned stores dominated the distribution network. By 1900, Singer had over 800 stores in the US.

Price-based marketing agreements among channel members

The medieval philosophy of the just price and just wage is not unique to that time period. Freidman (1984, 198) reported that similar price thinking existed in Talmudic times.

> The Talmud was afraid that too many intermediaries would result in high prices. Thus, in Israel, one was not permitted to make a profit as a middleman on commodities which were deemed necessary for life. These included such items as wines, oils, and various types of flour. These products were supposed to be sold directly from the producer to

the consumer in order to keep prices low (p. 199) ... The Talmud strongly believed in maintaining fair prices. Thus, it developed the following rules ... If the overcharge is less than one sixth, the sale is considered valid and the overcharge may be kept ... If the overcharge is exactly one sixth, the sale is still valid, but the overcharge must be returned. If the overcharge is more than one sixth, the sale is null and void (p. 202) ... Those middlemen who have virtually no overhead are allowed only a one-sixth profit over the cost of the item. Other intermediaries, such as retailers, who sell small quantities and have many expenses, are permitted to make a one-sixth profit on total cost, including the retailer's own labor ... more profit – even 400 percent on luxury items such as perfumes.

Moving forward to consider nineteenth-century pricing practices, consumer credit, then known as retail instalment selling, has a fascinating history, especially in France. Singer may have been the first US manufacturer to offer instalment selling plans to consumers. Others followed, as discussed by Lynn (1957) including makers of pianos, farm equipment and numerous other goods. However, its level of popularity in nineteenth-century France was unprecedented, perhaps because it was not manufacturer-initiated but rather retailer-initiated. The story begins with J.F. Crépin, a photographer, who decided in 1856 to sell 20 photos paid over time with one franc as a down payment. He had so many customers that he could not keep up with the demand. He then developed a marketing agreement with a number of retail merchants whereby consumers got credit tokens (vouchers) allowing them to buy merchandise on credit in participating stores. Georges Dufayel took over the credit business after Crépin died and by the 1870s, Dufayel transformed consumer instalment selling into a French national institution. Over 400 stores including many department stores accepted Dufayel's vouchers. Goods purchased required a 20 per cent down payment and Dufayel clients repaid the rest in small weekly instalments. In Paris alone, 3,000 clerks were employed to handle the orders and another 800 went out each day to collect repayments. By the end of the nineteenth century, there had been over 3 million Dufayel customers and there were credit branches in every large French town. By 1907, three out of every seven working-class families in Paris were doing business with Dufayel (Williams, 1982; Coffin, 1994). Dufayel also built a truly magnificent store to handle his credit business. At the time, Dufayel became the first department store to sell on credit, while others accepted cash only. The Dufayel instalment plan was so successful that it attracted rival credit firms. It was the beginning of the consumer credit era. The Parisian-based La Samaritaine may have been the first department store to organize its own credit company in 1913. Perhaps this explains why many department stores and other retailers were reluctant to accept credit cards, other than their own, decades after banks first issued such cards.

Fixed prices presented a problem for both merchants and customer, according to Williams (1982). Merchants were abusing customers who shopped in their stores using credit vouchers. Too often they were paying far more for the goods than they would have if they paid cash like other customers. The store had to pay a commission when redeeming the vouchers and as a result retail prices were raised accordingly by as much as 40 per cent in some cases. Store clerks were even told to hide retail prices when a customer was targeted as one having credit vouchers.

Cash payment either to retailers and other members of the channel was uncommon prior to the twentieth century for a number of reasons. The scarcity of money was one. Also many buyers were farmers and they lacked the means to pay until their crops were sold later in the year. Price haggling between buyers and sellers was the norm. With the rise of the department store after the 1850s, cash only became a more common practice. Department stores were

195

large urban retail institutions located in the downtown core of cities. They catered to tens of thousands and sometimes even hundreds of thousands of customers on some days. Price haggling was just not possible for such stores and cash payment was also the most desirable method of completing the sale. Clearly marked fixed prices were the department store norm.

But fixed pricing was known in Europe in the eighteenth century. For example, Jarry (1948, 81) presents an illustration of an ad dated 25 October 1824 (perhaps a handbill) for a Parisian store called La Belle Jardinière on opening day, informing the public that the store had fixed prices. A.T. Stewart's first small store in the 1820s used fixed pricing, long before he did the same at his 1846 Marble Palace, the very first department store located in New York City. Westerfield (1915, 346) goes even further back in time and says that fixed prices on merchandise were in effect in 1712–13 in a dry goods and clothing store, dismissing the myth that the department store was the original user of this pricing practice.

Marked prices on tags attached to merchandise was even less common than fixed prices, even during the credit craze in France in the nineteenth century. But the practice was encouraged by the 1855 Paris world fair, the first world fair to mandate price tags on all products on display. This practice allowed retailers to have at least two sets of prices, the ones marked on tags and the lower ones at which they were prepared to sell. This practice allowed suppliers (or manufacturers) to suggest the prices retailers should charge, some going so far as to put the suggested retail price on the package, a practice that began in the early 1900s. It was, however, still up to the retailer to decide the final price using the suggested price as a reference point. Some retailers using marked prices developed secret price marks useful in indicating what the real price was. The marked pricing practice has a long history and is still with us today, with the regular price shown when merchandise is on sale or in markdowns. Today's consumers cannot decipher the secret price code on tags as some could a century ago, leaving them to wonder if indeed they are getting a bargain.

Before the retail price maintenance movement of the 1890s, manufacturers allowed retailers to price their branded goods below their advertised prices (Yamey, 1952). Few manufacturers objected to the price-cutting habit of some retailers. Today, this is called loss leader selling, a practice of selling branded goods at low prices to attract customers. The politics of distribution gave rise to some retailers putting pressure on manufacturers to enforce minimum retail prices because price cutters were allegedly using unfair trade practices. Yamey (1952) concluded that the history of RPM was not the result of manufacturers being overly concerned about the reputational damage done to their brands by retail price cutting but because some retailers, notably small ones, objected to the loss of business and viscerally disliked price competition. It was a period of social activism with widespread support for the notion of fair living wages for small retailers. RPM was not, at least initially, part of a manufacturer's branding and advertising strategy, as it became later in the 1910s, and still clandestinely remains, even though RPM is now illegal.

Strasser (1989) described the resale price movement in the US as if it had originated in the 1910s, neglecting to mention that retail price competition on branded merchandises existed decades earlier. In any case, US manufacturers realized the market power of their brands and capitalized on this power by adopting a RPM policy, referring to it as 'fair trade'. This allowed them to control the subsequent price of their brands even after they sold them, a policy of price fixing, even though they had given up 'not only title to the goods but any right to govern the sale that middlemen made to a third party' (Stresser, 1989, 269).

RPM was an alliance between manufacturers and small retailers, each group being well represented by their own trade groups while the well-being of consumers was ignored. It was a weapon used against mass retailers, notably department stores and mail order catalogue retailers, because of their refusal to respect the agreed price. From the start, RPM touched upon antitrust issues dealing with patents and trademarks. Over the next half century, countless books, articles and legal opinions were written on the topic with more laws passed especially in the 1930s (Robinson Patman Act of 1936; Miller Tydings Act of 1937). Eventually, the Consumer Goods Pricing Act of 1975 made it illegal to use price maintenance agreements among manufacturers and resellers in interstate commerce. It would be near impossible in this chapter to summarize all the jurisprudence and marketing implications of this practice, one which began among channel members at the turn of the twentieth century. Similarly, slotting allowances, basically fees retailers charge suppliers for shelf space, and advertising allowances, which are payments made by manufacturers (and sometimes wholesalers) to retailers for various types of sales promotional effort are other channel marketing practices which had their origin at the turn of the turn of nineteenth century and they are as controversial as RPM. One also cannot do justice to their history within the space available. Unlike RPM, slotting allowances, despite numerous studies by both legal experts and government-commissioned reports, are still practised today because they have not been found to be illegal unfair trade practices (FTC, 2003).

Chandler (1977) discussed two business practices of significant importance in the distributive trades. One is gross margin — sales revenue minus cost of goods sold. The other is the rate of inventory turnover or 'the number of times stock on hand was sold and replaced within a specified time period' (p. 223). He added that 'the concept of stock-turn only appeared in American marketing after the coming of the railroads had permitted the rise of the modern wholesaler' (p. 223). The inventory turnover concept is an accounting method developed specifically for the distributive trades, especially wholesaling because, 'stock-turn was, indeed, an effective measure of the efficiency of a distributing enterprise, for the higher the stock-turn with the same working force and equipment, the lower the unit cost and the higher the output per worker and facility' (Chandler, 1997, 233). Chandler adds, 'I know of no example of a pre-railroad merchant using that term' (1997, 233). This important concept explains why wholesalers need to manage their inventory to succeed because inventory carrying costs can account for up to 50 per cent of total costs (Stern and El-Ansary, 1977). Similarly, retailers also need to manage their inventory carrying costs. Successful retailers appear to be those that can master well their overall wholesaling activities, including inventories. The gross margin concept is also an essential managerial tool. However, accounting historians might know more as to when, why and how gross margins were first used, one that even today remains a strong profitability measure, one many retailers prefer to turnover. Gross margin per unit sale is an easier concept for small retailers to grasp. Stock turnover rates require more sophisticated financial data and cannot be applied on a per unit product basis but rather on overall retail profitability calculated per accounting period.

Conclusions

Marketing practices among channel members were indeed present not only in ancient times but also in pre-twentieth-century Europe and America (Shapiro and Doody, 1968). The evolution of these practices has not received enough attention except when discussed by business and social historians either in the context of the historical development of the economy or the business practices of certain firms, notably large consumer goods manufacturers. Marketing practices tying channel members together are sometimes similar to consumer marketing practices but more often than not they differ radically. Moreover, consumer marketing practices are by definition interdependent and interrelated to some degree with those aimed at various channel members, a fact that is often not recognized.

Some marketing practices were mentioned in this chapter but not discussed in any great detail due to space limitations. Others were not even mentioned, notably those dealing with the supply channel. A channel of distribution focus presents a golden opportunity to bring back into academic marketing the study of the supply channel, the other half of marketing. After all, logistics service providers have been in business for millennia and have long employed marketing practices, agreements and partnerships that have linked them interorganizationally with other channel members.

The marketing practices employed in channels are often subject to antitrust laws and other regulatory enforcement rules that are unlike those focusing on the consumer. Price fixing, predatory and discriminatory pricing, exclusive dealings, tied contracts, territorial and customer restrictions, resale price maintenance, reciprocity, refusals to deal, functional and quantity discounts, licensing agreements, vertical integration, slotting and promotional fees, full line forcing, and dual distribution are among the topics discussed in Stern and Eovaldi (1984), a channels textbook covering the legal implications of such marketing practices. Most laws affecting the actual conduct of business are, in fact, laws aimed at the marketing practices employed by various businesses involved in the distribution of goods and services.

Business and social historians have done a remarkable job documenting the role played by marketing in the evolution of business in our market economy. They have contributed a descriptively rich and detailed account of what business did during the last century and even earlier. These authors have done the research expected of the best professional historians.

> They have delved into archives to study correspondence, business documents, pictures, transcripts of interviews, and promotional ephemera (e.g., coupons, trading stamps, illustrated trade cards). They have mastered thick runs of trade newspapers and magazines as well as available company histories and relevant academic studies.
>
> *(Fullerton, 1991, 84)*

Despite this tremendous academic achievement, examples of the multitude of marketing programmes and interorganizational agreements that previously governed relationships among channel members are most likely still hidden away in archival collections. Such documents deserve to be unearthed and studied.

However, a case can be made for looking forwards as well as backwards. Unprecedented changes have occurred in distribution in the last 30 or more years, the full impact of which is still being felt with digital marketing. Yet academic marketing has largely ignored the changes in the interorganizational networks among channel members, preferring instead to look at such topics as the social and media networks of consumers and how these networks affect brand perceptions. These are interesting topics but not any more so than the changes which have occurred and are still occurring within channels of distribution. After all, a multitude of economic participants other than the consumer exist in society.

The channel domain is a vast and expanding field with numerous subfields and topics which can be studied individually and historically. Channels do nothing less than bring our society's mix of goods and services to the marketplace. This provisioning function makes them an indispensable part of the marketing process. The channel domain thus emerges as an ideal alternative to an almost exclusive focus on the behaviour of the ultimate consumer.

References

Albion, R. (1939) *The Rise of New York Port*, Charles Scribner's Sons, New York.

Atherton, L. (1949) *The Southern Country Store, 1800–1860*, Louisiana State University Press, Baton Rouge, LA.

Beckman, T., and Davidson, W. (1967) *Marketing* (8th edition), Ronald Press, New York.

Berlow, R. (1971) 'The development of business techniques used at the fairs of Champagne from the end of the twelfth century to the middle of the thirteenth century', *Studies in Medieval and Renaissance History*, 8, 3–31.

Brown, M., Applebaum, W., and Salmon, W. (1970) *Strategy Problems of Mass Retailers and Wholesalers*, Richard D. Irwin, Homewood, IL.

Carus-Wilson, E.M. (1967) *Medieval Merchant Venturers Collected Studies*, Methuen, London.

Carver, T.N. (1917) 'Standardization in marketing', *Quarterly Journal of Economics*, 31/2, 341–444.

Chandler, A.D., Jr. (1977) *The Visible Hand: The Managerial Revolution in American Business*, Harvard University Press, Cambridge, MA.

Chatelain, A. (1971) 'Lutte entre colporteurs et boutiquiers en France pendant la première moitié du XIXe siècle', *Revue d'histoire économique et sociale*, 49/3, 359–84.

Cochrane, R. (1966) *Measures for Progress: A History of the National Bureau of Standards*, US Department of Commerce, Washington, DC.

Coffin, J. (1994) 'Credit, consumption, and images of women's desires: Selling the sewing machine in late nineteenth-century France', *French Historical Studies*, 18/3, 749–83.

Cummings, E. (1897) 'Co-operative Stores in the United States', *Quarterly Journal of Economics*, 11/3, 266–79.

Davidson, W. (1961) 'Marketing channels and institutions', *Business Horizons*, 4 (Feb.), 84–90.

Davis, N.Z. (1960) 'Sixteenth-century arithmetics on business life', *Journal of the History of Ideas*, 21/1, 18–48.

De Roover, R. (1958) 'The concept of the just price: Theory and economic policy', *Journal of Economic History* (18 Dec.), 418–34.

Dixon, D.F. (1982) 'The historical origins of the channel concept', in M. Harvey and R. Lusch (eds), *Marketing Channels: Domestic and International Perspectives*, Center for Economic and Management Research, University of Oklahoma, Norman, OK, pp. 146–51.

Dixon, J.F., Cann, J., and Renfew, C. (1968) 'Obsidian and the origins of trading', *Scientific American*, 219/3, 38–46.

Elisseeff, Vadime (ed.) (2000) *The Silk Roads: Highways of Culture and Commerce*, Berghahn Books, New York.

Ericson, J., and Earle, T. (eds) (1982) *Contexts for Prehistoric Exchanges*, Academic Press, New York.

Federal Trade Commission (2003) *Slotting Allowances in the Retail Grocery Industry: Selected Case Studies in Five Product Categories*, FTC, Washington, DC.

Finkelstein, J., and Thimm, A. (1973) *Economists and Society: The Development of Economic Thought from Aquinas to Keynes*, Harper & Row, New York.

Franklin, A. (1894) *Les magasins de nouveautés*, Librairie Plon, Paris.

Freidman, H. (1984) 'Ancient marketing practices: The view from Talmudic times', *Journal of Public Policy and Marketing*, 3/3, 194–204.

Fullerton, R. (1991) 'Book reviews: Strasser's *Satisfaction Guaranteed* and Tedlow's *The Story of Mass Marketing in America*', *Journal of Marketing*, 55 (July), 84–5.

Gide, C. (1924) *Les sociétés coopératives de consommation*, Librairie du Recueil Sirey, Paris.

Gide, C. (1929) 'La C.G.C.', *Revue d'économie politique*, 43, 13–43.

Godley, A. (2006) 'Selling the sewing machine around the world: Singers international marketing strategies, 1850–1920', *Enterprise and Society*, 7/2, 266–314.

Gras, N. S. B., and Larson, H. (1939) *Casebook in American Business History*, Appleton-Century-Crofts, New York.

Hollander, S. (1964) 'Nineteenth century anti-drummer legislation in the United States', *Business History Review*, 38 (Winter), 479–500.

Hood, J., and Yamey, B. (1957) 'The middle-class cooperative retailing societies in London, 1864–1900', *Oxford Economic Papers*, 9, 309–22.

Hubbard, E. (1909) 'A.T. Stewart', *Little Journeys to the Homes of Great Business Men*, vol. 2, *The Roycrofters*, East Aurora, New York, pp. 329–55.

Huvelin, P. (1897) *Essai historique sur le droit des marchés et des foires*, Arthur Rousseau, Paris.

Jack, A. (1957) 'The channels of distribution for an innovation: The sewing machine industry in America, 1860–1865', *Explorations in Entrepreneurial History*, 9 (Feb.), 113–41.

Jarry, P. (1948) *Les magasins de nouveautés: Histoire rétrospective et anecdotique*, André Barry et fils, Paris.

Jones, E. (1905) 'The manufacturer and the domestic market', *Annals of the Academy of Political and Social Science*, 25 (Jan.), 1–20.

Khalaf, S.G. (2015) 'Phoenicia', available online: http://phoenicia.org/trade (accessed Mar. 2015).

King, C. (1913) 'Municipal markets', *Annals of the American Academy of Political and Social Science*, 50 (Nov.), 102–17.

Lévy-Bruhl, H. (1933) 'La noblesse de France et le commerce à la fin de l'ancien régime', *Revue d'histoire moderne*, 8/2, 209–35.

Ligt, L. de (1988) 'Ancient periodic markets: Festivals and fairs', *Athenaeum*, 66, 391–416.

Livesay, H., and Porter, Glenn (1972) 'The financial role of merchants in the development of U.S. manufacturing, 1815–1860', *Explorations in Economic History*, 9, 63–87.

Lopez, R., and Raymond. I. (1955) *Medieval Trade in the Mediterranean World*, Columbia University Press, New York.

Lynn, R. (1957) 'Installment credit before 1870', *Business History Review*, 31/4, 414–24.

McCammon, B. (1970) 'Perspectives for distribution programming', in L. Bucklin (ed.), *Vertical Marketing Systems*, Scott, Foresman & Co., Glenview, IL, pp. 32–51.

McCammon, B., and Bates, A. (1965) 'The emergence and growth of contractually integrated channels in the American economy', in P. Bennett (ed.), *Marketing and Economic Development*, American Marketing Association, Chicago, IL, pp. 465–515.

McCammon, B., and Little, R. (1965) 'Marketing channels: Analytical systems and approaches', in G. Schwartz (ed.), *Science in Marketing*, Wiley, New York, pp. 321–85.

Mitchell, Ian (2007) 'The changing role of fairs in the long eighteenth century: Evidence from the north Midlands', *Economic History Review*, 60/3, 545–73.

Moore, E. (1985) *The Fairs of Medieval England: An Introductory Study*, Pontifical Institute of Medieval Studies, Toronto.

Mulvihill, D. (1987) 'Middle East merchants of the fourteenth century as viewed by IBN Khaldun', in T. Nevett and S. Hollander (eds), *Marketing in Three Eras*, Michigan State University, East Lansing, MI, pp. 23–31.

Origo, I. (1957) *The Merchant of Prato*, Alfred A. Knopf, New York.

Porter, G. (1980) 'Marketing', in G. Porter (ed.), *Encyclopedia of American Economic History*, vol. 1, Charles Scribner's Sons, New York, pp. 386–96.

Porter, G., and Livesay, H. (1971) *Merchants and Manufacturers: Studies in the Changing Structure of Nineteenth Century Marketing*, Johns Hopkins Press, Baltimore, MD.

Rubinow, I.M. (1905) 'Premiums in retail trade', *Journal of Political Economy*, 13/4, 574–86.

Savary, Jacques (1675) *Le Parfait negociant*, J. Guignard Fils, Paris.

Shapiro, S.J., and Doody, A. (eds) (1968) *Readings in the History of American Marketing: Settlement to Civil War*, Richard D. Irwin, Homewood, IL.

Shaw, Arch (1916) *An Approach to Business Problems*, Harvard University Press, Cambridge, MA.

Spufford, M. (1984) *The Great Reclothing of Rural England: Petty Chapmen and their Wares in the Seventeenth Century*, Hambledon Press, London.

Stern, L., and El-Ansary, A. (1977) *Marketing Channels*, Prentice-Hall, Englewood Cliffs, NJ.

Stern, L., and Eovaldi, T. (1984) *Legal Aspects of Marketing Strategy*, Prentice Hall, Englewood Cliffs, NJ.

Strasser, S. (1989) *Satisfaction Guaranteed: The Making of the American Mass Market*, Pantheon Books, New York.

Tamilia, R.D. (2011) 'The timeless intellectual contributions of Donald F. Dixon', *Journal of Historical Research in Marketing*, 3/1, 33–52.

Tamilia, R.D., and Reid, S. (2007) 'Technological innovation and the rise of the department store in the nineteenth century', *International Journal of Technology Marketing*, 2/2, 110–39.

Tosdal, H. (1957) *Selling in our Economy: An Economic and Social Analysis of Selling and Advertising*, Richard D. Irwin, Homewood, IL.

United States Industrial Commission (1901) *Report of the Industrial Commission on Trusts and Industrial Combinations, 13,* Government Printing Office, Washington, DC, pp. 197–200.

Verlinden, C. (1963) 'Markets and Fairs', in M. Postan, E. Rich and E. Miller (eds), *Cambridge Economic History of Europe*, vol. 3, Cambridge University Press, pp. 119–53.

Vidal, P., and Duru, L. (1911) *Histoire de la Corporation des Marchands Merciers,* Honoré Champion, Paris.

Westerfield, R. (1915) *Middlemen in English Business Particularly Between 1660 and 1760,* Yale University Press, New Haven, CT.

Williams, R. (1982) *Dream Worlds: Mass Consumption in Late Nineteenth–Century France*, University of California Press, Berkeley, CA.

Yamey, B. (1952) 'The Origins of Resale Price Maintenance', *Economic Journal,* 62 (Sept.), 522–45.

11
A history of advertising and sales promotion

Fred K. Beard

Introduction

Advertising may have more than its share of historical works. Histories date to the nineteenth century (Sampson, 1874), and general historical texts were written in the 1920s, 1950s, 1980s, 1990s and 2000s. The 1980s and 1990s were especially productive decades for advertising historians.

Schwarzkopf (2011), who reviewed studies published between 1980 and 2010 and synthesized the findings with several of the classic historical works, concluded that much advertising history is limited by at least two methodological-theoretical norms: 'Americanization' and 'Modernization'. America, as Schwarzkopf (2011, 534) observed,

> is talked up by historians into the embodiment of a new stage in the development of humanity, a stage dominated by modern consumer capitalism. With the takeover of European culture by the American advertising industry, thus goes the story, history had finally arrived at the level of a globally shared consumerist consciousness.

This chapter presents an integrative history that seeks to avoid these theoretical and philosophical limitations. First, rather than focusing on a supposedly 'modern' era, the narrative attempts a more comprehensive analysis of advertising's history in order to identify developmental trends and themes in advertiser beliefs and practices over the long term. As one historian and practitioner observed, 'Over the centuries, advertising has experienced changes in the proportioning of its ingredients, in direction, in application, but something of the first advertisement survives in the latest, and there will be traces of it in the last' (Wood, 1958, 502).

Second, the chapter directly avoids the Americanization paradigmatic limitation by synthesizing cross-cultural and global research findings. Although there is little doubt that the American advertising industry influenced other countries largely during the twentieth century, important themes include the extent to which media development, industry structures, professional practices and creative expression developed independently from

American influence. Important and related themes include how economic, political and legal contexts have also influenced developments throughout the world.

Third, this chapter offers a brief history of sales promotion. Sales promotion encompasses short-term marketing tactics targeting both consumers and the trade that often supplement advertising and personal selling. Although there is no indication in the literature regarding when the term sales promotion first came into use, one of the earliest definitions is that of the Committee of Definitions of the American Marketing Association, in 1950. Despite contemporary expenditures that rival those of advertising, a search revealed only one journal article (Wolofson, 2012) and one book (Lloyd and Spedding, 2009) on sales promotion history. This chapter, thus, contributes a comprehensive historical overview and synthesis of the marketing sub-disciplines of advertising and sales promotion. Indeed, as Church (1999) suggested, the study of advertising becomes almost inseparable from marketing in modern times.

Approach

The search for sources began with a list of more than 3,000 works, originally compiled for a study of the most influential contributions to advertising's literature. The list contained numerous works devoted to advertising history, including all the most widely cited, general histories (e.g. Fox, 1984; Lears, 1994; Marchand, 1985; Pope, 1983; Presbrey, 1929; Rowsome, 1970; Schudson, 1984). However, also present were several earlier works, including some with an international scope (Foster, 1967; Hindley, 1884; Leachman, 1950; Rivers, 1929; Turner, 1952; Wood, 1958). These sources were then augmented with a database search, with the goal of locating additional books, book chapters and refereed journal articles focusing on relevant topics specifically outside the scope of the Modernization and Americanization paradigms.

Periodization

The a priori periodization scheme began with Schwarzkopf's (2011, 539) observation that lacking are 'more integrative analyses of medieval, early-modern and contemporary advertising communications'. Thus, the scheme relies on classical and European historiographical approaches as well as major events in advertising's history. It identifies 'Medieval' advertising as developments occurring prior to the end of the Middle Ages and, in particular, German goldsmith Johannes Gutenberg's introduction of printing to Europe around 1449. 'Early-Modern' advertising refers to a period defined by many as the end of the Middle Ages to the start of the industrial revolution, roughly the late fifteenth to the late eighteenth century. The 'Late-Modern' period refers to the nineteenth century, the 'Contemporary' period refers to the 1900s to the 1950s, and 'Post-Modern' advertising consists of the remaining years of the twentieth century and beginning of the twenty-first. This final period includes two key events: advertising's 'Creative Revolution' and the digital revolution that began during the last decade of the twentieth century (Tungate, 2013). A comparison of the periodization scheme to several long-view advertising histories – previously summarized by Church (1999) and Hollander *et al.* (2005) – is shown in Figure 11.1.

Figure 11.1 Advertising history periodizations

	Year	Pre-1449	1450s–1799	1800s	1900s to 1950s	1960s to 2010s
Current		Medieval advertising and sales promotions	Early-modern advertising and sales promotions	Late-modern advertising and sales promotions	Contemporary advertising and sales promotions	Post-modern advertising and sales promotions
Fox	1984	19th-century prehistory			1890–1920: Emergence of agencies / 1920–1929: Advertising boom / 1930–1945: Depression, reform, WWII / 1945–1960: Second boom	1960–1970: Creative revolution / 1970–1980: Return to hard sell
Pope	1985	1700–1870: Rudimentary			Late 19th–early 20th century: Growth of national advertising and rise of full-service agencies / 1915–1925: Truth in advertising / 1955–1970: Increasing segmentation and agency specialization	1970–1980s: Revival of truth in advertising
Pollay	1985				1900–1920: Emergent era / 1930–1940: Experimentation / 1940–1950: Emergency / 1950–1965: Subsiding sizzle	
Gross and Sheth	1989				1890–1915: Labour saving / 1915–1940: Labour and time saving / 1940–1965: Efficiency and leisure time	1965–1990s: Time saving
Leiss et al.	1997				1880–1930: Product Idolatry / 1930–1960: Product iconology	1960–1980: Narcissism / 1990s: Totemism

Medieval advertising (pre-1449)

Period overview

Historians approaching advertising from an institutional perspective define it as 'market information' (Carey, 1989; Rotzoll *et al.*, 1989). They have also concluded there was little need for advertising in societies based on the traditional worldview, such as this period's medieval and feudal societies. Others argue advertising is an ancient form of communication and point to 3,000-year-old Babylonian bricks and tablets bearing cuneiform letters and pictures of grain, cattle and slaves for sale; painted signs in the ruins of Pompeii; and early Egyptian street criers (Foster, 1967; Presbrey, 1929; Tungate, 2013). There was also a mature and fairly sophisticated approach to branding via images and visual trademarks in China – which advertising historians have claimed as part of their field during this period (Eckhardt and Bengtsson, 2010). However, with no printing press and limited literacy among consumers, most commercial messages consisted of forms of identification, such as the names of merchants and manufacturers indicating what they sold or made (e.g. Goldsmith, Wheelright, Fletcher), as well as early trademarks.

Media development, industry structures, professional practices and creative expression

The earliest 'media' consisted of criers and 'barkers', who were present in ancient Carthage, Egypt, Greece and Italy (Presbrey, 1929; Wood, 1958). Dan John Lydgate (1370–1450), a monk of the Benedictine Abbey of Bury St Edmund's, was the first to mention the ubiquitous town criers of London (Hindley, 1884). Such criers were sometimes local merchants themselves, while others, favoured for their agreeable voices and elocutionary abilities, roamed early Greek and European towns, sometimes equipped with horns or accompanied by musicians.

Among the first visual media was the shop sign or signboard. Roman signs consisted of whitened areas (called *albums*) on the walls of forums, houses and marketplaces. These created a medium for written messages, in black or red, or sculptured inscriptions announcing gladiatorial combats and circuses. Signboards were also used to announce public events in Athens; however, in England, they were mainly restricted to inns until the twelfth or thirteenth century (Presbrey, 1929). The earliest recognized signboard is the Roman 'bush', which hung above wine shops. It continued in England until the sixteenth century (Rivers, 1929), when many taverns and inns began displaying coats of arms or other heraldic devices, dating from the use of baronial homes as inns. The first written announcements are traced to Egypt, where, as early as 1100 BCE, aristocrats dictated offers of rewards for runaway slaves to a scribe, who would then publicly post them (Presbrey, 1929). In medieval Europe, in the absence of trademark laws and facing the threat of counterfeited stamps of origin, some manufacturers developed conspicuous product characteristics, such as a unique fabric weave or pewter that resonated at a certain pitch (Eckhardt and Bengtsson, 2010).

Some historians argue that, for the most part, advertising progressed very little beyond its most basic function – providing information. Presbrey (1929), however, argues that Roman announcements about gladiatorial combats and circuses were also persuasive in intent. There is also some evidence that affluence and discretionary income in the medieval marketplace led to opportunities for people to satisfy wants and not just needs and, thus, encouraged more persuasive advertising. Limited research on the emergence of brands and use of trademarks possibly 9,000 years ago in China also suggests they provided a basis for status seeking and stratification in response to social needs (Eckhardt and Bengtsson, 2010).

Research offers limited insight into how the earliest advertisers viewed creative expression. Effective town criers were preferred for their pleasing voices, and the criers themselves favoured loud volume, music and other spectacular means for attracting attention. Moreover, even during this period, advertisers recognized the value of fine art. Tavern keepers in England paid high prices to prominent members of the Royal Academy to paint their signs (Presbrey, 1929). Moreover, as Laird (1998, 130) concluded, many signs, trademarks and promotions, for hundreds of years, 'gave little or no information about the product but attempted to evoke emotional responses'.

Economic, political and legal contexts

The distinction between informative and persuasive advertising can be found in the economics literature as early as the 1920s (Veblen, 1923) and 1930s (Burns, 1936). Both roles for advertising – and its recognized progenitor, salesmanship – are linked during this period to specialization in agriculture, crafts and arts, and the existence of marketplace economies (Foster, 1967; Presbrey, 1929). Moreover, as markets became more competitive, there was a greater incentive to advertise (Berg and Clifford, 2007). China had a sophisticated marketplace economy dating as early as the Han Dynasty (206 BCE–220 CE), which occurred several hundred years earlier than in Europe and shifted focus from individuals to consumer classes (Eckhardt and Bengtsson, 2010).

Political and legal contexts influenced commercial communications during this period. In China, during the Tang Dynasty (618–906), government regulations required products to be stamped with manufacturers' names to ensure quality, and these were enforced with lawsuits (Eckhardt and Bengtsson, 2010). French criers, as early as 1141, often held government charters, formed their own corporations or unions, and were restricted in number. In thirteenth-century Paris, tavern keepers were required by law to use criers (Presbrey, 1929).

Predominantly aural and visual forms of commercial communication have been frequently linked to a lack of literacy (Wood, 1958). Referring to a symbol used to represent a brand of sewing needles during China's Song Dynasty (960–1127), Eckhardt and Bengtsson (2010, 215) noted that 'Because the primary target market for the needles was women with limited literacy, the rabbit was an important symbol that could facilitate brand recognition.' As similarly observed by Presbrey (1929, 7): '*written* advertising came soon after the spread of literacy in ancient Rome, only to disappear with the decline in ability to read that followed and lasted through centuries of the Dark Ages'.

Sales promotion

Although rarely mentioned in the literature, sales promotions were not unknown during this period. The Romans favoured lotteries. There are signs offering point-of-purchase discounts in Pompeii (Lloyd and Spedding, 2009) and London theatrical performances were promoted 'by means of fantastic procession' (Presbrey, 1929, 14).

Early-modern advertising and sales promotion (1450s–1799)

Period overview

This period begins with Johannes Gutenberg's invention of a metal alloy soft enough to cast and hard enough to endure, which made movable type and widespread printing in Europe possible. William Caxton, London's first printer, printed what is believed to be Europe's first English-language advertisement, promoting his first book. This advertisement can be viewed online as part of the Bodleian Library collection at the University of Oxford (www.bodleian. ox.ac.uk/bodley/finding-resources/special). The first known advertisement in a newsletter, regarding the curative properties of a plant, appeared in a German news book in 1591 (Rivers, 1929). At about the same time in Japan, merchants were posting flyers on the pillars of Shinto shrines, Buddhist temples, fences and gateposts, and inserting advertisements into books (Tungate, 2013).

The term 'advertisement' was first used in 1655, when it took the place of 'advices', which had previously supplanted the term 'siquis'. This term came from ancient Rome, where announcements often began with the words 'Si quis', meaning 'if anybody' or 'if anyone' (Frederick, 1925; Presbrey, 1929). In seventeenth-century France, doctor and journalist Théophraste Renaudot established a *bureau des addresses et des recnotres* and France's first newspaper, *La Gazette* (Tungate, 2013). In eighteenth-century England and France there was a proliferation of new consumer goods and personal services and the emergence of a consumerist culture (Berg and Clifford, 2007), which has been linked to advertising in news-sheets (*affiches*) and other periodicals. Across the Atlantic, Benjamin Franklin was the first to consider advertising as a primary source of newspaper revenue (Foster, 1967).

Media development, industry structures, professional practices and creative expression

Criers remained important throughout this period in Europe and the American colonies (Frederick, 1925). Brands proliferated in both China and Europe, with place names often becoming associated with certain products as consumer satisfaction spread via word-of-mouth (Eckhardt and Bengtsson, 2010). In Europe, simple marks of origin were established by the trade guilds. They lacked broader symbolic associations, however, until the seventeenth century, when woodblock printing and other illustration methods began to link goods with producers (Ciarlo, 2011). One of the earliest symbols was the *Tabakmohr* (Tobacco Moor), which was associated with tobacco in all Western European nations and the American colonies for several hundred years (Ciarlo, 2011).

English tradesmen were using 'tackups' and handbills by the end of the fifteenth century. They spread widely as printing became available and were posted in taverns, town halls and even cathedrals (Frederick, 1925). Announcements for quack nostrums were among the first handbills circulated around London during the 1500s. The increasingly elaborate and artistic signs devised by the English guilds continued to be an important advertising medium. Many exhibited the work of some of the period's most famous artists, such as Hogarth and Holbein (Frederick, 1925).

The first newspaper to print an advertisement was either the *Mercurius Britannicus*, in 1625 (Presbrey, 1929; Wood, 1958), or London's *Weekly News* (Frederick, 1925), in 1632. The first regularly published newspaper in the North American colonies appeared in 1704 (*The Boston News-Letter*), but it was 1778 before the first daily newspaper (*The Pennsylvania Packet*) was published (Frederick, 1925). The first paid advertisements in the colonies were published in the third issue of the *News-Letter*, dated 1–8 May 1704. By the mid-1700s many newspapers in England and the colonies existed primarily to carry advertising. Some historians have referred to these publications as 'advertising sheets' (Presbrey, 1929). Although there were no daily newspapers in England outside of London, many were thriving in Dublin, Ireland and all of them carried advertising (Wood, 1958). During the late 1700s, many newspaper editors disdained advertising but accepted it because readers wanted information about products, ship landings and cures (Foster, 1967).

The use of non-periodical media and printed ephemera grew during this period. Venetian Aldus Manutius published the first home shopping catalogue in 1496, although another didn't appear until 1667 (Lloyd and Spedding, 2009). The most well-known and earliest types of printed advertisement to combine images and text were shop bills, trade cards and bill heads. In Europe and the North American colonies, their use increased from the early seventeenth century, peaked in the mid-eighteenth century, and continued for another two centuries (Laird, 1998). Advertising trade cards were an early means for educating consumers about new products that provided ease and comfort, although they were also prized as souvenirs and gifts (Berg and Clifford, 2007).

Similar to other craftsmen and tradesmen, those involved with advertising formed guilds and established protectionist policies (Hindley, 1884). London printers, for instance, adopted the first advertising code, agreeing to wait two weeks before pulling down competitors' handbills (Foster, 1967). More important were the public registries, which occurred coincidentally with early periodicals. Inspired by Frenchmen and essayist Michel de Montaigne, Englishmen Sir Arthur Gorges and Sir Walter Cope hoped to set up a registry office in 1611. Here, buyers and sellers would register their offers and requests, and copies would be distributed to branch offices. Such 'offices of entry' and accompanying periodicals were successfully established by Parisian Théophraste Renaudot, in 1630, and Englishmen Henry Walker, in 1649, and Marchmont Nedham, in 1657 (Presbrey, 1929).

Historians report that most advertisers well into the eighteenth century mainly intended to provide customers with information. Trade cards, shop bills and bill heads, in particular, were intended to reach current patrons, remind and encourage them to return, and to disseminate information to prospective customers (Berg and Clifford, 2007). However, advertisers as early as the seventeenth century also hoped to differentiate themselves with, for example, the novelty of their tavern signs (Presbrey, 1929). Moreover, some historians have concluded that the goals of some advertisers also involved persuasion. Presbrey (1929, 32) observed that shop bills 'developed from what was merely an ornamented business card into an advertisement which illustrated the wares, often in great detail, and grew into a persuasive selling message'. English essayist Joseph Addison confirmed that, by 1759, a clutter of newspaper advertisements was detracting from the drawing power of mere novelty and announcement, thus encouraging extravagant promises, beauty appeals and appeals to 'mother-love' (as cited in Presbrey, 1929, 70). Benjamin Franklin similarly utilized vanity, comfort, fear and health appeals to advertise the Franklin Stove in the 1740s (Wood, 1958).

Creatively, historians report that print advertisers soon recognized the importance of visuals for attracting attention. Graphic elements such as two-line initial letters, all-capped first words, and the pointing finger were the first elements employed by John Houghton in his *Whitson's Merchants' Weekly* in the late seventeenth century. However, the use of visuals in newspaper advertisements during the eighteenth century and into the first quarter of the nineteenth century, with the exception of book and curative advertisements, declined (Berg and Clifford, 2007), partly due to paper shortages and the necessity of conserving space (Presbrey, 1929). One of the most important developments for attracting attention and arousing interest was the headline, in frequent use by 1760 (Presbrey, 1929).

Economic, political and legal contexts

Signs of a flourishing consumer culture and the possibility for social mobility in China continued during the sixteenth century, well ahead of Europe. Product and service consumption during this period, with the exception of some national brands in China, was predominantly local or regional. During the eighteenth century, commercialized economies characterized by new systems of distribution, competition, the activities of salesmen and basic marketing methods were spreading across Europe (Church, 1999). Advertising in Europe and the American colonies was often associated with the arrival of exotic, foreign goods. The first ad for tea, for instance – 'That excellent, and by all physicians approved, China drink' – was published in England in 1658 (Rivers, 1929, 15). As Berg and Clifford (2007, 156) noted in regards to this period's trade cards: 'Advertising teaches consumers about new goods, how to use them and desire them. It transmits skills in identifying networks of goods and the lifestyles that frame them.'

Legal and regulatory contexts were also important during this period. In England, the Royal Mail refused to deliver advertising, forcing advertisers to post their handbills anywhere they could. In the late 1600s, advertising in England was brought under monopoly control by way of royal patents and licensing; in Paris, no one was allowed to open a tavern without displaying the bush on its sign, signifying the sale of wine (Rivers, 1929). Moreover, shop signs were severely restricted in both London and Paris by the mid-1760s, having been deemed a public nuisance (Presbrey, 1929). In 1712, Queen Anne's government in England placed a tax on newspapers and advertisements, which was levied for nearly 150 years. In 1765, King George III taxed newspaper advertising in the American colonies (Wood, 1958). Both the tax and the turmoil surrounding the American Revolution slowed the growth of newspaper advertising (Presbrey, 1929).

Sales promotion

Little has been reported regarding the use of sales promotion during this period. However, lotteries – a type of promotion involving the awarding of prizes determined by chance in exchange for a purchase or fee – were popular in England as early as 1569. Price promotions were also common, and bakers are said to have avoided fines for selling underweight bread by including the 'Baker's Dozen' of 13 for the price of 12 (Lloyd and Spedding, 2009).

Late-modern advertising and sales promotion (1800s)

Period overview

Historians agree that advertising in many countries during the nineteenth century was stimulated by urbanization, the mass production of consumer goods, geographic and social mobility, the spread of consumer culture and the rise of the newspaper. North American advertisers were clearly influential during this period, although there were other prominent pioneers, such as France's Charles-Louis Havas and Germany's Rudolf Cronau. During the second half of the nineteenth century, international campaigns for products such as Germany's Liebig's Extract of Meat and Great Britain's Pears Soap were becoming prevalent.

Many nineteenth-century businessmen remained sceptical regarding the reputability and value of advertising (Ciarlo, 2011; Laird, 1998; Marchand, 1985; Wood, 1958). Consequently, agents promoted advertising through their trade journals, associations and clubs, as well as by expanding services to include copy and art (McGovern, 2006; Schudson, 1984). At the same time, many manufacturers of consumer goods in the US were seeking to create national markets and wrest control of their distribution channels from jobbers and merchants (Beard, 2011).

Many contemporary sales promotion tactics appeared during the nineteenth century. The first in-pack premium was likely a Canadian cigarette card, and US advertisers such as the Quaker Company, Procter & Gamble, and C.W. Post used 'money off new purchase coupons', free and self-liquidating premiums, field marketing and point-of-purchase promotions (Lloyd and Spedding, 2009).

Media development, industry structures, professional practices and creative expression

Much of the media-related progress in the nineteenth century is also explained by advancements in printing technology. Rotation presses and the halftone process enabled cheaper production and the pictorial advertisement (Ciarlo, 2011). In Germany, chromolithography made the widespread use of advertising stamps (*reklamemarken*) possible. Some criers, such as the 'coster-monger' (fruit seller), were still at work in the streets of London (see Figure 11.2). Outdoor advertising expanded beyond wooden signs and painted messages, thanks to the lithography printing process (Foster, 1967) and, in the late 1800s, electricity.

Display advertising, as opposed to the 'want-ad style', appeared in the form of theatrical bills, handbills, direct mail circulars and in novels early in this period in Great Britain (Presbrey, 1929). However, newspaper advertisements in Great Britain, Germany and the US rarely included illustrations beyond simple woodcuts, even after presses and engraving processes made it easily possible (Ciarlo, 2011). As Presbrey (1929, 96) observes regarding this trend, many publishers doubted that 'an acceptance of the nuisance of innumerable type sizes, broken-column rules and 'vulgar screeching' would bring enough additional revenue

Figure 11.2   The coster-monger, source: Hindley, 1884, 35

to warrant a surrender' to the desires of advertisers. Bold display advertising was common in France, however, in the early 1850s (Presbrey, 1929). Mass circulation and penny papers, born in the US in 1825, encouraged greater use of advertising whenever and wherever they appeared (Ciarlo, 2011). Inspired by the American papers, for instance, the two main Italian newspapers, *Corriere della sera* and *Il Secolo*, became Italy's first national media for the dissemination of consumer culture (Arvidsson, 2003).

One of the most significant developments of this period was the arrival of the first mass medium that advertising substantially created – magazines (Foster, 1967). In Great Britain and the US, magazines got a boost with the steady growth in mail order retailing and direct mail advertising (Laird, 1998), which, in turn, expanded tremendously thanks to favourable postal rates. Mail order and direct mail catalogues for major department stores were important media in both the US and France during the latter part of the nineteenth century. Presbrey (1929) concluded that the quality of printing required by the mail order houses had a positive influence on advertising design in other media, including the use of colour.

Finely engraved bill heads and shop bills were used, as they had been during earlier periods, to wrap purchases, record transactions and for public posting (Laird, 1998). Job printers also competed with periodical media by creating ephemera with high-quality typesetting, engraving and lithography (Laird, 1998). A flourishing tradition of poster advertising appeared in England, France and Italy. France's Jules Chéret and England's Aubrey Beardsley substantially influenced the work of American poster artists, whose work also appeared in outdoor and magazine advertising (Wood, 1958). The artistic quality of posters also had a positive influence on other display advertising and their continued development was boosted by the refusal of newspapers to print visuals (Presbrey, 1929; Wood, 1958). In 1890s Germany, chromolithographic printing encouraged the widespread use of posters, trading cards and the *reklamemarken* (Ciarlo, 2011). Towards the end of the nineteenth century, the importance of job printers and their ephemera declined with the rise of periodical media and the growing influence of agency copywriters. Streetcar advertising emerged as an important medium, thanks substantially to American Barron G. Collier.

One of the most important developments in several countries was the steady professionalization of advertising agents. Evolving from the seventeenth-century public registries, advertising brokers were at work in England by 1800 (Presbrey, 1929). The first advertising agent was likely England's William Tayler in 1786 (Nevett, 1977). Although most agents represented a single newspaper, at least one, Charles Barker, was functioning as a true advertising agent as early as 1812, booking insertions in newspapers specified by his clients, negotiating rates and giving advice on advertising problems (Nevett, 1977).

In the US, most early agents were predominantly brokers, in some cases, buying space in bulk for resale to clients; soliciting advertising on behalf of newspapers; and, occasionally, collecting advertising fees plus a newspaper-paid commission (Wood, 1958). Since advertisers didn't know the rates they were paying or the circulation they were receiving and the publishers didn't know what the agents were collecting, the practice was fraught with dishonesty (Foster, 1967). During the first half of the nineteenth century in France, most newspapers also sold their advertising space to brokers, considering the selling of space to be undignified (Presbrey, 1929). By the end of the period, broker agents were at work in Japan (Tungate, 2013), and many agencies in Germany were overseeing advertising from conception to design, printing and distribution (Ciarlo, 2011). The American Newspaper Publishers' Association put an end to the space brokerage business in the US in 1867 (Foster, 1967). During the same year, an English court ruled that the advertising agent was in fact the agent of the advertiser (Nevett, 1977).

Many advertisers in Great Britain, Germany, and the US up to the mid-nineteenth century said they favoured informational and dignified advertisements intended to generate sales or brand awareness and were critical of the 'circus-style', with its link to the period's 'Barnumesque' creative expression. However, the professional tension between such advocates of rational advertising and the spectacular, often entertainment-oriented advertising designed to attract attention and trigger emotional responses continued throughout this period (Beard, 2004; Ciarlo, 2011). By 1865, retail advertisers had also discovered the emotional value of creating a sense of urgency (Laird, 1998), and some advertisers were attempting to persuade consumers to act on their impulses and desire for risk-taking (Wolofson, 2012). Some historians have also concluded that, by the end of the nineteenth century, US advertisers had redefined abundance and were successfully encouraging consumers to define themselves through commodity consumption (Fox, 1984; Leach 1994; McGovern, 2006). As Lears (1994) has suggested, the desire for a transformation of the self often served as a foundation for the appeal of consumer goods.

Whereas retailers had always targeted certain customers, an elementary appreciation for segmentation emerged, such as J. Walter Thompson's use of magazines to reach middle- and upper-class women (Foster, 1967). Many newspapers in the US also began in the 1890s to vary their design and content to appeal to women (Laird, 1998). Other later and emergent professional practices were the transfer of copywriting duties from advertisers and freelance 'literary men' to agency copywriters, the use of rudimentary market surveys and analyses, and the tracking of advertising effectiveness (Fox, 1984; Laird, 1998; Tungate, 2013).

Perhaps the most influential approach to message strategy was the 'reason why', often attributed to Albert Lasker, John E. Kenney and Claude Hopkins. Tactically, a visual communication revolution occurred in Europe and the US during the second half of the nineteenth century (Ciarlo, 2011). In France, Czech-born Alfons Maria Mucha is credited with the launch of the Art Noveau poster style. In the US, influential agency man Ernest Elmo Calkins also advocated the use of powerful visuals to attract attention and arouse interest (Tungate, 2013). In Great Britain, pictorial art in advertising received another boost in 1866 when Thomas A. Barratt used Sir John Millais's painting 'Bubbles' for Pears soap. The importance of trademarks also increased after the 1870s, as products were increasingly sold in consumer-sized units and it became more important to identify and differentiate them (Laird, 1998).

Advertising agency professionals throughout Europe and in the US all struggled similarly to overcome negative attitudes towards their emergent profession. Efforts on the part of US agency men F. Wayland Ayer and George Rowell helped disassociate agencies from shady practices and affirmed their loyalty had shifted from newspaper to marketer (Foster, 1967). Advertising professionals in Germany took a slightly different approach, attempting to legitimize their profession by emphasizing advertising's aesthetic worth and by, first, elevating British and American practices and, second, claiming familiarity with them (Ciarlo, 2011).

Economic, political and legal contexts

Production of goods in many countries surpassed local consumption and competition increased. New types of retail distribution and the shifting of marketplace leadership from wholesalers to retailers and then to manufacturers also encouraged both increased advertising of national brands to create new consumers for products they'd never purchased before, as well as increased retail advertising in Great Britain, Germany and the US (Ciarlo, 2011;

Foster, 1967; Presbrey, 1929; Tungate, 2013; Wood, 1958). Elsewhere, such as Italy, however, national markets emerged more slowly (Arvidsson, 2003).

In Great Britain, the tax on advertising was repealed in 1862, leading to a great increase in newspaper space. Legal controls gradually increased over the nineteenth century in Great Britain with the passage of Acts that banned obscene advertisements and regulated, among other practices, sandwich-board men, the placement of posters, the use of horns and other noisy instruments by the remaining criers (Hindley, 1884), and the advertising of quack nostrums. In 1879, magazines in the US were granted favourable mailing privileges and circulations climbed tremendously (Wood, 1958). In the late nineteenth century, Germany established new laws on unlawful competition that were also used to regulate advertising truthfulness (Ciarlo, 2011).

Sales promotion

What eventually became known as the twenty-first century's experiential marketing, promotions that enable consumers to experience a product or brand by way of personal contact, began with the exhibitions, road shows and stunt publicity tactics of the nineteenth century (Lloyd and Spedding, 2009). Claude Hopkins also relied on publicity stunts, famously ordering a giant cake to be displayed in the window of a department store to promote a butter substitute (Tungate, 2013). Benjamin Talbot Babbitt is credited with inventing the coupon in 1850 (Lloyd and Spedding, 2009), and Coca-Cola's John Pemberton offered the first coupon in the US in 1887 (see Figure 11.3). Babbitt is also credited with being the first to wrap products in lithographed pictures that were themselves valuable premiums (Foster, 1967; Wolofson, 2012). Premiums were widely employed in Great Britain, Germany and the US. These included lithographed pictures, reusable product containers, badges, dishes and crockery. Wolofson (2012, 791) proposed that premiums appealed 'not to reason, but to the heart, to the emotions, to sentiment, to good will on the basis of implied acquaintanceship'.

Warranties and guarantees were also frequently used during this period. Department stores in the US offered merchandise guarantees, with the goals of ensuring quality prior

Figure 11.3   First Coca-Cola coupon, 1887, source: www.grocery.com/coupons

to the more widespread distribution of well-known brands and to attract customers from neighbourhood and small-town stores (Laird, 1998). Loyalty programmes in the form of trading stamps appeared in Great Britain in 1851 and in the US in 1896. Lord & Thomas's John E. Kennedy and Claude Hopkins integrated free samples with advertising campaigns (Wood, 1958), and John E. Powers employed free trials to sell retail goods on behalf of Wanamaker's department stores (Presbrey, 1929).

Advertisers not only used sales promotions, they often did not distinguish much between them and advertising. As Presbrey (1929, 226) reported: 'All of [P. T.] Barnum's efforts – news-column publicity, posters, handbills, newspaper advertising, parades and street stunts – he grouped under the one word "Advertising."' Similarly, 1870s novelty advertising – 'commercial messages disguised as useful or decorative objects', including calendars, rulers, match holders, pocket mirrors, games and ashtrays – was described as 'a clever bit of advertising' in the trade literature of the period (Laird, 1998, 88).

Contemporary advertising and sales promotion (1900s to 1950s)

Period overview

Internationally, the full-service advertising agency reached maturity during the first half of the twentieth century. Many historians emphasize the contributions of entrepreneurs in the US to the continued professionalization of advertising and agencies, although they also point to the influence of others internationally – such as France's Marcel Bleustein, China's Carl Crow, Spain's Pedro Prat Gaballi and Australia's George Herbert Patterson (Tungate, 2013).

National advertising expanded significantly in many countries and important new product categories emerged almost continuously. Secondary factors contributing to growth during the first three decades of the twentieth century include single-price selling, the development of department stores and supermarkets, nationally branded products, mail order merchandising and market research (Church, 1999). The period is also distinguished by the application of the social and behavioural sciences to advertising planning and practice. Advertising and its advocates in Germany (Ciarlo, 2011), Great Britain, France (Howard, 2008) and the US also faced major backlashes against its quantity and qualitative content, as advertising 'creep' and 'clutter' led to messages being placed on almost every conceivable surface. This period is also distinguished by the emergence of magazines, radio and then television as major national media.

After the Second World War, sales promotion expanded greatly in Great Britain and the US. Henry Ford employed the first auto rebates in 1914, character licensing appeared, prize contests became national events and premiums were widely used in numerous product categories (Lloyd and Spedding, 2009).

Media development, industry structures, professional practices and creative expression

Advances in photomechanical printing and photography caused a continued decline in non-periodical media and ephemera and a reduced dependence on printers and engravers (Laird, 1998). During the inter-war period, French, German and Italian poster designers contributed significantly to avant-garde art (Arvidsson, 2003). In 1930s Shanghai, the *yuefenpai*, posters combining advertising images and calendars, evolved to become more traditional posters without a calendar (Zhao and Belk, 2008).

215

Newspaper advertising usage in Japan caught up with much of the rest of the industrialized world during the first three decades of the twentieth century, as did use of posters, handbills, magazines and non-periodical media (Gardner, 2006). Advertising in French newspapers and magazines, however, lagged behind many other countries until after the Second World War in regards to its volume, production quality and creativity (Pope, 1983), due in part to lower levels of consumption, predominantly regional versus national markets and brands, paper shortages and the continuing belief that advertising wasn't 'respectable'. Magazines remained a dominant advertising medium in Italy into the 1950s, often emphasizing the link between status and consumption (Arvidsson, 2003).

In the US, radio quickly enabled advertisers, despite early scepticism (McGovern, 2006), to reach mass audiences. Although commercial radio on the BBC (British Broadcasting Corporation) was banned in Great Britain in 1923 due to founding father John Reith's belief that the new medium should be free of political interference and commercial pressure (BBC, 2014), advertisers could place commercials on airwaves beamed in from Luxembourg and Normandy (Lloyd and Spedding 2009). In France, commercial radio began in December of 1921, but was nationalized and became non-commercial, as was radio in Italy until 1977. French radio advertising, however, expanded substantially in the 1930s. Japanese radio also began in the mid-1920s, and was soon organized into the national *Nippon hoso kyokai* (Japan Broadcasting Corporation, or NHK), modelled after the BBC.

Television advertising in the US was born on 1 July 1941, the day the Federal Communications Commission allowed TV stations to transmit commercial broadcasts. Unlike radio, both advertisers and the public initially accepted commercial television. Commercial television began in Great Britain in 1955 and in Italy at about the same time, but with an odd collection of commercials known as *Il Carosello* (Arvidsson, 2003). As with radio, French television was under government control and there was no advertising until 1968.

Although some agencies were still representing certain publications (Presbrey, 1929), the profession was well established in Great Britain, Germany and the US. In China, Carl Crow established an advertising brokerage in 1918, published the first periodical circulation guide, and employed bill posters in 60 cities (Tungate, 2013). Although French advertising professionals (*publicitaires*) established associations and trade groups in the 1920s to promote and reform advertising, development lagged behind many other countries until the 1950s (Pope, 1983). Agencies and the industry overall in Italy also progressed more slowly because many companies had their own advertising departments, media commissions were small or non-existent and rates were not fixed (De Iulio and Vinti, 2009).

By opening branch offices, US agencies succeeded in controlling European advertising after the Second World War, with France the only significant exception (De Iulio and Vinti, 2009). During the 1920s and, especially, following the war, the adoption of American practices – full-service agencies, consumer-orientation, marketing research and strategic planning – spread to many countries in Europe (De Iulio and Vinti, 2009). Many French, German and Italian practitioners, however, remained somewhat critical of the American approach and adapted it to their own social, legal, cultural and economic conditions and artistic traditions (Ciarlo, 2011; De Iulio and Vinti, 2009). The European artistic tradition with modernist design principles also influenced designers in the US, as some practitioners migrated there between the 1920s and the Second World War (De Iulio and Vinti, 2009; Tungate 1997). Advertising practitioners in most industrialized countries worked to promote and establish the legitimacy of their profession, gain patrons and establish codes and guidelines (Laird, 1998).

Regarding the roles and functions of advertising, the belief continued that advertising's primary role was to sell products directly by informing or in some cases educating prospective buyers about how to live better lives (Laird, 1998; McGovern, 2006). However, by the second decade of this period, advertisers increasingly advocated a more sophisticated view of an intermediary role, emphasizing that effective advertising needed to persuade (Beard, 2004), increasingly via strong competitive claims and psychological and emotional appeals (Wood, 1958).

Growing competition for accounts and their clients' sales (Laird, 1998) led to theory development and a greater reliance on research (McGovern, 2006). One of the most successful advocates of reason-why advertising, Claude Hopkins, preached the importance of tracking effectiveness in his influential book, *Scientific Advertising*. In the US, scientific advertising of the non-Hopkins type was rooted in the work of behavioural psychologist John B. Watson. The Germans, however, followed a different path with psychology entering the field from industrial psychology (Ciarlo, 2011), and Italians favoured the 'theory of suggestion' advocated by French psychologists Octave-Jacques Gérin and Charles Espindel (Arvidsson, 2003). Towards the end of this period, the limitations of quantitative methods and a European tradition of consumer research encouraged a global interest in motivation research. The adoption of scientific advertising, psychology, empirical research and strategic marketing contributed to a debate between advertising as science versus art, or at least craft (Fox, 1984), in France, Germany, Italy and the US.

As the announcement advertising of the late nineteenth century increasingly gave way to the belief it should inform and persuade, professional debate and experimentation in creative expression turned to the most appropriate ways to accomplish it. Some historians suggest many advertisers during the first three decades of the twentieth century continued to favour a product-focused, descriptive and rational approach due, in part, to embarrassment over the frequently dishonest 'bombast and ballyhoo', circus-style entertainment and patent medicine advertising of the nineteenth century (Beard, 2004; Laird, 1998; Leiss *et al.*, 1997; Rowsome, 1970). The 'Truth Well Told' motto of the H.K. McCann Company and the 'reason-why' are consistent with this view. However, a more artistic sell was also established in the US by the early 1900s, following the acknowledged value of emotional appeals and a decreased emphasis on price (Laird, 1998). This view was represented by the 'atmospheric' style of Theodore F. MacManus and the image-based approach of Earnest E. Calkins (Beard, 2004). By the 1950s, the 'American method', pioneered and expounded by agency JWT, was founded on the belief that advertising should show 'the product and its intended users in real-life situations (or at least what was represented as real life in the idealized rhetoric of advertising)' (Arvidsson, 2003, 70). This approach and similar creative executions based on it, such as slice-of-life appeals and tactics, spread widely across Europe, Africa and South-East Asia.

Economic, political and legal contexts

Advertising historians broadly agree that economic and cultural factors and social transformations continued to alter the criteria for consumption in many countries (Howard, 2008), leading advertisers during this period to emphasize the consumption of goods as an end in itself (Schwarzkopf, 2011). National markets and a common consumer culture expanded greatly during this period, although they were delayed somewhat until the 1950s in Italy and France (Arvidsson, 2003). Consumers also did not respond to advertising in Great Britain and France as they apparently did in the US because of lower incomes and greater differences in standards of consumption between rural and urban consumers (Frederick, 1925; Presbrey, 1929). Some suggest these factors explain most of the differences in the presumed influence of advertising and consumption between the US and other countries (Frederick, 1925). The economic role of advertising as a barrier to entry was openly acknowledged by 1910 (Laird, 1998).

Politically, advertising in the US got a boost when a 1918 tax made it a deductible business expense. Also in the US, public desire and political will to control advertising of patent medicines, dishonest advertising and other fraudulent practices produced numerous new laws between 1906 (the Pure Food and Drug Act) and 1938 (the Wheeler-Lea Amendments to the Federal Trade Commission Act of 1914). In France in 1940 and 1941, the Loi contre l'alcoolisme led to a ban on advertising for all distilled alcohols (Howard, 2008). In Germany, in 1932, the Zugabeverodnung ('free gift decree') effectively banned almost all sales promotions, and Great Britain's 1934 Betting and Lotteries Act impacted sales promotions by outlawing lotteries and restricting prize competitions that did not rely on the exercise of a substantial degree of skill.

Sales promotion

The extensive use of premiums by companies such as the Quaker Oats Company and the Kellogg Company in the US continued during this period. The use of 'coupon plans', such as Babbitt's Bab-O soap wrappers, was also widespread in Great Britain and the US. At the Lord & Thomas agency in Chicago, Claude Hopkins frequently combined mail order advertising, coupons, premiums and free or cheap samples (Fox, 1984).

Two important categories of promotions to appear were incentive or motivation programmes (promotions mainly used to motivate employees and the sales force) and loyalty programmes. In Great Britain, 'Father of Incentives' Elton F. MacDonald produced the first catalogue in 1927 (Lloyd and Spedding, 2009). Branded articles and gifts were widely used in France by the Belle Epoque marketers of aperitifs in the 1930s (Howard, 2008). Marketers favoured both loyalty schemes and coupons during the 1930s because they were cheaper than price-cutting and more difficult to copy (Lloyd and Spedding, 2009). Perhaps this period's single most important loyalty tactic proliferating widely during the 1950s and 1960s in Great Britain, Ireland and the US was trading stamps.

Post-modern advertising and sales promotion (1960s to 2010s)

Period overview

Much of the industrialized world experienced favourable economies in the 1960s and consequential increases in advertising. Marketers and their agencies developed increasingly fragmented approaches to market segmentation. Advertising took a turn creatively and, to a certain extent, internationally with the arguably short-lived 'Creative Revolution'. By the 1980s, American-style, post-modern consumer cultures were fully in place throughout much of the industrialized world, including Spain and Italy (Arvidsson, 2003; Tungate, 2013).

A global advertising industry had fully emerged by the end of the 1970s, and during the 1980s the industry consolidated due to agency acquisitions and mergers. Most of the largest companies such as the UK's Saatchi & Saatchi, Japan's Dentsu and the US's Young & Rubicam and Omnicom Group evolved by the turn of the century to become global communications groups integrating marketing services far beyond advertising, including direct response, public relations, sales promotion and digital marketing (Arndorfer et al., 2005; Tungate, 2013).

Elsewhere, however, advertising and agencies matured more slowly, such as in the 1960s and 1970s in Brazil (Tungate, 2013) and Italy (Ciarlo, 2011). The emergence of Integrated Marketing Communications in the 1980s, the internet, digital and mobile media, and new forms of promotional content, such as 'branded entertainment', substantially distinguishes this final period. The use of sales promotion also expanded greatly in the UK and US during the 1960s (Lloyd and Spedding, 2009), as specialist promotions consultancies began assuming responsibilities from advertising agencies and corporate marketing units and many new, often technology-driven tactics appeared.

Media development, industry structures, professional practices and creative expression

Well established in the US during the previous period, television advertising expanded greatly in Italy (Arvidsson, 2003), Germany (Tungate, 2013) and France during the 1980s. However, by the early 1990s, due to increasing globalization, the deregulation of the European telecommunications industry (Tungate, 2013), and rising internet and mobile phone penetration, the effectiveness of traditional advertising-supported media, especially television, was increasingly challenged by influential industry figures, such as Edwin L. Artzt, chairman-CEO of Procter & Gamble Co. (Arndorfer *et al.*, 2005).

Advertising agencies continued their international expansion and consolidation throughout the 1960s and 1970s, following the lead of McCann-Erickson's Marion Harper Jr. and his creation of the Interpublic holding company in 1960. Major international agencies, such as Japan's Dentsu in 1979, expanded to China in the 1970s as part of China's 'Open Door' policy (Tungate, 2013). Other trends in the agency business were the emergence of sales promotion consultancies in the 1960s in the US and UK (Lloyd and Shedding, 2009) and independent media-planning agencies (Tungate, 2013).

One of the most important transitions in professional practices evident among the sources was the proliferation of what has been defined as the 'orientation' stage of the marketing concept and its emphasis on establishing mutually beneficial exchange relationships between consumers and producers. Some argue that this stage had initially emerged following the Second World War, but that its influence in many countries greatly expanded during the 1950s and 1960s (Arvidsson, 2003; Keith, 1960). Others included the expansion of the agency practice of teaming art directors with copywriters, the adoption of account planning and the increasing influence of television commercial testing (Fox, 1984). The spread of psychographic, or lifestyle, research in the US, Italy and elsewhere (Arvidsson, 2003) also occurred, coincidentally with a greater emphasis in the 1970s and 1980s on segmentation by lifestyle settings and activities and message appeals based on themes of leisure, health, self-expression and references to group identification (Church, 1999; Leiss *et al.*, 1997). The emphasis on selling goods as the means for enabling and inspiring new ways to live a modern life continued (Arvidsson, 2003).

The belief that advertising was influenced internationally by Americanization was most prevalent in regard to professional practices during this period. Some, however, have argued that this influence was occasionally rejected, the practices criticized and was neither overwhelming nor uniform, with Italy (De Iulio and Vinti, 2009) and France (Guérin, 1965) the best examples. In some countries the criticism of American practices reflected the decades-old debate over whether a reliance on empirical research limited the artistic and creative character of advertising (De Iulio and Vinti, 2009).

Regarding creative expression, advertisers in some countries increasingly targeted youth markets during the 1960s and 1970s, and then young, upwardly mobile consumers in the

1980s (Arvidsson, 2003). Pollay's (1985) important descriptive history showed that late twentieth-century print advertisements in the US returned to an emphasis on product attributes, similar to those at the beginning of the century. The creative influence of London agencies flowed back towards Madison Avenue during this period, and European-inspired cubism, constructivism and the Dutch artistic movement called De Stijl influenced creative design in the US (Tungate, 2013). The most important event regarding creative expression was, of course, the Doyle Dane Bernbach-inspired Creative Revolution. Although it expanded to other countries such as Great Britain, Italy and Spain, some historians argue it wasn't slavishly copied (Tungate, 2013). In the 1990s, Japanese advertisers developed a uniquely short, noisy, politically correct format of television commercial that avoided Western themes of sex, politics and religion (Tungate, 2013).

Economic, political and legal contexts

The well-established relationship between advertising and capitalistic, free-market economic activity dating from the earliest period was perhaps most convincingly confirmed with the return of advertising and agencies to the People's Republic of China in the late 1970s. As then-premier Wan Li stated in 1987: 'Advertising links production and consumption. It is an important part of the economic activities of modern society. It has become an indispensable element in the promotion of economic prosperity' (cited in Tungate, 2013, 238).

In the US, Congress passed more than 25 Acts directly affecting advertising between 1960 and 1972 (Miracle and Nevett, 1993). Also in the US, advertising to children, severely restricted in the EU and elsewhere, came under attack in the 1970s, and tobacco advertising in the broadcast media was banned. Important legal events during this period included more aggressive action by the US Federal Trade Commission over false advertising claims, the UK's Lotteries and Amusements Act of 1976, and the French legislation of the Loi Evin and Loi Sapin, which forbade most tobacco and alcohol advertising and fixed media rates (Tungate, 2013). In Singapore, the government cracked down on advertising posters containing images of youthful rebellion, as well as other Western themes deemed inappropriate. At the end of 2002 and beginning of 2003, almost all tobacco advertising and promotions were banned in the UK (Lloyd and Spedding, 2009).

Advertising and sales promotion professionals' efforts to establish regulatory codes grew greatly during the 1970s. In the UK, the Committee of Advertising Practice (CAP) established both the British Code of Advertising Practice and the Advertising Standards Authority (ASA) in 1961–2, and the first code of practice regarding sales promotions was established in 1971 (Legh, 1986). In 2004, the regulation of all media advertising, sales promotion and direct marketing communications came under the ASA/CAP system. In the US, the major associations collaborated with the Council of Better Business Bureaus to establish the National Advertising Review Council in 1971. However, the UK's attitude towards sales promotion regulation diverged sharply and more favourably from its European neighbours during the 1960s (Lloyd and Spedding, 2009).

Sales promotion

Free-standing sales promotion consultancies by the end of this period were controlling expenditures rivalling those of advertising. However, whereas consultancies were common in the UK by the 1980s, there were no national companies in the US. One of the first global campaigns, the famous Esso Tiger tail, took place during the 1960s, when a UK-based promotion was integrated with a US agency-inspired advertising campaign ('Put a Tiger in Your Tank'). Lloyd and Spedding (2009) report that more than 3.5 million tiger tails were sold in the US in just five months. Other important innovations included 'instant win' sweepstakes in the 1960s and the use of promotions to support brand images in the 1970s.

The use of promotions, especially on-pack price promotions and coupons, grew in the UK with the energy crisis and ensuing recession of the 1970s (a trend frequently noted by marketers and by historians). Many marketers favoured the quick and apparently cheaper solutions as many female consumers began to question the recommended retail prices of widely advertised, national brands (Lloyd and Spedding, 2009). During the 1970s and 1980s, the use of sales promotion for non-fast-moving consumer goods expanded. American Airlines launched the first frequent-flyer programme in 1981, and the first gift card appeared in 1994. The use of research for both developing and evaluating the effectiveness of sales promotion campaigns and tactics also increased. Motivation programmes grew in the 1980s (Lloyd and Spedding, 2009), as did a new voucher tactic, which consisted mainly of free hotel accommodations, holiday packages and 'experiences' (e.g. cruises, lifestyle classes and adventures).

Technology also impacted sales promotion during this final period, with phone-in promotions frequently used in the 1980s, followed by voicemail, email, texting and eventually web-based promotions. Experiential marketing expanded greatly, including in-store sampling and product demonstrations. By the end of this period, marketers were employing truly extraordinary experiential promotions, such as Red Bull's sponsorship of the world's highest sky dive (23 miles) on 14 October 2012. Some suggest sales promotions had always been predominantly employed in the UK and in the US until the 2000s. Since then, marketers in Asia, Brazil, Korea and India have all launched major international promotions, thanks in part to the internet, satellite television, mobile phones and, more recently, the penetration of social networks (Lloyd and Spedding, 2009).

Conclusion

Many historians have concluded that advertising is a mainly twentieth-century phenomenon, an inevitable consequence of modernity's march towards rationalization, industrialization and free-market capitalism as they emerged and evolved in most Western countries and cultures. It has also been suggested that much of advertising's historiography has been influenced by this Modernist paradigm. This chapter's synthesis confirms that advertising existed much earlier, that it came into use for similar reasons, and that much the same pattern of reasons occurred across the globe, including among the ancient civilizations of the Middle and Far East. Economically, even during the earliest period, advertising was linked to trade specialization, affluence and discretionary income, marketplace economies, competition and new forms of goods distribution. Other important themes in the development of advertising and related forms of commercial communications are the use of trademarks; advertising's early use with persuasive intent; the importance of spectacle; the appearance and evolution of early aural and visual media; the influence of technology on media development; the use of fine art; the use of emotional appeals, and appeals to social status; and the regulation of advertising practices and practitioners, often with the goal of consumer protection.

This chapter's synthesis was also driven by the possibility that advertising's history has been limited by the deeply internalized methodological-theoretical norm of 'Americanization'. Historians do confirm the influence of American professional practices and consumer culture during the twentieth century. The widespread adoption of a marketing orientation, marketing research, segmentation, the creative team, agency specialization and professionalization, JWT's strategic approach, and a heavy reliance on the broadcast media were mainly American contributions to contemporary and post-modern advertising. However, a broader view of advertising and sales promotion history calls into question the existence of a globally shared, advertising-induced consumerist culture and, more important, the role of US advertising professionals in creating and sustaining it. Findings show that industry structures, professional practices and creative expression often evolved independently from American influence, both before and during the twentieth century. Influences flowing from Europe to the US include an early European consumer culture, advertising-supported print media and ephemera, poster design and other creative approaches and traditions, and the practices of the early advertising agent. The findings show that some US theories and practices were, in fact, often adapted according to various economic, social, legal and cultural conditions. Resistance among advertisers and advertising professionals elsewhere focused on creative expression, the roles of strategic planning and empirical research, advertising theory and advertising's status as art versus science.

Writings on the history of sales promotion are sparse. However, the synthesis here with historical works on advertising supports some interesting conclusions. First, consumers have long favoured both the tangible benefit of promotions that provided value and those that offered entertaining spectacle. Second, findings show that advertising and sales promotion overlapped a great deal. Many of the most influential late modern and contemporary advertising pioneers such as P.T. Barnum, Claude Hopkins and John E. Kennedy contributed to developments and the widespread use of both marketing sub-disciplinary tools. Indeed, sales promotion did not fully evolve as a specialized sub-discipline, with its own independent practitioners and consultancies, until the 1970s. Third, both advertising and sales promotion tactics were influenced similarly, and continue to be, by advancements in media technology.

Despite the recent volume of historical works devoted to advertising, the findings confirm that further research is called for. Obviously lacking are analyses of ancient, modern and contemporary advertising and sales promotion for many countries and cultures across the globe. Other topics of historical interest include the contemporary adoption of agency practices such as media planning and buying, consumer acceptance of and resistance to various message appeals and tactics and how these helped shape consumerism and long-term developments in advertising, and the relationships between advertising and consumers and how societies have chosen to manage both the promotion and consumption of potentially harmful products, such as the patent medicines of the nineteenth century, alcohol, cigarettes, fast food, video games and gambling (Schwarzkopf, 2011). Indeed, tack-ups and handbills for curatives and quack nostrums were among the very first advertisements, and the post-modern advertising of direct-to-consumer prescription drugs and health-related products remains a matter of significant controversy.

References

Arndorfer, J.B., Atkinson, C., Bloom, J., Cardona, M.M., Endicott, R.C., Goldsborough, R.G., Halliday, J., Hanas, J., Macarthur, K., McDonough, J., Neff, J., Oser, K., and Thompson, S. (2005) 'The biggest moments in the last 75 years of advertising history', *Advertising Age*, 76/13, 12–20.

Arvidsson, A. (2003) *Marketing Modernity: Italian Advertising from Fascism to Postmodernity*, Routledge, London.

BBC (2014) *The BBC Story*, available online: www.bbc.co.uk/historyofthebbc/resources/factsheets/1920s.pdf (accessed Oct. 2014).

Beard, F.K. (2004) 'Hard-sell "killers" and soft-sell "poets": Modern advertising's enduring message strategy debate', *Journalism History*, 30/3, 141–9.

Beard, F.K. (2011) 'Competition and combative advertising: An historical analysis', *Journal of Macromarketing*, 31/4, 386–401.

Berg, M., and Clifford, H. (2007) 'Selling consumption in the eighteenth century: Advertising and the trade card in Britain and France', *Cultural and Social History*, 4/2, 145–70.

Burns, A.R. (1936) *The Decline of Competition: A Study of the Evolution of American Industry*, McGraw-Hill Book Co., Inc., New York.

Carey, J.W. (1989) 'Advertising: An institutional approach', in R. Hovland and G.B. Wilcox (eds), *Advertising in Society*, NTC, Lincolnwood, NJ, pp. 11–26.

Church, R. (1999) 'New perspectives on the history of products, firms, marketing, and consumers in Britain and the United States since the mid-nineteenth century', *Economic History Review*, 52/3, 405–35.

Ciarlo, D. (2011) *Advertising Empire: Race and Visual Culture in Imperial Germany*, Harvard University Press, Cambridge, MA.

De Iulio, S., and Vinti, C. (2009) 'The Americanization of Italian advertising during the 1950s and 1960s: Mediations, conflicts and appropriations', *Journal of Historical Research in Marketing*, 1/2, 270–94.

Eckhardt, G.M., and Bengtsson, A. (2010) 'A brief history of branding in China', *Journal of Macromarketing*, 30/3, 210–21.

Foster, G.A. (1967) *Advertising: Ancient Marketplace to Television*, Criterion Books, New York.

Fox, S. (1984) *The Mirror Makers: A History of American Advertising and its Creators*, Vintage Books, New York.

Frederick, J.G. (1925) 'Introduction: The story of advertising writing', in J.G. Frederick (ed.), *Masters of Advertising Copy*, Frank-Maurice Inc., New York, pp. 13–42.

Gardner, W.O. (2006), *Advertising Tower: Japanese Modernism and Modernity in the 1920s*, Harvard University Press, Cambridge, MA.

Guérin, R. (1965) 'Coca-colonisation', *Vente et Publicité* (Apr.), 23.

Hindley, C. (1884) *A History of the Cries of London*, Charles Hindley [The Younger], London.

Hollander, S.C., Rassuli, K.M., Jones, D.G.B., and Dix, L.F. (2005) 'Periodization in marketing history', *Journal of Macromarketing*, 25/1, 32–41.

Howard, S. (2008) 'The advertising industry and alcohol in interwar France', *Historical Journal*, 51/2, 421–55.

Keith, R.J. (1960) 'The marketing revolution', *Journal of Marketing*, 24/3, 35–8.

Laird, P.W. (1998) *Advertising Progress: American Business and the Rise of Consumer Marketing*, Johns Hopkins University Press, Baltimore, MD.

Leach, W. (1994) *Land of Desire: Merchants, Power, and the Rise of American Culture*, Vintage, New York.

Leachman, H.B. (1950) *The Early Advertising Scene*, Leachman, Wood Dale.

Lears, T.J.J. (1994) *Fables of Abundance: A Cultural History of Advertising in America*, Basic Books, New York.

Legh, F. (1986) 'Half a century of professional bodies in sales promotions', *European Journal of Marketing*, 20/9, 27–40.

Leiss, W., Kline, S., and Jhally, S. (1997) *Social Communication in Advertising*, Routledge, New York.

Lloyd, C., and Spedding, K. (2009) *Beyond Redemption: The First Ever History of Sales Promotion*, Sales Promotion Publishing, London.

McGovern, C.F. (2006) *Sold American: Consumption and Citizenship, 1890–1945*, University of North Carolina Press, Wilmington, NC.

Marchand, R. (1985) *Advertising the American Dream: Making Way for Modernity, 1920–1940*, University of California Press, Berkeley, CA.

Miracle, G.E., and Nevett, T. (1993) 'A comparative history of advertising self-regulation in the U.K. and the U.S.', *European Journal of Marketing*, 22/4, 7–23.

Nevett, T. (1977) 'London's early advertising agents', *Journal of Advertising History*, 1/1, 15–17.

Pollay, R.W. (1986) 'The distorted mirror: Reflections on the unintended consequences of advertising', *Journal of Marketing*, 50/2, 18–36.

Pope, D. (1983) *The Making of Modern Advertising*, Basic Books, New York.

Presbrey, F. (1929) *The History and Development of Advertising*, Doubleday, Garden City, NY.

Rivers, H.W. (1929) *Ancient Advertising and Publicity*, Krochs, Chicago, IL.

Rotzoll, K., Haefner, J.E., and Sandage, C.H. (1989) 'Advertising and the classical liberal world view', in R. Hovland and G.B. Wilcox (eds), *Advertising in Society*, NTC, Lincolnwood, NJ, pp. 27–41.

Rowsome, F., Jr. (1970) *They Laughed When I Sat Down: An Informal History of Advertising in Words and Pictures*, McGraw-Hill, New York.

Sampson, H. (1874) *A History of Advertising from the Earliest Times*, Chatto & Windus, and Piccadilly, London.

Schudson, M. (1984) *Advertising: The Uneasy Persuasion*, Basic Books, New York.

Schwarzkopf, S. (2011) 'The subsiding sizzle of advertising history: Methodological and theoretical challenges in the post advertising age', *Journal of Historical Research in Marketing,* 3/4, 528–48.

Tungate, M. (2013) *Ad-land: A Global History of Advertising*, 2nd edn, Kogan Page, London.

Turner, E.S. (1952) *The Shocking History of Advertising!* Michael Joseph, London.

Veblen, T. (1923) *Absentee Ownership*, B.W. Huebach, New York.

Wolofson, W.A. (2012) 'Wishful thinking: Retail premiums in mid-nineteenth-century America', *Enterprise and Society,* 13/4, 790–831.

Wood, J.P. (1958) *The Story of Advertising*, Ronald Press, New York.

Zhao, X., and Belk, R. (2008) 'Advertising consumer culture in 1930s Shanghai', *Journal of Advertising,* 37/2, 45–56.

12

History of selling and sales management

Thomas L. Powers

Introduction

A review of the evolution and development of selling and sales management provides an important perspective on marketing history. Perhaps no other area within the marketing profession has such a long history and rich tradition (Beckman *et al.*, 1957, 427). Unlike many other aspects of marketing, selling in one form or another has existed since the early development of civilization (Butler, 1918, 44–5). There are several aspects of selling and sales management that are discussed in this chapter. These include sales professionalism, organizational issues and the use of technology. Tracing the early historical development of selling and sales management represents a daunting task as relatively few records exist. Written documentation is limited as the practice and history of selling had mostly been communicated verbally throughout its history until the modern era (Powers *et al.*, 1987). Fortunately, as we draw closer to the present time there is a better documented history, making the task easier and providing us with a richer perspective. The literature reviewed here is based on three primary areas: general historical works, books and articles from the popular business press, and the academic marketing literature.

In order to cover the evolution of selling and sales management, the chapter is divided into four sections that reflect the development of this topic. The first section, 'Selling through the millennia' examines selling activities from the ancient and classical world to the industrial revolution. The second section, 'The emergence of modern sales and sales management' begins with the developments spawned by the industrial revolution, leading to the modern era of selling at the dawn of the twentieth century. This is followed by an overview of the rapid growth of selling through the 1920s and the effects of the Great Depression. 'The continued development of the field' discusses how the mobilization in World War II influenced the practice of selling and sales management. This is followed by a discussion of the impact of the rapidly expanding economy in the post-war period and, and lastly 'Conclusions and looking ahead' examines the major influences on sales activities in the latter part of the twentieth and early twenty-first centuries.

Selling through the millennia

Personal selling is considered to be the oldest form of marketing activity (Beckman *et al.*, 1957, 427). The earliest known form of personal selling is that of a 'peddler' who encompassed the selling and inventory-holding function of a modern merchant. They appeared at the same time as the limited manufacture of goods began its initial development. The peddler, also referred to as an 'itinerant merchant', can be considered the originator of retail merchandising. They controlled the merchandising that existed outside of town centres. Peddlers went from tribe to tribe, town to town, and from country to country displaying their wares (Butler, 1918, 45–8). They travelled between villages bartering their wares for forms of currency which could in turn be used to purchase additional wares while making a profit. Some peddlers also plied their trade as a means of acquiring land. Centuries ago peddlers were often landless younger sons, as the eldest son typically inherited the father's estate (Heichelheim, 1957, 237).

A key role of peddlers was to balance supply and demand, much in the function of a modern marketplace (Converse and Huegy, 1946, 636). Peddlers balanced surpluses and shortages during this time, resulting in increased trade between geographic areas (Durant, 1954, 160). Fixed location markets developed when farmers and herders brought excess output to trade for items they were unable to produce themselves. Soon, merchant middlemen appeared, freeing producers from extended stays in the city. Middlemen also helped facilitate trade by arranging to export goods if surpluses threatened to decrease prices or to import goods if shortages were pending. The middleman tried to outdo competitors through more attractive display of samples, additional services such as delivery and reduced prices (Heichelheim, 1957, 87). The development of improved vessels helped to facilitate trade around the Mediterranean Sea. The Phoenicians, situated on the eastern Mediterranean shore between the fertile Nile region of Egypt and the cities of the northern Mediterranean basin, took advantage of this development. In addition, rather than simply landing and trading on the quay, they walked into a town and peddled their wares directly to the populace. Homer wrote of Phoenicians selling from door-to-door, and canvassing housewives. Traders were organized as groups, with a chief merchant and his underlings operating on a daily wage or commission basis (Powers *et al.*, 1987).

The Aegean Sea was another focus of trade, in this case by the Greek peoples. The abundance of Aegean harbours facilitated the development of trade and industry (Starr, 1974, 187). Selling practices developed during this time to include the establishment of laws governing trade and the creation of merchant wholesalers. An example of the ancient commercial legal system was when Alcibiades is said to have bought a team of horses on behalf of Diomedes, but failed to deliver the goods. Court proceedings ensued, indicating that a system of commercial law was in force (Dryden and Clough, 1937, 12). The development of coinage improved the efficiencies of trade. Lydia in 670 BCE was the first city to issue government-backed coinage. The Dorians, who settled at Argos, followed suit and before long Aeginetan 'tortoises', marked with the island's symbol, became the first official coinage in continental Greece. The impact of coinage on trade was as momentous as the effects that came from the introduction of the alphabet (Durant, 1966, 205).

Sellers were specialized by activity and went by different titles. Foreign traders in Greece were known as *emporoi* and *naucleroi*, while domestic traders were called *kapeloi*. The *naucleroi* was a shipowner who traded on his own account but also carried other merchants and their goods. The *emporoi* was a travelling merchant and in some cases travelled with the *naucleroi* (Dixon, 1995). The *kapeloi* bought goods from producers or from importers (Heichelheim, 1968, 66). The *kapeloi* town economy or market was fully formed by 400 BCE. The growth of towns as centres of population and trade gave craftsmen and traders a market to buy raw materials and sell goods (Clough and Cole, 1946, 25). City markets became subdivided with different goods in specific areas, for example, meat in one area and grains in another. This fostered competition and enabled customers to make quick comparisons. The specialization of the Greek retail merchants is extensive with 115 known *kapeloi* occupations, ranging from fishing tackle to purgatives. Men did not have a monopoly on selling jobs or trade. Some of the descriptions, such as 'pea soup woman', were distinctly feminine (Heichelheim, 1968, 66).

The Roman Empire saw further sales developments. Paid agents were a common sight. Commissions became popular because this form of payment increased the motivation of agents as they were not paid until the investor received his return (Durant and Durant, 1968, 55–7). The fall of Rome in 476 CE saw the rise of Islamic traders who elevated the merchant to a position of honour. The first regions to come into contact with Islamic merchants were those on the northern coasts of the Mediterranean. Florence, Venice and other merchant cities learned business procedures from these people. Terms such as tariff, traffic and risk are directly traceable to the Islamic traders (Lieber, 1968). Larger organizations dissolved with the collapse of Rome and the salesperson reverted to a role played centuries before. The economic activity of Europe reached a low point in the eighth, ninth and tenth centuries (Clough and Cole, 1946, 23). One of the first signs of a commercial reawakening was the development of merchant markets and fairs. Saints' bones, pieces of the cross and furs provided interest and variety to the normal types of goods available at fairs (Baldwin, 1968, 88–96). The salesperson was an important feature of these fairs. The salesperson was auctioneer, trader, lecturer and entertainer. He was worldly, wise and an object of intense interest to the general populace. This entertainment aspect of the salesperson would be seen later in the form of the nineteenth-century drummer. The businesspeople of the Middle Ages who engaged in trade often operated individually, however, partnerships did develop during this period (Clough and Cole, 1946, 465–7). Alliances were formed with wealthy patrons who financed sales trips in hopes of increasing their own treasure (Baldwin, 1968, 6–9).

By the eleventh century a trade revival had begun that can be illustrated by a brief example. The life of St Godric of Finchal was chronicled by Monk Reginald of Durham (Baldwin, 1968, 6–9). Originally written to praise Godric's decision to abandon business to become a religious hermit, the record is valuable to understanding selling at this time. Godric began by peddling lowpriced trinkets in England. These were bought in larger towns, and then sold door-to-door in rural areas. Godric's initial sales territory was the manorial estates dotting the countryside. Moving on to more lucrative markets, he abandoned the home market to sell to forts, castles and cities. He travelled widely, visiting Scotland and Flanders. In a few years Godric went from a shepherd to a respected man of substance. Eventually he gave up this life to become a religious recluse. Despite his final rejection of wealth, Godric's story is a forerunner of the more modern notion of quick success through a sales career. This story is also an early example of the notion that selling is the opposite of a pious existence.

The discovery of the new world and the development of trade with the colonies expanded commerce to new levels. The later development of steam power, iron construction and the screw propeller led to a further increase in international trade (Clough and Cole, 1946, 465–7). The problem of ground transportation remained a major obstacle for early manufacturing during the American colonial period (1492–1763). The problem of sales and distribution exceeded that of production during this period. By 1800, several thousand peddlers were working in New England, many of whom would accumulate enough money on the road to become merchants or traders (Scull, 1967, 25–6). Travelling salespeople in the colonial period were usually welcomed and often invited to stay overnight with families to share the latest news from other parts of the country (Christ and Anderson, 2011). A second type of salesperson who appeared in the early half of the eighteenth century was a greeter or 'drummer' employed by suppliers and manufacturers. Drummers were given this name because of their use of drums to generate attention as they greeted arriving retail buyers at train stations, ship docks or hotels (Christ and Anderson, 2011).

The expansion of the railroad system caused a great increase in the number and presence of travelling salespeople (Spears, 1995, 1). Often, these individuals were colourful, wearing brash clothing and bringing news of the outside world to the small towns that they visited (Spears, 1995, 82–5). In the 1880s, the publication *Commercial Travelers Magazine* was created to serve this market of individuals. These individuals serviced independent retailers as wholesalers, bringing goods and news to smaller towns from larger urban centres. This process is thought to have contributed to the material culture of American society (Strasser, 1989, 5). The presence of drummers also created a cultural perception of the selling profession that was in some cases positive and in some not. In the painting *The Drummer's Latest Yarn* by Archibald M. Willard that was based on an actual event in 1891, a portly drummer is depicted telling a humorous story on a train with an audience of several people listening. Some people are enchanted, some are disgusted, but all are affected by the drummer's tale (Spears, 1995, 113–14). Publications during this period used the *drummer* term in the title of collections of jokes and stories such as *Drummers Yarns* and *New Drummer Jokes*. The presence of drummers was short-lived, however. In the nineteenth century manufacturers sold their goods to wholesalers, who in turn used travelling salesmen (Friedman, 2004, 56–7). By 1900, retail chains that bought directly from suppliers and sold directly to customers became commonplace (Spears, 1995, 1). By this time a greater level of sales professionalism based on a scientific approach was becoming prevalent, slowly replacing the quick wits and an occasional sleight of hand approaches used by the drummers (Spears, 1995, 110).

The move to greater professionalism of personal selling developed after the industrial revolution with the corresponding increase in manufactured goods that required that demand be generated (Christ and Anderson, 2011). The independent peddlers and drummers were soon giving way to canvassers and agents who worked in a more direct fashion with the producer of the goods they were selling (Friedman, 2004, 37). The growth of urban markets after 1850 resulted in the development of more contemporary marketing practices and institutions (Silk and Stern, 1963). Branch sales offices in the 1860s were established by I.M. Singer and Company which produced the Singer sewing machine. These branch offices ensured that the company could control the selling and demonstration of the product. Other advances were made by Proctor & Gamble that pioneered the use of preselling their products by running advertisements on a regular basis in the 1880s (Silk and Stern, 1963).

Emergence of modern sales and sales management

The selling profession saw numerous developments in the late nineteenth and early twentieth centuries. The overall business was changing, with ever larger firms creating product differentiation, brand identities and expanded direct sales networks (Harris, 2008; Koehn, 1999). Large manufacturers of branded consumer goods desired closer control over their sales forces, resulting in formal sales organizations that included the use of sales managers (French and Popp, 2008). The professional salesperson soon replaced wholesale drummers as formally trained salespeople. As described at the World's Salesmanship Congress of 1916, 'the days of the backslapping, hard drinking drummer were over' (Friedman, 2004, 3). Both college and non-college courses on sales instruction was developed to aid in this effort. Education through correspondence schools played a major role in this process. In some cases sales education by correspondence was such a large business that it spawned enterprises like the Sheldon School founded by A.F. Sheldon. Not only was the Sheldon School a major force in sales training, but it also emphasized ethics and customer service as part of the selling process (Tadajewski, 2011).

The early understanding of salesmanship had been often considered a matter of keeping one's foot in the door (Agnew and Houghton, 1941). These correspondence schools taught what we would now consider the basics of a modern sales method such as predetermined sales talks, defined territories and methods of compensation (Friedman, 1998). In addition, motivational methods such as contests, sales conventions and motivational messages became commonly used (Friedman, 1998). During this period increased training and the use of standardized management procedures became common (Macbain, 1905, 9–16). New transportation methods including trains, streetcars and automobiles gave salespeople mobility they had never before experienced. They were able to cover more territory quickly, which increased salaries and personal efficiency (Scull, 1967, 213–15). The salesperson who primarily worked alone was replaced by one who took advice from the organization that employed him (Doubman, 1939, 22–23). This resulted in companies having to develop a new kind of leader – the sales manager, whose primary task was the supervision of salespeople (Bartels, 1976, 80). The sales manager became responsible for controlling the activities of salespeople in many cases over a large geographic area. Modern communication methods such as the telephone made this new sales management possible on a daily basis, despite the large distances involved. As company sales forces grew and began to implement modern sales techniques, larger firms found it necessary to separate the sales function and develop systematic means of selecting, training, motivating and controlling salespeople (Macbain, 1905, 9–16). In many cases these sales departments eventually became equal to those of manufacturing (*Business Week*, 1950).

Salespeople were often shown their firms' advertising at national meetings. It was a major part of their job to then carry the advertising messages about the products to the merchants to whom they would then be selling. Salespeople attended workshops to learn how to make displays and would share this knowledge in creating store window displays for their clients (Strasser, 1989, 195). The creation of new ways of selling opened up new areas of academic inquiry including industrial psychology (Friedman, 2004, 6). As sales and sales management methods became more established and widely adopted by large organizations, it became necessary to formalize sales training. The teaching of selling followed banking and finance as subjects taught in colleges. These courses were considered to be more directly applicable to business problems of the day. In 1902, college courses related to selling were offered for the first time and expanded rapidly in the following decade. The University of Michigan offered the first course with a selling component: The Distributive and Regulative Industries of the United States taught by Professor E.D. Jones of the Economics Department. The course description included 'the various ways of marketing goods, of the classification, grades, brands employed, and of the wholesale and retail trade' (Maynard, 1941, 382–4). The Marketing of Products, taught at the Wharton School of the University of Pennsylvania by W.E. Kruse, was described as 'The methods now practiced in the organization and conduct of the selling branch of industrial and mercantile business' (Maynard, 1941, 383). Ohio State began a programme in sales education with J.E. Hagerty teaching The Distribution of Products (Hagerty, 1936). Paul T. Cherington of the Harvard School of Business Administration taught Commercial Organization and Methods in 1908 (Hagerty, 1936). In 1916, the Ohio

State University developed a course on Salesmanship which was devoted exclusively to the subject (Bartels, 1976, 23). Several periodicals related to the selling profession were also developed during this time. These included *Industrial Distribution* (1911), *Stores* (1912), *Selling Digest* (1915), and *Business Marketing* (1916).

It should be kept in mind that the changes that were occurring in the US had parallels throughout the world. The development of sales techniques was not limited to the US. Research has found that there were books written in Polish for US Polish-speaking individuals who wanted to learn selling methods. Not only did these books contain sophisticated business skills, but also served to further the acculturation of immigrants into the US business environment (Witkowski, 2012). Efforts in other countries were also made to increase the professionalism of selling through training and education. England saw the development of a Sales Managers' Association in 1911, as well as the publication of *Sales Promotion* in 1928 (Walker and Child, 1979).

Despite the newly developed college courses the vast majority of training was 'on-the-job' and centred on prepared or 'canned' presentations (Dawson, 1970; Fullerton, 1988). This practice proved to be very effective as many firms achieved great sales success by having their salesmen memorize these canned talks (Bartels, 1976, 86). This practice was commonly incorporated into early sales manuals that became very popular in the early 1900s as attempts were made to standardize selling procedures (Macbain, 1905, 32–8). Percival White published a number of books including his landmark *Scientific Marketing Management* (1927) that represented a revolution in marketing practice similar to Frederick Taylor's work in the field of management (Jones and Tadajewski, 2011). White's ethically based and customer focused perspective stood in stark contrast to the 'supersalesmanship' that he took issue with (Jones and Tadajewski, 2011). Incorporating modern management into personal selling, C.W. Hoyt published *Scientific Sales Management* (1929) where he presented the case for standardized methods as developed in management by Frederick Taylor. He discussed the 'canned' sales talk in his text, based on the belief that the sales manager should incorporate the practices of the most successful salespeople (Hoyt, 1927). Not all of the successful salespersons and managers agreed with Hoyt. Some early sales manuals stressed a more problem-solving, consultative approach (Fullerton, 1988). Several early leaders in selling recognized the value of developing customers as opposed to dealing with the customers in a canned manner. Ben Affleck, President of Universal Portland Cement, believed in solid training combined with personal examples and positive encouragement for his sales force. He emphasized teamwork, standardization and minimum interference from higher authority (Crissey, 1928). The early period of the twentieth century also saw the development of charitable efforts by members of the sales profession. In 1910, J.W. Binder, the New York sales manager for Red Cross Stamps used 1,800 volunteer salesmen to run their annual stamp campaign. The result of this effort was the sale of over 4,200,000 Red Cross seals (Binder, 1911).

Advances were also made during this period in the management and organization of field sales people. In 1912, Marshall Field & Company hired William Mann into their sales department. Through his success in several large sales campaigns, Mann rose to be General Manager of Marshall Field by 1919. Much of that success was the result of his organization and management of the sales department. He developed 15 territories, each headed by a territorial manager. These managers were expected to use all the tools of modern sales management practice. These salespersons were organized into three groups; one to handle big businesses and large sales volumes, one for large areas and special product lines, and the third to handle 'piece goods' such as hosiery and handkerchiefs who worked smaller town merchants. Mann organized the company towards the total support of the selling effort by developing younger and bolder people to guide the sales effort of the firm (*Sales Management*, 1919).

During the 1920s, salespeople became seen as a key to economic development, which contributed to the profession being glamorized (Dawson, 1970; Tosdal, 1957, 88–9). The development of radio and improvements in transportation gave sales people an opportunity to improve and innovate sales methods and philosophies (Scull, 1967, 240–1). Many firms developed formalized training programmes for their salespeople which resulted in some firms exclusively hiring college graduates (Curtis, 1926). During this period books and articles on selling flourished describing how companies could use various techniques to increase sales (Hall, 1924). Many of these documents included stories of unprecedented sales increases (Rollins and Pulliam, 1926). The sales literature of this period was rich in ideas and procedures, many of which are still practical today. These include supervisory practices by sales managers (Deupree, 1924), the importance of sales knowledge of products and the characteristics of successful salespeople (Hoyt, 1927). There were also a number of new periodicals developed during this period. These include the introduction of *Sales Management* in 1918. *Opportunity Magazine* appeared in 1923 and the *Journal of Retailing* in 1925. In addition, the development of direct selling led to the publication of *Mail Trade* in 1929.

Advertising had traditionally supported personal selling, however, it took on a different role in 1922, with the first use of radio advertising (Scull, 1967, 240–1). It is interesting to note that advertising was considered a selling function during this period (Beckman *et al.*, 1957, 434–5). By 1930, the number of persons employed in sales was at an all-time high, having gone from 600,000 people in 1900 to over 2 million people by 1930 (*Abstract of the 15th Census of the United States*, 1930, 316). Selling was clearly identified as being an important element in creating demand and maintaining a high standard of living for the country. The term 'science' was increasingly used related to selling with such terms as 'science of salesmanship' and 'scientific salesmanship' (Frederick, 1937, 33). Sales management changed as well with additional responsibilities beyond supervision being added to the sales management role, including recruiting, selecting, training and compensating (Dawson, 1970).

The 1930s marked a profound change for the sales profession. The stature of salespeople declined, and in some cases the profession was actually blamed for the Great Depression (Powers *et al.*, 1988). A theme of this period was that proper selling methods and approaches could overcome economic events, and many successful examples were provided to give hope to others. A 1931 article in *Sales Management* stated 'that in practically every line of business there are a few companies that have blazed straight through the depression with strong sales campaigns and come out with records that make 1929 look like only a fair year after all' (Hahn, 1931). *Sales Management* concluded that this explained why 'sales-minded' individuals were going into company presidencies in place of managers with financial or legal backgrounds (Hahn, 1931). To overcome the effects of the Great Depression, sales techniques included researching the needs of the buyer and being at the purchasing manager's office well before the time that they normally saw salespeople (Hahn, 1931). Evaluating the productivity of salespeople, eliminating unprofitable territories and selling only to profitable customers reflected this new approach to selling during this economically difficult period (Hatch, 1930).

The depression was seen as a force that told buyers to hold onto their money (Lothrop, 1930). To some the depression was so discouraging it caused salespeople to assume that business could not be won, even to the point of not bothering to show their lines to customers. Different approaches were tried to encourage salespeople during this period. An example of a motivational technique was to include a printed sales message on the expense report form of which the sales manager wanted their salespeople to be aware. The salesperson would

231

be sure to see the message and hopefully pass it on to their customers (Lothrop, 1930). Other firms sent one new idea to salespeople each month in the hope that they would be able to use it as an opening line with customers. Cards were sometimes sent to salespeople daily, with a message or a slogan that hopefully would stimulate the seller. The required numbers of daily sales calls were increased and territories were exchanged to give salespeople new customers and selling experiences (Lothrop, 1930). Aggressive selling became more commonplace in some instances, with practices such as door-to-door selling that sometimes involved questionable ethics (Scott, 2008).

Despite the pressures of making sales during the depression the concept of the professional salesman saw continued development. This thinking was widely discussed both inside and outside the selling profession. Popular magazines such as *The Saturday Evening Post* described this new individual as one who did extensive planning before a sales contact, sometimes spending weeks in the field to understand a customer's need (Sprague, 1933). This also applied to business-to-business selling and meant that not only the needs of the dealer must be addressed, but also the needs of their customer (Sprague, 1933). With customers in short supply every effort had to be made to cater to those available (Fullerton, 1988). The literature of the period reflects an emphasis on professional selling with admonitions made to compete 'not with the smartest, slickest, salesman, but with the best service, quality and prices' (Frederick, 1937, 33). This represented a continued effort to operate on a higher ethical plane that no longer had 'caveat emptor' as a guiding philosophy (Doubman, 1939, 22–3). Firms researched buying motives of customers and designing new or redesigning existing products to suit consumer needs (*Automotive Industries*, 1932; Sheldon and Arens, 1932). An increase in professional advertising activities also occurred during this period with the use of market and media research, and copy testing (Fullerton, 1988).

The 1930s saw books and other written material on selling which stressed themes of efficient sales management methods in light of the depressed economy. The *Industrial Arts Index* of 1930 listed 22 books on salesmanship plus hundreds of articles. Some of this written material was relatively light-hearted, citing common mistakes in selling in a humorous format (DeArmond, 1939). Other published material detailed the new selling which included concepts such as selling the services that products performed as opposed to the product itself (Read, 1931). Because of the need to stimulate sales wherever possible, tools were developed to obtain marginal business and to identify areas that were not producing their potential sales. In an article in the *Journal of Marketing*, Wellman (1939) outlined detailed procedures for determining sales potentials utilizing linear regression. By following this procedure they suggested that firms could identify areas that were producing marginal sales and thus be able to allocate selling resources into that area. In another article in the *Journal of Marketing*, Applebaum (1943) explained procedures for developing sales quotas for retail stores. It must be kept in mind that the *Journal of Marketing* was very practitioner-focused, unlike the academic focus of the present time. Despite these challenges *Fortune* magazine described 'The Great American Salesman' as being larger than life and chiefly responsible for the development of the modern world's economic system (*Fortune*, 1940).

Continued development of the field

The 1940s saw radical disruptions in the selling profession but set the stage for later developments leading to selling's contemporary focus. Conversion to a war-based economy created a shortage of consumer goods and a reduction in the number of salespeople needed to sell them. After the war pent-up consumer demand led to a brief period where selling was not essential to business success due to existing shortages of many goods. This boom period soon ended, causing firms to hire and train more salespeople than ever before. The previous buyer's market of the 1930s had transformed into a seller's market in the 1940s where limited production of many consumer goods required minimal selling effort. At the same time, the introduction of new products, which typically required a greater selling effort to introduce their benefits, slowed to a near halt. This resulted in a decline in the number of professional salespeople who were employed (*Business Week*, 1941). As noted at the time, 'salesmen are fast becoming the forgotten men of the defense program' (*Fortune*, 1942). Salespeople were sometimes absorbed into other areas, such as market research and expediting. Industries, such as automobiles and appliances, that were virtually curtailed by the war effort left it to their salespeople to seek opportunities elsewhere (*Fortune*, 1942).

Following World War II, sales forces had to be increased, training had to be done on a larger scale, and sales and promotion budgets had to be increased. For the first time salespeople were recruited on a large scale from the ranks of college graduates. Often firms would test potential hires to measure a person's sales aptitude (*Business Week*, 1945). There was also an increased call to raise selling to a 'professional status' that would help convey the broader social benefits of the profession. It was thought that this would make it easier to employ a greater number of properly selected and adequately trained men (Maynard and Nolen, 1950, 11). Despite the conversion in this period to a post-war consumer driven economy, the communication and transportation infrastructure that salespeople faced was much the same as it was decades before. Travel by train in a Pullman, or sleeping car, was the norm and very time-consuming. For an extra fare, someone could get an express trip from Chicago to San Francisco on the Southern Pacific Railroad which was only a 40-hour trip (DeArmond, 1939). The types of salespersons and the equipment that they used can help us visualize the nature of selling during this period. Sales positions were broken down into several categories that included driver salesperson, inside sales, outside sales, missionary salesperson, sales engineer and the creative salesperson who sold intangibles such as insurance (Stanton and Buskirk, 1969, 104–5). During this time salespeople became differentiated by job title and by the type of equipment they used. Nystrom (1948, 699–704) detailed the equipment used in selling during this period that ranged from business cards, samples, models, swatches, visual equipment, statistics and graphs, photographs, slides, filmstrips to moving pictures.

The late 1940s saw a reduction in pent-up demand which led to a post-war recession. The idea that salespeople were not doing their jobs, and that the recession could be 'sold out of', recurred. Questions like 'what's the matter with American salesmanship?' (*Fortune*, 1949) became commonplace as the feeling became widespread that salespeople were again at fault for the latest recession. In some cases there were calls for a return to high-pressure sales, perhaps hoping that this would cause a resurgence of better times. This aggressive selling was portrayed citing successful examples of 'super salesmen' (*Fortune*, 1947). Eureka Williams Corporation, maker of the Eureka vacuum cleaner, began to sell packages to convert coal to oil furnaces. To promote the programme salespeople promoted a '3 and 3' programme which consisted of a guaranteed three hour time limit to do the work and three years to pay for it. The three hour period was designed to increase business in winter months. To make it even more appealing, customers were offered free movie tickets to use while the work was being performed (*Business Week*, 1947, 54, 56). Other firms, such as Philco, created contests for dealer appliance salespeople that awarded points that could be converted into prizes as an effort to push their products over the competition's (*Business Week*, 1947, 85). By 1950, the number of salespeople employed in the field reached 3.3 million, representing a five-fold increase from 1900 (*Census of Population*, 1950, 285; *Abstract of the 12th Census of the United States*, 1900, 25).

Although the dominant character and practice of the sales profession had largely developed by this time there were numerous events in the second half of the twentieth century that would continue to evolve the science of selling. A continued acceptance of a customer focus was part of this trend (McKitterick, 1974). Although the customer focus had developed earlier (White, 1927), the older 'hard sell' perspective on selling was still reflected in some of the literature of the period (Friedman, 2004, 251; Maxwell, 1950). During this time, sales and sales management activities were considered to be more aligned with the overall strategy and goals of the organization (Lazer, 1971, 381). Consistent with this thinking, scholars saw sales management as an organizational issue, and not a separate concern (Crissy and Kaplan, 1969, 18–21; Davis and Webster, 1968, 4–5). Similar to the advent of radio advertising in the 1920s, television advertising had a great impact on selling in the 1950s. Retailers now took a secondary role to manufacturers who were able to reach consumers direct (Scull, 1967, 259–60).

Conclusions and looking ahead

There are numerous aspects that have been discussed in this overview of the history of selling and sales management including professionalism, organization and technology. These elements have converged, creating a markedly different sales landscape in the late twentieth and early twenty-first century. In terms of professionalism, increased levels of education and training have occurred not just with salespeople but with organizational buyers as well. More sophisticated buyers, in turn, have created the need for more sophisticated selling procedures. Other trends in the personal selling environment, such as advances in technology, customer relationship management and globalization have placed a premium on training programmes designed to develop knowledgeable and effective sales managers (Deeter-Schmelz *et al.*, 2002; Jones *et al.*, 2005; Magrath, 1997; Marshall and Micheals, 2001). Similar to what was occurring a century before, college and university training remains an important component of salesperson training, however, on-the-job training continues to be the most common form (Powers *et al.*, 2010). Numerous issues have become a focal point of the selling and sales management process. These include developing improved selling skills (Rentz *et al.*, 2002), assessing salesperson perspectives on sales management effectiveness (Deeter-Schmelz *et al.*, 2008) and sales management leadership styles (Butler and Reese, 1991).

Changes in the expectations of buying organizations have likewise had a major impact on the sophistication of selling (Marshall *et al.*, 2003). The concentration of sales into a smaller number of retailers has increased their power and negotiating ability over the seller. There is a growing sophistication and aggressiveness of purchasers (Piercy and Lane, 2011, 20) that also has an impact on the increased role of salespeople in their own organizations. There is growing evidence that the sales function has a greater influence over business decisions, and that sales is increasingly having a strategic emphasis (Piercy and Lane, 2011, 20). The focus on production quality during this time also sharpened the focus on buyers and sellers. Buyers increasingly expect sellers not only to have quality products but to hold the entire selling effort to a higher standard (Cron and DeCarlo, 2009, 12–19). The traditional practice of using multiple suppliers has been replaced by a fewer number of suppliers to reduce transactional costs for the buyer. This has placed a corresponding premium on the sales function maintaining the buyer–supplier relationship over time (Cron and DeCarlo, 2009, 121). Cost for the seller has also been a concern. Outsourcing has seen a renewed focus, and the make or buy decision is increasingly being used in the approach to outsourcing the sales function from company personnel to manufacturer's representatives (DeCarlo, 2011).

Strategic buying and selling, as opposed to focusing on 'overcoming objections' and 'closing the sale', has become the norm. The long evolving customer focus that has its origins in the nineteenth century has evolved into solution selling that addresses the comprehensive long-term needs of the buyer (Epp and Price, 2011; Marshall *et al.*, 2003). In business-to-business selling sales teams are increasingly used as opposed to an individual salesperson. This process allows for multiple contacts between buyers and sellers and enhances the transfer of capabilities and communications (Cron and DeCarlo, 2009, 172). This is also part of a longstanding trend towards relational and consultative sales approaches that had its origins much earlier in the development of professional selling (Tadajewski, 2009). This 'service centred' view of the selling process has placed a premium on customized offerings (Cravens *et al.*, 2011, 81). Closely related to this is the advent of 'customer solutions' as a means of competitors differentiating themselves from one another (Tuli *et al.*, 2007). Customer solutions are based on an integrated combination of goods and services to meet a customer's business needs (Tuli *et al.*, 2007). A solution seller typically provides services to design, integrate, operate and finance products or systems during their life cycles (Davies *et al.*, 2006). This represents a full extension of the early notion that a salesperson should identify and fulfil customer's needs (Sprague, 1933). Customer solutions have been widely used as a selling practice in business-to-business and business-to-consumer markets (*Journal of Transportation*, 2010; *Biotech Business*, 2007).

The role and development of technology continues to have a profound impact on selling and sales management (Marshall *et al.*, 2003). These advances in communication and data processing have driven many new practices that include customer relationship and supply chain management. These activities involve the selling function and expand selling's reach into other areas of the business. They have created a proliferation of media, channel and customer contact points that more fully integrate buyers and sellers (Day, 2011; Ramani and Kumar, 2008). The ability to communicate electronically via numerous new methods and technologies has created and facilitated numerous changes and advancements to the selling process, with many more likely to occur (San Martin *et al.*, 2012). Countless salespeople work from home offices and are members of virtual teams. These individuals and processes are a great distance in time and method from the classic *kapeloi*, peddler and drummer, however, they remain the key to matching supply with demand and overcoming distances, both geographic and commercial, between buyer and seller.

References

Abstract of the 12th Census of the United States (1900) Arno Press, New York.
Abstract of the 15th Census of the United States (1930) Arno Press, New York.
Agnew, H. E., and Houghton, D. (1941) *Marketing Policies*, McGraw Hill Book Company, Inc., New York.
Applebaum, W. (1943) 'A case history of sales quotas', *Journal of Marketing* (pre-1986), 7/3, 200.
Automotive Industries (1932) 'GM query seeks buying reasons', 67 (9 Aug.), 82.
Baldwin, S. (1968) *Business in the Middle Ages*, Cooper Square Publishers Inc., New York.
Bartels, R. (1976) *The History of Marketing Thought*, Grid Inc., Columbus, OH.
Beckman, T.N., Maynard, H.H., and Davidson, W.R. (1957) *Principles of Marketing*, Ronald Press Co., New York.
Binder, J.W. (1911) 'Commercial sales methods applied to charity', *Printers' Ink*, 74/8, 17–20.
Biotech Business (2007) 'Novozymes opens Iowa center for ethanol/biofuel research', 20/5, 1.
Business Week (1941) 'Selling in a defense economy' (2 Aug.), 60.
Business Week (1945) 'Quiz for salesmen' (23 June), 81–3.

Business Week (1947) 'Fighting seasonal slumps' (15 Nov.), 54, 56.

Business Week (1947) 'Push money hit' (22 Nov.), 85.

Business Week (1950) 'Marketing men take over at GE' (24 Apr.), 30–2, 34, 36.

Butler, J.K., Jr, and Reese, R.M. (1991) 'Leadership style and sales performance: A test of the situational leadership model', *Journal of Personal Selling and Sales Management*, 11/3, 37–46.

Butler, R.S. (1918) *Marketing Methods*, Alexander Hamilton Institute, New York.

Christ, P., and Anderson, R. (2011) 'The impact of technology on evolving roles of salespeople', *Journal of Historical Research in Marketing*, 3/2, 173–93.

Clough, S.B., and Cole, C.W. (1946) *Economic History of Europe*, D.C. Heath & Co., Boston, MA.

Converse, P.D., and Huegy, H.W. (1946) *The Elements of Marketing*, Prentice-Hall, New York.

Cravens, D.W., Le Meuner-Fitzhugh, K., and Piercy, N.F. (eds) (2011) *The Oxford Handbook of Strategic Sales and Sales Management*, Oxford University Press, New York.

Crissey, F. (1928) 'Back in 1896 Ben Affleck got a job selling cement and he is still selling it', *Sales Management* (14 Apr.), 579.

Crissy, W.J.E., and Kaplan, R.M. (1969) *Salemanship*, John Wiley & Sons, Inc., New York.

Cron, W.L., and DeCarlo, T.E. (2009) *Dalrymple's Sales Management*, John Wiley & Sons, Inc., Hoboken, NJ.

Curtis, A.D. (1926) 'We stopped taking chances on our future executives', *Sales Management*, 11, 704–7.

Davies, A., Brady, T., and Hobday, M. (2006) 'Charting a path toward integrated solutions', *Sloan Management Review*, 47/3, 39–48.

Davis, K.R., and Webster, F.E. (1968) *Sales Force Management*, Ronald Press Co., New York.

Dawson, L.M. (1970) 'Toward a new concept of sales management', *Journal of Marketing*, 34/2, 33–8.

Day, G.S. (2011) 'Closing the marketing capabilities gap', *Journal of Marketing*, 75/4, 183.

DeArmond, F. (1939) 'The selling game', *Nation's Business* (Aug.), 29.

DeCarlo, T.E. (2011) 'Management of a contracted sales force', in D.W. Cravens, K. Le Meuner-Fitzhugh and N.F. Piercy (eds), *The Oxford Handbook of Strategic Sales and Sales Management*, Oxford University Press, New York, 201.

Deeter-Schmelz, D.R., Goebel, D.J., and Kennedy, K.N. (2008) 'What are the characteristics of an effective sales manager? An exploratory study comparing salesperson and sales manager perspectives', *Journal of Personal Selling and Sales Management*, 28/1, 7–20.

Deeter-Schmelz, D.R., Kennedy, K.N., and Goebel, D.J. (2002) 'Understanding sales manager effectiveness: Linking attributes to sales force values', *Industrial Marketing Management*, 31/7, 617–26.

Deupree, R.R. (1924) 'The kind of sales manager who builds an organization that endures', *Sales Management* (May), 977–79, 1011.

Dixon, D.F. (1995) 'Retailing in classical Athens: Gleanings from contemporary literature and art', *Journal of Macromarketing*, 15/1, 74.

Doubman, R.J. (1939) *Salesmanship and Types of Selling*, Appleton Century Crofts, Inc., New York.

Dryden, J., and Clough A.H. (1937) *Plutarch's lives of Themistocles, Pericles, Aristides, Alcibiades, and Coriolanue, Demos-Thenes and Cicero, Caesar and Antony*, P.F. Collier & Son Corp., New York.

Durant, W. (1954) *Our Oriental Heritage*, Simon & Schuster, New York.

Durant, W. (1966) *The Life of Greece*, Simon & Schuster, New York.

Durant, W., and Durant, A. (1968) *The Lessons of History*, Simon & Schuster, New York.

Epp, A.M., and Price, L.L. (2011) 'Designing solutions around customer network identity goals', *Journal of Marketing*, 75, 36–54.

Fortune (1940) 'The great American salesman' (Feb.), 72–5, 164, 166, 168, 170, 172, 174, 176.

Fortune (1942) 'But what's to become of the salesman?' (May), 84–7, 126–9.

Fortune (1947) 'Pepsi-Cola's Walter Mack' (Nov.), 127–31, 178, 181, 182, 184, 187–8, 190.

Fortune (1949) 'What's the matter with American salesmanship' (Sept.), 67–9, 180, 182, 184.

Frederick, J.G. (1937) *Modern Salesmanship*, Garden City Publishing Co., Garden City, NY.

French, M., and Popp, A. (2008) 'Ambassadors of commerce: The commercial traveler in British culture', *Business History Review*, 82/4, 1800–1939.

Friedman, W.A. (1998) 'John H. Patterson and the sales strategy of the National Cash Register Company, 1884 to 1922', *Business History Review*, 72/4, 552–84.

Friedman, W. A. (2004) *Birth of a Salesman: The Transformation of Selling in America*, Harvard University Press, Cambridge, MA.

Fullerton, R.A. (1988) 'How modern is modern marketing? Marketing's evolution and the myth of the "production era"', *Journal of Marketing*, 52/1, 108–25.

Hagerty, J.E. (1936) 'Experiences of an early marketing teacher', *Journal of Marketing*, 1/1, 20–7.

Hahn, A.R. (1931) 'Is any business worth any more than its sales plan?', *Sales Management*, 26 (Sept.), 454.

Hall, R.S. (1924) 'Why some salesmen never have to worry about price competition', *Sales Management* (Mar.), 679–80.

Harris, H.J. (2008) 'Inventing the U.S. Stove Industry, c.1815–1875: Making and selling the first universal consumer durable', *Business History Review*, 82/4, 701–9.

Hatch, C.H. (1930) 'Four ways to plug the leaks in profits during 1930', *Sales Management*, 4 (Jan.), 18, 20, 47–8.

Heichelheim, F.M. (1957) *An Ancient Economic History*, vol. 1, tr. J. Stevens, A.W. Sijthoff, Leiden, Holland.

Heichelheim, F.M. (1968) *An Ancient Economic History*, vol. 2, tr. J. Stevens, A.W. Sijthoff, Leiden, Holland.

Hoyt, C.W. (1927) 'Why every salesman should have and use a standard sales manual', *Sales Management* (6 Aug.), 213–14.

Hoyt, C.W. (1929) *Scientific Sales Management Today*, Thoemmes Press, London.

Jones, D.G.B., and Tadajewski, M. (2011) 'Percival White (1887–1970): Marketing engineer', *Marketing Theory*, 11/4, 455.

Jones, E., Dixon, A.L., Chonko, L.B., and Cannon, J.P. (2005) 'Key accounts and team selling: A review, framework, and research agenda', *Journal of Personal Selling and Sales Management*, 25/2, 181–98.

Journal of Transportation (2010) 'Air services, other; Atlas Air Worldwide Holdings, Inc. reports strong second-quarter earnings'. August 21, p.51. https://www.atlasair.com/holdings/archive.asp?Pressid=10758

Koehn, N. F. (1999) 'Henry Heinz and brand creation in the late nineteenth century: Making markets for processed food', *Business History Review*, 73/3, 349–93.

Lazer, W. (1971) *Marketing Management: A Systems Perspective*, John Wiley & Sons, Inc., New York.

Lieber, A.E. (1968) 'Eastern business practices and medieval European commerce', *Economic History Review*, 21/2, 230–43.

Lothrop, L. (1930) 'Nine plans to give salesmen who say business is rotten', *Sales Management* (13 Sept.), 380–1.

Macbain, A.L. (1905) *Selling: The Principles of the Science of Salesmanship*, The System Co., New York.

McKitterick, J.B. (1974) 'What is the marketing management concept?', in R.E. Karp (eds), *Issues in Marketing*, Irvington Publishers, New York, pp. 8–18.

Magrath, A.J. (1997) 'From the practitioner's desk: A comment on personal selling and sales management in the new millennium', *Journal of Personnel Selling Sales Management*, 17/1, 45–7.

Marshall, G.W., and Micheals, R.E. (2001) 'Research in selling and sales management in the next millennium: An agenda from the AMA Faculty Consortium', *Journal of Personnel Selling Sales Management*, 21/1, 15–17.

Marshall, G.W., Goebel, D.J., and Moncrief, W.C. (2003) 'Hiring for success at the buyer–seller interface', *Journal of Business Research*, 56/4, 247–55.

Maxwell, J.Q. (1950) *Birth of a Salesman*, Stern Printing Co., Atlanta, GA.

Maynard, H.H. (1941) 'Marketing courses prior to 1910', *Journal of Marketing*, 6/1, 382–4.

Maynard, H.H., and Nolen, H.C. (1950) *Sales Management*, Ronald Press Co., New York.

Nystrom, P. H. (1948) *Marketing Handbook*, Ronald Press Co., New York.

Piercy, N., and Lane, N. (2011) 'Strategizing the sales organization', *Strategic Sales and Strategic Marketing*, Routledge, New York.

Powers, T.L., DeCarlo, T.E. and Gupte, G. (2010) 'An update on the status of sales management training', *Journal of Personal Selling and Sales Management*, 30/4, 319.

Powers, T.L., Koehler, W.F., and Martin, W.S (1988) 'Selling from 1900–1949: A historical perspective', *Journal of Personal Selling and Sales Management*, 8, 11–21.

Powers, T.L., Martin, W.S., Rushing, H., and Daniels, S. (1987) 'Selling before 1900: A historical perspective', *Journal of Personal Selling and Sales Management*, 7/3. 1–7.

Ramani, G., and Kumar, V. (2008) 'Interaction orientation and firm performance', *Journal of Marketing*, 72/1, 27.

Read, G.H. (1931) *The New Salesmanship*, Associated Authors: Chicago, IL.

Rentz, J.O., Shepherd, D.C., Tashchian, A., Dabholkar, P.A., and Ladd, R.T. (2002) 'A measure of selling skill: Scale development and validation', *Journal of Personal Selling and Sales Management*, 22/1, 13–21.

Rollins, H.T., and Pulliam, C.P. (1926) 'A quarter century of modest growth, then we increase sales $1,500,000 in a single year', *Sales Management*, 10, 241–4, 296.

Sales Management (1919) 'How the wheels go around in big sales organizations, 2-Marshall Field and Company (Wholesale)', 1/10, 181–2.

San Martin, S., López-Catalán, B. and Ramón-Jerónimo, M.A. (2012) 'Factors determining firms' perceived performance of mobile commerce', *Industrial Management & Data Systems*, 112/6, 946-963.

Scott, P. (2008) 'Managing door-to-door sales of vacuum cleaners in interwar Britain', *Business History Review*, 82/4, 761-784,786.

Scull, P. (1967) *From Peddlers to Merchant Princes: A History of Selling in America*, Follett Publishing Co., Chicago.

Sheldon, R., and Arens, E. (1932) *Consumer Engineering: A New Technique for Prosperity*, Harper, New York.

Silk, A.J., and Stern, L.W. (1963) 'The changing nature of innovation in marketing: A study of selected business leaders, 1852–1958', *Business History Review* (pre-1986), 37/3, 182.

Spears, T.B. (1995) *100 Years On the Road: The Traveling Salesman in American Culture*, Yale University Press, New Haven, CT.

Sprague, J.R. (1933) 'Supersalesmanship-1932 model', *Saturday Evening Post* (Jan.), 7, 21, 31–3.

Stanton, W.J., and Buskirk, R.H. (1969) *Management of the Sales Force,* Richard D. Irwin, Homewood, IL.

Starr, C.G. (1974) *A History of the Ancient World*, Oxford University Press, New York.

Strasser, S. (1989) *Satisfaction Guaranteed: The Making of the American Mass Market*, Pantheon Books, New York.

Tadajewski, M. (2009) 'Competition, cooperation and open price associations: Relationship marketing and Arthur Jerome Eddy (1859–1920)', *Journal of Historical Research in Marketing*, 1/1, 122–43.

Tadajewski, M. (2011) 'Correspondence sales education in the early twentieth century: The case of the Sheldon School (1902–39)', *Business History*, 53/7, 1130.

Tosdal, H.R. (1957) *Selling in our Economy*, Richard D. Irwin, Inc., Homewood, IL.

Tuli, K.R., Kohli, A.K., and Bharadwaj, S.G. (2007) 'Rethinking customer solutions: From product bundles to relational processes', *Journal of Marketing*, 71/3, 1–17.

US Census (1976) *Census of Population, 1950: Characteristics of the Population*, Arno Press, New York.

Walker, D.S., and Child, J. (1979) 'The development of professionalism as an issue in British marketing', *European Journal of Marketing*, 13/1, 27.

Wellman, H.R. (1939) 'The distribution of selling effort among geographic areas', *Journal of Marketing*, 3, 225–41.

White, P. (1927) *Scientific Marketing Management: Its Principles and Methods,* New York, Harper & Brothers.

Witkowski, T. (2012) 'Marketing education and acculturation in the early twentieth century: Evidence from Polish language texts on selling and salesmanship', *Journal of Historical Research in Marketing*, 4/1, 97–128.

13

In search of macromarketing history
Eighteenth-century England as a case in point

Stanley Shapiro

The invitation was both overwhelming and compelling. Contribute a chapter on 'the' history of macromarketing to this publication. But does macromarketing even have a history in the traditional sense of that term? If so, where do you begin and how do you finish within the allotted length?

It didn't take too long to conclude that any meaningful contribution would have to be illustrative focusing on a particular time, a specified geographic area and a designated set of topics rather than exhaustive. But what time period and what country? For a variety of reasons, but primarily to provide considerable distance from the present while still having access to an extensive literature, the chosen focus of this study became, and has remained, a history of macromarketing in eighteenth century England.

But what are the topics to be considered when examining the history of macromarketing in any country during any given time period? To answer this question, we must turn to the themes or areas for which the *Journal of Macromarketing* now has section editors. These include Consumer Culture Theory, Sustainability, Quality of Life, Ethics and Distributive Justice, Marketing Systems, Marketing and Development and, of course, Marketing History. Each of these topics or themes will be explored in this investigation of macromarketing in eighteenth-century England. Another important, but currently less generally recognized, macromarketing theme, the politics of distribution, will also be examined.

The approach taken in this chapter focuses on these macromarketing themes as they can be detected within the 100-year period in question. However, a 100-year history of macromarketing is not being provided. The distinction just made is an important one. While developments relevant to macromarketing can fairly easily be discussed within a historical context, I have concluded that a traditional, broad-brush, from the beginning to the end of any given period, macromarketing history cannot be written. Macromarketing issues are both too limited in scope and at the same time far too intertwined with a myriad of other social, economic and political issues. This is true not only for eighteenth-century England but for other periods as well, even periods where there is far less disagreement among historians either as to what really happened or why it happened.

But is the eighteenth century as traditionally defined the appropriate time period for analysis? Scholars disagree as to whether the century itself should be the historical focus or if starting investigations earlier and/or ending them later would be more appropriate, with opinions reflecting, understandably, what different authors were investigating. For present purposes the focus will be on the traditional definition though attention will be called, as well, to some important developments that began before 1700 but came to a head within the eighteenth century or ended not too long after 1800, for example, the abolition of the slave trade in 1807.

There is nothing unique about this temporal uncertainty. Though there is rarely, if ever, an easy answer to the periodicity question, it is a question that must always be answered (Hollander *et al.*, 2005). The best we can do before writing any macromarketing history, and this only after a reasonably detailed introductory survey of the existing literature, is to make an informed, but obviously still very subjective, decision as regards the time period, or periods, that will become the focus of that study.

Macromarketing and the industrial revolution

The literature, far too much of it directly contradictory, on the nature, the causes, the importance in both the short and long run, and the societal impact of the industrial revolution is beyond voluminous. That revolution has been repeatedly re-examined by successive generations of both economists and historians for close to 200 years. The extent of that literature is reflected in the large number of sources identified as either required, recommended or historically relevant by instructors (Tomory, 2011; Maw, 2014) and the bibliographies prepared by those teaching courses (Koot, 2012a) on the industrial revolution.

There are, fortunately, literature reviews that provide as much of an introduction to that subject as macromarketers require. Griffin (2010) has provided one such especially useful overview. She shows how different points of view have first risen and then fallen in relative academic popularity as the decades from 1830 to 2000 have gone by. Griffin ends her review with some observations on the intellectual confusion that now prevails.

> Whilst most agreed that an industrial revolution had taken place, none could agree over exactly what it was. The possibilities of 'take-off', or rapid economic growth had been safely ruled out, but this still left plenty of possibilities. Was it, as Crafts had suggested, a switch of economic activity from agriculture to industry and services? What was the role of those great inventors and their inventions – the steam engine, the power loom, the railways? Was the focus on the more dramatic technological innovations misplaced; should the industrial revolution be located instead in the sphere of domestic industry and female and child labour? How did the switch from wood to coal fit into the picture? And how did changes in household demand over the eighteenth century feed into the process of industrialisation? By the close of the twentieth century, the centrality of the industrial revolution to Britain's history was firmly established, but an embarrassment of definitions undermined its value as a concept more powerfully than any of the more overt attacks it had had to endure in the preceding one hundred years.
>
> *(Griffin, 2010, 15)*

A review essay by Clark (2012) further highlights the still raging conflicts and the range of arguments being advanced in much of the current literature. Clark considers explaining the industrial revolution to be the ultimate elusive prize in economic history, one that has been a fruitless scholarly pursuit for generations. But fruitless or not, seven more books on the causes of that revolution were published between 2007 and 2010, literature that Clark divides into three broad categories. The first of his categories explains the industrial revolution in terms of the existence in England of the 'positive incentives' (i.e. cheap coal, technological advances and/or high wages vis-à-vis other European countries) which powered that revolution. The second category grounds that same revolution in the arrival of a particular culture or ideology, be that enhanced rationality drawing upon the Enlightenment (Mokyr's position, 2010) or enhanced social status for entrepreneurs and the activities they had always carried out (McCloskey, 2010). Finally, Clark maintains, there are hybrid 'historical materialists' who 'locate the Industrial Revolution in a particular set of values, but think of values as themselves subject to material or demographic forces' (Clark, 2012, 86).

The dimensions of development that are of most interest to macromarketers are those related to marketing's role in that development. As is revealed by the range of readings assigned for Lecture Seven of the Leeds University course (Maw, 2014), very different views have been expressed as to whether or not either export demand, a topic discussed in the following section, or increased domestic consumption made a substantial contribution to the industrial revolution and to Britain's subsequent commercial hegemony.

A case for increased domestic demand being an important factor is made by de Vries (1994) who argues that an industrious revolution in the first half of the eighteenth century preceded the industrial revolution. That position, and its marketing relevance, is first spelled out in the abstract de Vries prepared for his journal article on the subject.

> The industrious revolution was a process of household-based resource reallocation that increased both the supply of marketed commodities and labor and the demand for market-supplied goods … a household-level change with important demand side features that preceded the Industrial Revolution, a supply-side phenomenon.
>
> *(de Vries, 1994, 249)*

He then goes on to explain, first in his article, and then in considerably more detail in a book that followed (de Vries, 2008), that the household level change in question involved a willingness to work longer hours and a move towards more of that labour being urban employment rather than farm-based. This new employment pattern was one that, fortunately, would be producing increasing quantities of the same commodities that households were coming to desire.

The industrious revolution concept has won a certain degree of acceptance among economic historians. Indeed, some believe that the same shift to longer hours and urban labour in order to be able to purchase more goods and services was also a twentieth-century developmental engine (Bauer and Yamey, 1957, 152–5). That said, one research team (Clark and van der Werf, 1998) has argued that what evidence there is suggests no such increase in working hours actually took place in the first half of the eighteenth century. Another study (Allen and Weisdorf, 2011) concluded that while there was some evidence urban labourers did over time begin to work longer than was required to purchase a traditional market basket of goods, this did not hold true for agricultural workers.

One also finds specific examples of marketing-driven economic development related to import replacement. The items replaced included a wide variety of luxury goods in high demand, goods long imported from Asia but subsequently produced in England. Berg (2004) spells out, for a number of such goods, how English suppliers were able over time to learn both how to produce and to market items of equivalent quality. But while they imitated Asian consumer goods, 'the British techniques, based on the use of coal and a whole range of substitute "indigenous" materials and alloys, were distinctive and the goods were new products' (Berg, 2004, 130).

Eighteenth-century English trade: from a macromarketing perspective

Though not quite as extensive as that on the industrial revolution, there is no shortage of material dealing with, or of controversies regarding, eighteenth-century England's foreign trade. But for present purposes, the key issues are: (1) how did the volume and pattern of foreign trade change over the eighteenth century; (2) what was the impact of Britain's mercantilist policies; and (3) how much of a contribution did eighteenth-century foreign trade actually contribute to England's economic growth?

Thomas and McCloskey (1981) maintain that between 1700 and 1800 both British imports and British exports increased by over 500 per cent while re-exports increased by a factor of nine; between 1700 and 1740 the rate of growth was relatively slow, that rate doubled between 1740 and 1770 and between 1770 and 1800 it was three times that between 1700 and 1740; and although England's foreign trade at the beginning of the eighteenth century was primarily with Europe, by the end of the century, with the exception of re-exports, Europe's relative importance had significantly declined because of the growth of colonial markets, The overall economic impact, on either Britain's colonies or the home country, of the Navigation Acts that required enumerated colonial exports only be shipped to England was not all that great. 'The strongest effect between commerce abroad and industry at home was from industrialization to commerce, not the reverse. ... Trade was the child of industry' (Thomas and McCloskey, 1981, 87–102).

Price (1989) discusses the interrelationship between the growing domestic demand for American and Asian consumer goods and North European raw materials, the growing market in Northern and Western Europe for re-exports of American and Asian consumables, and of the growing protected market for British manufactures in the American colonies and Africa. He closes by calling attention to the institutional and systemic legacy of that greatly increased volume of trade.

> But the commercial dynamism of the eighteenth century left behind something arguably more significant than specific markets for specific products – namely, an infrastructure of great utility to the entire economy in the ensuing era of rapid industrialization and attendant export growth. By infrastructure I mean not merely roads, canals, docks, waterworks, and other physical improvements, but also the myriad commercial and financial institutions, including banks, clearinghouses, insurance companies, Lloyd's exchange, and the stock exchange of course, but also commercial practices and law, commercial education, an improved postal system, to say nothing of the human capital and good will created by the worldwide experience of hundreds, even thousands, of firms.
>
> *(Price, 1989, 283–4)*

North Atlantic trading patterns have been extensively studied with the major focus of attention being the triangular nature of the slave trade. Ships would leave England loaded with weapons, textiles, a variety of other manufactured goods and rum. Upon arrival in

Africa, these items were traded for slaves, a process that could take between a week and four months. The ships then crossed the Atlantic, a six- to eight-week journey during which a significant proportion of the slaves tightly packed in below decks might die. Upon arrival, the slaves were sold in the Caribbean or the Americas. On the third and final leg, the trip back to England, the slave traders brought sugar, cotton and other agricultural products produced with slave labour.

Richardson's 'British Empire and the Atlantic Slave Trade' (1998) provides a more complete discussion of the triangular trade. Even greater detail is provided by Morgan (2001) in *Slavery, Atlantic Trade and the British Economy 1660–1800*. Richardson's review of Morgan's work (2002) is also well worth reading as it relates that study to the aforementioned 'how important' and 'how much of a contribution did trade make' debates.

> For Morgan, the real significance of Atlantic trade lay in its impact on institutional change, regional and city growth, and the expansion of new industries whose dependence on export markets for sustained growth was evident even before the close of the eighteenth century. Recognizing that claims that slavery and sugar made a substantial contribution to British capital accumulation have yet to be proven (p. 95), he nevertheless argues that slave-based Atlantic trades made 'an important, though not decisive, impact on Britain's long-term economic development', though as much for their stimulus to industrial, commercial and financial innovation as for 'their direct impact on capital investment and national income'.
>
> *(Richardson, 2002)*

But slaves and sugar were by no means the only products sent to North America by English merchants. Breen (2004) advances the intellectually fascinating thesis that it was not political thought but rather consumer politics that shaped American independence. For present purposes, however, our interest is in the marketing channels or systems that served North America rather than the revolutionary impact of colonial consumer culture. In Breen's own words, a 'chain of acquisition' associated with that consumer culture, a chain that reached all the way back to England, provided ever increasing amounts of goods and credit to eighteenth-century colonial retailers. 'Each link in these expanding networks sustained expectations of reciprocity, which achieved a certain legitimacy through a commercial language of shared interests and mutual respect' (Breen, 2004, 119). Though temporarily severed by the Revolutionary War, these links were almost immediately thereafter reforged and England once again traded extensively with its former colonies.

As regards eighteenth-century trade with Asia, the historical focus has been on the activities of the English East India Company. Bowen (2002) spells out the trade practices, supply chains and marketing initiatives that provided the Company with its late eighteenth-century exports. The volume of the Company's export trade significantly increased during the second half of that century with the China trade, far less important than trade with India in the 1750s, becoming by the 1790s somewhat more important. Between 1756 and 1800 as a whole, wool textiles accounted for more than half of all Company exports to Asia, metal raw materials for over a quarter and 'general merchandise' for just under 20 per cent. Though contracts were awarded using a tender process, only suppliers 'well connected' with Company Directors were likely to have their bids accepted.

How the Company, along with others trading with Asia, was provided with the products they imported into Europe is discussed in even greater detail in K.N. Chaudhuri's *The Trading World of Asia and the English East India Company 1660–1760* (1978).

The Company history extends through a description of the pattern of commercial settlements in Asia as Chaudhuri describes the various methods of acquiring goods. In Bengal a system of brokers and middlemen was used to contract textile production, while in China goods were purchased onboard ships commanded by supercargoes. He provides quantitative analysis on the long-term fluctuations in the volume of imports and exports and in the 'terms-of-trade.' He describes the politics of foreign trade in Mughal India, the Company's pursuit of trading privileges and the private trade of the Company's servants. The shipping schedule, the export of treasure – nearly every aspect of trade with Asia is addressed.

(Hejeebo, 2002)

Detailed examination of the marketing practices employed by English textile merchants and merchant manufacturers exporting to Europe in the second half of the eighteenth century reveals well developed marketing channels. One also finds a surprising degree of travelling salesman based promotional sophistication, of awareness of customer preferences and, above all else, of responsiveness to both the product quality and the time of delivery requirements of these foreign customers (Smail, 1997).

An equally perceptive study sets the British iron trade, broadly defined, within a system of commodity flows that extended around the Northern hemisphere. It describes that trade as one of 'the great engines of the Atlantic economy', bringing semi-processed materials from the Baltic and spewing forth a variety of manufactured products, including chains for Caribbean slaves and harpoons for American whalers. The market required to produce such diversity, it is further argued, was in fact a series of interdependent but distinct and unique specialty markets (Evans *et al.*, 2002).

Quality of life and distributive justice

Quality of life, standards of living and income distribution are topics that must be considered when examining the macromarketing history of any given country. The data available on these issues in eighteenth-century England leave, by present standards, much to be desired. Nevertheless, it is possible to find publications that throw some light and even more heat on these issues.

Whether and, if so, to what extent the industrial revolution led to improved living standards between 1770 or so and the mid-nineteenth century is another one of those issues endlessly debated by different schools of thought. In this case the two sides have become known as 'the optimists' (yes, living standards did improve) and 'the pessimists' (they did not!). The argument has raged for decades, both sides having over time become more sophisticated and increasingly quantitative in their analyses of source documents. A useful abridged introduction to literature representative of the two positions, Lindert and Williamson (1983) being the optimistic source and Feinstein (1998) the pessimistic one, is provided by Koot (2012b). Of course, the previously discussed differences between de Vries and his critics also have earlier eighteenth-century standard-of-living implications.

The almost complete absence in the eighteenth century of the kind of data we now rely upon to provide contemporary estimates of 'standards of living' and 'quality of life' is, of course, the reason for this still continuing dispute. Records on how much people were paid are fragmentary at best with no accompanying information available as to the often very significant additional but non-cash benefits to which various categories of workers were entitled. The information available on changes in GNP over the century are based on 'best guestimates'. What is known regarding the prices paid for food over the eighteenth century also reveals very significant regional differences, so national estimates conceal more than they disclose (Daunton, 1995).

There were also important regional differences in family, as opposed to individual, income, with this due primarily to differences in what was being produced in each community. Some industries provided ample employment opportunities for women and children but others did not. Poor laws in the eighteenth century were also an important, and relatively generous for the period, source of income, occasionally for some and repeatedly for others (Daunton, 1995). And in London, then the greatest city in the world, we find those 'down and out' making a marginal living sweeping roads, selling matches, singing ballads, performing all sorts of menial labour, begging and relying on charity (Hitchcock, 2004).

After having chronicled all these and numerous other problems in trying to answer the question, Daunton concludes:

> the standard of living probably rose most rapidly in the earlier eighteenth century, for food output grew faster than population, allowing food prices to fall and real incomes to rise. A period of faster population growth followed, coinciding with slower expansion of agricultural output, which put pressure on food prices. Many workers found that their wages did not keep pace because of the increased supply of labour and real per capita income grew more slowly or even fell.
>
> *(Daunton, 1995, 438)*

There is even less, in fact almost no, eighteenth-century information available on the kind of subjective indicators that today let us generalize about the changes in quality of life or 'well-being' over immediately past decades. Was it a conscious decision, for example, to work fewer hours in the later eighteenth century or, when average hours of employment declined, was that because there were too many workers or not enough work? Looked at another way, we have no way of knowing either the value of or the degree of interest in increased leisure time during that period (Daunton, 1995).

As for income distribution, the major determinant of distributive justice, Lindert concludes that all throughout the eighteenth century the top 10 per cent of English households controlled about 80 per cent of the wealth and received at least 45 per cent of the annual income, with the 'best tentative guess' being a likely further rise in income inequality between 1750 and 1815 (Lindert, 1994).

The food riots of the eighteenth century and the related concept of 'the moral economy' are other quality-of-life-related topics of interest to macromarketing. The notion of the moral economy was one first introduced by E.P. Thompson in a paper designed to highlight the 'real' motivating force behind the eighteenth century's food riots (1971). These riots took place, he maintained, because merchants were no longer respecting the unwritten laws that had long governed the operation of markets.

> It is, of course true that riots were triggered off by soaring prices, by malpractices among dealers, or by hunger. But those grievances operated within a popular consensus as to what were legitimate and what were illegitimate practices in marketing, milling, baking, etc. This in its turn was grounded upon a consistent traditional view of social norms and obligations, of the proper economic functions of several parties within the community, which, taken together, can be said to constitute the moral economy of the poor. An

outrage to these moral assumptions, quite as much as actual deprivation, was the usual occasion for direct action.

(Thompson, 1971, 79)

Over time Thompson's 'moral economy' thesis has gained a considerable degree of scholarly acceptance. However, a dissertation-based article by Williams (1984) questions the moral economy's relevance to the English food riots of 1766. Instead, Williams argues, these riots were generated by a combination of post-Seven Years War economic recession, governmental incompetence and atypical weather patterns, all impacting on each other and on an evolving market economy. He concludes that Thompson, with his focus on conflict between the gentry and the peasant class and on how past experience shapes future marketplace expectations, failed to pay adequate attention either to emerging marketing systems or to the involvement of both small-scale local manufacturers and marketing middlemen in the food riots of 1766.

Two more contemporary publications are also essential reading for anyone interested in food riots. An edited collection by Randall and Charlesworth (1996) discusses not only a number of eighteenth-century food riots but also the market culture of the time and the manner in which eighteenth-century markets were regulated. Bohstedt (2010) focuses more specifically on food riots but over a 300-year time span and with considerable attention also being paid to the relevance of Thompson's moral economy argument.

Distribution and distributive systems

A macromarketing history should not be unduly concerned with how any given store was managed at a specific point in time. However, macromarketing does have a very legitimate interest in how retail institutions, retailing practices and entire distributive systems evolved over time. But since the authors of such studies are almost all professional historians who quite understandably base their generalizations on specifics, some of the material of greatest macro value also has a significant micro or managerial dimension. That is especially true of the available literature on eighteenth-century retailing.

How did distributive networks operate in the eighteenth century and how did they change over the course of that century? Considerable insight into the marketing channels of the period, along with a position in favour of the view that 'significant change in retailing did occur over the eighteenth century', a position that earlier had been disputed, is found in two of the most recent of a long line of publications by Jon Stobart. In *Sugar and Spice: Grocers and Groceries in Provincial England 1650–1830* (2013), Stobart largely focuses on the people from which contemporaries purchased such goods – the grocers whose increasingly complicated supply networks allowed them to sell a range of imported goods to an ever-widening group of consumers. 'Stobart tells a global story through a particular lens, in order to demonstrate how the supply of goods such as tobacco, tea, coffee and chocolate shaped the retail practices and spaces of early modern Britain' (Smith, 2014). Somewhat earlier, Stobart and Hann (2004) had argued that in North-West England significant change in eighteenth-century retailing had indeed taken place.

> The eighteenth century was a period when the practices, geography and distribution of retail activity experienced profound change. If the retail trade was already widespread and sophisticated at the turn of the eighteenth century, the following decades witnessed the spread of new retailing and shopping practices; the emergence of new forms of retail

space, and the proliferation of fixed shops, especially in the burgeoning manufacturing towns. Whether these amounted to a retail revolution remains a moot point, but they underline the position of the eighteenth century as a bridge between the traditional and the modern, in retailing as much as manufacturing.

(Stobart and Hann, 2004, 94)

A somewhat earlier study by Fowler (1998) of retailing in central southern England had reached a similar conclusion, 'that retail distribution underwent a significant transformation in the eighteenth century'. Fowler also cited as evidence the relative decline of markets, fairs and itinerant traders and the increasing importance of specialized retailers operating out of fixed locations. There was also growing acceptance, Fowler argues, of the new retailing practices that Stobart and Hann were to find in the North-West; fixed pricing, the use of loss leaders, the promotion of cash, the tightening of credit and the introduction of branded goods.

But retail distribution, of course, took place at the very end of the distribution chain. Perhaps the most distinguishing feature of eighteenth-century English marketing from a macromarketing perspective was the revolution in transport modes, methods and costs that contributed to the development of a truly national market. Specialization of labour helped to make economies of scale in production possible but so did the development of an increasingly effective system of both collecting the raw materials required for manufacturing and of dispersing the products subsequently produced. Transport-related technological improvements of all sorts contributed to the creation of a truly national eighteenth-century market with first the turnpikes built by chartered turnpike trusts and then, in the later part of the century, the construction of canals being by far the most important of these developments (Daunton, 1995, 285–307).

Annual fairs served as distributive hubs throughout the eighteenth century, becoming only somewhat less important as the century wore on. Each September, at Sturbridge Fair, retail goldsmiths, turners, milliners, mercers, drapers, pewterers, haberdashers, wholesale grocers, iron merchants and brasiers, all these trades and many others came together, some to buy and others to sell.

There was iron and brass from Birmingham, tools and knives from Sheffield, stockings from Nottingham and Leicester, and the last day was given over to horses. Among all this activity, Sturbridge specialized in two commodities, wool from Lincolnshire was sold to manufacturers in East Anglia; and hops from Kent and Surrey were sold to Northern brewers.

(Daunton, 1995, 321)

And what about fixed location, permanently operating city markets, what is known about their role, operations and importance in the eighteenth century? A study by Colin Smith (2002) of London's central markets answers these questions for that dominating metropolis. The scope of this study, based on the author's dissertation (Smith, 1999), discusses products, locations and regulation in considerable detail. Smith's description of what went on in the 'typical' London market is especially deserving of note.

Collectively, formal markets traded a wide range of goods; agricultural raw materials (livestock, hay, coal, hides and leather, grain, fish, cloth); fresh produce (fruit, vegetables, herbs, and flowers); processed foodstuffs (malt meal, butter, soup, ginger bread); and household goods (such as tallow, earthenware, and hardware). Tropical, imported commodities such as tea and sugar were subject to more private marketing arrangements, as were certain high-value domestic products such as honey, hops, and lace. Eighteenth century London markets typically comprised a backbone of 'shops' for butchers, fishmongers and poulterers; a 'country market' for higglers and farmers' wives, a 'green market' for garden stuffs; perhaps also a market for hay and straw ... Other shops (fixed or enclosed retail outlets) were found both within and without the market place. Indeed, the presence of fixed retailers and wholesalers – vintners, turners, oilmen, grocers, cheesemongers, and others – muddled distinctions between what was traded inside and outside markets.

(Smith, 2002, 34–5)

Since marketing is indeed society's provisioning technology, then the challenge of provisioning cities in eighteenth-century England becomes another obvious topic of macromarketing interest. The Smith dissertation provides some insight into this process for London, but its focus, as indicated above, is on changes in the relative importance of central markets over time. Blackman (1963) had earlier discussed in considerable detail the long established links between Sheffield's public markets, the sources of the agricultural products sold at those markets and the food supply of that city. However, far more detail on the same subjects is provided in Scola's *Feeding the Victorian City: The Food Supply of Manchester 1770–1870* (1992).

Both Blackman and Scola start by focusing on the late eighteenth century and end their analyses well beyond our period of interest. However, both their starting point descriptions and their turn of the century observations are for present purposes obviously relevant. Scola was especially concerned with how the standard of living of the English working class, as reflected in the kinds and quantity of the food they consumed, had, or had not, improved over the century in question. Such an improvement took place, Scola concluded, but not until well into the nineteenth century.

The politics of distribution

The Politics of Distribution (1955) was the title of Palamountain's study of how in the 1930s small retailers, feeling their very existence threatened by the development of much larger chain stores, sought to obtain a measure of legislative protection. They extensively lobbied for passage of the Clayton Act and the Robinson-Patman Act at the Federal level and for 'fair trade' laws at the state level, laws that would allow for the setting of a minimum price below which no retailer might offer a given product. But while the term itself is a relatively new one, interesting examples of the politics of distribution can also be found in eighteenth-century England.

Mother Gin

'The Mother Gin Controversy' was an early effort to restrict the alcohol consumption of the laboring classes and the unemployed. The first (fairly) recent discussion of this controversy appears in a paper read by Peter Clark in 1987 to the Royal History Society. That 'the politics of distribution' was to be the focus of that paper is revealed in its opening paragraph.

During the second quarter of the eighteenth century there were successive waves of public agitation over the spirits trade – in 1726, 1728–29, 1735–38 and again in 1748–51

... Parliament in this period enacted a series of measures to deal with the problem. The most dramatic and draconian of these was the 1736 Gin Act, which was hurried through Parliament in a few weeks and threatened to close down the spirits trade overnight. The Act, with secondary legislation in 1737 and 1738, caused such a landslide of protest and opposition in the capital that it had to be abandoned and later repealed. In this paper I want to concentrate on the 1736 Act, looking at its background and aftermath. As we shall see, the controversy raises important questions not only about the organisation of the drink trade and consumption patterns in the early eighteenth century, but also about the social and political processes of legislation, the activity of interest groups, the attitude of government, and the problems of enforcement.

(Clark, 1988, 63)

Abolition of the slave trade

How much did the type of activism we associate with the 'politics of distribution' contribute to the ending of the slave trade in 1807? That parliamentary decision to abolish a long-established and still quite profitable trade had economic and political as well as moral dimensions. As has already been made clear, economic historians rarely agree either on what happened in the eighteenth century or on why it did, or did not happen. That certainly is the case as regards the motivating force behind, after a two-decade-long struggle, an overwhelming parliamentary vote in favour of abolition.

To commemorate the 200th anniversary of that vote, a journal entitled, appropriately enough, *Parliamentary History* published a special issue that re-examined this event. In his contribution to that special issue Professor Seymour Drescher, one of the academic giants of slavery studies, traces the 20-year history of abolitionist activism and agitation culminating in the 1807 vote (Drescher, 2007). That his paper does indeed deal with the politics of distribution, c.1800, is made quite clear in one of its opening paragraphs.

Within this broader process abolition came to occupy a distinctively innovative position. As we shall see, it combined new techniques of propaganda, petitioning and association with the organizational networking techniques of mercantile and manufacturing lobbyists. Between its emergence as a national political movement in 1787 and the internationalization of slave trade abolition at the end of the Napoleonic wars, political abolition became a pioneering organization in mobilizing hitherto untapped groups as actors for philanthropic and social reform. The movement's fortunes in Parliament during those three decades were also emblematic of the difficulties entailed in converting public pressure into law and policy.

(Drescher, 2007, 42)

But was the repeal really a victory for evangelically inspired activism or did, as some historians claim, economic factors, especially the economic decline of the British West Indian planter, in large part explain Parliament's willingness to ban the trade? Richardson (2007), in that same special issue, discusses this controversy but then devotes the remainder of his paper to offering a third explanation. He argues that the determining factor was neither a victory for the morally driven nor a decline in the British West Indian economy, a decline that most economic historians now believe never occurred. Rather it was the development of a new reigning mindset, a mindset favouring free markets over mercantilism, as regards the forms of economic organization and regulation that would from then on best serve British interests.

But neither Richardson's explanation nor the humanitarian thesis has yet gained universal acceptance. More than 30 years after initial publication of Drescher's *Econocide: British Slavery in the Era of Abolition* (1977) James Walvin wrote quite positively about that book's still current relevance (2011). Nevertheless, he maintained Drescher had, in over a third of a century of his research, never been able to explain why Parliament had voted for abolition given the now established profitability of British West Indian trade. This eighteenth-century controversy remains another one of the many from that period which continues to this day.

Macromarketing, consumer culture and consumption

The Birth of a Consumer Society, the Commercialization of Eighteenth Century England (McKendrick *et al.*, 1982) was a landmark study that helped to refocus scholarly attention on the consumer culture of the period.

> The key claim made ... was that eighteenth century ... England... underwent a revolutionary transformation that saw the creation of a mass market in consumer goods and the emergence of modern spending patterns based on consumption for pleasure rather than need. The desire to acquire was not new, its authors argued, but more people than ever could enjoy the experience of buying material goods. Rising population and incomes unleashed the drive to emulate which permeated down through the social order, creating markets which could then be further developed by innovations in marketing techniques.
>
> *(White, 2006, 93–4)*

Though the volume has a much broader geographical and chronological focus, many of the contributions to *Consumption and the World of Goods* (Brewer and Porter, 1993) focus on the lives, the belongings and the purchasing habits of eighteenth-century English consumers. Also noteworthy is the editors' response in their Introduction to social critics from the left who feared that highlighting the history of consumption would 'underwrite market economics and the politics accompanying it'. They reject this position, arguing instead 'that our understanding of the development of western societies will remain dramatically impoverished unless we confront the fact that such polities, uniquely in world history, have come to revolve around the mass consumption of goods and services' (p. 3). The editors close by maintaining 'it is imperative that we investigate in the most comprehensive way the links connecting this material culture (one often highly and increasingly inegalitarian) to the political and social systems with which it has become symbiotic' (Brewer and Porter, 1993, 3).

The preceding position is intellectually important in its own right. It also provides all the justification required, and then some, for consumer culture's fairly recent, c.2000, acceptance as a priority macromarketing theme. And with consumer culture have come many of the critical marketers who have recently associated themselves with macromarketing, bringing with them a far less positive view of 'free markets' in general and neoliberalism in particular than one finds reflected in the 'developmental' stream of macromarketing thought (Mittelstaedt *et al.*, 2014).

Brewer and Porter tried, but failed, to protect subsequent eighteenth-century studies of consumer culture from further social criticism. White's review article (2006) on the 'consumption turn' in eighteenth-century British history criticizes much of the recent literature on eighteenth-century consumption, including the sources and authors mentioned above, for reflecting a 'free market' ideological bias and downplaying, if not completely ignoring, the very real problems of the economically disadvantaged during that period.

Additional information of relevance to macromarketing comes from more specialized consumer culture studies. Not only are the items consumed, their end users and the final transactions discussed in such studies but so also are entire marketing channels, supply chains and, to some extent, entire marketing systems. Much of Maxine Berg's published work, for example, focuses not only on eighteenth-century consumers and the luxury goods they owned but also on the marketing channels, originally international but over time increasingly domestic, through which such goods had reached these consumers.

> These new products, regarded as luxuries by the rapidly growing urban and middling-class people of the eighteenth century, played an important part in helping to proclaim personal identities and guide social interaction. Customers enjoyed shopping for them; they took pleasure in their beauty, ingenuity or convenience. All manner of new products appeared in shop windows; sophisticated mixed-media advertising seduced customers and created new desires. This unparalleled 'product revolution' provoked philosophers and pundits to proclaim a 'new luxury', one that reached out to the middling and trading classes, unlike the elite and corrupt luxury of old.
>
> *(Berg, 2005, abstract)*

But not everyone in eighteenth-century England had the means to take pleasure in wearing luxury goods purchased from high-end shops. Nevertheless, both farm labourers and the growing urban workforce still found it possible to gain 'second hand' access to clothing and other consumer goods. By doing so, they became familiar with and obtained a taste for both domestically produced and imported products. 'Through the aegis of the second hand trade consumerism was stimulated on the widest scale throughout Britain, and the flexible marketing practices combining barter, sale, and exchange permitted a level of consumerism within the whole society unattainable by cash sales only' (Lemire, 1988, 24). This closing statement is preceded by as detailed description as possible, given the paucity of surviving documentation, of the marketing channels and practices used in the collecting, sorting and dispersing of second hand clothing.

Sustainability

Sustainability as such is a twentieth-century concept. One of the central concerns long associated with that concept is the challenge of feeding a rapidly growing global population. But that concern as such is not a new one. The Reverend Malthus, writing in England in 1798 and at 32 years of age a product of the last third of the eighteenth century, felt that unless controlled either by positive checks ('the whole train of common diseases and epidemics, wars, pestilence, plague and famine') or by 'preventive checks' on procreation (celibacy, delayed marriage and abstinence), the growth in population would outstrip food supplies. And because such a policy ran counter to 'preventive', fewer births thinking, Malthus was opposed to poor relief payments being linked to the number of children in the family (Daunton, 1995, 4–5).

Malthus maintained that uncontrolled population growth must inevitably lead to higher prices because of increased demand, to falling wages because of the glut of labour and to a standard of living declining to subsistence levels. The cause of the problem, he argued, was the fact that unless checked, positively or preventively, the population would geometrically double (1, 2, 4, 8, etc.) every 25 years while the food supply during the same period would only increase arithmetically (1, 2, 3, 4, etc.). And because of this 'population trap', Malthus assumed any continued improvement in the standard of living was impossible (Daunton, 1995, 4–6).

Malthus was a controversial figure during his life time and Malthusian-like arguments have both repeatedly resurfaced and been just as vigorously challenged since his death in 1834. What actually happened to the English standard of living during the second half of his life remains a subject of controversy. But while that standard may or may not have gone up, few have argued that it actually went down despite a very significant population increase over the period (Clark, 2012). In the short run at least, the Malthusian trap had failed to snap.

A concluding observation

The preceding sections have examined eighteenth-century England in an effort to provide a macromarketing perspective on that time and place. But what has been learned from this experience as regards who should be writing future macromarketing histories? I believe that a macromarketing scholar would not be the best choice unless he or she already had considerable prior knowledge of both the time period and the geographic region of interest. Such a history can be written without such prior knowledge or expertise but only after a very significant expenditure of both time and effort. One also finishes with a nagging fear that some really important sources might not have been uncovered.

Given the voluminous literature in any time period associated with each of the various macromarketing themes, a form of intellectual outsourcing might well be in order. Why not begin by undertaking a relatively straightforward and far less demanding task familiarizing an economic or social historian specializing in the particular time period and region of concern with macromarketing's various areas of interest? Possibly, but not necessarily, joined by someone from the sub-discipline of macromarketing, that individual could then utilize already existing time and place expertise in exploring macromarketing issues and concerns during the period in question far more easily than could those with no prior knowledge of the relevant literature.

References

Allen, R.C., and. Weisdorf, J.L. (2011) 'Was there an "industrious revolution" before the industrial revolution? An empirical exercise for England, c.1300–1830', *Economic History Review*, 64, 715–29.

Bauer, P.T., and Yamey, B.S. (1957) *The Economics of Underdeveloped Countries*, University of Chicago Press, Chicago, IL.

Berg, M. (2004) 'In pursuit of luxury: Global history and British consumer goods in the eighteenth century', *Past and Present*, 182, 85–142.

Berg, M. (2005) *Luxury and Pleasure in Eighteenth-Century Britain*, Oxford University Press, Oxford.

Blackman, J. (1963) 'The food supply of an industrial town, a study of Sheffield's public markets, 1780–1900', *Business History*, 5, 83–97.

Bohstedt, J. (2010) *The Politics of Provisions: Food Riots, Moral Economy and Market Transition in England 1500–1850*, Ashgate, Farnham.

Bowen, H.V. (2002) 'Sinews of trade and commerce: The supply of commodity exports to the East India Company', *Economic History Review*, 55/3, 446–56.

Breen, T.H. (2004) *The Marketplace of Revolution: How Consumer Politics Shaped American Independence*, Oxford University Press, Oxford.

Brewer, J., McKendrick, N., and Plumb, J.H. (eds) (1982) *The Birth of a Consumer Society,* Europa, London.

Brewer, J, and Porter, R. (eds) (1993) *Consumption and the World of Goods in the Eighteenth Century,* Routledge, London.

Chaudhuri, K.N. (1978) *The Trading World of Asia and the English East India Company, 1660–1760,* Cambridge University Press, Cambridge

Clark, G. (2012) 'Review essay: *The Enlightened Economy: An Economic History of Britain, 1700–1850* by Joel Mokyr', *Journal of Economic Literature,* 50/1, 85–95.

Clark, G., and van der Werf, Y. (1998) 'Work in progress? The industrious revolution', *Journal of Economic History,* 58, 830–48.

Clark, P. (1988) 'The Mother Gin controversy in the early eighteenth century', *Transactions of the Royal Historical Society,* 38, 63–84.

Daunton, M.J. (1995) *Progress and Poverty: An Economic and Social History of Britain, 1700–1850,* Oxford University Press, Oxford.

de Vries, J. (1994) 'The industrial revolution and the industrious revolution', *Journal of Economic History,* 54, 249–70.

de Vries, J. (2008) *The Industrious Revolution: Consumer Behavior and the Household Economy, 1650 to the Present,* Cambridge University Press, Cambridge.

Drescher, S. (1977) *Econocide: British Slavery in the Era of Abolition,* University of Pittsburgh Press, Pittsburgh, PA.

Drescher, S. (2007) 'Public opinion and Parliament in the abolition of the British slave trade', *Parliamentary History,* 26/suppl., 42–65.

Evans, C., Jackson, O., and Ryden, G. (2002) 'Baltic iron and the British iron industry in the eighteenth century', *Economic History Review,* 55/3, 642–65.

Feinstein, C.N. (1998) 'Pessimism perpetuated: Real wages and the standard of living in Britain during and after the Industrial Revolution', *Journal of Economic History,* 58/3, 625–58.

Fowler, C. (1998) 'Changes in provincial retail practice during the eighteenth century with particular reference to Central Southern England', *Business History,* 40, 37–54.

Griffin, E (2010) *A Short History of the British Industrial Revolution,* Palgrave Macmillan, London.

Hejeebo, S.H. (2002) 'Review of K. N. Chaudhuri, *The Trading World of Asia and the English East India Company, 1660–1760,* available online: http://eh.net/book_reviews/the-trading-world-of-asia-and-the-english-east-india-company-1660-1760/ (acessed Nov. 2014)

Hitchcock, T. (2004) *Down and Out in Eighteenth Century London,* Bloomsbury, London.

Hollander, S.C., Rassuli, K.M., Jones, D.G.B., and Dix, L.F. (2005) 'Periodization in marketing history', *Journal of Macromarketing,* 25/1, 32–41.

Koot, G.M. (2012a) 'Aspects of the Industrial Revolution in Britain: Bibliography', available online: http://www1.umassedu/ir/resources (accessed Nov. 2014)

Koot, G.M. (2012b) 'The standard of living debate during Britain's industrial revolution', available online: http://www1.umassedu/ir/resources (accessed Nov. 2014)

Lemire, B. (1988) 'Consumerism in preindustrial and early industrial England: The trade in second hand clothes', *Journal of British Studies,* 27 (Jan.), 1–24.

Lindert, P.H. (1994) 'Unequal living standards', in R. Floud and D. McCloskey (eds), *The Economic History of Britain since 1700,* vol. 1, *1700–1860,* Cambridge University Press, Cambridge, pp. 357–86.

Lindert, P.H., and Williamson, J.G. (1983) 'English workers' living standards during the industrial revolution: A new look', *Economic History Review,* 36/1, 1–25.

Maw, P. (2014) 'Reading list: Britain and the industrial revolution', available online: https://leeds for life/leedsac.uk/ Broadening/Modules/Hist. 2135 (accessed Nov. 2014).

McCloskey, D. (2010) *Bourgeois Dignity: Why Economics Can't Explain the Modern World,* University of Chicago Press, Chicago, IL.

McKendrick, N., Brewer J., and Plumb, J. H. (1982),*The Birth of a Consumer Society: Commercialization of Eighteenth Century England,* University of Indiana Press, Bloomington, IN.

Mittelstaedt, J.D., Shultz, C.J., II, Kilbourne, W.E., and Peterson, M. (2014) 'Sustainability as megatrend: Two schools of marketing thought', *Journal of Macromarketing*, 34 (Sept.), 253–64.

Mokyr, J. (2010) *The Enlightened Economy, an Economic History of Britain 1700–1850*, Yale University Press, New Haven, CT.

Morgan, K. (2001) *Slavery, Atlantic Trade and the British Economy, 1660–1800*, Cambridge University Press, Cambridge.

Mui, L.H., and Mui, H.C. (1989) *Shops and Shopkeeping in Eighteenth Century England*, McGill-Queens Press, Montreal.

Palamountain, J.C., Jr. (1955) *The Politics of Distribution*, Harvard University Press, Cambridge, MA.

Price, J.M. (1989) 'What did merchants do? Reflections on British overseas trade, 1660–1790', *Journal of Economic History*, 49, 267–84.

Randall, A., and Charlesworth, A. (eds) (1996) *Markets, Market Culture and Popular Protest in Eighteenth Century England Britain and Ireland*, Liverpool University Press, Liverpool.

Richardson, D. (1998) 'The British Empire and the Atlantic slave trade, 1660–1807', in P.J. Marshall, A. Low and W. Louis (eds), *The Oxford History of the British Empire*, vol. 2, *The Eighteenth Century*, Oxford University Press, Oxford, pp. 440–464.

Richardson, D. (2002) 'Review of *Slavery, Atlantic Trade and the British Economy, 1660–1800* by K. Morgan', *Reviews in History* (review 259), wavailable online: www.history.ac.uk./reviews (accessed Nov. 2014).

Richardson, D. (2007) 'The ending of the British slave trade in 1807', *Parliamentary History*, 26/suppl., 127–40.

Scola, R. (1992) *Feeding the Victorian City: The Food Supply of Manchester, 1770–1870,* Manchester University Press, Manchester.

Smail, J. (1997) 'Demand has shape: Exports, entrepreneurs, and the eighteenth century economy', *Business and Economic History*, 26 (Winter), 354–64.

Smith, C.S. (1999) 'The market place and the market's place in London, c1660–1840', unpublished PhD thesis, University of London, available online: http://discovery.ucl.ac.uk, 1318007 (accessed Oct. 2014).

Smith, C.S. (2002) 'The wholesale and retail markets of London, 1660–1840', *Economic History Review,* 55/1, 31–50.

Smith, K. (2014) 'Review of *Sugar and Spice: Grocers and Groceries in Provincial England 1650–1830* by Jon Stobart', *Reviews in History,* Review 1453, available online: www.history.ac.uk./reviews (accessed Jan. 2015).

Stobart, J. (2013) *Sugar and Spice: Grocers and Groceries in Provincial England 1650–1830*, Oxford University Press, Oxford.

Stobart, J., and Hann, A. (2004) 'Retailing revolution in the eighteenth century? Evidence from North-West England', *Business History*, 46, 171–94.

Thomas, R.P., and McCloskey, D.N. (1981) 'Overseas trade and empire 1700–1860', in R.C. Floud and D.N. McCloskey (eds), *The Economic History of Britain since 1700*, vol. 1 (1st edn), Cambridge University Press, Cambridge, pp. 87–102.

Thompson, E.P. (1971) 'The moral economy of the English crowd', *Past and Present*, 50 (Feb.), 76–136.

Tomory, L. (2011) 'History 436 topics in European history: The industrial revolution', available online: www.mcgill.ca/history/sites (accessed Nov. 2014).

Walvin, J. (2001) 'Why did the British abolish the slave trade? "Econocide" revisited', *Slavery and Abolition*, 32/4, 583–8.

White, J. (2006) 'Review essay: The "consumption turn" and eighteenth century British history', *Culture and Social History*, 3, 93–104.

Williams, D.E. (1984) 'Morals, markets and the English crowd in 1766', *Past and Present,* 114 (Feb.), 56–73.

14

US antitrust law and the practice of marketing

Ross D. Petty

If history repeats itself, and the unexpected always happens, how incapable must Man be of learning from experience.

George Bernard Shaw

Introduction

Today, there are two categories of laws dealing with the propriety of business conduct: competition law (antitrust law in the US) and unfair competition law. The former deals with conduct that is likely to lead to, or cause the continuation of, a market-dominating monopoly position by one or more firms. The latter includes conduct that is considered wrongful regardless of whether the conduct may lead to market power in the economic sense. Current examples of unfair competition torts that enable injured parties to bring civil lawsuits against the alleged 'tortfeasor' include knowingly inducing another to break a binding contract with a third party, bribing another firm's agent, disparagement (sometimes called trade libel), fraud and misappropriation of someone else's trade secrets or trade identity. The misappropriation of someone else's trade identity has evolved into modern trademark law (see Chapter 6).

In contrast, antitrust or competition law in most countries has been enforced by the government. As discussed below, the US has been the exception to this rule as the number of private lawsuits filed by allegedly injured parties seeking treble damages has risen dramatically in the second half of the twentieth century. Marketing practices under antitrust law can generally be divided into three areas of concern: exclusion (monopolization or attempted monopolization – Sherman Act section 2), collusion (agreements that unreasonably restrain trade – Sherman Act section 1) and distribution (the application of exclusion and collusion vertically across the distribution channel rather than horizontally vis-à-vis rivals). The relationship between these three areas can be illustrated by Figure 14.1.

This chapter examines the historical evolution of US antitrust law and its impact on the practice of marketing. US antitrust law is important for three reasons. First, the US is

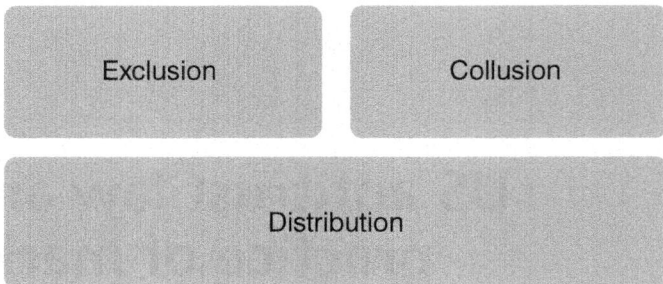

Figure 14.1   Types of antitrust cases

a large market so many companies based outside the US sell products in the US and are subject to its laws. Second, US antitrust law is important because it provided the initial model for other countries. After the First World War some countries adopted or strengthened their antitrust laws (often now called competition laws). In 1923, Canada introduced the Combines Investigation Act and in 1926 France reinforced its basic competition provisions from the 1810 Napoleonic Code. After the Second World War, the Allies, led by the United States, introduced tight regulation of cartels and monopolies in occupied Germany and Japan (it was widely believed that the predominance of large cartels supported the war effort in those countries).

More recent antitrust statutes, including former communist countries after the fall of the USSR and Mexico, tend not to follow US antitrust statutes, preferring instead the statutory model provided by the 1957 Treaty of Rome that established the European Economic Community. However, a third reason US antitrust law is important at a global level is that US courts have analysed many common antitrust situations for nearly 125 years and other countries look to these decisions particularly if they have no relevant prior court decisions of their own (Handler *et al.*, 1997, 20–5).

The remainder of this chapter is organized into time periods to examine developments in US antitrust law and their impact on the practice of marketing. These periods, similar to those in other antitrust histories, are designed to reflect significant changes in antitrust policy (Hollander *et al.*, 2005).

Prehistory

The condemnation of monopoly, at least in land ownership, dates back at least to the Old Testament when Isaiah 5: 8 declared: 'Woe unto those that join house to house, that lay field to field, till there be no room, and ye be made to dwell alone in the midst of the land.' In addition, the ancient Romans also enacted anti-monopoly laws at various times.

Antitrust interest in the United States dates back at least to 1773 and the Boston Tea Party (see Chapter 15 for coverage of EU competition law and marketing). This protest is famous for opposing taxation without representation but also can be interpreted as people objecting to monopolization of commerce within the colonies by a single foreign company – the British-East India Company. This interpretation of the Tea Party is consistent with the condemnation of monopolies (except for innovations for a short period of time) in 1641 by the Massachusetts colonial legislature. Indeed, several states proposed that the federal bill of rights prohibit Congress from granting monopolies (Letwin, 1965, 59–60).

While no federal antimonopoly law was enacted during these formative years, the US did inherit English common (judge-made) law. By the early seventeenth century, England condemned royal grants (called patents) when the result was a monopoly although parliamentary monopoly grants were still allowed. Even before that time, the English courts condemned 'Engrossing, Forestalling and Regrating'. While judicial definitions of these three terms were neither well understood nor consistent from decision to the decision, the three terms were mostly used together to condemn the purchasing of necessary goods (such as food) with the plan to resell the goods at a higher price (see Chapter 15 for coverage of EU competition law and marketing). In modern parlance, these terms condemned 'cornering the market' by purchasing all sources of supply of a particular good and then raising the price of those goods (Adler, 1917). Controlling the market supply and raising prices continues to be a fundamental antitrust concern.

Thorelli (1955, 36–7) argues that these concepts were not relied upon after the middle of the nineteenth century even though they were later discussed in at least one early antitrust decision (*Standard Oil of New Jersey v. US*, 1911). Rather he argues the concept of combinations and conspiracies in restraint of trade or to monopolize trade became well known in state common law during the second half of the nineteenth century. The concept held that such combinations (such as 'pooling' sales to a joint selling agent and 'gentlemen's' agreements not to compete on price) were against public policy and therefore unenforceable when one party of the combination breached the agreement and was sued for breach of contract by another party. Thus as one early marketing scholar noted, 'The common law's support of the right to compete was primarily responsible for changing economic life' away from privilege (Lyon, 1936, 101). While the substantial majority of such agreements were declared invalid, some were held to be reasonable so the underlying contract was enforced (Thorelli, 1955, 40–8). Of course, no one knows how many such agreements were simply followed for some time by the agreeing parties.

In the nineteenth century, the United States' North American neighbours enacted antimonopoly laws before the US. The Mexican Constitution of 1857 explicitly prohibited monopolies and practices that that affected free participation in the marketplace. This was a reaction to the prior Spanish empire that tended to favour monopolies for companies based in Spain. Despite this language and newer laws, Mexican economic policy until the mid-1980s established state-owned monopolies and protected politically powerful cartels and often included governmentally fixed prices (Slottje and Prowse, 2001).

In 1889, Canada enacted what is considered the first modern national competition statute: the Act for the Prevention and Suppression of Combinations formed in restraint of Trade. This Act made it a criminal offence punishable by fines and up to two years imprisonment to unduly prevent or lessen competition by conspiracy, combination, agreement or arrangement, if the collaborative conduct also constituted a common law restraint of trade. Monopolization and mergers were not covered until 1910 and after revisions, the entire statute was declared unconstitutional in 1921 leading to the post-First World War Canadian statute of 1923 (Duhaime, 2012).

US antitrust before the Sherman Act of 1890

During the later 1800s, the US experienced an industrial revolution that led to a dramatic increase in the production of goods. The creation and use of the corporate business form enabled firms to attract a broad range of investor/owners to raise more capital beyond what was possible with partnerships. Large-scale production facilities became financially

Ross D. Petty

Table 14.1 Antitrust state cases

Year	State	Trust	Result
1888	Louisiana	Cotton oil	Enjoined from doing business in state because it was acting like a corporation, but not incorporated.
1889	New York	Sugar	River Sugar Refining Corp. charter repealed – violated its charter by not independently conducting business.
1889	California	Sugar	American Sugar Refining Corp. forfeits right to be a corporation by not being independent and by participating in a monopoly.
1890	Nebraska	Whiskey	Nebraska Distilling Corp. loses its charter because it is not authorized to terminate its own existence by transferring all assets to the trust. Contract joining the trust also void because it creates a monopoly.
1892	Ohio	Standard oil	Ohio Standard ordered to cease its connections with the trust because monopoly is against state policy.

feasible leading to advancements in mass-production techniques and technology. These mass-produced goods were sold nationally using advertising in the new national medium of magazines and shipped over newly completed railroads. This development of large-scale manufacturing oversaturated the developing national market, leading to price declines. Businesses attempted to address this overcapacity by loose agreements such as 'pools' and 'gentlemen's agreements' but as noted above such agreements were often not enforceable under state law.

To address this issue of unenforceability, some firms turned to joint ownership rather than a mere agreement to coordinate actions of independent firms. The Standard Oil Trust secretly formed in 1882 among some 40 firms and individuals required all the firms and owners to relinquish control of all assets to the trust which was run by a board of nine trustees (Thorelli, 1955, 76–7). This trust served as a model for trusts in other industries allowing such trusts to limit the output of all their plants in order to maintain price levels (McCraw, 2008, 1–2). Arguably, the trust converted collusion among competitors to market domination by a single large firm.

However state governments challenged corporations that joined trusts for giving up their autonomy which states held corporations were not authorized to do. Additionally some states recognized that trusts were monopolies that were contrary to state public policy. Table 14.1 lists several of these early 'antitrust' state cases (Thorelli, 1955, 48–50, 79–82).

The result of these challenges was two-fold. First, trusts reorganized as large single corporations (Thorelli, 1955, 82–4). Second, in 1889, the New Jersey legislature was the first to authorize one corporation to own shares in another that enabled the creation of companies that owned interests in a substantial majority of firms in an industry (Limbaugh, 1953). Other states soon followed the New Jersey 'holding company' law in their efforts to attract taxable incorporations. Companies found that the acquisition of another corporation's stock in order to gain control of that corporation was easier and less costly than attempting a merger (called 'fusion') and was less subject to lawsuits by dissident shareholders (Thorelli, 1955, 216–17).

The federal government and several states reacted to the trust issue with the introduction of several anti-monopoly bills in 1888. Although Senator Sherman's proposal was rewritten by Senator Edmunds and criticized for being vague and therefore likely to be ineffective, Congress enacted the rewrite in 1890 with little enthusiasm. Republicans supported it because they also sought a 'pro-trust' tariff increase (Dickson and Wells, 2001). By 1890, at least 14 states had inserted anti-monopoly provisions into their state constitutions and 13 states had passed antitrust legislation. Six states did both (May, 1987; Thorelli, 1955, 155). Maine and Kansas enacted the first laws that condemned 'all arrangements, contracts, agreements, trusts or combinations'. Texas followed only by Mississippi in 1890 took a more specific approach, declaring trusts to be illegal and defining trusts as combinations of 'capital, skill or acts ... for various specific improper purposes' (*California v. Van de Kamp,* 1988). State interest in controlling monopolies did not end with the enactment of the Sherman Act in 1890. By 1915, most states had enacted their own state anti-monopoly legislation (Davies, 1916).

Passing and enforcing the Sherman Act 1890–1917

In contrast to the rest of the world, the trust question was important in the US political discussions both before and after the federal enactment of the Sherman Act in 1890. Many argued that trusts raised prices by restricting competition and output. Trust defenders generally argued they were result of success in the free market – part of the American dream, everyone should have the right to decide how to use their own property – and that trusts developed economies of scale and therefore were a lower cost form of doing business than small firms that lacked scale economies.

Despite the state and private lawsuits discussed above, many felt that the legal system was not able to sufficiently curtail trust activity. When states attacked corporate charters, trusts simply reorganized. As holding company laws became more widespread, such corporate charter attacks could be based only on vague arguments that monopolies violated public policy. In addition, the common law condemnation of combinations in restraint of trade served only as a defence to judicial enforcement of the combination contract. It did not allow customers who paid an above-market price because of the trade restraint to sue to enjoin the trade restraining conduct or obtain damages caused by it. The Sherman Act was politically promoted as the solution to the trust problem.

Section 1 of the Sherman Act (26 Stat. 209) declared illegal (in the form of a misdemeanour) 'every contract, combination in the form of trust of otherwise or conspiracy in restraint of trade'. Section 2 similarly condemned any persons who 'monopolize, or attempt to monopolize or combine or conspire with any other person or persons to monopolize any part of the trade or commerce among the several States'. Section 7 authorized private lawsuits and treble damage awards by anyone injured by Sherman Act violations.

Initial enforcement efforts

During the period between 1890 and 1903, the US government brought 23 Sherman Act cases (Jones, 2004, 410) while state governments brought around a dozen cases, and private parties brought a significantly larger number of lawsuits against various restraints of trade (Thorelli, 1955, 265–6, 477–99). Attention was naturally focused on Supreme Court decisions involving the new law. With the exception of preventing workers from collusively organizing unions, federal courts were not initially sympathetic to the antitrust goals of the Sherman Act. Of the five non-labour cases decided before 1897, the government only obtained one injunction. For example, in *US v. E.C. Knight Co.* (1895) where the government challenged the acquisition of four smaller firms jointly producing about 33 per cent of all sugar in the US by the American Sugar Refining Company that produced 65 per cent of refined sugar in the US, the majority of the Supreme Court affirmed dismissal of the case. They held that the acquisition of manufacturing capacity through mergers did not constitute monopolizing commerce among the states because Sherman Act did not reach the acquisition of property by corporations organized under state law. Justice Harlan dissented, arguing goods produced were then shipped in interstate commerce and based on English and American common law court decisions this should be condemned as a restraint of trade. This opinion led to the enactment of over a dozen state merger laws within the next two years (Bittlingmayer, 1985, 88–9).

This reluctance to find violations turned around with the Supreme Court decision in *US v. Trans-Missouri Freight Ass'n.* (1897) where a Court majority held that the Sherman Act did apply to railroads despite the creation of the Interstate Commerce Commission in 1887. The majority ruled that the agreement (collusion) among independent railroads to maintain prices was illegal. Justice White dissented, arguing that every contract restrained trade to some degree but only unreasonable agreements should be deemed illegal. Two years later in *Addyston Pipe & Steel Co v. US* (1899), the Court affirmed that the bid-rigging cartel among six cast iron pipe producers controlling between one-fifth and one-third of nation's supply also restrained trade in interstate commerce and the cartel did not charge reasonable prices. The appellate court decision authored by future President and later Supreme Court Justice William Howard Taft argued that ancillary restraints of trade reasonably related to legitimate purposes of the joint enterprise would be lawful. In an early discussion of distributional antitrust issues, at least one legal commentator suggested *Addyston* also might condemn exclusive territories if assigned to subsidiaries since bids were territorially allocated (Bittlingmayer, 1985, 103).

These three Court decisions told businesses that they were at antitrust risk if operating as a collusive trust of independent businesses but that a complete consolidation into a single market-dominating firm was outside the scope of antitrust laws. This belief contributed to a wave of mergers in the late 1890s that ultimately involved approximately 50 per cent of US manufacturing capacity, with many of the resulting merged firms enjoying market shares of over 50 per cent (Bittlingmayer, 1996, 379).

1905–1914: antitrust takes off

A lull in antitrust enforcement occurred from December 1897 to March 1902 when only one Department of Justice antitrust case was filed (Bittlingmayer, 1996, 380; Thorelli, 1955, 405). But then in 1903, President Teddy Roosevelt formed the Bureau of Corporations, an investigatory agency within the Department of Commerce and Labor and the Antitrust Division within the Department of Justice, each with its own budget (Letwin, 1965, 240–4; Bittlingmayer, 1996, 382). Between 1905 and 1914, Justice filed 130 antitrust cases, nearly 70 per cent challenging horizontal conspiracies. The Department litigated about half of these and won about 60 per cent including settlements. Half of these cases were criminal prosecutions and eight cases ordered divestiture (Posner, 1970).

In *Northern Securities Co. v. United States* (1904), where one company owned a majority of stock in two purportedly independent railroad companies effectively creating a merger of those two railroads, a narrow 5-4 majority upheld an order requiring the company to divest its shares in the railroads (Letwin, 1965, 182–237). Thus, nine years after its *E.C. Knight* decision placed acquisitions even in highly concentrated industries outside the scope of the

Figure 14.2   Sherman Act back from the dead cartoon (1904), source: http://thebreakingtime.
typepad.com/the_breaking_time/2010/07/nation-vs-corporation.html

Sherman Act, the Supreme Court finally held that a merger could violate the Sherman Act.
The Court continued down the divestiture path in 1911 when it upheld divestiture decrees
in two famous cases involving market dominating trusts: *Standard Oil of New Jersey v. US*
and *U.S. v. American Tobacco Co.* (1911). The former controlled 95 per cent of domestic oil
refining and the latter produced 95 per cent of domestic plug tobacco.

In *Standard Oil*, the Court announced its famous rule of reason that, despite statutory
language seemingly condemning all restraints of trade, only unreasonable restraints actually
violated the Sherman Act (May, 2007, 48–54). Chief Justice White's opinion reviewed the
history of monopolies in England, the common law condemnation of 'forestalling, engrossing
and rebating' and the evolution of the common law concept of restraints of trade to conclude
that, under the Sherman Act, courts must necessarily exercise their judgment to determine if
an alleged restraint of trade is unreasonable. Consistent with Judge Taft's opinion in *Addyston
Pipe*, reasonableness predominantly would be determined by whether the combination
could control the market and raise prices (May, 2007, 48–56). The decision became known
for condemning Standard Oil's price cutting and driving rivals out of the market or to join
the combination. McGee (1958) notes that Standard Oil seldom priced below cost, often
enjoyed lower costs than rivals and most of its price wars seemed to be local in nature (and
less expensive for it than a national price war seeking to drive rivals out of business). Rather
than force others to exit, Standard Oil appears to have signalled to rivals that they would be
better off joining the firm, which many did (cf. Heil and Langvardt, 1994).

The *American Tobacco* case was about price wars too but since tobacco products were among
the first to develop strong brands, the case also became known for the use of a 'fighting
brand', appropriately named 'Battle Ax', in price wars while the long-term brands maintained
prices to help cover the price war losses (see Fig. 14.3). *Standard Oil* also contained allegations
of the use of bogus independent companies so both cases arguably involved both price and
product tactics.

Also in 1911 there was a clear holding in distributional antitrust. The Supreme Court
declared vertical price fixing (resale price maintenance, RPM) to be per se illegal in *Dr.*

Figure 14.3 Battle Ax, source: *Oakland Tribune* (1906), www.weirduniverse.net/blog/comments/you_are_discharged

Miles Medical Co. v. John D. Park & Sons Co. (1911). Dr Miles argued that its trade secret formula and trademark-protected brand name gave it a legal monopoly over its product that authorized it to set terms of trade such as price at the retail level. However, the Supreme Court majority held that a trade secret was not a Congressional grant of rights like a patent and the contract was essentially a sale contract so that the seller lost all rights to the product. Therefore, trying to set retail prices was per se illegal. In dissent, Justice Holmes pointed out that changing to a consignment contract so that the medicines were not sold to retailers but only consigned to them with ownership being retained by the manufacturer would make the holding easy to circumvent for manufacturers who could afford not to get paid until dealers sold the product (Peritz, 2007, 77–88).

The following year, the Supreme Court further limited market dominating businesses by holding in *U.S. v. Terminal Railroad Association* (1912) that an association of rival railroads that had a virtual monopoly to the St Louis terminal could not prohibit non-member railroads from terminal access and must offer equal terms to all railroads (Kovacic and Shapiro, 2000, 46). That same year, in contrast to its minimization of property rights associated with trade secrets in *Dr. Miles*, the Court deferred to the grant of a patent in a tying case. A.B. Dick required customers of its patented mimeograph machine to use its unpatented ink. It sued a distributor of a competitor's ink for contributory patent infringement on the grounds the distributor knew that this would induce the customer to violate the terms of the contract that permitted it to use the patented product. The Court held that tying arrangements based on a patent should be considered reasonable under the Sherman Act (Hovenkamp, 1994, 57). So apparently manufacturers could not dictate retail prices but they could require customers to buy an unpatented second product in order to get a patented first product.

While the Supreme Court affirmed divestiture orders in both *Standard Oil* and *American Tobacco* and appeared tough against vertical price fixing, it was widely viewed as favouring

Figure 14.4 Dr. Miles Nervine, 1904, source: www.pinterest.com/fhamptonmoore/medical-quackery-and-patent-medicines

business because of its announced rule of reason. Indeed, the divested oil and tobacco entities continued to enjoy regional dominance and exercised 'sharp tactics' against independent firms (Peritz, 1996, 60–64). Because some feared the rule of reason adopted in *Standard Oil* had weakened the Sherman Act and the wave of mergers stimulated in part by a belief that the antitrust laws could prohibit trusts among independent firms, but would tolerate asset acquisitions and holding companies, antitrust became an important issue in the 1912 presidential election. Roosevelt, famous as a 'trust buster', argued that only bad trusts should be condemned. However his major opponent, Woodrow Wilson, argued that anti-competitive practices, not just trusts and monopolies, needed to be regulated.

Augmenting the Sherman Act

Once elected, Wilson persuaded Congress to transform the Bureau of Corporations into an expert antitrust regulatory agency through enactment of the Federal Trade Commission Act (1914). In the same year, Congress also enacted the Clayton Act to tighten rules against anti-competitive mergers and interlocking directorates, price discrimination, tying and exclusive dealing. In contrast to the Clayton Act's condemnation of specific anti-competitive practices, the FTC was formed to exercise expert judgement under the rule of reason to identify and condemn unfair methods of competition that had not previously been identified (Hovenkamp, 1994, 56–7). However, the Supreme Court would soon note that the words 'unfair methods of competition' under the FTC Act were 'clearly inapplicable to practices never heretofore regarded as opposed to good morals because characterized by deception, bad faith, fraud or oppression, or as against public policy because of their dangerous tendency unduly to hinder competition or create monopoly' (*FTC v. Gratz*, 1920, 427). While this language clearly restricted the FTC, the Commission adapted by pursuing what today would be called competitive torts under common law unfair competition law (such as fraudulent advertising, bribery of other firm's agents, passing off, etc.).

By this time, marketers should have realized that fixing prices or dividing markets with competitors was illegal collusion, as was fixing retail prices with retailers. The newly enacted Clayton Act prohibited price discrimination, tying and exclusive dealing but only when such practices substantially lessened competition or tended to create a monopoly in any line of commerce. The required competitive analysis complicated the predictability of the legality of these sorts of practices. Furthermore, all three Clayton Act practices listed above could have either horizontal effects against competition or rivals of the firms using these tactics or vertical effects on competition among firms at other levels of the distribution channel.

However, the US entry into the First World War would effectively suspend the antitrust laws during the war and lead to a new era of business-government cooperation and business 'associationalism' (Keller, 1981, 74). Business had come to understand that tight combinations such as trusts and cartels had antitrust risks, so firms experimented with loose combinations, often called associations, that would try to effectively restrict competition but not violate the law (Hawley, 1981, 154). Associations were viewed as a new third form of economic organization with unique economic virtues (Peritz, 1996, 75).

Judicial deference to business and cooperative competition, 1918–1936

Arguments that the rule of reason was pro-business appeared justified when the Supreme Court refused to find antitrust liability against two market-dominating firms: United Shoe (1918) with 90 per cent market share of shoe machinery production and U.S. Steel (1920) with over 60 per cent market share of steel production (Keller, 1981, 75). Indeed in *U.S. v. U.S. Steel* (1920), the Court found no liability despite occasional price-fixing efforts that had largely not been successful. The firm had discontinued these efforts and some competitors voluntarily chose to follow U.S. Steel's price leadership (which was not illegal). U.S. Steel's market share had declined from over 80 per cent in 1910 to about 40 per cent in 1920 (Kovacic and Shapiro, 2000, 48). The Supreme Court even allowed a price-fixing agreement among members of the Chicago Board of Trade that set the price for grain that was to be delivered overnight at the prior day's closing price. In its 1918 decision, the Court did not apply the per se illegal analysis but instead under the rule of reason found this price-fixing to be reasonable since no attempt was made to actually change prices away from the market price (Crane, 2007, 111).

The Court also recognized freedom of choice in contracting despite antitrust concerns. In *U.S. v. United Shoe Machinery Co.* (1918), the Court by bare majority permitted United Shoe to include restrictive conditions in its 17-year leases of its patented shoe manufacturing machinery. These conditions included: using each machine to full capacity; leasing other machines from United Shoe as more work became available; not using any other machines or output from other machines; requiring lessees to use specified United Shoe supplies; requiring lessees to assign rights for machinery improvements to United Shoe and lastly lessees that breach any of lease provisions agree to return machines and pay a return charge. Similarly, in *U.S. v. Colgate & Co.* (1919), the defendant was allowed to announce its policy of not dealing with discount retailers and then refuse to deal with those who did not comply. Although RPM was per se illegal according to the *Dr. Miles* case, refusals to deal were declared legal even though it would allow manufacturers to essentially declare RPM policies so long as they did not negotiate to form an agreement with dealers (Page, 2008, 6–7).

Cooperative 'competition?'

These new court decisions allowing greater economic freedom for business in part reflected then current thinking in support of business–government and business–business cooperation. When the US entered the First World War, this thinking became explicit policy. Exemptions from the antitrust laws were enacted such as the Webb-Pomerene Act (1918) exempting export associations and the Capper-Volstead Act (1922) for agricultural co-operatives. The War Industries Board under President Wilson encouraged the formation of trade associations to exchange information and stabilize markets, with about 1,000 associations formed by 1920. The courts initially viewed trade association information exchanges, particularly pricing and output information, with suspicion. However, in a series of decisions in the early 1920s, the Supreme Court permitted voluntary trade association exchanges of information (Duddy and Revzan, 1947, 593).

During this time of antitrust relaxation, marketing emerged as a new discipline in the 1920s and marketing books during this time period generally saw increasing discussion of antitrust concerns (e.g. compare Butler, 1917; Duncan, 1921, with Converse, 1921; Clark, 1922). In contrast, antitrust activity slowed. The Antitrust Division's budget fell from fell from $270k in 1914 to $81k in 1919 so it focused on mergers and consent decrees. It negotiated 112 consent decrees by 1932, making consent decrees the preferred enforcement mechanism compared to criminal litigation (Keller, 1981, 76).

In the decade of the 1920s, Justice initiated an average of 12.5 antitrust cases per year (Posner, 1970, 366). The FTC also was not very active on the antitrust front, averaging only about ten restraint of trade cases (not including deception or competitive torts) per year in the 1920s (Posner, 1970, 369). The Supreme Court augmented its 1920 holding that the FTC could not define unfair methods of competition beyond traditional common law offences, by holding in 1927 that the FTC did not have authority to order divestiture in merger cases (*FTC v. Eastman Kodak Co.* 1927; Kovacic and Shapiro, 2000, 48–9). By the 1930s more than 90 per cent of the FTC's complaints involved deceptive practices rather than antitrust (Keller, 1981, 76).

The FTC also embraced business government cooperation and business 'associationalism' by sponsoring trade practice conferences in the 1920s (peaking in 1929 with 50 conferences) where executives from single industries would meet to discuss and promulgate codes of fair conduct (McCraw, 1984, 151–2; Meese, 2013, 281–3). Claudy (1920) provided a first-hand report on the FTC's hearings with the California Raisin Growers Association and how the FTC might tell the association not only what not to do but also what to do to stay within legal boundaries. However in 1930, the Department of Justice noticed that some of these trade practice rules contained provisions that restricted price competition, so the FTC began both revising parts of existing rules and curtailing the number of trade practice conferences that it would host (Gaskill, 1936, 120–2).

A new deal for antitrust

Although the Supreme Court in 1927 once again declared unadorned price-fixing agreements were per se illegal (*U.S. v. Trenton Potteries Co.* 1927: Kovacic and Shapiro, 2000), the great stock market crash of 1929 caused many to feel antitrust was a failure and the government needed to more actively orchestrate commerce. For this reason, Congress passed the National Recovery Act in 1933 that contained an antitrust exemption and authorized the code authority to formulate codes for the control of price, output and non-price competition. According to a recent study, 450 of the 650 codes prepared before this Act was declared unconstitutional in

1935 sought to affect prices and output (Keller, 1981, 92). Given the breadth of this activity, it is not surprising that the NRA and trade practices were popular subjects in the marketing literature of this period (Witkowski, 2010; Converse, 1936). For example, Brand (1935) attempted to distinguish trade association price exchange programmes that would be pro-competitive from those that would enable illegal price-fixing and Compton (1934) described the experiences of the lumber industry in formulating codes of practice.

Courts were sympathetic to trade associations during the 1930s. In *Appalachian Coals, Inc. v. U.S.* (1933), the Court judged a regional joint sales agency under rule of reason and held with one dissent that it was reasonable because it might allow them to survive in a depressed industry. Three years later, the Court considered antitrust charges against a national trade association of 18 large sugar refiners that collectively produced 70–80 per cent of the sugar sold in the US. While the Court found liability, foreshadowing a revitalized interest in antitrust, it only prohibited 47 specific unfair methods of competition and did not order dissolution (Peritz, 1996, 136–7; *Sugar Institute Inc. v. U.S.*, 1936).

Retail chain stores and pricing

Perhaps the last gasp of trade 'associationalism' was the lobbying by small businesses, particularly retailers, to address concerns about large chain stores – a dominating antitrust issue by the mid-1930s. The fear was that such chains were exerting leverage over manufacturers in order to gain price concessions to enable them to undersell small retailers (Haring, 1935). After an FTC report, two statutes were enacted to address these issues.

The first was the Robinson Patman Act of 1936 that made three changes in the price discrimination provisions of the Clayton Act. First, to address the issue of large retail chain stores directly, the new statute added liability for buyers who knowingly induced or received a prohibited discrimination in price. Second, the RP Act added an alternative injury provision that made price discrimination illegal when it would injure, destroy or prevent competition with any person who either grants or knowingly receives the benefit of the discrimination in price. Third and most controversially, the RP Act eliminated the justification for quantity discounts but left the cost justification defence, following FTC policy that quantity discounts should be cost justified (Peritz 1996, 149–53). The marketing literature offered multiple articles on the implications of the Act for various types of marketers including distributors, wholesalers and retailers (e.g. Engle, 1936; Stevens, 1937; Cassady, 1947; Robbins, 1959).

The second statute was the Miller-Tydings Resale Price Maintenance Act of 1937 that would allow manufacturers to practise RPM in states where it was legal (Peritz, 1996, 153–6). By April 1937 under this new law, 33 states had passed laws legalizing RPM within state borders (Kelley, 1937, 48). Forty-six states would legalize RPM at one time or another until the repeal of Miller-Tydings in 1975 30 years after the FTC went on record to advocate for the repeal (Hovenkamp, 1994, 394; Grether, 1941, 1947).

1936–1976: expansive antitrust and per se illegality

As confidence in trade associations and economic planning as a form of market organization faded in the mid-1930s and the NRA was declared unconstitutional in 1935, President Franklin Roosevelt turned to advisers who favoured more rigorous antitrust enforcement as a method stimulating economic recovery. Economists at the University of Chicago advocated in favour of antitrust enforcement within free markets as preferable to market planning (Kovacic and Shapiro, 2000, 49). The Antitrust Division and the FTC ended up suing many associations for anti-competitive codes of conduct that they had previously reviewed and allowed.

This so-called Second New Deal started vigorous antitrust enforcement. From 1940 through 1949, the Antitrust Division brought 382 cases, winning 304. A 1948 note in the *Journal of Marketing* cautioned that using a trade association to fix prices horizontally or vertically would be illegal and that distributing price lists among members would be risky, but the risk could be reduced if circulation of price lists was anonymous, not mandatory, and if there was 'no tendency toward current identity [of products] or prices' (Meyers, 1948, 380). Customer or territorial allocation and attempts to create a group boycott through the association also would be illegal but it would likely be permissible to circulate technical research and offer lobbying and arbitration services as well advocating the elimination of misrepresentations by members. Lastly, a 1949 Supreme Court decision signalled an expansive interpretation of exclusive dealing under section 3 of the Clayton Act to condemn an exclusive dealership scheme that covered less than 7 per cent of the market (Curran, 1950).

This period would see a rise in private antitrust lawsuits that would dramatically outnumber the number of federal filings. Up until this time, private lawsuits had not been a significant component of antitrust enforcement. From 1890 to 1940, 175 private damage antitrust lawsuits proceeded to final adjudication and the plaintiffs won in only 13 (National Committee, 1955, 378). But for the decade of the 1940s, 826 private antitrust lawsuits were filed, far exceeding the number of government cases (Salop and White, 1988, 4). That is not to say that private plaintiffs were as successful as the government. For example, between 1952 and 1958 private plaintiffs recovered damages in only 20 of 144 reported cases and obtained a favourable settlement in another 25 per cent of cases (Bicks, 1959, 11). In a study of cases filed, the 1950s saw over 500 government antitrust cases filed but over four times as many private antitrust lawsuits. By the 1960s and 1970s between 48 and 100 government cases were filed each year with the number of private filings increasing from just below 400 in 1961 to over 1,000 per year in the 1970s. Roughly three-quarters of the private antitrust lawsuits are settled (presumably with the plaintiffs obtaining some relief). In litigated cases defendants won more than twice as often as plaintiffs (Salop and White, 1988, 4, 11).

This increase in private antitrust lawsuits was undoubtedly stimulated by the expansionist view of antitrust law taken by the Supreme Court during this period as illustrated in Table 14.2. The only decision in Table 14.2 that is not from the Supreme Court is the 1945 Second Circuit opinion in ALCOA. The Supreme Court justices had too many conflicts of interest to hear the case, so they let the Second Circuit hear the appeal instead. The Supreme Court was quick to confirm the analysis of the ALCOA decision the following year when it decided *American Tobacco*.

The cases cited in Table 14.2 show an expansion in antitrust liability. Many practices were declared per se illegal, meaning they could be condemned without considering whether they tended to lessen competition. For other practices, the burden of proving a possible lessening of competition was reduced to a simple analysis of sales or market share that permitted condemnation of practices that affected relatively small market shares.

This long list of cases finding antitrust liability suggests a high legal risk for any horizontal or vertical agreements from price-fixing to territorial allocation to group boycotts. Single-firm exclusionary activities such as price cutting, even with prices above costs, tying and pre-emptive expansion also likely would be condemned. Co-operative associations of small competitors found themselves at risk for violating per se rules, but the Court also allowed small firms to recover damages even if competition was not harmed. Robbins (1959) noted that the 1940s embodied expansive enforcement of the Robinson-Patman against price

Table 14.2 Expansion in antitrust liability

Case name	Decision
Interstate Circuit, Inc. v. U.S. (1939), 306 U.S. 308	Affirmed the finding of horizontal price fixing among movie theaters based on circumstantial evidence rather than the confession of one or more conspirators.
U.S. v. Socony Vacuum Oil Co. (1940), 310 U.S. 150	Collusion among major oil companies to purchase distressed oil to stabilize prices is illegal horizontal price fixing.
Fashion Originators' Guild v. FTC (1941), 312 U.S. 457	Illegal for clothing producers collectively agree not to deal with companies that make or sell with "knock-offs."
U.S. v. Aluminum Co. of America (ALCOA), (2nd Cir. 1945), 148 F.2d 416	Held ALCOA liable for monopolization of the virgin aluminum ingot market (obtaining 90% market share) by seizing every opportunity to expand capacity before any rival could enter.
American Tobacco Co. v. U.S. (1946), 328 U.S. 781	Affirmed convictions of executives for collusion and monopolization based on the power to exclude competition and raise prices not proof that they accomplished these goals.
Int'l Salt Co. v. U.S. (1947), 332 U.S. 392	Tying is per se illegal when lessor must agree to buy second product (salt) in order to lease patented salt tablet machines.
FTC v. Morton Salt Co., (1948), 334 U.S. 37; (Curran, 1950).	Extensive quantity discounts that enable chain stores to receive a lower price on table salt than wholesalers who sell to retailers tends to lessen competition = illegal price discrimination.
Standard Oil Co. v. United States, (1949), 337 U.S. 293	Exclusive dealing contracts with independent gasoline dealers held to violate the Clayton Act because they foreclosed $58m. in sales (6.7% of market) which is substantial.
Lorain Journal Co. v. United States, (1951), 342 U.S. 143	Monopoly local newspaper refuses to sell advertising to firms who advertise on new radio station = attempt to monopolize.
Timken Roller Bearing Co. v. U.S. (1951), 341 U.S. 593	Allocation of markets & price fixing among competitors who formed a joint trademark licensing scheme are per se illegal.
Kiefer-Stewart Co. v. Seagram & Sons, Inc., (1951), 340 U.S. 211	Liquor producers conspired to set wholesale price ceilings (RPM) & refused to sell non-compliers – violates Sherman Act rejecting the defense that price ceilings are pro-competitive.
Northern Pacific Railway v. U.S. (1958), 356 U.S. 1; (Edwards, 1950, 662)	Railroad land sales contingent on agreement by the buyer to use railroad for all transportation and shipping needs held illegal tie-in despite lack of market power in real estate market.
U.S. v. United Shoe Mach. (1954), 330 U.S. 806	Affirmed 10-year lease of shoe making machines requiring full capacity use and higher early cancellation fees if switch to rival machines resulting in 85% market share is monopolization.
Klor's v. Broadway–Hale Stores, Inc. (1959), 359 U.S. 207	Group boycott of small retailer by large chain and ten appliance manufacturers per se illegal even if competition is robust after small retailer is eliminated.
United States v. Parke, Davis & Co., (1960) 362 U.S. 29	Pharmaceutical firm that uses wholesalers and retailers to find, initiate discussions & terminate discounters goes beyond its right to announce its RPM policy & terminate discounters.
Simpson v. Union Oil Co. of Cal., (1964), 377 U.S. 13	Gasoline supplier can't coercively impose RPM by leasing retail location, consigning gas & terminating discounters.

Case name	Decision
FTC v. Borden Co., (1966), 383 U.S. 637; (Werner, 1969)	Borden sold identical evaporated milk under its own label and as private label for different prices = illegal price discrimination.
FTC v Brown Shoe Co., Inc., (1966), 384 U.S. 316; (Werner, 1969)	In exchange for exclusive benefits, shoe marketer induced hundreds of dealers (1% of the market) into exclusive dealing = incipient violation of antitrust laws violating FTC Act.
U.S. v. General Motors Corp., (1966), 384 U.S. 127; (Werner, 1969)	Illegal for GM to use location clauses in franchise agreement to prohibit dealers from selling to discounters in different locations.
Utah Pie Co. v. Cont'l Baking Co. (1967), 386 U.S. 685; (Werner, 1969)	Above cost local price cutting by national bakery illegal under Robinson-Patman Act.
U.S. v. Arnold Schwinn & Co. (1967), 388 U.S. 365; (Werner, 1969)	Territorial restrictions upon dealers in case where bicycles are sold rather than merely consigned are per se illegal.
United States v. Sealy, Inc. (1967), 388 U.S. 350; (Werner, 1969)	Sealy owners-trademark licensees allocated territories which constitute per se horizontal collusion when prices also are fixed.
Albrecht v. Herald Co. (1968). 390 U.S. 145	Maximum vertical price fixing (RPM) is per se illegal.
U.S. v. Container Corp. of Am. (1969), 393 U.S. 333; (Werner, 1977)	Even infrequent and irregular exchanges of price information among association members are still per se illegal.
U.S. v. Topco Associates, Inc. (1972), 405 U.S. 596; (Werner, 1977)	Exclusive territories for the sale of private label products produced by a cooperative association of about 25 regional supermarket chains are per se illegal.
U.S. v. U.S. Gypsum Co. (1978), 438 U.S. 422; (Werner, 1978)	Price information exchange in oligopolistic industry to verify meeting competition defense is not per se illegal, but still is highly suspect.

discrimination, but in the 1950s, courts shifted the burden of proving competitive injury to the plaintiffs and were more likely to recognize the meeting competition and cost justification defences.

During this time period mergers (both between competitors and between firms at different levels of the same distribution chain) were so commonly condemned that, in a 1966 opinion, a dissenting Supreme Court Justice famously complained that the only consistency he could find in Supreme Court merger decisions is that the 'government always wins' (Kovacic and Shapiro, 2000, 51). Most mergers are not particularly interesting for the practice of marketing, but two are worth mentioning as expansive government victories. First, in *U.S. v. Du Pont de Nemours & Co.* (1956), over a rigorous dissent, a majority of the Court held that DuPont's 1919 purchase of a 23 per cent interest in the General Motors corporation was an illegal merger because it led to DuPont becoming a major supplier to GM of paint finishes (two-thirds of GM's needs) and fabrics (half GM's needs) (Edwards, 1950,

662–3). Another expansive merger decision affirmed the FTC's condemnation of the asset acquisition by P&G, the national market leader in soaps, detergents and cleaners, of Clorox, the market leader in bleach. The Supreme Court agreed with the FTC that the combination would substantially lessen competition because economies of scale in advertising would raise barriers to entry in the bleach industry and P&G was the most likely entrant into the bleach industry and a potential competitor monitored by Clorox before the acquisition (Armentano, 1982, 252–62).

There were few significant setbacks in the Supreme Court for this reign (or perhaps rain) of antitrust liability. In 1954, the Supreme Court held in a private case that the plaintiff had to prove more than 'conscious parallelism' in order to show an agreement to restrain trade because rivals naturally watch and often follow rivals' pricing (Kovacic and Shapiro, 2000, 50). A second setback was the government case against DuPont alleging it had monopolized the market for cellophane. DuPont successfully persuaded the trial and Supreme Courts that the market was not just cellophane but flexible wrapping materials and DuPont only commanded 17.9 per cent of that market which was too small a market share to constitute monopolization (Armentano, 1982, 118–19). The Supreme Court also held that a 20-year exclusive contract to provide all the coal needed by Tampa Electric was not anti-competitive because it foreclosed less than 1 per cent of the regional market for coal (*Tampa Elec. Co. v. Nashville Coal Co.*, 1961). Finally in 1979, the Court held that a large buyer could pressure a seller into offering a price discount if the seller acted in good faith to meet competition. The meeting competition defence would apply to both (*Great Atlantic & Pacific Tea Co. v. FTC* 1979). This last decision occurred in an era when the Court more actively applied the rule of reason (Werner, 1982).

1975–present: the return of the rule of reason

The rule of reason never returned for horizontal collusion such as price-fixing, bid-rigging and market allocations. Instead during this period such conduct generally was treated as per se illegal and often criminally prosecuted with increasing penalties. For all other practices, the Supreme Court required some form of rule of reason analysis that looked at likely market effects of the challenged practices on competition. This modern period arguably begins in 1975 when the Supreme Court examined a minimum fee schedule enacted by the Virginia State Bar Association and declared it in violation of the Sherman Act under the rule of reason rather than being per se illegal. The 'learned professions' were entitled to rule of reason analysis (*Goldfarb v. Virginia State Bar*, 1975). Since then occasional unusual situations of alleged horizontal collusion also have been analysed under rule of reason.

In the same year, Congress repealed the Miller-Tydings Act of 1937 that had allowed states to enact laws permitting RPM. In repealing Miller-Tydings, Congress and President Ford recognized that state laws permitting RPM caused consumers to pay higher prices for many products. Repeal would mean that throughout the country RPM would be considered per se illegal. This harsh treatment of RPM would continue until a 2007 Supreme Court decision overturned 91 years of antitrust law by declaring that even minimum RPM would no longer be considered per se illegal. It would now be examined under the rule of reason (*Leegin Creative Leather Products, Inc. v. PSKS, Inc.*, 2007).

The road to this dramatic 2007 decision began 30 years earlier when the Supreme Court overturned another of its own decisions that was just ten years old. In *Continental TV v. GTE Sylvania Inc.* (1977), the Supreme Court overruled its *Arnold Schwinn* decision and declared that non-price vertical restraints would be examined under the rule of reason and found reasonable if there was robust inter-brand competition (Werner, 1978). The Court was persuaded by so-called Chicago School economists' arguments about possible efficiencies of non-price vertical restraints. The *Sylvania* decision was written broadly to discuss all forms of non-price vertical restraints and has generally been interpreted that way.

Tying and exclusive dealing may have vertical effects that would be analysed under the rule of reason according to *Sylvania* to see if inter-brand competition was robust or if not, to see if intra-brand competition was unreasonably restrained. These practices also may have horizontal exclusionary effects upon competitors. For example, the Supreme Court examined the effects of a tying or exclusive dealing arrangement where a hospital contracted with just one firm for all anaesthesiology services. The Court held under the rule of reason that the plaintiff failed to prove there were distinct markets for hospital and anaesthesiology services or that there was any anti-competitive effect on the market for this alleged restraint of trade (*Jefferson Parish Hosp. Dist. v. Hyde*, 1984).

Similarly, price discrimination by a firm might affect its rivals (often called predatory pricing or primary line injury) or other firms in the distribution channel such as dealers (secondary line injury). Predatory pricing must be proven to be below some appropriate level of cost and the complaining party also must prove that recoupment of the predation losses is likely by the post-predation exercise of market power (*Brooke Group Ltd. v. Brown & Williamson Tobacco Corp.*, 1993). Secondary line cases, particularly those brought by the government, have become rare. The only FTC case since 1990 was a settlement with McCormick which controlled 90 per cent of supermarket spice sales. The FTC complaint alleged that McCormick provided discounts to select supermarkets to the disadvantage of other supermarkets. By 3-2, the Commission accepted the consent decree and the dissent argued the case was one of possible primary not secondary line injury (Gavil *et al.*, 2002, 769–71). Of the 100 private secondary line injury cases brought between 1990 and 2000 only three found liability and awarded damages to the disfavoured dealer (Bulmash, 2012).

The peak of private antitrust litigation was 1977. The return of the rule of reason adds both expense and uncertainty to private antitrust lawsuits. In addition, 1977 also was the year, the Supreme Court (in separate decisions) both banned indirect purchasers from suing for damages from anti-competitive practices and required plaintiffs to prove antitrust injury flowing from a decrease in competition rather than the rigours of robust competition (Bauer, 2001). Starting in 1986, the Supreme Court began to encourage summary dismissal of antitrust complaints if proof of any required case element seemed implausible or the theory of the case was implausible based on the pleadings. Finally, legal trends outside of antitrust law have contributed to the expense and risk of private antitrust litigation. So-called 'junk science' experts may be challenged, which is usually directed at antitrust plaintiff's experts and at least partially successful in excluding testimony 40 per cent of the time. Even the simple rise in business use of email contributes to the costs of discovery in antitrust cases (Kolasky, 2012). These factors all contribute to the continuing decline of private antitrust actions.

Conclusion

By the end of the first quarter-century under the Sherman Act, courts had figured out antitrust law consistent with modern policy. Price-fixing and bid-rigging (and market divisions) by competitors were illegal. Since these practices necessarily are anti-competitive, there is no need to conduct a time-consuming analysis of likely competitive effects. All other practices must be judged under the rule of reason to determine if within the specific market context they are likely to allow the exercise of market power to restrict output and raise prices.

After reaching these simple conclusions, continuing political debate led to experimentation. The Clayton Act was proposed to condemn some practices without market analysis but the final statute was amended to include a likelihood of lessening competition standard. Cooperative antitrust largely through trade associations was tried and seemed to work during wartime but not during the Great Recession. The alternative of free market plus antitrust then came to the forefront and led to antitrust expansion and the development of per se rules to condemn some practices with no (or little) market analysis for likely competitive effects. However antitrust was then criticized for over-reaching and in the past 40 years or so, antitrust law has worked its way back to its origins: with few exceptions horizontal collusion among rivals is generally illegal without further analysis and all other practices are judged under the rule of reason. Back in a 1985 article in the *Journal of Marketing*, Ray Werner (1985, 105) intimated that the future of antitrust might be 'less restraining' but also suggested that marketers still needed to continue to pay attention to antitrust – 'a field both technical and complicated'. Antitrust history should help marketers understand what is likely to be legal versus illegal since this history does indeed appear to be repeating.

References

Adler, E.A. (1917) 'Monopolizing at common law and under section two of the Sherman Act', *Harvard Law Review*, 31/2, 246–70.

Armentano, D.T. (1982) *Antitrust and Monopoly: Anatomy of a Policy Failure*, John Wiley & Sons, New York.

Bauer, J. P. (2001) 'The stealth assault on antitrust enforcement: Raising the barriers for antitrust injury and standing', *University of Pittsburgh Law Review*, 62/3, 427–52.

Bicks, R.A. (1959) 'The Department of Justice and private treble damage actions', *Antitrust Bulletin*, 4/1, 5–15.

Bittlingmayer, G. (1985) 'Did antitrust policy cause the great merger wave?', *Journal of Law and Economics*, 28/1, 77–118.

Bittlingmayer, G. (1996) 'Antitrust and business activity: The first quarter century', *Business History Review*, 70/3, 363–401.

Brand, C.J. (1935) 'A public policy as to open price plans', *American Marketing Journal*, 3/1, 84–91.

Bulmash, H. (2012) 'An empirical analysis of secondary line price discrimination motivations', *Journal of Competition Law and Economics*, 8/2, 361–97.

Butler, R.S. (1917) *Marketing Methods*, Alexander Hamilton Institute, New York.

Cassady, R. (1947) 'Legal aspects of price discrimination: Federal law', *Journal of Marketing*, 11/3, 258–72.

Clark, R.E. (1922) *Principles of Marketing*, Macmillan Co., New York.

Claudy, C.H. (1920) 'Federal Trade Commission may say "do" instead of "don't"', *Printers' Ink*, 110/3, 85–8.

Compton, W. (1934) 'Trade practices in fair competition', *American Marketing Journal*, 1/2, 85–90.

Converse, P.D. (1921) *Marketing Methods and Policies*, Prentice Hall, New York.

Converse, P.D. (1936) *Essentials of Distribution*, Prentice Hall, New York.

Crane, D.A. (2007) 'The Story of *United States v. Socony-Vaccum*: Hot oil and antitrust in the two new deals', in E. Fox and D. Crane (eds), *Antitrust Stories*, Foundation Press, New York, pp. 91–119.

Curran, K.J. (1950) 'Exclusive dealing and public policy', *Journal of Marketing*, 15/2, 133–44.

Davies, J.E. (1916) *Trust Laws and Unfair Competition*, Government Printing Office, Washington, DC.

Dewey, D. (1990) *The Antitrust Experiment in America*, Columbia University Press, New York.

Dickson, P.R., and Wells, P.K. (2001) 'The dubious origins of the Sherman Antitrust Act: The mouse that roared', *Journal of Public Policy and Marketing*, 20/1, 3–14.

Duddy, E.A., and Revzan, D.A. (1947) *Marketing: An Institutional Approach*, McGraw-Hill Book Co, New York.

Duhaime L. (2012) '1889: Canada wheels out the world's first competition statute', *Canadian Legal History,* available online: www.duhaime.org/LawMuseum/CanadianLegalHistory/LawArticle-1420/1889-Canada-Wheels-Out-the-Worlds-First-Competition-Statute.aspx (accessed Aug. 2013).

Duncan, C.S. (1921) *Marketing: Its Problems and Methods,* D. Appleton & Co., New York.

Edwards, C.D. (1950) 'Trends in enforcement of the antimonopoly laws', *Journal of Marketing,* 14/5, 657–65.

Engle, N.H. (1936) 'Implication of the Robinson-Patman Act for marketing', *Journal of Marketing,* 1/2, 75–81.

Gaskill, N.B. (1936) *The Regulation of Competition,* Harper & Brothers, New York.

Gavil, A.I., Kovacic, W.E., and Baker, J.B. (2002) *Antitrust Law in Perspective: Cases, Concepts and Problems in Competition Policy,* Thomson-West, St Paul, MN.

Grether E. T. (1941) 'Current trends affecting pricing policies', *Journal of Marketing,* 5/3, 222–3.

Grether, E.T. (1947) 'The Federal Trade Commission versus resale price maintenance', *Journal of Marketing,* 12/1, 1–13.

Handler, M., Pitofsky, R., Goldschmid, H.J., and Wood, D.P. (1997) *Cases and Materials Trade Regulation,* Foundation Press, Westbury, NY.

Haring, A. (1935) 'The fight to control retail prices', *American Marketing Journal,* 3/1, 78–83.

Hawley, E.W. (1981) 'Antitrust and the association movement: 1920–1940', in *National Competition Policy: Historians' Perspectives on Antitrust and Government-Business Relationships in the United States,* Federal Trade Commission, Washington, DC, pp. 98–142.

Heil, O.P., and Langvardt, A.W. (1994) 'The interface between competitive market signaling and antitrust law', *Journal of Marketing,* 58/3, 81–96.

Hollander, S.C., Rassuli, K.M., Jones, G.B., and Dix, L.F. (2005) 'Periodization in marketing history', *Journal of Macromarketing,* 25/1, 32–41.

Hovenkamp, H. (1994) *Federal Antitrust Policy: The Law of Competition and its Practice,* West Publishing Co., St Paul, MN.

Jones, C.A. (2004) 'The growth of private rights of action outside the US: Exporting antitrust courtrooms to the world: Private enforcement in a global market', *Loyola Consumer Law Review,* 16/4, 409–30.

Keller, M. (1981) 'The pluralist state: American economic regulation in comparative perspective', in T.K. McCraw (ed.), *Regulation in Perspective: Historical Essays,* Harvard University Press, Cambridge, MA, pp. 56–94.

Kelley, P.C. (1937) 'Recent price-regulating legislation', *Journal of Marketing,* 2/1, 46–51.

Kolasky, W. (2012) 'Antitrust litigation: What's changed in twenty-five years?', *Antitrust,* 27/1, 9–17.

Kovacic, W.E., and Shapiro, C. (2000) 'Antitrust policy: A century of economic and legal thinking', *Journal of Economic Perspectives,* 14/1, 43–60.

Letwin, W. (1965) *Law and Economic Policy in America: The Evolution of the Sherman Antitrust Act,* University of Chicago Press, Chicago.

Limbaugh, R.H. (1953) 'Historic origins of anti-trust legislation', *Missouri Law Review,* 18/3, 215–48.

Lyon, L.S. (1936) 'The trade practice problem', *American Marketing Journal,* 3/1, 97–102.

McCraw, T.K. (1984) *Prophets of Regulation,* Harvard University Press, Cambridge, MA.

McCraw, T.K. (2008) 'Antitrust: Perceptions and reality in coping with big business', Harvard Business School, Case no. 9-391-292.

McGee, J.S. (1958) 'Predatory price cutting: The Standard Oil (N.J.) case', *Journal of Law and Economics,* 1 (Oct.), 137–69.

May, J. (1987) 'Antitrust practice and procedure in the formative era: The constitutional and conceptual reach of state antitrust law 1880–1918', *University of Pennsylvania Law Review,* 135/3, 495–593.

May J. (2007) 'The story of *Standard Oil Co. v. United States*', in E. Fox and D. Crane (eds), *Antitrust Stories,* Foundation Press, New York, pp. 7–59.

Meese, A.J. (2013) 'Competition policy and the Great Depression: Lessons learned and a new way forward', *Cornell Journal of Law and Public Policy*, 23/2, 255–336.

Meyers, E.S. (1948) 'Some observations on trade associations and the Law', *Journal of Marketing*, 12/3, 379–81.

National Committee (1955) *Report of the Attorney General's National Committee to Study the Antitrust Law*, U.S. Government Printing Office, Washington, DC.

Page, W.H. (2008) 'The ideological origins and evolution of U.S. antitrust law', *Issues in Competition Law and Policy*, 1, 1–17.

Peritz, R.T. (1996) *Competition Policy in America: History, Rhetoric, Law*, Oxford University Press, Oxford.

Peritz, R.T. (2007) '"Nervine" and knavery: The life and times of *Dr. Miles Medical Company*', in E. Fox and D. Crane (eds), *Antitrust Stories*, Foundation Press, New York, pp. 61–90.

Posner, R.A. (1970) 'A statistical study of antitrust enforcement', *Journal of Law and Economics*, 13/2, 365–419.

Robbins, W.D. (1959) 'A marketing appraisal of the Robinson-Patman Act', *Journal of Marketing*, 24/1, 13–21.

Salop, S.C., and White, L.J. (1988) 'Private antitrust litigation: An introduction and framework', in L.J. White (ed.), *Private Antitrust Litigation: New Evidence, New Learning*, MIT Press, Cambridge, MA, pp. 3–60.

Slottje, D.J., and Prowse, S.D. (2001) 'Antitrust policy in Mexico', *Law and Business Review of the Americas*, 7/3, 405–15.

Stevens, W.H.S. (1937) 'An interpretation of the Robinson-Patman Act', *Journal of Marketing*, 2/1, 38–45.

Thorelli, H.B. (1955) *Federal Antitrust Policy: Origination of an American Tradition*, Johns Hopkins Press, Baltimore, MD.

Werner, R.O. (1969) 'Marketing and the United States Supreme Court, 1965–1968', *Journal of Marketing*, 33/1, 16–23.

Werner, R.O. (1977) 'Marketing and the U.S. Supreme Court, 1982–1984', *Journal of Marketing*, 41/1, 32–43.

Werner, R.O. (1978) 'The 'new' supreme court and the marketing environment, 1975–1977', *Journal of Marketing*, 42/2, 56–62.

Werner, R.O. (1982) 'Marketing and the United States Supreme Court, 1975–1981', *Journal of Marketing*, 46/2, 73–81.

Werner, R.O. (1985) 'Marketing and the supreme court in transition, 1982–1984', *Journal of Marketing*, 49/3, 97–105.

Witkowski, T.H. (2010) 'The marketing discipline comes of age', *Journal of Historical Research in Marketing*, 2/4, 370–96.

Legal references

Addyston Pipe & Steel Co v. United States (1899) 175 U.S. 211.

Appalachian Coals, Inc. v. U.S. (1933), 288 U.S. 344.

Brooke Group Ltd. v. Brown & Williamson Tobacco Corp. (1993) 509 U.S. 209.

California v. Van de Kamp (1988) 46 Cal.3d 1147 (Supreme Court of California).

Continental TV v. GTE Sylvania Inc. (1977) 433 U.S. 36.

Dr. Miles Medical Co. v. John D. Park & Sons Co. (1911) 220 U.S. 373.

FTC v. Eastman Kodak Co. (1927) 274 U.S. 619.

FTC v. Gratz (1920) 253 U.S. 421.

Goldfarb v. Virginia State Bar (1975) 421 U.S. 773.

Great Atlantic & Pacific Tea Co. v. FTC (1979) 440 U.S. 69.

Jefferson Parish Hosp. Dist. v. Hyde (1984) 466 U.S. 2.

Leegin Creative Leather Products, Inc. v. PSKS, Inc. (2007) 551 U.S. 877.

Northern Pacific Railway v. U.S. (1958) 356 U.S. 1.
Northern Securities Co. v. United States (1904) 193 U.S. 197.
Standard Oil of New Jersey v. U.S. (1911) 221 U.S. 1.
Sugar Institute Inc. v. U.S. (1936) 297 U.S. 553.
Tampa Elec. Co. v. Nashville Coal Co. (1961) 365 U.S. 320.
U.S. v. American Tobacco Co. (1911), 221 U.S. 106.
U.S. v. Colgate & Co. (1919), 250 U.S. 300.
U.S. v. Du Pont de Nemours & Co. (1956), 351 U.S. 377.
U.S. v. E.C. Knight Co. (1895), 156 U.S. 11.
U.S. v. Terminal Railroad Association (1912), 224 U.S. 383.
U.S. v. Trans-Missouri Freight Ass'n. (1897), 166 U.S. 290.
U.S. v. Trenton Potteries Co. (1927), 273 U.S. 392.
U.S. v. United Shoe Machinery Co. (1918), 247 U.S. 32.
U.S. v. U.S. Steel (1920), 251 U.S. 417.

15

EU competition law and the practice of marketing

Andrew D. Pressey

Competition has been both God and devil in Western civilization. It has promised and
provided wealth and economic progress; it has also altered the distribution of wealth,
undermined communities and challenged moral codes.

(Gerber, 1998, 1)

Introduction: protecting Prometheus

Competition law (termed antitrust law in the United States) refers to legislation that protects
markets from abuses by dominant firms and practices that restrict competition. Competition
law in the European Union (EU) is chiefly administered under Articles 81 and 82, established
under the Treaty of Rome in 1957, which mirror the American Sherman Act of 1890 and
the Clayton Act of 1914, that prohibits acts such as vertical restraints and cartels (including
market sharing and price-fixing), and monopolies and market abuses by dominant actors
(including exclusive dealing and price discrimination). These laws are designed to protect
consumers from powerful corporations, encourage competition and prohibit any agreements
undertaken between companies that may adversely affect trade between member states that
prevents, restricts or otherwise distorts competition. Competition policy and regulation
in the EU is complex; while the EU has centralized competition law, policy and courts,
it simultaneously maintains nationally distinct competition laws for member states that
maintain distinct national competition agencies. This chapter focuses on the evolution of
competition law in the EU and its earlier incarnations.

This chapter examines the complex historical foundations and evolution of competition
laws across Europe to the present regulatory environment and its impact on marketing
practices. EU competition law is important for several reasons. The EU is a major trading
area and companies based outside the EU but operating within its borders will be subject to
its competition laws, where the risk of violating competition law in the EU by businesses
is perceived to be greater than any other region of the world (Hylton and Deng, 2007).
The EU also has an established tradition of investigating market abuses; although not
as established as antitrust prosecutions in the US, which have been undertaken for over
a century, investigations have nevertheless been taking place since the late 1950s. Finally,

some countries have looked to the EU model of competition law when creating their own regulatory bodies and laws governing competition (Gerber, 1999a). Competition law should also be a topic of interest to marketers in Europe. Much marketing management work places marketers in boundary-spanning roles (Wilkie and Moore, 1999) and managers may lack awareness or unknowingly breach the law pursuing firms' objectives (Bush and Gelb, 2005; LeClair, 2000). Indeed, recent studies have established a link between marketing practices and infringements of competition law in Europe (Ashton and Pressey, 2011; 2008).

This chapter dismisses the widespread myth that the foundation of competition law in the EU was simply through the importation of US antitrust laws to post-war Germany, and points to a tradition of creating laws to protect markets in Europe for over two millennia. We also note that, while marketing scholarship in the US has an established tradition of evaluating the impact of antitrust laws on marketing practices that can be traced to the first marketing journals published in the 1930s, there was no parallel tradition in Europe, which largely continues to this day. We question why this might be the case, particularly when, as we shall see, certain marketing practices have infringed competition laws from thirteenth-century England to contemporary prosecutions of price-fixing cartels.

This chapter is organized in the following way. After this introduction we briefly examine the historical background to competition law in Europe from ancient Rome to late nineteenth-century Austria. Next, we look at the evolution of competition law between the two world wars (1918–45). We then examine the period between 1945 and 1957, which witnessed the introduction of the European Economic Community in 1957, and the introduction of standard competition laws regulating competition among the participating nations. Next, we look at the period between 1958 and 1984, which saw the cautious deployment of competition law across an expanded European Community. We then examine the period from 1985 to the present and focus on the European Union's emphasis on prosecuting cartels that operate across Europe and the role that marketing managers are seen to be playing. Finally, a concluding section dispels the myth that competition law was an American import to post-war Germany that later dispersed across the EU, and questions why European marketing scholars have effectively disregarded the impact of competition laws on marketing practices whereas their American counterparts have an established history of debating the impact of antitrust laws on marketing.

A brief history of competition law in Europe: ancient Rome to late nineteenth-century Austria

Laws governing trade and competition have an ancient history among European countries. In the Roman city-state c.50 BCE, under the Lex Julia de Annona ('the emperor's law of the price of grain'), laws were enacted to control the price and distribution of corn, with fines levied on anyone interfering with trade (Wilberforce, 1966). Later, the Ius Commune ('common law') evolved in the late medieval period based on the study of Roman law and was popular in some Western European nations (Gerber, 1994). Under the Ius Commune, three precepts were outlined: (i) transactions and markets should be subject to notions of fairness, (ii) the notion of a 'just' or 'fair' price for any transaction, and finally (iii) the prohibition of monopolistic control or market manipulation (Gerber, 1998). The Ius Commune created a tradition in Europe that markets and transactions were subject to normative regulations and assessments of justice from as early as the twelfth century, as well as the notion of 'unfair competition', and continued to have a strong influence on legal systems in Continental European countries until the arrival of modern legal precepts in the nineteenth century (Piotrowski, 1933; Zimmermann, 1990).

Later, in the late third and early fourth centuries CE, the Roman Emperor Diocletian decreed that certain everyday goods should have a maximum price and any transgressors of a tariff system would be subject to the death penalty (Wilberforce, 1966), in an attempt to introduce fiscal policies in the wake of troubles across the Empire. Later, under the reign of Emperor Justinian I of the Byzantine Empire in the sixth century, a compendium of earlier Roman law was produced in an attempt to codify the legal apparatus of the time, ultimately forming the 50-volume artefact *Justinian's Digest* that would strongly influence legal education and training for centuries. Across Europe as a whole, however, trade laws failed to evolve (or at least we have limited records of laws and lawmaking during the period) after the collapse of the Western Roman Empire, leading to the period of the Dark Ages from the sixth to the thirteenth centuries, an era synonymous with economic and cultural regression. Not until the later Middle Ages and the advent of the *lex mercatoria* ('merchant law') – 'a transnational set of norms and procedural principles, established by and for commerce in (relative) autonomy from states' (Michaels, 2007, 448) – did commercial laws begin to regain popularity and importance across Europe. European economic expansion from the medieval period through trade between major centres within Europe (Carman, 2005) called for some common rules for the regulation of trade between merchants who required expedient restitution. The *lex mercatoria* represented a collection of commercial law employed by artisans across Europe enforced by merchant courts on principal trade routes and acted as a major catalyst in the expanding trade between countries. Economic expansion across Europe was fuelled by the growth of the guilds (coalitions of artisans in common trades – the trade associations of their day), improvements in educational institutions, banking systems and improvements in agricultural methods and surplus output (Carman, 2005). With economic growth, however, came a growth of market abuses of monopoly powers.

As trade increased, medieval guilds were created to protect what were nascent industry interests, and became an accepted part of the economic landscape: 'in 1180 no fewer than nineteen such adulterine, gilds [sic] were reported in London alone' (Salzman, 1914, 225). In time, however, they effectively created monopolies with shortages in craftsmen (Kopp and Landry, 1997). This was compounded by the Black Death spreading across Europe in 1348, killing a significant number of the population and its artisans (Biddle, 1995), leaving guilds and tradesmen to inflate prices (Arterburn, 1927). With the stranglehold on key markets by guilds and powerful merchants and complaints of excessive prices, regulation was introduced to curb monopolistic powers. For example, laws were introduced in England under the Statute of Labourers of 1349, to regulate prices and overcharging and delimit certain key conditions of trade (see Kopp and Landry, 1997, for an insightful discussion of early marketing and commercial regulatory measures). Also under Edward III, attempts were made to curtail the power of trade arrangements between merchants, as the statute outlined:

> we have ordained and established, that no merchant or other shall make Confederacy, Conspiracy, Coin, Imagination, or Murmur, or Evil Device in any point that may turn to the Impeachment, Disturbance, Defeating or Decay of the said Staples, or of anything that to them pertaineth, or may pertain.
>
> *(Green, 2004, 17)*

Clearly within some European countries, competition laws have a lengthy and separate history of their own. For example, drawing on England as an example, regulations designed to restrict monopoly powers predate the Norman invasion of 1066 (Wilberforce, 1966). An interesting example in this regard are the powers that King Edward the Confessor held to curb the practices of engrossing and forestalling as recorded in the Doomsday Book (Pollock and Maitland, 1898). These represented '[t]he earliest attempts in English Law to regulate trade' (Herbruck, 1929, 365), which could be traced to Anglo-Saxon laws. Engrossing and forestalling (the terms are often used interchangeably) were essentially marketing offences, and, as such, are worth briefly dwelling on here. First mentioned in the statute books of England in 1266 (Herbruck, 1929), forestalling and the related offence of engrossing refers to the act of stopping other traders on their way to market either through buying up their goods (usually foodstuffs), dissuading other traders from going to market, or else persuading others trading to artificially raise their prices, all with the motive of subsequently raising prices in the marketplace and increasing profits – a form of localized monopoly by some unscrupulous traders in medieval county markets in England (Britnell, 1987; Chisholm, 1911), and some of the earliest examples of price-fixing cartels. Related to this was the practice of regrating, where traders would procure other traders' goods for sale at the same or nearby markets (Blackstone, 1809).

Successive English monarchs introduced further regulations to curb market abuses. For example, under the reign of Henry III, laws were passed to control the prices of ale and bread in the 1200s, the Statute of Labourers was introduced under Edward III in the 1300s, as noted, while Henry VIII attempted to stabilize fluctuating prices in the wake of foreign imports in the 1500s. Henry's daughter, Elizabeth, faced with the advent of significantly expanded trade prospects through the discovery of the new world and its rich resources, reigned over a period of monopoly abuses in the late 1500s largely caused through the award of royal grants (essentially patents) to certain parties. The issue of the regulation of monopoly power would be a thorny issue under succeeding sovereigns, particularly as the tax revenues derived from them rendered them a positive phenomenon to some monarchs (Wilberforce, 1966). Some later observers were even doubtful that England would ever be free of major restraints of trade. For example, Adam Smith (1776 [2001], 614) observed:

> To expect indeed that freedom of trade should ever be entirely restored in Great Britain is as absurd as to expect that Oceana or Utopia should ever be established in it. Not only the prejudices of the public, but what is much more unconquerable, the private interests of many individuals, irresistibly oppose it.

Returning to the context of early regulation across other parts of Europe, numerous countries can point to examples of early legislation designed to reduce monopoly power. For example, in late thirteenth-century Bohemia, under Wenceslas II, the *constitutiones juris metallici* was introduced to curb the monopoly power of traders of ore, while in the sixteenth-century Holy Roman Empire under the reign of Charles V, legislation was introduced to avert commercial losses to monopoly powers, and in fourteenth-century Florence edicts eschewing certain monopolies were put in place.

These early contributions to competition law aside, as competition began to create considerable wealth and taxation revenues in Europe, towards the close of the nineteenth century attitudes towards the protection of market competition began to take hold in a way that had not previously been present in European consciousness. While a US conception of antitrust was being introduced in the form of the Sherman Act (1890), and later the Clayton Act (1914), in order to curb the influence of major American corporations, in Europe at the end of the nineteenth century, Austria with its liberal politics, administrative systems and intellectual tradition emerged as an important catalyst for subsequent European competition laws. Although its role in European competition laws has been largely overlooked by legal scholars (Gerber, 1998), Austria in the 1890s set the agenda for modern competition laws and thinking about market regulation. Although to some the setting of Austria as a major spur to modern EU competition law might seem surprising, in the late nineteenth century, much of Europe's intelligentsia were based in Austria. This included Sigmund Freud, Arnold Schoenberg, Gustav Mahler, Eugen Böhm-Bawerk, Carl Menger and Ludwig Wittgenstein, who were shaping European thinking about music, the human psyche, economics, philosophy and market control (Gerber, 1998). Vienna – as the capital of the Austro-Hungarian Empire – was a 'bastion of tradition [that] could also be a forcing-house for modernity' (Emmerson, 2013, 102), but also 'unique in Europe for its aesthetic cultivation, personal refinement and psychological sensitivity' (Schorske, 1980, 298).

The rise of European competition law standards in Austria can be attributed to its tradition of liberalism and mechanisms of economic control combined with 'new and creative thinking about the uses of law' (Gerber, 1998, 43). Following a series of resounding military defeats (to France in 1859 and then to Prussia in 1866), a parliamentary democracy was ushered in with a liberal leadership that witnessed a decline in the power of Emperor Franz Joseph. Considerable economic growth followed in the seven years between the defeat at the hands of Prussia and 1873 when a crippling economic depression took hold. The broad public consensus held that the liberal leadership had allowed unfettered competition – the source of their economic melancholy. The view that 'unrestrained competition was folly' (Gerber, 1998, 49), and had resulted in the devastating depression of the 1870s, led to key changes to legislation in the last decade of the nineteenth century.

Liberal Austrian scholars began to explore the notion of using the law to administer the process of competition (Gerber, 1998). Under legal scholars such as Adolf Menzel new competition laws were designed chiefly to curb the power of industrial cartels who could artificially raise prices to customers (the only country in Europe at that time to have such legislation). Policy-makers were particularly conscious of the experiences of the US where 'whole branches of industry and commerce have been monopolized' (Menzel, 1895, 44, in Gerber, 1998, 56), and feared the same problems taking root in the Austrian economy. The new competition laws proposed in the late 1890s were presented as a fundamental political problem for society to tackle, and a new administrative office was proposed to oversee cartel activity and compel firms to release commercial data (such as pricing data) that could be collated in order to understand the influence of individual cartels and the potential harm they might be causing. It was argued that some cartels might be permitted to continue provided they caused no tangible public harm. Political factions within the Austrian parliament could not agree on the legislation, despite multiple attempts to introduce a cartel law by the government, and the law was never enacted. Legal scholars in Austria had proposed a radically new way of thinking about market regulation, and despite these failures to provide a new legal and administrative approach to regulate the Austrian economy, the ideas put forward at this time were to become 'the original core of the European competition law tradition' (Gerber, 1998, 43). A counterpoint to this thinking is looking at how market regulation was viewed in other parts of Europe at the time. One such example is Germany. It is interesting to note that Austria's neighbour was actually enthusiastic about the existence of cartels. The German Imperial Court made the following ruling in 1897:

> If prices continue to remain so low that economic ruin threatens entrepreneurs, their union [industry cartels] appears not merely as a rightful exercise of self-preservation, but rather as a measure of serving the interests of the whole as well.
>
> *(Fear, 1996, 9, in Wells, 2002, 5)*

As a final comment, it is important to note that the evolution of modern European competition laws in the late nineteenth century paralleled those introduced in the United States at approximately the same time; but US antitrust norms had less of an influence on European competition law thinking than is commonly believed (Gerber, 1998). This belief can largely be attributed to the perceived wisdom around the framing of European competition law principles in the 1950s, as we shall see later. In case of point, the reverse may actually be argued. In the US in 1911, Chief Justice White drew parallels between the Sherman Act and sixteenth-century English common laws on 'engrossing' (the acquisition of significant quantities of certain goods in order to raise prices) and other restraints of trade in presiding over the landmark case of *Standard Oil of New Jersey v. United States* (1911), in which the Supreme Court distinguished between 'reasonable' and 'unreasonable' restraints of trade, later expanded upon in the Clayton and Federal Trade Commission Acts (1914) (Freyer, 1992). It is certainly the case that US antitrust laws did influence later thinking on competition laws in Europe but to a limited extent in the early twentieth century. For example, while Austrian legal scholars were fully aware of the experiences of policy-makers in the US, the US antitrust law model was rejected on the basis of its perceived inflexibility and unwieldy nature due to its dependence on the normal court system, which was viewed as ineffective in dealing with the problems of powerful trusts (Gerber, 1998).

While Europe at this time may well have been a continent amidst an 'era of new strategies' (Hobsbawm, 1987, 99, in Gerber, 1998, 63) and thinking concerning social and economic problems, the onset of hostilities with the outbreak of the First World War in 1914 saw the regulation of markets and potential corporate abuses become a distant second to war efforts across Europe.

Competition policy between the World Wars (1918–1945): the seeds of European competition law

After hostilities had ceased in 1918, competition law began to permeate peacetime Europe, with a particular focus on curbing cartels. It was Germany, more than Austria, however, that took over the mantle of progressive thinking regarding competition law. Where Austrian legislators had failed to usher in a general law to restrict the monopoly powers of price-fixing cartels in the 1890s, Germany introduced a cartel law in 1923 – the first European country to do so. Post-war Germany would become a focal point for European policy-makers for its reformist competition laws. The German attempt to control cartels, including the creation of a 'Cartel Court', however, has largely been viewed as ineffective in curbing cartels, and its powers were significantly reduced in the wake of adverse market conditions in 1929 (Gerber, 1998).

Undoubtedly the greatest (and largely) unregulated practice between the world wars was the proliferation of international cartels – agreements between firms to fix prices, allocate markets, regulate production and share commercial information – that restrain competition in markets. Although international cartels had certainly existed prior to 1914, during wartime in countries such as Germany where they became a tool of government in controlling industrial production; immediately after the war cartels were useful to countries in restoring their economies. Market conditions across Europe also encouraged collusive behaviours between firms of all European nations and governments frequently supported these practices, or at least accepted their necessity. Over-supply in certain key markets (such as steel), deflation and the destabilization of currencies, encouraged exporting firms to collaborate in practices such as market-sharing agreements that would 'impose order on their industries and to insulate themselves, as much as possible, from the risks of operating in a disturbed world' (Wells, 2002, 9). For example, an estimated 3,000 cartels were in operation in Germany alone at the end of the 1920s (Gerber, 1998, 141). The global depression at the end of the 1920s fortified the need for industry leaders to control markets and inure themselves to the harsh economic realities they faced. Against this background, many political leaders across Europe believed that cartels were a progressive method of economic organization, thus leaving market regulation in Europe largely in the hands of business interests.

Hence, at the onset of the Great Depression of 1929 that led to a global depression lasting well into the 1930s, European countries had very little appetite for competition law. Indeed, '[i]nternational cartels filled part of the vacuum left by government inaction' (Wells, 2002, 9). This was aided by commentators in academia and members of government who felt that cartels helped limit 'destructive' competition; politicians, scholars and business leaders were largely sympathetic to international cartels, believing that that such partnerships among European firms of differing nationalities who were traditional competitors would actually help sustain peace with such interwoven economic interests. For example, in his book *The United States of Europe*, Édouard Herriot (1930, 169–70) commented that '[t]he [international] cartel is a sign of progress, uniting national economies that were previously hostile'. Indeed, when a number of inefficient British steel manufacturers joined an international steel cartel in 1935, British Prime Minister Stanley Baldwin commented that 'I make bold to say that in four or five years the [British] steel industry will be second to no steel industry in the whole world' (Hexner, 1946, 243). Many others concurred with this affirmative view of cartels:

> [International cartels] are expected to help bridge over the enmities created or inflamed by the War or at least to mitigate their disastrous influence upon the economy of the different nations and on the world economic order.
>
> *(Liefmann, 1932, 153)*

> It is a striking fact that public opinion, which had in pre-war times in many countries been hostile to the exploitation of monopolistic power by cartels, now become almost all over Europe rather unanimous in acknowledging cartels as unavoidable, or even necessary, outcomes of modern economic development.
>
> *(Pribram, 1937, 5)*

As a consequence of the environmental factors outlined above, between the First and Second World Wars, most governments endorsed cartel proliferation, leading to their general acceptance, in response to fears of 'destructive competition' (Wells, 2002). For example, when the League of Nations organized the World Economic Conference in 1927, the meeting held in Geneva explored both the pros and cons of cartels and global economic issues and suggested a number of policy solutions. Their final report concluded that in some industries (under certain economic conditions) cartels might be advantageous, ensuring that dramatic fluctuations did not occur in production and helping maintain price stability. Some international cartels were even created by governments themselves, in markets such as rubber and sugar (Hexner, 1946). The prevailing view recognized that, while cartels might harm individual consumers, they had a positive influence in stabilizing international economic conditions by encouraging cooperation between business concerns and thus encouraging European and world peace. Given the modern view of competition law in Europe such views might seem surprising; however, as Gerber (1998, 160) notes, '[l]ess than a decade after the horrors of the First World War, this idea had considerable force'.

It is interesting to briefly reflect on the purpose of marketing in such highly self-regulated industries where competition is effectively suspended. In such circumstances the marketing concept becomes practically redundant, particularly if powerful business interests – in major commodity markets (such as steel) – create cartels that decide which markets to allocate to manufacturers and other conditions of trade such as prices. It is important to note, however, that cartels did not proliferate in all areas of the European economy. In some industries – e.g. the markets for consumer goods products such as confectionary, soap and cigarettes – marketing played a pivotal role in creating and promoting distinct brands to consumers in an attempt to foster customer loyalty (Wells, 2002). In industries where cartels did operate across Europe, marketing efforts between firms could often be merged and rationalized to reduce costs, as was the case for one sub-cartel in the market for steel, which managed the market for steel rails prior to the Second World War (Wells, 2002).

At the outbreak of hostilities in 1939, international cartels were a prolific force in the global economy (Wells, 2002). During the Second World War antitrust prosecution largely stalled in Europe and the US as governments heavily regulated domestic markets in terms of production and prices as part of the war effort, but towards the end of hostilities European governments and Washington began to concern themselves with peacetime political and economic issues. Considerable optimism towards curbing abuses by large corporate interests in the post-war world took hold in ways that it had not previously. The experiences of the war had demonstrated to policy-makers that governments could effectively regulate markets (Gerber, 1998). Post-war economic harmony would help maintain peace and avoid costly conflicts to both economy and society experienced in the global conflicts in the first 50 years of the twentieth century. The assessment that international cartels could be a force for economic good in stabilizing volatile market conditions and encouraging political and economic harmony between the wars was now considered faulty and injurious to society. Indeed, the considerable growth in economic and military power afforded to Germany between the wars was believed to have been facilitated in part by the participation of its companies in international cartels, as Borkin and Welsh (1943, 14) observed: 'during the past twenty years, this cartel device has been the first line of German assault'. Not only had international cartels assisted Hitler's preparations for war, they had artificially raised prices and limited employment and output. In short, they had prevented the global economy from fully realizing its economic potential.

Although some commentators and business leaders still believed that cartels could be a post-war force for good, such views were beginning to look anachronistic at the end of hostilities. The vision of Europe at peace with its political and economic machinery would clearly take a very different turn, and one that eschewed monopoly powers, perhaps best captured by Henry Wallace, Vice President of the US, who maintained that '[t]he international monopolists should be conspicuous by their absence at the peace table' (Wallace, 1943, 754). Views of economic governance, particularly cartels, had taken a dramatic turn with the inter-war experience of cartels and monopolies and the rise of the Nazi war machine; clearly a Europe at peace would have to tackle monopoly power and 'big business'. Indeed, an article in the *New Republic* in 1944 reflected this necessity: 'when we have finally achieved victory, we shall still have to face the big Corporate International of cartels' (1944, 199–200, in Wells, 2002, 91). Attitudes towards market regulation across Europe had reversed, and the inter-war period in Europe had witnessed the slow development of a shared set of basic ideas concerning the regulation of competition (Gerber, 1998) that would result in a 'model' of competition law in the post-war period that would administratively control the harmful conduct of powerful (and dominant) companies (or the 'abuse' model of competition), in contrast to the American 'prohibition' model where issues of monopolization are prominent (Gerber, 1999b).

This period witnessed the emergence of dedicated marketing journals with the two forerunners to the *Journal of Marketing* (*JM*) – the *American Marketing Journal* (*AMJ*) and the *National Marketing Review* (*NMR*), published from 1934 until 1936, ultimately combining to form the *JM* in 1936; these collectively provide an interesting barometer as to the consideration of antitrust in early marketing scholarship. A wealth of papers dealing with key antitrust legislation in the form of the Sherman Act, Robinson-Patman Act and Clayton Act, as well as other related regulatory issues are evident in the early volumes of the *AMJ* and *JM*. Public policy matters were an early pressing issue for marketing scholars (Savitt, 2011; Witkowski, 2010); throughout the mid-1930s and early 1940s, American scholars engaged on issues related to antitrust and the regulation of competition in the *AMJ* and *JM* (see e.g. Compton, 1934; Haney, 1934; Brand, 1935; James, 1935; Engle, 1936; Stevens, 1937; Bain, 1941; Grether, 1944). This record strongly suggests that American scholars were highly conversant with antitrust laws concerning a variety of practices such as antitrust and fair trade practices (Compton, 1934), price discrimination (Stevens, 1937), collusive agreements between firms (Bain, 1941), and price controls and monopoly powers (Grether, 1944), among many other issues. Evidently scholars – and many practitioners – comprehended that certain marketing practices might act as restraints of trade (such as collusive agreements like price-fixing between firms) and were strongly prohibited in the public interest. Wilson Compton's article on fair trade and marketing in the first volume, second issue, of the *American Marketing Journal* perhaps sums this up best:

> It is not mere moralizing to say not only that business must accept the public interest as a decisive factor, but also that it must be content with profits which are earned and which are not taken away from somebody else. Therein is the essence of fair trade practice as we hope it will be manifested in the new economic age. [We need the] ... development of a deliberate spirit and purpose of commercial honor and the education of a new understanding of business as essentially an enterprise in public service.
>
> *(Compton, 1934, 87, 90)*

The *JM* incorporated a 'Legal Developments in Marketing' section that ran for a number of decades in various guises, which often included reference to court rulings on antitrust cases of the day that carried implications for marketing practice, as well as scholarly articles dealing with the intersection between antitrust laws and marketing, indicating that consideration of the antitrust laws and marketing was thriving in the US. Sadly, we have no European equivalent consideration of competition laws (e.g. the *European Journal of Marketing* was launched in 1967, and to date is yet to publish a meaningful contribution on competition law and marketing practices), nor can we find European scholars dealing with substantive issues of competition law in the *AMJ*, *NMR* or *JM*. But our brief evaluation of US colleagues' views suggests that American scholars were much more engaged with issues of antitrust and marketing practices than their European counterparts during this period (and indeed since).

1945–1957: the aftermath of the war and the Treaty of Rome – the road to reform and European harmonization

The post-war world was one in need of reconstruction on many fronts, and many of the necessary wartime provisions, such as the creation of powerful industry advisory committees in the US, had to be reflected upon in the light of the antitrust laws. Although in the US, during the war, industry committees had played an important role in advising government departments on allocating supply and prices, the proliferation of trade associations after the conflict had the capacity of being 'potentially embarrassed under the antitrust laws', as Ernest S. Meyers writing in the *JM* observed (Meyers, 1948, 379), particularly if they fixed prices or engaged in other restraints of trade. Meyers was not isolated in framing marketing practices against antitrust laws; a post-war reflection on marketing practices and antitrust continued well into the 1950s and 1960s in the pages of the *JM* (see e.g. Edwards, 1950; Barrett *et al.*, 1954; Buggie, 1962; Manischewitz and Stuart, 1962). Concerns by agencies such as the Federal Trade Commission related to the concentration of economic power and potentially injurious monopoly power, or 'bigness and the regulation of marketing' (Edwards, 1950, 190). Clearly US scholars understood the importance of avoiding practices that were injurious to competition such as price-fixing, the allocation of business and customers, and selling below cost to drive out competitors in the post-war economy, and were clear on certain illegalities that are not reflected in European marketing scholarship. While American scholars and policy-makers were reminding themselves of the antitrust laws and business practices that regulated pre-war commerce, however, Europe was only beginning to embrace similar ideals.

As hostilities ceased in 1945, the Allied powers turned their attention to administrative and political controls in Europe, particularly in occupied Germany, with a vision of the continent at peace. Competition laws and provisions played a significant role in these reforms. There was a gradual reduction in trade barriers, beginning under the Treaty of Paris in 1951, with the formation of the European Coal and Steel Community (ECSC) – the forerunner to the modern EU and the origins of EU competition law – which removed trade barriers in the markets for steel, iron and coal, between France, Germany, Italy and the Benelux countries (Belgium, the Netherlands, and Luxemburg). Conceived in the hope that this would prevent powerful cartels emerging in these markets, particularly by German companies, some sceptical American policy-makers and members of the government, however, feared that without the inclusion of antitrust provisions the ECSC would simply be 'a clever cover for a gigantic European cartel for coal and steel producers' (Acheson, 1969, 383–4). The French policy-maker Jean Monnet, who was central to the drafting of the ECSC accord, invited American economist and former member of the State Department Raymond Vernon to insert text into the ECSC agreement that would strongly prohibit cartels and assuage fears in Washington. The involvement of Vernon in the framing of the ECSC rules of trade is probably responsible for the myth that competition law was imported wholesale to Europe by the Americans by way of Germany in the aftermath of the Second World War (Gerber, 1999b). Consequently the ECSC anti-cartel agreement represented 'Europe's first strong anti-cartel law' (Duchene, 1994), and was essentially framed by way of Washington. Although prior to the 1950s, attitudes to cartels in Europe and particularly Germany had been somewhat ambivalent, 'after 1950, it was part of an idealistic and generally popular program to build a united Europe and overcome the continent's sad history of war' (Wells, 2002, 174), by seeing their eradication.

The dissemination of competition laws across Europe was strongly facilitated by the middle of the decade, where under the Treaty of Rome in 1957, six European countries agreed to abolish trade barriers between themselves, which created the supranational institution the European Economic Community (EEC). Competition law was introduced as part of the treaty to regulate trade between the member countries, and designed to encourage peace across Europe and counter the significant power of American firms. The EEC's first president, Walter Hallstein, commented that the goal of 'the transformation of the market relations in the European Community as a whole was to build a new giant big enough in a world of giant powers' (Freyer, 2006, 282). Clearly this giant would need to operate against a system of fair and firm rules that regulated trade not only between member countries but also provided rules of competition for the foreign firms accessing European markets that would address restrictive practices and cartels, and market abuses by dominant firms. Article 3(1)(g) of the Treaty of Rome formed one of the central precepts of the EEC agreement through the creation of 'a system ensuring that competition in the internal market is not distorted' (Buch-Hansen and Wiger, 2010, 28).

Articles 81 and 82 of the Treaty of Rome (numbered as Articles 85 and 86 under the treaty, but later renumbered under the Treaty of Amsterdam in 1997), were introduced to provide a framework for market regulation between member states that essentially provided the 'Rules of Competition' (Buch-Hansen and Wiger, 2010, 28), which could be enforced through the European Court of Justice (ECJ). The first of these, Article 81, akin to the American Sherman Act (1890), relates to vertical restraints and cartels, which prohibits:

> all agreements between undertakings, decisions by associations of undertakings and concerted practices which may affect trade between Member States and which have as their object or effect the prevention, restriction or distortion of competition within the common market …
>
> *(European Commission, 2015)*

This Article strongly prohibits practices such as market sharing and price-fixing as 'hard core' offences. Article 82 relates to monopolies and market abuses by dominant actors, including exclusive dealing and price discrimination, reminiscent of the Clayton Act (1914) in the US. Article 82 also regulates mergers and acquisitions between firms that are deleterious to trade within EEC member states. Under the provisions outlined in the Treaty of Rome, marketers should have understood that price-fixing and other restraints of trade were now strongly prohibited practices across the EEC. The apparatus to prosecute firms, however, was significantly underfunded.

While competition laws regulating trade in European countries predate the activities in the aftermath of 1945 as demonstrated, the US played a peerless supporting role in post-Second World War market regulation not just in Europe but globally. In addition to the involvement of influential figures such as Raymond Vernon in the ECSC, for example, other US mechanisms (such as aid under the Marshall Plan that included prohibitions on international cartels) were beginning to lead to a post-war consensus on the terms of trade emerging to some extent between the US, Europe and Japan. As Wells (2002, 205) observes:

> Without American encouragement and example, officials abroad probably would not even have thought to restrict cartels, and business, left to its own devices, no doubt would have continued to rely on them.

1958–1984: the cautious deployment of competition law across the EC

On 19 March 1958, the first EEC Parliamentary Assembly took place, and attention across Europe's capitals turned from post-war reconstruction to economic growth as Europe witnessed a period of growth and stability continuing until the early 1970s. Described subsequently as the 'Golden Age' of the world economy (Hobsbawm, 1994), manufacturing output doubled during this period (Gerber, 1998). Despite the competition law articles set out under the Treaty of Rome in 1957, competition law enforcement across the EEC was at an embryonic phase and officials often lacked experience and rarely adopted a proactive role (Buch-Hansen and Wiger, 2010). Against this period of economic expansion, the EEC was also sympathetic to much of domestic European industry throughout the 1960s and 1970s as it faced powerful competition from American and Japanese firms, affording favoured treatment to some sectors.

The 'crisis years', from the initial oil shock experienced in 1973 to a global recession that lasted well into the 1980s, witnessed recession across Europe (as well as economic crises across much of the world with declining production levels and rising unemployment) and a partial hiatus to the enforcement of competition laws within the EU. 'Crises cartels' in certain industries such as sugar, textiles, motorcars, shipbuilding, as well as coal and steel, were even tolerated in the EU, as attempts were made by business leaders to curb production surpluses and avoid ruinous competition (Tsoukalis and da Silva Ferreira, 1980), while government subsidies to industries in dire circumstances were frequently accepted. During this period many breaches of EU competition law were overlooked and even tolerated by the authorities, as Buch-Hansen and Wiger (2010, 31) note:

> Despite the large-scale tide of restrictive agreements, concentrations, and protectionist national subsidies, the [European] Commission repeatedly ignored significant breaches of EC competition law that risked being politically controversial, and focussed on relatively minor matters instead.

This is not to suggest that the economic recession resulted in a complete cessation of competition law prosecution across Europe. A series of major cases were heard during this period across a diverse range of markets which saw the European Court of Justice (ECJ) become bolder in cases of market abuse including *Continental Can* (1973), *Commercial Solvents* (1973), *United Brands* (1978), *Hoffman-La Roche* (1979) and *Michelin* (1983).

In *Continental Can v Commission*, the ECJ had to decide whether a corporate acquisition of a competitor could constitute an abuse under Article 82, where the merger would effectively see one company (Continental Can) eliminate a competitor. The Court ruled that Continental Can had abused their dominant market position, a significant ruling as it demonstrated that under Article 82 the Court could not only inhibit practices where organizations wielded market power that constituted a market abuse but also where companies took steps to increase their market power. The case also demonstrated that Article 82 was not only able to target practices where consumers were damaged directly, but also instances where changes in competitive structure could be detrimental to consumers. In *Commercial Solvents v Commission*, the Court took a similar line to the *Continental Can* case, where it ruled that the US firm Commercial Solvents through its dominant position had caused a market abuse by its refusal to supply a key raw ingredient to a competitor, which was subsequently unable to compete effectively under Article 82 of EU law. This latter case demonstrated that the Court was concerned with consumer welfare caused by the removal of a competitor from the market.

In the case *United Brands v Commission* (1978), the ECJ determined that the US firm United Brands Company (UBC), which held a dominant position in the European market for bananas, had abused its dominant position by imposing a variety of conditions on European wholesalers, including obliging them to refrain from stocking bananas that were not branded by UBC and restricting them in supplying certain customers. The Court ruled that the practices by United Brands damaged consumer welfare since it limited competition in the market and allowed UCB to charge 'excessive' prices.

Hoffman-La Roche v Commission (1979) represented a landmark case in that the pharmaceutical company Hoffman-La Roche was deemed to have abused its dominant market position under Article 82 through undertaking exclusive purchasing agreements with its largest buyers in return for a loyalty rebate (so-called 'fidelity rebates'). The ECJ ruled that the purchasing agreement had afforded Hoffman-La Roche the ability to raise prices in the future through driving competitors out of the market.

In *Michelin v Commission* (1983), the ECJ looked into the practices of the tyre manufacturer Michelin, which held a dominant position in the European market for new replacement tyres for heavy vehicles. Michelin granted its major customers a variable discount in return for meeting annual sales targets (although Michelin did not employ an exclusive purchasing agreements as in the case of Hoffman-La Roche). The ECJ ruled that under Article 82 the loyalty rebate scheme had restricted buyer freedom to select their preferred source of supply and limited access to the market from competitors.

Competition law was also firmly back on the agenda within some European countries during this period. For example, the UK introduced its first competition law in 1948. The Monopolies and Restrictive Practices (Inquiry and Control) Act 1948, which was initially somewhat lacking in legislative 'bite' (owing to apprehensions by policy-makers about 'meddling' too severely in monopoly and restrictive practices about which little was known), would ultimately in time yield 'a formidable and complex competition law system' (Gerber, 1998, 215). Under the Act, the Monopolies and Restrictive Practices Commission (which reported to the President of the Board of Trade) was given powers to investigate markets where a powerful supplier (monopoly) or a powerful buyer (monopsony) operated against the 'public interest'. Hence, the new law and its regulatory body initially adopted an educational role following an administrative system of competition law (in contrast to the US system), that surprised some business leaders in its thinking. As Allen (1968, 84–85, in Gerber, 1998, 216) observed:

> the businessmen who appeared before the commission, at any rate in the early days, expressed surprise and indignation that their practices should be scrutinized, let alone condemned as pernicious. 'Why', asked typical witnesses before the commission, should a firm or group of firms be adversely criticized for practices which were common to a great part of industry and had been actively encouraged by the Government a short time ago?

The earliest investigations of the Monopolies and Restrictive Practices Commission (although admittedly few in number initially) identified certain restrictive practices that were viewed as endemic in British industries, including group boycotts and collective discrimination (Gerber, 1998). Research has also demonstrated that certain marketing practices were linked to all major areas of market abuses beginning in the 1950s. For example, Ashton and Pressey (2008) linked problematic marketing practices to a compendium of illegal market abuses including excessive prices, price discrimination, predation, illegal discounts, vertical restraints and refusal to supply. The UK experience, as in many other European countries as well as the EC itself, set competition law adoption and understanding on an upward trajectory that would yield an effectual system of competition law over time.

By the early 1980s, in addition to centralized EU competition laws, most European nation states had competition laws in place; as Kingman Brewster wryly observed in an update of his 1958 study: 'America no longer has a monopoly on antitrust' (Atwood and Brewster, 1981, 4). Given, however, the major economic problems that European countries had faced in the previous decade, EU-wide competition law and powers had been wielded cautiously. A return to economic growth experienced in the EU in the 1980s would witness a change in competition law priorities and enforcement; as the following section demonstrates, this led to a focus on the pursuit of price-fixing cartels across the EU that had previously operated largely unfettered.

1985–present: cartel 'busting' in the EU and the role of marketing managers

Although, as Wells (2002, 5) notes, 'collusion among businesses is no doubt as old as trade itself', it is only relatively recently in the EU that the prohibition of cartels has been undertaken with such apparent zeal. Indeed, since the mid-1980s, the detection and prosecution of international cartels has formed the most pressing regulatory issue of the EU. This unprecedented targeting of cartels is in stark contrast to the earlier stance of leniency and even support of many cartels operating in Europe (Buch-Hansen and Wiger, 2010).

The EU currently pursues 'a blanket prohibition on vertical agreements that restrict competition' (Lafontaine and Slade, 2005, 11), which refers to an agreement between two or more independent firms who collude to control the terms of business in a particular market (Dick, 1996), such as price-fixing, allocating customers and markets, and sharing sensitive commercial information. The anti-cartel stance presented in the EU is one of the strongest in the world, as former Competition Commissioner for the EU Mario Monti observed: 'Cartels are cancers on the open market economy, which forms the very basis of our [European] Community. By destroying competition they cause serious harm to our economies and consumers' (Monti, 2001, 14).

In an attempt to reveal greater numbers of cartels operating across the EU a Leniency Notice was introduced in 1996, and subsequently revised in 2002 and 2006, based on game theoretical principles (i.e. the prisoners' dilemma model). This encouraged companies to divulge collusive behaviour, by offering a sliding scale of fines based on the order in which actors divulged their involvement in a cartel and provided evidence against partners; the greatest incentive is provided for the first company to come forward for they frequently receive no fine in return for disclosing wrongdoing – an initiative modelled on successful anti-cartel measures introduced earlier in the US.

Cartels 'involving secret meetings amongst rivals', regarded as 'not only the archetypical violation of antitrust law', but the 'archetypical inter-firm organization of crime' (Faulkner et al., 2003, 515), have been detected and prosecuted in the EU in markets for supplies of bananas, marine containers, vitamins and car glass, among many other industries. Since the emphasis placed on cartel detection in the EU from the mid-1980s, record fines have been handed down in the last decade (McGowan, 2010). But what, if any, has been the role of marketing managers in such illegal endeavours?

Table 15.1 Marketing and sales manager involvement in European cartels by industry: 1990–2009

Year	Case
2009	Marine hoses
2008	Banana suppliers, paraffin/candle waxes
2007	Flat glass, professional videotape producers
2006	Synthetic/butadiene rubber, copper fittings, methacrylates/acrylic glass, hydrogen peroxide
2005	Rubber chemicals, industrial bags, monochloroacetic acid
2004	Choline chloride, needles, copper plumbing tubes
2003	Industrial copper tubes, organic peroxide, sorbates
2002	Speciality graphite, methyglucamine, plasterboard, fine art auction houses, methionine
2001	Zinc phosphate, citric acid, vitamins, graphite electrodes
2000	Amino acids
1999	Seamless steel tubes
1994	Marine containers, cartonboard, PVC, cement

Source: Ashton and Pressey (2012)

In a content analysis of 56 international cartels detected by the European Union (EU) competition law agency (the Directorate General for Competition) between 1990 and 2009, Ashton and Pressey (2012) find evidence of marketing and sales managers participating in just under half (approximately 43 per cent) of cartels operating in Europe during the period on behalf of their firms, and in numerous major markets (see Table 15.1). Interestingly, marketing and sales managers are rarely the most senior managers within these conspiracies, intimating that such middle managers are being metaphorically 'thrown under the bus', as corporations and senior managers divert attention from the firms' and senior managers' failings (Robson, 2010). Research examining how cartel offences are presented in the media, reveals this organizational practice, where firms' attribute blame to middle managers and imply these employees have a lower morality than senior staff, is not uncommon (Siltaoja and Vehkaperä, 2010).

While successfully prosecuted cartel cases involving sales and marketing managers remained relatively few in the 1990s as Table 15.1 illustrates, such cases have risen considerably since the early 2000s. The practices of sales and marketing managers in these cases has been to demonstrably collude with competitors to exchange sensitive commercial information related to sales, agree to fix prices and share customers and markets across the EU and sometimes globally, not just involving firms based in the EU but also between corporate allies in Japan, North America and the EU (Ashton and Pressey, 2012). While the detection rate of international price-fixing cartels and the involvement of marketing executives continues to rise, the scale of cartel fines has also witnessed a dramatic increase in the last decade (Buch-Hansen and Wiger, 2010).

Although international cartels have constituted a major focus of the EU in recent years, other important competition law cases have been heard. For example, in the major case *British Airways v Commission* (2003), the Court of First Instance (CFI) found that British Airways' marketing agreements under its rewards scheme chiefly to major travel agents (who in addition to receiving a sales commission would also receive a payment in return for achieving a certain volume of sales, essentially fidelity rebates), constituted a restriction of competition by limiting key market intermediaries (i.e. travel agents) by preventing customers to attain supplies from rival companies under Article 82.

From the emergence of a modern European competition law beginning at the end of World War II, by the 2000s, the prevailing view of global regulatory power and jurisdictions estimates that currently in the EU '...for large enterprises "antitrust risk" – the risk of violating some competition law provision – is substantially higher in the European Union than anywhere else' (Hylton and Deng, 2007, 314–315); Prometheus has never been so well protected.

Conclusions

As we have seen, European competition law was not simply a US import to post-war Germany that later permeated Europe under the expansion of the EEC and EU. Such views are overly-simplistic and faulty. While European competition laws have undoubtedly benefitted from input from the US and its system of antitrust, competition law and market regulation in Europe has a lengthy history, with its origins in ancient Rome, the establishment of some common trade laws across Europe in the Middle Ages, as well as ancient laws in countries such as England designed to curb the practices of engrossing and forestalling in medieval marketplaces, that can then be traced over subsequent centuries through to late nineteenth-century Vienna where scholars began to rethink the administration of competition laws. Why, then, has the view that European competition laws are merely an imitation of US antitrust laws gained such traction? Further, why have European marketing scholars effectively disregarded the impact of competition laws on marketing practices?

The answer to the first question perhaps lies partly in the reality that post-Second World War European countries did draw on the laws and experiences of the US when framing their competition laws, as did the Treaty of Rome (1957) with the introduction of Articles 81 and 82, which are strongly reminiscent of two important American antitrust laws in the Sherman Act (1890) and the Clayton Act (1914). But parallels to these latter laws can be found many hundreds of years earlier in medieval European countries and even ancient Rome; ultimately, Europe has its own competition law tradition (Gerber, 1999b). Just as American antitrust thinking has influenced legal concepts in European competition law, European countries have influenced American legal systems of antitrust. Writing in the *Michigan Law Review* in 1929, Wendell Herbruck observed that: 'The earliest attempts in English Law to regulate trade are to be found in the enactments against forestalling, regrating and engrossing and in them, it has been asserted, is the basis of our [US] modern legislation against monopolies and combinations in restraint of trade' (Herbruck, 1929, 365).

The answer to the second question is rooted in how modern competition laws have evolved in Europe versus the US. Competition law in the EU has an image of a 'bland one in which laws seem to be without significant political or intellectual foundations', which as a consequence is 'not a very inspiring one' (Gerber, 1999b, 18). It stems from the expansion of the EU and its administrators in Brussels, and a system that brings to mind bureaucracy and administration. In contrast, antitrust laws in the US are part of the '"American way" that tolerated big business but preserved a measure of competition among even the largest firms' (Wells, 2002, 27). The consolidation of commercial power in the US happened relatively quickly between the 1850s and the end of the nineteenth century and led to public concerns over monopoly power and influence over markets that was undemocratic. As a consequence, antitrust laws in the US can be traced to late nineteenth-century efforts by policy-makers to encourage economic freedom and emancipation, a central facet of the American story. Further, as historian Richard Hofstadter (1964 [1996], 195–6) observed:

> But in America competition was more than a theory: it was a way of life and a creed. From its colonial beginnings through most of the nineteenth century, ours was overwhelmingly a nation of farmers and small-town entrepreneurs – ambitious, mobile, optimistic, speculative, anti-authoritarian, egalitarian, and competitive.

There is no comparative tradition in Europe, where new thinking concerning competition laws grew out of new ways of market administration in 1890s Vienna, 1920s Germany and then being significantly boosted in post-war Europe as part of the creation of a new agenda for competition. The US antitrust history of 'trust-busting' and economic freedom, and redress through the courts for certain prohibited acts, is a much richer story in comparison to the administration of competition law on market abuses by committee in Brussels. Hence, commentary on the antitrust laws in the US by marketing scholars contributes to an established discourse on economic freedom and democracy, whereas in Europe it contributes to a debate on administration, bureaucracy and Brussels. The growing recent evidence demonstrating that certain marketing practices may be strongly linked to some aspects of market abuse (see e.g. Ashton and Pressey, 2012, 2008, 2011) may provide some stimulus for future interest.

References

Acheson, D. (1969) *Present at the Creation: My Years in the State Department*, Norton, New York.

Arterburn, N.F. (1927) 'The origin and first test of public callings', *University of Pennsylvania Law Review*, 75/5, 411–28.

Ashton, J.K., and Pressey, A.D. (2008) 'The regulatory perception of the arketing function: An interpretation of UK competition authority investigations 1950–2005', *Journal of Public Policy and Marketing*, 27/2, 156–64.

Ashton, J.K., and Pressey, A.D. (2011) 'The regulatory challenge to branding: An interpretation of UK competition authority investigations 1950–2007', *Journal of Marketing Management*, 27/9–10, 1027–58.

Ashton, J.K., and Pressey, A.D. (2012) *Who Manages Cartels? The Role of Sales and Marketing Managers within International Cartels: Evidence from the European Union 1990–2009*, Centre for Competition Policy, Working Paper, 12–11, Centre for Competition Policy, University of East Anglia, Norwich,

Atwood, J.R., and Brewster, K. (1981) *Antitrust and American Business Abroad* (2nd edn), vol. 1, McGraw Hill, Colorado Springs, CO.

Bain, J.S. (1941) 'The Sherman Act and "the bottlenecks of business"', *Journal of Marketing*, 5/3, 254–58.

Barrett, E.W., Boyd, H.W., Forbush, D.R., and Westfall, R. (1954) 'The Automatic Canteen Co. case and buyer's liability under the Robinson-Patman Act', *Journal of Marketing*, 18/3, 246–54.

Biddle, W. (1995) *A Field Guide to Germs*, Henry Holt & Co., New York.

Blackstone, W. (1809) *Commentaries on the Laws of England*, vol. 4 (15th edn), Blackstone, London.

Borkin, J., and Welsh, C.A. (1943) *Germany's Master Plan: The Story of Industrial Offensive*, Sloan & Pearce, New York.

Brand, C.J. (1935) 'A public policy as to open price plans', *American Marketing Journal*, 3/1, 84–91.

Britnell, R.H. (1987) 'Forstall, forestalling and the Statute of Forestallers', *English Historical Review*, 102, 89–102.

Buch-Hansen, H., and Wiger, A. (2010) 'Revisiting 50 years of market-making: The neoliberal transformation of European competition policy', *Review of International Political Economy*, 17/1, 20–44.

Buggie, F.D. (1962) 'Lawful discrimination in marketing', *Journal of Marketing*, 26/2, 1–8.

Bush, D., and Gelb, B.D. (2005) 'When marketing practices raise antitrust concerns', *MIT Sloan Management Review*, 46/4, 73–81.

Carman, J.M. (2005) 'The impact of trade on the rapid economic development in Western Europe, 1000 to 1200', Proceedings of the Conference on Historical Analysis and Research in Marketing, California State University Long Beach, Long Beach, CA.

Chisholm, H. (ed.) (1911) 'Engrossing', *Encyclopædia Britannica* (11th edn), Cambridge University Press, Cambridge.

Compton, W. (1934) 'Trade practices in fair competition', *American Marketing Journal*, 1/2, 85–90.

Dick, A.R. (1996) 'When are cartels stable contracts?', *Journal of Law and Economics*, 34/1, 241–83.

Duchene, F. (1994) *Jean Monnet: The First Statesman of Interdependence*, W.W. Norton & Co., London.

Edwards, C.D. (1950) 'Further comments on bigness and the regulation of marketing', *Journal of Marketing*, 15/2, 190–8.

Emmerson, C. (2013) *1913: The World Before the Great War*, Random House, London.

Engle, N.H. (1936) 'Implications of the Robinson-Patman Act for Marketing', *Journal of Marketing*, 1/2, 75–81.

European Commission (2015) Article 81 of the EC Treaty, available online: http://ec.europa.eu/competition/legislation/treaties/ec/art81_en.html (accessed June 2015).

Faulkner, R.R., Cheney, E.R., Fisher, G.A., and Baker, W.E. (2003) 'Crime by committee: Conspirators and company men in the illegal electrical industry cartel', *Criminology*, 41/2, 511–54.

Freyer, T. (1992) *Regulating Big Business: Antitrust in Great Britain and America, 1880–1920*, Cambridge University Press, Cambridge.

Freyer, T. (2006) *Antitrust and Global Capitalism, 1930–2004*, Cambridge University Press, Cambridge.

Gerber, D.J. (1994) 'The transformation of European Community competition law', *Harvard International Law Journal*, 35/1, 97–147.

Gerber, D.J. (1998) *Law and Competition in Twentieth Century Europe: Protecting Prometheus*, Oxford University Press, New York.

Gerber, D.J. (1999a) 'The U.S.–European conflict over the globalization of antitrust law: A legal experience perspective', *New England Law Review*, 34/1, 123–43.

Gerber, D.J. (1999b) 'Europe and the globalization of antitrust law', *Connecticut Journal of International Law*, 14/15, 15–25.

Green, N. (2004) 'The road to conviction: The criminalisation of cartel law', in Barry E. Hawk (ed.), *Annual Proceedings of the Fordham Corporate Law Institute Conference on International Antitrust Law and Policy*, Fordham Corporate Law Institute, New York, pp.13–28.

Grether, E.T. (1944) 'Long run postwar aspects of price control', *Journal of Marketing*, 8/3, 296–301.

Haney, L.H. (1934) 'The dangers of price fixing', *American Marketing Journal*, 1/1, 34–40.

Herbruck, W. (1929) 'Forestalling, regrating and engrossing', *Michigan Law Review*, 27/4, 365–88.

Herriot, É. (1930) *The United States of Europe*, Viking Press, New York.

Hexner, E. (1946) *International Cartels*, London: Sir Isaac Pitman & Sons, New York.

Hobsbawm, E. J. (1994) *The Age of Extremes: A History of the World, 1914–1991*, Pantheon, New York.

Hofstadter, R. (1964[1996]) *The Paranoid Style in American Politics and Other Essays*, Harvard University Press, Cambridge, MA.

Hylton, K.N., and Deng, F. (2007) 'Antitrust around the world: An empirical analysis of the scope of competition laws and their effects', *Antitrust Law Journal*, 74/2, 271–341.

James, C.C. (1935) 'The one-price policy and cut-throat competition', *American Marketing Journal*, 2/3, 193–5.

Kopp, S.W., and Landry, M. (1997) 'The tangled roots of regulation in marketing: A history of the common calling', Proceedings of the Conference on Historical Analysis and Research in Marketing, Kingston, Ontario.

Lafontaine, F., and Slade, M. (2005) 'Exclusive contracts and vertical restraints: Empirical evidence and public policy', Advances in the Economics of Competition Law conference, Rome (June).

LeClair, D.T. (2000) 'Marketing planning and the policy environment in the European Union', *International Marketing Review*, 17/3, 193–215.

Liefmann, R. (1932) *Cartels, Concerns and Trusts*, D.H. MacGregor, New York.

McGowan, L. (2010) *The Antitrust Revolution in Europe: Exploring the European Commission's Cartel Policy*, Edward Elgar, Cheltenham.

Manischewitz, D.B., and Stuart, J.A. (1962) 'Marketing under Attack', *Journal of Marketing*, 26/3, 1–6.

Meyers, E. S. (1948) 'Some observations on trade associations and the law', *Journal of Marketing*, 12/3, 379–81.

Michaels, R. (2007) 'The true lex mercatoria: Law beyond the state', *Indiana Journal of Global Legal Studies*, 14/2, 447–68.

Monti, M. (2001) 'Why should we be concerned with cartels and collusive behaviour?', in Anita Sundberg (ed.), *Fighting Cartels – Why and How?*, Swedish Competition Authority, Stockholm, pp. 14–22.

Piotrowski, R. (1933) *Cartels and Trusts: Their Origin and Historical Development from the Economic and Legal Aspects*, Porcupine Press, Philadelphia, PA..

Pollock, F., and Maitland, F. W. (1898 [1968]) *The History of English Law*, vol. 2, Cambridge University Press, London.

Pribram, K. (1937) *Cartel Problems: An Analysis of Collective Monopolies in Europe with American Application*, Hein, Buffalo, NY.

Robson, R.A. (2010) 'Crime and punishment: Rehabilitating retribution as a justification for organizational criminal activity', *American Business Law Journal*, 47/1, 109–44.

Salzman, L.F. (1914) *Henry II*, Oxford University Press, London.

Savitt, R. (2011) 'What they wrote about World War II: *The Journal of Marketing* 1939–1946', Proceedings of the Conference on Historical Analysis and Research in Marketing, New York.

Schorske, C.E. (1980) *Fin-de-Siècle Vienna: Politics and Culture*, Alfred A. Knopf, Inc., New York.

Siltaoja, M.E., and Vehkaperä, M.J. (2010) 'Constructing illegitimacy? Cartels and cartel agreements in Finnish business media from critical discursive perspective', *Journal of Business Ethics*, 92/4, 493–511.

Smith, A. (1776 [2001]) *An Enquiry into the Nature and Causes of the Wealth of Nations*, book 4, *Of Systems of Political Economy*, Electric Book Co., London.

Stevens, W.H.S. (1937) 'Federal price legislation', *Journal of Marketing*, 1/4, 326–33.

Tsoukalis, L., and da Silva Ferreira, A. (1980) 'Management of industrial surplus capacity in the European Community', *International Organization*, 34/3, 355–76.

Wallace, H.A. (1943) 'What we fight for, "Each Age Demands a New Freedom"', delivered before a meeting sponsored by the Chicago United Nations Committee to Win the Peace, Chicago, IL, 11 Sept.

Wells, W. (2002) *Antitrust and the Formation of the Postwar World*, Columbia University Press, New York.

Wilberforce, R. (1966) *The Law of Restrictive Practices and Monopolies* (2nd edn), Sweet & Maxwell, London.

Wilkie, W.L., and Moore, E.S. (1999) 'Marketing's contribution to society', *Journal of Marketing*, 63, 198–218.

Witkowski, T.H. (2010) 'The marketing discipline comes of age, 1934–1936', *Journal of Historical Research in Marketing*, 2/4, 370–96.

Zimmermann, R. (1990) *The Law of Obligations: Roman Foundations of the Civil Law Tradition*, Juta & Co., Cape Town.

Legal references

Case 6/72, *Europemballage v. Commission* [1973] ECR 215 (*Continental Can*).
Cases 6 & 7/73, *Istituto Chemioterapico Italiano S.p.A and Commercial Solvents Corp. v. Commission* [1973] ECR 357.
Case 27/76, *United Brands v. Commission* [1978] ECR 207.
Case 85/76, *Hoffman-La Roche & Co. AG v. Commission* [1979] ECR 461.
Case 322/81, *Nederlandse Banden-Indsutrie Michelin NV v. Commission* [1983] ECR 3461.
Case T-219/99 *British Airways plc v Commission* [2003] ECR II-5917.
Standard Oil Co. of New Jersey v. United States (1911) 221, U.S., p.1.

16

More than froth and bubble

Marketing in Australia, 1788–1969

Robert Crawford

Introduction

In 1843, an article headed 'Lord's-Day Marketing' appeared in the *Sydney Morning Herald*. It reported on the Sydney City Council's plan to open the markets 'for buying and selling' on Sunday mornings. The *Sydney Morning Herald* was outraged. It angrily declared that such a proposal would 'pollute the city revenue with the unrighteous gains derived from Sabbath stalls and shambles' (p. 2). However, this article stands out less for its vehement stance than its headline, which features what appears to be the first use of the term marketing in the Australian press. Significantly, marketing here refers to the practices of buying and selling. Such ambiguous use of the term continued through to the 1890s, when references to marketing increasingly referred to the production and distribution of goods and wares rather than the act of purchasing.

Despite its longevity and evolving status, marketing in Australia has attracted little attention from local historians. This shortcoming owes more to the focus of historians than any absence of marketing practices in Australia. In their account of the politics of consumption in Australia, Nikola Balnaves and Greg Patmore (2011, 146) contend that local labour historians have focused on 'the politics of production rather than of consumption'. Together with social, business and economic historians, labour historians have viewed 'consumption as an outcome of production'. For radical historians, this stance is further entrenched by an ideological opposition to the practice of consumption (Balnaves and Patmore, 2011, 146). This situation has hardly been aided by the myopic state of business history in Australia. Aside from some pioneering efforts (Fleming *et al.*, 2004; Johns and van der Eng, 2010; Ville, 1998), business history in Australia generally has focused on 'the particular while ignoring the larger context of the private sector economy' (Merrett, 2001). However, the cultural turn in Australian historiography has seen increased attention being paid to the processes of consumption. Shopping and consumers have attracted significant attention (Kingston, 1994; Humphery, 1998; McLeod, 2007; Bailey, 2014). Other accounts have sought to position consumption within a broader context that encompasses the manufacturing, retailing and the media industries (Crawford *et al.*, 2010, 4–5). While these accounts have certainly recognized the presence of marketing and its role in promoting and enhancing a consumer society in Australia, they offer little critical examination of marketing, let alone its evolution. The notable exception is Amanda McLeod's (2007) *Abundance*, which suggests that marketers and consumers shared a symbiotic relationship. However, in focusing on the Long Boom spanning the late 1950s to the early 1970s, McLeod's study neglects the marketing practices and skills that had evolved since the eighteenth century.

Few marketing scholars have attempted to address the historians' shortcomings. Claiming that '[m]arketing has never been a particularly well respected discipline in Australia', John H. Roberts and Chris Styles (2001, 106) first contend that historical factors underpin this problematic image. Australia's economy had long been dependent on primary industries. Its distance from international markets along with the adoption of protectionist policies effectively restricted competition and the need for innovative marketing practices. Looking at the post-Second World War period, Roger Layton (1981, 159) similarly attributes Australians' lack of interest in marketing to economic factors. For Layton, Australia's booming economy and growing population meant that it 'was, and still is, "the lucky country," in which it is not hard to do well enough to get by'. Roberts and Styles further identify Australian cultural norms as another factor inhibiting marketing's development. Australians, they argue, possessed a '"cut the bull shit" mentality', which meant that marketing was viewed 'as froth and bubble rather than a systematic way of ensuring alignment between productive capability and user needs' (2001, 107). Australian consumers thus considered marketing 'manipulative and exploitative', while industry leaders contemptuously viewed 'marketers ... as extraneous to real, tangible value creation; a group that refused to be accountable but still insisted on its own importance' (2001, 107). While these factors certainly affected the growth and development of marketing in Australia, a closer inspection reveals that marketing practices had long been utilized by a range of Australian authorities, organizations and businesses.

Drawing on the Marketing Association of Australia and New Zealand's (2015) definition of marketing as 'the activities that facilitate and expedite satisfying exchange relationships in a dynamic environment through the creation distribution, promotion, and the pricing of products (goods, services, and ideas)', this chapter addresses the gap within Australian historical and marketing studies by undertaking a broad-ranging examination of the growth and development of marketing and marketing practices in Australia. Specifically, this chapter focuses on retailing, advertising, market research and professional education. These fields not only reflect the multiplicity of agents and practices involved in marketing, they also provide an opportunity to develop a broader overview of marketing's evolution in Australia. Rather than following the conventional narrative that situates marketing's emergence in the period of the Long Boom of the 1950s and 1960s, this chapter traces the evolution of marketing practices back to the eighteenth century, when Australia was still a fledgling penal colony, and follows their evolution through to the economic boom of the 1950s and 1960s. Over this timeframe, the growing affluence of Australian society progressively led to the expansion and diversification of local marketing practices. In turn, the development of such practices, as well as the growing number of individuals employed to implement them, gave rise to a professional marketing industry. By undertaking a long-term overview of Australian marketing practices, this chapter will demonstrate that marketing in Australia evolved gradually in response to broader social, cultural and economic factors as well as the innovative practices being implemented across different marketing fields.

New markets

Founded on the shores of Port Jackson in January 1788, the colony of New South Wales (NSW) was the British Empire's first Australian settlement as well as its furthest colony. Eight months earlier, the First Fleet had set out form Portsmouth carrying provisions for establishing a new penitentiary-cum-colony. Upon landing, these provisions were distributed via the government's Commissariat Store. With a monopoly over the entire colony and regulated by the military government, the store meant that there was initially little need for marketing practices. However, this situation was temporary. As conditions began to improve, administrators paid greater attention to the development of a civil society whilst entrepreneurial colonists identified new, emergent markets.

At the beginning of 1790, Sydney was on the verge of starvation. After two years of unsuccessful crops, the Commissariat Store's provisions had almost run out. Disaster was only averted when the Second Fleet arrived in June 1790. Over the coming decade, settlers found better soil inland. These settlers established the colony's first public markets at nearby Parramatta. A formal market soon followed in Sydney, on the same site where an informal market had already been operating (Karskens, 2009, 172). By 1803, the *Sydney Gazette & New South Wales Advertiser* was reporting that the markets were plying a healthy trade: 'Yesterday came in several market boats from Kissing Point, with a small supply of vegetables, a quantity of very fine potatoes, poultry, &c. Vegetables were not so cheap as last week' (*Sydney Gazette & New South Wales Advertiser*, 1803, 4).

The public markets were not the only alternative to the government stores. As the number of ships moving through Port Jackson increased, so too did the flow of goods and manufactured wares from other parts of the Empire. Officers of the NSW Corps were instrumental in this trade. In addition to buying the entire cargo from trading ships landing in the colony, they also dispatched ships to import speculative consignments. As the officers' code of honour prevented them from retailing their wares, they sold them wholesale to a range of dealers – from soldiers to convicts (Karskens, 2009, 172). The officers' monopoly loosened as private merchants arrived in the colony (Karskens, 2009, 172–3). Together with emancipist traders, such as Simeon Lord, these merchants successfully lobbied the Governor to gain direct access to the ships and established their own mercantile operations (Hainsworth, 1967).

The on-selling of goods acquired from wholesalers fuelled the colony's retail sector (Kingston, 1994, 9). Commencing trade a month after the arrival of the Second Fleet, Sydney's first brick-built shop was presumably selling some of the wares picked up by the Second Fleet's crew (Barnard, 2015, 10). By the time it commenced publication in 1803, *Sydney Gazette & NSW Advertiser* discovered a ready market of local retailers and dealers eager to advertise their wares. The newspaper's reports of thefts and burglaries also indicate the presence of a healthy black market. The General Muster of NSW conducted in 1814 revealed the scale of the local retail trade. While the census only lists 10 shopkeepers, it also counts 52 shoemakers, 26 dealers, 22 butchers, 19 tailors, as well as 10 merchants and one market keeper. Such figures, however, pale in comparison to the number of landholders/settlers (882) and labourers (725) working in the colony's primary industries (Baxter, 1987). Early retailers conducted their trade from the front room of their homes. As Grace Karskens notes, they 'were indistinguishable from houses: they had no large doors nor large plate or multi-paned window to show off the wares' (1997, 22). Increasing trade led shop owners to expand their premises and embellish their shop frontages. Retailers also clustered around the busy marketplaces (Kingston, 1994, 16).

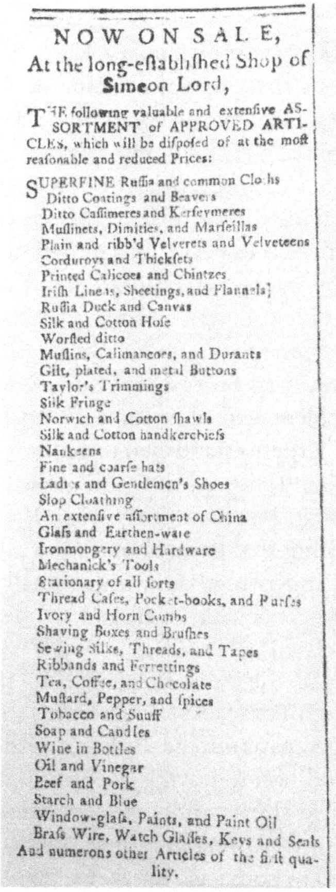

NOW ON SALE,
At the long-eſtabliſhed Shop of
Simeon Lord,

THE following valuable and extenſive ASSORTMENT of APPROVED ARTICLES, which will be diſpoſed of at the moſt reaſonable and reduced Prices:

SUPERFINE Ruſſia and common Cloths
Ditto Coatings and Beavers
Ditto Caſſimeres and Kerſeymeres
Muſlinets, Dimities, and Marſeillas
Plain and ribb'd Velverets and Velveteens
Corduroys and Thickſets
Printed Calicoes and Chintzes
Iriſh Linens, Sheetings, and Flannels
Ruſſia Duck and Canvas
Silk and Cotton Hoſe
Worſted ditto
Muſlins, Calimancoes, and Durants
Gilt, plated, and metal Buttons
Taylor's Trimmings
Silk Fringe
Norwich and Cotton ſhawls
Silk and Cotton handkerchiefs
Nankeens
Fine and coarſe hats
Ladies and Gentlemen's Shoes
Slop Cloathing
An extenſive aſſortment of China
Glaſs and Earthen-ware
Ironmongery and Hardware
Mechanick's Tools
Stationary of all ſorts
Thread Caſes, Pocket-books, and Purſes
Ivory and Horn Combs
Shaving Boxes and Bruſhes
Sewing Silks, Threads, and Tapes
Ribbands and Ferrettings
Tea, Coffee, and Chocolate
Muſtard, Pepper, and ſpices
Tobacco and Snuff
Soap and Candles
Wine in Bottles
Oil and Vinegar
Beef and Pork
Starch and Blue
Window-glaſs, Paints, and Paint Oil
Braſs Wire, Watch Glaſſes, Keys and Seals
And numerons other Articles of the firſt quality.

Figure 16.1 Advertisement in *Sydney Gazette & New South Wales Advertiser*, 24 April 1803, 4

Advertisements in the *Sydney Gazette & New South Wales Advertiser* reveal the growing number of retailers, dealers and auctioneers trading in the city. The size of Simeon Lord's operations meant that he was one of the colony's largest advertisers. Stating the products on offer and the place where they could be obtained, Figure 16.1 illustrates the standard advertisement of the time. Others found innovative ways of differentiating themselves. By identifying the ships that delivered their wares, retailers intimated that they were offering the latest imports – particularly clothing and other fashionable items (*Sydney Gazette & New South Wales Advertiser*, 1803, 4). Local manufacturers like potter Samuel Skinner sought to counter the bias towards imported items by referring to price and quality: 'THE FOLLOWING ARTICLES, Now on Sale at his Shop, with the annexed low Prices, he begs leave to recommend as by no means inferior to the Workmanship of the most eminent Potteries in the Mother Country' (*Sydney Gazette & New South Wales Advertiser*, 1803, p.3).

By the 1830s, the quality of shops in Sydney and Hobart was improving. A correspondent for the *Australian* proclaimed Sydney's 'shops that would do credit to London itself; where … you may produce anything convenience requires … from the clumsiest Dutch toys to the exquisite manufactures of China and Japan' (1828, 3). However, a competing newspaper felt a need to correct this impression. The *Monitor* (1828, 3) agreed that there 'are a few houses and showy shops in George-Street' but observed that 'they stand so far asunder, and the intermediate spaces are occupied with shops and houses of such a different description, that the effect is not quite so imposing'. It also claimed that a 'lady from London wishing to ornament her own person or her drawing-room, would not find in our shop one article in six she might require'. A more common comparison likened Australian shops to those in England's larger provincial towns (Kingston, 1994, 17).

Shop owners were developing their own networks both within the colonies and across the Empire. John Muston's drapery illustrates these networks. Landing in Hobart in 1834, Muston maintained a close correspondence with his Birmingham-based supplier, Joseph James. From the very outset, Muston sought to convince his partner that colonial consumers were discerning and that the 'idea so prevalent at home that low goods are the only ones in demand for this colony *is a most mistaken one*' (cited in Toplis, 2013, 116). Fashion provided an opportunity for colonists (free-settler and emancipist alike) to differentiate themselves from convicts (Maynard, 1994, 150–1). In highlighting his English connections, Muston inferred that his imported wares were the latest fashion from 'Home'. Yet despite Muston's promises to the public and his admonishment of his supplier, the quality of exported materials remained an abiding issue, as well as their erratic supply. Muston therefore diversified his business, branching into manufacturing clothes (Toplis, 2013, 123). Examining the demise of Muston's venture in 1836, Alison Toplis (2013) identifies deeper problems relating to his marketing practices. As many free settlers continued to buy their wares directly from England, Muston had targeted the middle-class consumer. However, the middle class in 1830s Hobart was simply too small. Muston's offer of credit was also problematic. While this was an expected practice for this class of consumer, Muston's mounting debts suggest that some wealthy ex-convicts had not entirely dispensed with their recidivist ways (Toplis, 2013, 121). Ironically, the marketing strategies deployed by Muston would become the mainstays of Australian retailing practice over the second half of the nineteenth century.

Organising the market

In the 1850s, the Australian colonies experienced significant changes. The transportation of convicts to NSW formally ceased in 1850 and in 1853 for Van Diemen's Land (Tasmania). NSW was partitioned, resulting in two separate colonies – Victoria in the south and Queensland in the north. By 1859, each of the Australian colonies (except Western Australia) had been granted limited self-government. However, it would be the discovery of gold in NSW and then Victoria that would have the most profound impact on the colonies. Waves of fortune seekers ventured to the gold fields to try their luck. The colonies profited both from the wealth generated by gold and the rapid increase in population. Moving on from their convict origins, the colonies' political, social and economic development created new commercial opportunities for enterprising retailers.

For the first half of the nineteenth century, the development of Australia's retail sector had been impeded by a combination of distance, rudimentary transportation links, an undeveloped manufacturing sector and a scattered population (McArthur, 2013, 454). However, over the second half of the century, these barriers were progressively overcome. Technology in the form of the steam engine and the telegraph reduced distances. Local manufacturing also expanded, particularly in Victoria, where protectionist policies had been adopted. Both Melbourne and Sydney not only boasted large populations, but possessed a burgeoning middle class that increasingly had the means and desire to consume. Such conditions facilitated the emergence of the department store.

Australia's initial department stores had commenced in the first half of the century as individual dress makers (David Jones, Farmer's), drapers (Anthony Hordern & Sons, Buckley & Nunn) and ironmongers (Lassetter's, Harris Scarfe). Growing custom led them to diversify their goods and recast themselves as emporiums or universal providers. From the 1880s, a new wave of emporiums opened across Australia (Fitzgerald's, Foy & Gibson, Marcus Clark). By the 1900s, they had adopted the term department store from the United States. The growing number of universal stores clamouring for the consumer's attention generated interest in marketing strategies. In addition to keeping a close eye on local competitors, proprietors also kept close tabs on overseas developments, notably in London and New York, through visits and reports in the local and imported press, though there was often a time lag between Australian developments and those in the leading commercial centres.

The department stores' marketing practices and initiatives both reflected and reinforced the notion that shopping was now a leisure activity undertaken by middle-class women – a trend that Australians had observed at Macy's in New York and, later, Selfridge's in London. Shopping thus became a 'feminine speciality', where '[s]urroundings were designed to educate and to flatter the taste and sensibilities of the shopper – fittings, decorations, furniture, arrangements and, obviously, goods' (Kingston, 1994, 26). Completed in 1887, the renovated David Jones building in Sydney had thus been 'built in an Italian Classic style, to accentuate the nature of the merchandise offered inside' (Miller and Merrilees, 2013, 175). Shop windows performed a similar function. Carefully arranged by trained window dressers, the store's front windows sought to 'create an "atmosphere"' that entertained and enticed onlookers (Reekie, 1993, 91–2). Alongside promises of a vast range of goods, the department store's emphasis on cash trade and clearly marked prices appealed to middle-class consumers (Kingston, 1994, 42). Knowing the actual cost of items facilitated the shopping process. Consumers could shop to a budget. Marked prices also prevented any embarrassing misunderstandings at the cash register and eliminated the prospect of being overcharged by unscrupulous sales staff.

Once inside, 'destination retailing' strategies sought to keep customers and maximize their likelihood of spending money (McArthur, 2013, 459). Aside from its functional role, technology symbolized the department store's modernity. David Jones's electric lights dazzled and intrigued whilst facilitating consumers' capacity to see the store's wares. Hydraulic lifts likewise entertained shoppers as they provided greater access to the store's different departments (Miller and Merrilees, 2013, 175). Figure 16.2 illustrates Anthony Hordern's 'Palace Emporium', which boasted a refreshment room 'capable of seating at once 300 to 350 persons', where customers could enjoy locally made drinks and confectionary 'purchased from the best houses abroad' (*Town and Country Journal*, 1906, 34). Lavatories for customers were a somewhat less dramatic addition to the store's offerings, but in cities where there were few public amenities, they were most welcome (Kingston, 1994, 29). However, the arrival of the department stores was not universally celebrated. In 1897, Melbourne's *Advocate* reported on overseas concerns about department stores – from their impact on smaller competitors to their de-skilling of staff and driving down of wages (*Advocate*, 1897, 12).

As Australian cities expanded, the department stores increasingly worked to overcome the tyranny of distance. While some department stores hoped that sales, range of goods and in-store marketing efforts would continue to draw in the suburban and regional consumers, others ventured out beyond the city. Opening outlets in the suburbs offered consumers a convenient alternative to travelling into the central business district (Kingston, 1994, 39). Home delivery added further convenience to the shopping process. Anthony Hordern's

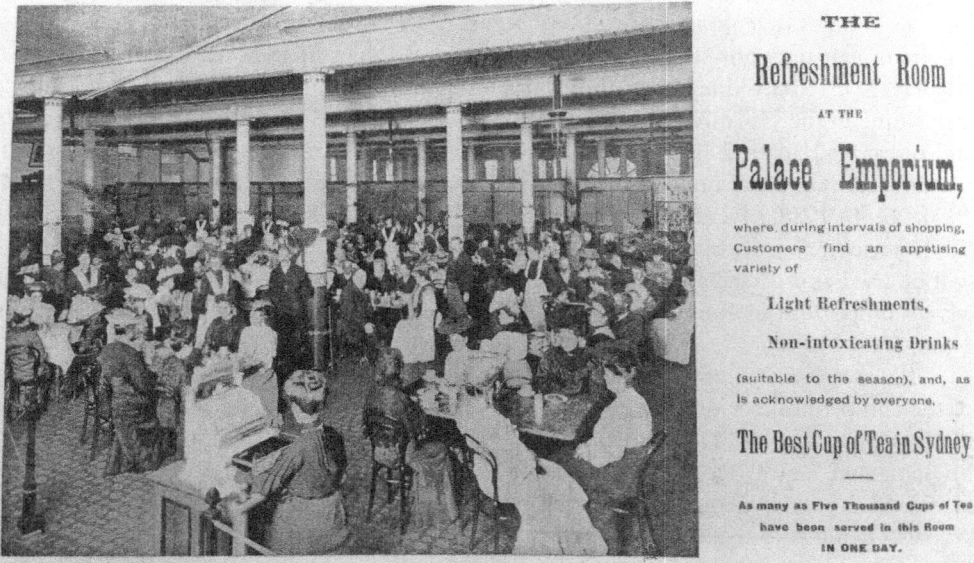

Figure 16.2 The New Palace Emporium on Brickfield Hill, Sydney, Anthony Hordern & Sons, Sydney, c.1907, 8.

home delivery service, for example, had grown from a single horse in the 1870s to a fleet of motorized vehicles at the turn of the century (*Hordernian Monthly*, 1938, 118). Mail order similarly reached out into the suburbs and beyond. Australians had long been accustomed to ordering goods via mail with David Jones's first catalogues appearing in the 1850s (Waller, 1992). The growth of American mail order operations such as Montgomery Ward and, later, Sears Roebuck did not go unnoticed. In 1884, the catalogue for Anthony Hordern's contained a modest 14 pages – by the turn of the century, it spanned no less than 600 pages (Webber and Hoskins, 2007, 10). Department stores developed other initiatives. David Jones offered to send approved clients parcels of goods for a free trial. Those who bought more than £2 worth would be spared the cost of returning the remaining items by post (O'Neill, 2013, 61). In addition to its catalogue, the Marcus Clark store created sample rooms in large regional centres that were manned by travelling salesmen (Pollon, 1989, 234).

Reaching the mass market

The federation of the Australian colonies in 1901 formed the Australian Commonwealth and created a new national market. Free trade between the new States was enshrined in the constitution. After protracted debates, the Commonwealth adopted protectionist policies to safeguard local manufacturers. However, it would be First World War that stimulated the growth and development of a national market. The war had dramatically exposed Australia's meagre manufacturing capabilities. Adopting the mantra 'men, money, and markets', Prime Minister Stanley Bruce sought to stimulate national growth and production during the 1920s. Such conditions would also prove to be a boon to local marketers and marketing practices.

Over the 1920s, the large department stores continued to expand their services and facilities. Sales appealed to consumers' purse strings whilst large promotions such as 'Empire

Shopping Week' and 'Buy Australian' stirred their hearts. The expansion of services to include lounges, telephone bureaus and information services (covering public transport, entertainment and sight-seeing) all worked to keep customers in the store longer than before (Reekie, 1993, 107). Sidney Myer, the proprietor of the Myer Emporium, was spending much of his time in the US, buying wares and closely studying the latest American developments and research (Barber, 2008, 46). Department stores were also expanding other operations. Wartime shortages had underscored the need to manufacture their own products (Wolfers, 1980, 20). In 1928, Myer bought a four-storeyed building in Adelaide's King William Street 'for factories making furniture, women's garments, underclothing, etc., and the ground floor will be used as a garage and despatch department ... This will mean that the top floor of Myers Emporium in Rundle-street ... will be available for additional showrooms' (*Daily News*, 1928, 1).

The department stores' expansion of services and operations not only reflected the intensity of the competition between stores; they also reveal an important shift in the perception of the consumer market. Department stores now spoke of dealing with a mass market and implemented new practices to meet its needs. Escalators and less cluttered show spaces facilitated the flow of consumers through the store (Kingston, 1994, 56). Greater attention was also being paid to the role of salesmanship and the ways in which the application of scientific principles could improve it. Complementing the implementation of more formal training schemes for staff, trade journals and educational manuals offered advice on the latest sales techniques, store layout and customer management (Reekie, 1993, 47–8: Miller, 2006).

The need to motivate the mass market to visit their premises prompted the department stores to allocate greater resources to advertising. Speaking at the University of Melbourne in 1928, Myer's general manager underscored advertising's centrality: 'Advertising is to a business what vitamins are to health. With the cessation of advertising, the complex machinery of retail marketing would be slowed down and unemployment would become rife' (*Argus*, 1928, 9). While the larger department stores such as Myer and David Jones had their own advertising units, a growing number of retailers and manufacturers were outsourcing their advertising needs to advertising agencies.

Australia's first advertising agencies emerged in the second half of the nineteenth century to sell newspaper space to advertisers. Of these, the largest was Gordon & Gotch, which progressively grew from being a local Melbourne agency to selling space to advertisers across the Australian colonies and the Empire (Wallace, 1972). By the turn of the century, a new wave of advertising agencies was offering to create, illustrate and insert advertisements on the client's behalf. In Sydney, the first 'full-service' advertising agencies were the Weston Company (established c.1901) and Thomas A. Miller (1902). Hugh Paton established the Paton Advertising Service in Melbourne in 1904. For these pioneering advertising agencies, the first task was to persuade prospective clients to pay for their services. Reflecting on his early days, Paton (1914, 17) recalled how he approached 'leading Melbourne firms and begged them to allow me to write their advertisements. They gazed at me in consternation and doubted whether I was in my right senses.'

As their livelihood depended on advertising's growth, the full service agencies set about improving the advertising's reputation as a marketing tool. Figure 16.3 reveals agencies practising what they preached – that it pays to advertise. Following in the wake of the 'truth in advertising' movement waged by the Associated Advertising Clubs of America from the 1880s to the early 1910s (Jones *et al.*, 2000), the Ad Club of Victoria was formed in 1914 with the object of working 'for truth and honesty in advertising and advertising methods' (*Bendigo Advertiser*, 1914, 10). Similar issues were discussed four years later, when Brisbane

Figure 16.3   *Ad Writer*, 1(1), March 1909, 6

played host to the inaugural Convention of Australian Advertising Men (*Proceedings*, 1918). Participants came from the retail and media industries as well as the agencies. Such diversity revealed the growing importance being attributed to advertising and its marketing role. However, H.E. Wilson's call for retail managers to give their 'wholehearted' support to agencies indicated that the relations between retailers and advertising agents were still in their infancy. Significantly, Wilson suggested that fellow 'ad men' also needed to identify 'a word that would adequately express his sphere of occupation in a store or big houses'. Agencies, it seems, already considered themselves to be engaging in marketing practices – even if they lacked the right work for it (*Brisbane Courier*, 1918, 4).

Over the course of the 1920s, the intensifying competition within Australia's expanding retail and manufacturing sectors saw more businesses engaging advertising agencies. Speaking on the growth of advertising at the 1920 Ad Men's Convention, H.E. Poole pointed out that 'the newspaper, the catalogue, the cinema, electric sign, circular letter, and poster' were all being used by advertising agencies to 'capture an audience of millions' (*Evening News*, 1920, 5). The formation of national advertising bodies and the publication of various trade journals revealed the agencies' expansion as well as their commitment to professionalising advertising. As advertisers were funding this growth, they too moved to protect their interests by forming the Association of Australian National Advertisers in 1928. Agencies also increased their self-promotion efforts. Their assertions that modern advertising was a science rather than an art, for example, resonated with clients who wanted to see a return on investment. Echoing the claims being made in retailing circles, advertising practitioners asserted that psychology enabled them to reach into the mind of the mass market and to understand how it behaved (Crawford, 2008, 51–5). Such insights and skills would become integral to the agencies' survival when the economy collapsed.

Threats to the market

The Depression hit Australia hard. As retailers, manufacturers and advertising agencies watched consumption levels plummet, they were forced to reconsider their operations as well as their relationship with the consumer. While this crisis inevitably produced knee-jerk responses, it also resulted in a greater level introspection that led these industries to adopt a more holistic view of marketing practices and their improvement.

As sales stalled, advertising came under pressure to perform. Many advertisers simply cut their advertising expenditure. Hoping to demonstrate the importance of advertising, the advertising industry organized another national convention in 1931. W.R. McFerran told delegates that the advertising industry had more to offer than mere advertisements: 'In Britain and the United States … advertising leaders had been called in to help the nation with advertising, sales and marketing problems, and they had gladly given their services' (*Sydney Morning Herald*, 1931, 13). Australia, he lamented, 'preferred to hand over the work to some worn-out politician'. His call was ignored and agencies were left to find their own way out of this crisis.

Although immediate savings could be made by slashing advertising budgets, retailers and manufacturers could not adopt a similar strategy in their sales operations. Sales strategies therefore needed to be analysed in order to ascertain what improvements could be made. Eager to develop a better understanding of their profession, a group of concerned sales managers in Sydney formed the Institute of Sales and Business Management in 1932. Its main aims were to 'formulate standards, so that sales and business management may be exercised as a profession; to raise the status of management; to develop the status and technique of sales and business management' and to establish educational programmes (*Sydney Morning Herald*, 1932, 8). The Institute proposed to establish a library, undertake research and organize regular lectures with a view to promoting the 'interchange of views, experiences, and results of investigations' (*Sydney Morning Herald*, 1932, 8). The lecture series reflected the Institute's aspirations. Early speakers included Ernest Fisk, the director of Amalgamated Wireless, A.H. Martin from the Department of Psychology at University of Sydney, and Herbert Lloyd, a member of New South Wales Legislative Assembly. Topics would assume a more practical focus, moving from industrial psychology to the use of graphs in presentations. The Institute became a national organization with branches opening in Melbourne (1932), Brisbane (1932, reopened 1939) and Adelaide (1939). Membership was also broadened, with salesmen being permitted in 1933. Recognizing the breadth of roles covered under the umbrella of sales and business management, the Institute established specific divisions to focus on particular aspects of marketing. An 'ad man's' division was formed in 1934. The following year saw the addition of an executives' division and a general division.

Market research provided another means by which manufacturers, retailers and their agencies could improve the efficacy of their marketing practices and strategies. As Daniel Oakman's (1995) survey of the evolution of market research and William McNair's (1978) interviews with market research pioneers demonstrate, market research played a key role in establishing marketing's professional credentials. The prospect of deploying science to identify, measure and analyse issues pertaining to clients' sales and consumers appealed to advertising agencies. Introduced to the concept in 1927, members of the Western Australian

Institute of Advertising heard that market research could help explain the success or failure of a product and it could 'discover the likes and dislikes of the public, and the attitudes of retailers and wholesalers towards a new product' (*Daily News*, 1927, 2).

The pioneer of market research in Australian advertising circles was J. Walter Thompson (JWT). When commencing its Australian operations in 1929, JWT sold market research as a point of difference. An advertisement for the agency thus explained that 'Successful advertising campaigns are now built on actual knowledge of market conditions. Campaigns so constructed rarely fail' (*Newspaper News*, 1931, 3). JWT's inaugural local appointment in 1929 was Rudolph Simmat, who had recently worked for the psychological department of Rowntree & Co. in the UK. Simmat's first task was to develop a statistical overview of the Australian market, which would be forwarded to New York. Consumer surveys were then undertaken on behalf of Pond's Cream, Flit insect spray and Lux soaps. The agency also undertook research on dealers and retail distribution structures and patterns (Simmat, 1978, 5–6). William McNair replaced Simmat in 1932. In addition to undertaking research for JWT clients, McNair set about conducting the first surveys of radio audiences. Discovering that 'present attempts to measure the Australian radio audience have not been altogether successful' (1937, 248), McNair undertook his own study and published his findings as *Radio Advertising in Australia*. As his radio audience surveys were attracting attention from other agencies and their clients, McNair persuaded JWT to establish his department as a separate operation (McNair, 1978, 18–19). Sylvia Ashby was another alumna of JWT's research department. After three years with JWT, Ashby went to London, where she spent three years working at Charles W. Hobson. Her employer actively encouraged her interest in market research and she 'made useful contacts with English and American researchers' (Ashby, 1978, 9). Ashby returned to Australia in 1936 and duly established the Ashby Research Service, Australia's first market research firm. It was a bold venture for anyone, let alone a young woman. Given her contacts in London, it is likely that she was aware of the achievements of such pioneering women in the field as Pauline Arnold (Jones, 2013) and hoped to emulate their success in Australia. It would be a tough start. Ashby later recalled that the independent research agency's first years were frustrating as 'business executives … appeared to know little and to care even less' about market research (1978, 9). She nevertheless plugged away, challenging the prevailing sexism and ageism and 'convincing know-it-all executives that market research could give them marketing information they didn't already have' (p.12). By 1939, the Ashby Research Service held accounts with various major advertisers and media companies.

Australia's economy had been gradually improving when the Second World War broke out in 1939. In contrast to the Depression, consumers now had money to spend but rationing and restrictions left them with few choices. Advertising's wartime duty was to keep brand names alive (Crawford, 2008, 101–17). As newsprint shortages restricted print advertising, many advertisers looked to radio. However, the size of radio audiences remained unclear. Growing out of JWT's research department, the McNair Survey Pty Ltd sought to measure radio audiences. Demand for accurate figures also gave rise to a competing research firm, Anderson Analysis of Broadcasting. Their methodological differences – McNair opted for interviews whilst Anderson used diaries – revealed them to be pioneers in approach as much as marketing services (Balnaves and O'Regan, 2011, 28–32). The impact of such research was also being felt in other ways. Newspapers discovered the importance of research in generating news, commissioning opinion polls to ascertain public views on contemporary political, economic and social issues (Goot, 2010).

By late 1945, the outlook for Australia's retailers, manufacturers, advertising agencies, and market researchers looked positive. They had withstood an economic collapse and a global war. Such crises had necessitated a rigorous self-assessment, which provided them with a clearer understanding of their marketing practices. Moreover, they were gaining a clearer understanding of consumer activities and motivations. These experiences and insights would prove indispensable in the post-war era.

The rise of the marketing professional

As the wartime austerity measures lifted, it was widely assumed that the shift from a seller's market to a buyer's market was but a matter of time (Crawford, 2008, 39–54). The eagerly anticipated shift finally materialized in the mid-1950s. In this crowded market, competition for the consumer's attention intensified and marketing practices became more important than ever before. Increased investment of time and money on marketing practices and strategies not only saw their expansion; it resulted in the emergence of the marketing professional.

Advertisements depicting the post-war era as the age of affluence had already been commonplace during the Second World War. As Australia moved into the post-war period, advertising agencies sought to maintain this excitement by urging clients to prepare for the new age. They also recognized that the imminent buyer's market opened new opportunities beyond advertising. Speaking in 1960, J.J. Mullins of the Advertising Association of Australia urged Australian advertising agencies to expand their services.

> In Australia, agencies, with a few notable exceptions, still do not appear to have accepted the marketing concept. The last available analysis … indicates that about 90 per cent of agency turnover is in media advertising and only about 10 per cent in printing and miscellaneous activities connected with marketing. The proportion has not changed very much over the last five years and it seems to imply that most Australian advertisers do not use their agencies for promotional and marketing purposes.
>
> *(Mullins, 1960, 10)*

Various agencies were alert to the issues that Mullins raised. Research was emerging as an integral part of the modern post-war agency. In 1959 Canny, Paramor & Canny announced that its desire 'to find out what makes people buy' had led it to form 'a separate research subsidiary'. Such initiatives signalled an intention to do more than mere advertising. A few months later, Nichols-Cumming went a step further when it announced that it would be forming a marketing development department. The agency explained that:

> It is planned to build this department, not with advertising men, but with businessmen who have proved their ability as sales managers and marketing men in companies in all sorts of fields. Their business is to understand marketing trends, margins, price structure in general, new products and new markets, and the reorganisation of sales staffs.
>
> *(Advertising, 1959b)*

The emphasis on marketing within agency ranks reflected broader trends. In 1959 McCann-Erickson entered Australia. *Advertising* correctly predicted that the 'advent of McCann-Erickson may have the effect of accelerating interest in marketing among Australian agencies' as it was a world leader 'in establishing the complete creative advertising-marketing service' (*Advertising*, 1959a, 22).

Over the course of the 1960s, advertising campaigns were increasingly informed by research findings. Agencies also worked to identify and address their clients' marketing issues – ranging from product development and packaging to consumer attitudes and behaviours. While research would remain an abiding part of agency practice, the agencies' expansion into the marketing field would be more short-lived. Already in the mid-1960s, Australians were commenting on American trends that saw agencies being confined to creative work (*Newspaper News*, 1966, 1). This trend would become more discernible in Australia in the 1970s, as a new generation of trained marketing professionals entered the advertisers' ranks.

At the Institute of Sales and Business Management, it was becoming clear that its diverse members shared a common interest in marketing. The Institute's lecture series in 1956 revealed that its focus was still on the 'practical techniques and methods from ... top executives', with presenters covering a broad range of marketing topics, including the selection and training of salesmen, television advertising, packaging, and the conduct of sales meetings (*Argus*, 1956, 17). By this stage, the Institute's changing focus led it to shorten its title to the Institute of Business Management. Along with the new title came a new publication, *Sales Management in Australia*, which provided another opportunity for members to familiarize themselves with the latest developments in the sector. As the definition of marketing solidified and practitioners increasingly came to identify their work with it, the Institute adopted a new title, the Institute of Sales and Marketing Executives, in 1965. Similarly retitled, the Institute's journal (now *Sales and Marketing in Australia*) also reflected the members' embrace of marketing. A decade later, the Institute's conceptualization of marketing practice resulted in another name change for the organization and its publication. Reflecting the prevailing view that marketing practice went beyond sales, the Institute's members adopted their current title, the Australian Marketing Institute, in 1975, and accordingly rebadged their journal *Marketing* (*Rydge's Marketing*, 1975).

The growing interest in marketing practices and strategies generated further business for market researchers. Already in 1948, JWT's Lloyd Ring Coleman was urging Australian advertisers to invest more in research. Coleman (1948) warned that competition was no longer local – American firms entering Australia could call on the large and well-established marketing strategies from their home markets. Australians appeared to take heed of Coleman's warning. The condescension that market research had encountered in the 1930s was being replaced by a more positive attitude. David Bottomley's *Introduction to Market Analysis* revealed this shift. First published in 1959, this pioneering Australian text on market research identified the five phases of incorporating research into a business's operations. Initially sceptical of market research, firms would reluctantly undertake research. The next phase would see a small but regular allocation of funds for research. This would be followed by the appointment of a market research manager. Securing greater amounts to support research, market research managers were in a position to plan ahead. The final phase saw the market research manager's activities being 'properly integrated into his company's operations' (Bottomley, 1964, 29). This outline not only identified where market researchers sat in relation to their clients – it also offered hope.

Bottomley's text was published by the Market Research Society of Australia (MRSA). Established in 1955 as a forum for market researchers to meet and to improve professional standards, the Society embodied the growing importance attributed to market research (Bottomley, 1964,. i). The advertising industry as a whole was interested in market research. In 1964, the 'extension of interest in marketing, including sales and distribution, media advertising, stores promotion, etc.' led the Australian Association of National Advertisers to publish *Marketing Terms and Definition in Common Use in Australia* (1964) to assist its members' understanding of contemporary marketing practices.

The growth of the market research industry over the 1950s and 1960s was reflected in the number of research firms. Where the Ashby Research Service had claimed to be the only independent market research firm at the end of the Second World War, the Australian Association of National Advertisers' guide, *Marketing Research,* identified 47 firms, organizations and institutions involved in market research in 1968 (pp. 4–5). The breadth of current market research practice was illustrated in the range of facilities and services on offer. These included statistical market research, consumer buying habits, packaging tests, advertisement testing, media research, motivational research, public relations and public opinion polls. The size of the industry was also revealed in the MSRA's *Directory of Market Research Organizations* (1966) The largest firms such as Anderson Analysis, the Ashby Research Service, Beacon Research Company and the McNair Survey employed 30–70 full-time staff with a further 150–250 trained supervisors and interviewers collecting the data.

Educating the marketing professional

Education played an integral role in the emergence of Australia's marketing professionals. In their 1947 text for prospective marketing professionals, the authors of *Marketing and Selling* emphasized education: 'Only by a thorough and constant study of the entire distributive machine can adequate and effective plans be developed and applied to the distribution problems of the future. These are the reasons why business today demands trained salesmen' (Hemingway Robertson Institute, 1947, vii). Such calls were hardly new. Education had been cited as a primary reason for the establishment of the Institute of Sales and Business Management in 1932 (*Sydney Morning Herald*, 1932, 8).

The Institute of Sales and Business Management's interest in education went beyond concerns about the state of training. As the first courses on advertising and salesmanship had been available to Australians since 1910, various practitioners could already claim that they had been trained (Ellis and Waller, 2011, 115). The Institute's discourse on education had therefore been as much about public recognition of their professional status as it was about practical training. Efforts to establish such recognition had commenced in the early 1920s when the Victorian Institute of Advertising Men unsuccessfully approached the Faculty of Arts at the University of Melbourne to establish a course on advertising (Ellis and Waller, 2011, 116).

Although the University of Melbourne had rejected the Victorian Institute's proposal, its newly established Faculty of Commerce recognized the growing importance of marketing. In 1929 it offered an elective subject on marketing that covered 'the marketing function in relation to other economic functions; … retail marketing; … the determination of price; the marketing of primary products; … psychology in marketing; market research; advertising; [and] salesmanship' (Ellis and Waller, 2011, 116–17). The subject would remain unchanged until 1944. As business paid greater attention to marketing issues, so too did educators. Over the 1950s and 1960s, marketing courses were being delivered by numerous technical colleges and institutes of technology across the country (Sheedy, 2007, 2–4, 8–10). Such competition ultimately led the Australian Marketing Institute to abandon its training schemes. In 1963, the University of NSW entered the marketing education field when it announced that it had sourced sufficient funding from industry to appoint the nation's first chair in marketing. 'The man being sought for the chair', reported *Newspaper News*, 'will have proven practical ability as well as academic qualifications. The post might go to an Australian in the US who has a wide marketing background plus a knowledge and understanding of the Australian market' (*Newspaper News*, 1963, 1). The University of NSW's marketing department started teaching students in 1966 and produced its first graduates in 1969. Observing that 'All of the graduates had been approached with offers from industry, many from foreign owned companies' (*Newspaper & Advertising News*, 1969, 1), the trade press recognized that this new generation of marketing professionals was destined to have an impact on industry and, indeed, the professional status of the marketing sector.

Conclusion

As Australia moved into the 1970s and 1980s, marketing had become more than a range of practices; it was emerging as a profession. Business invested in it; retail and communication industries understood it; higher education institutions formally taught it; and the consumer was fully immersed in it. From the vantage point of the 1970s and 1980s, it is perhaps unsurprising that past efforts to 'facilitate and expedite satisfying exchange relationships' through marketing seemed to pale in comparison. However, this chapter has revealed that this view of the marketing's past is a somewhat blinkered one. Marketing practices in Australia have long been implemented by an assortment of authorities, organizations, companies and agencies. From the entrepreneurial officers of the NSW Corps in the eighteenth century to the professional marketing executives of the mid-twentieth century, marketing in Australia progressively grew in size and scope to service increasingly affluent Australians who were eager to consume.

In many ways, the prevailing sense that marketing only really emerged in Australia in the post-Second World War decades reflects the fluidity of the term marketing over the past century. Practitioners had long lacked a clear term that collectively covered the multitude of practices that were deployed to engage consumers. Surveys of marketing history have therefore struggled to see these practices as something more than isolated, sporadic and incoherent actions undertaken by discrete firms. The efforts to professionalize marketing-related fields would ultimately address this perspective. As Australia's advertising and retail sectors sought to improve their own practice, they developed a more comprehensive overview of where they sat in relation to other related industries. Recognition of this bigger picture triggered a deeper understanding of marketing and a more nuanced approach to implementing and expanding marketing practices. Professional organizations and formal education in the field similarly reinforced these perspectives, whilst expanding knowledge and awareness of marketing practices as well as the number of individuals involved in marketing.

As the post-war economic boom ended in the 1970s, Australia's marketing industry found itself in a new position. Observing that these conditions saw management become 'much more sensitive to the role of marketing', Layton notes that 'organizations were changed to introduce marketing as a major functional component, and the logic of the marketing concept became part of accepted management thinking' (1981, 159). This new period of growth and development appeared to signal a fundamental break from the past. However, as this study has revealed, these developments might be better understood as the next chapter in a much longer history of marketing in Australia.

References

Advertising: The Magazine of Marketing (1959a) 'Basic relationship aides US advertising' (June), 22–3.
Advertising: The Magazine of Marketing (1959b) 'Research expansion at Nichols-Cumming' (Nov.), 25.
Advocate (1897) 'Department stores' (14 Aug.), 12.

Argus (1928) 'Retail marketing' (2 Aug.), 9.

Argus (1956) 'Back to school for sales executives' (7 July), 17.

Ashby, S. (1978) 'The twenties and thirties – Sylvia Ashby', in W.A. McNair (ed.), *Some Reflections on the First Fifty Years of Market Research in Australia*, Sydney, Market Research Society of NSW, pp. 8–14.

Australian (1828) 'Sydney in 1828' (13 Aug.), 3.

Australian Association of National Advertisers (1964) *Marketing Terms and Definition in Common Use in Australia*, AANA, Sydney.

Australian Association of National Advertisers (1968) *Marketing Research: A Guide to Facilities and Services*, AANA, Sydney.

Bailey, M. (2014) 'Retailing and the home in 1960s Sydney', *History Australia*, 11/1, 59–81.

Balnaves, M., and O'Regan, T. (2011) *Rating the Audience: The Business of Media*, Bloomsbury Academic, London and New York.

Balnaves, N., and Patmore, G. (2011) 'The politics of consumption and labour history', *Labour History*, 100, 145–65.

Barber, S.M. (2008) *Your Store Myer: The Story of Australia's Leading Department Store*, Focus, Sydney.

Barnard, E. (2015) *Emporium: Selling the Dream in Colonial Australia*, National Library of Australia, Canberra.

Baxter, C.J. (ed.) (1987) *General Muster of New South Wales, 1814*, Australian Biographical and Genealogical Record, Sydney.

Bendigo Advertiser (1914) 'Ad. Club of Victoria' (20 June), 11.

Bottomley, D. (1964) *Introduction to Market Analysis* (rev. edn), Market Research Society of Australia (Victorian Division), Melbourne.

Brisbane Courier (1918) 'Advertising convention' (5 Sept.), 4.

Coleman, L.R. (1948) 'The potential of the home market', in *Meeting the Buyer's Market*, Institute of Industrial Management, Melbourne, pp. 58–77.

Crawford, R. (2008) *But Wait, There's More … : A History of Australian Advertising, 1900–2000*, Melbourne University Press, Carlton, Victoria.

Crawford, R., Smart, J., and Humphery, K. (2010) 'Introduction', in R. Crawford, J. Smart and K. Humphery (eds), *Consumer Australia: Historical Perspectives*, Cambridge Scholars Press, Newcastle-upon-Tyne, pp. 1–10.

Daily News (1927) 'Institute of Advertising' (9 Dec.), 2.

Daily News (1928) 'Big Adelaide purchase' (12 Oct.), 1.

Ellis, R., and Waller, D. (2011) 'Marketing education in Australia before 1965', *Australasian Marketing Journal*, 19/2, 115–21.

Evening News (1920) 'Growth of advertising' (31 Aug.), 5.

Fleming, G., Merret, D., and Ville, S. (2004) *The Big End of Town: Big Business and Corporate Leadership in Twentieth Century Australia*, Cambridge University Press, Cambridge.

Gibson, R.W. (1966) *Directory of Market Research Organizations*, AIM Secretariat, Melbourne.

Goot, M. (2010) '"A worse importation than chewing gum": American influences on the Australian press and their limits – The Australian Gallup Poll, 1941–1973', *Historical Journal of Film, Radio and Television*, 30/3, 269–302.

Hainsworth, D.R. (1967) 'Lord, Simeon (1771–1840)', *Australian Dictionary of Biography*, Canberra, National Centre of Biography, available online: http://adb.anu.edu.au/biography/lord-simeon-2371/text3115.

Hemingway Robertson Institute (1947) *Marketing and Selling: Part 1 – principles of selling*, Dept. of Distribution, Hemingway Robertson Institute, Melbourne.

Hodernian Monthly (1938) 'The Delivery', 15/5, 118–20.

Humphery, K. (1998) *Shelf Life: Supermarkets and the Changing Cultures of Consumption*, Cambridge University Press, Cambridge.

Johns, L., and van der Eng, P. (2010) 'Networks and business development: Convict businesspeople in Australia', *Business History*, 52/5, 812–33.

Jones, D.G.B., Richardson, A.J., and Shearer, T. (2000) 'Truth and the evolution of the professions: A comparative of "Truth in Advertising" and "True and Fair" financial statements in North America during the progressive era', *Journal of Macromarketing*, 20/1, 23–35.

Jones, D.G.B. (2013) 'Pauline Arnold (1894–1974): Pioneer in market research', *Journal of Historical Research in Marketing*, 5/3, 291–307.

Karskens, G. (1997) *The Rocks: Life in Early Sydney*, Melbourne University Press, Carlton, Victoria.

Karskens, G. (2009) *The Colony: A History of Early Sydney*, Allen & Unwin, Sydney.

Kingston, B. (1994) *Basket, Bag and Trolley: A History of Shopping in Australia*, Oxford University Press, Melbourne.

Layton, R. (1981) 'A review of marketing literature in Australia', *Journal of Marketing*, 45/2, 159–60.

McArthur, E. (2013) 'The role of department stores in the evolution of marketing: Primary source records from Australia', *Journal of Historical Research in Marketing*, 5/4, 449–70.

McLeod, A. (2007) *Abundance: Buying and Selling in Postwar Australia*, Australian Scholarly Publishing, Melbourne.

McNair, W.A. (1937) *Radio Advertising in Australia*, Angus & Robertson, Sydney.

McNair, W.A. (1978) 'The Twenties and Thirties – W.A. McNair', in W.A. McNair (ed.), *Some Reflections on the First Fifty Years of Market Research in Australia*, Market Research Society of NSW, Sydney, 15–21.

Marketing Association of Australia (2015) 'Marketing defined', available online: www.marketing.org.au/?i=Xn3dEjHBZ5M=&t=jZS6ngCVPug=.

Maynard, M. (1994) *Fashioned from Penury: Dress as Cultural Practice in Colonial Australia*, Cambridge University Press, Cambridge.

Merrett, D. (2001) 'Business history', in G. Davison, J. Hirst and S. MacIntyre (eds), *The Oxford Companion to Australian History*, Oxford University Press, Melbourne and New York, pp 102–4.

Miller, D. (2006) 'Strategic human resource management in department stores: An historical perspective', *Journal of Retailing and Consumer Services*, 13, 99–109.

Miller, D., and Merrilees B. (2013) 'Historical ambidextrous marketing: Antipodean perspectives 1876 to 1915', *Proceedings of the sixteenth Biennial Conference on Historical Analysis and Research in Marketing*, Copenhagen Business School, Available online: http://faculty.quinnipiac.edu/charm/CHARM%20proceedings/CHARM%20article%20archive%20pdf%20format/Volume%2016%202013/MIller%20Merrilees%20CHARM%202013%20Proceedings.pdf.

Monitor (1828) 'The Monitor' (23 Aug.), 3.

Mullins, J.J. (1960) 'Marketing services will expand in next decade', *Newspaper News*, 5 (Feb.), 10, 32.

Newspaper & Advertising News (1969) 'First marketing graduates get their degrees' (2 May), 1.

Newspaper News (1931) (Apr.), 3.

Newspaper News (1963) 'University gets "Go" sign to fill marketing chair' (6 Sept.), 1.

Newspaper News (1966) 'No Australian advertising' (25 Nov.), 1.

O'Neill, H. (2013) *David Jones' 175 Years*, NewSouth, Sydney.

Oakman, D. (1995) 'Researching Australia: A history of the market research industry in Australia', MA dissertation, Monash University.

Paton, H. (1914) 'Early reflections of Melbourne advertising', *Ad Club Magazine*, 1/1, 17.

Proceedings and Resolutions of the First Australian Convention of Advertising Men (1918) Queensland Institute of Advertising Men, Brisbane.

Pollon, F. (1989) *Shopkeepers and Shoppers: A Social History of Retailing in New South Wales*, Retail Traders' Association of New South Wales, Sydney.

Reekie, G. (1993) *Temptations: Sex, Selling and the Department Store*, Allen & Unwin, St Leonards, NSW.

Roberts, J.H., and Styles, C. (2001) 'Australia's competitive advantage: Gaining the marketing edge', *Australian Journal of Management* (26 Aug.), 105–20.

Rydge's Marketing (1975) 'How the AMI plans to celebrate 50 years' (July), 27.

Sheedy, K. (2007) *Evolution through Innovation: A History of Marketing Education at Monash*, Monash University, Melbourne.

Simmat, R. (1978) 'The Twenties and Thirties – Rudolph Simmat', in W.A. McNair (ed.), *Some Reflections on the First Fifty Years of Market Research in Australia*, Market Research Society of NSW, Sydney, pp. 5–7.

Sydney Gazette & New South Wales Advertiser (1803) 'In addition to the extensive assortment at the Universal Warehouse' (17 Apr.), 4.

Sydney Gazette & New South Wales Advertiser (1803) 'Earthen-ware – manufactory – Pitt's Row, Sydney' (9 Oct.), 3.

Sydney Gazette & New South Wales Advertiser (1803) 'Sydney Wharf' (11 Dec.), 4.

Sydney Morning Herald (1843) 'Lord's-Day marketing' (27 July), 2.

Sydney Morning Herald (1931) 'Advertising' (12 Mar.), 13.

Sydney Morning Herald (1932) 'Institute formed' (28 July), 8.

Sydney Morning Herald (1932) 'Sales and business' (11 Aug.), 8.

Toplis, A. (2013) '"[No] spot in the whole world offers the advantages to the capitalist which these colonies do …": Setting up a draper's shop in Van Diemen's Land during the 1830s', *Family and Community History*, 16/2, 113–27.

Town and Country Journal (1906) 'Anthony Hordern and Sons' (14 Nov.), 34.

Ville, S. (1998) 'Business development in colonial Australia', *Australian Economic History Review*, 38/1, 16–41.

Wallace, K. (1972) 'Gotch, John Speechly (1829–1901)', *Australian Dictionary of Biography*, National Centre of Biography, Australian National University. Available online: http://adb.anu.edu.au/biography/gotch-john-speechly-3644/text5677.

Waller, D. (1992) 'Shopping by post: The early development of mail order in Australia', *Journal of Direct Marketing Association*, 8/1, 24–38.

Webber, K., and Hoskins, I. (2007) *What's in Store? A History of Retailing in Australia*, Powerhouse Publishing, Sydney.

Wolfers, H. (1980) 'The big stores between the wars', in J. Roe (ed.), *Twentieth Century Sydney*, Hale & Ironmonger, Sydney, 18–33.

17

Marketing history in Britain

From the ancient to internet eras

Richard A. Hawkins

Introduction

Marketing has played an important role in the economic development of the first industrial nation. However, although many different aspects of Britain's marketing history have been explored in the academic literature, as yet no one has written an overview monograph. Furthermore there are gaps in the literature, most notably an absence of case studies relating to Scotland, which was politically independent from the rest of Britain until 1707. Indeed, in this chapter the term 'Britain' refers to the geographical entity and will encompass all of the various political entities that have existed on the island since 43 CE.

Ancient marketing: 43–410 CE

For several centuries much of the island of Britain was a province of the Roman Empire. Nevett (1982, 3–5) suggests the Romans made extensive use of advertising, including advertisements written or inscribed on walls and shop signs. Temin (2013, 100) observes that Roman merchants also 'lessened the threat of adverse selection and moral hazard by using dependents and friends as agents, and through use of a peer-monitored information network, lawsuits, and guilds that were more trustworthy than individuals'. He suggests that there may not have been a more complex and effective system during the next sixteen centuries. Potter and Johns (1992, 143, 203) also suggest by the third century small British towns were engaged in the mass production of table and cooking ware, which would imply the manufacturers were engaging in marketing.

Medieval and pre-modern marketing: 410–1700

Fullerton (1988, 121–2) suggests the antecedents of modern marketing fall within a period beginning approximately in 1500 and ending in 1750. He observes that early capitalist entrepreneurs were unable to create a mass market but did succeed in creating markets for luxury goods. This section adopts a longer period than Fullerton, ending earlier at the beginning of the eighteenth century.

After the collapse of Roman rule in Britain the civilized society they had established collapsed. Nevett (1982, 5–7) suggests that the conditions that had previously provided opportunities for advertisers no longer existed. He suggests the revival of advertising in Britain is linked to the renewed growth of urban settlements and points to the fortified burghs established by Kings Alfred the Great (871–99) and Edward the Elder (899–924) to protect parts of England from Viking raids. Whyte (1995, 54–5) notes that in Scotland there were no Roman towns to provide continuity of urban society, and nothing similar to the fortified burghs in England. In Scotland, comparable burghs do not emerge until the twelfth century. Nevett points to the use of shop signs and town criers in medieval English towns as precursors of modern advertising. Medieval merchants probably also made use of handwritten announcements which they displayed on walls in public places. Casson and Lee (2011, 16–17) have observed that there was a noteworthy proliferation of formal markets and fairs in the period 1050–1330, alongside an expansion of population, production and exchange. Shops emerged in the later thirteenth century. However, contrary to the traditional view argued by Jeffreys (1954, 1–6), that modern retailing is determined by the evolution of fixed shops replacing markets, fairs and itinerant tradesmen, Casson and Lee (2011) suggest that the distinction between markets and shops is not always unambiguous. Shops could be found both within and outside the marketplace. Nonetheless, Berry (2002, 378) observes that from the early medieval period to about 1690 local markets dominated retailing in provincial England. Lythe and Butt (1975, 32) note that in Scotland the sheriffdoms, of which the royal burghs were the centres, had a monopoly of trade and this explains why rural fairs and markets are absent from the kingdom until the late seventeenth century.

The invention of printing in the second half of the fifteenth century was the first disruptive technology to be employed in marketing. Printed notices gradually displaced handwritten ones. Voss (1998, 738) suggests that William Caxton printed the first English advertisement in 1477. He also shows that by the second half of the sixteenth century prefaces inserted by printers, publishers or authors can be found in a wide variety of publications. These prefaces were often used for diverse forms of advertising promoting the written word. Printing also made possible the development of the newspaper. The first consecutively numbered publications appeared in London in the 1620s. Known by various names including newsbooks, they had small circulations and were relatively expensive items affordable only by the literate elite. Nevett (1982, 8) suggests the earliest surviving example of a newsbook advertisement is from 1622. Very few early newsbooks have survived. But it would appear that a growing number were published during the next few decades. The early advertisements appear to have been for books, real estate and patent medicines. By 1657 permission was given for the first publication devoted entirely to advertisements (Nevett, 1982, 7–9). Church (2000, 627) argues that modern advertising from a literary perspective emerged in the late seventeenth century because 'advertising differs from simple announcement by substituting rhetoric for unadorned information'.

After the restoration of the English monarchy in 1660 following the Interregnum of 1649–1660 there was an attempt to introduce censorship with the Printing Act of 1662. The legislation led to the widespread publication of illegal newsletters until it lapsed in 1695. Nevett observes that in the seventeenth century newspaper advertising was a relatively minor advertising medium. He argues retailers would have used shop signs as their main form of marketing. The printed poster was another common form of advertising in the second half of the seventeenth century (Nevett, 1982, 9–14).

Beginning of modern marketing: 1700–1850

The transport revolution of the eighteenth and nineteenth centuries, the development of a national network of canals followed by a nationwide network of railways, helped build a national market for the first time for all categories of goods. During the same period Britain started to build an extensive overseas empire. Belich (2009) has argued the white settlement colonies which formed part of this expanding empire constituted a 'Greater Britain'. The introduction of steam-powered shipping reduced the cost of ocean transportation, allowing British firms to expand into both Greater Britain and other British imperial markets. Fullerton (1988, 122) suggests that the period 1750 to 1850 is when modern marketing in Britain began: 'this period marked the beginning of pervasive attention to stimulating and meeting demand among nearly all of society'.

Berry (2002, 385–6, 389–90, 392) notes that there was little idea of specialization in marketing and sales techniques in the late seventeenth century. This changed during the eighteenth century as retailers began to become increasingly aware of the importance of salesmanship. In the eighteenth century retailers negotiated prices with their customers and offered credit. There were some exceptions, many books, pamphlets and news-sheets had the prices printed on them. However, by the last quarter of the eighteenth century, new retailing practices of cash-only sales combined with fixed prices were being pioneered.

Nevett (1982, 20–2) suggests that the principal form of advertising in the eighteenth century was billposting. While few examples have survived, he notes that bills were used to advertise patent medicines. Much more evidence of newspaper advertising has survived. The eighteenth century saw a ten-fold increase in the number of newspaper titles from 25 to 258. During this century the first daily newspaper was founded, the *Daily Courant*. Whereas in the seventeenth century newspaper publication had been centred in London, as the eighteenth century advanced newspapers began to be printed and read outside London, especially in industrializing Central and Northern England. The government sought to curtail the expansion of the press with the Stamp Act of 1712 which placed a duty ½d. or 1d. on newspapers depending on the size of the printed sheet, as well as a flat rate tax of 1s. on every advertisement. In 1757 the stamp duty was raised to 1d. regardless of size and the advertisement tax was doubled to 2s. Although newspapers were a relatively expensive item in the eighteenth century, it would appear that they were widely read except by the poor and illiterate. Those of modest means did not need to purchase a newspaper because many coffee houses made newspapers available to their customers to read with their coffee. Advertisers were able to place advertisements aimed at both the wealthy and those of modest means. So advertisements began to appear for products such as soap, tobacco, cheap brandy and patent medicines, as well for country estates and expensive books (Nevett, 1982, 15–19). However, Nevett (1982, 20) observes that while advertisements for some categories of consumer goods appear in eighteenth-century newspapers, their incidence tended to be fairly low. Common foods and beer were seldom advertised, while luxury products, for example tea and coffee, ceased to be advertised once they were no longer novelties. He also observes that from the early eighteenth century newspaper advertising provides evidence of the emergence of the practice of branding of products such as ink powder, polishes, blackings, sauces and patent medicine (Nevett, 1982, 21–4). Mitchell (2014, 43–4) provides examples from the eighteenth century of retailers advertising their wares in provincial newspapers. Robinson (1963, 51–2) also provides an example of a manufacturer, Matthew Boulton of Birmingham, who advertised ormolu in the London press in the 1770s (Boulton also used the postal service to contact potential customers using private letters).

During the eighteenth century there was an expansion of fixed shop retailing, in particular for the upper class. By the end of the century luxury and semi-luxury retailers were making carefully targeted use of display and advertising methods. But the lower classes stayed loyal to traditional forms of retailing such as markets and peddlers (Mitchell, 2014, 1–2). Mitchell (2014, 17) observes that it seems likely that during the seventeenth century approximately 40 per cent of markets in English towns specialized in some product or group of products while at the same time providing a centre for the sale of necessities of life and other basic goods. In his case study of London markets, Smith (2002, 41–2) notes that in the capital before the nineteenth century contemporary entrepreneurs and observers rarely concerned themselves with the distinction between retail and wholesale markets. However, he notes that the number of 'wholesaling' markets trebled in London between 1660 and 1840. Mitchell (2007, 550) argues that in provincial England fairs were significant during the eighteenth century and early nineteenth century for agricultural marketing and retailing, although many of them were in gradual decline by the beginning of the 1800s. Hawkers and peddlers filled a market niche later taken in the nineteenth and twentieth centuries by mail order catalogue companies and in the twenty-first by online retailers. Although in eighteenth-century England they were greatly outnumbered by fixed shopkeepers (Mitchell, 2014, 69), they helped widen the market for consumer goods, in particular textiles, clothing and hardware. They reached consumers geographically remote from shops, or who preferred to purchase goods on their doorstep. Mitchell (2014, 64) shows that in the eighteenth century some peddlers would hire rooms in the towns they visited, distributing printed handbills advertising their goods, or placing advertisements in local newspapers. There is evidence (Mitchell, 2014, 69) that by the late eighteenth century some sectors of manufacturing saw hawkers and peddlers as a vital part of their distribution chain. Indeed during the first half of the nineteenth century a growing number of textile and clothing peddlers surrendered some of their independence by becoming agents of a particular firm.

Lythe and Butt (1975, 138) observe that at the beginning of the Union with England fairs and markets rather than shops were the main form of retailing in Scotland. However, by 1725 shops had largely displaced fairs and markets in urban communities although the latter retained their place in rural communities. Lythe and Butt further observe that the great increase in the number and variety of shops in urban Scotland was most marked from the mid-eighteenth century and by the 1820s was a feature of rural Scotland too. From the 1830s they observe that multiple retailers increased in number and non-fixed prices gradually ceased to be a feature of retail trade in Scotland. They also note that, while the Fenwick Weavers' Society founded the first Scottish retail co-operative in 1769 in opposition to employers' truck stores, the most significant period for retail society formation in Scotland was the 1850s and 1860s. Notwithstanding these initiatives on the part of workers, truck shops survived and, in spite of government legislation, continued to dominate retailing in Scottish mining and iron-working districts into the mid-nineteenth century (Lythe and Butt, 1975, 139, 142–3).

Berg and Clifford (2007, 146) observe that newspaper advertising was 'only a small part of a wider world of commercial promotion, display and printed advertisements'. They refer to the wide variety of advertising media employed, which included street posters, shop signs, trade catalogues, manuals, almanacs, town directories and histories, handbills, letterheads and insurance policies. In particular they suggest that the trade card or bill head 'was the earliest widely circulated form of advertising combining image and printed text, and [that] it was more central to pre-nineteenth century advertising than were newspapers and newssheets'. Berg and Clifford (2007, 146, 166) challenge the assumption that pre-nineteenth-century advertising was primitive and argue that 'they very effectively combined visual and textual devices to attract and to challenge "active" readers and consumers'.

The growth in Britain's population during the industrial revolution was accompanied by urbanization. As towns and cities experienced rapid growth in this period former agricultural labourers were unable to continue growing or making the things they required to feed, clothe and house themselves. Mitchell (2014, 10, 102, 111) has observed that there is no doubt that both more consumer goods and a much wider variety of them were available to a wider range of people in the early nineteenth century than at the beginning of the eighteenth. He also notes that retailers displayed an increasingly wide range of sophisticated techniques to attract consumers. These included advertisements in newspapers and published town guides, trade cards and window displays. Mitchell argues that they were also able to target different parts of the potential market by focusing on, for example, price, credit availability, quality or customer service. Strachan (2007, 14) suggests that there were significant innovations in advertising techniques and a progressively refined range of marketing techniques in the late eighteenth and early nineteenth centuries. In addition to the techniques used by retailers, Strachan notes that advertisers made their products separate and distinct. Newspaper advertising was supplemented by a range of secondary marketing techniques including extensively disseminated handbills, advertising carts, roadside advertisements, wall posting and wall painting.

During the first half of the nineteenth century Britain saw the development of larger shops, alternative forms of retail space like arcades and bazaars and the forerunners of department stores (Mitchell, 2014, 129–300). The first arcades and bazaars date back to the period immediately after the conclusion of the Napoleonic wars (Mitchell, 2014, 140). However, Mitchell (2014, 151) observes that there was little difference between the language of a typical shop advertisement in the 1780s and one from the 1830s. Purvis (1992, 107–11) also notes the proliferation of co-operative retail stores in England during the 1820s and 1830s. More were founded in the years immediately before the foundation of the well-known Rochdale Equitable Pioneers Society of 1844. These often short-lived stores were committed to fair trade and also paid dividends to their customers.

The French Revolution which began in 1789 led to a period of political repression in Britain. As Table 17.1 shows, this resulted in both an increase in the taxes applied to newspapers in 1797 and the introduction of a new paper duty in 1803.

While the number of advertisements in stamped newspapers increased from 511,258 in 1800 to 1,902,322 in 1848, Nevett (1982, 26–7) suggests that the effect of the increased duty

Table 17.1 Changes in newspaper taxation, 1797–1861

	1797	1803	1815	1833	1836	1853	1855	1861
Newspaper Stamp Duty	3½d.		4d.[1]		1d.[2]		Abolished	
Advertisement Duty[3]	3s. 0d.		3s. 6d.	1s. 6d.		Abolished		
Paper Duty[4]		3d.			1½d.			Abolished

Notes:
1 effectively 3d. net
2 ½d. extra for supplements
3 levied at a flat rate on each advertisement
4 per lb.

Source: A.P. Wadsworth (1955) *Newspaper Circulations 1800–1954*, Manchester, Norbury, Lockwood & Co., as cited in Nevett (1982, 25)

may have been to divert advertising to illegal unstamped newspapers or alternative media such as placards and circulars. Newspaper advertising was also influenced by the business cycle. In addition to longstanding advertisers such as patent medicine manufacturers, publishers and booksellers, other businesses began to place advertisements in the press, for example, company promoters inviting applications for shares in newly floated companies (Nevett, 1982, 15–40). Advertisement for branded grocery products began to appear in this period, for example, James Schweppe's imported mineral waters from 1793; Robinson's Patent Barley Water from 1824; Crosse & Blackwell's Soho Sauce from 1833, Huntley and Palmer's Superior Reading Biscuits from 1842, and Horniman & Co.'s tea from 1852.

Nevett observes that the taxation of newspaper advertising during the first half of the nineteenth century was one of reasons for the popularity of posters as an alternative advertising medium. Posters were also popular because newspapers did not permit large advertisements or illustrations. Furthermore posters could be organized, produced and installed much more quickly than the placement of advertisements in newspapers. The over-sticking of posters led to the employment by advertisers of sandwich board men and horse-drawn advertising carts (Nevett, 1982, 53–61).

During this period new types of marketing also arose. French and Popp (2008, 793) have noted the emergence of the commercial traveller, or bagman, in the late eighteenth century. The travellers were often employed by merchants, although from the beginning some were employed directly by manufacturers. They might supply products directly or carry samples in order to stimulate orders from retailers, and they were normally responsible for collecting payments.

The growth in advertising in this period led to the emergence of professional intermediaries between the advertisers and the publishers known as advertising agents. Nevett suggests that William Taylor was the first recorded British advertising agent, who was in business as early as 1786. In the early nineteenth century advertising agency firms were established in London. By 1819 an advertising agent was in business in Edinburgh as well (Nevett, 1982, 61–6).

Era of institutional development: 1850–1914

Fullerton's (1988, 122) third era of modern marketing's historical development for Britain begins in 1850. He describes this period as one in which the super-structure of modern marketing was built. However, the outbreak of the First World War marks a more decisive dividing point than the beginning of the Great Depression in Fullerton's suggested periodization.

This era began with the Great Exhibition of 1851 at the specially built Crystal Palace in Hyde Park, London, which showcased Britain's economic progress. It represented an unparalleled marketing opportunity for British business. Richards (1991, 21–2, 36–7) argues it marked a decisive watershed. It marked the beginning of a process of 'commodification', one consequence of which was that goods acquired a potentially enhanced attraction to middle-class consumers. However, Church (2000, 641) argues that patterns of consumption before and after the exhibition invalidate Richards's argument.

Another important development was the nationalization of the telegraph in 1868–70 after which the service was delivered by the Post Office. The telegraph has been described as the Victorian internet (Standage, 1998) because it allowed for the first time the almost instantaneous long-distance transmission of information. Telegraphy should have strengthened the provincial press by allowing them obtain their own news from London and publish and distribute their newspapers before the metropolitan newspapers had been delivered to the provinces by train. However, as Silberstein-Loeb (2009, 759–88) shows, a price cartel controlled telegraphy, service was poor and exorbitant rates were charged for telegrams. Post-nationalization the Post Office charged low rates for telegrams because priority was given to the social importance of distributing news widely throughout the country. In 1870 the principal provincial newspaper publishers founded the Press Association (PA) to prevent competition in news provision which would have raised costs. The PA was to achieve an effective monopoly in the provision of news to the provinces. The number of daily newspapers published outside London increased from 79 to 211 between 1870 and 1900.

The measures taken by the government to create a more permissive environment for the press resulted in a big increase in both the number of newspapers and advertisements during the second half of the nineteenth century. Manufacturers of repeat purchase household products became some of the most prolific advertisers (Nevett, 1982, 67–86). Illustrated advertisements began to appear at the end of the 1870s in new weekly illustrated newspapers such as *The Graphic,* and in the late 1880s in magazines such as the *Illustrated London News.* Benson (1994, 145) suggests some late nineteenth-century advertisers sought to associate their products with the strongest of national symbols, the royal family. With or without permission, they exhibited the royal warrant, printed royal testimonials, put pictures of royalty alongside those of their products and attempted to include members of the royal family in their publicity stunts.

From the 1880s there was a significant reduction in the cost of paper with the substitution of rags or esparto grass by imported wood pulp (Cox and Mowatt, 2014, 25–6). This allowed upmarket newspapers to increase their pagination together with the introduction of cheaper mass market daily newspapers with illustrated advertisements such as the *Daily Mail* in 1896, the *Daily Express* in 1900 and the *Daily Mirror* in 1903. During the first decade of the twentieth century upmarket newspapers such as *The Times* also introduced illustrated advertisements.

Advertisers continued to employ other forms of advertising media. In the 1870s large-scale use of lithography became commercially viable for the first time to allow the production of long runs of colour posters. The introduction in 1855 of a ½d. postal rate for circulars led to the extensive use of duplicated letters in the last quarter of the nineteenth century. Telegrams were also used for advertising campaigns during this period (Nevett, 1982, 86–99). Schwarzkopf (2008, 175) also observes that in 1876–7 the British government issued a million handbills to promote government savings schemes, life insurance and annuities. This was the beginning of central government advertising in Britain.

Mitchell (2014, 11) argues that the middle decades of the nineteenth century are a key watershed in the history of retailing. This is not because the eighteenth century was not dynamic or often modern, but because retailing was essentially structured to meet the needs of a commercial rather than an industrial society. In the decades immediately prior to 1850 there were some significant signs of structural change and radical innovation affecting the scale of individual retail businesses and the way in which they were organized. The really radical developments, such as the spread of multiple and department stores, the increasing importance of branding and the emergence of the mass consumer market were, however, essentially a feature of the second half of the nineteenth century. Fitzgerald (1995, 19, 26, 67) observes that by the last quarter of the nineteenth century even working-class consumers were abandoning retail markets and travelling salesmen in favour of fixed shops. This is also reflected in a big expansion in the number of co-operative stores between 1850 and 1914. The Industrial and Provident Societies Act of 1852 provided a specific legal status for the co-operative societies that founded these stores (Purvis, 1992, 111–30).

The rise of multiple stores was accompanied by packaged branded consumer goods. Companies became responsible for making sure that their brands were stocked by retailers. From the 1870s firms like Rowntree began to increase the numbers of their travelling salesmen. Other methods were used to market packaged goods. In the 1890s Rowntree began to use trading stamps. Each tin of its Elect cocoa contained a trading stamp. Stamps equivalent to the purchase of 6 lb. entitled the purchaser to a free box of Rowntree's chocolates and gums. Rowntree also included coupons in its newspaper advertising that could be exchanged for a 2 oz. sample tin of Elect (Goodall, 1986, 32–3).

The second half of the nineteenth century saw the beginnings of mass production and the development of branding (Mitchell, 2014, 174). The legal recognition of trademarks in Britain in 1876 (Duguid *et al.*, 2010, 13) led to the development of numerous branded and mass-produced goods, which offered consumers consistent quality and standardized shape and size. In turn these types of goods led to the development of mass marketing in Britain. Different types of marketing strategies were employed. For example, the cigarette company, Wills, introduced collectors' cards in 1887 in order to encourage smokers to purchase its cigarettes. Schwarzkopf (2010, 168–70) notes that advertising agencies only began to play an active role in the mass marketing process at a relatively late stage. Before 1914 most advertising agencies restricted their role to the placement of their clients' advertisements in print media. Other professionals such as trademark and patent agents specialized in the creation of brands.

The development of marketing in this period was not restricted to tangible goods. Shin (2014, 188, 191) suggests that from the 1860s Britain's railway companies began to develop sophisticated advertising and publicity techniques. He (Shin, 2014, 203) argues that Britain's railway was one of the pioneers 'in setting the standard of marketing an intangible commodity – travel – through advertising and branding'.

During the first half of the nineteenth century advertisers who wanted to use printed media for business to business advertisements were restricted to trade cards, daily and weekly press, magazines and books. During the second half of the nineteenth century trade journals began to emerge to fill the gap. Tweedale (2014) suggests *The Ironmonger*, first published in 1859, was later claimed with some justice to be the first British trade newspaper. By the end of the nineteenth century there were trade journals covering a wide variety of manufacturing, wholesale, retail and financial sectors. At the same time during the late 1880s two specialist national daily newspapers were founded to serve the business community, the *Financial News* in 1884 and the *Financial Times* in 1888 (Kynaston, 1988).

There were also changes in other types of marketing during this period. French and Popp (2008, 790–1) have noted that the number of commercial travellers increased from 20,730 in 1871 to 98,428 in 1911. A number of manufacturers brought marketing in-house and employed travellers direct, but other businesses continued to use wholesalers and agents in addition to employing their own travellers. French and Popp observe that in 1900, as in 1800, travellers were primarily a feature of the grocery, drapery and hardware sectors, whereas wholesale agencies continued to be significant in the marketing of iron products, jewellery, rubber and tinplate.

Era of consolidation: 1914–1945

Contrary to Fullerton (1988) this chapter suggests the period of the two World Wars and the period in between is a distinct period of consolidation. During the First World War there was a significant reduction in commercial advertising as a result of shortages of newsprint which led to newspapers with fewer pages. However, the government made significant use of advertising during the war to promote army recruitment and the sale of the war loan (Nevett, 1982, 138–44). The war also led to a greater appreciation of working-class consumers. For example, Fitzgerald (2005, 522) observes that during the war production was focused on the less expensive commodities of cocoa and chocolate bars. He further notes that 'The growth in the "working class" market was linked to a perceived need for advertising based on illustrations, emotional appeals, personalities and storylines, all of them able, furthermore, to "make a strong appeal to the cinema-going type of mind."'

Fitzgerald (1995, 5–7) has observed that the 'new' sectors emerging in the twentieth century, in particular those in the electrical, motor car, chemical, food, drink and tobacco industries, as the 'old' staples of textiles, coal, engineering, shipbuilding and steel declined, devised marketing and advertising methods to assist them in securing and retaining customers and to promote consumer demand. He (1995, 34) also argues that after the First World War, 'advertising became more sophisticated and professional, and depended less on the "push" effects of shop displays and discounts and more on the "pull" effects of press and poster campaigns'. Scott and Newton (2012) also provide an example from the financial services sector where marketing and advertising was employed in the successful development of nationwide building societies in this period. Fitzgerald (2005, 512, 521, 527) points in the case of tangible goods to the replacement of an extensive 'scatter-gun' approach to marketing 'with intensive, targeted and highly promoted best sellers', which allowed firms to give pre-eminence to the needs of customers and consumers. Fitzgerald shows that a single company's distribution and advertising policies could transform a sector, as in the case of Cadbury which created a mass market for confectionery in the 1920s centred on the product, Cadbury's Daily Milk, characterized by high levels of personal consumption for the majority of the population. His history of the confectionary manufacturer, Rowntree, provides another example of how changes in marketing methods could transform companies in these 'new' sectors. By the 1930s Rowntree was an innovator in market research, product development and branding. Fitzgerald points to a revolution for many consumer goods manufacturers in which the commercial world was turned upside down and marketing considerations dominated the production function. Although the marketing revolution had its origins in the inter-war period the 'half-cycle' was not completed until the 1950s, which Fitzgerald argues was the first decade of mass consumerism in Britain (Fitzgerald, 1995, 5–7).

The inter-war period saw a big increase in the use of instalment plans known as hire purchase (HP) to sell consumer durables. The total number of HP agreements grew from 6 million in 1924 to 24 million in 1936. HP sales had begun in the second quarter of the nineteenth century and although they were originally restricted to wealthier consumers, by the 1860s working-class households were able to use HP to purchase sewing machines and, by the 1900s, pianos. Scott (2009, 802–27) shows in his case study of inter-war furniture retailing that HP was key to widening the market for new furniture. Furniture retailers made HP a central part of their inter-war newspaper advertising following the initial success of Drage's 'Mr. Everyman' campaign.

In the years immediately before the First World War several American advertising agencies established branch offices in London (West, 1988, 472). Schwarzkopf (2009, 8–20; 2010, 179–184) shows that during the inter-war period one of these American advertising agencies, J. Walter Thompson (JWT), began to offer additional services to its British clients, such as market research and brand planning. From 1927 JWT helped Lever Brothers reinvent Lux soap as one of Britain's first lifestyle brands. British advertising agencies also began to offer brand management to their clients during this period. The value of powerful and emotive brands began to be recognized, and so too was the value of legal protection of brands. During the inter-war period British businesses lobbied government to modernize the trademarks legislation. They eventually achieved their goal with the enactment of the 1937 and 1938 Trade Marks (Amendment) Acts. However, Schwarzkopf (2007, 23–57) argues it would be wrong to see the establishment of British branch offices by these agencies as part of an Americanization process. He observes that in fact until at least the 1950s British agencies enjoyed a competitive advantage over their American competitors because of their capacity to take advantage of the ethos of 'British culture', which significantly hindered the expansion of the American agencies in Britain.

The inter-war years saw the development of new advertising media in addition to traditional ones such as the press and posters. One of these was the cinema. However, advertising appears to have met with resistance from the cinema industry. During this period the government also made use of cinema advertising. From 1928 the Empire Marketing Board (EMB) produced a number of films to promote the produce of the British Empire. They were only partially successful. After the disbandment of the EMB in 1933 its film unit was transferred to the General Post Office (GPO). The GPO was to produce a wide variety of short advertising films promoting its work and products (Heller, forthcoming). Schwarzkopf (2012, 171–92) also shows that during the inter-war period British government departments and public sector organizations such as the EMB and GPO engaged in market and consumer research.

Another new advertising medium was radio. However, the British government had established a monopoly radio broadcaster in 1922, the British Broadcasting Corporation (BBC), funded by radio set licence fees. The British government was opposed to commercial radio stations funded by advertising (USBFDC, 1932, 5–9, 20). However, in 1932 Leonard Plugge founded the International Broadcasting Company (IBC), which was to broadcast regular sponsored programmes with the assistance of French commercial stations such as Radio Normandie. The following year they were joined by Radio Luxembourg which had been granted a government charter in 1931. Britain's newspapers chose to support the BBC by declining to publicize commercial programmes. In response IBC launched its own listings magazine, *Radio Pictorial*, in 1934. Advertising agencies, in particular JWT and the London Press Exchange, also produced sponsored radio programmes broadcast from France and Luxembourg. Commercial radio became an increasingly important medium for the advertising of consumer products during the remainder of the 1930s (Street, 2006, 97–186). The outbreak of the Second World War resulted in the suspension of commercial radio for its duration.

Shin (2014) has shown how railway companies pioneered the marketing of the intangible commodity, travel, before 1914. Heller (2010, 200–4; BBC, 1990) shows that other companies continued to pioneer the marketing of travel in the inter-war period, in particular Shell-Mex Ltd. Shell realized in the inter-war period that in order to create demand for its petroleum products it had to first create the desire and need to travel, by car on land and airplane in the air. Like many other 'new' industries in this period Shell was very creative in its publicity and marketing. For example, to boost air travel it sponsored record-breaking flights within the British Empire. It also made two aviation film documentaries during the 1930s. Shell's director of advertising, Jack Beddington, in an era before design manuals and codes of practice, also commissioned modern art for posters promoting the British countryside and famous landmarks. While this art had nothing to do with petrol it did promote travel and sightseeing. The advertising was aimed at the rich and the affluent middle class. To please them Shell did not disfigure the countryside with advertising billboards. Instead Shell affixed the posters to the sides of their trucks which carried petrol in cans. The cans were essential in era where petrol filling stations were few and far between. From the mid-1930s Beddington also commissioned an acclaimed series of county guidebooks for motorists (BBC, 1990; Schwarzkopf, 2008, 75–7; Heller, 2010, 200–4).

French (2008, 353–4) observes that the numbers of commercial travellers in the inter-war years continued to grow. There were 138,426 in 1931. He quotes a report from 1937 in the *Daily Express* as describing commercial travelling as an 'overcrowded occupation'. Nonetheless, even businesses which adopted new marketing techniques, continued to regard travellers as important. French (2008, 367–8) observes that advertising agencies contended that their services complemented the traveller's knowledge of markets and role in stimulating orders. After 1920 travellers began to provide additional services to retailers on behalf of manufacturers such as advice on products, display and sales techniques.

Notwithstanding the constraints of the wartime economy many businesses continued to advertise their products during the Second World War to maintain brand loyalty (Nevett, 1982, 169). For example Bovril, a meat extract, was advertised extensively in the national press as well as in the regional and local press. In addition, as in the First World War, the government made extensive use of marketing to further the war effort, as for example Watkiss Singleton (2014, 217–31) shows in the case of the National Savings Movement. The war effort was also supported by commercial advertising. Some of Bovril's advertisements, for example, encouraged consumers to forgo their product in order to 'put every penny in national savings' (*Portsmouth Evening News*, 1941).

Era of post-imperial adjustment: 1945–1992

Fullerton (1988, 122) suggests that the period from 1930 to the late 1980s was one of further development, refinement and formalization of institutions and practices that were developed earlier. Although he argues this period began at the same time in Britain as in the United States, in fact in terms of economic development Britain lagged behind the United States in per capita income by at least ten years in 1930. Furthermore Britain suffered a significant loss of productive capacity during the Second World War, causing it to fall even further behind the United States.

Britain emerged from the Second World War heavily in debt. Much of its productive capacity had been destroyed by aerial bombardment during the war. As a result the second half of the 1940s and the early 1950s was a period of austerity. Rationing of food continued until 1954. From 1945 the British Empire was dissolved and replaced by the British Commonwealth – an organization bringing together Britain, the self-governing white settlement colonies and the growing number of former imperial possessions. However, it did not prove possible to create a viable trading bloc. Instead, in 1973 the Britain joined the European Economic Community (EEC) and redirected much of its foreign trade to the ever expanding customs union.

Nevett (1982, 178) observes that from an advertising perspective the years 1952–4 marked a return to normality because this was when controls ended not just on food, but on coffee, tea, biscuits, sugar, confectionery, eggs and petrol. Furthermore, restrictions on hire purchase agreements were lifted in July 1954, providing a boost to the sales of white goods such as radios, televisions, refrigerators and washing machines. Corley (1987, 75–6) notes the remarkable growth in national demand for consumer durables. By 1960 almost two in three British households possessed a television set and almost one in three a motor car.

The national press remained a very effective advertising medium throughout the austerity period. Advertisers also took advantage of the resumption of transmissions to Britain by

Radio Luxembourg in 1946. In 1955 newspaper publishers lifted the ban they had imposed on commercial radio listing 22 years earlier. But after 1955 many of Radio Luxembourg's shows moved with their hosts to the new commercial regional independent television (ITV) stations. Radio Luxembourg then focused on niche youth-focused popular music programming. It progressively lost its audience from the mid-1960s, and its English language service finally went off the air in 1992 (Street, 2006, 199–200).

The economic revival was accompanied by a significant increase in the pagination of both newspapers and magazines. However, newsprint rationing and restrictions on the size of newspapers remained in place until December 1956. Prior to the abolition of newsprint control there was insufficient space available for advertisers in the national press. The provincial press was a very costly alternative in terms of cost per thousand readers if employed for a national campaign. This explains why advertisers enthusiastically embraced the newly launched ITV in September 1955 (Nevett, 1982, 184–90). Rowntree was one of these advertisers and within a short period almost every one of its major brands was being advertised by television. The company found its early use of advertising to be entirely successful (Fitzgerald, 1995, 444, 454).

The 1950s also saw the introduction of self-service retailing in Britain. This trend was reinforced with the progressive removal by the government of resale price maintenance from 1956. The result was a more competitive retail market in which small inefficient independent retailers were unable to compete with multiple retailers. In 1963 the grocery chain store Tesco sought to undermine individual resale price maintenance by the introduction of 'Green Shield Stamps', trading stamps which could be exchanged for gifts. Cadbury and Macintosh temporarily stopped supplying their products to Tesco, followed by Rowntree the following year. Fitzgerald notes that Rowntree had historically overlooked the dividends and discounts provided by the Co-operative (Fitzgerald, 1995, 474, 476, 482–3, 486–8). Tesco continued to give the trading stamps to its customers after the final demise of individual retail price maintenance in 1966 (after 1966 only book publishers could legally enforce minimum prices under the Net Book Agreement which dated back to 1900). Many other retailers followed Tesco's example and adopted trading stamps. However, the significant cost of providing trading stamps led to their demise from the late 1970s (*The Times*, 1977).

Notwithstanding the increase in advertising during the 1950s, Carson (1968, 34–6) has noted there was less recognition of marketing by industry, organizationally as well as operationally. This was due to a number of factors which included the continuance of some rationing into the 1950s, the existence of a resilient seller's market in most industries until the end of the decade, overseas captive markets protected by the British Commonwealth and political and economic ties, reconstruction of war damage caused by aerial bombardment, the actual or threatened nationalization of certain industries, and a failure to recognize social change resulting from the war. Carson's survey of a sample of British firms during the period 1961 to 1966 showed a marked move to establish unified marketing departments but, even in 1967, 25 out of the 54 firms in his sample had yet to be convinced of the need for change. Carson's view that British industrial marketing lagged behind that of the United States is at least in part supported by Tweedale's (1992, 115–16) case study of the Ferranti Computer Group between 1949 and 1963. He observes 'Amateurish marketing techniques, inappropriate sales strategies and poor coordination between R & D and marketing', although he also notes that these faults did not contribute to the failure of Ferranti's computer department.

Between 1955 and 1990 commercial television captured a significant share of total British advertising expenditure. In response the newspaper and magazine sectors had to reorganize and rationalize. Roy Thomson, a Canadian who had acquired the *Sunday Times* in 1959, adopted a different strategy. In February 1962 he introduced a 'revolutionary development in colour advertising', the full-colour *Sunday Times Magazine*, which was offered free with the Sunday newspaper. Although advertisers were slow to embrace this new medium, it later became one of the notable publishing successes of this period (Nevett, 1982, 184–7). Commercial television responded with the introduction of programmes in color in 1969 (*Financial Times*, 1969b). By the autumn of 1973, 93 per cent of the British population could receive good-quality ITV colour pictures (*Financial Times*, 1973). Industry research suggested that colour TV advertisements generated a significantly higher recall than black and white (*Financial Times*, 1969a). By the end of the 1970s colour television set ownership exceeded that of black and white sets (*Financial Times*, 1986).

Another foreign investor in the British newspaper industry, Australian Rupert Murdoch, had an even bigger impact. In 1981 Murdoch acquired *The Times* and *Sunday Times* from Thomson Newspapers. Murdoch believed Britain's newspaper industry was suffering from outmoded labour practices linked to powerful trade unions. In 1985 he opened a new printing plant at Wapping in East London and defeated the print workers' unions the following year after a prolonged dispute. The result was a significant reduction in the cost of newspaper production not just for Murdoch, but for the whole industry. This allowed for a significant increase in newspaper pagination and advertising space. During the late 1980s Britain's national press also began to invest in full-colour presses to try to win back advertisers lost to television (Cox and Mowatt, 2014, 120).

It has been noted above commercial radio had ceased to be significant after 1955 as an advertising medium. However, in 1972 the Sound Broadcasting Act allowed the establishment of local commercial radio stations funded by advertising in Britain for the first time. Nonetheless, commercial radio remained confined to large urban centres until the 1980s (Nevett 1982, 190–1).

The growing concentration of the retail trade from the 1950s increased the bargaining power of the major retailers at the expense of the manufacturers. The retailers also sought to capitalize on their growing power by improving the quality of their private label goods while continuing to offer a cheaper alternative to manufacturers' branded goods. Miskell's (2010, 215, 230) case study of Unilever shows it responded with market segmentation and product differentiation strategies. By the 1980s it was spending four times as much on marketing as on R&D.

Since 1945 there has been a significant growth in foreign ownership of British business. The advertising industry was no exception. American-owned advertising agencies' share of agency billings rose from 13 per cent in 1938 to 42 per cent in 1970. However, the rise of a new wave of British-owned agencies in the 1970s, most notably Saatchi & Saatchi, played a stimulating role in encouraging British agencies to expand overseas. By 1987 the American agencies' share of billings had been reduced to 22 per cent (West, 1988, 470, 478–83).

In addition to the growth of foreign ownership, multinationals increased their share of many sectors of the British economy in this period. Not surprisingly they embraced international marketing methods, in particular corporate identity. Corporate identity means strict control of every aspect of the corporation's image of which the corporate logo is a central part. As part of the adoption of this method Shell, for example, commissioned Raymond Loewy, the French-American industrial designer, to redesign its logo in 1971. The logo became a unifying device to give all of Shell's diverse activities cohesion. In an era where big multinationals had become increasingly similar, where the product appeared to be the same, a strong corporate image could be used to gain a competitive edge. So it was rigidly controlled with strict rules governing its use: by 1990 manuals running to four volumes dictated how Shell's image was to be applied and maintained (BBC, 1990).

Era of the Single European Market and online marketing, 1992 to present

One of the goals of the founders of the EEC was economic and political union. A major step towards economic union took place after 1 January 1993 when all of the internal border controls on trade were removed. The EEC was renamed the European Union (EU). Britain's national market was subsumed into a single European market which, by 2014, comprised 28 EU member states with 507 million people, as opposed to a British market of 64 million people.

During the same period a number of disruptive technologies have had a significant impact on marketing within Britain. From the early 1980s many British retailers began to replace traditional cash registers with laser scanning checkouts. The data from the barcodes of each product scanned at the checkouts were uploaded onto the in-store computers. Among the many benefits was instant stock control (*Financial Times*, 1979). Later the internet allowed in-store computers at multiple stores to be linked to a central computer at the retailers' headquarters allowing the collection of metadata. A further innovation is the collection by some retailers of metadata on individual customers by offering them loyalty cards. The Tesco Clubcard, introduced in 1995, was a pioneer (*Financial Times*, 1995). These cards allow retailers to monitor their customers' expenditure so that they can, as in the case of Tesco, engage in highly focused personalized marketing.

The worldwide web has transformed marketing in Britain in a number of other ways. First, it has transformed and continues to transform the economics of the British press. Newspaper circulation was already in decline before the 1990s. The availability of free news on the web – in some cases provided by newspapers in the form of a web-based version of their print edition – has further contributed to the circulation decline. A significant proportion of advertising has migrated online – particularly advertising placed in regional and local newspapers before the 1990s. The revenue from online newspaper advertising has failed to compensate for declining revenue from print advertising. Furthermore, whole categories of online advertising no longer use newspapers as a medium, with advertisers either advertising on their own websites or specialist websites. Many local and regional newspapers have ceased publication. Before the worldwide web, media rates were based on scarce distribution, whereas there is now unlimited and low-priced online advertising space (Suich, 2014, S3). Second, the worldwide web has transformed retailing since 1990 and continues to do so. Web search engines such as Google and social media sites such as Facebook have become significant new advertising media for British business. The worldwide web has also become a marketplace for goods and services. Initially online retailing in Britain was restricted to the sale of items such as airline tickets, train tickets, hotel rooms, books, CDs and DVDs. The American online retailer Amazon, founded in 1995, has captured a significant share of British markets for the latter three items. It also benefited from the abolition of the Net Book Agreement in 1997. Hundreds of bricks and mortar book stores and CD/DVD stores have gone out of business. Internet booking webpages have to a significant extent displaced bricks and mortar travel agencies and package holiday operators. The new online providers are able to market their products to their customers directly using their email accounts. But Isaacson notes that online marketplaces such as Amazon.co.uk have recreated the type of artisanal cottage industry found in Britain before the industrial revolution (*Financial Times*, 2015). The late 1990s also saw the start of internet grocery shopping. By 2003 Tesco's online division, Tesco.com, had become one of the most profitable internet retail businesses in the world (*The Times*, 2003).

Since the start of an economic crisis in 2008 there has been a significant change in the retailing sector. The giant out of town shops have lost business to online shopping, which is now provided by most major retailers, and in addition, discount retailers and convenience stores too. While the grocery retailers seem likely to survive with a mixed bricks and mortar and online retailing business model, in some sectors such as electrical goods it would appear bricks and mortar retailing is no longer viable.

There have also been changes in television transmission technology which have had a significant impact on its use as an advertising medium. Since the early 1990s the advertising-funded free to air TV channels have progressively lost audience share to multi-channel commercial television delivered by satellite and cable. The mid-2000s saw the introduction of internet streaming of free to air television. Then from 2008 to 2012 the switch from analogue to digital free to air television brought multi-channel television to all British TV viewers (*Daily Telegraph*, 2012). While multi-channel TV allows advertisers to target niche markets, no single TV programme is able to attract the huge national audiences of the 1960s, 1970s and 1980s.

Conclusion

In the mid-2010s there was significant political uncertainty regarding Britain's continued membership of the EU, as well as Scotland's future within the British political union. This potentially has major implications for marketing in Britain, as does the disruption caused by the continued evolution of the worldwide web. Olins (2014, 123–31) also suggests that the decline of the cultural hegemony of the West in the early twenty-first century is beginning to be reflected in the successful marketing of branded goods and services by emerging market companies in Western markets such as Britain. The aftermath of the economic crisis of 2008 has left many of their British competitors in a very weak position to meet this challenge.

References

Belich, J. (2009) *Replenishing the Earth: The Settler Revolution and the Rise of the Anglo-World, 1783–1939*, Oxford University Press, Oxford.

Benson, J. (1994) *The Rise of the Consumer Society in Britain, 1880–1980*, Longman, London.

Berg, M., and Clifford, H. (2007) 'Selling consumption in the eighteenth century: Advertising and the trade card in Britain and France', *Cultural and Social History*, 4/2, 145–70.

Berry, H. (2002) 'Polite consumption: Shopping in eighteenth-century England', *Transactions of the Royal Historical Society*, 6th ser. 12, 375–94.

British Broadcasting Corporation (BBC) (1990) *Design Classics: Shell Logo*. Broadcast on 10 July.

Carson, D. (1968) 'Marketing organization in British manufacturing firms', *Journal of Marketing*, 32/2, 34–9.

Casson, M., and Lee, J.S. (2011) 'The origin and development of markets: A business history perspective', *Business History Review*, 85/1, 9–37.

Church, R. (2000) 'Advertising consumer goods in nineteenth-century Britain: Reinterpretations', *Economic History Review*, 53/4, 623–45.

Corley, T.A.B. (1987) 'Consumer marketing in Britain, 1914–60', *Business History*, 29/4, 55–83.

Cox, H., and Mowatt, S. (2014) *Revolutions from Grub Street: A History of Magazine Publishing in Britain*, Oxford University Press, Oxford.

da Silva Lopez, T., and Duguid, P. (eds) (2010) *Trademarks, Brands, and Competitiveness*, Routledge, New York and London.

Daily Telegraph (2012) 'Switching off ... analogue television comes to an end' (24 Oct.), 14.

Duguid, P., da Silva Lopez, T., and Mercer, J. (2010) 'Reading registrations: An overview of 100 years of trademark registrations in France, the United Kingdom, and the United States', in T. da Silva Lopez and P. Duguid (eds), *Trademarks, Brands, and Competitiveness*, Routledge, London, pp.9–30.

Financial Times (1969a) 'Marketing through colour TV' (24 June), 26.

Financial Times (1969b) 'Colour set market poised for growth' (7 Nov.), 37.

Financial Times (1973) 'ITV colour for 93% of UK' (28 Sept.), 2.

Financial Times (1979) 'Start of a supermarket laser check-out revolution' (12 Oct.), 31.

Financial Times (1986) 'Vital statistics come to life' (9 Jan.), 1.

Financial Times (1995) 'The faithful shopper' (16 Feb.), 18.

Financial Times (2015) 'Opinion: Walter Isaacson: Luddites fear humanity will make short work of finite wants' (4 Mar.), 11.

Fitzgerald, R. (1995) *Rowntree and the Marketing Revolution, 1862–1969*, Cambridge University Press, Cambridge.

Fitzgerald, R. (2005) 'Products, firms and consumption: Cadbury and the development of marketing, 1900–1939', *Business History*, 47/4, 511–31.

French, M. (2005) 'Commercials, careers, and culture: Travelling salesmen in Britain, 1890s–1930s', *Economic History Review*, 58/2, 352–77.

French, M., and Popp, A. (2008) '"Ambassadors of Commerce": The commercial traveler in British culture, 1800–1939', *Business History Review*, 82/4, 789–814.

Fullerton, R.A. (1988) 'How modern is modern marketing? Marketing's evolution and the myth of the "production era"', *Journal of Marketing*, 52/1, 108–25.

Goodall, F. (1986) 'Marketing consumer products before 1914: Rowntree and Elect Cocoa', in R.P.T. Davenport-Hines (ed.), *Markets and Bagmen: Studies in the History of Marketing and British Industrial Performance, 1830–1939*, Gower, Aldershot and Brookfield, VT, pp. 16–56.

Heller, M. (2010) 'Corporate brand building: Shell-Mex Ltd. in the interwar period', in T. da Silva Lopez and P. Duguid (eds), *Trademarks, Brands, and Competitiveness*, Routledge, New York and London, pp. 194–214.

Heller, M. (forthcoming) '"Outposts of Britain": The General Post Office and the birth of a corporate iconic brand, 1930–1939', *European Journal of Marketing*.

Jeffreys, J.B. (1954) *Retail Trading in Britain, 1850–1950: A Study of Trends in Retailing with Special Reference to the Development of Cooperative, Multiple Shop and Department Store Methods of Retailing*, Cambridge University Press, Cambridge.

Kynaston, D. (1988) *The Financial Times: A Centenary History*, Viking, London.

Lythe, S.G.E., and Butt, J. (1975) *An Economic History of Scotland*, Blackie, Glasgow and London.

Miskell, P. (2010) 'Unilever's (other) brand wars: Retailers, private labels, and struggles for supremacy within product supply chains', in T. da Silva Lopez and P. Duguid (eds), *Trademarks, Brands, and* Competitiveness, Routledge, New York and London, pp. 215–233.

Mitchell, I. (2007) 'The changing role of fairs in the long eighteenth century: Evidence from the north midlands', *Economic History Review*, 60/3, 545–73.

Mitchell, I. (2014) *Tradition and Innovation in English Retailing, 1700 to 1850*, Ashgate, Farnham.

Nevett, T.R. (1982) *Advertising in Britain: A History*, Heinemann, London.

Olins, W. (2014) *Brand New: The Shape of Brands to Come*, Thames & Hudson, London.

Portsmouth Evening News (1941) 'Bovril Advertisement' (20 Nov.), 1.

Potter, T.R., and Johns, C. (1992) *Roman Britain*, University of California Press, Berkeley and Los Angeles, CA.

Purvis, M. (1992) 'Co-operative retailing in Britain', in J. Benson and G. Shaw (eds), *The Evolution of Retail Systems, c.1800–1914*, Leicester University Press, Leicester, pp. 107–134.

Richards, T. (1991) *The Commodity Culture of Victorian England: Advertising and Spectacle, 1851–1914*, Stanford University Press, Stanford, CA.

Robinson, E. (1963) 'Eighteenth-century commerce and fashion: Matthew Boulton's marketing techniques', *Economic History Review*, 16/1, 39–60.

Schwarzkopf, S. (2007) 'Who said 'Americanization'? The case of twentieth century advertising and mass marketing from an American perspective', in J.C.E. Gienow-Hecht (ed.), *Decentering America*, Berghahn Books, New York and Oxford, pp. 23–72.

Schwarzkopf, S. (2008) 'Respectable persuaders: The advertising industry and British society, 1900–1939', PhD. thesis, Birkbeck College, University of London.

Schwarzkopf, S. (2009) 'Discovering the consumer: Product innovation, and the creation of brand loyalty in Britain and the United States', *Journal of Macromarketing*, 29/1, 8–20.

Schwarzkopf, S. (2010) 'Turning trademarks into brands: How advertising agencies practiced and conceptualized branding, 1890–1930', in T. da Silva Lopez and P. Duguid (eds), *Trademarks, Brands, and Competitiveness*, Routledge, New York and London, pp. 165–193.

Schwarzkopf, S. (2012) 'Markets, consumers, and the state: The uses of market research in government and the public sector in Britain, 1925–1955', in H. Berghoff, P. Scranton and U. Spiekermann (eds), *The Rise of Marketing and Market Research*, Palgrave Macmillan, New York, pp 171–192.

Scott, P. (2009) 'Mr Drage, Mr Everyman, and the creation of a mass market for domestic furniture in interwar Britain', *Economic History Review*, 62/4, 802–27.

Scott, P., and Newton, L.A. (2012) 'Advertising, promotion, and the rise of a national building society movement in interwar Britain', *Business History*, 54/3, 399–423.

Shin, H. (2014) 'The art of advertising railways: Organisation and coordination in Britain's railway marketing, 1860–1910', *Business History*, 56/2, 187–213.

Silberstein-Loeb, J. (2009) 'The structure of the news market in Britain, 1870–1914', *Business History Review*, 83/4, 759–88.

Smith, C. (2002) 'The wholesale and retail markets of London, 1660–1840', *Economic History Review*, 55/1, 31–50.

Standage, T. (1998) *The Victorian Internet: The Remarkable Story of the Telegraph and the Nineteenth Century's On-Line Pioneers*, Walker & Co., New York.

Strachan, J. (2007) *Advertising and Satirical Culture in the Romantic Period*, Cambridge University Press, Cambridge.

Street, S. (2006) *Crossing the Ether: British Public Service Radio and Commercial Competition, 1922–1945*, John Libbey, Eastleigh.

Suich, A. (2014) 'Special report: Advertising and technology', *The Economist*, 412/8904, S1–S12.

Temin, P. (2013) *The Roman Market Economy*, Princeton University Press, Princeton, NJ, and London.

The Times (1977) 'Trading stamps: The grocery giants brace themselves for a price war' (3 June), 17.

The Times (2003) 'Supermarket's four pillars lift it above rivals' (17 Nov.), 26.

Tweedale, G. (1992) 'Marketing in the second industrial revolution: A case study of the Ferranti Computer Group, 1949–63', *Business History*, 34/1, 96–127.

Tweedale, G. (2014) *The Ironmonger: The King of Hardware Trade Journals*, self published, Manchester.

United States Bureau of Foreign and Domestic Commerce (USBFDC) (1932) *Trade Informaion Bulletin 787: Broadcast Advertising in* Europe, Government Printing Office, Washington, DC.

Voss, P.J. (1998) 'Books for sale: Advertising and patronage in late Elizabethan England', *Sixteenth Century Journal*, 29/3, 733–56.

Watkiss Singleton, R. (2014) '"Doing Your Bit": Women and the National Savings Movement in the Second World War' in M. Andrews and J. Lomas (eds), *The Home Front in Britain: Images, Myths and Forgotten Experiences since 1914,* Palgrave Macmillan, Basingstoke, pp. 217–231.

West, D. (1988) 'Multinational competition in the British advertising business, 1936–1987', *Business History Review*, 62/3, 467–501.

Whyte, I.D. (1995) *Scotland before the Industrial Revolution: An Economic and Social History, c.1050–c.1750*, Longman, London and New York.

18

Pre-Confederation Canadian marketing history

Leighann C. Neilson and Delphin A. Muise

Introduction

In 2017 the Dominion of Canada will celebrate its 150th birthday. While Canada is still a relatively young country by world standards, trade by Europeans within the geographic areas now encompassed by Canada dates back to at least the 1500s. Many good and popular economic histories of Canada over this time period exist (e.g. Bliss, 1987; Norrie and Owram, 1991); however, these have been written primarily by historians and/or economists and therefore tend not to focus on matters of interest to marketing historians. Partly due to the nature of extant historical records and partly because the researchers have come from disciplines other than marketing, factors such as the marketing mix, marketing strategy and the marketing system tend not to be discussed in detail.[1]

In the review which follows, we have been guided by Church's and Godley's (2003, 1) definition of 'modern marketing' as

> the characteristics of persistent, systematic, and increasingly widespread marketing methods adopted by businesses ... In addition to selling ... the term includes advertising, branding, pricing, promotion, market research, and product planning and development ... 'Modern marketing' also encompasses increasingly complex distribution systems.

This definition nicely encompasses the so-called 4 Ps of marketing (price, product, promotion and place) while leaving the door open to discussion of the aggregate marketing system. Wilkie and Moore (1999, 204) describe the aggregate marketing system as 'extend[ing] from extraction of raw materials/crops ... through many levels of value creation to end consumption and disposition in far-off locales'. Importantly for the discussion which follows, what Wilkie and Moore (1999) term the 'classic' functions of distribution – transportation, storage, financing, risk-bearing and selling – are all included in the aggregate marketing system. We may not see evidence of all of these functions in any one firm, however, across the discussion we find many 'historical analogues' (Carlos and Lewis, 2002) and antecedents of 'modern marketing' practice and the aggregate marketing system in Canada. In particular, the

333

effects of what are commonly termed 'external influences', such as political, economic, social and technological forces, on individual businesses and whole industries can be observed.

After providing some basic but necessary historical context, we present a story of Canadian marketing from the time of sustained European interest to the era of Confederation. Due to space restrictions, some topics have of necessity been left out. Thus while the discussion encompasses some of the 'staples' industries, such as fishing, the fur trade and the coal industry in Nova Scotia, treatment of other staples, such as timber from New Brunswick (MacNutt, 1949; Wynn, 1981) and Upper Canada (McCalla, 1987), shipbuilding in maritime Canada (Fischer, 1979; Sager and Fischer, 1982) and wheat from central Canada, has to be left for another time. It is hoped that this chapter will provide the foundation for additional research, including research efforts tracking marketing history post-Confederation.

The historical Canadian context

Canadian history prior to Confederation can be divided into three broad phases, each about a century long and each characterized by a different aspect of its social, economic and political history. As well, each represents a different phase of community development through the exploitation and marketing of a variety of staples. The first two phases were conducted in the context of a struggle between the British and the French for supremacy in various trading ventures – in a way acting out in North America their competition for political and economic advantage in Europe. All colonies were developed for the profit of imperial powers, but differing circumstances could redefine the extent to which their regulation would be seen as a necessary extension of imperial economies.

Phase one was more exploratory than settlement oriented, dominated largely by private individuals who sometimes acted as agents of their sponsoring European states, in the Canadian situation mostly France and England. Between roughly the 1490s, when John Cabot and then Jacques Cartier first identified and mapped the resources of Newfoundland and the Gulf of Saint Lawrence, and the 1660s, the European footprint in what would become Canada was relatively light, assuming we discount the European diseases that devastated much of the native population they encountered along the Atlantic seaboard. In Newfoundland and Québec, although officially discouraged, small, tentative settlements resulted from merchant-driven ventures trading for furs or harvesting the great cod resources of the north-west Atlantic. Any settlements were tolerated as a necessary investment for better exploiting staples to profit the empire.

The second phase – roughly from the mid-1660s through the conquest of New France by the British in 1763 and the subsequent American Revolution, concluded in 1783 – featured direct intervention of the European powers to compete for advantage in North America. Establishment of Royal Government and military reinforcement of New France was paralleled by the British granting of monopoly privileges to the Hudson's Bay Company (HBC). The HBC theoretically controlled upwards of two-thirds of the eventual Canadian land-mass, supported with modest military outposts to control the Bay itself. Competition for the furs of that vast interior was supported on both sides by alliances with various native nations, who exchanged furs for increasingly sophisticated European goods. On the eastern seaboard, competition in the cod fishery was increasingly conducted by European nations who were also competing for advantage at home. The fishery did not require extensive transportation networks on land, so settlement and management of colonial populations was not a priority. The importance of the fishery to France was signalled when they insisted on retaining Cape Breton Island, following their losses in the wars that culminated in the

Treaty of Utrecht (1713). Renamed Ile Royale, the French would establish the largest single military presence in the continent at Fortress Louisbourg, designed to defend their rights in the fishery and serve as an entrepôt for trade between France and Canada, as well as direct trade with the French West Indies.

The third phase – roughly from the 1780s through the 1870s – was conducted in the context of a British Imperium, established after withdrawal of the French in 1763. The essential characteristic of the period was the struggle for various levels of self-determination on the part of the colonists. At the height of its power following victories all across the world, Britain managed its empire to defray the costs of running and defending the colonies and to maximize profits for British merchants. The older American colonies pushed back against these attempts to regulate their economy, resulting in the American Revolution and a total reordering of the North American community. The remnants of the empire would eventually become Canada, now tasked with maintaining a British presence against America's determination to eventually control the continent. A self-defensive protectionist economic environment would privilege British North American access to British markets in exchange for providing a secure source for the fish and timber that would be central to the newly reconfigured empire's survival.

Both France and England had operated their colonies in North America according to an economic theory later labelled 'mercantilism'. Mercantilism holds that there is a fixed amount of wealth in the world. A nation's wealth, therefore, depends on it accumulating as much of that wealth as possible in a zero-sum game (Pinkus, 2012). A basic component of mercantilism was the accumulation of precious metals which could be used for paying soldiers and purchasing arms and ships. 'If gold and silver could not be obtained directly … it had to come indirectly, through a favourable balance of trade, which allowed [the empire] to accumulate gold' (Norrie and Owram, 1991, 24). To accomplish this goal, the agricultural and industrial self-sufficiency of colonies was promoted while trade and commerce was restricted to vessels from the same nation, a complex system encoded in a series of 'Navigation Acts'. 'Colonies contributed to a positive payments balance by providing raw material not available in the home country, by absorbing its processed products, and by acting as a training ground for its navy and merchant marine' (Norrie and Owram, 1991, 24). In this manner, specie supposedly circulated within instead of between empires.

What this meant was that Canadian interests were held to be subordinate to the interests of the 'mother' country. As Reid (1953, 18) has commented,

> The mercantilist theories prevalent in France during the seventeenth and eighteenth centuries made it inevitable that Canadian masts and boards, tar and hemp, wheat and fish should be preferred to similar products from foreign countries; while the prohibition of trade between New France and the English colonies to the south strengthened the reliance of the colonies upon the mother country for manufactured goods.

Colonies were not to develop industrial expertise of their own to compete with that of the mother country (Norrie and Owram, 1991). Therefore, Louisbourg was dependent on Canadian provisions, with many ships stopping there on their return voyage from Québec (Miquelon, 1975), just as New France was dependent on trade with France (Reid, 1953).

Various authors argue that mercantilism was never a conscious strategy of any government (Norrie and Owram, 1991) and that belief in the mercantilist doctrine was always tempered with an eye to strategic advantage in any international competitive circumstances (Pinkus, 2012). Further, Canadian historians disagree about the extent to which mercantilism hindered the growth and prosperity of New France, with some authors pointing instead to geographic factors and the lack of entrepreneurial talent.

> French mercantilism, because of its rigidity, gave only feeble encouragement to the expansion of New France; but not all the weaknesses of the economy of the Saint Lawrence Valley may be ascribed to colonialism. Some of them were inherent in the Canadian geographical context and others, just as fundamental, came from the very mentality of the colonists. The initiatives taken by the metropolis to stimulate economic progress, and sometimes to allow Canadians a greater participation in large-scale trade, met with little response among the population.
>
> *(Fernand Ouellet, 1966, 14, cited in Bosher, 1994, 78)*

Regardless, in the discussion which follows a familiarity with the concept is helpful to understanding how various industries developed and the restrictions on practice faced by early Canadian marketers.

The staples trade

One of the fundamental theories encountered in the study of Canadian economic history, and thus Canadian marketing history, is the staples thesis, popularized by Harold Innis in his 1930 book, *The Fur Trade in Canada*. The staples thesis argued that the stages of colonial development depended on the exploitation of a succession of key primary resources – fish, fur, timber and agricultural products such as wheat. 'The characteristics of the staples, from the technology of their production to the social infrastructures needed to support them, set the pattern of economic and political development of the colony' (Norrie and Owram, 1991, 4). The staples thesis fits hand-in-glove with mercantilist policies. Trade in staples was seen to be dependent on the mobilization of labour, capital and in some instances production techniques imported from Europe in order to extract raw materials on a resource periphery for shipment to distant markets (Harris, 2010). Furthermore, the model that was established with one form of staple could be replicated with minor variations in other staples markets. Thus while the fur trade was dependent on native rather than imported labour to hunt and process a resource that was widely distributed across a land mass rather than concentrated in offshore fishing ranges, the key feature was foreign capital investment designed to meet the demands of foreign markets (Harris, 2010).

Some critics of the staples school of thought point to the way that important industry sectors, and even whole regions of the country, disappear from the discussion once they no longer fit within the staples argument (Norrie and Owram, 1991). Other critics have demonstrated that regional economies, such as that of Ontario, grew and diversified before staples such as wheat became important; historical evidence demonstrates that such supposedly 'key primary resources' may, in fact, have represented only a small proportion of provincial income (McCalla, 1985). More recently, historians such as Béatrice Craig (2009, 4) have argued that the focus of staples theorists on international markets has caused local and regional markets to be overlooked as 'engines of growth and development in their own right'. One result is that agricultural production and locally focused markets have been either overlooked or considered in a negative light because of their comparatively low participation in international trade.

In summary, although the staples thesis has met with much criticism, it continues to be useful, if only for drawing our attention to industries and thus markets worthy of historical research. While in this chapter we do focus on exports to international[2] markets we also recognize that much local trade occurred and include discussion of this where possible.

The fishery (sixteenth century to eighteenth century)

Ships from many countries took part in the early years of the cod fishery off the east coast of Canada. Cod was highly valued because it helped meet consumer demand for a quality meat substitute. A major influence on demand was religious practice.

> There was a desperate need for a cheap source of protein in a time when beef was a luxury. Also, demand was enhanced considerably by contemporary religious doctrine. Various religious holidays were marked by the Roman Catholic Church as meatless. As holy observance multiplied, so, too, did the number of meatless days. With Lent, the fast days associated with various saints, Fridays, and other 'fish days,' this number could be considerable. Altogether, in the sixteenth century, about one in three days was declared to be 'meatless.' The result was a tremendous demand for fish.
>
> *(Norrie and Owram, 1991, 40)*

France was interested in the Atlantic Canadian fishery to meet her own needs, whereas England sought to meet the needs of the Spanish market for dry fish through the expansion of its fishing industry in Newfoundland (Innis, 1937; Janzen, 1998). The French fishery originated from seaports such as La Rochelle, Rouen, St Malo, Nantes and Le Havre where a long tradition of fishing in the Atlantic, along with well-developed technologies and commercial practices, had existed. These technologies and practices could be applied in the Canadian fishery (Harris, 2010; Norrie and Owram, 1991).

For their part, British fishermen found they could catch more fish than they could transport back to market, thus the use of 'sack ships' was implemented. 'Sack ships' were usually larger than fishing ships and carried fewer crew, making it more economical for them to transport the catch to markets in Portugal and Spain. They left port once the season was well under way, in June or July, planning to arrive when sufficient quantities of salted fish were ready for purchase and transport without delay. They set sail loaded with supplies such as biscuit, fabric, clothing, shoes and sundry items like buckles, buttons, thimbles and pins (Janzen, 1998), which they sold to the master of the fishing ship who then resold them to the crew (Pope, 1996).

Sack ships acquired cargo through two means: either the fish had been purchased on consignment via arrangements made before the season began or arrangements were made once the sack ship arrived in Newfoundland (Janzen, 1998). Earlier in the trade, the first method was preferred, but by the early eighteenth century the small, resident population in Newfoundland had grown and was dependent on the sack ships to transport their products to market and provide dry goods and other essential supplies (Crowley, 1989; Janzen, 1998). The goal of the sack ships was to be among the first to reach the markets in Spain, when prices were highest, thus they sought multiple sources of supply in addition to those for which they had contracted.

From the perspective of Great Britain, the Newfoundland fishery was seen as a training ground, producing seamen for the British merchant marine and Royal Navy (Whiteley, 1969). A shore fishery conducted by persons settled in Newfoundland was opposed by British mercantile interests (Norrie and Owram, 1991) and officially discouraged in favour of migratory fishers who returned to Britain in ships laden not only with fish but more importantly with experienced seamen. The trade conducted by the sack ships, therefore, had an important outcome for Newfoundland – by purchasing the catch of the tiny resident population they sustained it and allowed it to exist.

The fishery was regulated to promote British interests over local interests or those of independent businessmen. Trade among Newfoundland settlers, French merchants based in St Pierre and Miquelon and New Englanders after 1783 was considered illicit; active measures were taken to disrupt such trade because it was seen as 'taking away the wealth of England' (Crowley, 1989, 381; Whiteley, 1969). The residential fishery was a disruptive force – it increased the competition and complexity of the market by providing a market for goods from New England. The New England traders brought flour, pork, tobacco, molasses, sugar, lime juice and rum, selling these goods in Newfoundland at prices lower than those that English merchants could profitably offer. As a result, some of the English fishing ships along with some Newfoundland residents 'were liable to find themselves with unsold fish, which made it difficult to pay their men's wages and to order supplies for the next year' (Crowley, 1989, 319).

The practice of extending credit also created problems – an issue we will return to in the discussion of merchants below. Newfoundland residents often hired their crews from Britain, paying them in wages rather than a share of the catch. It was not uncommon for men to contract for two seasons, wintering over in Newfoundland. These fishermen 'were liable to ruinous debt to their employers because they bought goods from them on credit before their wages became due' (Crowley, 1989, 318). Further, during the winter, their employers sold them provisions, including alcohol, at 'extortionate' rates. Moore (1982) argues that in years when catches were small, some proprietors earned more from rum sales to their indebted employees than they did from the fish they caught. As a consequence the fishermen found themselves owing more than they could earn and unable to repay their debts. When the fishermen could not repay their employers, the employers could not pay the merchants who had supplied them with goods for the fishery and the whole network was subject to collapse.

In summary, the east coast fishery was multinational and multilateral, but essentially involved the import of capital, labour and technology and the export of product and profit. Although the fishery was considered to be high risk, it could also be high reward. Norrie and Owram (1991, 43) cite returns as high as 79 per cent for a four- to six-month investment. Although on a small scale and heavily discouraged by Great Britain, we can see evidence of entrepreneurial activities associated with the most basic function of marketing – exchange (Bagozzi, 1978). The terms under which provisions were sold led to complex debt arrangements and not infrequently consumers were unable to meet their financial obligations[3] – a negative aspect of the marketing system which has received recent attention (Besharat et al., 2014; Soll et al., 2013; Wilkie and Moore, 1999).

The fur trade (seventeenth to nineteenth century)

The fur trade occupies an important place in the Canadian imaginary; not only does the beaver loom large as an official emblem of Canada, but so too does the romantic figure of the voyageur. The fur industry emerged to meet the demands for luxury products in Paris. At the same time, it stimulated demand for European goods among native communities (Innis, 1937). The fur trade provides a fascinating example of an extensive, integrated supply chain; for the Hudson's Bay Company the supply chain stretched from the Pacific to Labrador and included hundreds of standardized trading posts (Harris, 2010). Of further interest to marketing historians are the roles played by native peoples as both middlemen and demanding consumers, along with the efforts expended by the HBC to develop products to meet their requirements.

The market for beaver was the primary driving force for the fur trade. Expanding trade during the eighteenth century reflected the growth of the European hat and felting industry, based primarily on beaver pelts (Carlos and Lewis, 2002). Other skins, such as mink, marten, lynx, fox, and ermine, were used for ladies fashions but beaver was the most adaptable and used pelt (Morse, 1961b). Norrie and Owram (1991, 78) estimate that animal pelts 'accounted for more than 90 percent of the exports of New France well into the eighteenth century'. (Though for most of the period we are looking at, the Canadian fur trade was but a fraction of the value of the cod fishery of France and England; and the latter was much less susceptible to the vagaries of the fashion cycle.)

Both the French and the English were involved in the fur trade in Canada. The French were trading through Montréal and Québec City from the early 1600s (Carlos and Lewis, 2002), with the Hudson's Bay Company, headquartered in London, establishing its first posts in the 1670s. Subsequent to the signing of the Treaty of Utrecht in 1713, the area covered by HBC was defined as British, but economic rivalry with the French continued until the end of the French Empire in Canada in 1763. After this, English and Scottish merchants operating out of Montréal also posed competition until the company they formed, the North West Company, merged with HBC in 1821. After the merger, the fur trade experienced a period of expansion from 1821 to 1849 (Hammond, 1993).

In the early days of the fur trade, during the seventeenth century, both the HBC and Montréal fur trade let the Indians come to them (Morse, 1961b). Indian tribes living in close proximity – the Swampy Cree near the HBC's York Factory base of operations and primarily the Huron, but to some extent the Ottawas and Nipissings, for Montréal – would act as intermediaries. In contrast to the popular conceptualization of native peoples foolishly trading valuable furs for a few coloured beads, a number of scholars have instead presented Indians as experienced traders, skilled negotiators and consumers who demanded quality products which suited their way of life and personal preferences (Carlos and Lewis, 2002; Rich, 1960). Rich (1960) emphasizes that the Indians who traded with both the French and the English/HBC jealously guarded their role as middlemen (Norrie and Owram, 1991). The Assiniboine and Cree who brought furs to the HBC trapped very few of the furs themselves. Instead, they traded European goods to other tribes residing at a greater distance from York Factory for all the furs they needed for trade (Rich, 1960). As skilled negotiators, the Indians played the English and French against each other, claiming French goods were superior when bargaining with the English and vice versa when negotiating with the French (Ray, 1988).

The Indians had been receiving French trade goods for a considerable time before the English established their trading posts in the late 1660s. Therefore, the HBC was at a competitive disadvantage. Not only had the French developed considerable experience dealing with the Indians, but the Indians had 'grown accustomed to the French merchandise' (Ray, 1988, 135), in a clear case of first mover advantage leading to customer preference formation (Carpenter and Nakamoto, 1980). HBC attempted to obtain goods with which the Indians were already familiar either by sourcing them from French suppliers or by obtaining samples of French trade goods and attempting to have English manufacturers produce them. Their efforts were not always successful. The Indians sought light-weight goods that were both durable and could stand up to the climate, but English manufacturers had little experience designing for Canadian conditions (Ray, 1988).

Carlos and Lewis (2002) along with others argue that Indian traders were not willing to accept just any goods in trade; goods had to meet their standards and preferences. Metal goods such as guns, hatchets, scrapers, knives and ice chisels were important trade items but were often rejected by Indian traders because they were prone to failure in the extreme climate of Canada. Guns, for example, were inclined to explode if snow got into the barrel. Both Carlos and Lewis (2002) and Ray (1988) document the extensive written correspondence between HBC officials in Canada and the governors back in England regarding the need to adapt metal products to the cold winter conditions of Canada.

Carlos and Lewis (2002, 309) provide evidence of other product failures – pearl beads which met with rejection due to their colour, shape and size; blankets of the right shape, colour and construction but six to nine inches too short; twine that suffered from inconsistency in thickness being both too thick and too thin in places; kettles that were too small and poorly shaped given their weight. These product failures were not the result of negligence or a lack of care. For example, HBC made extensive efforts to obtain the 'best Brazil tobacco' that could be acquired in European markets in order to satisfy the demands of the Indian traders (Ray, 1988). Furthermore, the London directors of the company were diligent in seeking out goods they hoped would appeal to Indian traders and frequently sent samples to Canada to test the market (Carlos and Lewis, 2002). Instead, what we see here is a learning process between trading partners located in very different cultures and geographies. Over time, the goods chosen by Indian traders shifted from what Carlos and Lewis (2002) termed 'producer goods' like guns, powder and knives used for hunting game to 'luxury' items, such as tobacco, alcohol, beads, cloth and jewellery, indicating both their acculturation to European goods and growing sophistication as consumers.

As middlemen, the Huron played a leading role in the fur trade until 1649. In that year, the Iroquois launched a successful assault on the Huron, causing their dispersal and disrupting the balance of power. Although they threatened other tribes who might have taken over the middleman role, the Iroquois were never able to gain the same dominant position once occupied by the Huron. Instead, the French took over the role themselves, and as Norrie and Owram (1991, 69) report, 'Over the next 30 years ... tremendous expansion of the French presence and influence took place'. This vertical integration by the French Canadians led to markedly different supply chain strategies between the two competitors. While the HBC continued to wait for native peoples to bring furs to their forts on the waterfront, the French Canadians moved directly into the interior of the country, collecting furs from tribes at further and further distances from Montréal (Carlos and Lewis, 2002). The French recognized the need to eliminate the middleman many years before the HBC did and it gave them a competitive advantage – by going inland and trading with the tribes who actually trapped the furs, 'they took all the best and lightest furs, leaving only the heavy and poor-quality skins to come down to the Bay' (Rich, 1960, 40).

In order to execute their strategy, the Montréal fur trade[4] made use of Canada's inland waterways. Given the distances to be travelled and the fact that part of the waterway would only be free from ice for five months, both 'ends' of the supply chain moved towards the middle. The journey of the Montréal voyageurs started in Lachine, just above Montréal, in early May. Large canoes capable of carrying up to 3 tons each, and necessitating 10 to 12 paddlers, carried trading goods consisting of hunting equipment, woollen clothing, blankets, metal cooking vessels and utensils, needles, awls and thread (Morse, 1961b). After an eight-week journey, during which they traversed much of contemporary Ontario, they arrived at Grand Portage on Lake Superior.[5] Meanwhile, smaller canoes capable of carrying about half of what the Montréal canoes carried but better suited to western waterways, started moving east from Lake Athabasca, carrying furs. Along the way, other fur-laden canoes would join the procession. Crews from Grand Portage sometimes met the western canoes at Fort St Pierre on Rainy Lake in mid-July in order to give their western partners time to return and distribute trade goods before freezing set in (Morse, 1961a). In this manner, a distance of approximately 3,000 miles (4,800 km) was traversed yearly; trading goods moved west and furs moved east.

One outcome of the expansion of the fur industry by the French was oversupply. 'Between 1675 and 1685, exports of furs doubled. By the late 1690s, they doubled again. Inevitably, the price declined' (Norrie and Owram, 1991, 80). However, instead of fewer furs being supplied, more were offered. In part, this was due to the response of the native suppliers.

> Many of them were nomadic, and accumulation of goods presented real difficulties. Extra pots, pans, or whatever, could be burdensome during the journeys from place to place. There was, in other words, a fixed number of goods desired by many Indian bands. The higher the price for their furs, the fewer the furs that would be necessary to supply their wants. In times of lower prices, however, more would be needed and more would be supplied.
>
> *(Norrie and Owram, 1991, 80)*

Eventually the French government did enact measures to balance supply with demand, however, the effects were not immediately felt and in some years pelts were sold in France at a loss (Norrie and Owram, 1991).

For their part, the HBC maintained a competitor orientation (Armstrong and Collopy, 1996), focusing their attention on their European rivals and attempting to trade in such a manner as to dissuade the Indians from trading with their competitors. HBC took aggressive measures to fend off new competition. When American trapping parties threatened the company's ability to harvest beaver in the Oregon territory in 1820s, HBC sent Métis and Iroquois trappers to harvest the beaver directly, bypassing local native communities. In the words of Governor Simpson, 'The greatest and best protection we can have from opposition is keeping the country closely hunted' (quoted in Hammond, 1993, 17), thereby denying their competition access to raw materials. When the American Fur Company entered the English market for muskrat in 1834, HBC changed its shipping schedule in order to beat the arrival of American furs to market (Hammond, 1993).

The HBC was also proactive in its strategies to overcome cultural differences that stood in the way of trade (Carlos and Lewis, 2002). The response of the Indian tribes to price changes caused similar problems for the HBC to those experienced by the French. The company considered offering higher prices in the hopes of attracting a larger supply of furs. However, the opinion of seasoned traders was that Indians would provide fewer furs if the prices given were increased – sufficient only to purchase enough commodities until the next year/trading cycle. In Rich's (1960, 49) opinion, the Indians were 'hardened enough traders to exploit competition and an alternative market, but un-European in their reaction to better prices'. Rather than rely on price as an incentive, the British introduced new trading goods in an effort to increase trade in specific pelts that were in high demand in the London market (Carlos and Lewis, 2002).

Another important obstacle to overcome was language differences. HBC started sending 14-year-old boys to learn the trade and the Cree language. One of these boys, Henry Kelsey, became a distinguished trader who, after mastering the Cree language, prepared a Cree dictionary which was sent back to London. The company printed copies of the dictionary and sent them to its posts (Carlos and Lewis, 2002). But perhaps a more important influence was the intermarriage of male traders from both the French and English sides with native women. Although discouraged by the HBC, which employed its men on seven-year indentured contracts, it became commonplace. By the early decades of the nineteenth century much of the trade beyond the established forts on the Bay was being conducted by this new Métis nation, the offspring of these country marriages (Brown, 1980; Friesen, 1984; Van Kirk, 1980).

HBC managers employed sophisticated marketing techniques. They learned to recognize cycles in wildlife availability and managed the supply of product to market accordingly. In years when the harvest of skins was great and a collapse in wildlife population was expected in the next year, the company held back some of its products, expecting prices to rise during times of shortage in supply (Hammond, 1993). Although beaver pelts were the best known of the products HBC supplied to the European market, managers sought to diversity their product portfolio and other products found a market as well.

> There were military contracts for bear skins; cutlers bought deer horns or stag horns for pen knife handles; and dentists used "sea horse teeth" (walrus tusks) to make dentures … Isinglass, a pure gelatin extracted from the sturgeon's float bladder, helped clarify wine and beer. Feathers, such as the down of the trumpeter swan, sold for powder puffs.
> *(Hammond, 1993, 15)*

The company's factors forwarded samples of various forms of wildlife in order to determine their worth in European markets. Once such samples reached London, the company researched their relative quality, value, potential markets and potential competitors. Some items were sold at auction so that the company could directly assess buyer response (Hammond, 1993). When the market for beaver collapsed in the 1840s, as the silk hat gained favour with consumers, HBC sought other uses and markets for its flagship product. They experimented with shaving and dyeing beaver pelts to resemble fur seal pelts. Finally, in an attempt to harvest value in the decline stage of the product lifecycle, beaver pelts were shipped to the US, where the beaver hat was still in vogue and a test shipment was sent to China, although the latter effort met with disappointing results (Hammond, 1993).

In summary, the fur trade provides an interesting illustration of the need to adapt to the conditions of international trade. The Montréal-based traders adapted their processes to the Canadian geography and used vertical integration to turn their supply chain into a competitive advantage. The HBC demonstrated the core tenet of the marketing concept by listening to the needs and wants of its consumers/trading partners (Webster, 1988). In a typical year, Indian traders could select from 60 to 70 different trading goods (Carlos and Lewis, 2002). Furthermore, the company conducted quite a bit of product development, seeking new uses for its products and exploring the market potential of new products.

The effects of the fur trade were far-reaching. Ray (1988, 146) goes so far as to call the Indian traders agents of technological change, since 'the tempering and casting of metal had to be improved to produce knives, hatchets, kettles, ice chisels, and guns that were less prone to breaking in the severe cold'. But probably the biggest impact that the fur trade had on Canada was that it established 'east-west thinking'; 'As Harold Innis states in his *The Fur Trade in Canada*: "It is no mere accident that the present Dominion coincides roughly with the fur-trading areas of northern North America"' (Morse, 1961b, 74–5).

The coal industry (nineteenth century)

Coal was slower to evolve as a staple than some other products, mostly because there was little perceived demand. Coal was available in abundance in Britain and France; its relatively high bulk in relation to value did not encourage transatlantic trade. During Louisbourg's occupation in the first half of the eighteenth century coal was taken from the cliffs in nearby Port Morion to heat public buildings and it was used in the forges there. A certain amount of casual exploitation by New England traders looking for a return cargo occurred where the coal was easily available on the cliffs.

After sporadic but under-capitalized initiatives following the American Revolution various Halifax merchants determined to test American markets along the Atlantic Seaboard. The continued control over the resource by the imperial government kept leases short-term, thereby inhibiting possibilities for increasing revenue from royalties paid directly to the local government. In the 1820s, the smaller scale of the earlier years was replaced by demands for more long-term leases to encourage investment. Halifax merchants led by Samuel Cunard pressed for a monopoly in exchange for promises of royalty money that would help defray the costs of government (Langley, 2005).

In the midst of these negotiations a British firm, the General Mining Association, sought and was awarded by the imperial government a controversial 99-year exclusive lease of all coal and other minerals of the province. Recognizing the controversy their monopoly caused, the General Mining Association allied itself with the Cunard family of Halifax as their agents for the disposition of coal in Halifax and for the marketing of Nova Scotia coal in Boston, New York and Philadelphia. Convincing American consumers that the Nova Scotia coal was equivalent in quality to Newcastle coal being brought out to America as ballast was one of their chief tasks. Sub-agents were engaged in all the principal port cities along the American seaboard and the success of the coal industry was guaranteed (Gerriets, 1991, 1992).

The combination of experienced British mine managers, who recruited hundreds of skilled British miners, and the acumen of Halifax businessmen propelled the industry into a dramatic expansion. What had been little more than a cottage industry, with mostly surface workings, became an extensive deep underground mining operation at several sites in Cape Breton Island and on mainland Nova Scotia in Pictou and Springhill. A yearly output of something less than 20,000 tons spiralled to 100,000 tons during the first decade of the Mining Association's tenure. With American markets established and expanding in the 1840s and 1850s the demand for free trade in coal was accomplished with the Reciprocity Treaty of 1854 between the British North American colonies and the United States. By the end of its ten-year span output would approach a million tons per annum, virtually all of it going to established and carefully developed American markets.

The success of the coal industry was entirely about successful marketing. Doubts about the quality of the Nova Scotia coal had to be overcome with a variety of demonstrations before likely customers. And the industry could only succeed with careful cultivation of that market over time through maintaining the quality and supply of coal to long-term buyers. The coal industry would soon become the most important single industry in Nova Scotia, its royalties subject to fierce debates in the legislature over the legitimacy of the British conferred monopoly. The monopoly was finally broken in 1857, allowing new entrepreneurs from the United States and other parts of Nova Scotia into the industry. The end of the American Civil War prompted a turn to a protective regime there, which soon excluded Nova Scotian coal from that market. After a short pause, the Nova Scotian politicians in the new Canadian nation were advocating retaliatory tariffs to protect

Canadian markets for Canadian coal, which responded to the new opportunities that arrived with railroads and Confederation.

The merchants

Merchants played important roles during all three historical periods in pre-Confederation Canada (Acheson, 1969; Bosher, 1994). Miquelon (1975) identifies the resident factor, or agent, as the most important of the merchant groups in New France, because without them the business of companies based in France could not be enacted in Canada, while Acheson (1969, 414) argues that, in the early nineteenth century, wholesale importers in York (Toronto), 'carried the whole burden' of the region's balance of trade. While there are many case studies in the literature,[6] the examples which follow serve to illustrate four major points. First, the occupation of merchant has historically encompassed a broader scope of activities and ventures than how we understand the term today. Second, to be successful merchants operated within a broad network built on trust and commitment that could be even more extensive than our current conceptualization of business-to-business relationship marketing (Morgan and Hunt, 1994). Third, while the two most important duties of factors and merchants were composing their orders for the following season's goods and the decisions they made about the extension of credit (Miquelon, 1975), it was the granting of credit which had a crucial impact on the economy. And finally, through their support for mercantilism and investments in commercial ventures, merchants may have delayed the expansion of industrial development.

David Kirke and his family provide an early example of the range of functions performed by merchants. They settled in Newfoundland in 1638 after Kirke received a patent from the crown to collect taxes (Pope, 1996). Kirke-owned ships 'engaged in new trading practices: selling supplies brought out from England, buying fish on the spot, [and] arrang[ing] the export of cargoes to England' (Bliss, 1987, 28). He established Newfoundland's first tavern and after his death, his widow, Sara, and their sons managed 12 boats and employed more than 60 men. Kirke thus combined his official function of tax collection with his own entrepreneurial activities in the fishing and service industries, import/export trade and ship-owning. This pattern would be repeated many times over the years by other merchants.

Today, we tend to think 'retail' first when we hear the term 'merchant', but this was not always so. Merchants in Saint John, New Brunswick, characteristically performed a range of commercial functions including

> the importing and wholesaling of produce, the export of fish and wood products, the transport of other people's goods, the purchase of staples produce on other people's accounts, the sale and auction of other people's goods, private banking, and acting as agents or directors for chartered banks, fire, marine and life insurance companies.
>
> *(Acheson, 1979, 4)*

Probably no one merchant combined all of these functions; the most successful focused their efforts on three or four of these activities. In York in the 1820s, the typical entrepreneur was both a wholesale importer and retailer, performing five key functions: 'retailer to the consuming public; wholesale importer both for personal retail purposes and for re-sale to shopkeepers; flour and ash speculator to local farmers; flour and ash exporter to the Montréal market; and financier' (Acheson, 1969, 408). As the business community expanded, new business owners adopted specialized roles, but those who fulfilled the traditional roles dominated the business community (Acheson, 1969).

In their seminal article, Morgan and Hunt (1994) developed a model of relational exchanges which exist at the core of relationship marketing. They argued that the 'new' relationship marketing was part of a then-developing network paradigm, 'which recognizes that global competition occurs increasingly between networks of firms' (p. 20). The merchants of New France provide additional evidence that relationship marketing has a much longer history than originally thought (Tadajewski, 2009; Tadajewski and Saren, 2009). As Bosher (1994, 373) explains,

> The business associates of a typical Québec merchant in the eighteenth century might include a score of variously employed friends in France, Canada and perhaps the West Indies; formal business partners in La Rochelle and Bordeaux; and a dozen or more agents in other French and Spanish ports, including Saint-Malo, Nantes, Bayonne, Rouen, Santander, Bilbao, Cap Français (Saint-Domingue) and one of the Martinique ports. He was part of a large trans-Atlantic circle including perhaps royal officials, minor noblemen and other landowners, military or naval officers, as well as bankers and merchants. How all these people assisted him is not always recorded in archival sources, but the more we study such circles, the more we see them as associations for mutual advancement and profit.

Family connections were particularly important, with some families 'choos[ing] to live partly on one side of the Atlantic and partly on the other in order to facilitate their trans-Atlantic trade' (Bosher, 1994, 7). Whenever possible, merchants sought to employ their relatives as clerks, partners and agents. 'Loyalty and trust, supreme elements in all business relations, were doubly vital in the seventeenth and eighteenth centuries when cash was scarce and trade depended on a sophisticated network of credit' (Bosher, 1987, 30). Merchants' families sought upward social mobility, with marriage between families being used as a means of cementing business relations based on trust and common purpose. Within New France, wholesale and shipping merchants (*négociants*) ranked higher on the social scale than shopkeepers (*marchands*) and thus marriage into the families of military officers, royal officers or magistrates by family members of merchants was seen as more acceptable (Bosher 1994, 373).

Bosher argues that religious affiliations were the most important to New France merchants. 'Catholic, Protestant, and Jewish merchants traded freely together, but they seldom formed partnerships and even more rarely intermarried ... Religious groups were, then, more persistent and fundamental than we are accustomed to think' (Bosher, 1987, 43). The Protestant Huguenots were largely driven out of the Canada trade from 1685 to 1730. From 1713 to the 1740s, most of the trade was in the hands of Roman Catholics. The place of Catholics in official French society was privileged – only Catholics could obtain royal appointments, financial posts, and only the families of Catholic merchants could intermarry with officials, financiers and magistrates (Bosher, 1987). Not only could Catholics, therefore, obtain competitive advantage over their business rivals in terms of exploiting their relational networks, but the Catholic clergy represented a profitable market segment.

From the 1730s onward, the Huguenots started to reclaim and increase their share of the market until the British conquest in 1763 (Bosher, 1987). One of the essential differences between the two religious groups when it came to the conduct of business was the composition of their relational networks. While the typical Catholic merchant would be related to priests, officials, military officers and financiers, all within Bourbon royal society, the typical Huguenot merchant was related to other merchants in Amsterdam,

London, Hamburg, Geneva and Boston (Bosher, 1987), a more international network. Thus, marketing practice was dependent on building and maintaining a variety of relationships from an early date in Canada.

The importance of trust in business relationships can be linked directly to the system of credit that was employed. Whether in eighteenth-century New France or in early nineteenth-century Upper Canada the shortage of specie in circulation meant that direct exchange of imports for exports was preferred. Because of the unfavourable balance of Canadian exports, importers and merchants sometimes had to be paid with promissory notes (Acheson, 1969; Bosher, 1987; Reid, 1953). In New France, merchants usually opened current accounts with one another, with their suppliers and with local tradesmen (Bosher, 1987). 'Credit by current accounts was short-term, being in principle settled on an annual basis; low-risk, being confined to stable business friends, and most important of all, it was reciprocal. Debit and credit transactions were continually cancelling each other out' (Miquelon, 1975, 8).

Moore (1982) relates the history of Jacques Rolland, a young entrepreneur who established a shop in Louisbourg in 1742. Rolland spent a summer in Louisbourg conducting business on behalf of his employer Mervin et fils before proposing that company advance him the stock to establish his own shop. He would retail Mervin goods year-round, repaying his suppliers out of his profits. The firm had consigned merchandise to local retailers in the past but the death of their local agent presented an opportunity for Rolland. He was able to establish trade credit with the Mervins, and through them to stock his shop with many goods including bolts of fabric from France, Spain, Holland and Britain, sewing materials (needles, pins, thread, buttons, clasps), yarn for knitting, ribbons, beads, costume jewellery, ready-to-wear items such as capes, breeches and shirts, men's, women's and children's shoes and slippers, gloves, mittens, stockings, hats, and various household and personal items such as pencils, corkscrews, tobacco, knives, combs, and soft cover books, including those designed for the instruction of young children (Moore, 1982, 95–7).

The value of the goods which arrived on the ships in April 1743 totalled about twice what Rolland's yearly salary would have been as an employee. He was granted credit under the usual terms – interest free until the end of September of the same year. He in turn, offered credit to those customers he assessed as worthy until the end of the fishing season. Unfortunately for Rolland, the summer of 1743 was one of the worst ever for fishing. As a result, his customers could not repay him and he, in turn, was forced to ask his supplier, Mervin et fils, to consider converting his debt into a longer term loan with interest. In the end, the Mervins declined to do so. Rolland's personal effects along with the remainder of his stock were sold at public auction in order to satisfy his creditors and he left Louisbourg bankrupt.

As discussed above, the granting of credit to fishermen by their employers could have negative effects (Crowley, 1989). This case illustrates the network effects of a downturn in the supply of a staple. It also demonstrates the wide range of manufactured products, sourced from international markets, which trade brought to residents. Dealing in a wide variety of merchandise was one way to reduce risk – the hope was that losses on some goods would be recouped through the sale of others (Bosher, 1987). But the maintenance of a large assortment of goods was also linked to the credit system. Credit was extended in return for volume purchase. Like Rolland, Québec merchants Havy and Lefebvre stocked a wide range of goods so that a customer might satisfy all his needs at their warehouse. Having made a large purchase, the customer often paid for only half and was given credit for the remainder (Miquelon, 1975). In the agricultural economy of 1820 York, farmers were likely to pay much of their debt to local merchants in the form of flour. They were frequently given premiums of up to 7 per cent for exchanging their flour and ashes for goods rather than specie, a practice which ate into the margin of merchants who aimed to achieve a net profit of 15 per cent on the sale of their goods (Acheson, 1969). Merchants in York typically replenished their stock at least two, if not three, times per year. The goods they brought in would be sold within a short time frame of four to five months. However, most of this would be sold on credit, and it would be a least a year before final payment could be expected. In the meantime, the merchant would need to restock (Acheson, 1969). Thus we see the merchant's dilemma and the importance of credit-granting to the marketing system of the time.

Merchants exercised influence in other areas as well. In his study of the 'Great Merchants'[7] of Saint John, New Brunswick, Acheson (1979) asks if, 'by virtue of their influence within the political framework of the colony and their control of the principal sources of capital, merchants were able to promote or inhibit certain kinds of [economic] development'. If so, 'then their role in determining the economic destiny of the city [and the surrounding area] ... was as important as the presence or absence of any specific resource' including staples (Acheson, 1979, 7). Acheson is here contributing to the debate regarding the role of the nineteenth-century merchant in Canada – whether merchants promoted or retarded the development of an industrial base under local control.[8] In making his case based on the merchants of Saint John, Acheson identifies them as ship-owners rather than shipbuilders, an important distinction also made by Sager and Fischer (1982). Ship-owners speculated in the purchase and sale of ships or used them to move goods, often as part of the West Indies trade. Shipbuilders were closer in spirit to manufacturers. Acheson demonstrates how these merchants were not risk-averse, they made substantial investments in industries which they considered essential to the economic well-being of their core businesses, 'Financial institutions, transportation links, resource exploitation and urban development ... enable[d] them to facilitate trans-Atlantic trade and dominate a hinterland extending for 200 miles around the city' (Acheson, 1979, 11). Their single most important investment was land and several of the great merchants owned significant amounts of land in the Saint John area as well as in Nova Scotia, Maine, New York and Upper Canada. While they considered shipbuilding and wood and fish processing to be important elements of their commercial systems, most of the leading merchants did not invest in secondary industries prior to 1840. The great merchants dominated the Chamber of Commerce, which, as a result, took no position on the requests from the manufacturing industry for support in their quest for tariff protection. The great merchants were not able to control the destiny of the province single-handedly and thus by the 1850s and 1860s, the manufacturing sector in New Brunswick experienced rapid growth and by 1871 the provincial economy was becoming increasingly diversified. However, Acheson (1979, 27) concludes, 'the influence of the great merchants delayed this development by two critical decades'.

Sutherland (1978) looks at eighteenth- and early nineteenth-century development strategy of merchant community in Halifax, identifying a group of 'great merchants' similar to Acheson's. He notes that, after the 1780s, Loyalist merchants saw Halifax emerging as a second Boston,

> thriving on the West Indies carrying trade and functioning as chief commercial entrepôt within the Maritimes. Implementation of this development program demanded the elimination of competition from 'old' New England, a task colonial lobbyists believed could be accomplished through the application of mercantilist restrictions against American business enterprise.
>
> *(Sutherland, 1978, 2)*

Following the War of 1812, Halifax merchants became increasingly involved in staples production, particularly fish and timber. They lobbied for a redefined form of mercantilism. The merchants still wanted a privileged position in trade with Britain and other imperial dependencies, but now they wanted to be able to trade directly with European countries in order to reduce the cost of their inputs, subsidies on imported salt for the fisheries, bounties to encourage the production of high-quality salted cod, and support for the building of canals to facilitate trade with interior Nova Scotia (Sutherland, 1978). As directors of banks, marine and fire insurance companies, and owners of steamship lines and newspapers, few of these merchants showed an interest in manufacturing. Sutherland concludes that Halifax merchants weren't drawn into investment in mass production facilities because, first, they lacked access to a populous, integrated regional market, and second, the imperial government was opposed to protective tariffs that might have encouraged colonial industry. Instead, Halifax merchants displayed a preference for commercial over industrial ventures, and began to see their future as linked to an integration of maritime and St Lawrence colonies (Sutherland, 1978).

In general, the great merchants were aligned with the empire and privileged access to British markets. 'Many Halifax merchants believed that as mercantilism collapsed, so disappeared their port's prospects for further survival' (Sutherland, 1978, 14). However, a larger number of more localized merchants were looking to free themselves from restraints to buy in the cheapest markets and sell in the highest, no matter where they were located. Increasingly, such issues revolved around the relationship with the more powerful economy emerging in the United States.

Conclusion

British North America's circumstances shifted both politically and economically between 1860 and 1880. America's Civil War brought on a wave of nationalism which installed a protectionist and revenue-seeking regime, which virtually excluded Canadians from their markets. The British, fearful of the rising cost of imperial management and the new military might of the Americans, were determined to reduce their financial and military responsibilities for their North American colonies. The realignment of the colonies was propelled forward by their individual exposure to the vagaries of changing economic circumstances, as well as a political crisis in the United Province of Canada, where French and English seemed unable to form a stable government. While the subsequent Confederation of the colonies, formalized by the British North America Act of 1867, would take most of a decade to complete, a new Dominion of Canada from sea to sea would be accomplished.

What was to be the guiding principle of the new nation? Principally, it was an economic union to defend themselves from American protectionism. In the first instance there was an attempt to renegotiate some form of reciprocal trade agreement in natural products, such as wheat, timber and coal, with the Americans. When that failed, debate revolved around the alternatives and – in the midst of a sharp economic crisis during the 1870s – the idea of a firm nationalist stand to include broad tariff protection for Canadian-based industries against both their American and British competitors. The new 'National Policy' was soon given substance as Canadian merchants and entrepreneurs pushed to render the country independent of foreign imports of the widest array of consumer goods. The new manufacturing economy was largely derivative of American and British technologies and know-how, but the brands were defiantly Canadian and the markets soon spread across the whole country. While exports would continue to drive large areas of the economy, incentives would promote Canadian-made goods. Extensive industrialization over ensuing decades occurred in every sector, from textiles through to farm machinery and various refined foods, etc. A massive trans-Canadian rail network would ensure that no matter where the products were produced they would be available everywhere.

Canadian business cannot boast of pioneering new forms of enterprise or developing unique managerial methods; its business practices have typically been derived from those of French, British or American trading partners (Bliss, 1987). In fact, trade depended to such a large degree upon credit extended by merchants and financiers in the 'mother' country that Miquelon (1975, 21) sees it as a 'natural occurrence' that 'brought with it the whole European apparatus of promissory notes, personal bonds, mortgages, the taking of interest, and redress through the courts for commercial causes'. Instead, the factors which distinguish Canadian business include: (1) its relatively small population, especially in comparison to the neighbours to the south; (2) the tendency for that population to cluster along the 8,891 km (5,525 miles) border with the United States; (3) the immense size of the country, second only to Russia, with a total area of 9.9 million square kilometres (3.8 million square miles; (4) the difficulty of conducting business in a harsh climate; (5) the historical reliance on natural resource extraction/production and export trade (Norrie and Owram, 1991); and (6) a competitive strategy based on working with or through government, which again distinguishes Canada from the US (Bliss, 1987).

Notes

1 We owe a debt of gratitude to Robert Tamilia and Stanley Shapiro for their 2011 bibliography on Canadian marketing, *References on the History of Canadian Marketing Found in Textbooks, Journals and Other Sources from the Seventeenth Century to Present*, which can be accessed on the CHARM website: www.charmassociation.org. An abbreviated and annotated version was published in the *Journal of Historical Research in Marketing* (see reference list for citation information).

2 In agreement with Cunningham and Jones (1997), we suggest that the existence of international trade or commerce presupposes the actuality of international marketing practice. However, if we accept Fisk's (1907, 6, cited in Cunningham and Jones, 1997, 89) definition of 'international commerce' as 'commercial dealings between nations' then we need to qualify this to a certain extent by recognizing the nature of the exchanges which took place. During the French and English regimes, trade was conducted among colonies of an empire, rather than between independent nations (Bosher, 1987; Miquelon, 1975; Norrie and Owram, 1991). Some coastal trade, such as the servicing of Newfoundland outport villages, operated within the colony. And in spite of attempts to control and direct trade to maximize advantage to European competitors, the reality is that there was extensive smuggling and competition among the colonists, who persisted in pursuing their own interests with or without the benediction of their colonial masters (Sutherland, 1975). This form of coastal trade, between Atlantic Canada, the territories still claimed by France and New England post-1783, could be considered 'international'.

3 The discussion of consumer debt issues in the late seventeenth century is particularly interesting given the state of consumer indebtedness in Canada today. The ratio of household debt to income increased to a 'record high' in 2014. The ratio of household debt to disposable income reached 163.3% (Marr, 2015) compared with a ratio of 66% in 1980 (Chawla and Uppal, 2015).

4 The years 1770 to 1820 mark the peak period for the Montreal-based fur trade (Morse, 1961a).

5 After 1803, they used Fort William instead because Grand Portage became American property.

6 See e.g. Eric Sager's study of St John, Newfoundland merchants, Gerry Panting's discussion of the growth and decline of merchandising in Yarmouth, Nova Scotia, and Lewis Fischer's biography of Charlottetown entrepreneur James Peake; all in Fischer and Sager (1979). Cariou (2004) discusses the nineteenth-century tailoring trade in Montreal through the example of Gibb & Co., while Miquelon (1975) provides a detailed account of Havy and Lefebvre, factors for Robert Dugard & Co. of Rouen, France.

7 Acheson focuses on 40 'Great Merchants' out of a population of 800 individuals who held the legal status of merchant. The criteria he used to identify the great merchants was 'ownership of significant shipping, wharfing and waterfront facilities, directorships of important financial agencies, public esteem and influence as manifested in the press and in public documents, public service and personal wealth' (Acheson, 1979, 7).

8 For a thorough review of the debate up to Acheson's time, see MacDonald (1975).

References

Acheson, T.W. (1969) 'The nature and structure of York commerce in the 1820s', *Canadian Historical Review*, 50/4, 406–28.

Acheson, T.W. (1972) 'The national policy and the industrialization of the Maritimes, 1880–1910', *Acadiensis*, 1/2, 3–28.

Acheson, T.W. (1979) 'The Great Merchants and Economic Development in St. John 1820–1850', *Acadiensis*, 8/2, 3–27.

Armstrong, J.S., and Collopy, F. (1996) 'Competitor orientation: Effects of objectives and information on managerial decisions and profitability', *Journal of Marketing Research*, 23 (May), 188–99.

Bagozzi, R.P. (1978) 'Marketing as exchange: A theory of transactions in the marketplace', *American Behavioral Scientist*, 21/4, 535–56.

Besharat, A., Carrillat, F.A., and Ladik, D.M. (2014) 'When motivation is against debtors' best interest: The illusion of goal progress in credit card debt repayment', *Journal of Public Policy and Marketing*, 33/2, 143–58.

Bliss, M. (1987) *Northern Enterprise: Five Centuries of Canadian Business*, McClelland & Stewart, Toronto.

Bosher, J.F. (1987) *The Canada Merchants, 1713–1763*, Clarendon Press, Oxford.

Bosher, J.F. (1994) *Business and Religion in the Age of New France, 1600–1760: Twenty-Two Studies*, Canadian Scholars' Press Inc., Toronto.

Brown, J.S.H. (1980) *Strangers in Blood: Fur Trade Families in Indian Country*, University of British Columbia Press, Vancouver.

Cariou, G. (2004) 'Enduring roots: Gibb and Co. and the nineteenth century tailoring trade in Montreal', in A. Paul (ed.), *Fashion: A Canadian Perspective*, University of Toronto Press, Toronto, pp. 182–202.

Carlos, A.M., and Lewis, F.D. (2002) 'Marketing in the land of Hudson Bay: Indian consumers and the Hudson's Bay Company, 1670–1770', *Enterprise and Society*, 3 (June), 285–317.

Carpenter, G.S., and Nakamoto, K. (1989) 'Consumer preference formation and pioneering advantage', *Journal of Marketing Research*, 26 (Aug.), 285–98.

Chawla, R.K., and Uppal, S. (2015) 'Household debt in Canada', Statistics Canada, 75-001-X, available online: www.statcan.gc.ca/pub/75-001-x/2012002/article/11636-eng.htm (accessed June 2015).

Church, R., and Godley, A. (2003) 'The emergence of modern marketing: International dimensions', *Business History*, 45/1, 1–5.

Craig, B. (2009) *Backwoods Consumers and Homespun Capitalists: The Rise of a Market Culture in Eastern Canada*, University of Toronto Press, Toronto.

Crowley, J.E. (1989) 'Empire versus truck: The official interpretation of debt and labour in the eighteenth-century Newfoundland Fishery', *Canadian Historical Review*, 70/3, 311–36.

Cunningham, P., and Jones, D.G.B. (1997) 'Educator insights: Early development of collegiate education in international marketing', *Journal of International Marketing*, 5/2, 87–102.

Fischer, L.R. (1979) '"An engine, yet moderate": James Peake, entrepreneurial behaviour and the shipping industry of nineteenth century Prince Edward Island', in L.R. Fischer and E.W. Sager (eds), *The Enterprising Canadians: Proceedings of the Second Conference of the Atlantic Canada Shipping Project*, Memorial University of Newfoundland, St John's, pp. 97–118.

Fischer, L.R., and Sager, E.W. (eds) (1979) *The Enterprising Canadians: Proceedings of the Second Conference of the Atlantic Canada Shipping Project*, Memorial University of Newfoundland, St John's.

Fisk, G.M. (1907) *International Commercial Policies*, Macmillan Co., New York.

Friesen, G. (1984) *The Canadian Prairies: A History*, University of Toronto Press, Toronto.

Gerriets, M. (1991) 'The impact of the General Mining Association on the Nova Scotia coal industry, 1826–1850', *Acadiensis*, 21/1, 54–84.

Gerriets, M. (1992) 'The rise and fall of a free-standing company in Nova Scotia: The General Mining Association', *Business History*, 34/3, 16–48.

Hammond, L. (1993) 'Marketing wildlife: The Hudson's Bay Company and the Pacific Northwest, 1821–49', *Forest and Conservation History*, 37/1, 14–25.

Harris, C. (2010) 'The spaces of early Canada', *Canadian Historical Review*, 91/4, 725–59.

Innis, H.A. (1930) *The Fur Trade in Canada: An Introduction to Canadian Economic History*, Yale University Press, New Haven, CT.

Innis, H.A. (1937) 'Significant factors in Canadian economic development', *Canadian Historical Review*, 18/4, 374–84.

Janzen, O.U. (1998) 'A Scottish sack ship in the Newfoundland trade 1726–27', *Journal of Scottish Historical Studies*, 18/1, 1–18.

Langley, J.G. (2005) 'Samuel Cunard 1787–1865: "As fine a specimen of a self-made man as this western continent can boast of"', *Journal of the Royal Nova Scotia Historical Society*, 8, 92–115.

McCalla, D. (1985) 'The internal economy of Upper Canada: New evidence on agricultural marketing before 1850', *Agricultural History*, 59/3, 397–416.

McCalla, D. (1987) 'Forest products and Upper Canadian development, 1815–46', *Canadian Historical Review*, 68/2, 159–98.

MacDonald, L.R. (1975) 'Merchants against industry: An idea and its origin', *Canadian Historical Review*, 56/3, 263–81.

MacNutt, W.S. (1949) 'The politics of the timber trade in colonial New Brunswick, 1825–40', *Canadian Historical Review*, 30/1, 47–65.

Marr, G. (2015) 'Canada household debt ration hits new record of 163.3%', *Financial Post* (12 Mar.), available online: http://business.financialpost.com/personal-finance/debt/canada-household-debt-ratio-hits-new-record-of-163-3 (accessed June 2015).

Miquelon, D. (1975) 'Havy and Lefebvre of Quebec: A case study of metropolitan participation in Canadian trade, 1730–60', *Canadian Historical Review*, 56/1, 1–32.

Moore, C. (1982) *Louisbourg Portraits: Life in an Eighteenth-Century Garrison Town*, Macmillan of Canada, Toronto.

Morgan, R.M., and Hunt, S.D. (1994) 'The commitment-trust theory of relationship marketing', *Journal of Marketing*, 58 (July), 2–38.

Morse, E.W. (1961a) 'Voyageurs' highway: The geography and logistics of the Canadian fur trade', *Canadian Geographical Journal*, 62/5, 148–61.

Morse, E.W. (1961b) 'Voyageurs' highway: The Canadian fur trade. Its logistics, and contribution to Canadian development', *Canadian Geographical Journal*, 63/2, 64–75.

Norrie, K., and Owram, D. (1991) *A History of the Canadian Economy*, Harcourt, Brace, Jovanovich Canada Inc., Toronto.

Ouellet, F. (1966) *Histoire économique et social du Québec, 1760–1850: Structures et conjonctures*, Fides, Montreal and Paris.

Panting, G. (1979) 'Cradle of enterprise: Yarmouth, Nova Scotia, 1840–1889', in L. R. Fischer and E.W. Sager (eds) *The Enterprising Canadians: Proceedings of the Second Conference of the Atlantic Canada Shipping Project*, Memorial University of Newfoundland, St John's, pp. 253–71.

Pinkus, S. (2012) 'Rethinking mercantilism: Political economy, the British Empire, and the Atlantic world in the seventeenth and eighteenth centuries', *The William and Mary Quarterly*, 69/1, 3–34.

Pope, P. (1996) 'Adventures in the sack trade: London merchants in the Canada and Newfoundland Trades, 1627–1648', *The Northern Mariner*, 6/1, 1–19.

Ray, A.J. (1988) 'Indians as consumer in the eighteenth century', in R. Fisher and K. Coates (eds), *Out of the Background: Readings on Canadian Native History*, Copp Clark Pitman Ltd., Toronto, pp. 134–49.

Reid, A.G. (1953) 'General trade between Quebec and France during the French regime', *Canadian Historical Review*, 34/1, 18–32.

Rich, E.E. (1960) 'Trade habits and economic motivation among the Indians of North America', *Canadian Journal of Economics and Political Science*, 26/1, 35–53.

Sager, E.W. (1979) 'The merchants of Water Street and capital investment in Newfoundland's traditional economy', in L.R. Fischer and E.W. Sager (eds), *The Enterprising Canadians: Proceedings of the Second Conference of the Atlantic Canada Shipping Project*, Memorial University of Newfoundland, St John's, pp. 75–95.

Sager, E.W., and Fischer, L.R. (1982) 'Atlantic Canada and the age of sail revisited', *Canadian Historical Review*, 58/2, 125–50.

Shapiro, S.J., and Tamilia, R.D. (2011) 'The history of Canadian marketing: From the seventeenth century to World War II: An annotated bibliography', *Journal of Historical Research in Marketing*, 3/3, 402–22.

Soll, J.B., Keeney, R.L., and Larrick, R.P. (2013) 'Consumer misunderstanding of credit card use, payments, and debt: Causes and solutions', *Journal of Public Policy and Marketing*, 32/1, 66–81.

Sutherland, D. (1975) 'Halifax 1815–1914: "Colony to Colony"', *Urban History Review*, 1975/1, 7–11.

Sutherland, D. (1978) 'Halifax merchants and the pursuit of development, 1783–1850', *Canadian Historical Review*, 59/1, 1–17.

Tadajewski, M. (2009) 'The foundations of relationship marketing: Reciprocity and trade relations', *Marketing Theory*, 9/1, 9–38.

Tadajewski, M., and Saren, M. (2009) 'Rethinking the emergence of relationship marketing', *Journal of Macromarketing*, 29/2, 193–206.

Van Kirk, S. (1980) *Many Tender Ties: Women in Fur-Trade Society in Western Canada, 1670–1870*, University of Manitoba Press, Winnipeg.

Webster, F.E., Jr. (1988) 'Rediscovering the marketing concept', *Business Horizons*, 31 (May–June), 29–39.

Whiteley, W.H. (1969) 'Governor Hugh Palliser and the Newfoundland and Labrador Fishery, 1764–1768', *Canadian Historical Review*, 50/2, 141–63.

Wilkie, W.L., and Moore, E.S. (1999) 'Marketing's contributions to society', *Journal of Marketing*, 63 (special issue), 198–218.

Wynn, G. (1981) *Timber Colony: A Historical Geography of Early Nineteenth Century New Brunswick*, University of Toronto Press, Toronto.

19

A history of modern marketing in China

Zhihong Gao

Introduction

While China's history dates back to as early as 4500 BCE, the imperial period started in 221 BCE with a unified Qin Dynasty and ended with the collapse of the Qing Dynasty in 1911. Politically, China opened a modern chapter in 1912 with the founding of the Republic of China, which was succeeded by the People's Republic of China (PRC) on the mainland in 1949. However, it would be inaccurate to periodize the development of modern marketing in the country solely based on these epochal milestones.

According to Lin (2015), the traditional economy is one that developed without the influence of modern science and technology. Skinner (2001) posits that modern markets occur only when a marketing system is linked by efficient transport to external efficient systems of production. Following this logic, I define modern marketing as marketing that utilizes modern manufacturing, transportation, and communication technologies to achieve economic efficiency, and traditional marketing as marketing that does not possess these characteristics.

The ending of the First Opium War in 1842 marked a turning point in Chinese history. Before 1842 traditional marketing dominated. Afterwards, unequal treaties with foreign powers forced the Qing government to open its port cities to foreign businesses, and some Chinese elites turned to the West in their search for solutions to China's woes. Therefore, it was during the late Qing period that, together with modern industry, transportation and communication, modern marketing first took root in China (Bergère, 2009; Cochran, 1980). The same period also witnessed the birth of Chinese nationalism (Fairbank and Goldman, 2006), a direct product of China's humiliating interaction with the West and a predominant theme of China's modern history. Thus, it is more productive to consider 1842 as the starting point of modern marketing in China and treat the late Qing and the Republican period together. Although the Chinese Communist Party (CCP) has been ruling mainland China since 1949, its regime can be further divided into two periods of divergent practices, with the year of 1978 as the dividing line: between 1949 and 1977, Communist China was committed to socialist economic development, anti-capitalism and anti-imperialism; since 1978 it has been gradually opening up its economy to capitalist development and globalization. For these reasons, this chapter will periodize the development of modern marketing in China into three periods: the Late Qing and Republican period (1842–1949), the Communist Mao period (1949–77), and the Post-Mao period (1978–present). The first period is further divided into the Late Qing period and the Republican period.

Before we discuss these periods, it is helpful to outline the state of traditional marketing in China. Imperial China was an agrarian economy of vast regional differences, an autocratic state with bureaucratic administration and a Confucian culture of conservatism and anti-commercialism (Fairbank and Goldman, 2006). Yet, it had a well-developed traditional marketing system with elaborate hierarchical networks of standard, intermediate and central markets, which not only enabled the flow of merchandise throughout the system but also functioned as social systems where marriages were arranged, religious affiliations organized, and class structure solidified (Skinner, 2001). Licensed by the state and serving primarily courtiers, officials and wealthy landowners, some merchants handled interregional trade through extended family networks, became conspicuous consumers themselves and joined the gentry class by buying land and cultivating literati lifestyles (de Pee, 2010; Esherick and Rankin, 1990; Finnane, 2003). By the early nineteenth century, China remained a self-sufficient agrarian economy with a huge but largely poor population, and its international trade was limited to exports such as silk and tea and imports such as silver and opium (Fairbank and Goldman, 2006). Against this background, China – defeated by the British in 1842 and forced to open some of its ports to foreigners – was reluctantly thrust into the turbulent tide of globalization and modernization.

Marketing during the Late Qing and Republican period: 1842–1949

Chinese nationalists remember the Late Qing and Republican period as 'China's century of humiliation' because of the many invasions, unfair treaties and concessions that foreign imperialists inflicted upon the country. The period was also associated with perennial corruption, rebellions, revolutions, warlords, boycotts, wars and devastation (Fairbank and Goldman, 2006). On the other hand, it was an era of capitalist development, modernization and globalization, as new ideas, media, technologies and institutions from the West were introduced into the once-isolated Middle Kingdom and fundamentally changed the Chinese way of life (Bell, 1999). Modern marketing took roots in China in this complex context.

The Late Qing period (1842–1911)

The late Qing period witnessed the appearance of modern transport such as steamers and the railway, improved roads to industrial production centres, the introduction of mass media such as newspapers and magazines, and the growth of treaty ports (Fairbank and Goldman, 2006; Skinner, 2001). Treaty ports were governed by unfair treaties between China and foreign powers, where foreign governments could establish concessions and exercise extraterritorial jurisdictions. Shanghai grew from a population of 700,000 in 1865 to 1,300,000 in 1910 (Bergère, 2009; Fairbank and Goldman, 2006). The population of Hankou, a treaty port on the Yangtze River in central China, increased from 181,000 in 1888 to 590,000 in 1911 (He, 2010).

China did not experience rapid industrialization during the Late Qing period due to the government's suspicion of Western technology (Fairbank and Goldman, 2006). In 1885 there were 16 machine-explored coal mining enterprises and 23 metal ore enterprises in the country, and in 1895 there were 21 modern arsenal and navy construction enterprises – these projects were all sponsored by the state (He, 2010). Shanghai had 108 modern industrial businesses in 1894 with a combined capital of $30 million but most of them were foreign-owned (Bergère, 2009). There were 11 foreign-funded modern factories in Hankou by 1895 (He, 2010). In his study on businessmen in Hangzhou during the period, Yin (2014) records 42 factories established in the city by the Chinese between 1894 and 1911, majority of which produced cotton products, foods, soaps, candles, matches or cigarettes. In the late nineteenth century, foreign imports into China grew in both volume and variety. In 1893, 'miscellaneous goods', including cigarettes, matches and cotton products, constituted 30 per cent of the value of total imports (Bergère, 2009). The rapid growth of imports produced a strong detrimental effect on China's domestic industries (He, 2010).

Foreign companies during the Late Qing period relied largely on local Chinese merchants as their agents to distribute their products in China (Chan, 2001). Hence, coming from prominent families with a Confucian-learning, bureaucratic-office-seeking tradition, many Chinese compradors of foreign businesses made their fortune by serving as the nexus between the Chinese and the foreign, and between the old and the new (Bell, 1999). Meanwhile, new professions, such as industrialists, teachers, journalists, engineers, medical doctors, independent writers and artists, began to emerge in large cities (Fairbank and Goldman, 2006), and these in turn became consumers of both Western ideas and products. Retailing flourished in cities. By the 1860s there were specialty shops in Shanghai that sold Western goods, and in the 1890s there were 28 foreign tooth powder brands on the market (Nakajima, 2012). According to government statistics, Hankou in 1909 had more than 4,800 stores selling all kinds of products (He, 2010).

Advertising experienced development together with new technologies and mass media. The first lithographic printing shop appeared in Shanghai in 1876 (Cahan, 2006). *Shenbao*, an influential newspaper, was founded in 1872 in Shanghai by an Englishman (Tsai, 2010) and carried product advertisements (Si, 2011). Magazines witnessed steadily rising readership from the 1870s (Nakajima, 2012). The British-American Tobacco Company (BAT) started to widely disseminate its advertising in China in the 1890s, and it set up its own print shops with imported printing presses in 1905 to produce advertisements (Cochran, 1980).

In summary, modern marketing took root in China during the Late Qing period but did not experience substantial development. This was due to the Qing government's conservative attitude towards new technologies and commercial activities. It was during the Republican period that modern marketing entered a golden age in China.

The Republican period (1912–1949)

China during the Republican period was marked by tremendous divides between cities and rural areas, between coastal regions and inland regions, and between the rich and the poor. Today researchers are mesmerized by the cosmopolitan, glamorous facets of Chinese port cities such as Tianjing and Shanghai in the early 1900s, even though the majority of the Chinese at the time – including urban residents – lived in poverty. For example, in Shanghai a floor area of 718 square feet and 8,077 cubic feet of space usually housed eight families with 24 persons (Lu, 1999). Chinese smokers had to give up cigarettes in summer in order to buy melons because they could not afford both (Crow, 1937/2008). In 1930 the average Beijing household spent 70 per cent of its income on food, and low to middle income families on average had 3 pieces of summer clothing, 1.5 pieces of fall and spring clothes, and 2.4 pieces of winter clothing per person (Dong, 2003).

While the traditional marketing system continued to dominate China's rural areas, the Republican period witnessed the rapid growth of some consumer goods industries, including cotton mills, flour mills, as well as cigarette, paper and match manufacturing (Fairbank and Goldman, 2006). Relying heavily on networks of personal relations, Chinese merchants and capitalists from the same localities monopolized certain lines of business and favoured mutual obligations in their business transactions (Crow, 1937/2008; Bergère, 2009). Imports flooded the Chinese market: textile, flour, rice, sugar, alcohol, cooking oil, baking soda, seafood, cigarettes, metal products, chemicals, items for daily use (kerosene, paper, pens, hats, glass, clocks, umbrellas, tooth powder, tools for barbers, eye glasses, new-style buttons), equipment for hospitals and schools, vehicles and parts, photographic and musical instruments, foreign films, laundry machines, Kotex sanitary napkins, hormonal birth control agents, cornflakes, antiseptic soaps, deodorants and Parisian hosiery (Crow, 1937/2008; Dong, 2003; Bergère, 2009). This long list suggests that rich Chinese at the time already participated in a global consumer culture. To compete with imports, Chinese companies offered products of equal or even superior quality at lower prices (Dong, 2003), and they were big imitators of trademarks (Crow, 1937/2008, 219). Some Chinese brand names at the time – such as Airplane firecrackers, Aviation cigarettes, Football wool products and Boy Scouts textile machinery – reflected the appeal of Western modernity to the Chinese (Cahan, 2006). Chinese businesses also utilized segmentation and targeting: one shoe shop in Beijing, Nei Lian Sheng, targeted the rich and powerful, while another, Tianchengzhai, provided for the needs of ordinary folk (Dong, 2003). Given widespread poverty, cigarette marketers sold individual cigarettes to the poor (Cochran, 1980).

The development of marketing during the Republican period was facilitated by China's modernizing transportation system. Beijing was accessible by train from almost all the major cities in the country by 1935 (Dong, 2003). Most imports arrived at major Chinese seaports and then were moved to the interior by wholesalers (Bergère, 2009). In his meticulous study of the long rivalry between BAT and China's Nanyang Brothers Tobacco Company (Nanyang), Cochran (1980) provides some interesting details on how BAT managed its supply chain and distribution system in China. Once established in China, instead of importing raw materials from the United States (US), BAT taught Chinese farmers to grow American tobacco with free American seeds as well as initial financial support from the company, which inevitably made these farmers dependent on the company. It also linked tobacco purchasing with manufacturing, distributing and advertising through a decentralized system of eight regional offices that could adapt easily to local situations. For distribution, it recruited influential local Chinese merchants to serve as regional agents with exclusive distribution rights, while its foreign employees served as inspectors, overseers and advisers to these Chinese merchants. It further instituted a hierarchy of distributors consisting of regional dealers, sub-dealers and itinerant vendors who travelled around in the countryside to set up mobile cigarette concessions. Even though much of China's interior was still inaccessible by modern transport, BAT managed to distribute its products all over the country by combining modern means such as trains and steamboats with traditional options such as caravans, boats, mules, horses and camels. Evidence suggests that, to compete with foreign companies, many Chinese capitalists also incorporated vertical integration into their operation (Bell, 1999; Cochran, 1980).

In major cities retailing stratified to serve different market segments. There were 12,000 shops in Beijing in 1935, with foreign retailers (British, French, American, Russian and Japanese) handling imports and serving foreign customers, department stores and specialty stores catering to rich Chinese, and outdoor temple markets and street stands selling cheap handcraft products to the lower class (Dong, 2003). The rise of modern department stores, such as Wing-on, Sincere and Dah Sun, in Shanghai is well documented by researchers. According to Chan (1999), these department stores were located in Western-style buildings equipped with elevators, air-conditioning, heating, basement shopping arcades and in-house broadcasting stations to play music and announce sales. Sincere alone boasted four floors of shopping areas, 300-plus salesmen, and over 10,000 items of consumer goods, the majority of which came from Europe, Japan and North America. Branding themselves as symbols of modernity through fixed prices, stylish product displays and friendly service, these stores even introduced purchase by correspondence and home delivery in the 1920s (Bergère, 2009). In contrast to these upscale department stores, most retailers in China at the time were small and ill funded. Crow (1937/2008) describes a typical Chinese indoor shop as 12 feet wide and 18 feet deep, 'windowless and doorless so that the whole front was open for the display of goods in the daytime and closed by shutters at night. In the back was a small stone-paved court-yard separating the shop from the kitchen, and above were several sleeping-rooms' (Crow, 1937/2008, 33). Such shops were usually very specialized, incurred low fixed expenses and maintained very low inventory.

Thanks to the development of modern media such as newspapers, magazines and radio, advertising experienced impressive growth during the Republican period. By 1931 there were nine daily newspapers in Shanghai, 15 in Tianjing, 21 in Beijing, and 11 in Guangzhou; *Shenbao* was distributed nationally with a circulation of more than 100,000 in 1931 (Tsai, 2010). There were over 200 magazines in 1933 (Bergère, 2009). In major Chinese cities consumers were exposed to advertising in a variety of media, such as newspapers, radio, magazines, and outdoors; in a variety of forms, such as sign boards, wall paintings, neon lights, cigarette cards, scrolls, handbills, calendars, wall hangings, packing cases, cotton canvas covers for the tops of carts and vests for rickshaw pullers and mats for their rickshaws; and in all kinds of places, including temple walls, city gates, houseboats, ship sails, water tanks, military headquarters, schools and private residences (Barlow, 2008; Cochran, 1980). Most of the print ads targeted the new professional middle class in major cities, and the advertised products were marketed as symbols of progress and modernity. Sex appeal was widely used to sell all kinds of products, including beer, cigarette, insurance and medicine. Initially, foreign brands directly imported their ads from home markets. For example, BAT first put up posters depicting American historical figures such as George Washington and Abraham Lincoln as well as white women as pin-ups, which were called 'hairy person pictures' by the Chinese (Cochran, 1999). Later on, foreign brands learned to adapt their advertising to the Chinese taste (Crow, 1937/2008). Overall, commercial arts of this period represented a hybrid of Chinese and Western influence (Cahan, 2006).

There were two types of ad agencies during this period: foreign agencies of British, Japanese and American origin, and Chinese domestic agencies. Carl Crow Inc., established in 1918 by an adventurous American, was the most well-known foreign agency at the time. It employed a dozen staff, owned a network of 15,000 billboard sites throughout China, served famous clients such as Buick, Pond's, Colgate, Eastman Kodak and California Raisin; it famously induced all the Chinese movie stars to use the toilet soap it advertised and used star testimonials in its newspaper ads, which pictured Hollywood and Chinese stars together but gave more space to Chinese stars (French, 2008). There were some successful Chinese agencies as well. For example, C.P. Ling, which was founded by Lin Zhenbin, a US-educated adman, handled major accounts such as Ford, GM, Coca-Cola, Philip Morris, ASPRO, KLIM milk powder, Parker Pen and Pan American World Airlines (Barlow, 2008). Leading agencies offered a full range of services, including creative work, media placement, marketing research and promotion management, and to overcome language problems in advertising modern products such as cars, Carl Crow even compiled a complete glossary of car-related terms and cajoled a Chinese association of car dealers to officially endorse it (Crow, 1937/2008).

Attracted by the huge size of the Chinese market and facilitated by big budgets, major foreign advertisers spared no efforts in their marketing promotion. BAT opened a school in lithography to teach its workers, hired Chinese artists to invent calendar-poster advertising, reached tie-in agreements with a wide range of businesses to do place-based advertising and invested in one of the best modern motion picture studios outside the US as well as a large network of movie theatres to showcase its products through movies (Cochran, 1980, 1999). In addition, promotional methods, such as contests, sweepstakes, rebates, discounts and free samples, were frequently used to boost sales (Cochran, 1980, 1999; Crow, 1937/2008). To build its relationship with the government, BAT sponsored documentaries to promote political figures, including warlords (Johnson, 2012, 160). In its long battle against Nanyang, BAT resorted to methods such as price wars, trademark lawsuits, exclusive dealing arrangements, false advertising and public relations campaigns to play on the rival's alleged connection to Japan (Cochran, 1980). On their side, Chinese companies played the card of nationalism and frequently mobilized all of Chinese society to boycott foreign products; foreign companies also experienced more strikes by their workers (Benson, 1999; Cochran, 1980; Gerth, 2003; Tsai, 2010).

The Chinese government during the Republican period played an ambivalent role in the rivalry between Chinese and foreign businesses. Restrained by unfair treaties, the tax system of the Chinese government exempted foreign companies and products and levied heavy taxes on Chinese businesses to fund its military initiatives (Bell, 1999; Cochran, 1980). While the Nationalist government promoted economic nationalism and supported boycotts against foreign products and especially those from Japan, it initiated government control of some industries, which led to bureaucratic capitalism and large-scale corruption among government officials (Bell, 1999; Benson, 1999; Fairbank and Goldman, 2006). It also collaborated with foreign businesses out of self-interest. Chinese local government frequently suppressed labour unrest on behalf of foreign capitalists; as rewards for being its major financial prop, the Nationalist government allowed BAT to operate outside treaty ports and granted it major tax concessions (Osterhammel, 1984).

Lack of protection for local industries led to the dominance by foreign businesses, which owned 73.8 per cent of China's total industrial capital by 1936 (Cheng, 1964). China's budding capitalist development was disrupted by the Sino-Japanese War between 1937 and 1945 as well as the civil war between the Nationalists and the Communists that followed. More importantly, the national crisis brought about by the Japanese invasion pushed the Nationalist government to embrace a planned socialist economic system that emphasized state-owned enterprises and heavy industry, which laid the ideological and institutional foundation for Communist China's state monopoly after 1949 (Bian, 2005).

Marketing during the Mao period: 1949–1977

After taking control in 1949, the Communist regime implemented drastic measures of socialist transformation to modernize China. The Chinese economy experienced rapid growth between 1949 and 1957 due to significant investment in heavy industry and infrastructure (Fairbank and Goldman, 2006). Notably, the new government expanded existing railroad and highway networks to facilitate inter-regional trade (Lippit, 1966). However, misguided policies on agriculture and commerce soon led to insufficient supply of agricultural and consumer products, so that Chinese living standards in both cities and rural areas actually declined after 1957 (Ash, 2006). More importantly, in implementing its Marxist view of marketing, the regime adopted radical policies to curtail the role of the market in the economy (Solinger, 1984). Regular political campaigns against traditional and bourgeois values ushered in a socialist culture against materialism and hedonism. Socially, the country witnessed the rise of women in the labour force, changing family structure, shifting loyalty from kinship to the state and the celebration of youth power.

Although the Communist regime embraced the value of egalitarianism, income stratification and varied living standards remained a reality during the Mao period. First, almost 80 per cent of the Chinese population still lived in rural areas, and the urban–rural divide remained significant due to government policies favouring urban workers. Chinese peasants lived largely on the margin of subsistence, had less access to consumer goods, had a lower total energy intake per capita per annum and consumed much less vegetable oil, sugar, and animal proteins than their urban counterparts (Ash, 2006). Urban workers also enjoyed many fringe benefits, such as free medical care, childcare, subsidized housing and pensions. Stratification was present among the urban population as well; workers in heavy industry were better paid than those in light industry (Chen and Galenson, 1969). In addition, different ranks were entitled to different levels of income, housing, transportation, dining facilities and even office furniture 'in a fashion strangely suggestive of New York corporation executives rather than revolutionary and ostensibly egalitarian leaders' (Barnett, 1966, 17). This noted, the entire Chinese population lived a rather austere life at the time, and equality largely characterized the consumption of people from the same work unit.

Given the severe shortage of agricultural and consumer goods, the Communist government discouraged consumption through low salaries, forced purchase of saving bonds and large-scale rationing programmes. A wide range of products from food items to soap and cloth, and from pots and pans to bicycles, were subject to rationing, and the allotment an individual received varied according to age, types of work and geographic location (Cheng, 1964; Huenemann, 1966). The Chinese on average spent two-thirds of their income on food and other essentials, such as clothing and fuel (Ash, 2006). According to Chen and Galenson (1969), the annual consumption of cotton cloth per worker was merely 4.3 metres in Beijing in 1964. Durable consumer goods were very expensive: a bicycle cost at least 130 yuan, a radio 40 yuan and the cheapest wristwatch 100 yuan in 1975, while the average monthly salary was about 50 yuan (Chen and Galenson, 1969; Solinger, 1984).

The Communist regime finished its socialist transformation of the economy in 1956 by taking over bureaucratic capital and foreign enterprises, nationalizing the banking system and turning private firms and factories into state companies and co-operatives. After 1956 industrial production was largely monopolized by the state; however, it was inefficient and fragmented due to an over-emphasis on state planning and local self-reliance. For example, in the mid-1970s, China had over 130 motor vehicle manufacturers producing over 120 makes, with at least one produced in each province (Lyons, 1987). China's foreign trade during this period was also monopolized by the state and conducted according to a state plan. Its trade partners included Western countries such as Australia, Canada, France, the United Kingdom and West Germany, as well as fellow socialist countries (Chen and Galenson, 1969).

The supply and distribution system during the Mao period also suffered from inefficiency and fragmentation. The state classified goods into three categories: Category I goods were allocated by the State Planning Commission and Category II goods by the various industrial ministries, while Category III items were regulated by local governments and could be freely traded. The first two categories included all vital industrial and agricultural goods and were subject to 'unified purchase and distribution' by the state according to the state plan at state-determined prices (Koziara and Yan, 1983). The procurement of agricultural products was controlled by the All-China Federation of Supply and Marketing Cooperatives, a national agency, and its branches at different levels throughout the country – farm products constituted nearly 75 per cent of all national consumer goods at the time (Cheng, 1964). The distribution of light-industry products was controlled by the Ministry of Commerce, while heavy industrial products were supplied through the industrial bureaucracy and hence not available in the marketplace (Solinger, 1984). Under the Ministry of Commerce, each of many state companies was dedicated to dealing with a specific line of products: one for grain, one for cotton, one for general goods (department store types), one for salt, and so on. The state's purchase and allocation plans dictated the flow of products from factories to state commercial companies within various geographical jurisdictions (Solinger, 1984). Such an arrangement was plagued by severe vertical conflicts between factories and commercial units, and between supply and demand. In one case cited by Solinger (1984), Shanghai's factories came up with 40 new products in one year, but only one made it to the market because the commercial and industrial departments could not agree on the prices of those new products (Solinger, 1984, 209). In such a system of insufficient supply, a pulling strategy played a major role, and numerous purchasing agents were employed by companies to locate goods (Koziara and Yan, 1983). Hoarding by enterprises at various levels became a serious problem, and practices such as underground bartering, exchange of goods for favours and bribery were prevalent (Solinger, 1984).

Retailing during this period had its share of problems, including mismatches between market demand and supply, stockpiles, sellouts, storage and sanitation problems, waste, crowded shops, long queues, problematic shop hours and forced purchase of shoddy products (Skinner, 2001; Solinger, 1984). Because of supply shortages, employees of retail outlets often took advantage of their access to products for personal benefit (Solinger, 1984). The retail network in cities usually consisted of a few department stores and many small state-owned shops which specialized in a product line. In his account of vegetable markets in Chinese cities in 1977, Skinner (1978) observes that most of the vegetables consumed by the Chinese urban population were produced within the bounds of the municipality, and that storage and delayed marketing were a common tactic to even out seasonal supply. One of the largest general food stores in Beijing had a floor space of 6,650 square metres, employed 320 workers and served 40,000 customers a day; in comparison, many food markets were housed in cramped or antiquated structures, and there were also dedicated small vegetable shops and stalls scattered around residential areas for the convenience of shoppers (Skinner, 1978). While all prices were fixed by state companies, the average mark-ups by Chinese vegetable retailers ranged from 13 to 37 per cent: in the city of Nanjing, the purchase price on average was 7.1 cents per 500 grams, the wholesale price 7.4 cents, and the retail price was 8.0 cents (Skinner, 1978). In rural areas, the Communist regime disrupted the traditional marketing system by reducing the number and frequency of market fairs and by imposing restrictions on who could participate and what could be sold and bought there – during some radical periods it instituted a total ban on market fairs (Skinner, 1985). Meanwhile, rural stores operated by the All-China Federation of Supply and Marketing Cooperatives, a state firm that controlled the flow of goods between cities and villages, were frequently out of stock (Solinger, 1984). Most important, in minimizing the role of periodic market fairs, the state seriously interrupted the basic rhythms of peasant life around such fairs, took away the essential venue for peasants to socialize and hence led to both psychological shock and social deprivation in rural areas (Skinner, 2001, 108).

As free market competition played a minimal role in the Chinese economy, advertising did not experience much development during the Mao period. Initially, the Communist regime tolerated its existence but imposed clear guidelines on acceptable images and styles in advertising. State-controlled media gave large discounts to government organs, state enterprises and advertisers deemed beneficial to socialist transformation, and untruthful and excessive advertising was singled out for criticism (Gerth, 2013). As a result, Chinese advertisements during this period gradually lost the vibrancy and individuality that characterized advertising in the Republican era. Most interestingly, compared to the bourgeois females in calendar posters from the 1930s, the females in Chinese advertisements during this period were depicted as healthy, happy, productive members of the labour force. Symbols of industrial modernity such as modern bridges, radio towers, dams and factories appeared in the background of advertisements to highlight socialist achievements. During the Cultural Revolution, advertising largely disappeared from people's daily life, although advertising for Chinese firms which specialized in foreign trade continued and was characterized by a clean and striking design aesthetic (Cahan, 2006).

If we consider socialist propaganda a special form of advertising that promotes socialist values and ideas instead of materialism and consumption, then we have to admit that socialist propaganda during this period was very successful in utilizing all the available media to mobilize the Chinese populace. According to Liu (1971), there were 6 million loudspeakers in China in 1964, so that wired radio stations and local broadcasting reached 95 per cent of the population, including those in isolated areas. Chinese socialist propaganda used techniques such as hyperbole, repetition, testimonials, symbolic communication and rituals participated in by the masses (Mittler, 2012), which are also staples of commercial advertising. Popular propaganda posters were painted by well-known artists who had created the famous calendar posters of the 1930s and thus represented a continuity of Chinese artistic tradition (Mittler, 2012, 17).

With anti-imperialism as part of its core ideology, the Communist regime perceived foreign businesses in China as exploitative. They were accused of keeping technical knowledge from Chinese employees, collecting exorbitant profits, resorting to unfair commercial practices, understating outputs and evading taxes (Shai, 1996, 51). Instead of direct expropriation, the government implemented a series of measures, including heavy taxation, enforced subscription to government loans, restrictive labour legislation and employee agitation, to slowly pressure foreign companies to withdraw from China (Shai, 1996). In the case of BAT, unable to sell its products in China, the company was coerced into relinquishing its property to the Chinese government in 1952 – the occasion was celebrated as 'the great joy in life' by Chen Yuu-Chieh, a top executive of Nanyang, who became a model patriotic capitalist in the new regime (Cochran, 1980, 200). While most Western companies left China by the late 1950s, some managed to stay and profit by collaborating with the regime. For example, the Hongkong and Shanghai Banking Corporation (HSBC) played an important role in helping finance China's foreign trade, and, in return, the Chinese government channelled considerable business to HSBC's Shanghai branch, so that its profits in China gradually increased over the years – even during the Cultural Revolution (Lu, 2008).

When Mao Zedong died in 1976, the country was materially deprived, psychologically scarred and politically disillusioned. After a brief power struggle, Deng Xiaoping-led reformists took control of the government and worked to reorient the Chinese economy. Hence, Chinese society took a sharp turn from their socialist past and plunged into a frenzied pursuit of money and material possessions.

Marketing during the post-Mao period

China embarked on market-oriented reform in 1978 to open up its economy and improve productivity through material incentives (Naughton, 1995). After 1992 it implemented further measures to establish a market economy and to reform the pension, housing and health care systems which had been the safety nets of state workers (Naughton, 2006). China joined the World Trade Organization in 2001 and became the world's second largest economy in 2010. Politically, the Chinese government remains a one-party, authoritarian regime, even though it has adopted measures to address rising social problems, such as corruption, income inequality, environmental deterioration and social dissatisfaction (Lewis and Xue, 2003). As Chinese socialist ideology has lost its relevance in a market economy, nationalism has surged and become the new unifier of the Chinese (Gries, 2004).

Since 1978 Chinese people have witnessed rising incomes, more access to consumer goods and improving living standards. The average annual consumption of rural and urban households rose from 138 and 405 yuan in 1978 to 7,409 and 22,880 yuan in 2013, respectively; in 1990 there were 59.04 TV sets and 0.34 air-conditioners per 100 urban households, and by 2010 the numbers rose to 137.43 and 112.07, respectively (China Statistics Bureau, 2014). The country saw the emergence of an affluent middle class, many of whom have benefited from their connections to the state (Fleischer, 2010). China's new rich are status conscious and prefer global brands adapted to their own tastes and traditions (Gerth, 2010). On the other hand, China's economic reform has led to substantial income inequality and disadvantaged groups such as peasants, migrant workers and the unemployed urban poor (Cheng, 2014; Fleischer, 2010; Khan and Riskin, 1998). Meanwhile, bombarded by commercialism and materialism, the Chinese – both the privileged and disadvantaged – feel empty and exhausted, longing for more meaningful connection with others (Hessler, 2010; Loyalka, 2012).

The Chinese market today offers an abundance of products and brands. The competitive landscape varies significantly across sectors. Some industries, such as telecommunication services, cigarette manufacturing and utility services, continue to be monopolized by state companies. For the household appliances market, Chinese domestic brands dominate the overall market share due to their competitive prices and large distribution networks, while foreign brands hold advantages in the high-end category because of their new technology and status appeal. For personal care products such as toothpaste and shampoo, multinational giants prevail by heavily marketing their global brands or acquiring leading local brands. For example, Colgate held 24.6 per cent, Procter & Gamble's Crest 23.8 per cent, Unilever's Zhonghua 16.7 per cent, of the toothpaste market share in 2013 – Unilever acquired the Zhonghua brand, which, ironically, means 'China' in Chinese, through a joint-venture with the Shanghai Toothpaste Factory in 1994; some Chinese local toothpaste brands have managed to carve out small market shares by extolling the Chinese medicinal ingredients of their products (IBISWorld, 2014a). In comparison, leading internet services companies in China are largely home-grown, private enterprises, and foreign capital investment is concentrated within a few major players, so that it accounts for 1.5 per cent of the enterprises but makes up 23.8 per cent of the industry's revenue (IBISWorld, 2014b). Overall, many Chinese domestic brands are not competitive due to short-term profit orientation, inconsistent quality and lack of investment in product research and development (R&D) – rather than designing their own products, they frequently copy or counterfeit the leader of the market (Chin, 2010; Gillette, 2010). Realizing these problems, some Chinese companies have begun to increase their R&D investment. For example, Chery, a privately owned Chinese car manufacturer, has established R&D partnerships with companies in Italy, Austria, UK and

Israel (Chin, 2010). Huawei, a Chinese network equipment manufacturer, spent about $4.7 billion, or 13 per cent of its total revenue, on R&D in 2012 (Osawa, 2013). Meanwhile, not all foreign marketers in China are success stories. There are many cases of failures and losses because of strategic misjudgement, inability to adapt, ineffective public relations, culturally incompatible management styles and direct clones of home-market models (Pu and Que, 2004). As corruption is a rampant issue in China, some foreign companies have also been accused of using bribery to solicit business (Voreacos, 2013).

The Chinese supply and distribution system has experienced transformational growth since 1978. The auto industry offers a good example. To meet government quotas of local content, joint ventures such as Shanghai Volkswagen (SVW) and Shanghai-General Motors (SGM) – established in 1984 and 1997, respectively – helped their local suppliers to partner with their global suppliers, so that the local suppliers were able to quickly upgrade their technologies, product lines and services (Chin, 2010). Today, Shanghai GKN Drive Shaft Co. – founded in 1988 and partially owned by GKN Driveline International GmbH of Germany – purchases its raw and supplemental materials mainly from domestic suppliers and its lubricating oil and grease from Germany; its customers are major car makers such as SVW, SGM, FAW-Volkswagen, Chery, Dongfeng Honda, Nissan, B-BMW, HN-Mazda, and Guangzhou Honda, which in turn have pressured and helped the company and its local suppliers to improve their supply chain management, including adopting environmentally friendly practices (Liu et al., 2011). This positive case noted, some foreign companies had to adapt their supply chain management to the Chinese situation. To maintain a consistent global image, premium cosmetic brands such as Estee Lauder imported their products from Europe; to lower production costs, ensure quality and protect intellectual property, mass-market brands such as Maybelline and Olay chose to have their core operations located outside China and non-core operations, such as the manufacturing of packaging materials and basic ingredients, outsourced to Chinese manufacturers (Wu et al., 2008). Still, there were many cases where local suppliers became competitors of foreign brands. The most recent example came from Foxconn, the manufacturer of Apple's iPhones and iPads: squeezed by rising labour and raw material costs as well as low purchasing prices from its global customers, the company decided to market its own brand of cellphone to improve its profitability (Luk, 2014).

The procurement of agricultural products in China has also evolved over the years after the government removed its quota and price control as part of its market-oriented reform package. Now the market plays a major role in the supply of such products, so that large end purchasers, such as supermarket chains, food processors, juice manufacturers and wine makers exercise great influence (Stringer et al., 2008; Zhou, 2011). In one case, sweet potato farmers in Sichuan were linked to the production chain in three ways: through employment by the processing enterprise either as employees with full benefits or as seasonal workers; through participation in a production base established through a contract between the local township and the processing enterprise; or through land lease to the processing enterprise (Lingohr, 2007). In cases of cash crops such as grapes and apples, agents or arbitrageurs with strong local ties – often village cadres or influential elites – played an important role in the system, and, most interestingly, their contracts with purchasing companies were usually oral agreements based on mutual trust (Zhou, 2011). Although the Chinese government has encouraged the development of large agri-businesses, the Chinese agricultural sector continues to be dominated by small farmers (Waldron et al., 2010), which creates serious food safety challenges (Stringer et al., 2008).

As part of its reform package, the Chinese government gradually liberalized retailing by reinstituting free markets, allowing individuals to run retail outlets and opening the sector to foreign capital. Today the Chinese retail sector is intensely competitive. Consumers in cities have access to a variety of retail outlets to meet their shopping needs, which range from upscale shopping malls to small specialty stores, from supermarket chains to morning markets and street vendors. Supermarket chains alone include local players, such as China Resources Enterprise, Lianhua, Hualian and Wumart, as well as international companies, such as Walmart, Carrefour, RT-Mart of Taiwan, Lotus of South Korea and Auchan of France, all of which entered China in the 1990s (IBISWorld, 2013a). The retail sector is becoming even more competitive with the booming of online shopping, which grew at an annual rate of 58.9 per cent between 2009 and 2014 (IBISWorld, 2014c). With easy access to the internet through computers and mobile phones, Chinese consumers in cities buy all kinds of products online, including toilet paper and condiments as well as luxury bags and premium cosmetics, because of lower prices and convenient delivery. Alibaba, founded in 1999 by a school teacher in his small apartment, has dominated China's online shopping scene with 80 per cent of the market share in 2012: its marketplace platforms such as Taobao.com and Tmall tailor to Chinese culture by offering free basic services to both buyers and sellers and by establishing mechanisms that foster trust between buyers and sellers (*The Economist*, 2013).

Advertising reappeared in China in 1979 and has been developing at a rapid speed ever since: the total Chinese ad spending was 10 million yuan in 1979 and reached 424 billion yuan, or $68.36 billion, in 2013 (IBISWorld, 2013b; China Statistics Bureau, 2001). Since its start in 1997, Chinese online advertising has also experienced fast growth, reaching 75.31 billion yuan in total revenue in 2012 (iResearch, 2013). Structurally, the affiliates of global advertising conglomerates such as Saatchi & Saatchi, Leo Burnett and Dentsu constituted 9.2 per cent of the total agencies but collected 21 per cent of the total revenue (IBISWorld, 2013b). Concentrated in Beijing, Shanghai and Guangzhou, large joint-venture agencies served both multinational clients and large domestic clients, playing a prominent role in upgrading Chinese advertising standards and practices (Po, 2006).

The styles and appeals of Chinese advertisements have also evolved over the years. Advertisements in the early 1980s were simple in design with a strong focus on the product (Yu and Deng, 1999). Gradually, sex appeal, testimonials, and celebrity endorsements became staples. The most popular TV commercials in the late 1980s and 1990s relied on soft sell and catered to the Chinese propensity for sentimentalism and nostalgia (Yu and Deng, 1999). In addition, Chinese creatives frequently drew inspiration from Chinese traditional cultural elements and developed ads with distinctive Chinese style and aesthetics. This theme has continued after 2000 and even influenced the advertisements of foreign brands from time to time. For their part, foreign advertisers had a tentative start in the 1980s and early 1990s but grew rapidly afterwards. When cosmetic brand Maybelline first advertised on Chinese television, it directly imported its commercials from the US; later on, it employed Chinese models in its ads while sticking to a standardized global slogan. Some advertisers saw the need to adapt to regional differences in China (Po, 2006). McDonald's 'Manly Man' Campaign in 2012 had different versions for the Northern, Yangtze Delta and Guangdong markets, with each version depicting the stereotypical traits of men from that region. Meanwhile, advertisers and agencies, including foreign operators, have voluntarily contributed to the government's public service advertising programme over the years, which serves as a new propaganda tool of the state (Stockmann, 2013).

Chinese marketing has apparently experienced impressive development since 1978. To a large extent, the Chinese government has directly engineered its development, though its active role is frequently paradoxical in its consequence. It adopted favourable policies to attract foreign capital and even helped foreign businesses suppress labour strikes from time to time, yet it expected and required foreign businesses to contribute to its nation-building project by transferring their newest technology to their Chinese partners (Chin, 2010). It instructed the Chinese media to promote domestic brands and target foreign companies for scrutiny (Gao, 2012). Managing the economy at the macro-level, it used subsidies and policy tools to foster domestic companies (Gerth, 2010), which actually hurt the long-term competitiveness of these companies. Again, the experience of the auto sector offers a good example. Government policy requirements for technology transfer and local content helped the sector modernize in a short period, but its measures to protect the domestic auto market from imports also enabled the few early joint-ventures to charge high prices and reap huge profits, thus providing disincentives for further R&D investment and technology upgrades; as a result, China's domestic auto industry still lacks competitiveness in the global market (Chin, 2010).

Conclusion

Covering over one and a half centuries, this chapter presents a brief review of the development of modern marketing in China. Some recurring themes and valuable insights emerge from this gallop through history. First, it is apparent that, in spite of the unique political-economic contexts, Western-style modernization dominated Chinese development in each period. What differentiates the three periods is the manner and degree that modernization was achieved: during the Late Qing and Republican period, the process was first thrust upon the Chinese by foreign imperial powers and confined to treaty ports and large cities; the Mao Communists put emphasis on heavy industry with the aim of surpassing the West in their industrial output, even though they chose to reject foreign capital altogether and pursue national development through central planning and self-reliance; the post-Mao reformists invited foreign capitalists back into China, hoping that foreigners would help China modernize while filling their own pockets. To some degree, the post-Mao reformists succeeded in what the regimes of the first two periods failed in terms of industrialization and modernization, even though at very high social and environmental costs. Most important, Western-style marketing is not ideology-free – in utilizing foreign capital for nation-building, the Chinese government became an enabler of transnational capitalism rather than a limit to it, thus contradicting its socialistic ideology (Dirlik, 2005).

Similar to the global scene, where capitalism and nationalism grew up side by side (Smith, 1998), nationalism was another constant theme of marketing during the three periods, although its expression varied from time to time. Given the weakness of the Late Qing and Republican regimes, Chinese nationalism manifested mainly in the bitter rivalry between Chinese and foreign businesses as well as in boycotts and labour strikes against foreign commercial interests at the grassroots level. Exercising enormous state power, the Mao Communists drove out foreign businesses and practised economic sovereignty and self-reliance. The post-Mao period saw Chinese nationalism expressed in both government policy and grassroots agitation. Today, Chinese officials, intellectuals, business professionals and many ordinary Chinese sincerely subscribe to economic nationalism and aspire to build a strong, prosperous Chinese nation, and foreign companies in China are often perceived to be exploitative profiteers. Given this aspect of salient Chinese ideology, the effect of nationalism on marketing in China will likely intensify in the future.

The history of marketing in China also confirms that globalization has a long history – Chinese elites in the early 1900s already enjoyed the bounty offered by a vibrant global consumer culture. Key marketing concepts, such as vertical supply chain integration, segmentation and glocalization, were successfully practised by multinational marketers in their expansion in China long before they entered marketing textbooks. Similarly, the competition between foreign and local businesses invariably involved standard tactics and tools such as imitation, trademark lawsuits, price wars, PR campaigns, as well as illegal means such as bribery. It is true that the success of a company in a host country depends on its making the right strategic decisions at the right time. However, its long-term fate is ultimately determined by uncontrollable geo-political factors, which is perhaps another important lesson that marketers can learn from the modern history of China.

References

Ash, R. (2006) 'Squeezing the peasants: Grain extraction, food consumption and rural living standards in Mao's China', *China Quarterly*, 188, 959–98.

Barlow, T.E. (2008) 'Buying in: Advertising and the sexy modern girl icon in Shanghai in the 1920s and 1930s', in A.W. Weinbaum *et al.* (eds), *The Modern Girl around the World: Consumption, Modernity, and Globalization*, Duke University Press, Durham, NC, pp. 288–316.

Barnett, A.D. (1966) 'Social stratification and aspects of personnel management in the Chinese Communist bureaucracy', *China Quarterly*, 28, 8–39.

Bell, L.S. (1999) *One Industry, Two Chinas: Silk Filatures and Peasant-Family Production in Wuxi County, 1865–1937*, Stanford University Press, Stanford, CA.

Benson, C. (1999) 'Consumers are also soldiers: Subversive songs from Nanjing Road during the New Life Movement', in S. Cochran (ed.), *Inventing Nanjing Road: Commercial Culture in Shanghai, 1900–1945*, East Asia Program, Cornell University, Ithaca, NY, pp. 91–132.

Bergère, M. (2009) *Shanghai: China's Gateway to Modernity*, tr. J. Lloyd, Stanford University Press, Stanford, CA.

Bian, M.L. (2005) *The Making of the State Enterprise System in Modern China*, Harvard University Press, Cambridge, MA.

Cahan, A.S. (2006) *Chinese Label Art 1900–1976*, Schiffer Publishing, Atglen, PA.

Chan, K.Y. (2001) 'A turning point in China's comprador system', *Business History*, 43/2, 51–72.

Chan, W.K.K. (1999) 'Selling foods and promoting a new commercial culture: The four Shanghai premier department stores on Nanjing Road, 1917–1937', in S. Cochran (ed.), *Inventing Nanjing Road: Commercial Culture in Shanghai, 1900–1945*, East Asia Program, Cornell University, Ithaca, NY, pp. 19–36.

Chen, N., and Galenson, W. (1969) *The Chinese Economy under Communism*, Aldine Publishing, Chicago, IL.

Cheng, C. (1964) *Communist China's Economy, 1949–1962*, Seton Hall University Press, South Orange, NJ.

Cheng, Z. (2014) 'Layoffs and urban poverty in the state-owned enterprise communities in Shaanxi Province, China', *Social Indicators Research*, 116, 199–233.

Chin, G.T. (2010) *China's Automotive Modernization: The Party-State and Multinational Corporations*, Palgrave Macmillan, New York.

China Statistics Bureau (2001) *Twenty Years' of Chinese Advertising*, China Statistics Press, Beijing.

China Statistics Bureau (2014) *National Statistics: Population*, China Statistics Bureau, Beijing.

Cochran, S. (1980) *Big Business in China: Sino-Foreign Rivalry in the Cigarette Industry, 1890–1930*, Harvard University Press, Cambridge, MA.

Cochran, S. (1999) 'Transnational origins of advertising in early twentieth-century China', in S. Cochran (ed.), *Inventing Nanjing Road: Commercial Culture in Shanghai, 1900–1945*, East Asia Program, Cornell University, Ithaca, NY, pp. 37–60.

Crow, C. (1937/2008) *400 Million Customers*, Earnshaw Books, Hong Kong.

de Pee, C. (2010) 'Purchase on power: Imperial space and commercial space in Song-Dynasty Kaifeng, 960–1127', *Journal of the Economic and Social History of the Orient*, 53/2, 149–84.

Dirlik, A. (2005) *Marxism in the Chinese Revolution*, Roman & Littlefield, Lanham, MD.

Dong, M.Y. (2003) *Republican Beijing: The City and its Histories,* University of California Press, Berkeley, CA.

Esherick, J.W., and Rankin, M.B. (1990) *Chinese Local Elites and Patterns of Dominance*, University of California Press, Berkeley, CA.

Fairbank, J.K., and Goldman, M. (2006) *China: A New History,* Harvard University of Press, Cambridge, MA.

Finnane, A. (2003) 'Yangzhou's "modernity": Fashion and consumption in the early nineteenth century', *Positions*, 11/2, 395–425.

Fleischer, F. (2010) *Suburban Beijing: Housing and Consumption in Contemporary China,* University of Minnesota Press, Minneapolis, MN.

French, P. (2008) 'Foreword', in C. Crow, *400 Million Customers*, Earnshaw Books, Hong Kong, pp. v–x.

Gao, Z. (2012) 'Chinese grassroots nationalism and its impact on foreign brands', *Journal of Macromarketing*, 32/2, 181–92.

Gerth, K. (2003) *China Made: Consumer Culture and the Creation of the Nation*, Harvard University Asian Center, Cambridge, MA.

Gerth, K (2010) *As China Goes, So Goes the World: How Chinese Consumers are Transforming Everything*, Hill & Wang, New York.

Gerth, K. (2013) 'Compromising with consumerism in socialist China: Transnational flows and internal tensions in "socialist advertising"', *Past and Present*, suppl. 8, 203–32.

Gillette, M. (2010) 'Copying, counterfeiting, and capitalism in contemporary China', *Modern China*, 36/4, 367–403.

Gries, P.H. (2004) *China's New Nationalism: Pride, Politics, and Diplomacy*, University of California Press, Berkeley, CA.

He, Y. (2010) 'Prosperity and decline: A comparison of the fate of Jingdezhen, Zhuxianzhen, Foshan and Hankou in modern times', *Frontiers of History in China*, 5/1, 52–85.

Hessler, P. (2010) *Country Driving: A Journey through China from Farm to Factory*, Harper, New York.

Huenemann, R.W. (1966) 'Urban rationing in Communist China', *China Quarterly*, 26, 44–57.

IBISWorld (2013a) 'Supermarkets in China', Industry Report 6512.

IBISWorld (2013b) 'Advertising agencies in China', Industry Report 7440.

IBISWorld (2014a) 'Toothpaste and toothbrush manufacturing in China', Industry Report 2673.

IBISWorld (2014b) 'Internet services in China', Industry Report 6020.

IBISWorld (2014c) 'Online shopping in China', Industry Report 6220.

iResearch (2013) 'China online advertising revenue impressively increases 46.8%', available online: www.iresearchchina.com/views/4712.html (accessed June 2014).

Johnson, M.D. (2012) 'Propaganda and censorship in Chinese cinema', in Y. Zhang (ed.), *A Companion to Chinese Cinema*, Wiley-Blackwell, Oxford, pp. 153–78.

Khan, A.R., and Riskin, C. (1998) 'Income and inequality in China: Composition, distribution and growth of household income, 1988 to 1995', *China Quarterly*, 154, 221–53.

Koziara, E.C., and Yan, C. (1983) 'The distribution system for producers' goods in China', *China Quarterly*, 96, 689–702.

Lewis, J.W., and Xue, L. (2003) 'Social change and political reform in China: Meeting the challenge of success', *China Quarterly*, 176, 926–42.

Lin, M. (2015) 'The characteristics of China's traditional economy', in C. Chow and D.H. Perkins (eds), *Routledge Handbook of the Chinese Economy*, Routledge, London, pp. 1–20.

Lingohr, S. (2007) 'Rural households, dragon heads and associations: A case study of sweet potato processing in Sichuan Province', *China Quarterly*, 192, 898–914.

Lippit, V.D. (1966) 'Development of transportation in Communist China', *China Quarterly*, 27, 101–19.

Liu, A.P.L. (1971) *Communications and National Integration in Communist China*, University of California Press, Berkeley, CA.

Liu, X., Wang, L., Dong, Y., Yang, J., and Bao, C. (2011) 'Case studies of green supply chain management in China', *International Journal of Economics and Management Engineering*, 1/1, 22–34.

Loyalka, M.D. (2012) *Eating Bitterness: Stories from the Front Lines of China's Great Urban Migration*, University of California Press, Berkeley, CA.

Lu, H. (1999) '"The seventy-two tenants": Residence and commerce in Shanghai's Shikumen Houses, 1872–1951', in S. Cochran (ed.), *Inventing Nanjing Road: Commercial Culture in Shanghai, 1900–1945,* East Asia Program, Cornell University, Ithaca, NY, pp. 133–86.

Lu, Q. (2008) 'Government control, transaction costs, and commitment between the Hongkong and Shanghai Banking Corporation and the Chinese government', *Enterprise and Society*, 9/1, 44–69.

Luk, L. (2014) 'Foxconn recrafts its future', *Wall Street Journal* (28 June), B3.

Lyons, T.P. (1987) *Economic Integration and Planning in Maoist China*, Columbia University Press, New York.

Mittler, B. (2012) *A Continuous Revolution: Making Sense of Cultural Revolution Culture*, Harvard University Asia Center, Cambridge, MA.

Nakajima, C. (2012) '"Healthful goods": Health, hygiene, and commercial culture in early twentieth-century Shanghai', *Twentieth-Century China*, 37/3, 250–74.

Naughton, B. (1995) *Growing Out of the Plan,* Cambridge University Press, Cambridge, UK.

Naughton, B. (2006) *The Chinese Economy: Transitions and Growth,* MIT Press, Boston, MA.

Osawa, J. (2013) 'Huawei's best-kept secret: An army of engineers', *Wall Street Journal* (1 July), A1.

Osterhammel, J. (1984) 'Imperialism in transition: British business and the Chinese authorities, 1931–37', *China Quarterly*, 98, 260–86.

Po, L. (2006) 'Repackaging globalization: A case study of the advertising industry in China', *Geoforum*, 37, 752–64.

Pu, H., and Que, Y. (2004) 'Why have some transnational corporations failed in China?', *China and World Economy*, 12/5, 67–79.

Rawski, T.G. (1989) *Economic Growth in Prewar China*, University of California Press, Berkeley, CA.

Shai, A. (1996) *The Fate of British and French Firms in China, 1949–54: Imperialism Imprisoned*, Macmillan, Oxford.

Si, J. (2011) 'Reprinting Robert Morrison's dictionary: Producers, literary audience, and the English language market in nineteenth-century Shanghai', *Frontiers of History in China*, 6/2, 229–42.

Skinner, G.W. (1978) 'Vegetable supply and marketing in Chinese cities', *China Quarterly*, 76, 733–93.

Skinner, G.W. (1985) 'Rural marketing in China: Repression and revival', *China Quarterly*, 103, 393–413.

Skinner, G.W. (2001) *Marketing and Social Structure in Rural China*, Association for Asian Studies, Ann Arbor, MI.

Smith, A.D. (1998) *Nationalism and Modernism,* Routledge, London.

Solinger, D.J. (1984) *Chinese Business under Socialism: The Politics of Domestic Commerce, 1949–1980*, University of California Press, Berkeley, CA.

Stockmann, D. (2013) 'Greasing the reels: Advertising as a means of campaigning on Chinese television', *China Quarterly*, 208, 851–69.

Stringer, R., Sang, N., and Croppenstedt, A. (2008) 'Producers, processors, and procurement decisions: The case of vegetable supply chains in China', *World Development*, 37/11, 1773–80.

The Economist (2013) 'Alibaba, a trailblazing Chinese internet giant, will soon go public', available online: www.economist.com/news/briefing/21573980-alibaba-trailblazing-chinese-internet-giant-will-soon-go-public-worlds-greatest-bazaar (accessed June 2014).

Tsai, W. (2010) *Reading Shenbao: Nationalism, Consumerism and Individuality in China 1919–37*, Palgrave Macmillan, London.

Voreacos, D. (2013) 'China's bribery culture poses risks for multinationals', *Bloomberg News* (21 Nov.), available online: www.bloomberg.com/news/2013-11-21/china-s-bribery-culture-poses-risks-for-multinationals.html (accessed June 2014).

Waldron, S., Brown, C., and Longworth, J. (2010) 'A critique of high-value supply chains as a means of modernising agriculture in China: The case of the beef industry', *Food Policy*, 35, 479–87.

Wu, T., Wang, W., Tang, C.S., Liu, D., Gao, F., and Fang, C. (2008) 'How do foreign cosmetics companies align their supply chains and distribution channels in China?', *International Journal of Logistics Research and Applications*, 11/3, 201–28.

Yin, T. (2014) *Research on Businessmen and the Early Modernization of Hangzhou*, Zhejiang University Press, Hangzhou, China.

Yu, H., and Deng, Z. (1999) *Contemporary History of Chinese Advertising*, Hunan Science and Technology Press, Hunan, China.

Zhou, A. (2011) 'The autumn harvest: Peasants and markets in post-collective rural China', *China Quarterly*, 208, 913–31.

20

Towards marketing management

German marketing in the nineteenth and twentieth centuries

Ingo Köhler and Jan Logemann

Introduction

Marketing, it was long held, did not play an important role in the development of business and the economy in Germany. German companies were said to be focused on production and quality and nineteenth-century German entrepreneurs like Werner von Siemens voiced their disdain for advertising, for example, as an unnecessary and even frivolous burden on a company's budget (Berghoff, 2007a, 15). This 'producerist perspective' (Blaich, 1982) assumed that a company's products and their quality should speak for themselves and that there was no need to actively create consumer goods markets. Such attitudes were not unique to Germany, but they were pronounced in a market in which investment goods long trumped consumer goods and domestic markets often took the back seat to exports. The producerist perspective was thus thought to have prevailed in Germany well into the twentieth century.

German industry has the reputation of a late comer in the marketing game, fully embracing the concept only by the 1960s and 1970s. Marketing was long discussed as an element foreign to German business, imported from abroad. The debate about marketing in Germany is thus heavily intertwined with debates about the 'Americanization' of German industry in the twentieth century (Schröter, 2005). Both contemporaries and the historiography have paid close attention to American developments and transfers. In general, however, German business history long ignored marketing questions, thus contributing to the producerist bias in the literature. One prominent exception is the history of advertising which saw a number of publications during the 1990s as consumer history emerged as a field in Germany (Reinhardt, 1993; Borscheid and Wischermann, 1995; Lamberty, 2000; Swett *et al.*, 2007). The history of marketing thought also saw a number of early publications (Jones, 1992; Hansen and Bode, 1999).

Over the past 15 years, however, marketing history has seen an increase which a number of surveys and edited volumes can attest (Wischermann, 2003; Kleinschmidt and Triebel, 2004; Berghoff, 2007a; Borscheid, 2009). This new literature on German marketing history paints a very different, much more vibrant picture by drawing on developments within companies and in the retail sector as well as in finance, market research or graphic design.

In this chapter we will take stock of these new research findings and trace the development of marketing in Germany since the late nineteenth century. We will pay attention to a wide range of factors that fall into what today is called the 'marketing mix', including advertising and public relations (promotion), pricing and credit schemes (price), product design and engineering (product) and retailing and distribution (place), as well as different forms of market research. While integrated and scientifically grounded concepts of marketing management were, indeed, rarely found in Germany prior to the 1970s, the literature now shows a broad array of developments since the late nineteenth century that defy the myth of a marketing-averse German business culture.

The emergence of modern marketing practices in late nineteenth century

Many German economists at the end of the nineteenth century were highly critical towards consumption which was widely regarded as a 'destruction of value' rather than a satisfaction of needs (Nonn, 2009). The economic value of creating markets – for individual companies or the economy as a whole – was not widely understood (Rossfeld, 2004, 25). Advertising posters were frequently met with elitist disdain or even outright hostility, attacked as eye-sores in urban and rural landscapes (Spiekermann, 1995). Yet, a number of developments since about 1850 allow us to talk of the beginnings of a marketing orientation among German companies. Producers no longer waited for consumers to seek out their wares, but began to think about how to bring their goods to the market. In some markets, as Fullerton (2012) has shown for the book trade, we even find early forms of segmentation. By 1900, Germany had become a nascent consumer society in which some companies not only advertised, but also experimented with ways to create markets and to entice consumer demand.

The rise of advertising was a central feature of this process during the second half of the nineteenth century. In the wake of rapid urbanization and the economic growth spurts of the *Gründerboom* (1867–73) and of the 1890s, large and anonymous urban markets emerged that demanded new forms of business communication. Reinhardt (1993) has shown how early advertising agencies (*Annoncen-Expeditionen*), which primarily brokered advertising space in newspapers, became a fixture in the German market from the 1870s. Of some prominence were also advertising pillars (so-called *Litfassäulen*) which became part of the urban landscape of Berlin and other metropolitan centres already by the late 1850s (Lamberty, 2000). In general, these early advertising efforts still rested on simplistic and linear conceptions of market communication, aimed merely at making a product known. They were not yet part of any larger corporate strategy. Such efforts would emerge only after the turn of the century as both design and psychological considerations came to play a bigger role in the advertising industry (Reinhardt, 2003). Advertising posters and print ads became increasingly artistic and aimed to lure consumers towards new consumption experiences. Coffee and chocolate advertisements of the time, for example, frequently played on the colonial imagination and displayed a fascination with the exotic (Ciarlo, 2011).

Early advertising was often less the domain of producers than that of retailers, and the creation of a modern infrastructure of distribution was a necessary corollary to the growing marketing orientation of producers (Haupt, 2003). As elsewhere in Europe and the United States, the advent of department stores as a new retailing format that captured the imagination of contemporaries has received considerable attention in the literature (Crossick and Jaumain, 1999). While department stores and their display windows certainly helped to mould the desires of consumers during the imperial era, other forms of retailing also contributed to the transformation of distribution. Spiekermann (1999) has argued that the emergence of a vibrant retailing sector formed the 'basis of the consumer society' in late nineteenth-century Germany. The rationalization and modernization of small stores (often already organized in chains or consortiums such as EDEKA) laid the foundation for new forms of brand-name marketing in Germany. Consumer co-operatives, finally, were an indispensable part of the modernizing retail sector prior to World War I. With over 2 million members, consumer co-operatives were among the largest mass organizations of their time and had a significant impact on reshaping distribution chains (Nonn, 1996).

Retailers did not only impact advertising and distribution, they also helped introduce early forms of consumer credit. Credit financing, long seen as atypical for German consumption styles, was already quite prevalent in the last decades of the nineteenth century. Mail order businesses such as Bial & Freund began to offer consumer durables from gramophones to typewriters on instalment payments by the turn of the century, and the American Singer Manufacturing company offered its sewing machines to German customers by hire purchase (Logemann and Spiekermann, 2010; Spiekermann, 1999). Especially in the furniture and piano trade, hire purchase was a widely used form of accessing new markets. The rise of credit marketing, however, was also widely criticized by other retailers and many social commentators, prompting regulatory action. The Hire-Purchase Act of 1894 regulated the new market for credit sales, which would remain comparatively small in Germany for much of the twentieth century. Nonetheless, consumer credit became a permanent fixture in the marketing activities of both German companies and retailers.

Consumer goods producers became especially marketing-oriented by the late nineteenth century. The emergence of the so-called *Fabrikantenhandel* shows the interest of many producers in organizing and controlling sales themselves and in eliminating middlemen by employing company salesmen or by creating nationally advertised brand goods (Blaich, 1982). Rossfeld (2007) took the example of Swiss chocolate firms such as Suchard and Tobler to show that their global success did not simply depend on technical innovations and product quality, but also on aggressive marketing strategies that involved pricing (rebates), packaging, sales organization and widespread advertising. The Cologne candy manufacturer Stollwerck is another example of innovative marketing through sales agents and early vending machines which provided a new technology for accessing anonymous urban mass markets (Epple, 2010). Marketing efforts, however, were not limited to such classic consumer goods as chocolate or coffee. The chemical industry as one of the leading sectors of the second industrialization in Germany also depended on new approaches towards their customers. New synthetic dye stuffs, for example, needed new markets and applications that companies were eager to suggest (Engel, 2009). Many chemical companies introduced departments for customer education which instructed potential buyers in new printing techniques for aniline dyes. This allowed textile firms without integrated research laboratories to participate in the innovation cycle initiated by the chemical industry and significantly expanded their markets (Streb, 2004).

The establishment of nationally recognizable brands to replace anonymous bulk goods was the central development for these new marketing trends. Brands such as Odol mouthwash (produced by Ligner in Dresden), Continental bike tyres, Kupferberg sparkling wine, Dr Oetker baking powder, Bahlsen cookies or Pelikan pens were now frequently promoted by advertising departments within the company (Borscheid, 2009, 84). These products were part of an increasingly differentiated consumer society by the early 1900s, recognizable icons of a new era and cultural 'media' in and of themselves (Gries, 2003). The iconography of the brands was now carefully devised not only by advertisers, but also by product and graphic designers who shaped products, brand and company logos for the consumer market.

German marketing history is heavily intertwined with the development of modern design trends. Advertising posters for companies such as Priester matches or Pelikan ink by graphic designers including Ludwig Hohlwein in Munich or Lucian Bernhard in Berlin remained a genre between art and commerce. Especially after 1905, the clean and bold look of the *Sachplakat* poster managed to capture viewers' attention and signalled a sense of modernity that was welcomed by many consumer goods producers (Reinhardt, 1993, 49–76). At the same time, consumer goods were increasingly influenced by design movements such as the Werkbund (founded in 1907) which brought artists and companies together in order to improve aesthetics and achieve recognizable brand images in an era of mass production (Ottomeyer, 1996; Schwartz, 1996a).

Most influential for the integration of design into broader marketing strategies were the efforts of designer Peter Behrens at the leading electric company AEG. As a design consultant, Behrens not only got involved in the design of the company's logos and products, he also shaped AEG's advertising and external communication as well as the internal communication down to the design of offices and shop-floor interiors (Buddensieg and Rogge, 1984; Schwartz, 1996b). Behrens's approach had many students, but his vision of a holistic corporate identity geared towards the consumer marketplace was still the exception rather than the norm by World War I. While advertising, retailing, financing, sales and design had seen a great deal of innovation by the early twentieth century, these innovations remained often haphazard. A full-fledged marketing mindset had not yet emerged in most German companies.

Towards professional marketing: the inter-war years

Marketing efforts in the inter-war years were marked by a continuity of many of the trends sketched above, but also by a series of severe disruptions to which companies and retailers had to respond, from the war economy to hyperinflation and the Great Depression – which hit Germany with nearly as much severity as the United States. Economic histories of early twentieth-century Germany have typically emphasized the 'special path' the country took. Its 'organized capitalism' defined by interest groups and influential banks as well as legally sanctioned cartels hampered the kind of competitive marketplace that spurred on the development of marketing in the United States (e.g. Abelshauser, 2005). Indeed price and service cartels in many sectors of the economy meant that marketing strategies of German companies were embedded in a unique economic context, in some industries syndicate cartels even pooled the sales of goods for the entire market into one organization. This did not translate, however, into a complete lack of managerial innovation on the part of German firms prior to World War II (Chandler, 1990). On the contrary, even the (much maligned) German family firms frequently developed modern managerial structures that also left room for the evolution of marketing approaches (Fear, 2005).

A push towards professionalization was the defining characteristic of the inter-war years in many areas of German marketing. This was most pronounced in the field of advertising. Observers at the time noted the increasing prominence of advertising as a cultural form and as a feature of modern urban life in the metropolitan centres of Weimar era Germany. Advertising in display windows, newspapers and magazines and on billboards became augmented by the spread of neon light fixtures, cinema, sky-writing and ultimately radio advertising. Metropolitan places such as Berlin's Alexanderplatz were increasingly shaped by an accelerated and vibrant but at times also crass and unruly commercial life (Ward, 2001;

Borscheid, 2004, 320–6). In order to foster this boom in advertising and to rein in its more excessive and carnivalesque elements, German advertisers increasingly sought to organize and regulate their profession. Once the immediate scarcity of the post-war and inflation years had been overcome, advertisers argued for a stronger incorporation of their profession within company decision-making processes and at the same time pushed for better professional credentials. Large professional organizations such as the Verein Deutscher Reklamefachleute (VDR) had already emerged during the imperial era and now dedicated training programmes began to follow. While university-based advertising research remained underdeveloped, the first correspondence course in advertising was established already in 1919 and soon augmented by other offerings to improve professional standards from educational seminars to periodicals like *Seidels Reklame* (Hirt, 2013).

The German advertising profession grew to about 50,000 full-time professionals by the mid-1930s, either working independently, for advertising agencies or for corporate advertising departments (Schug, 2009, 361). Traditional agencies (*Annoncen-Expeditionen*), such as the large Berlin firm of publisher Rudolph Mosse, increasingly expanded their portfolio of services. They were spurred on by competition from American firms coming to the German market such as J. Walter Thompson (since 1927) or McCann (since 1928). As full-service agencies, these firms offered advertising pretests and market analyses to their customers that many German advertisers resisted. German inter-war advertisers commonly emphasized intuition, gut feeling and the artistic genius of advertising artists over market data and scientific analysis (Schug, 2003, 2007; Ross, 2007). American firms at times struggled when they applied their experience derived from domestic markets to consumers overseas (Schug, 2005), yet the trend in German advertising as well slowly moved away from the artistic *Sachplakat* towards the text-heavy and psychology-laden advertising copy of American pedigree (de Grazia, 2005, 250–60).

Still, the close interaction between art and commerce fostered by the *Werkbund* was developed further during the inter-war years, now with a decisively modernist bent. Packages for cigarettes and other branded goods, for example, frequently betrayed a fascination with new art forms such as Dada. Novel forms of graphic art such as the photomontage became a prominent feature in advertising, as evidenced by the work of Herbert Bayer at the Dorland agency (Brüning, 2004). Bayer was one of many commercial artists who had emerged from the modernist Bauhaus school for design in Dessau, whose artists left their mark on product design for many German companies during the 1920s and 1930s (Schwartz, 2006). Well known is the cooperation between designer Wilhelm Wagenfeld and Schott glass-works in Jena. These modernist design forms became characteristic for upscale consumer goods in inter-war Germany and reflected a professional concern among designers at the Bauhaus and elsewhere to produce 'good design' for a commercial mass market.

Professionalization also entailed the development of early consumer research in Germany, albeit at a much slower pace than in the United States. Advertising reception and studies in 'psychotechnics', pioneered by German-American psychologist Hugo Münsterberg, found a growing reception at universities such as Mannheim and Cologne (Regnery, 2003). In Vienna, the Wirtschaftspsychologische Forschungsstelle, founded by Paul Lazarsfeld, began to conduct increasingly sophisticated market surveys for Austrian, Swiss and also German companies by the early 1930s (Fullerton, 1994; Logemann, 2013). The perhaps most lasting institutional innovation at the time was Wilhelm Vershofen's Institut für Wirtschaftsbeobachtung der Fertigware in Nuremberg which would make the city a leading centre for consumer research for decades to come (Bergler, 1959). While only in its infancy, professional marketing research (*Absatzforschung*) emerged during the inter-war years and began to make its way into the business practices of German retailers and consumer goods producers.

Retailers organized ever more effectively after the crises of war and inflation – in part to modernize and rationalize the trade and in part to ward off competition from a growing number of chain-stores, large department stores and efficiently organized consumer co-operatives (Spiekermann, 1999). Retailers increasingly relied on consumer credit to market new consumer goods. Subsidiaries of American sales-financing firms had arrived during the 1920s to promote automobile sales and were soon joined by German consortiums such as GEFI which backed credit-financed retail sales. The so-called 'Königsberg system' of credit checks helped the (still limited) advance of new consumer durables into German households between the wars (Logemann, 2011). As with advertising, however, overly 'indulgent' forms of consumption and marketing experienced public scolding and legislative push-back. In particular, the opulence of large department stores, but also credit financing schemes and new sales devices such as rebates or giveaways were targets of public criticism at the time (Briesen, 2001; Torp, 2011).

Not to be deterred by this cultural backlash, consumer goods companies attempted to exploit the growing culture of consumerism and to draw on the nascent professional expertise in the marketing field. Already in 1922, by one estimate, over 150 German firms had departments that were devoted to psycho-technics and applied psychology (Friebe, 2007, 82). Firms that marketed relatively new branded goods to a mass market were often ahead of the curve in consumer research – e.g. Berlin Leo-Werke, maker of Clorodont toothpaste. The company established a market research division during the early 1930s and collaborated with schools and dentists to promote tooth-brushing among German children (Gasteiger, 2010, 38). Another famous example is the tobacco company Reemtsma which relied on the expertise of renowned marketing expert Hans Domizlaff to promote its cigarette brands. Domizlaff's much discussed branding strategies involved elements of segmented marketing with a carefully designed mix of luxury and mass market brands, but also entailed the use of rebates, trading cards and elaborate package designs (Jacobs, 2008).

Like Behrens's work at AEG prior to the war, Domizlaff and his *Markentechnik* (brand technics) capture in some ways the spirit of what Friebe (2007) has called the 'conservative revolution' in inter-war German marketing. Domizlaff's understanding of brand images and of the need to win public trust through public relations were quite modern and his rejection of the advertiser as a boisterous mountebank reflected the professionalizing ethos of the time. On the other hand, his celebration of creative genius, his focus on advertising, and his dismissal of systematic research mark the difference from later forms of modern marketing management. More important perhaps, Domizlaff conceived of his audience very much in terms of an irrational and malleable mass which could be influenced for commercial and political ends. At the 1929 world advertising congress in Berlin, Domizlaff advocated a conception of 'social marketing' (Schwartzkopf, 2009) which betrayed an uneasy propensity for political propaganda.

The 'Nazi marketplace': marketing in dictatorship and war

Any discussion of marketing in 1930s Germany needs to acknowledge the proximity of inter-war commercial practices to the political propaganda of the Nazi state. Some have gone so far as to call Joseph Goebbels a political 'brand technician' in the sense of Domizlaff's *Markentechnik* (Voigt, 1975, cited in Friebe, 2007, 92) and both, indeed, drew heavily on the mass psychology of Gustave le Bon. Nazi propaganda relied on some of the same poster art traditions that mark the inter-war years and modern marketing technologies such as radio advertisements were famously employed in the service of state and party promotion. Commercial interests, by the same token, quickly seized on Nazi symbolism, using Swastikas and images of Hitler to sell goods and services, until the state cracked down on the unlicensed sale and promotion of 'Nazi kitsch' in May 1933 (Betts, 2004).

Marketing during the Nazi era was embroiled in contradictions. On the one hand, Nazi ideologues advanced scathing critiques of the competitive liberal marketplace (associated with Weimar Germany as well as the United States) with unregulated advertising, out-of-control credit and frivolous consumption. Official rhetoric called for an orderly marketplace with quality goods and organized economic actors (Wiesen, 2011). On the other hand, the popular appeal of mass consumption did not elude the party leadership. Promises of consumption – of radios and automobiles as *Volksempfänger* (people's receivers) or *Volkswagen* (people's cars) for average German households – soon became part of the state's propaganda repertoire. Berghoff's (2001) characterization of 'enticement and deprivation' captures the 1930s attempt to create a virtual image of a consumer society which in reality (and especially with intensified war preparations after 1936) fell very much short of its promises (König, 2004).

The advertising field mirrors this overall ambivalence of the Nazi years. A 1933 law regarding the advertising business regulated this sector of the economy and led to the dismissal of advertisers of Jewish descent or critical political persuasion. It created a state-related oversight structure, the Werberat (advertising council), which soon tried to regulate business practices (Swett, 2009). This included attempts to further professionalize and to enforce 'truth in advertising', but also entailed efforts to 'Germanize' the language and appearance of newspaper advertising (Berghoff, 2003). Like Jewish-owned businesses, the American agencies in the German market were soon forced out or changed ownership (Schug, 2003). However, while advertising language was now often infused with the ideology and symbolism of the Nazi regime, business – until the war – very much continued on as before. Swett (2013) emphasizes that the advertising industry was hardly under tight direction of the regime, but evolved in many ways in parallel with Western countries when it came to new trends in copy and style. Consumer research also made significant strides in 1930s Germany with the establishment of the Gesellschaft für Konsumforschung in Nuremberg which conducted nationwide consumer surveys for marketing purposes after 1934 (Feldenkirchen and Fuchs, 2009; Wiesen, 2011).

Both retailers and consumer goods companies engaged in a similar give-and-take with the new regime. Many retailers benefited from the elimination of competition as Jewish-owned stores suffered from boycotts or were 'aryanized', i.e. forced to change ownership (e.g. Bajohr, 1997). Consumer co-operatives, too, were expropriated, but neither department stores nor other features of modern consumer marketing, such as retail credit, disappeared during the 1930s. Wiesen (2011) notes the continuity of business as usual for German companies under the new regime, though many firms were now eager to market their goods as assets to the Nazi *Volksgemeinschaft*. The state's emphasis on health and (racial) hygiene quickly meshed with Bayer's attempts to sell medicine, Henkel's interest in cleaning supplies or the promotion of 'nerve-calming' decaffeinated coffee by Kaffee HAG (Wiesen, 2011). For marketing during the Nazi era, 'racist utopia and commercial utopia went hand in hand' (Wiesen, 2011, 19).

Wartime marketing has recently received attention in the literature. Both Wiesen (2011) and Swett (2013) emphasize the increasing control over advertising and business practices by the state after 1939. Controlling individual consumption attained new urgency and industry and government collaborated in promotional campaigns designed to alter consumer behaviour in face of scarcity and rationing. By the same token, the continued marketing of everyday luxuries such as tobacco and coffee was deemed essential to the war effort by the state (Petrick-Felber, 2015). Yet companies also pursued their own interests, especially as the fortunes of war turned after 1942; they increasingly sought to distance themselves and their brands from the regime. One central goal of wartime advertising strategies was to keep currently unavailable brands alive in the public consciousness. The continuity provided by these marketing efforts for Nivea skin cream or Persil detergent, along with many other products, would help pave the way for the resurgence and success of these brands in the post-war economic boom period (Swett, 2013).

'Americanization'? The discovery of the consumer after World War II

Germany did not become a mass consumer society in the full sense until the post-wa era. Scholars now identify the late 1950s as a break-through point at which the post-war 'economic miracle' affected the consumption standards of the majority of the population and we begin to detect a shift from a seller's market to a buyer's market, with important ramifications for the history of marketing. When we discuss the transformation of German marketing in these decades, furthermore, we do this in the context of the Cold War division of the country (Crew, 2003). While there has been some intriguing recent research on marketing and product design under the conditions of a planned economy in socialist East Germany (e.g. Ciesla and Poutrus, 1999; Gries, 2003; Rubin, 2008; Patterson, 2013), we will focus our subsequent discussion on West German developments alone.

Following the war, the 'Americanization of West German industry' (Berghahn, 1986) was said to have thoroughly taken hold. To be sure, 'Americanisms' in advertising or popular culture as well in the rationalization of industrial processes were already widely discussed in the Weimar era (Nolan, 1994). Scholars, however, have traced the reception of American production and management methods especially in the wake of the Marshall Plan and its productivity missions. This went hand-in-hand with the post-war proliferation of a new consumption regime which provided an economic corollary to America's new political empire (de Grazia, 2005). While the American example was undeniably important for post-war discussions regarding marketing and consumption, however, recent publications have cautioned that there was no wholesale importation of American methods. Instead, German companies were very selective in what they appropriated; they adapted to their specific needs, and the overall structure of the consumer marketplace remained quite different from the American case with regard, for example, to Germany's export orientation, or its retail and financing structures (Kleinschmidt, 2002; Logemann, 2012).

The dialogue with the American model could be traced across the marketing spectrum. The retailing sector made the new affluence of the 1950s most tangible to German consumers. Larger, modernized stores provided increasingly unhampered access to a wide variety of branded goods (Jessen and Nembach-Langer, 2012). Downtown department stores witnessed dramatic expansions and lived through their 'golden age' in the immediate post-war decades (Banken, 2012). While traditional stores and consumer co-operatives continued to dominate the retail landscape into the 1960s, self-service 'supermarkets' following an American model began to spread (Langer, 2013). Credit financing, too, saw an expansion, with banks and even the traditional German savings banks (*Sparkassen*) moving into the sector, yet credit use and credit marketing was much more limited than in the United States (Ellerbrock, 2004; Stücker, 2007; Logemann, 2011). Despite innovations such as self-service stores and the success of mail-order shopping catalogues from Quelle and Neckermann, the limits of American-style mass consumer marketing remained clear in 1950s and 1960s Germany, whether it came to credit financing, to checks on aggressive pricing or to unlimited night and weekend shopping.

The advertising industry demonstrates the continued uneasiness with American marketing styles after the war. The field felt renewed competition from American firms and larger German agencies adopted the full-service model with exclusive clients in various industries (Schröter, 1997). While the advertisements were frequently more dull and conservative than those of the Weimar era, overall advertising expenses rose by a factor of eight during the 1950s, touting a growing array of branded goods in new media such as television (Zimmermann, 2004). Still, this did not amount to an 'Americanization' of the profession, which continued to harbour resentments against what was portrayed either as the crass materialism, manipulative psychology or the uninspired 'nose-counting' of Madison Avenue. Many successful German advertisers such as Hanns Brose were open to new trends, but ultimately saw themselves as traditional, yet creative self-made men. Brose, like Domizlaff, had advocated concepts of advertising as public relations in a social context during the Nazi years. Now, after the war, he campaigned with like-minded admen of the WAAGE circle to use advertising in support of the post-war 'social market economy'. They were, however, no cheerleaders of an unbridled, competitive market economy (Schindelbeck, 1995; Hirt, 2013).

The continuity of inter-war traditions was prominent in other fields of marketing as well. Product design efforts in the post-war years clearly connected back to Weimar modernity. A new design school in Ulm partly benefited from the expertise of émigrés returning from the United States, but the 'international style' of design prominent, for example, in Braun electronic products or the work of Otl Aicher and other influential graphic and product designers, clearly built on a long indigenous tradition (Selle, 1987). According to Betts (2004), modernism in design became the 'aesthetic signature' of many companies and consumers in post-war Germany. Similarly, the market research sector received external input from émigrés such as Ernst Dichter, who began to offer his motivational analyses to companies in Germany and Europe by the 1950s (Schwarzkopf and Gries, 2010). Yet, German research firms such as Allensbach and the GfK emphasized the independent traditions of marketing research and *Absatzlehre* in Germany (Feldenkirchen and Fuchs, 2009; Brückweh, 2011). Still, their work contributed to an overall shift in how marketing experts in Germany thought about consumers during the post-war decades. Slowly departing from Domizlaff's conception of consumers as an irrational mass, German marketers – like their American counterparts – increasingly recognized consumer motivations as psychologically and sociologically constructed (Gasteiger, 2010).

So, when and how did German companies set out in earnest to find and win over the 'consumer'? According to Sabel (1982), many firms could largely afford to ignore consumers until the end of the 1960s. Market conditions were favourable as boom-era companies navigated a seller's market with little competition, a strong, fairly homogeneous demand and a still relatively basic structure of consumer needs. The production orientation from the era of the cartels and syndicates survived in the minds of many. The wake-up call came only after two decades of post-war reconstruction when consumer markets became increasingly saturated, differentiated, and stratified. By the end of the 1960s, marketing management rapidly became integrated into management practice, prompting a radical 'marketing revolution' (Sabel, 1982) with a thorough shift in business mentality towards a consumer orientation. Much like Tedlow a few years later, Sabel viewed change in business strategies as a function of broader shifts in the market; and much like their peers in the US or the UK,

German business historians since the 1990s have tirelessly pointed out the shortcomings of such linear development models which nonetheless continue to enjoy currency in many business administration textbooks (Kleinschmidt and Triebel, 2004; Berghoff, 2007b).

Today, a number of case studies detailing the marketing practice of German companies exist. Read side-by-side, the dramatic unevenness of the 'marketing revolution' becomes apparent. While changes in the market did lead companies to adopt new management strategies, their reactions and innovations varied by economic sector (Erker, 2007). Producers of everyday consumer goods such as hygiene products, cosmetics or fashion were confronted with market saturation phenomena earlier than durable goods producers of household appliances and cars. Beiersdorf, maker of Nivea skin cream, had already been a branding pioneer during the 1920s and again was one of the early adaptors after the war (Schröter, 1995). Even within one specific sector, a recent study on the automobile industry suggests, we find significant variation with regard to the speed and the manner with which new marketing methods were implemented (Köhler, 2012).

Many German companies retained patriarchical management styles and hierarchical organizational structures throughout the 'miracle years'. Strategic decisions were based upon the skills and experiences of local factory management, the perspective of the production engineers and on a belief in quality products 'Made in Germany'. The introduction of new marketing concepts frequently depended on isolated initiatives by individuals or on business contacts to American firms. Kleinschmidt (2002) and Hilger (2004) have traced a transatlantic knowledge transfer in marketing back to the early 1950s. Entire delegations of German managers travelled to the United States to study the intensive advertising competition on the American market with an ambivalent mix of disdain and fascination. In addition, the return of advertising firms like J. Walter Thompson and McCann Erickson to the European market led to new forms of cooperation (Schröter, 1997). Volkswagen presents a case in point; the company initially ran its irreverent 'beetle' ad campaign developed by Doyle Dane Bernbach in the United States and, after 1962, adapted it to the domestic market in Germany (Vaillant, 1995; Rieger, 2013).

One important precondition for the success of new marketing strategies in German companies was their compatibility with existing market conditions and management traditions. With regard to international advertising, this meant a 'translation' of language and iconography to the local market which opened up opportunities for smaller German agencies. Marketing concepts, Kleinschmidt (2012) stresses, could not simply be copied from the American example. Adaptation always entailed a hybridization of marketing knowledge which affected both German and American advertisers. This very phenomenon of convergence processes also applied to the development of marketing methodology. The success of new methods during the 1950s and 1960s rested on the compatibility of 'American' innovations with 'German' traditions in consumer and advertising research that had emerged since the 1920s with the inter-war notion of *Absatzwirtschaft*. Now American gurus of motivation research offered German companies new psychological tools to motivate consumers to buy. Yet this concept still conformed to a traditional, producer-oriented and rather one-dimensional conception of markets. If even desires could be 'produced', companies had to pay only marginal attention to actual consumers (Kronenberg and Gehlen, 2012).

Towards the practice of modern, scientific marketing after 1965

As long as the boom in demand continued, successes in sales did as much to pre-empt fundamental reforms towards modern marketing management as did sceptical attitudes.

The methods of motivation research were regarded as manipulative, unscientific, as well as useless by many managers (Hansen and Bode, 1999; Hilger, 2004). New advertising agencies and company ad departments sprang up everywhere during the 1950s and 1960s, along with a new professional elite of advertisers and marketing experts. However, they were in many ways 'ignored prophets' (Hirt, 2013) who constantly felt the need to vie for recognition and respect from upper management. For marketing to become an integrated management strategy meeting the many challenges of the period following the boom, another developmental step was required. The 20-year transition from the early stages of marketing management to its full-fledged establishment by the 1970s was an evolutionary process of scientization and professionalization.

Perhaps the decisive step in marketing's development from operative advertising to strategic management was the inclusion of the behavioural sciences into the methodological toolkit (Hansen and Bode, 2007). By the mid-1960s, influences of American 'behavioural marketing' were combined with approaches from cognitive and social psychology which had been developed within Germany. Mannheim-based independent market researcher Bernt Spiegel mustered a great deal of attention with his psychological market models which sought to map the brand image of BMW cars within a social field of consumer attitudes and perceptions (Köhler, 2012). Aided by new forms of systematic representative surveys, semantic differentials and comparative associations, this approach succeeded reliably in measuring and revealing those product qualities which influenced consumer decision-making.

Such sophisticated image analyses finally freed marketing from the stigma of being 'speculative' rather than 'scientific'. They furthermore offered companies a methodology to effectively segment markets and to strategically place their products. As image analyses spread from the auto industry to other consumer goods sectors they provided an important stimulus for the expansion of market research in Germany (Silberer and Büttner, 2007). Consumer typologies which had long been based on simplistic categories of income and profession were augmented by multidimensional analyses of consumer desires. This kind of expert knowledge was now offered by a growing array of market research and polling institutes, including the GfK, Infratest or the Institut für Demoskopie Allensbach. At the end of the 1960s, marketing and consumer research had become a booming field and an academic discipline in its own right at German universities as well (Berghoff, 2007b).

Companies themselves also began to expand or create specialized market-research departments. Existing advertising departments were recast as marketing departments and given control over strategic decision-making with regard to long-term market developments and image policies. In a series of often contested episodes of organizational restructuring, marketing moved beyond its limited sales function towards an element of integrated control (Köhler, 2008). This entailed a fundamental change in the way managers conceived of markets. According to the logic of a consumer perspective, the goal was no longer primarily to manipulate demand in order to enhance sales, but rather to engineer and produce products from the start with consumer demand in mind. In this way, products were increasingly seen as media in a reciprocal exchange of meanings and attitudes between consumers, companies and stakeholders (Gries, 2003; Wischermann, 2003; Bruhn, 2004).

This paradigm shift from producer to consumer orientation, however, was less a 'revolution' than an incremental process. Even as consumer markets tightened noticeably by the late 1960s, many companies still believed they could manage sales through simple image adjustments. Management trusted they 'understood' developments in the consumer markets, relying on the trend of 'trading up' towards higher-priced, more prestigious goods to continue as it had throughout the decade. Only the crises of inflation, stagnation and soaring oil prices during the early 1970s truly confronted German managers with the complicated reality of a developed and highly diverse mass consumer society (Köhler, 2007). Much like they had in the United States a few years before, the public and political debates over 'consumerism' and a nascent consumer rights movement also helped to reshape the market perception of German companies and sensitized them to importance of social changes for their own strategic decisions (Gasteiger, 2009; Kleinschmidt, 2004, 2006). As uncertainty about economic and social developments grew, so did the demand within companies for new forms of marketing expertise.

Increasingly sophisticated market and social prognoses offered to fill this void and led to a boom in marketing research for German companies. Consulting agencies and in-house marketing experts developed market segmentation concepts that built on Inglehart's theories of changing values or Well's activities-interests-opinions model and other new approaches from the social sciences and communication studies. By the mid-1970s, the Sinus Institute and the market research agency Compagnon offered consumer typologies based on milieus and lifestyles, which promised to provide companies with insights into differentiated consumer preferences and to enable targeted marketing towards specific consumer segments. Computerized data analysis, furthermore, significantly increased the representativeness and precision of panel and image studies demographics (Hansen and Bode, 1999, 235).

Integration became the new mantra of marketing management in Germany. The image targets devised by marketing planners became a guide for overall management strategies. This meant that the previously separate areas of market research, advertising, product policy, public relations as well as sales planning and controlling were brought together under the rubric of marketing. As had been demanded by many American and German marketing experts since the 1920s, the internal value-chain of many companies was reversed and geared towards consumer perceptions and desires. Product portfolios were expanded to match the increasingly diverse spread of consumer typologies and preferences (Schröter, 1995; Köhler, 2010). Pricing, advertising and service strategies now became focused on target groups with increasingly fine-grained gradations and differences in the marketing mix. Integration processes also affected the area of business communication. Concepts of corporate design and corporate identity, as devised already by Behrens for AEG at the beginning of the century, were now adopted by more and more German companies trying to improve long-term consumer relations in competitive markets through an intensive and consistent image design. As had been common in the United States, packaging, sales and service stations, company letterhead as well as advertising messages were harmonized to achieve a uniform corporate image. Again, marketing management drew on advertising psychology to project an integrated and holistic image of the company to consumers.

Conclusion

Overall, the history of modern marketing in Germany was characterized by several severe caesurae. Specific political and economic contexts of war, reconstruction or dictatorship contributed to a comparatively lagged development of mass consumption and of a corresponding marketing orientation in contrast to the speedier and somewhat more even process in the United States. While the German 'laggards' benefited from transfers of marketing concepts and methodologies especially after World War II, however, they did not become time-delayed copies of their American counterparts. The continuities of a significant indigenous marketing tradition – which also impacted the American development through numerous émigrés – left their mark into the post-war era. Recent research shows that the convergence in retailing and financing practices, in advertising strategies, product design or marketing management entailed transatlantic transfers, mutual influences, as well as parallel developments which in the German case drew on traditions dating back to the imperial era.

To this day, it remains common in Germany to conceive of marketing as being little more than a glorified new advertising strategy. German business history has only just begun to discover the gradual but fundamental shift towards integrated marketing management as a major caesura during the last third of the twentieth century. The traditional preoccupation with 'quality', however, remains a unique aspect of German marketing debates as 'quality' has now become a central element of sophisticated modern image strategies. This should not simply be dismissed as a relic of an outdated producer-oriented mindset, which celebrated quality as the guarantor of success (Berghoff, 1997). Instead it is an expression of a business culture of a heavily export-dependent economy. 'Made in Germany' has been consciously developed as a brand to be marketed globally with a quality image since at least the inter-war era. To this day, this has influenced the corporate identity and marketing of German firms in the global marketplace and has provided them with a competitive edge (Kühschelm et al., 2012).

References

Abelshauser, W. (2005) *The Dynamics of German Industry: Germany's Path toward the New Economy and the American Challenge*, Berghahn Books, New York.

Bajohr, F. (1997) *'Arisierung' in Hamburg: die Verdrängung der jüdischen Unternehmer 1933–1945*, Christians, Hamburg.

Banken, R. (2012) '"Everything that exists in capitalism can be found in the department store": The development of department stores in the Federal Republic of Germany, 1949–2000', in R. Jessen and L. Langer (eds), *Transformations of Retailing in Europe After 1945*, Ashgate, Arnham, pp. 147–62.

Berghahn, V. (1986) *The Americanisation of West German Industry, 1945–1973*, Cambridge University Press, Cambridge.

Berghoff, H. (1997) *Zwischen Kleinstadt und Weltmarkt: Hohner und die Harmonika 1857–1961*, Schöningh, Paderborn.

Berghoff, H. (2001) 'Enticement and deprivation: The regulation of consumption in pre-war Nazi Germany', in R. Daunton and M. Hilton (eds), *The Politics of Consumption*, Berg, Oxford, pp. 165–84.

Berghoff, H. (2003) '"Times change and we change with them": The German advertising industry in the "Third Reich"', *Business History*, 46, 128–47.

Berghoff, H. (ed.) (2007a) *Marketinggeschichte: Die Genese einer modernen Sozialtechnik*, Campus, Frankfurt.

Berghoff, H. (2007b) 'Marketing im 20. Jahrhundert. Absatzinstrument – Managementphilosophie – universelle Sozialtechnik', in Berghoff (ed.), *Marketinggeschichte: Die Genese einer modernen Sozialtechnik*, Campus, Frankfurt/M. and New York, pp. 11–58.

Berghoff, H., Scranton, P., and Spiekermann, U. (eds) (2012) *The Rise of Marketing and Market Research*, Palgrave Macmillan, New York.

Bergler, G. (1959) *Die Entwicklung der Verbrauchsforschung in Deutschland und die GfK bis zum Jahre 1945*, Laßleben, Kallmünz.

Betts, P. (2004) *The Authority of Everyday Objects: A Cultural History of West German Industrial Design*, University of California Press, Berkeley, CA.

Blaich, F. (1982) 'Absatzstrategien deutscher Unternehmen im 19. und in der ersten Hälfte des 20. Jahrhunderts', in H. Pohl (ed.), *Absatzstrategien deutscher Unternehmen – Gestern – Heute – Morgen*, Steiner, Wiesbaden, pp. 5–46.

Borscheid, P. (2004) *Das Tempo-Virus: Eine Kulturgeschichte der Beschleunigung*, Campus, Frankfurt.

Borscheid, P. (2009) 'Agenten des Konsums: Werbung und Marketing', in H. Haupt and C. Torp, *Die Konsumgesellschaft in Deutschland 1890–1990: Ein Handbuch*, Campus, Frankfurt, pp. 79–96.

Borscheid, P., and Wischermann, C. (eds) (1995) *Bilderwelt des Alltags: Werbung in der Konsumgesellschaft des 19. und 20. Jahrhunderts*, Steiner, Stuttgart.

Briesen, D. (2001) *Warenhaus, Massenkonsum und Sozialmoral: Zur Geschichte der Konsumkritik im 20. Jahrhundert*, Campus, Frankfurt.

Brückweh, K. (ed.) (2011) *The Voice of the Citizen Consumer: A History of Market Research, Consumer Movements, and the Political Public Sphere*, Oxford University Press, Oxford.

Bruhn, M. (2004) 'Der Streit um die Vormachtstellung von Marketing und Public Relations in der Unternehmenskommunikation: Eine unendliche Geschichte?', *Marketing. Zeitschrift für Forschung und Praxis*, 26, 71–81.

Brüning, U. (2004) 'Herbert Bayers Neue Linie: Standardisierte Gebrauchsgraphik aus dem Studio Dorland', in S. Hansen and A. Schug (eds), *Moments of Consistency*, Transcript, Bielefeld, pp. 192–204.

Buddensieg, T., and Rogge H. (1984) *Industriekultur: Peter Behrens and the AEG, 1907–1914*, MIT Press, Cambridge, MA.

Chandler, A. (1990) *Scale and Scope: The Dynamics of Industrial Capitalism*, Belknap Press, Cambridge, MA.

Ciarlo, D. (2011) *Advertising Empire: Race and Visual Culture in Imperial Germany*, Harvard University Press, Cambridge, MA.

Ciesla, B., and Poutrus, P. (1999) 'Food supply in a planned economy', in K. Jarausch (ed.), *Dictatorship as Experience*, University of North Carolina Press, Chapel Hill, NC, pp. 144–62.

Crew, D. (ed.) (2003) *Consuming Germany in the Cold War*, Berg, Oxford.

Crossick, G., and Jaumain, S. (eds) (1999) *Cathedrals of Consumption: The European Department Store, 1850–1939*, Ashgate, Aldershot.

de Grazia, Victoria (2005) *Irresistible Empire: America's Advance through twentieth-Century Europe*, Belknap Press, Cambridge, MA.

Ellerbrock, K.-P. (2004) 'Konsumentenkredit und ‚Soziale Marktwirtschaft', in C. Kleinschmidt and F. Triebel (eds), *Marketing: Historische Aspekte der Wettbewerbs- und Absatzpolitik*, Klartext, Essen, pp. 105–33.

Engel, A. (2009) *Farben der Globalisierung: Die Entstehung moderner Märkte für Farbstoffe 1500–1900*, Campus, Frankfurt.

Epple, A. (2010) *Das Unternehmen Stollwerck: Eine Mikrogeschichte der Globalisierung*, Campus, Frankfurt.

Erker, P. (2007) 'Die Macht der Unterscheidung: Markenstrategie und Märktedynamik am Beispiel von Continental und Dachser', in H. Berghoff (ed.), *Marketinggeschichte*, Campus, Frankfurt, pp. 296–322.

Fear, J. (2005) *Organizing Control: August Thyssen and the Construction of German Corporate Management*, Harvard University Press, Cambridge, MA.

Feldenkirchen, W. and Fuchs, D. (2009) *Die Stimme des Verbrauchers zum Klingen bringen: 75 Jahre Geschichte der GFK Gruppe*, Piper, München.

Friebe, H. (2007) 'Branding Germany: Hans Domizlaff's Markentechnik and its Ideological Impact', in P. Swett, J. Wiesen and J. Zatlin (eds), *Selling Modernity*, Duke University Press, Durham, NC, pp. 78–101.

Fullerton, R. (1994) 'Tea and the Viennese: A pioneering episode in the analysis of consumer behavior', in T. Allen and D. John (eds), *Advances in Consumer Research*, Association for Consumer Research, Provo, UT, pp. 418–21.

Fullerton, R. (2012) 'The historical development of segmentation: The example of the German book trade 1800–1928,' *Journal of Historical Research in Marketing*, 4, 56–67.

Gasteiger, N. (2009) 'Konsum und Gesellschaft: Werbung, Konsumkritik und Verbraucherschutz in der Bundesrepublik der 1960er- und 1970er-Jahre', *Zeithistorische Forschungen/Studies in Contemporary History*, 6, 1–12 (online).

Gasteiger, N. (2010) *Der Konsument: Verbraucherbilder in Werbung, Konsumkritik und Verbraucherschutz 1945-1989*, Campus, Frankfurt.

Gries, R. (2003) *Produkte als Medien: Kulturgeschichte der Produktkommunikation in der Bundesrepublik und der DDR*, Leipziger Univ.-Verlag, Leipzig.

Grube, N. (2011) 'Targeting and educating consumers in West Germany: Market research by the Allensbach Institute up to the 1970s', in K. Brückweh (ed.), *The Voice of the Citizen Consumer*, Oxford University Press, Oxford, pp. 75–95.

Hansen, U., and Bode, M. (1999) *Marketing & Konsum: Theorie und Praxis von der Industrialisierung bis ins 21. Jahrhundert*. Vahlen, Munich.

Hansen, U., and Bode, M. (2007) 'Entwicklungsphasen der deutschen Marketingwissenschaft seit dem Zweiten Weltkrieg', in H. Berghoff (ed.), *Marketinggeschichte*, Campus, Frankfurt, pp. 179–204.

Haupt, H.-G. (2003) *Konsum und Handel: Europa im 19. und 20. Jahrhundert*, Vandenhoeck & Ruprecht, Göttingen.

Hilger, S. (2004) *Amerikanisierung' deutscher Unternehmen: Wettbewerbsstrategien und Unternehmenspolitik bei Henkel, Siemens und Daimler-Benz (1945/49–1975)*, Steiner, Stuttgart.

Hirt, G. (2013) *Verkannte Propheten? Zur "Expertenkultur"(west-)deutscher Werbekommunikatoren bis zur Rezession 1966/67*, Leipziger Universitätsverlag, Leipzig.

Jacobs, T. (2008) *Rauch und Macht: das Unternehmen Reemtsma 1920 bis 1961*, Wallstein, Göttingen.

Jessen, R., and Nembach-Langer, L. (2012) *Transformations of Retailing in Europe After 1945*, Ashgate, Farnham.

Jones, D.G. Brian (1992) 'Die Deutsche Historische Schule: Begründerin des nordamerikanischen Marketingdenkens', *Marketing Zeitschrift für Forschung und Praxis*, 14, 5–12.

Kleinschmidt, C. (2002) *Der produktive Blick: Wahrnehmung amerikanischer und japanischer Management- und Produktionsmethoden durch deutsche Unternehmer 1950–1985*, Akademie Verlag, Berlin.

Kleinschmidt, C. (2004) '"Konsumerismus" versus Marketing: Eine bundesdeutsche Diskussion der 1970er Jahre', in Kleinschmidt and F. Triebel (eds), *Marketing*, Klartext, Essen, pp. 249–60.

Kleinschmidt, C. (2006) 'Konsumgesellschaft, Verbraucherschutz und Soziale Marktwirtschaft: Verbraucherpolitische Aspekte des Modell "Deutschland" (1947–1975)', *Jahrbuch für Wirtschaftsgeschichte*, 1, 13–28.

Kleinschmidt, C., and Triebel, F. (eds) (2004) *Marketing: Historische Aspekte der Wettbewerbs- und Absatzpolitik*, Klartext, Essen.

Köhler, I. (2007) 'Marketing als Krisenstrategie: Die deutsche Automobilindustrie und die Herausforderungen der 1970er Jahre', in H. Berghoff (ed.), *Marketinggeschichte*, Campus, Frankfurt, pp. 259–95.

Köhler, I. (2008) 'Marketingmanagement als Strukturmodell: Der organisatorische Wandel in der deutschen Automobilindustrie der 1960er bis 80er Jahre', *Zeitschrift für Unternehmensgeschichte*, 53, 216–39.

Köhler, I. (2010) 'Overcoming stagnation: Product policy and marketing in the German automobile industry of the 1970s', *Business History Review*, 84, 53–78.

Köhler, I. (2012) *Die Neuvermessung des Automobils. Gesellschaftswandel und das Marketingmanagement der deutschen Autoindustrie in den 1960er Jahren,* Habil. Georg-August-University Göttingen.

König, W. (2004) *Volkswagen, Volksempfänger, Volksgemeinschaft: 'Volksprodukte' im Dritten Reich,* Schöningh, Paderborn.

Kronenberg, C., and Gehlen, B. (2012) '"Der Versager des Jahres": Marketingorientierung, Corporate Governance und die Krise der Gebrüder Stollwerck AG 1970/71', in I. Köhler. and R. Rossfeld (eds), *Pleitiers und Bankrotteure: Geschichte des ökonomischen Scheiterns vom 18. bis 20. Jahrhundert*, Campus, Frankfurt, pp. 317–40.

Kühschelm, O., Eder, F.X., and Siegrist, H. (eds) (2012) *Konsum und Nation: Zur Geschichte nationalisierender Inszenierungen in der Produktkommunikation*, Transcript, Bielefeld.

Lamberty, C. (2000) *Reklame in Deutschland 1890–1914: Wahrnehmung, Professionalisierung und Kritik der Wirtschaftswerbung*, Duncker & Humblot, Berlin.

Langer, L. (2013) *Revolution im Einzelhandel: Die Einführung der Selbstbedienung in Lebensmittelgeschäften der Bundesrepublik Deutschland (1949–1973)*, Böhlau, Cologne.

Logemann, J. (2011) 'Americanization through credit? A transnational and comparative history of consumer credit in Germany, 1860s–1960s', *Business History Review*, 85, 529–50.

Logemann, J. (2012) *Trams or Tailfins? Public and Private Prosperity in Postwar West Germany and the United States*, University of Chicago Press, Chicago, IL.

Logemann, J. (2013) 'European imports? European immigrants and the transformation of American consumer culture from the 1920s to the 1960s', *GHI Bulletin*, 52, 113–33.

Logemann, J., and Spiekermann, U. (2010) 'The myth of a bygone cash economy: Consumer lending in Germany from the nineteenth century to the mid-twentieth century', *Entreprises et Histoire*, 59, 12–27.

Nolan, M. (1994) *Visions of Modernity: American Business and the Modernization of Germany*, Oxford University Press, New York.

Nonn, C. (1996) *Verbraucherprotest und Parteiensystem im wilhelminischen Deutschland*, Droste, Düsseldorf.

Nonn, C. (2009) 'Die Entdeckung der Konsumenten im Kaiserreich', in H. Haupt and C. Torp, *Die Konsumgesellschaft in Deutschland 1890–1990: Ein Handbuch*, Campus, Frankfurt, pp. 221–31.

Ottomeyer, H. (1996) 'Kommunikation durch Design', in S. Bäumler (ed.), *Die Kunst zu werben: Das Jahrhundert der Reklame,* DuMont, Cologne, pp. 228–40.

Patterson, P. (2013) 'The bad science and the black arts: The reception of marketing in socialist Europe', in H. Berghoff, P. Scranton and U. Spiekermann (eds), *The Rise of Marketing and Market Research*, Palgrave Macmillan, New York, pp. 269–89.

Petrick-Felber, N. (2015) *Kriegswichtiger Genuss: Tabak und Kaffee im Dritten Reich*, Wallstein, Göttingen.

Regnery, C. (2003) *Die Deutsche Werbeforschung 1900–1945*, Monsenstein, Münster.

Reinhardt, D. (1993) *Von der Reklame zum Marketing: Geschichte der Wirtschaftswerbung in Deutschland*, Akademie Verlag, Berlin.

Reinhardt, D. (2003) 'Zeitgenössische Ansätze der Marktkommunikation durch Werbung vom Kaiserreich zur Bundesrepublik', in C. Wischermann (ed.), *Unternehmenskommunikation deutscher Mittel- und Großunternehmen*, Ardey, Münster, pp. 41–56.

Rieger, B. (2013) *The People's Car: A Global History of the Volkswagen Beetle*, Harvard University Press, Cambridge, MA.

Ross, C. (2007) 'Visions of prosperity: The Americanization of advertising in interwar Germany', in P. Swett, J. Wiesen and J. Zatlin (eds), *Selling Modernity*, Duke University Press, Durham, NC, pp. 52–77.

Rossfeld, R. (2004) 'Unternehmensgeschichte als Marketinggeschichte,' in C. Kleinschmidt and F. Triebel (eds), *Marketing*, Klartext, Essen, pp. 17–39.

Rossfeld, R. (2007) *Schweizer Schokolade: Industrielle Produktion und kulturelle Konstruktion eines nationalen Symbols 1860–1920,* Hier + Jetzt, Baden.

Rubin, E. (2008) *Synthetic Socialism: Plastics and Dictatorship in the German Democratic Republic*, UNC Press, Chapel Hill, NC.

Sabel, H. (1982) 'Absatzstrategien deutscher Unternehmen seit 1945', in M. Pohl (ed.), *Absatzstrategien deutscher Unternehmen: Gestern – Heute – Morgen*, Steiner, Wiesbaden, pp. 47–66.

Schindelbeck, D. (1995) '"Asbach Uralt" und "soziale Marktwirtschaft": Zur Kulturgeschichte der Werbeagentur in Deutschland', *Zeitschrift für Unternehmensgeschichte,* 40, 235–52.

Schröter, H. (1995) *Erfolgsfaktor Marketing: Der Strukturwandel von der Reklame zur Unternehmenssteuerung*, Bergakademie, Freiberg.

Schröter, H. (1997) 'Die Amerikanisierung der Werbung in der Bundesrepublik Deutschland', *Jahrbuch für Wirtschaftsgeschichte*, 91/1, 93–115.

Schröter, H. (2005) *Americanization of the European Economy: A Compact Survey of American Economic Influence in Europe since the 1880s*, Springer, Dordrecht.

Schwartz, F. (1996a) *The Werkbund: Design Theory and Mass Culture Before the First World War*, Yale University Press, New Haven, CT.

Schwartz, F. (1996b) 'Commodity signs: Peter Behrens, the AEG, and the trademark', *Journal of Design History*, 9, 153–84.

Schwartz, F. (2006) 'Utopia for sale: The Bauhaus and Weimar Germany's consumer culture', in K. James-Chakraborty (ed.), *Bauhaus Culture: From Weimar to the Cold War*, University of Minnesota Press, Minneapolis, MN, pp. 115–38.

Schwarzkopf, S. (2009) 'What was advertising? The invention, rise, demise, and disappearance of advertising concepts in nineteenth and twentieth century Europe and America' *BEH Online,* 7. http://www.thebhc.org/sites/default/files/schwarzkopf.pdf

Schwarzkopf, S., and Gries, R. (eds) (2010) *Ernest Dichter and Motivation Research: New Perspectives on the Making of Post-War Consumer Culture*, Palgrave Macmillan, New York.

Schug, A. (2003) 'Wegbereiter der modernen Absatzwerbung in Deutschland: Advertising Agencies und die Amerikanisierung der deutschen Werbebranche in der Zwischenkriegszeit', *WerkstattGeschichte*, 34, 29–51.

Schug, A. (2005) 'Missionare der globalen Konsumkultur: Corporate Identity und Absatzstrategien amerikanischer Unternehmen in Deutschland im frühen 20. Jahrhundert', in W. Hardtwig (ed.), *Politische Kulturgeschichte der Zwischenkriegszeit 1918–1939*, Vanderhoek & Ruprecht, Göttingen, pp. 307–42.

Schug, A. (2007) *'Deutsche Kultur' und Werbung: Studien zur Geschichte der Wirtschaftswerbung 1918–1945*, Diss. Humboldt-Univ., Berlin.

Schug, A. (2009) 'Werbung und die Kultur des Kapitalismus', in H. Haupt and C. Torp (eds), *Die Konsumgesellschaft in Deutschland 1890–1990: Ein Handbuch*, Campus, Frankfurt, pp. 355–69.

Selle, G. (1987) *Design-Geschichte in Deutschland: Produktkultur als Entwurf und Erfahrung*, DuMont, Cologne.

Silberer, G., and Büttner, O. (2007) 'Geschichte und Methodik der akademischen Käuferforschung', in H. Berghoff (ed.), *Marketinggeschichte*, Campus, Frankfurt/M. and New York, pp. 205–30.

Spiekermann, U. (1995) 'Elitenkampf um die Werbung: Staat, Heimatschutz und Reklameindustrie im frühen 20. Jahrhundert', in P. Borscheid and C. Wischermann (eds), *Bilderwelt des Alltags*, Steiner, Stuttgart, pp. 126–49.

Spiekermann, U. (1999) *Basis der Konsumgesellschaft: Entstehung und Entwicklung des modernen Kleinhandels in Deutschland 1850–1914*, Beck, Munich.

Streb, J. (2004) 'Kundenberatung und Kundenausbildung als innovative Marketingstrategien der deutschen Chemieindustrie im 19. und 20. Jahrhundert', in C. Kleinschmidt and F. Triebel (eds), *Marketing*, Klartext, Essen, pp. 85–104.

Stücker, B. (2007) 'Konsum auf Kredit in der Bundesrepublik', *Economic History Yearbook*, 48, 63–88.

Swett, P. (2009) 'Preparing for victory: Heinrich Hunke, the Nazi *Werberat*, and West German Prosperity', *Central European History*, 42, 675–707.

Swett, P. (2013) *Selling under the Swastika: Advertising and Commercial Culture in Nazi Germany*, Stanford University Press, Stanford, CA.

Swett, P., Wiesen, J., and Zatlin, J. (2007) *Selling Modernity: Advertising in twentieth-Century Germany*, Duke University Press, Durham, NC.

Torp, C. (2011) *Konsum und Politik in der Weimarer Republik*, Vandenhoek & Ruprecht, Göttingen.

Vaillant, K. (1995) *Vom 'Ervolkswagen' zum Designer-Schmuckstück: Automobilwerbung in Publikumszeit-schriften (1952–1994)*, WZB discussion paper, Berlin.

Voigt, G. (1975) 'Goebbels als Markentechniker', in F. Haug (ed.), *Warenästhetik: Beiträge zur Diskussion, Weiterentwicklung und Vermittlung ihrer Kritik*, Suhrkamp, Frankfurt, pp. 221–6.

Ward, J. (2001) *Weimar Surfaces: Urban Visual Culture in 1920s Germany*, University of California Press, Berkeley, CA.

Wiesen, J. (2011) *Creating the Nazi Marketplace: Commerce and Consumption in the Third Reich*, Cambridge University Press, Cambridge.

Wischermann, C. (2003) 'Unternehmenskultur, Unternehmenskommunikation, Unternehmensidentität', in Wischermann (ed.), *Unternehmenskommunikation deutscher Mittel- und Großunternehmen*, Ardey, Münster, pp. 21–40.

Zimmermann, C. (2004) 'Marktanalysen und Werbeforschung der frühen Bundesrepublik: Deutsche Traditionen und US-Amerikanische Einflüsse, 1950–1965', in M. Berg and P. Gassert (eds), *Deutschland und die USA in der Internationalen Geschichte des 20. Jahrhunderts*, Steiner, Stuttgart, pp. 473–91.

21

History of marketing in India

Hari Sreekumar and Rohit Varman

Introduction

Contemporary concepts and practices of marketing, and the ideologies which impel these, originate from the social and economic contexts of the West, particularly the United States and Europe (Ellis *et al.*, 2011; Eckhardt *et al.*, 2013). As a consequence of this Western dominance, the marketing discipline became permeated with values such as individualism and rationalism (Ellis *et al.*, 2011). The Eurocentrism of much of marketing theory has resulted in knowledge pertinent to contexts such as India being overlooked (Varman and Saha, 2009; Varman and Sreekumar, 2015). In an early paper that appeared in the *Journal of Marketing*, Westfall and Boyd, Jr. (1960) suggested that marketing practices in India were not sufficiently 'developed', and called for a 'modernization' of marketing in India. In response to such criticism, marketing academics in India adopted theories and practices of marketing from the West, especially the US. Not surprisingly, these theories and practices were often far removed from the realities of the Indian economy and consumers (Varman *et al.*, 2011). This is particularly ironic because India, like many other parts of the world, has a rich history of markets and marketing. There is clearly a need to bridge this gap in our knowledge and understanding about the rest of the world. This chapter on history of marketing in India addresses this lacuna in the discipline.

While India as a nation-state is a relatively new entity, the broader geographical region referred to as 'India' in historical work comprises a large area that includes present-day Pakistan, Bangladesh, Afghanistan, Sri Lanka and even some of the south-east Asian countries such as Myanmar. Moreover, the region has a history of trade and commerce dating back more than 2,000 years. In providing an account of marketing history of such a vast area over such a long period, one faces the challenge of disentangling marketing history from the history of trade and business in general. In attempting to determine what constitutes marketing history, we have relied on Jones and Tadajewski's (2014) suggestion that marketing history includes advertising, retailing, marketing channels, product design and branding and consumer behaviour, but is not limited to these. We attempt to use the present state of marketing as a touchstone to look at business and trade events in the past, taking care to avoid an anachronistic reading of marketing history (Fullerton, 2011).

Periodization is one of the vexing problems that historians face. It is common to divide Indian history into ancient, medieval and modern periods. We concur with Thapar (2002) that these classificatory terms are arbitrary, more so given the emphasis on marketing activity. However, for purposes of simplicity and narrative ease, one has to follow some kind of periodization of events. We follow a chronological order in describing India's marketing history, by dividing the time period under consideration into three phases. In the first part, which we call the ancient and medieval period, we describe marketing practices from 2,000 years ago to the seventeenth century, when the British East India Company started operating in India. The colonial encounter changed the marketing system and consumption in considerable ways, and in the second part of our chapter we detail these changes. In the third part on the post-colonial period we briefly touch upon some of the developments in marketing after India's independence in 1947. We believe that this classification takes into account the points of inflection in India's society and economy with respect to market activities.

Markets in ancient and medieval India

The centres of marketing and selling

India has a fairly diverse geography and climate, and the nature of commercial activity in the littoral towns differed considerably from that in the interiors. The literature dealing with the ancient period suggests a primarily agricultural society that was not trade oriented (Hall, 1977). However, research also points to the diversity of soil and climate in the subcontinent which made trading a necessity in order to obtain goods that were not locally produced or available (Hall, 1977). Physical constraints in navigation meant that items such as spices, silks and pearls were easier to trade, given that these items did not weigh much and could be transported easily (Roy, 2012). Moreover, Roy (2012) points out that towns situated on coasts, or at places where the river met the coast, enjoyed advantages with regard to trade, since it was much easier to carry cargo through rivers and the sea, as compared to over land. The selling and buying activity in these sites was however more akin to that happening in a seasonal trade fair, rather than that of an established commercial centre (Roy, 2012).

Early records indicate that urban centres appeared in north India in the Gangetic plain, around the first millennium BCE, and the first century BCE period was marked by considerable economic growth and prosperity (Ray, 1985). Merchants obtained goods such as wheat, rice, clarified butter, sesame oil, cotton cloth and honey from ships that arrived in port through mutual agreement with merchants living in other regions, or directly from producers, and these goods were then sold in urban centres through retail outlets (Ray, 1985). Major ports such as Bharuch in western India and other ports along the Konkan coast in the south-west facilitated trade with the Persian Gulf (Ray, 1985). We thus find, many centuries ago, a fairly complex marketing network comprising producers, wholesale merchants, retailers and itinerant merchants, all of whom exchanged goods and services in major ports and urban centres.

Looking at the marketing centres of a later era, the Chola period, roughly from 850 to 1279 CE in south India, historians present an interesting account of regional commercial centres (Hall, 1975; Mukund, 2012). There were streets devoted to the sale of food grains, textiles, gold jewellery, copper ware and leather work (Mukund, 2012). There were specific marketing institutions such as *nagaram* or a commercial urban centre and guilds or collective bodies of traders and artisans that played important roles in this era. In a *nagaram* there were *kadai* (shops), *angadi* (markets) and *perangadi* (a big market in the inner city) (Mukund, 2012). Accordingly, unlike village exchanges that were primarily determined by patron–client relationships or the *Jajmani* system, transactions in a *nagaram* were market-based. By the twelfth century CE most *nagarams* were associated with merchant guilds that played a significant role in spreading markets to different parts of the region. Merchant guilds helped traders who did long-distance trade to share their risks, provide credit and to tide over short-term needs. Guilds were particularly useful for sellers to ward off physical dangers as they travelled through unprotected parts of the country in groups. The temples were another important integrative institution that attracted donations of gold, money, land and livestock, and contributed to the spread of markets in south India (Mukund, 2012). While *chetti* (merchants) gained legitimacy by donating, temple authorities circulated these donations in the local economies to support commercial activities. In this period, temples were also important institutional buyers of large quantities of oil, rice, lentils, spices, fruits, vegetables, flowers and aromatic substances (Mukund, 2012). Hall (1977) provides further evidence of the important economic role of temples in his analysis of inscriptions from the Chola period mentioning distribution of gold and livestock grants to the local shepherds. Thus, religion and markets were intertwined and strengthened each other in medieval India.

The present-day marketing system uses ports and harbours as points of contact with the outside world for the export and import of goods and commodities. This system depends on strong connections between the ports and their hinterlands, which is facilitated by local governments and nation-states. However, the port towns of the medieval period carried on selling and trade in a somewhat different manner. Hall (2010, 114) suggests what is referred to as a 'networked heterarchy', wherein the regional ports that were located near the coast would network with multiple other regional centres rather than with one omnipotent centre. Relationships between merchants thus operated across maritime boundaries, and even transcended language and cultural barriers, pointing to the prevalence of an unexpected level of what is now referred to as 'globalization'. This period also witnessed expansion in trade with other parts of Asia and Europe and contributed to increase in sales of food grains, spices, cotton and luxury goods such as silk, ivory and beryl (Mukund, 2012).

As in the contemporary world, urban centres were major sites for marketing transactions in early India. Cities could be port towns such as Puhar in south India or inland centres of religious or commercial importance such as Benares in north India. For rich descriptions of cities, we can refer to Kautilya's *Arthasastra*, considered to be a major ancient Indian treatise on politics, society and the economy. The *Arthasastra* is dated around the Mauryan period (320 to 185 BCE), and describes a city that is highly planned and ordered, with selling places for dealers in perfumes, flowers and toiletries and also storage areas for forest produce and other items (Chattopadhyaya, 1997). In contrast to the planned, orderly city of the *Arthasastra*, we have the city of Puhar which is described as a bustling urban centre with market squares, boulevards and streets where people belonging to different professions lived all together, constituting a hive of activity (Chattopadhyaya, 1997). The city is also characterized by an abundance of goods, a profusion of activities and the accompanying noise and cacophony, reminiscent of the bazaars and fairs of modern-day India. Mukund (2012) describes how gold, food grain, toddy (an alcoholic drink, made usually from palm sap) and textile sellers in the tenth century CE markets used flags of different colours to inform buyers about different qualities of goods sold. Thus, urban centres in early India were major centres of commercial activity in which markets and marketing flourished.

There were, however, some limitations. The spread of markets to rural areas was restricted because most Indian rulers accorded limited attention to physical infrastructure for long-distance trade (Tripathi and Jumani, 2007). Merchants had to move in convoys because of dangers of theft and violence. This was further complicated by political fragmentation of the region for large parts of its history which meant that there would be several provincial rulers and local chieftains who could extract taxes and duties for goods passing through their territories. In the absence of political integration and market fragmentation, prices of goods varied widely (Banerjee, 1999). In another account showing us some of the dysfunctional aspects of the marketing system in the fourteenth century CE, the courtier Barani describes what is assumed to be the city of Delhi, with its marketplaces, grain merchants and sellers (Sarkar, 2011). Barani decries the presence of swindlers, hoarders and cheats in the city against whom action has to be taken, which tells us that the darker side of markets, with illegal trade and selling practices, was very much a concern even in this period (Sarkar, 2011). Occupational and living patterns in cities also contributed to particular forms of marketing activity. For example, scholars suggest that during the Mughal king Akbar's time (later sixteenth century CE), the city was primarily seen as a place where craftsmen lived (Vanina, 1989). The preponderance of skilled craftsmen and artisans in cities, along with the domination of agricultural activities in villages, led to a marketing channel with a one-way flow of goods from villages to cities, since villagers could not afford to purchase the luxury commodities made by the city craftsmen (Vanina, 1989). In later years, with the advent of early forms of industrial production, during the eighteenth century, this one-way flow of goods was partially altered with the manufacture of mass-produced commodities in the cities, which were cheap, enabling affluent villagers to purchase them (Vanina, 1989).

With the spread of markets across much of urban India by the sixteenth century, merchants became increasingly powerful entities. Even in periods of powerful dynasties such as the Mughals, merchants continued to exercise influence in political decision-making and in funding wars of territorial expansion and courtly rituals (Bayly, 1983). Knowledge about trade and markets was complicated and certain caste groups, such as Khattris from Punjab, Agarwals, Oswals and Maheshwaris moving out of the dry lands of Rajasthan, started to become powerful in this period. Rulers devoted considerable attention to attracting rich merchants and competition among kings often took the form of tax exemptions (Timberg, 2014).

Our analysis of the sites of marketing exchange in early India reveals that marketing transactions happened in networks involving multiple actors such as merchants, itinerant sellers, craftsmen and farmers from villages, who exchanged or sold goods at locations such as urban centres, ports and cities. Goods were transported from producers to consumers through land by caravans, or through sea routes. Many of these ports and urban centres had some connections with the hinterland, and also with far-flung ports in foreign countries. Cities, with their myriad activities, businesses, cacophony and confusion were very much a part of the marketing system, providing a variety of goods to residents as well as visitors.

Systems of exchange

Given the lack of communication and control systems, we can safely assume that a centralized economy could not have existed in early India. Even in later periods such as the Mughal era (1526–1857), the emperor's hold over the economy, especially in the hinterlands, was tenuous (Moosvi, 1985). A common currency or coinage was difficult to implement in such conditions, and unsurprisingly, barter was a major mechanism of selling and trade. Goods in kind were also used as means of payment. Inscriptions from the time of Rajendra Chola, in the eleventh century CE, talk about the equivalence of various items for trading.

Furthermore, rice appears to have been a standard of value, which could be used to purchase other items such as spices, sugar, salt and luxury goods (Hall, 1977). Historians suggest that coinage emerged quite early in India, around the first millennium BCE (Ray, 1985). However, the state did not have a monopoly over the issue of coins, with multiple types of coins in existence at the same time, and local coins often being used in transactions (Ray, 1985). Early coinage facilitated redistributive activities such as land transfers, and purchase by wealthy patrons of items that were required for local temples, such as lamps and aromatics (Hall, 1999).

There is evidence in the literature of the prevalence of multiple currencies or modes of exchange in the same region. The Bengal Sultanate of the thirteenth to sixteenth century CE had two such currencies – a high value and relatively pure silver coin called *tanka*, which was used for trade and transactions with the government, and lower value cowry shells that were used for day-to-day transactions (Deyell, 2010). Furthermore, these currencies were serviced by an elaborate financial industry comprising mint masters, money-changers, brokers and accountants. In another instance of multiple currency circulation, in the Bahamani kingdom, in addition to the royally sanctioned coinage, the coins of the Vijayanagar kingdom were widely used, with recalcitrant money-changers even going to the extent of ignoring royal decrees prohibiting circulation of these coins (Wagoner, 2014). In his analysis of a later period, under Mughal rule, Habib (1969) describes the use of both cash and kind to pay for taxes imposed by the government. Habib (1969) takes a negative view of monetization and taxes, and argues that they led to impoverishment of the countryside and a one-way flow of resources to the capital region. Moreover, he contends that monetization could have led to adverse consequences for peasants by exposing them to widely fluctuating prices over which they had no control.

An increase in market activities due to long-distance trade created a need for credit notes or *hundis* issued by individual traders (Tripathi and Jumani, 2007). These credit notes were safer and easier to carry from one place to another as they could be cashed in distant places. *Hundi* was employed to make remittances, raise loans and to finance movement of goods from one place to another. Like any other era, this was a period in which market economy relied heavily on a moral economy for its functioning. Trade and credit relations over long distances were dependent on conceptions of caste, status and mercantile honour (Bayly, 1983; Ray, 2011). Market disputes were primarily settled through caste-based organizations and market committees, and excommunication of a buyer or a seller was the most potent way of punishing offenders. A large group of traders were Marwaris, who belonged to Rajasthan, and had developed extensive networks of institutions to support each other in their market operations. Marwaris developed institutions for easy loans, access to markets and created messes for market traders to get food and rest when they travelled. These messes were informal training schools and sites for networking for new traders – Timberg (2014) equated them with contemporary business schools for training in marketing and business management.

In sum, we can conclude that, while the use of standardized coins was prevalent in early India, it was limited in scope. Multiple coins, some of them locally issued, competed with the royal issues. There were also other means of exchange such as cowry shells and *hundi*. Coinage could have led to the establishment of market economy relationships between people, but some historians also suggest that they facilitated redistributive activities such as purchase of items to be used in local temples. Payments in kind and barter of goods coexisted with coins, especially in hinterlands and villages outside the metropolitan areas. Credit notes facilitated conduct of trade over long distances, and had the advantage of being safer and easier to transport, compared to coins or other valuables. Overall, we get the picture of a society that relied on a variety of means in order to engage in the process of buying and selling.

Consumption of goods and services

There are a few direct accounts of consumption goods from early India. Scholars have primarily described the items traded, bought and sold in ports, fairs and markets. From these descriptions, we can form a picture of the consumption goods used by people of this period. The *Jataka* tales are part of Buddhist literature, and are a collection of nearly 550 anecdotes and stories, dated between 300 BCE and 400 CE (Ashliman, 2004). Ray (1985), in his analysis of one of the *Jataka* stories, describes the employment of evaluators who would assess the value of horses, elephants, jewels and gold purchased by kings. These were presumably luxury items that were out of the reach of ordinary consumers. Ray (1985) also describes the goods available in weekly markets and fairs, where people could buy items such as grain, salt, spices, cooking vessels and coarse cloth, which were possibly goods for everyday consumption. We can infer from Hall's (1977) description of Chola inscriptions that goods such as cardamom seeds, pepper, mustard, lentils, cumin and sugar were bought by some consumers. Most of these were luxury goods that were purchased through the sale of surplus rice. Furthermore, we can infer that spices, cloth goods and woods such as sandal and cedar required higher payments, in the form of gold, whereas rice and beans were commodities of local exchange that were not handled by itinerant traders.

As Thapar (2002) points out, it is likely that life for an average consumer was quite difficult, with famines being common. Natural calamities had a considerably disturbing effect on consumers during the Mughal period. Moosvi (1985) describes the agrarian crisis of the seventeenth century during Aurangzeb's reign, when scarcity became so acute that there was an exodus of peasants from villages to urban centres, and there was a real threat of depopulation in the famine-stricken areas. The increase in monetization, exploitative taxation policies and failure of rains are believed to have contributed to the famine (Moosvi, 1985). Habib (1969) also documents exploitation of peasants by rulers that led to impoverishment of rural consumers. In contrast, Desai (1972) presents a more positive picture of the consumption levels of peasants and workers during Akbar's period (later sixteenth century) and concludes that food consumption levels were higher both among urban workers as well as peasants during this period as compared to the 1960s in independent India.

As in present times, the medieval city was seen as a site of conspicuous consumption, with the rich consuming luxury goods, and living in opulence. Abundance, gaiety and celebration through consumption are some of the key aspects of Puhar, south India, mentioned in literature (Chattopadhyaya, 1997). In the eighth century CE, urban consumers could access finer varieties of cotton woven by urban weavers, while those in the rural parts were primarily using coarse cotton cloth (Mukund, 2012). In cities in south India, there were streets selling textiles in which hundreds of perfumed *sari*s were stacked according to quality. These markets also sold silk and cotton fabrics, and wool from rat's hair for the colder months. These clothes were kept perfumed with incense that was particularly in demand in this period (Mukund, 2012). Some of the richer merchants were known for lavish lifestyles and Mukund (2012) notes that they lived in tall houses that were filled with expensive goods and artefacts. Interestingly, the present-day anxiety surrounding consumption and urban decadence is present in writings on the medieval Indian city, with apprehensions expressed about city life corrupting *dharma* (religion) and posing a threat to the way of life sanctioned

Table 21.1 Chronology of marketing institutions and practices in India

Era and time period		Key marketing features
Pre-Mauryan period	Middle of 1st millennium BCE (Ray, 1985)	Appearance of urban centres in north India, waning of sacrificial ritual leading to surplus cash for consumers, early coinage
Mauryan period	320 to 185 BCE (Roy, 2012)	Early trade routes through land and sea to transport natural resources, Arthasastra composed with normative prescriptions on business, selling, and trade
Satavahana period	First century BCE (Ray, 1985)	Emergence of external trade with Mediterranean regions, formation of artisan guilds specializing in making different goods
Chola period	850 to 1279 CE (Hall, 1975)	Specific sites such as nagarams established for marketing activity, temple as site of economic redistribution, use of flags to advertise, barter a dominant form of exchange
Mughal period	1526 to 1757 (Heesterman, 2004)	Emergence of powerful merchant communities, specialized production of goods in cities, one-way flow of goods from villages to cities, indigenous credit instruments such as hundi, occurrence of famines and agrarian crises
Initial encounter with Europe and early colonial period	1498 to 1857 (Robins, 2006)	Early encounter with the Portuguese, middlemen such as banians play an important role, specialized local markets such as haats, bazaars and gunges, early advertising in newspapers, Indian manufacturing capabilities diminish, railways increase market penetration
Later colonial period	1857 to 1947 (Authors' periodization)	The British Crown takes over Indian administration from the East India Company, the spread of British consumption goods such as tea and coffee, adoption of Western medicine and consumption practices, consumer anxiety at displacement of indigenous and 'Indian' consumption goods and habits
Post-colonial period	1947 to present day (Authors' periodization)	Centralized planning and state protection for industry in the post-independence period, low levels of consumer demand, economic liberalization in the nineties, emergence of Indian language advertising, media proliferation and rise of consumer culture, increasing economic inequality

by the scriptures (Chattopadhyaya, 1997). Upward mobility using consumption was possible during this period, with Durga (2001) describing how members of a lower caste could move up through gift-giving to temples.

In summary, our analysis of marketing activity in the early period shows that littoral towns played key roles in the economy as bustling sites of buying and selling. Major urban centres could be located inland too, but were often near the coast, or on the banks of a navigable river. The city was a major nerve centre of marketing activity with bazaars, shops, artisans and numerous others providing goods and entertainment to consumers. For ordinary consumers in the early period, many common present-day items such as spices and sugar were luxuries. Wealthy consumers had no such constraints, and consumed many luxury items. Famine and scarcity were common, and severely affected the lives of the poor. The ambiguity surrounding excessive consumption existed even in this period, with the city and its ostentation seen as potentially corrupting influences.

Colonial period

The early encounters of India with European colonizers started in the sixteenth and seventeenth centuries with the Portuguese. Later, by the eighteenth and nineteenth centuries, Britain had entrenched itself as a colonizer in India. The colonial encounter had wide-ranging effects on Indian industry, economy, marketing systems and consumption habits. In this section of the chapter, we provide an overview of the markets and consumption during the colonial period.

Local markets, merchants and the colonial state

Colonialism had a significant impact on living conditions and consumption patterns of Indian consumers of the time. Existing networks of production were changed, and consumption habits altered either due to the introduction of new products, or due to changes in economic circumstances. The earliest colonial encounter with the Portuguese was marked by the brutal violence of the colonizers in order to secure 'Christians and spices' (Hall, 1996, cited in Robins, 2006). Vasco Da Gama and his successors disrupted the longstanding tradition of free trade in the Indian Ocean area with the use of violence (Robins, 2006). In contrast, the East India Company, at least in its initial years in India, was motivated more by economic than political or evangelizing ambitions. Yet these economic ambitions also caused much misery and suffering among the Indian people (Bagchi, 2006; Habib, 2006).

Indian businessmen played an important role in the economy and markets during the colonial period. Several historians observe that Fateh Chand, who was a *Jagat Seth* or a rich banker and businessman in Murshidabad, supported Robert Clive in his victory over Siraj-ud-Daulah in 1757 in the Battle of Plassey that led to the foundation of British rule in India (Timberg, 2014; Tripathi and Jumani, 2007). Fateh Chand in 1757 was in charge of the Murshidabad mint and to a great extent controlled the money economy of Bengal (Timberg, 2014). In its early years in India, the East India Company had to rely heavily on local merchants, who acted as middlemen. The British were unaware of the local markets, languages, customs, weights and measures, and had to enlist the help of these middlemen to engage in transactions such as procuring cotton cloth from weavers (Chakrabarti, 1994). These middlemen were of various categories such as *banians, dewans, gomastahs, dalals* and *pykars*. The *banian* acted as an interpreter, and used local knowledge and skill to help the European as a partner in business. The *dewan* was a high-caste intermediary who was employed by the Company, and oversaw *gomastahs, dalals* and *pykars* who were subordinates. The *gomastah* was a salaried agent of the company, advancing money to *dalals* and *pykars*, who in turn provided these funds to producers of material such as weavers. The *dalal* was a broker who connected the producers and buyers of goods such as cotton cloth. The *dalal* received a small commission on successful transactions. *Pykars* purchased on behalf of the Company and were also independent traders and financiers (Chakrabarti, 1994). The influence of these middlemen can be understood from Robins's (2006) description of Nabakrishna Deb, one of the *banians* of Calcutta, who developed close relationships with Robert Clive (a powerful official of the East India Company) and Warren Hastings (the first Governor-General of India), and managed to amass a huge fortune. Chakrabarti (1994) suggests that far from being willing and pliable accomplices of the Company officials, these intermediaries often took advantage of the Company's ignorance of local conditions by engaging in tactics such as surreptitiously marking up prices, violating contract agreements and using advance funds procured from the British to make and sell cloth to the French, Dutch and other European traders. Merchants also played a critical role in the marketing of grain, a crucial commodity. Datta (1986) highlights the powerful role played by intermediary merchants in the channelling of grain from the countryside of Bengal to the urban areas. The merchant was motivated by two priorities that included maintaining control over the supply chain of grain so that the maximum amount could be sold or hoarded, and maximizing profit through manipulating the price differentials that existed between urban and rural areas (Datta, 1986). The supply chain of grain from its producers to the market was mediated by a network of agents which was so complex that even the colonial government could not infiltrate it and directly deal with the peasants (Datta, 1994).

There are conflicting interpretations of the role of *byapari* or merchants in this period (Bayly, 1983). In the accounts of the East India Company, the role of the merchant, while significant, was hardly a positive one. Accordingly, motivated by almost inhuman avarice, merchants often played the toxic role of exacerbating shortages of food grains and converting them into full-fledged famines. Datta (1994) describes the shocking ways in which merchants profited from grain scarcity, going to the extent of denying supply to food-deficient areas in order to profit by hoarding and high prices. Furthermore, the officials of the East India Company often worsened crisis situations by engaging in their own private grain trade, again to the detriment of consumers. Some other historians such as Bayly (1983) offer a nuanced view of merchants. Accordingly, merchants were embedded within the social context and their identities as pious credit-worthy Hindus were woven around conceptions of religion and credit. While making profits, merchants were also seen to be agents who contributed to the economy by supporting peasants, producers and artisans, and made donations to temples and royal courts.

With the spread of trade by the eighteenth century, local markets started becoming increasingly complicated and specialized. Datta (1986) describes three types of markets that engaged in local trade. These were *haats, bazaars* and *gunges*, and they differed in terms of the days of operation, types of trade and traders, and the commodities sold. The *haats* were markets that operated only on certain days, and were used by petty vendors and traders, who put up markets in available open spaces, and used flags to mark them. *Bazaars* were daily markets, but on certain days they could even be located in the *haats*. Besides established shopkeepers, there were also petty vendors who traded in these *bazaars*. In *gunges,* grains and other essentials were sold in bulk and this was a wholesale market. However, these *gunges* could have *haats* and *bazaars* located within them and goods available on retail as well (Datta, 1986).

Mukherjee (2011), in a description of the markets of eighteenth-century Bengal, suggests that urban markets were not isolated sites but were integrated well with rural areas. Markets were highly decentralized, and horizontally linked to other markets. Moreover, these markets often sprung up spontaneously, and were founded by people belonging to different communities, from noblemen to merchants. Mukherjee (2011) further observes that the number of such markets greatly increased during the eighteenth century, suggesting that local buying power was enhanced during this period.

The deepening of colonial rule in India also created specific market requirements for the colonizers. In 1780 an English newspaper, *Hicky's Bengal Gazette*, was started in Calcutta by a British trader James Hicky and became the first major vehicle for carrying print advertisements in the region (Chaudhuri, 2007). *Hicky's Gazette* printed many advertisements, mainly about auctions and goods for sale, and was also called the *Calcutta General Advertiser.* Chaudhuri (2007, 41) observes that, 'Hicky, the first practitioner of copywriting in India did a commendable job with the body copy of the advertisements he published. Whether he was trying to sell a horse or a sloop he realized that he had to breathe life into his words in order to persuade a prospective customer not to lose this wonderful opportunity!' These advertisements were close to what we see as classified display in contemporary newspapers in India. Although this newspaper closed down in 1782, there were several news publications in English and different Indian languages that subsequently started and carried advertisements for their clienteles. For example, Richard Johnston started *Madras Courier* in the south in 1785, which was followed by the *Weekly Madras Gazette* in 1795. In this short period of time print advertising improved substantially, with sharper typeface, improved images and layouts, and enhanced use of white space (Chaudhuri, 2007). Moreover, the eighteenth-century newspapers primarily carried advertisements on their front pages. Thus, print advertising in India took roots in the eighteenth century. In 1824 a publication by the name of *The Calcutta Gazette and Commercial Advertiser* was started with the sole idea of advertising. The second half of the nineteenth century also saw the setting up of industrial art schools to prepare professionals to create advertisements. Until the twentieth century there were no advertising agencies, and newspapers did all the pre-press work in their in-house advertising departments and were staffed with artists, block-developers, copy-writers and composers as they combined to produce advertisements.

In the early parts of the nineteenth century there were several aspects of the colonial rule that changed the competitive dynamics of markets, restricted the spread of Indian businesses and resulted in widespread increases in poverty levels in the region that had a negative impact on local markets (Habib, 2006). One of the biggest factors that contributed to the decline of local producers and sellers was competition from manufactured products from England. It was further exacerbated by a lack of government patronage and protection against foreign competition that manufacturers in Europe enjoyed for considerable periods of time (Bagchi, 2006). Moreover, until the middle of the 1830s, Indian manufacturers were made to pay higher duties than on the goods imported from Britain (Bagchi, 2006). By the 1840s India was transformed from being a substantial exporter of handloom textiles into a producer and exporter of primary goods (Banerjee, 1999).

Toward the late nineteenth century, the British had connected large parts of India with the railways. This new technology further altered markets. Dutta (2012) argues that railways enabled mass transport of agricultural produce safely across large areas, which meant that the market for produce was no longer local but regional, and even national. Moreover, older trading centres were located along rivers which were the earlier means of transport. These fell into disuse, and new centres located along the railway lines came into existence. A three-stage process evolved in the movement of rice and paddy to the market – first, the peasant sold it to itinerant traders or the village *haat* from where it reached the larger markets, and then on to regional sites of consumption (Dutta, 2012). However, this did not produce a unified national market of goods and there were considerable differences across rural and urban markets in terms of prices and availability of goods (Banerjee, 1999).

To summarize, during the colonial period, intermediaries or merchant middlemen played an extremely critical role in the marketing system. British company officials and independent traders were dependent on these middlemen. Some merchants engaged in unethical practices such as hoarding grain in order to maximize profits. The marketing system was highly decentralized with a profusion of markets of different types. The advent of new technology such as the railways opened up large parts of the country to the producing regions, and led to some consolidation but failed to create a national market with a high level of uniformity of prices and availability of goods. Local institutions such as the *bazaar* continued to play a critical role by linking up numerous small producers to end consumers.

Consumers and consumption

Although British rule in India prevailed from 1857 to 1947, its influence in the form of the East India Company dated back to 1618, when the Company entered into its first trade agreement with the Mughal Empire (Robins, 2006). In the early part of this period, there were two institutional buyers that contributed significantly to market activities. A large part of consumption in colonial India in the seventeenth and eighteenth centuries was centred on armies. Various princely states, rulers and the British spent considerable amounts of money on consumption by their armed forces (Bayly, 1983). Accordingly, 'military incomes bulked large against the background of trade and consumption in the ordinary periodic market or small fixed market (*gunj*). By comparison, the total demand generated by peasant families and by the means of urban population was tiny' (Bayly, 1983, 55). While an average consumer survived at the level of subsistence with low levels of consumption, the military-commercial establishment was a thriving circuit of consumption and profits in this period.

Royal courts in several parts of the country were significant consumers of luxury goods (Bayly, 1983). Kings spent considerable amounts of money on luxury goods for harems and courtesans. In addition, large sums of money were spent on ritual consumption in these royal courts. Some kings spent as much as 30 per cent of their incomes on festivals and ritual feasts. Kings also spent large amounts of money on jewellery and clothing. In this period, the Kashmir shawl had become a universal symbol of aristocracy. Kings in north India gave shawls of different grades to visitors, servants and supporters as honorific currency. In contrast to rulers, priests, most merchants and peasants emphasized frugality. Accordingly, conspicuous consumption in the forms of elaborate clothing, housing and rituals were frowned upon and seen to be unnecessary. It was primarily among the new military peasant conquerors such as Marathas and Sikhs in the 1770s and 1780s, who were beginning to control the north-western part of the region, that luxury consumption of the form associated with old Mughal royalties was witnessed. These rulers constructed palaces and indulged in elaborate court rituals of gift-giving to signal their presence (Bayly, 1983). This group was also a big consumer of artisanal products. Thus, institutional sales were the most important aspects of marketing in this period.

In the later years, luxury consumption in royal courts was severely curtailed by the British as they withdrew their support and increased their revenue collections from these rulers. The colonial state attempted to control and regulate the local economy in the area of fiscal policy by closing mints managed by these rulers that financed local consumption. This also contributed to a liquidity crunch and losses for several native mercantile communities, and to a decline in consumption for the poorer sections of the population (Bayly, 1983). Historians further argue that the colonial state made only limited attempts to standardize markets across the country. There were differences maintained across landlords and traders, and corporate trading agencies, instead of acting as price levellers to help consumers, reaped the benefits arising out of multiple prices of the same commodity (Banerjee, 1999).

In the period prior to the eighteenth century, there was a limited demand for European goods (Tripathi and Jumani, 2007). Local cotton was considered superior and Indian exports were dominant, with calicoes or Indian textile goods enjoying considerable price advantage in the British market. However, the industrial revolution and mechanization of production in England created a complete reversal of the situation in the early nineteenth century, with India being reduced to an exporter of raw cotton and an importer of cotton fabric (Bayly, 1983). While the rural population consumed coarse cotton fabric that was locally produced and was outside the market economy, the richer classes in urban India switched to British cotton goods in the nineteenth century. Habib (2006) notes that there were specialized centres of production for cloths of higher quality such as calico and muslin, and textiles with complex weaves and dyes. Moreover, Habib (2006) suggests that such textiles enjoyed the patronage of the richer classes in Indian cities, and experienced a sharp decline in demand as the result of the import of cotton goods from Britain. There were similar declines experienced by jute handloom weavers and woollen manufacturers in different parts of the country with the onset of cheaper industrially produced output from England that was adopted by the richer consumer groups. This popularity of foreign goods among the elite became a particular point of contest in the nationalist struggle when anti-colonial mobilizations in the late nineteenth and early twentieth centuries particularly focused on the rejection of foreign goods. British cloth was actively targeted by nationalists and was rendered dirty and impure (Bayly, 1986). A defining feature of the rejection of refined foreign cloth was support for the consumption of coarser homespun cloth, which became a symbol of resistance and national identity (Trivedi, 2003).

The arrival of the colonial powers led to wide-ranging changes in the consumption habits of Indian consumers. The British to a great extent, and the French and Portuguese to a limited extent, imparted some of their consumption habits to the Indian populace. As Robins (2006) points out, the East India Company's motives were primarily economic, and achieving political domination was a means to these economic ends. The connections formed by trade, sometimes voluntary and often coerced, introduced many new consumption goods into India. As Robins (2006, 109) eloquently puts it, 'mixed with slave grown sugar from the West Indies, the afternoon cup of tea perfectly expressed Britain's emerging empire of consumption'. These new consumption goods evoked mixed reactions. While they gained widespread acceptance among consumers, they also evoked anxiety at the displacement of old consumption goods and habits, anxieties that have outlasted the colonial experience and continue even into the twenty-first century. For example, Guha (2008) in his analysis of a colonial era literary work describes an exchange between a villager visiting Calcutta and a resident of the city. The villager expresses displeasure at the city residents who dress like foreigners, consume food prepared by Muslims (considered a taboo among religious Hindus), drink brandy and even read literature mainly in English and Persian. The city dweller seeks to alleviate the villager's anxiety by reassuring him that the Hindu way of life was still prevalent. Guha's (2008) account informs us about the cultural anxiety evoked among Indians, especially Hindus, by changes in consumption and lifestyle. Western medicine, which was introduced initially for the benefit of Europeans, quickly spread to the

Indian population, leading to indigenous medical systems such as *Ayurveda* coming under considerable strain (Panikkar, 1992). Meat eating, more problematically consumption of beef, became prevalent among some of the urban Hindus, leading to perceived shortages of milk, which was seen as a healthier food (Chatterjee, 1997). Tea and coffee were the other important additions to the Indian diet. In a fascinating account of the spread of coffee in Tamilnadu, Venkatachalapathy (2002) observes that coffee displaced the traditional *neeragaram* (water used to cook rice that was fermented and mixed with leftover vegetables and pickle) and became the drink of choice, even among the lower classes. Coffee became incorporated into the Tamil middle-class milieu, getting enmeshed in rituals of hospitality, as a drink to be served to guests and even as a sign of exclusion, through the use of metal tumblers with rims so that consumers could pour the coffee straight into their mouths without touching the glass, and avoiding caste pollution (Venkatachalapathy, 2002). The beverage also evoked anxiety, perceived as a Western product that infiltrated the pristine countryside, with even women finding it difficult to do without it (Venkatachalapathy, 2002).

As these accounts reveal, Indian consumers' encounter with the West was often marked by discomfort, suspicion and grudging acceptance. Even when it came to life-threatening illnesses and medical care, religious and caste customs prevailed over reasonable medical advice. While some communities such as the Parsis readily accepted Western medical practices, many of the Hindu castes, due to notions of ritualistic pollution and religious beliefs, refused to take medical advice or help even for serious issues such as childbirth and smallpox (Ramanna, 2000). The British contributed to this scepticism and hostility among the Indians by their dismissal of local knowledge and products as being uncivilized, even barbarian. For example, the British establishment was reluctant to accept that the tea plant could be found indigenously in Assam, and instead claimed that such a refined product as tea could originate only from China, and not from the fever-ridden jungles of Assam (Sharma, 2006). Even when evidence emerged that the tea plant could indeed be found in Assam, attempts were made to characterize the variant as savage and uncivilized, and not suitable to the delicate palette of consumers in London (Sharma, 2006). In the face of the onslaught of imperial reason and Western science, Indian consumption practices and traditions struggled to recast themselves as scientific and modern. These displacements contributed to boycott of Western goods in the early twentieth century as consumption and markets became important sites for enacting nationalism and freedom in colonial India.

In summary, the Indian encounter with Britain and other colonial powers resulted in changes in marketing systems and consumption habits. Middlemen played a vital, though not always positive role in the supply chain. Markets were highly decentralized and diversified, and the *bazaar* played a critical role in connecting supply centres in the countryside with sites of buying and consumption in the urban areas. Colonization resulted in many changes in the consumption habits of Indians, with the introduction of new goods and services such as tea, coffee and Western medicine. Cultural changes produced by these encounters resulted in considerable anxieties among consumers, with Western products appropriated into the local social and cultural milieu, or resisted and denigrated as being inferior to Indian goods and practices.

Post-colonial period

India secured independence in 1947 and although most of the marketing activities developed during the earlier periods continued, the change in administration led to modifications in the economy, enabling the country to move forward with economic policies more suited to its own interests. The state in the initial years after independence placed an emphasis on planning. There was a considerable stress on heavy industry and public sector enterprises. Nation-building was the priority, and private enterprises had to negotiate a complex system of licences and permits to function. This period also saw emphasis on small and medium enterprises, and several goods were exclusively reserved for these businesses as a form of state protection.

In the aftermath of colonialism, India was struggling with severe problems such as widespread illiteracy and poverty. Economic indicators were poor, and this reflected in the state of consumption. Westfall and Boyd (1960) point out that in India consumption expenditure in the 1960s was a mere US$54 per capita per annum, as compared to US$1664 in the United States. The stunted marketing system was partly due to the extremely low levels of consumer demand as a result of colonial plunder. In a survey conducted in a small town in the 1960s, Braunthal (1969) describes word of mouth as the primary means of access to information for Indian consumers. Accordingly, radio was a key source of communication, and a lack of access to newspapers was not only due to the inability to read, but also due to the inability to pay even the small price of a newspaper. Moreover, 96 per cent of consumers cited food scarcity as a critical problem facing India, indicating the extent of economic deprivation (Braunthal, 1969).

For a long period of time after independence, the state, with its emphasis on welfare measures, was guarded in its support for markets and marketing. In a 1966 coverage of an advertisers' meeting in the *Economic and Political Weekly*, the correspondent reports that advertisers were trying to persuade the government, led by then Prime Minister Indira Gandhi to allow commercial advertising on radio and TV, which was yet to be introduced in India. The reporter describes the Prime Minister's concern as to whether commercial TV would serve the national purpose, and then goes on to rather unimaginatively and myopically suggest that mass communication would be useful when there was mass consumption, which was not foreseeable in India in the near future (*Economic and Political Weekly*, 1966).

Since television was not available, newspapers, magazines and cinema halls were the outlets for advertising. Even in such a constrained environment, there were a large number of agencies. Banerjee (1968) reports that there were 279 advertising agencies with a turnover of INR 350 million, and J. Walter Thompson was the largest agency with over a third of the total turnover. In-house media planning and marketing research were also emerging in the field (Banerjee, 1968). However, the media continued to be weak, with Banerjee (1968) complaining that, in the absence of specialized trade publications, even engineering firms selling expensive machinery were forced to advertise in the daily newspapers, leading to a huge wastage.

The economic liberalization process started in the 1980s, and led to economic priorities shifting from a welfare state-oriented model, to a right-leaning approach favouring more business-friendly practices, which coincided with the development and consolidation of national television (Rajagopal, 1998). This increased growth rates but is also criticized for increasing inequality. For the marketing system, the biggest change has been the gradual transition from a controlled economy to a consumption culture with myriad marketing opportunities, albeit marked by persistent poverty and inequality. Television coupled with globalization had a significant impact on the advertising industry. It created a national market, with advertisers being able to reach rural areas. This led to advertising adopting new languages, moving away from Anglophone domination to copy being written in Hindi and regional Indian languages (Rajagopal, 1998). The last two decades are marked by the development of several marketing institutions, such as organized large-scale retailing, retail credit and e-marketing, with an increasing number of consumer goods and the spread of consumer culture (Varman and Belk, 2012; Venkatesh, 1994).

While some of the literature on economic liberalization and its impact on India has been unabashedly celebratory (e.g. Sheth, 2004), scholars have also raised concerns about rising levels of consumption, and the consequent environmental degradation (e.g. Guha, 2003). There are also concerns voiced in the literature about mass media fuelling consumer desires, and leading to an increase in materialism among poor consumers, many of whom cannot afford the luxury goods advertised on television (Varman and Belk, 2008). Writers such as Shrivastava and Kothari (2012) have severely criticized the neglect of the poor and economic degradation accompanying the neoliberal developmental agenda (also see Varman and Vikas, 2007; Varman *et al.*, 2012). While the neoliberal agenda has definitely produced a proliferation of consumer goods, and significant rises in standard of living for some consumers, it appears to have had the perverse effect of stagnation or further impoverishing the weaker sections, resulting in India achieving what Dreze and Sen (2013) aptly refer to as 'an uncertain glory'.

In conclusion, our study shows that Indian markets had a number of institutions, mechanisms and consumption goods that point to a fairly high degree of sophistication even in medieval times. Indian marketing evolved over a long period of time impelled by its specific historical experiences and institutional make-up. This chapter thus fills a significant gap in extant understanding of markets and marketing. As the neoliberal economic agenda leads to the expansion of marketization in India, this historical perspective will serve an important sense-making role in our understandings of markets and consumers.

References

Ashliman, D.L. (2004) *Folk and Fairy Tales: A Handbook*, Greenwood Press, Westport, CT.

Bagchi, A.K. (2006) *Perilous Passage: Mankind and Global Ascendancy of Capital*, Oxford University Press, New Delhi.

Banerjee, D. (1999) *Colonialism in Action: Trade, Development and Dependence in Late Colonial India*, Orient Longman, Hyderabad.

Banerjee, S. (1968) 'The advertising agency: A new service', *Economic and Political Weekly*, 3/21, M19–M23.

Bayly, C.A. (1983) *Rulers, Townsmen and Bazaars: North Indian Society in the Age of British Expansion: 1770–1870*, Oxford University Press, New Delhi.

Bayly, C.A. (1986) 'The origins of swadeshi (home industry): Cloth and society 1700–1930', in A. Appadurai (ed.), *The Social Life of Things*, Cambridge University Press, Cambridge, pp. 285–322.

Braunthal, G. (1969) 'An attitude survey in India', *Public Opinion Quarterly*, 33/1, 69–82.

Chakrabarti, S. (1994) 'Collaboration and resistance: Bengal merchants and the English East India Company, 1757–1833', *Studies in History*, 10/1, 105–29.

Chatterjee, P. (1997) 'Talking about our modernity in two languages', in *A Possible India*, Oxford University Press, New Delhi, pp. 263–85.

Chattopadhyaya, B.D. (1997) 'The city in early India: Perspectives from texts', *Studies in History*, 13/2, 181–208.

Chaudhuri, A. (2007) *Indian Advertising 1780 to 1950 AD*, Tata McGraw-Hill, New Delhi.

Datta, R. (1986) 'Merchants and peasants: A study of the structure of local trade in grain in late eighteenth century Bengal', *Indian Economic and Social History Review*, 23/4, 379–402.

Datta, R. (1994) 'Subsistence crises, markets and merchants in late eighteenth century Bengal', *Studies in History*, 10/1, 81–104.

Desai, A.V. (1972) 'Population and standards of living in Akbar's time', *Indian Economic and Social History Review*, 9/1, 43–62.

Deyell, J.S. (2010) 'Cowries and coins: The dual monetary system of the Bengal Sultanate', *Indian Economic and Social History Review*, 47/1, 63–106.

Dreze, J., and Sen, A. (2013) *An Uncertain Glory: India and its Contradictions*, Princeton University Press, Princeton, NJ.

Durga, K.P.S. (2001) 'Identity and symbols of sustenance: Explorations in social mobility of medieval south India', *Journal of the Economic and Social History of the Orient*, 44/2, 141–74.

Dutta, A.K. (2012) 'Rice trade in the "rice bowl" of Bengal: Burdwan 1880–1947', *Indian Economic and Social History Review*, 49/1, 73–104.

Eckhardt, G., Dholakia, N., and Varman, R. (2013) 'Ideology for the 10 billion: Introduction to globalization of marketing ideology', *Journal of Macromarketing,* 33/1, 7–12.

Economic and Political Weekly (1966) 'Much ado about TV', 1/8, 341.

Ellis, N., Fitchett, J., Higgins, M., Jack, G., Lim, M., Saren, M., and Tadajewski, M. (2011) *Marketing: A Critical Textbook*, Sage, New Delhi.

Fullerton, R.A. (2011) 'Historical methodology: The perspective of a professionally trained historian turned marketer', *Journal of Historical Research in Marketing*, 3/4, 436–48.

Guha, R. (2003) 'How much should a person consume?', *Vikalpa*, 28/2, 1–11.

Guha, R. (2008) 'A colonial city and its time(s)', *Indian Economic and Social History Review*, 45/3, 329–51.

Habib, I. (1969) 'Potentialities of capitalistic development in the economy of Mughal India', *Journal of Economic History*, 29/1, 32–78.

Habib, I. (2006) *Indian Economy 1858–1914*, Tulika, New Delhi.

Hall, K.R. (1975) 'The nagaram as a marketing center in early medieval south India', unpublished doctoral dissertation, University of Michigan.

Hall, K.R. (1977) 'Price-making and market hierarchy in early medieval south India', *Indian Economic and Social History Review*, 14/2, 207–30.

Hall, K.R. (1999) 'Coinage, trade and economy in early south India and its Southeast Asian neighbours', *Indian Economic and Social History Review*, 36/4, 431–59.

Hall, K.R. (2010) 'Ports-of-trade, maritime diasporas, and networks of trade and cultural integration in the Bay of Bengal region of the Indian Ocean: c.1300–1500', *Journal of the Economic and Social History of the Orient*, 53, 109–45.

Hall, R. (1996) *Empires of the Monsoon*, HarperCollins, London.

Heesterman, J.C. (2004) 'The social dynamics of the Mughal Empire: A brief introduction', *Journal of the Economic and Social History of the Orient*, 47/3, 292–7.

Jones, D.G.B., and Tadajewski, M. (2014) 'Proposal for Routledge Companion to Marketing History', unpublished manuscript.

Moosvi, S. (1985) 'Scarcities, prices and exploitation: The agrarian crisis 1658–70', *Studies in History*, 1/1, 45–55.

Mukherjee, T. (2011) 'Markets in eighteenth century Bengal economy', *Indian Economic and Social History Review*, 48/2, 143–76.

Mukund, K. (2012) *Merchants of Tamilakam: Pioneers of International Trade*, Penguin, New Delhi.

Panikkar, K.N. (1992) 'Indigenous medicine and cultural hegemony: A study of the revitalization movement in Keralam', *Studies in History*, 8/2, 283–308.

Rajagopal, A. (1998) 'Advertising, politics and the sentimental education of the Indian consumer', *Visual Anthropology Review*, 14/2, 14–31.

Ramanna, M. (2000) 'Indian attitudes towards Western medicine: Bombay, a case study', *Indian Historical Review*, 27/1, 44–55.

Ray, H.P. (1985) 'Trade in the Western Deccan under the Satavahanas', *Studies in History*, 1/1, 15–35.

Ray, R.K. (2011) 'Bazaar: Pulsating heart of the Indian economy', in M.M. Kudaisya (ed.), *The Oxford India Anthology of Business History*, Oxford University Press, New Delhi, pp. 3–48.

Robins, N. (2006) *The Corporation that Changed the World: How the East India Company Shaped the Modern Multinational*, Orient Longman, Hyderabad.

Roy, T. (2012) *India in the World Economy: From Antiquity to the Present*, Cambridge University Press, New Delhi.

Sarkar, N. (2011) 'An urban imaginaire, ca 1350: The Capital City in Ziya' Barani's Fatawa-I Jahandari', *Indian Economic and Social History Review*, 48/3, 407–24.

Sharma, J. (2006) 'British science, Chinese skill and Assam tea: Making empire's garden', *Indian Economic and Social History Review*, 43/4, 429–55.

Sheth, J. (2004) 'Making India globally competitive', *Vikalpa*, 29/4, 1–9.

Shrivastava, A., and Kothari, A. (2012) *Churning the Earth: The Making of Global India*, Penguin, New Delhi.

Thapar, R. (2002) *The Penguin History of Early India: From the Origins to AD 1300*, Penguin Books, New Delhi.

Timberg, T.A. (2014) *The Marwaris: From Jagat Seths to the Birlas*, Penguin, New Delhi.

Tripathi, D., and Jumani J. (2007) *The Concise Oxford History of Indian Business*, Oxford University Press, New Delhi.

Trivedi, L. N. (2003) 'Visually mapping the "nation": Swadeshi politics in nationalist India, 1920–1930', *Journal of Asian Studies*, 62/1, 11–41.

Vanina, E. (1989) 'Urban industries of medieval India: Some aspects of development', *Studies in History*, 5/2, 271–86.

Varman, R., and Belk, R.W. (2008) 'Weaving a web: Subaltern consumers, rising consumer culture and television', *Marketing Theory*, 8/3, 227–52.

Varman, R., and Belk, R.W. (2012) 'Consuming postcolonial shopping malls', *Journal of Marketing Management*, 28/1–2, 62–84.

Varman, R., and Saha, B. (2009) 'Disciplining the discipline: Understanding postcolonial epistemic ideology in marketing', *Journal of Marketing Management*, 25/7, 811–24.

Varman, R., and Sreekumar, H. (2015) 'Locating the past in its silence: History and marketing theory in India', *Journal of Historical Research in Marketing*, 7/2, 272–9.

Varman, R., and Vikas, R.M. (2007) 'Freedom and consumption: Toward conceptualizing systemic constraints for subaltern consumers in a capitalist society', *Consumption, Markets and Culture*, 10/2, 117–31.

Varman, R., Saha, B., and Skalen, P. (2011) 'Market subjectivity and neoliberal governmentality in higher education', *Journal of Marketing Management*, 27/11–12, 1163–85.

Varman, R., Skalen, P., and Belk, R.W. (2012) 'Conflicts at the bottom of the pyramid: Profits, poverty alleviation and neoliberal governmentality', *Journal of Public Policy and Marketing*, 31/1, 19–35.

Venkatachalapathy, A.R. (2002) '"In those days there was no coffee": Coffee-drinking and middle-class culture in colonial Tamilnadu', *Indian Economic and Social History Review*, 39/2–3, 301–16.

Venkatesh, A. (1994) 'India's changing consumer economy: A cultural perspective', *Advances in Consumer Research*, 21, 323–8.

Wagoner, P.B. (2014) 'Money use in the Deccan, c.1350–1687: The role of Vijayanagara Hons in the Bahmani currency system', *Indian Economic and Social History Review*, 51/4, 457–80.

Westfall, R., and Boyd, Jr., H.W. (1960) 'Marketing in India', *Journal of Marketing*, 25/2, 11–17.

22

Marketing history in Japan

Changes in channel leadership

Yumiko Toda

Introduction

Compared to the uniqueness of Japanese management practices such as seniority-based wage systems, lifetime employment, consensus decision-making (*ringi*) and the quality control movement (or 'QC Circles'), little attention has been paid to Japanese marketing practices and history (Lazer *et al.*, 1985; Toba, 1982). Lazer *et al.* (1985, 69) explain this by observing that it is difficult for international researchers to understand Japanese marketing because they lack an understanding of the culture, language, and history of Japanese business development. Shimaguchi (1978, 1) also wrote that Japan's distribution and marketing system has been considered an untouchable topic by Western academics because the field is so mysterious and complex.

Other reasons are found in Japan's own marketing research, which began when the Japan Society for the Study of Marketing History was established in 1988. Since then, historical studies on marketing have developed in earnest, centring on organization-level analyses. This research topic has a rather short history compared to other marketing research fields and remains underdeveloped. Moreover, while many books and articles on the history of Japanese marketing have been published in Japanese, relatively few studies have been presented to international conferences or journals.

This chapter reviews research on Japanese marketing and sketches an outline of its history. To simplify my approach to this complex topic, I focus on historical changes in channel leadership in Japanese marketing. This chapter contains three sections. The first covers the development of marketing practices before the Second World War. The dominant position of wholesalers will be discussed, and then the exceptional marketing activities of pioneering manufacturers will be explored. This section characterizes the marketing of this period as the 'wholesaler initiative' type of marketing. The second section discusses the development of marketing management between the mid-1950s to the mid-1980s, defining it as a 'manufacturer-leading' type of marketing. The last section details the growth of large-scale retailers and the new retailer-driven type of marketing that has dominated Japan since the 1990s.

Wholesaler initiative marketing before the Second World War

Dominant position of wholesalers

The end of the Edo period in the late 1860s brought Japan's 200-year isolation to a close. Japan opened itself to the world and the Meiji period (1868–1912) started. The new Meiji government took the initiative and encouraged new industries to catch up to and surpass the major US and European powers. The government established silk-reeling factories and spinning mills, as silk was one of Japan's staple exports, along with cotton yarn and textile products. In the late Meiji period, the government sought to strengthen industrialization by adopting Western technologies and developing heavy industries centred on steel production. Japan imported coal and iron ore from China and India and exported steel products, general machinery and military weapons. By the end of the Meiji period, Japan's industrial modernization had been largely accomplished.

On the other hand, foreign traders controlled overseas trade at the beginning of the Meiji period. The government established trading companies, or general wholesalers (later called *sogo shosha*), such as Mitsui & Company to strengthen Japanese import and export trade. These general wholesalers took important initiatives such as importing silk-reeling and spinning machines and iron ore and coal and helped develop Japan's light and heavy industries, furthering the economic policy of the Meiji government. As a broader range of industries developed and the number of imports and exports increased, wholesalers specializing in single product lines or parts of a line began to appear (Dowd, 1959, 260). By the end of the Meiji period, numerous specialty wholesalers were operating. The domestic market featured regional wholesalers, usually located in large trading centres such as Tokyo and Osaka, and local wholesalers operating in secondary trading centres. These were small-scale enterprises that limited their businesses to the immediately surrounding area (Arakawa, 1957, 59).

Wholesalers became specialized and subdivided into classes, deepening the complexity of Japan's distribution system. Dowd (1959) defines wholesaler types according to their products and locations, but the 'wholesaler' concept in Japan is much more complicated. The *ton-ya* is a Japanese wholesaler type, but it must be functionally distinguished from general and specialty wholesalers. The ton-ya generally had property rights over their distributed products, conducted stock and transport operations, took all the business risks and operated independently, without any exclusive contract with a manufacturer. Thus, the ton-ya performed all the trade and marketing functions, including physical distribution and demand–supply adjustment. On the other hand, general and specialty wholesalers focused on demand–supply adjustment; they neither performed physical distribution nor held property rights over manufacturers' products (Tajima and Harada, 1997, 200–4). General and specialty wholesalers acted as organizers in the supply chain (Toba, 1982, 7), while ton-ya engaged in all trade functions, especially in the domestic market. Ton-ya have a much longer history than do general and specialty wholesalers, having first appeared in the Edo period. Wholesalers in Japan were well-organized and formed well-developed and complex distribution systems centring on the Ton-ya system. Dowd (1959, 259) makes the striking observation that there were almost no direct sales by Japanese manufacturers, no matter how large, even of industrial commodities to industrial users. Manufacturers principally depended on wholesalers, and even large department store chains used them as their supply source (Dowd, 1959, 260). Toba (1982) claims that ton-ya and general and specialty wholesalers played important marketing roles in supplementing the manufacturers' inadequate distribution capacities. While manufacturers and chain stores engaged in marketing activities in the United States at this time, wholesalers played this role in Japan (Toba, 1982, 5).

Marketing conducted by Japanese manufacturers lagged far behind the American equivalent, when Japanese manufacturers were small and more interested in technological problems than in marketing (Dowd, 1959, 258). The uniqueness of Japan's marketing system and wholesalers was their huge distribution and marketing power during this period (Toba, 1982, 5).

Pioneering marketing practices

The new Meiji government also took the initiative in introducing Western culture. New products like milk, bread, Western confectionary and beer appeared on the market, while oil lamps became commonplace and the use of electric lighting began. From the Meiji through the Taisho (1912–26) period and until the start of the Second World War, elements of Western culture gradually penetrated Japan's daily life, including food, clothing, and housing (Maeda, 1977, 163). In addition, the urban development of social infrastructure and services such as transportation, railroads, water and sewerage systems, electricity and education spurred a rapid increase in the proportion of the population living in cities from the end of the Taisho to the beginning of the Showa (1926–89) period. Japan's standard of living had risen sharply through Westernization, urbanization and social infrastructure development by the mid-1930s (Kohara, 1994, 7–8). Urban white-collar workers who had received higher education, seen as the 'new middle class', played a central role in the changes in consumer life during the 1920s (Nihon Research Sogo Kenkyu-jyo, 1988, ch. 6).

The chemical and heavy industries achieved remarkable development through the 1910s to the 1920s, and Japan's pre-war economic growth was dominated by light industries centred on textiles. However, the consumer goods industries remained underdeveloped and exerted little impact on the national economy (Kohara 1994, 8). As mentioned, most consumer goods companies depended on wholesalers and retailers, though some innovative consumer goods manufacturers attempted to intervene in the distribution process, implementing sales practices to increase sales, prevent price slumps and control their brand image (Maeda, 1977, 164). Examples include Ajinomoto (who produced artificial flavouring), Calpis (who produced a condensed dairy beverage), Suntory and Kirin (who made wine, whiskey and beer), Kagome (who produced tomato ketchup), Janome (who produced sewing machines), Morinaga and Meiji (who produced Western confectionaries), Shiseido (who produced cosmetics), Lion and Kao (who produced soaps and toothpaste), and Matsushita Electronic (who made electrical products). These companies had much in common; their products were new, they used mass advertising in newspapers and magazines, and they evolved out of a partial dependence on traditional wholesalers by gradually selecting superior companies and organizing their own direct distribution channels. These marketing-oriented companies emerged before the Second World War despite lacking a concept of 'marketing' and without recognizing their innovations as such. Thus, some of the leading manufacturers in Japan's emerging consumer goods industry were clearly engaged in marketing practices, albeit in early stages of development. However, these pioneering marketing practices were the exception at the time. In general, wholesalers performed the marketing tasks, and many manufacturers depended on them to market their products during the pre-war period (Toba, 1982, 10).

Manufacture-leading marketing in the post-war period

Marketing as an idea imported from the United States

As mentioned in the previous section, pioneering manufacturers engaged in marketing as early as the 1920s and 1930s. Most practitioners were not even aware of the marketing concept before the Second World War. Marketing concepts were imported through the Japan Productivity Center (JPC), established in 1955 as a central industrial organization to promote the Productivity Movement (Japan Productivity Center, 1965). The Productivity Movement was initially started in the UK in 1948 with financial support from the US under the Marshall Plan. It aimed at economic recovery by learning advanced American business practices, and then the movement spread in European countries. Mr Kouhei Gohshi, the Chief of Japan Association of Corporate Executives, was inspired by the success of Productivity Movements in Europe and established the JPC in 1955 (Bando, 2014). The JPC consisted mainly of scholars and representatives of industrial organizations such as the Japan Business Federation, Japan Committee for Economic Development, Japan Chamber of Commerce and Industry, and Japan Management League. Through this movement, business principles and technologies developed in the US were introduced to industries in Japan. Marketing concepts were also imported as techniques for improving business productivity (Japan Productivity Center, 1957a, 1957b). In 1955, the JPC organized the Top Management Mission group consisting of practitioners, academics and public officials and dispatched them to the US to inspect American business practices (Japan Society for the Study of Marketing History, 1995). When Taizo Ishizaka, Chairman of the Japan Business Federation and head of mission, returned to Japan, he stated that 'marketing is a scientific method to resolve market problems, and Japanese companies need to learn the theory and principle of marketing more seriously and adopt them into their practices' (*Nikkei Shimbun*, 17 October 1955). His speech was widely reported in both general newspapers and technical journals, and 'marketing' became a catchphrase among practitioners. The following year, the First Marketing Mission was reorganized to concentrate on marketing practices (Yokota, 1987; Japan Society for the Study of Marketing History, 1995).

The teams imported two fundamental principles. First there was the idea of consumer-centrism, placing consumer demand at the centre of marketing activity as expressed by the phrase 'the consumer is king'. Second, managerial marketing emphasized scientific market research on consumer demand and the integrated management of marketing tools such as product planning, pricing policies, distribution channel management, and promotion policies, later conceptualized as the '4Ps marketing mix' (McCarthy, 1960).

The JPC held marketing seminars, invited prominent marketing scholars from the US to conferences as guest speakers, published marketing journals and even produced radio programmes featuring marketing lectures (Japan Marketing Association, 2007, 5–7). Through these efforts, marketing concepts spread rapidly through Japan's industries (Shirahige, 1967, ch. 4). Unlike the US, marketing was introduced in Japan intentionally rather than emerging spontaneously.

Practitioners driven to learn marketing principles soon realized that the marketing techniques learned from the US were quite similar to the pre-war business practices of pioneering Japanese companies mentioned in the previous section and that these in fact constituted marketing management practices. However, the American emphasis on the integrated management of the marketing mix offered a new perspective which Japanese industries eventually adopted.

Manufacturer-leading marketing in the post-war period

The pioneering pre-war marketing practices were suspended at the outbreak of the Second World War and during the post-war struggle for recovery, when the government aggressively promoted heavy chemical industrialization based on the mass production of durable consumer goods. Production facilities in the main industries were modernized and new industries emerged, including the production of artificial fibres, home electrical appliances and automobiles. Japan's mass production system made steady progress (Maeda, 1977, 172).

In the post-war period, Japan achieved rapid and remarkable economic growth, increasing its national income by the mid-1950s, with the economy recovering to 13 per cent above the pre-war baseline. The 1956 White Paper declared the end of the post-war period (Economic Planning Agency, 1956), and Japan's income level doubled between 1955 and 1960. This increase in income and narrowing income gaps led to changes in the national class-consciousness, with most Japanese coming to recognize themselves as belonging to the middle class.

These economic factors raised consumption levels and changed consumption patterns. A mass consumption culture was established around the end of the 1950s, with the consumption of electric appliances such as washing machines, refrigerators and black and white televisions dramatically increasing between the 1950s and 1960s. These three items were named as the *sanshu no jin-gi*, the three sacred imperial jewels. In addition, clothes made from newly developed chemical fibres such as nylon were available to most people at reasonable prices. Western clothing became more popular and fashionable. Throughout the 1960s and 1970s, the development of credit turned the '3Cs' (colour TVs, cars, and 'coolers', or air-conditioners) into the new 'sacred imperial treasures' symbolizing mass consumption in Japan. During the period of high economic growth from the mid-1950s to the beginning of the 1970s, consumption was no longer limited to the rich but was enjoyed by most Japanese. The advent of this mass consumption society was an essential factor in the development of Japanese marketing in the post-war era (Kohara, 1994, 70–1; Maeda, 1977, 173).

Marketing in the post-war period was developed most highly in the durable consumer goods industry, which used such marketing strategies as full-product lineups, frequent model changes, quality improvements, cost and price reductions derived from the scale advantages of mass production, exclusive manufacturer sales channels, mass advertising and adaptations of other promotional tools (Kohara, 1994, 141). Eventually, these practices spread to other industries, widely disseminating marketing management ideas. Since the late 1950s, manufacturers of durable goods have tended to strengthen their channel management strategies to secure stable sales and avoid severe price competition.

Prices were strictly regulated and business activities severely limited during the war, but the government lifted these controls in the late 1940s. Manufacturers of durable consumer goods, now allowed to operate freely, reorganized their marketing channels. Most still depended on independent wholesalers to sell their products, but some gradually organized their own sales companies (called *hansha*) in order to reinforce sales. Matsushita Electronic founded its own sales company in 1950, Toshiba in 1953 and Hitachi in 1955, establishing an exclusive marketing channel at the wholesale level and founding the basis of a mass sales system. For example, in 1955, Matsushita Electronic had 110 sales companies and 41 joint ventures with wholesalers and another 65 independent sales agents (Shirahige, 1967, 55). By 1965, Matsushita had reorganized, cutting ties with its joint ventures and independent sales agents, integrating all wholesaling functions into its own sales company (Kohara, 2010, 84).

Meanwhile, they also controlled retailing activities. Matsushita graded retailers according to the in-store share of the manufacturer's products. Retailers whose coverage of Matsushita merchandise (branded as 'National') exceeded 80 per cent were designated a National Shop; retailers with 50 to 79 per cent coverage were designated a National Shop Association (*National Tenkai*), and retailers with 30 to 49 per cent were deemed a National League Shop (*National Renmei-ten*). National Shops received favourable terms such as volume and other discounts for buying merchandise directly from Matsushita (Shirahige, 1967, 57). This direct retail control was called '*keiretsu* in the marketing channel'.[1] Manufacturers of automobiles, electric appliances, medicines, cosmetics and detergents adopted a similar vertical keiretsu system. These manufacturers did not invest capital in retail, as most were independent. Keiretsu in the marketing channel were deployed to avoid intense price competition by selling as a loss leader at extremely low prices and protect the manufacturers' brand image. The business practices of Matsushita and Shiseido serve as representative examples of keiretsu in the marketing channel.[2] Most of their products were sold at the same price across keiretsu retail stores. Keiretsu retailers cooperated with the manufacturers' strategic directions and followed their suggested retail prices, though they were not obliged to. In return, manufacturers maintained better relationships with keiretsu retailers and dealers and established win–win relationships throughout the 1950s and up to the mid-1980s. During the economic growth period, Japan enjoyed strong consumer demand for branded goods from these manufacturers, and retailers benefited from their cooperation with them.

Thus, channel management through keiretsu in the marketing channel and pricing strategies were integrated in order to maintain prices and protect the manufacturers' brand image. Still primitive in the pre-war period, keiretsu in the marketing channel spread widely across industries in the post-war period. As new products with identifiable brands entered the market and manufacturers advertised directly to consumers, manufacturers needed to secure stable marketing channels that they could manage to prevent prices from collapsing. Keiretsu in the marketing channel was an innovative way to shift competition from pricing to non-price factors such as branding and product differentiation.

These manufacturers began selling, distributing and marketing their products, functions which had been mainly carried out by wholesalers. The manufacturers reduced their dependence on wholesalers and executed their own marketing tasks according to their own marketing plans and strategies. The concept rapidly came to be recognized by business practitioners and scholars as manufacturer-leading activity. Manufacturers took over from wholesalers by initiating marketing and became leaders in marketing channels throughout the 1960s until the 1980s.[3]

Retailer-driven marketing since the 1990s

While keiretsu retailers organized by manufacturers developed in the cosmetics and electronic appliance sectors in the post-war period, some independent retailers developed nationwide store networks with self-service systems. These unique Japanese self-service stores were called *super* in Japanese, an abbreviation of 'supermarket' (Usui, 2014, 111). The leading company was Daiei, which was established in 1957 as a drug store and changed its name to 'Housewives' Store Inc.' in 1959. They expanded their inventory and started to sell common food, processed meat products, daily necessities, cosmetics, drugs, and clothing (Daiei, 1992). Self-service stores such as Daiei came to be called *general super* to distinguish them from self-service stores that sold only food, which were called *food super* (Usui, 2014, 120). In the middle of the 1960s, the Self-Service Discount Department Store (SSDDS) was introduced (Usui, 2014, 121). This was a self-service store offering a full range of products, as in a department store, at discount prices (Kitazato, 1962). Daiei opened Japan's first SSDDS in 1963 (Usui, 2014, 121).

Just one year before this first SSDDS opened, Tajima (1962) and Hayashi (1962) advocated the modernization of the Japanese distribution structure in a 'Distribution Revolution', a term coined by Tajima (1962) that became fashionable in the 1960s. The term denoted the elimination of intermediaries and wholesalers and the establishment of large-scale retailers of food and other consumer products in order to shorten and widen distribution channels (Nakanishi, 1981, 206). As noted, wholesalers' division into multiple classes complicated Japanese distribution. Moreover, Japan had a huge number of small retailers of food and other consumer products. Advocates of a distribution revolution assumed that a modernization of distribution channels in Japan could be achieved through the emergence of large-scale retailers and direct selling between them and large manufacturers. Daiei is a representative example of this distribution revolution. Revolution advocates argued that the inefficiency of the Japanese distribution system was caused by the complexity and multi-stage nature of the wholesaling system and predicted wholesalers' disappearance. National and regional *super* chains increased their share of retail sales from 9 per cent in 1964 to 24 per cent in 1979, while the traditional small retail stores' share decreased from 73 to 57.4 per cent over the same 15 years (Nakanishi, 1981, 206). Increasing the efficiency of Japan's distribution channels was a major issue among both marketing practitioners and academics throughout the 1960s and 1970s.

However, contrary to the advocates' expectations, wholesalers did not disappear, while SSDDS and food *super* grew throughout the 1970s and 1980s. According to Sumiya (2010), the number of wholesalers increased from 225,993 in 1960 to 255,974 in 1970. In some sectors, such as textiles, minerals, and metals, the numbers dropped, but these wholesaling sectors were not directly influenced by the growth of SSDDS and food *super* (Sumiya, 2010, 3–4). Sumiya (2010) explains that self-service stores such as SSDDS and food *super* lacked the funds needed to establish their own distribution centres or secure the capabilities and technological skills required to operate distribution functions such as inventory control and delivery management. As a result, they needed to depend on wholesalers or ton-ya. In fact, large-scale retailers realized that it was better to obtain help from ton-ya and coexist with them than to try to eliminate them. By the middle of the 1980s, a distribution revolution came to be regarded as unrealistic.

After the economic bubble burst in Japan at the beginning of the 1990s, high-volume specialty stores, such as drug stores, home electric appliance retailers and DIY stores, grew rapidly. This followed the deregulation of the Large-scale Retail Store Law, which had been established in 1972 in order to protect relatively small and mid-sized retailers from large-scale retailers entering the market (see Ishihara and Yahagi, 2004; Tajima and Harada, 1997). Home electronics appliance chain stores had been established as early as the 1960s and 1970s, but they did not greatly influence the distribution channels because the keiretsu system dominated these markets. During the chronic depression years of the 1990s and 2000s, however, high-volume sales specialty stores attracted consumers with their extremely low prices, and the Japanese retail industry experienced a remarkable fall in prices, known as 'price destruction'. During this period, a wide variety of discount stores emerged, with mass selling power (Kubomura, 1996, ch. 3). The SSDDSs emphasized wide product assortment, but specialty discount stores focused on assortment depth. Japanese consumers of the 1960s and 1970s had uniform and homogeneous demands, whereas consumers in the 1980s and 1990s had developed specific, unique and differentiated demands and sought a wide variety of product choices. These new consumers supported specialty discount stores. Furthermore, these stores directly negotiated with manufacturers and obtained extremely favourable terms, with massive buying and bargaining power over manufacturers, thereby reducing their dependence on wholesalers. The power balance between manufacturer and large retailer has been changing dramatically since the late 1990s,[4] resulting in a gradual decline in keiretsu in the marketing channel. The large retailers began to demonstrate leadership in Japan's distribution channels.

Moreover, along with the development of the information society from the beginning of the 1980s, self-service retailers have aggressively increased their use of information technology. Seven-Eleven Japan, a former subsidiary of Ito-Yokado, a leading SSDDS, introduced POS (point-of-sale) terminals in their convenience stores in 1982. These enabled retailers to collect sales information for any item. The system improved the efficiency by which customers could order the best-selling products and reduced lost sales opportunities through merchandise sales data. These data on best-selling product lines became useful not only for inventory control on the retail side but also for flexible production adjustments according to changes in consumer demand on the manufacturing side. In the 1990s, the POS system was widely diffused among SSDDS, food *super* and convenience stores. Other retailers recognized that access to POS data resulted in a competitive advantage and rapidly adopted related business models, such as Seven-Eleven's unit article management and Wal-Mart's retail link (Ishihara and Yahagi, 2004, 254).

Once retailers obtained POS sales data, the power relationships between manufacturers and retailers changed. Throughout the post-war period, as mentioned, manufacturers of consumer goods grew and acquired power over wholesalers and retailers. By the middle of the 1970s, SSDDS and food *super* had increased the number of their chain stores and gained strong buying power over manufacturers. Contrary to the prediction of the distribution revolution, these retailers had to depend on wholesalers for physical distribution throughout the 1970s and lacked the negotiation power to establish direct trade with large manufacturers. However, as retailers came to use POS and other information technologies to collect consumer information, they found it to be a most powerful weapon against large manufacturers by the end of the 1980s. Manufacturers had always held a superior position in the distribution channels, but they favoured keeping a close relationship with retailers in order to have access to POS data and became eager to offer the joint development of new products with retailers using that data. Strategic alliances for joint product development and joint supply chain management between manufacturers and retailers rapidly emerged in the 1990s. This tendency was discussed in terms of the power shift from manufacturer to retailer, with large-scale retailers recognized as the new captains of Japan's distribution channel (Tajima and Harada, 1997, 294–5). This phenomenon was also called the 'second distribution revolution' (Kubomura, 1996).

Large-scale retailers also began to lead their own brand development in the early 2000s. Among SSDDSs, Daiei had developed a Private Brand (PB) strategy as early as the mid-1960s to provide merchandise that was much cheaper than the manufacturers'. In general, PB products are 20 to 30 per cent cheaper than similar branded products. Other SSDDSs followed this strategy and introduced PB products. However, many large manufacturers hesitated to provide PB to emerging retailers because they had their own strong, high-quality national brands and refused to work as subcontractors. Therefore, SSDDSs had to request PB production from mid- or small-sized manufacturers. The resultant PB products were thus inferior to the leading manufacturers' brands in the 1960s. Furthermore, Daiei's PB products were cited as an example of the countervailing power that could be used against manufacturers, as Galbraith (1952) observes, leading to conflict between Daiei and major manufacturers such as Matsushita and Shiseido (cf. Usui, 2014). In the 1970s, Daiei introduced generic PB products, which were 15 per cent cheaper than Daiei's original PB products. The low quality of the original generic PB products had however given consumers a poor image of all PB products. Thereafter, Japan entered the favourable business era known as the 'bubble economy', when Japanese consumers preferred the manufacturers' brands to PB products. Retailers failed to establish a strong brand identity for PB products until the end of the 1980s.[5] As the bubble economy collapsed in the 1990s, SSDDSs had to fight with the many discounters that emerged and thus reduced the prices of manufacturers' branded products; they lacked the funds and human capacity needed to improve their skills and know-how and pursue a PB strategy.

By contrast, Seven-Eleven Japan, a major convenience chain store with 17,206 domestic and 37,004 overseas stores (in 2014), introduced a new concept to the PB strategy in 2007, symbolized by the new brand name 'seven premium'. The company emphasized PB products' value for money, not their low prices. As British retailers such as Marks and Spencer, Tesco and Sainsbury's have done, Seven-Eleven also introduced brand categories such as Seven-Premium Gold, which are of higher quality than the standard PB and manufacturers' lines and are more expensive. Since Seven-Eleven neither emphasizes low price nor engages in price competition, leading manufacturers willingly cooperate with Seven-Eleven by providing them with PB products. In this PB strategy, manufacturers can conduct joint product development with Seven-Eleven and work as partners instead of subcontractors. Other convenience store chains and SSDDSs have been following Seven-Eleven's business model since the mid-2000s, and the PB strategy has become a prominent issue among marketing scholars. Yahagi (1993, 1996) examines the history of PB strategy in Japan; Ohno (2010) analyses the mechanisms and rationales by which retailers conduct PB strategy, and Akikawa and Toda (2013) discuss supply chain management within the PB strategy for retail chain stores. Retailers following a PB strategy actively participate in the production process and give manufacturers detailed specifications for their PB products.

In recent years, chain store retailers have come to hold unprecedented power in distribution and marketing channels and have become channel leaders. Retailers have been demonstrating a strong ability to collect consumer information using information technology, a considerable buying power and a major capacity to lead product development as well. They are now supreme in Japan's distribution channels.

Conclusion

This chapter offers a brief review of Japanese marketing focusing on channels. Its roots took hold as early as the 1920s and 1930s, through practices that were not recognized as marketing until the concept was imported via the Top Management Mission to the United States in the mid-1950s. Throughout the post-war period, Japan experienced rapid economic growth, dramatically increasing its standard of living and giving birth to a mass consumption society. Manufacturers of durable consumer goods enthusiastically developed a channel system, the keiretsu in marketing channel. They worked with wholesalers and retailers to secure sales and avoided severe price competition by internalizing some of the wholesalers, establishing their own sales companies and organizing keiretsu retailers. The keiretsu were effective until large-scale retailers grew more powerful in the marketing channels. In the late 1980s and 1990s, large-scale retailers started using information technology such as the POS system as powerful tools for collecting consumer data and thus obtained massive negotiation power over leading manufacturers. Retailers also came to lead product development of PB products and become channel captains in the 2000s.

This chapter has focused on changes in Japanese channel leadership. Retailers have held hegemony since the 1990s. This somewhat simplified view of the historical dynamics of the power shifts in Japanese marketing indicates that wholesaler-initiative, manufacturer-leading and retailer-driven marketing types coexist in some industries and business environments and cannot be merged into a single type. Instead of seeking a single leader in the marketing channel, we should understand that research on the history of marketing in Japan has not been limited to manufacturing but has recognized the dynamism among distribution systems and marketing environments. The uniqueness of Japanese distribution channels lies in the originality of their management and other marketing practices.

Notes

1 The term *keiretsu* has two dimensions – horizontal and vertical. Vertical keiretsu includes 'keiretsu in production' (*seisan keiretsu*), exemplified by Toyota's JIT production system, and 'keiretsu in distribution', or 'keiretsu in the marketing channel' (*ryuhtsu keiretsu*), which includes the relationship between manufacturers and wholesalers and/or retailers (Usui, 2005, 309). In this section, 'keiretsu' refers to keiretsu in the marketing channel. For more detailed definitions of 'keiretsu,' see Usui (2005).
2 Some product categories, including soaps, cosmetics, men's shirts, medical products, and published books, were allowed by the Japan Fair Trade Commission (JFTC) to maintain their resale prices from 1953 to 1959. From the mid-1960s on, the JFTC gradually rescinded this designation, but that for cosmetics and medical goods remained until 1993. Cosmetic manufacturer Shiseido grew under the protection of the resale price maintenance. They had a good reason to manage keiretsu retailers – to legitimately maintain their retail prices.
3 Since the 1970s, Japanese companies have entered international markets. They organized keiretsu in the marketing channel domestically and similarly focused on securing stable marketing channels in foreign markets. Williamson and Yamawaki (1991) argue that Japanese companies' strategy of significant investment in distribution was a hidden advantage for them. See Kotler and Fahey (1982) regarding the development of international marketing by Japanese manufacturers.
4 Specifically, the fight for distribution channel supremacy between manufacturers and retailers dates back to the mid-1960s, when Daiei, a supermarket chain, expanded and thus triggered the distribution revolution. See Nakauchi (2007), Nakauchi and Mikuriya (2009), and Toda (2014) regarding the history of Daiei.
5 See Yahagi (1993, 1996) and Toda (2014) regarding the history of PB strategy in Japan.

References

Akikawa, T., and Toda, Y. (2013) 'Supply chain management for private brands: The case study of seven premium' [Puraibe-to Burando no Supply Chain Management, Seven Premium no Jirei Kousatsu kara], *Business Review*, 61/2 (Autumn), 144–56 (in Japanese).

Ando, Y. (1979) *Catalogue of Economic History in Modern Japan [Kindai Nihon Keizai-shi Yoran]* (2nd edn), Tokyo University Press, Tokyo (in Japanese).

Arakawa, Y. (1957) 'Small wholesalers in the cotton textiles marketing in Japan', *Annals of the School of Business Administration* (Kobe University), 1, 59–93.

Bando, M. (2014) 'The foundation of Japan Productivity Center and the development of productivity movement' [Seisansei Honbu no Setsuritsu to Undou no Tenkai], *Sanken Ron-Shu* (Kwansei Gakuin University), 41, 15–22 (in Japanese).

Daiei, Editorial Office of Company History (1992) *35 Years Record of the Daiei Group [Daiei Grupu 35 nen no Kiroku]*, Daiei Inc., Osaka (in Japanese).

Dowd, L.P. (1959) 'Wholesale marketing in Japan', *Journal of Marketing* 23 (Jan.), 257–62.

Economic Planning Agency (1956) *White Paper on the Growth and Modernizaton of Japanese Economy [Nihon Keizai Seicho to Kindaika]*, Economic Planning Agency, Tokyo (in Japanese).

Economic Planning Agency (1970) *White Paper on National Lifestyle [Kokumin seikatsu Hakusho]*, Economic Planning Agency, Tokyo (in Japanese).

Economic Planning Agency (1991) *The Consumer Behavior Survey* [*Shouhish Doukou Chousa Nenpo*], Economic Planning Agency, Tokyo (in Japanese).

Galbraith, J.K. (1952) *American Capitalism: the Concept of Countervailing Power*, Houghton Mifflin, Boston, MA.

Gordon, A. (2012) *Fabricating Consumers: The Sewing Machine in Modern Japan*, University of California Press, Berkeley, CA.

Hayashi, S. (1962) *Distribution Revolution: Products, Marketing Channels, and Consumers* [*Ryu-tsu Kakumei, Seihin, Ryu-tsu chaneru, Shouhisha*], Chu-ko Shin-sho, Tokyo (in Japanese).

Ishihara, T., and Yahagi, T. (2004) *Japanese 100-Year Distribution: Marketing Channels, Retailing and Public Policy Issues* [*Nihon no Ryutsu 100 nen*], Yuhikaku, Tokyo (in Japanese).

Ishikawa, K. (2011) *The Dynamics of Marketing in Japanese Automobile Industry* [*Waga-kuni Jidousha Ryutsu no Dynamics*], Senshu Daigaku Shuppan-kyoku, Tokyo (in Japanese).

Japan Marketing Association (2007) *Japan Marketing Association, 50 years of History* [*Nihon Marketing Kyokai, 50 nen no Ayumi*], Japan Marketing Society, Tokyo (in Japanese).

Japan Productivity Center (1957a) *Marketing: The Principles and Case Study* [*Marketing, Genri to Jirei*], Japan Productivity Center, Tokyo (in Japanese).

Japan Productivity Center (1957b) *The Report of the First Marketing Mission* [*Marketing Senmon Shisatsudan Houkokusho*], Productivity Report 19, Japan Productivity Center, Tokyo (in Japanese)

Japan Productivity Center (1965) *The Development of Japan Productivity Center for the Last 10 Years*, Japan Productivity Center, Tokyo (in Japanese).

Japan Society for the Study of Marketing History (1995) *Japanese Marketing: The Introduction and Development* [*Nihon no Marketing, Dounyu to Tenkai*], Dobunkan Shuppan, Tokyo (in Japanese).

Japan Society for the Study of Marketing History (2010) *Marketing of Japanese Companies* [*Nihon Kigyo no Marketing*], Dobunkan Shuppan, Tokyo (in Japanese).

Kitazato, U. (1962) 'A turmoil over the selling revolution in the USA: Emergence of large-sized discount department store', *Economist*, 28 (Aug.), 6–19 (in Japanese).

Kinoshita, A. (2010) 'Marketing of Onward, the branding and internalization of retailing function' [Onward no Marketing, Brand kouchiku to Kouri Kinou no Housetsu], in Japan Society for the Study of Marketing History (ed.), *Marketing of Japanese Companies* [*Nihon Kigyou no Marketing*], Doubunkan Shuppan, Tokyo, pp. 113–35.

Kohara, H. (1994) *History of Japanese Marketing, the Historical Structure of Modern Distribution System* [*Nihon Marketing-shi, Gendai Ryutsu no Shiteki Kouzu*], Chuo Keizai-sha, Tokyo (in Japanese).

Kohara, H. (2010) 'Marketing history of Panasonic (Matsushita Electronic Industrial Co.)', in Japan Society for the Study of Marketing History (ed.), *Marketing of Japanese Companies* [*Nihon Kigyou no Marketing*], Doubunkan Shuppan, Tokyo, pp. 76–94.

Kotler, P., and Fahey. L. (1982) 'The world's champion marketers: The Japanese', *Journal of Business Strategy*, 3/1, 1–13.

Kubomura. R. (1996) *The Second Distribution Revolution, Further Tasks Rest in the Twenty-first Century* [*Dai Niji Ryutsu Kakumei, 21seiki he no Kadai*], Nihon Keizai Shinbunsha, Tokyo (in Japanese).

Lazer, W., Murata S., and Kosaka, H. (1985) 'Japanese marketing: Towards a better understanding', *Journal of Marketing*, 49/2, 69–81.

McCarthy, E.J. (1960) *Basic Marketing: A Managerial Approach*, Richard, D. Irwin, Inc., Homewood, IL.

Maeda, K. (1977) 'Marketing', in M. Miyamoto and K. Nakagawa (eds), *Japanese Management: The History of Japanese Management* [*Nihon teki Keiei: Nihon Keiei-shi*], vol. 5, pp. 159–83 (in Japanese).

Maruyama, M. (2004) 'Japanese distribution channels, structure and strategy', *The Japanese Economy*, 32/3, 27–48.

Matsushita Electric, Inc. (1985) *50 years of History, Matsushita Electric, Inc., as a Pioneer of International Trade* [*Matsushita Denki Boueki 50 nen no Ayumi: Kaden Boeki no Pioneer wo Mezashite*], Matsushita Electric, Inc., Tokyo (in Japanese).

Nakanishi, M. (1981) 'Marketing developments in Japan', *Journal of Marketing*, 45 (Summer), 206–8.

Nakauchi, I. (2007) *My Discounting Philosophy* [*Waga Yasuuri Tetsugaku*], Chikura Shobo, Tokyo (in Japanese).

Nakauchi, J., and Mikuriya, T. (2009) *Nakauchi Isao, his Life and Distribution Revolution* [*Nakauchi Isao, Ryutsu Kakumei ni Shougai wo Sasageta Otoko*], Chikura Shobo, Tokyo (in Japanese).

Nihon Research Sogo Kenkyu-jyo (1988) *Historical Research of Living Standard* [*Seikatsu Suijyun no Rekishi Bunseki*], Sogo Kenkyu Kaihatsu Kiko, Tokyo (in Japanese).

Ohno, N. (2010) *PB Strategy: The Structure and Dynamics*, Chikura-shobo, Tokyo (in Japanese).

Shimaguchi, M. (1978) *Marketing Channels in Japan*, UMI Research Press, Ann Arbor, MI.

Shimizu, A. (1974) *Marketing Theory, Principles and Cases* [*Marketing Tsu-ron, Genri to Jirei*], Dobunkan Shuppan, Tokyo (in Japanese).

Shimokawa, H. (1990) *Marketing-The History and International Comparison* [*Marketing, Rekishi to Kokusai Hikaku*], Bunshin Do, Tokyo (in Japanese).

Shirahige, T. (1967) *The History of Japanese Marketing* [*Nihon Marketing Hatten-shi*], Bunkasha, Tokyo (in Japanese).

Sumiya, H. (2010) 'A Re-examination of the Theory for the Grounds of Existence of Wholesalers' [Oroshi-uri-shou Sonritsu Konkyo-ron no Saikentou], *Keiei Ronsyu*, 75 (Mar.), 1–14 (in Japanese).

Tajima, Y. (1962) *Distribution Revolution in Japan* [*Nihon no Ryu-tsu Kakumei*], Nihon Noritsu-Kyokai, Tokyo (in Japanese).

Tajima, Y., and Harada, H. (1997) *Introduction to Distribution Studies* [*Ryu-tsu Nyu-mon*], Nihon Keizai Shinbun-sha, Tokyo (in Japanese).

Takeda, S. (1985) *International Marketing of Japanese Companies* [*Nihon Kigyo no Kokusai Marketing*], Dobunkan Shuppan, Tokyo (in Japanese).

Toba, K. (1982) 'Modernization of distribution system in Japan' [*Nihon no Marketing, Sono Dentousei to Kindaisei ni tsuiteno ichi Kousatsu*], *Japan Business History Review*, 17/1, 1–21 (in Japanese).

Toda, Y. (2014) 'Historical analysis of alliance between Daiei and Marks and Spencer' [Daiei to Marks and Spencer no Teikeikankei ni kansuru Rekishi Kenkyu], *Ryutsu, Journal of Japan Society for Distributive Sciences*, 35 (Dec.), 33–51 (in Japanese).

Usui, K. (2005) 'An original early version of the 'Keiretsu' retail store: Marketing of Western-style sweets by Morinaga before the Second World War in Japan', in Proceedings of the 12th Conference on Historical Analysis and Research in Marketing, pp. 301–11.

Usui, K. (2014) *Marketing and Consumption in Modern Japan*, Routledge, New York.

Williamson, P.J., and Yamawaki, H. (1991) 'Distribution: Japan's hidden advantage', *Business Strategy Review*, 2/1, 85–105.

Yahagi, T. (1993) 'Change of distribution channels' [Ryutsu Gendai-shi], in Nihon Keizai Shinbun-sha (ed.), *History of Modern Distribution*, Nikkei Shinbun-sha, Tokyo, pp. 119–49 (in Japanese).

Yahagi, T. (1996) 'The framework of PB strategy', in R. Kubomura (ed.), *The Second Distribution Revolution*, Nikkei Shinbun-sha, Tokyo, pp. 80–101 (in Japanese).

Yamamoto, Y. (1992) *Economic History of Modern Japan* [*Kindai Nihon Keizai-shi*], Minerva Publishing, Tokyo (in Japanese).

Yokota, S. (1987) 'A memorandum regarding the marketing mission in 1956, the historical material in the beginning of marketing in Japan' [Marketing Shisatsu Dan ni Kansuru Oboegaki], *Keiei Ronsyu* (Meiji University), 34/3–4, 115–35 (in Japanese).

Yoshino, M. (1971) *The Japanese Marketing System: Adaptation and Innovations*, MIT Press, Cambridge, MA.

23

A history of Danish advertising, market research, and retailing institutions: 1920–1960

Erik Kloppenborg Madsen

Introduction

This chapter deals with three marketing institutions which are well established in Denmark today, and with how they developed from 1920 to 1960: the advertising agency, the market research agency and the retailer. Advertising and of course retailing have a history which goes further back than 1920, but this period of time witnessed a profound transformation of these two trades. The traditional advertisement office from 1880 to 1920 developed into the independent 'fully developed creative advertising agency' over the period from 1920 to 1945, and retail business became revolutionized at the end of the period. The third trade, the market research agency, was brand new and made its entry in the late 1930s.

Together these new and/or transformed institutions paved the way from mass production to mass consumption in Denmark. As argued by Kjær-Hansen (1937), the importance of advertising for the development of mass consumption was comparable to the importance of the steam engine for the industrial revolution.

The amount of original research conducted in the field of Scandinavian marketing history in general and Danish marketing history in particular is quite sparse but a few relatively recent Danish contributions, indicating increased interest in the field, may be found. The following outline of the history of advertising, retailing and market research in Denmark is based on these sources and on the contemporary writings of authors from the period investigated.

The period under review was selected for two reasons: the accessibility of sources, to some extent, dictates the choice, but more importantly, the period from the end of World War I until the 1950s or early 1960s was characterized by profound institutional changes in the particular fields of marketing scrutinized in this chapter.

A substantial part of European research on marketing history relating to the period from 1920 to 1960 has been conducted under the heading of 'Americanization' (see e.g. Schröter, 2005; Iulio, 2009; Whelan, 2014; Fasce and Bini, 2015). This is also true of recent Danish contributions (e.g. Sørensen, 2011; M.B. Andersen, 2011; K.Ø. Andersen, 2011).

There is a general discussion (Schröter, 2005; Sørensen, 2011) about whether these institutional inventions and transformations should be seen as independent European –

including Scandinavian – modernization or rather as Americanization, i.e. as direct imitation, more or less selective adoption or as a kind of adaptation of local standards to American ideas. These issues are not of primary concern in this chapter, but the development of the new independent trades of advertising and market research was clearly influenced by American ideas. It is probably best understood and explained in the light of a functional understanding of the need or even necessity for modernization. The overall interpretation of the changes and developments described in this chapter is based on the modernization perspective.

This should not be taken to mean that American firms operating in the Scandinavian countries did not influence practice or that American intentions to influence European business practice did not exist. The European recovery programme, known as the Marshall Plan, proposed by the Truman administration, actually intended to influence the development and adoption of the American way in the Scandinavian countries. The recovery programme was not limited to material aid, but also, importantly, included the introduction of new ideas. The aim of the plan was aptly revealed by Paul Hofman, who was responsible for the programme from 1948, and who compared the 'American assembly line to the communist party line' (Schröter, 2005, 47). One might say that it was an activity in (what had not yet been coined) 'social marketing'. A quite substantial amount, 5 per cent of the recovery funds, was spent on the promotion of the Marshall Plan. Between 1949 and 1951, Denmark, for instance, saw three major pro-Marshall-Aid campaigns (Schröter, 2005). Among the promotional instruments used was the 'European Train', a mobile exhibition which visited the three Scandinavian countries in the early 1950s.

It follows that it is difficult, if not impossible, to treat the development of marketing in Scandinavia over the period from about 1920 to 1960 without mentioning the role of the US in that process. However, the term 'Americanization' has connotations of coercion, which is not part of the perspective in this study. Danish players participated voluntarily and actively in the process. The term of 'modernization' seems to fit better the overall perspective applied in this account of the institutional development in Denmark. The particular reason for this is the fact that the development of modern marketing as a new and expanding social institution concerned with organizing and managing the link between production and consumption occurred later in Scandinavia and Europe at large than it did in America. There was a time lag. Europeans, therefore, did not have to, and did not actually, invent everything from scratch but could look across the Atlantic and gain inspiration from practices already invented by the Americans. The impact from the US is quite clear and it is impossible to talk about the modernization of business in Europe, including Scandinavia, without considering the effect of American ideas and practices.

The process of learning from, or adapting to, American ideas in the economic realm developed in three waves (Schröter, 2005). The first wave from 1870 to 1945 brought Fordism and Taylorism to Europe. The second wave, during the period 1945 to 1975 – rebuilding Europe after the war – brought the Marshall Plan and a new economic boom, which meant not only taking mass production and mass consumption to a new level, but also, in particular, the introduction of self-service on a large scale and of other distributional innovations. The third wave since 1980 was characterized by ideas of deregulation and privatization.

From a marketing perspective, the two first waves, not least the second one, seem to be of special interest. They contain organizational and institutional changes strongly involved in the emergence of a European mass market (Schröter, 2005). These developments also caused extensive changes in retailing, consumer behaviour, advertising and market research in Denmark, Norway and Sweden. The time span over which these changes occurred in the Scandinavian countries does not differ significantly from that seen in the rest of Europe. In particular, the period from 1945 to 1975 (the second wave) also seems, in a Scandinavian context, to have been a time of extensive change and growth in marketing activities and marketing institutions. It should be kept in mind that an important difference between the three fields mentioned is that market research bureaus and creative advertising agencies were more or less brand-new institutions in society, which was not true of retailing. So while advertising and market research were activities which in themselves represented modern business conditions and an active part of the development, this was slightly different in the case of retailing because retailers had already existed for a long time. In fact, in some sense they became the victims of these developments. If the advertising agencies were the revolutionary rebels, the retailers, or at least some of them, represented the part of the marketing system which in the end became revolutionized.

In sum, the first half of the twentieth century witnessed extensive major changes in the field of marketing or, more correctly, marketing proper was established in Denmark during that period. New trades (some even aspiring to the status of not merely new trades but new professions proper) emerged: the independent advertising agency, the marketing, or market research, agency and, finally, the completely transformed trade of retailing.

Advertising

According to Kjær-Hansen (1958), the period from around 1880 to approximately 1945 saw a three-phase change and development in advertising intermediaries in Denmark: from being advertisement offices (*annonceekspeditioner*), c.1880–1920, they became creative advertising bureaus (*det kreative reklamebureau*), in 1920–45, and, from 1945 on, developed into 'the modern, fully developed advertising agency' (*det moderne reklamebureau*).

A closer examination of how and why advertising intermediaries transformed from advertisement offices into fully developed advertising agencies reveals that the transformation mirrors a change, not only in tasks and functions, but also in organizational structure. Originally, the function of the advertisement office was quite simple. Its task was to mediate between the buyer of advertising, i.e. the firm wanting to sell a product, and the seller of advertising, which was quite often a newspaper wanting to sell 'white space'. In the early days of the mediation trade, advertisement offices were paid by those who wanted their services, i.e. the sellers of advertisement space, the newspapers (Kjær-Hansen, 1958, 4–5). As business firms increasingly demanded better consultancy from advertising bureaus and more effective advertising, changes in the function of mediator were needed, however. In other words, the advertising trade had to become more skilled and competent. This led to a transformation of the trade during the first half of the twentieth century, as a result of which the buyer of advertising also paid for the service rendered by the agency. From a present-day perspective, this seems quite logical as the modern independent agency works in the interest of its client, the buyer of advertising.

Although advertisements were used in Denmark as early as 1735 (Agger, 1993), the period from 1880 to 1920 marks the beginning of the institutionalization in Denmark of advertising intermediaries (Kjær-Hansen, 1958). At the beginning of this period, two advertisement offices existed in Denmark. One was situated in Copenhagen, the capital and Denmark's largest city; and one in Aarhus, the second largest city. The first office began its activities as an advertisement office in Copenhagen in 1858 (Wolffs Reklamebureau A/S) and the second was established in Aarhus in 1880 (Weber & Sørensen Reklamebureau). The first Swedish advertisement office came into existence around 1870 (Kjær-Hansen, 1958). The Copenhagen office existed until 1991; the Aarhus office merged with another agency as late as in 2005.

From 1882 to 1920, the number of advertisement offices developed rapidly. In 1880, there were two offices in Denmark, namely the ones mentioned above, and in 1920, i.e. 40 years later, there were 122. The increasing number of advertising offices covers a hidden history in that actually 271 new bureaus were started during that period but 150 also closed down. So this development not only shows a marvellous 'Gründer' activity within the field but also testifies to the risky business conditions applying to the trade (Kjær-Hansen, 1958, 22).

In sum, the mediating activities performed by the advertisement offices marked only the beginning of the development process. The kind of mediation performed by these offices did not meet the needs of business and did not resemble what modern advertising agencies offer. They were very largely merely a special service invented by already existing newspapers and had not yet developed into proper advertising agencies.

The period after World War I, which Kjær-Hansen (1958, 26) has characterized as the 'industrialization of selling' period, saw a new development in the business of advertising: the advertisement offices, or some of them at least, became creative advertising bureaus. As standardized and mass-produced consumer goods, domestic as well as foreign brands, conquered consumer markets, and because mass production is conditioned by mass consumption, advertising was needed in order to expand consumption. This generated new tasks and required new skills in the trade; it had to have much more technical and creative skills and it needed knowledge of consumer psychology and an ability to handle large advertising campaigns because business firms increasingly needed technically as well as creatively competent advice in these respects. As the new requirements were well beyond the skills of the advertisement offices and the tasks they had performed until then, the creative advertising bureau emerged. Kjær-Hansen (1959, 29) estimates that, in Denmark, the period from 1921 to 1945 saw the following development in the number of such advertising bureaus: 18 in 1921, 19 in 1925, 23 in 1930, 33 in 1935, 36 in 1940 and 39 in 1945.

From the late 1930s, the development into the modern advertising agency was slowed by World War II, which created a seller's market. After the war, however, the trade developed further and the agencies broadened their scope, increasingly becoming consultants to firms in need of advice in the broad field of marketing. Their primary function as independent agencies was no longer that of selling empty space for the newspapers but, rather, to help firms in all matters regarding the selling of products. They became the experts on promotion and publicity, and the selling role which had characterized the old advertisement offices had now been completely 'replaced by consultants assisting the clients of the agency'. A new trade had emerged (Kjær-Hansen, 1958, 89).

Of course, the number of agencies – 39 in 1946, 45 in 1951 and 46 in 1956 – does not actually reflect the increase in selling activities and the volume of advertising from the 1950s on. In fact, advertising expenditure fell between the late 1930s and 1949. In 1935 advertising amounted to 1.4 per cent of national income and in 1948 to 1.0 percent. Comparison of the 1935 figures with the US figures at that time reveals that, in relative terms, the Danish percentage of national income spent on advertising was slightly less than half the percentage of national income spent on advertising in America, where total advertising expenditure amounted to 3 per cent of national income (Kjær-Hansen, 1949, 60) – that is, compared to the US, the Danish per capita spending on advertising was considerably smaller. Based on a calculation by Schröter (1998, 29) and mentioned in Schröter (2005), in 1960 Europe could be divided into three categories with the per capita expenditure of $64 in America as the benchmark. The highest spending European category clusters around US$20 and includes such countries as Switzerland ($28), the UK ($24) and Germany ($21) and the three Scandinavian countries – Sweden ($24), Denmark ($19) and Norway ($18).

The second cluster, the middle group spending around $10, includes among others Belgium ($12), the Netherlands ($11), France ($8) and Finland ($7). The third cluster, consisting of Portugal and Italy, spent less than $4 per capita. As we shall see later, these figures are consistent with the relatively quick adoption of market research in the Scandinavian countries.

If Kjær-Hansen's (1949) calculations are correct, then the structure of advertising (advertisements, printed matter, outdoor advertising, window displays, radio advertising, etc.) also seems to have differed from the American picture. A problem for comparison, however, is the fact that expenses on, for example, window displays were not included in the calculation of the American advertising figures and that, in the case of Denmark, about half the advertising expenditure (51.9 per cent) went to advertising media while about a quarter (25.2 per cent) was spent on window displays. From 1935 to 1948, the share of approximately three-quarters of total expenditure on these two media overall did not change in any significant way but, during that period, advertisement expenditure increased to 56.2 per cent while expenditure on window displays dropped to 18.9 per cent. Kjær-Hansen (1949) concluded that advertisements were indisputably the most important kind of advertising, and that, in this regard, advertisements in the daily newspapers played a key role. Advertisements in weekly magazines amounted, both in relative and absolute terms, to a minor sum while the remainder, the periodical press, reference books and so on, accounted for considerable sums. In terms of costs, advertising through displays, especially window displays, was the second most important form of advertising in Denmark. Film and lantern slide advertising was of much greater importance in Denmark than in other countries, although it only accounted for a modest sum. Outdoor advertising was without major importance and, by international standards, it was little used. Both with regard to total advertising expenditure and in comparison to the other countries, very little was spent on advertising management (Kjær-Hansen, 1949, 72).

During the period from 1935 to 1948, advertising was closely related to magazines, newspapers and window displays – not until the 1980s were commercial messages over radio or television allowed throughout Scandinavia. The question of how the general public or consumer, i.e. the targets of increased advertising, received these changes is difficult to answer. In the first issue of *Dansk Reklame* (Danish advertising), a Danish journal on advertising launched in 1927, the attitude of a prominent business leader towards advertising was quoted as, 'I detest advertising. [I] prefer to do without it and earn less … Denmark has no use for advertising' (Agger, 1995, 134). As a topic for political, cultural and social debate, advertising was generally ignored in the 1920s and 1930s.

In the 1940s, however, a sharp critique of the new institution was delivered by Theodor Geiger (1943), a professor of sociology, in his book *Kritik af Reklamen* (A critique of advertising), which thoroughly investigated this rapidly growing phenomenon. In a broad sense, Geiger's critique reflected a general public discomfort with the process of modernization in general and with the new institutions of marketing such as advertising and, later, systematic market research in particular – a discomfort which, more than ten years later, was reflected in the debate following the publication in Danish of Vance Packard's book *The Hidden Persuaders* in 1958. Commenting on the new market research ideas from America, Poul Henningsen, a prominent Danish intellectual, labelled Packard's book 'the most appalling reading a supporter of democracy can be confronted with' (quoted in M.B. Andersen, 2011, 267).

Geiger's book was much more sober in its tone of voice and based on thorough academic analysis. Nevertheless, it was a sharp rejection of modern advertising. Basically, Geiger perceived advertising in much the same vein as the prominent business leader mentioned above: it was an example of business excesses and not a functionally necessary institution linking mass production with mass consumption through the industrialization of selling as suggested by Kjær-Hansen.

Market research

Independent bureaus of market research did not emerge as a new and independent trade or profession until after independent advertising agencies had been established. There is some logic to this in that satisfying the demands of the creative function of the advertising agency required more knowledge about the consumer than had previously been the case. In a sense, market research gave the otherwise anonymous consumer a voice to which the firms and, on their behalf, the advertising agencies could listen (Schwarzkopf, 2011; M.B. Andersen, 2011, 269).

As regards Scandinavian consumers, they may have resembled European consumers in general in terms of the challenge of understanding them. From the marketer's point of view, it was not the over-satiated consumer but, rather, the recalcitrant one that posed a problem. 'A considerable number of Europeans resisted the purchase of mass-produced goods, considering them to be a denial of individuality' (Schröter, 2005, 112).

In Europe, the earliest institution of market research (Institut für Wirtschaftsbeobachtung der deutschen Fertigware in Nuremberg) dates back to the 1920s (Schröter, 2005, 111). But the development of market research in Europe varied in timing and extent (Schröter, 2005, 114). In Scandinavia, the first institution was established in Sweden in 1932, and in Denmark the earliest piece of market research was done by Haagen Wahl Asmussen, one of the pioneers in the field in the early 1930s (B. Rasmussen, 1979b). The number of market research firms in Denmark did not increase until after the 1950s.

In many cases, market research firms developed from advertising agencies. For example, the advertising agency Harlang & Toksvig Reklamebureau had plans even during the war to set up a market research agency. These plans resulted in the creation of INFORMA, Institut for Markedsanalyse (Institute for Market Research) (B. Rasmussen, 1979b). From a technical point of view, market research agencies developed under the strong influence of American marketing – and of ideas relating to opinion research. A substantial number of Danish market research and advertising agencies which saw the light in the 1950s did not, however, survive as independent firms for long, as they were acquired by some of the largest American advertising agencies only five to ten years later, namely, in the early 1960s (M.B. Andersen, 2011, 294).

In the mid-1950s (specifically, 1956), the number of market research firms in Europe was still quite limited, counting only 54 firms, and, in the case of Scandinavia, there were merely two in Norway, three in Denmark and five in Sweden (Schröter, 2005). There were also two in Finland. In sum, the Scandinavian share of market research firms – 10 out of 54 – was actually considerable if the size of the Scandinavian population compared to the total population of Europe is taken into account.

In addition to the establishment of national market research agencies in the Scandinavian countries, Europe witnessed other players entering the field. A.C. Nielsen, an American market research company, established subsidiaries in Europe, including one in Sweden, in the early 1950s. According to Schröter (2005, 113), the demand for the services needed came mainly from American subsidiaries or American-based companies trying to penetrate European markets. The American firms were already familiar with the use of statistical and general analytical methods and techniques and well instructed by their parent companies (Kapferer, 1956, 68).

The founding of ESOMAR (the European Society for Opinion Survey and Market Research) in Amsterdam in 1948 marked not only increased interest in market research in Europe but even aspirations of becoming, not just a new trade, but a new profession proper. Hélène Riffault, a French founding member, expressed this unequivocally: 'We wanted to show potential clients in Europe that we were a new profession which they needed, a profession with advanced technologies, discipline and ethical rules' (Downham, 1998, quoted in Schröter, 2005, 114). Wahl Asmussen, who conducted interview-based market research in the early 1930s, also founded the first Danish institution for opinion research in 1939, which was named 'Dansk Gallup Institut' (Danish Gallup Institute) in 1943.

In terms of staff and turnover, the agencies were generally of limited size. While the number of agencies rose from 11 in 1959, to 16 in 1964, 25 in 1969, 33 in 1974 and 35 in 1979, the number of employees (tenured staff) went from 71 in 1959, to 114 in 1964, 152 in 1969, 155 in 1974, to 222 in 1979 (based on W. Rasmussen, 1979). Approximately half the agencies performed market research and broad management consultancy tasks while the other half undertook market research tasks only. The overall turnover of the agencies was only a little more than the sales of a single large supermarket unit (about 7m Danish kroner) in 1964, for example (B. Rasmussen, 1979a). It obviously was not much of a trade but it was still new. Of total turnover 76 per cent came from private firms, consumer goods and media; 11 per cent was due to producers of industrial goods and 13 per cent to public authorities and concessionary companies. For the purpose of conveying an idea of the size and tasks of the major firms, the following agencies, which were all established before 1960 and still in existence 20 years later, are listed below.

- AIM A/S Institut for Meningsmåling (Institute for Opinion Research): founded in 1949, named AIM in 1961; taken over by T. Bak-Jensen A/S in 1971; sold to a group of people (AIM) in 1973; staff of 50 permanent employees and 250 part-time interviewers in 1979.
- Gallup Markedsanalyse A/S (Gallup Market Research): founded in 1939 as Dansk Institut for Måling af Den Offentlige Mening (Danish Institute for Public Opinion Research); its owner, Wahl Rasmussen, met with George Gallup in Berlin in the same year and was given permission to use the name 'Gallup' in Denmark; renamed Dansk Gallup Institut in 1943; staff of 30 permanent employees and 200 part-time interviewers in 1979.
- IFH-Research International A/S (Instituttet for Husholdningsanalyse) (Institute for Household Analysis): founded by Dansk Unilever A/S in 1947 in cooperation with Lintas, an advertising agency; mainly a research agency for Unilever-based firms until 1970; staff of 13 permanent employees and about 45 external employees in 1979.
- Lisberg Marketing ApS: founded in 1959; originally, primarily an advertising agency but developed into a broad management consulting firm also offering market research; staff of about 80 employees in 1979.
- A/S Markeds-Data: founded in 1952 by De Samvirkende Danske Købmandsforeninger (The Federation of Danish Merchant Associations) under the name of Købmands-Indeks (Merchant Index); renamed Markedsdata (Market Data) in 1958; specialized in retail selling and convenience goods; staff of 20 permanent employees and 30 external/ part time employees in 1979.
- OBSERVA Instituttet for Erhvervsanalyser og Markedsforskning (Institute for Business Analysis and Market Research): founded in 1956; ran Dansk Husmoder-Panel (Danish Housewife's Panel) from 1961; Dansk Husmoder-Panel replaced the former attempt at creating an Attwood Consumer Panel in Denmark; conducted interview-based market research (Consumption Index, quantitative and qualitative ad hoc analysis) and

panel-based market research (Dansk Husmoder Panel, Observa's Person-Panel, Dansk Landbrugs-Panel, Observa's distributions index); staff of 35 permanent employees and about 170 part-time employees in 1979.

The years shortly after 1945 were characterized by commodity shortages. As it was a seller's market, the need for detailed knowledge about consumers was quite limited. After 1945, a new type of market research, the Gallup technique, was introduced in Denmark. Interviews were adopted instead of questionnaires as was an approach based on judgemental sampling – quota sampling. The general purpose was the creation of a copy, a miniature version, of Danish society, which represented the population in general. Together with the consumer index, these techniques were the first American-inspired market research methods which came into use among a wide circle of market research agencies in Denmark (M.B. Andersen, 2011). Andersen draws this conclusion on the basis of three sources: *Det Danske Marked* (The Danish Market), a scientific journal; *Erhvervsliv* (Trade and Industry), a popular science magazine; and *Dansk Reklame* (Danish Advertising), a trade magazine. It should be noted that the spread of these new techniques in a Danish context was due not only to direct inspiration from American market research but also, to a very large extent, to relatively advanced market research in Sweden, which included methods for the measurement of advertising effects (M.B. Andersen, 2011, 271).

The quota sampling technique was an issue from the very beginning. One basic flaw was that when the quotas were defined, a large part of the remaining process, in particular the choice of respondents, was left to those who would conduct the interviews. These and other flaws led, among other things, to a controversy over the results of a Gallup survey in 1955, which is discussed below in the section on retailing.

The immediate competitor to quota sampling, namely probability sampling, was advocated by Leif Holbæk-Hansen (1950, 154–61), the Norwegian market researcher and later professor at the Norwegian School of Economics and Business Administration. Theoretically at least, probability sampling makes statistical uncertainty known. In practice, however, there is a difference between designed sample and achieved sample, and there are other problems such as samples spread over large geographical areas, which make data collection difficult and therefore very expensive. Even today, simple random sampling is not 'widely used in marketing research' (Malhotra *et al.*, 2012). The question of the advantages and disadvantages of the two methods dominated the debate in the mid-1950s, both methods having their problems. Quota sampling was easier and less expensive but probability sampling was generally considered the scientifically correct way of doing quantitative market research. Even so, probability sampling in practical use was also subject to criticism, mainly because relatively large samples were needed in order to reduce uncertainty. In general, the limits of these quantitative methods were not broadly acknowledged in much university teaching in Denmark until the early 1980s – or, rather, the alternative – qualitative research methods – were considered even more problematic.

Already in the mid-1950s, however, the advertising industry was quite prepared for the kind of market and consumer research which a new technique from the US called motivation research seemed able to deliver. *Dansk Reklame* published two articles in 1956 about motivation research by Thranow (1956) and Parrild (1956). Parrild (1956) noted that motivation research was a controversial phenomenon in the US. Even if there was considerable disagreement among people from market research and advertising about the value of these new qualitative methods, there was agreement about the need for better methods to understand consumer behaviour (M.B. Andersen, 2011, 280).

With a few early bird exceptions, the new trade of market research developed from the 1950s and onward. The number of agencies in Denmark increased from 11 in 1959 to 25 in 1969, mirroring the transition from a seller's market to a buyer's market in the 1950s and 1960s, which called for a better understanding of the consumer. The first general meeting of the Danish Market Association, which was held in December 1959 (B. Rasmussen, 1979b), marks the institutionalization of market research as a new profession.

Retailing

As a result of the second industrial revolution mass production became a reality in the early twentieth century, but in Denmark retailing did not really become tuned to this reality until 1950 nor to the fact that an increasing volume of branded goods from countries abroad were appearing on the Scandinavian market. As Kjær-Hansen (1960, 5–6) argued, the industrialization of production was not yet followed by the industrialization of selling.

In Denmark, the original form of retailing was the merchant's house, where trade in all kinds of goods took place and where customers were served from a relatively large area. It also included crafts-related retailing, where selling was strongly linked to production because the craftsmen (shoemakers, watchmakers, weavers, etc.) marketed the goods they themselves produced, but from around the late nineteenth century these craftsmen increasingly became small shopkeepers. From that time, for example, the production of footwear was increasingly carried out by large footwear factories, and the shoemakers, watchmakers and weavers increasingly became store managers and retailers, rather than craftsmen. The old merchant house was split up into specialized shops – some selling grocery products, and others selling hardware. This branch-related type of trade was predominant until the outbreak of World War I in 1914 (Kjær-Hansen, 1960). The industrialization of selling, reflecting the needs of market-expanding sales efforts due to mass production, did not really begin until 1920. It took some time until the structure of retail business eventually matched the needs of industrial production. In order to make selling more effective, retailers had to reconsider their assortment policy. The organization of retailing had to reflect the needs and wants of its customers rather than focus on supplier relations. According to Kjær-Hansen (1960, 9), this led to the replacement of the production or procurement-based product range with more sales-oriented assortments.

Interestingly, two opposing developments followed in the wake of this endeavour, a tendency towards specialization and a tendency towards integration. In the case of specialization, the shops had an ever diminishing product range. Clothing stores were divided into stores selling women's wear and others selling men's wear and, replacing grocery stores, tea, coffee, tobacco, soap and other specialized stores emerged. These stores developed alongside the specialized shops already in existence such as the baker, the butcher, fruit and vegetable stores, bookstores and so on. It was difficult, however, for these relatively small units to achieve economies of scale and efficient sales. As a result, integration of activities, through the combination of individual specialized stores or a variety of goods under the same roof, began to take place for the purpose of achieving economies of scale (Kjær-Hansen, 1960, 9).

In that regard, some important differences between shopping goods and convenience goods should be mentioned. The shopping goods area saw the development of section-divided stores – the beginning of what later became department stores. The same could not happen equally easily with respect to convenience goods because these goods were needed on a daily basis and were, therefore, strongly connected to people's residential situation. For this reason, grocery stores as well as other more specialized stores continued to be located in residential areas.

As ordinary people did not have cars at the time, the only way for these stores to achieve some economies of scale was by organizing buying and promotional activities in chain stores. This did happen in the 1920s and 1930s but only to a limited extent, which was at least partly due to regulatory restrictions on retailing. These restrictions did not hamper the consumer co-operative organization – FDB – which, in the late 1940s, became the first to establish self-service stores in Denmark.

The introduction of self-service stores was a contentious issue at the beginning of the 1950s. 'Supermarkets are not a form of store that can be transplanted to Denmark, maybe not to Europe at all so far' (quoted in Rostgaard, 2011, 239, from the report on a study tour in March and April 1952 on modern retail trade in the US – the participants in the trip were representatives from the retail business, consumer organizations and the shop workers' union). Only ten years later, self-service stores were widely accepted in Danish society.

According to Schröter (2005, 79), the first self-service store in Europe was opened by a storekeeper in the north German town of Osnabrück in 1938. In Sweden, the first self-service store opened in Stockholm in 1941. K.Ø. Andersen (2011) argues that Svenska Kooperativa Förbundet (The Swedish Cooperative Federation) established a self-service store in Sweden in 1946 and that Sweden was the first European country to adopt the concept of self-service. The two different time indications, 1941 and 1946, are both right because the general shortage of goods during the war resulted in lack of success and, as a result, quick cessation of activities started in 1941. In Norway, the first supermarket opened in 1960, and in Denmark, it started sometime after the end of World War II. As an experiment, the co-operative movement opened a self-service store in Copenhagen in 1947 (K.Ø. Andersen, 2011) and a complete self-service store was established in the city of Esbjerg in 1949. Actually, the local store manager from Esbjerg went on a study trip to Stockholm in 1948 (immediately after a study trip to the US) to visit representatives from the Swedish Co-operative Movement; and, before the opening of the self-service store in Esbjerg, two employees were sent on a three-month internship to the new self-service store in Stockholm (K.Ø. Andersen, 2011, 103).

The number of self-service stores increased dramatically in a very short time. In 1953, only four years after the introduction of the Esbjerg store, there were 117 self-service stores in Denmark. In 1959, the number had increased to 545, corresponding to about 7 per cent of the turnover in the range of goods suited for self-service (Rostgaard, 2011). These were evidently small compared to their American role model but, nevertheless, self-service was a fact and well received by consumers – and in the course of ten years they had undergone a transformation from a controversial issue to a fait accompli.

It is noteworthy that the co-operative movement was the frontrunner in the process of modernizing retail business in Sweden, Denmark and Norway and that much of their inspiration came from studying retail business in America. This is particularly evident in the Danish case, where FDB, The United Danish Co-operatives, participated in no less than 19 study trips to the USA between 1950 and 1955 (K.Ø. Andersen, 2011, 98) and where more than half of these trips related specifically to modern retailing.

The small private grocery stores, represented by De Samvirkende Købmandsforeninger i Danmark (The Co-operating Grocery Associations in Denmark), were more reluctant about the whole idea. In *Dansk Handelsblad,* 1949, a magazine published by the associations, the entire consumer co-operative movement and, by implication, its stores and outlets were accused of being 'socialists, introducing a state socialist version of trade and paving the road to a planned economy' (K.Ø. Andersen, 2011, 106).

At the time, the whole idea of self-service was a much contested issue. Rostgaard (2011) has an interesting interpretation of the issue at stake, one which adds new dimensions to the whole issue. The official point of view, represented by the Productivity Commission of Denmark's Ministry of Commerce, was that self-service meant rationalization of trade and cheaper goods. The core argument was the industrialization of retailing. The retail business itself pointed to increased turnover, more effective use of the workforce and, as a result, increased profits. The co-operative stores had a clear advantage in this regard, compared to the private stores, because they already had their own production facilities and, therefore, a more integrated system of distribution.

All these framings and perspectives, however, did not really include the voice of the consumer, the Danish housewife. As stated in Rostgaard (2011), much of the literature about retailing in the late 1940s and early 1950s was not well informed about the motivation of the housewife as a consumer. Insight into the topic was based on expert knowledge of a mainly managerial or economic nature but, in 1955, the Danish Gallup Institute carried out an investigation of 'What do housewives want from the retail trade'? The Gallup investigation was made on behalf of the Productivity Commission of the Ministry of Commerce and constituted one of the few sources of knowledge about the opinions of the housewives themselves on modern retailing (Rostgaard, 2011).

According to the Gallup investigation, 80 per cent of the respondents who actually did their shopping in self-service stores were quite satisfied. The reasons for their satisfaction were not just lower prices or timesaving but the fact that they could now make their own choice (without the intervention of a shop assistant) and pick the products they wanted: self-service stores 'are easier to shop in'; 'It is easier to remember when you see all the goods'; 'supply feels more free'; 'no pressure to buy'; 'free to recommend any specific items'; 'clean, everything is wrapped' – to the surprise of the investigators, lower prices were not an important issue (quotations from Rostgaard, 2011, 252). In a recent marketing management textbook (Kotler *et al.*, 2012, 757), the merits of self-service, 'the cornerstone of most retail operations', are primarily argued to be based on the customers' willingness to 'carry out their own "locate-compare-select process" to save money'. It seems that the 'locate-compare-select process' also has some intrinsic value in itself.

The report from the study trip in 1952 was concerned that the housewife might feel a bit uncertain without guidance from the grocer or the shop assistant but the Gallup investigation told a different story. According to Rostgaard's (2011) interpretation, the findings tell us that it was not, in fact, the self-service system as a rational way of distributing goods or the housewife's acceptance of the role model as a socially responsible buyer or consumer that was of importance. Instead, it was the concept of self-service itself – leaving room for unsupervised and autonomous choice – that appealed to the modern consumer. The time-saving aspect was also of importance because, during the 1950s, middle-class housewives became increasingly active on the labour market. So it also involved an element of emancipation from the traditional role of housewife. At least to some degree, this explanation is at odds with any more instrumental rational explanation of the merits of self-service.

Conclusion

The period from 1920 to 1960 was characterized by profound changes in the Danish marketing system. The second industrial revolution was followed by major changes in the distribution, advertising and market intelligence institutions in Denmark – a development process which Kjær-Hansen (1958) labelled 'the industrialization of selling'. Expanding the market in order to match mass production was much needed.

Denmark, and Scandinavia at large, saw the emergence and institutionalization of some brand new trades – the advertising agency and the market research agency. The advertising agency had its embryonic start in the late nineteenth century but changed and developed into its modern form in three phases from 1880 to 1945. Until the late 1930s, the market research agency was non-existent. The first market research agency in Denmark was established in 1939, but the shape of an independent trade did not really develop until the late 1950s. The third trade – retailing – also underwent major changes in the 1950s and, based on the perspective adopted in this chapter, it may represent the finishing touch in the gradual transition of Denmark into a modern mass consumption society. The co-operative movement was the frontrunner in the process of modernizing retail business, not only in Denmark but throughout Scandinavia. Both among the public and even among business people, there was some criticism and scepticism of the new institutions of advertising and market research but the notion of the recalcitrant consumer, suggested in Schröter (2005), did not really correspond to the way in which Danish consumers, i.e. Danish housewives, actually welcomed the transformation of the classical grocery store into larger self-service stores.

References

Agger, G. (1993) 'Fra fabrik til forførelse – om dansk reklames udvikling i perioden 1880–1920', in J.F. Jensen (ed.), *Reklame – Kultur,* Aalborg Universitetsforlag, Aalborg, pp. 129–64.

Andersen, K.Ø. (2011) 'FDB som amerikaniseringsagent in dansk detailhandel efter 1945' (FDB as Americanizer in Danish retail business after 1945), in N.A. Sørensen (ed.), *Det amerikanske forbillede? Dansk erhvervsliv og USA ca. 1920–1970*, Syddansk Universtitetsforlag, Odense, pp. 95–123.

Andersen, M.B. (2011) 'Forbrugeren på sigtekornet: Indførelsen af amerikanske markedsanalyse-teknologier i Danmark 1945–65' (The consumer in the crosshairs: The introduction of US market technologies in Denmark 1945–65), in N.A. Sørensen (ed.), *Det amerikanske forbillede? Dansk erhvervsliv og USA ca. 1920–1970.* Syddansk Universitetsforlag, Odense, pp. 267–303.

Fasce, F., and Bini, E. (2015) 'Irresistible empire or innocents abroad? American advertising agencies in post-war Italy', *Journal of Historical Research in Marketing*, 7/1, 7–30.

Geiger, T. (1943) *Kritik af Reklamen (A Critique of Advertising)*, Nyt Nordisk Forlag, Copenhagen.

Holbæk-Hansen, L. (1949) 'Nye samplingmetoder prøvet I Norden', *Det Danske Marked*, 8, 154–61.

Holbæk-Hansen, L. (1950) 'De vises sten i markedsforskningen: Indlæg om moderne samplings-metoder', *Det Danske Marked*, 9, 22–7.

Iulio, S. and Vinti, C. (2009) 'The Americanization of Italian advertising during the 1950s and the 1960s. Mediations, conflicts, and appropriations', *Journal of Historical Research in Marketing*, 1/2, 270-294.

Kapferer, C. (1956) *Market Research Methods in Europe*, Project 261, Paris: OEEC.

Kjær-Hansen, M. (1937) 'Videnskabelig kritik, svar til professor F. Zeuthen' (Scientific criticism, response to professor F. Zeuthen), *Nationaløkonomisk Tidsskrift*, 45, 106–25.

Kjær-Hansen, M. (1949) *Reklameforbruget i Danmark: En statistisk undersøgelse af det danske erhvervslivs absolute og relative reklameomkostninger (Advertising expenditure in Denmark: A statistical study of the absolute and relative advertising costs in Danish business)*, Einar Harcks Forlag, Copenhagen.

Kjær-Hansen, M. (1958) *Reklamebureauet i Danmark: En undersøgelse og vurdering af reklamenureauernes udvikling og placering i dansk erhvervsliv (The advertising agency in Denmark: A study and evaluation of the development and position of advertising agencies in the Danish business*), Einar Harcks Forlag, Copenhagen.

Kjær-Hansen, M. (1959) 'Revolution i detailhandelen', *Det Danske Marked*, 18, 193–204.

Kjær-Hansen, M. (1960) *Selvbetjeningsbutikkerne i Danmark: En analyse af den moderne udvikling i dagligvare-detailhandelen med særligt henblik på selvbetjeningssalget (Self-service stores in Denmark, an analysis of the modern development in the grocery retail sector with special emphasis on self-service sales)*, Handelsministeriets produktivitetsudvalg, Sekretariatet for Danmarks Erhvervsfond, Copenhagen.

Kjær-Hansen, M., and Olufsen P. (1974) *Reklamen i det 20. Århundredes Danmark (Advertising in the 20th-century Denmark)*, Nyt Nordisk Forlag, Copenhagen.

Kotler, P., Keller, K.L., Brady, M., Goodman, M., and Hansen, T. (2012) *Marketing Management* (2nd edn), Pearson Education, Harlow, Essex.

Malhotra, N.K., Birks, D.F., and Wills, P. (2012) *Marketing Research: An Applied Approach* (4th edn), Pearson Education, Harlow, Essex.

Parrild, S. (1956) 'Motivation research in marketing', *Dansk Reklame*, 7.

Rasmussen, B. (1979a) *En branche skabes: Markedsanalysens gennembrud og udvikling i Danmark 1959–1979*, Dansk Markesanalyse Forening, Copenhagen.

Rasmussen, B. (1979b) 'Dansk Markedsanalyse Forening 1959–1979', in B. Rasmussen (ed.), *En branche skabes: Markedsanalysens gennembrud og udvikling i Danmark 1959–1979*, Nyt Nordisk Forlag Arnold Busck, Viborg, pp. 11–49.

Rasmussen, W. (1979) 'Markedsanalyseinstitutter I Danmark 1959–1979', in B. Rasmussen (ed.), *En branche skabes: Markedsanalysens gennembrud og udvikling I Danmark 1959–1979*, Nyt Nordisk Forlag Arnold Busck, Viborg, pp. 50–66.

Rostgaard, M. (2011) 'Mrs. Consumer og fremvæksten af selvbetjeningsbutikker in Danmark', in N.A. Sørensen (ed.), *Det amerikanske forbillede?* Syddansk Universitetsforlag, Odense, pp. 239–65.

Schröter, H.G. (1998) 'Advertising in West Germany after World War II. A case of an Americanization', in H. G. Schröter and E. Moen (eds), *Une Américanisation des entreprises?* Entreprise et Histoire, Vol. 19, Editions Eska, Paris, pp. 15–33.

Schröter, H.G. (2005) *Americanization of the European Economy: A Compact Survey of American Economic Influence in Europe since the 1880s*, Dordrecht, Springer

Schwarzkopf, S. (2011) 'The consumer as "voter," "judge," and "jury": Historical origins and political consequences of a marketing myth', *Journal of Macromarketing*, 31/1, 8–18.

Sørensen, N.A. (2011) 'Det amerikanske forbillede?', in N.A. Sørensen (ed.), *Det amerikanske forbillede? Dansk erhvervsliv og USA ca 1920–1970*, Syddansk Universitetsforlag, Odense, pp. 7–17.

Thranow, I. (1956) 'Hvad er "Motivation Research"', *Dansk Reklame*, 7.

Whelan, B. (2014) 'American influences on Irish advertising and consumerism 1900–1960: Fashioning Irishwomen', *Journal of Historical Research in Marketing*, 6/1, 159–82.

24

The history of marketing in Russia

Karen F. A. Fox

Introduction

World interest in the Russian/Soviet economy focused on two major turning points in the country's history: the 1917 Bolshevik Revolution and creation of the Soviet Union, replacing capitalism with socialism; and the transition beginning in the mid-1980s from a country where marketing was anathema to one where marketing took on new scope and importance. Near the centenary of the 1917 Revolution, Russia again is in the spotlight. After decades of progress in marketing and standards of living, the Russian government has closed its markets to many imports, heightened internal control of mass media and education, linked the State to the Russian Orthodox Church and placed limits on political freedoms.

This chapter is a chronological presentation of Russia's marketing history, divided into periods: early Russian trade; the nineteenth century to World War I; the war, the Bolshevik Revolution, and the civil war, followed by the New Economic Policy (NEP); the Stalin era 1928–53, including World War II; the Soviet Union after Stalin; from *Perestroika* to 2000; and the period 2000–15.

Widely held myths about Russian marketing are that marketing was primitive before the twentieth century and that during the Soviet era there was no marketing at all. This chapter reveals a long history of trade and marketing in Russia chronologically to the present. Marketing refers to the activities involved in creating a good or service, in packaging, pricing and promoting it, and delivering it to selected markets. In the nineteenth century Russia experienced rapid development and modernization, production of a great variety of industrial and consumer goods and the establishment of elegant shops and department stores, amid an explosion of advertising signs, posters and mass media.

The twentieth century brought the jolt of civil and World Wars, and a revolution that ended with the Bolsheviks in total control of the newly formed Soviet Union. The 1917 Revolution and its aftermath broke the connections to the larger world and stunted the country's development for decades. The Soviet period saw not only wars and revolution, but also expropriations, starvation, destruction, terror and millions of deaths. The number of Soviet citizens who died due to war, repression and starvation under Stalin will never be known to the nearest million (Dyadkin, 1983; Naimark, 2010). Except for a brief period in the 1920s, the Soviet state outlawed capitalist marketing and replaced it with socialist substitutes. Modern marketing terminology and overt implementation of marketing principles largely disappeared, to be replaced by socialist terms and practices. Soviet consumers consistently experienced product shortages, poor quality and inadequate assortments, deficient retail infrastructure necessitating queuing and a reduced standard of living. Improvement efforts fell short, and led to the rise of illegal, black-market enterprises to fill the gaps.

Present-day Russia emerged from centuries of shifting boundaries. The 'Russian Empire' refers to the country from 1721 until 1917, which over centuries incorporated vast territories through alliance and conquest, containing more than 170 distinct nationalities. 'The Soviet Union' or the USSR refers to the country between the 1917 Revolution and 1991. During the Soviet period several areas of the Russian Empire were designated 'Soviet republics' and several adjoining countries were added under the same rubric. When the Soviet Union was disbanded the republics became independent, the former Russian Federative Socialist Republic became 'Russia' or the 'Russian Federation'.

In 1990 the Soviet Union covered one-sixth of the earth's land surface, and contained 288.6 million people (US Bureau of the Census, 1991, 1–2). The breakup of the Soviet Union in 1991 still left the Russian Federation the largest country in the world, but with half its former population. Distribution has been hampered by patterns of settlement, harsh climate and weak infrastructure, including warehousing. Other than rail, surface transportation remains dependent on an inadequate highway and secondary road network.

The term *torgovlya* – trade – was used for exchange of raw materials and goods throughout Russian history. In the 1970s the term 'marketing', written in Cyrillic, was borrowed directly into Russian. A marketing manager or marketing specialist is a *marketolog*. Advertising in Russian/Soviet use is *reklama*, from the Latin verb *reclamare*, meaning to call out. Some Soviet trade managers, particularly foreign trade specialists, read Western periodicals on marketing, retailing and advertising and even reprinted and distributed articles on these subjects translated into Russian, but such materials were often secured in restricted-access reading rooms (Fox *et al.*, 2008, 154). This chapter will use the term 'trade' when it was used historically (including most of the Soviet era), and use the term 'marketing' as it entered into use in the Soviet Union. The term 'marketing' also will be used to refer to tools and concepts of modern marketing, as many Western observers translated what they saw in the Soviet Union into marketing categories.

From 1917 Soviet-era trade/marketing was tightly controlled by the state, loosening only during the period of the New Economic Policy in the 1920s and the period of *perestroika* beginning in the late 1980s. The regime imposed the ideology and established structures and procedures for all aspects of trade, including advertising and foreign trade marketing. From diaries, reports, museum exhibits, archival materials, newspapers, posters, books, articles and other publications, this chapter describes Russian and Soviet trade, marketing activities and the challenges consumers faced in provisioning their lives and realizing their material aspirations.

Early Russian trade

A millennium ago Russian lands already were criss-crossed by important trade routes, along the Danube and Dnieper Rivers, connecting with the Black, Azov and Caspian Seas (Chulkov, 1788). The earliest active traders were Varangians (Vikings) to the north, seeking to trade with centres of wealth and high culture to the south, including Greek tribes and

Byzantium (Hodges, 1988). Novgorod, Kievan Rus' and the Grand Duchy of Moscow were early centres of political and economic power that ultimately came under the control of Moscow.

Novgorod ('new city') was unique: an independent republic, a wealthy city governed by powerful merchants and a trade hub for two major trade routes through Russian lands. A combined river and land corridor passed through Novgorod for trade between the Varangians in the north and the Black Sea; and another that followed the Volga River. In addition, Novgorod had the good fortune to be located at the north-western end of the Silk Road from China, and also controlled the trade of Russian furs to Europe. In the late twelfth century Novgorod became the eastern entrepôt of the most significant trade alliance of the era, the Hanseatic League, which stretched from London through the Baltic Sea and controlled much of the international trade in that network (Halliday, 2009). The Novgorod Republic eventually controlled a large territory from the Baltic Sea to the northern Ural Mountains.

Kievan Rus', surrounding present-day Kiev, became prosperous in the tenth century, exporting furs, flax, wax, honey and slaves, and importing spices, silk, precious stones and metal weapons (Magocsi, 2010, 96; Moss, 2005, 37). Kievan Rus' controlled three trade routes, providing access as far as Baghdad, Constantinople, Greek settlements and present-day Central Europe.

The Grand Duchy of Moscow conquered the Novgorod Republic in 1478 and consolidated its control over other lands, including the greatly weakened Kievan Rus'. From 1547 Tsar Ivan the Terrible became the ruler of Russia, and Moscow became the political and mercantile centre of Russian lands.

By the mid-sixteenth century some London merchants, recognizing the commercial potential of Russia, formed a joint-stock company, the Muscovy Company (also called the Russia Company), and received a royal monopoly over trade between England and Russia. First-person accounts from English sea captains often described Russian merchants and traders of the period as devious, crafty and dishonest, characterizations that endured for centuries afterward. Johan Kielberger, a merchant who travelled to Russia with an embassy of the king of Sweden in 1673–4, provided detailed lists of Russian exports and imports, with quantities and prices. From Europe Russia received such luxury goods as pearls, diamonds, silk and Venetian velvet (Kielberger, 1820).

Hellie listed the vast array of domestic and imported products available in seventeenth-century Russia, including price data for more than 1,500 commodities ranging from agricultural products to perfumes, spices and fabrics (Hellie, 1999). Rural peasants, most of the Russian population, engaged in agriculture, produced most of what was needed within the village or estate, and obtained a range of essential goods in the marketplace.

In 1697 Peter the Great took 300 associates to learn about technology and trade in Western Europe and England (Florinsky, 1964, 166). Peter's new capital St Petersburg, founded 1703, attracted industrial enterprises, trade workshops and markets, and replaced Moscow as the country's primary centre of foreign trade. By 1825 the city handled 70 per cent of the Russian Empire's imports and 50 per cent of its exports (Rieber, 1982, 22). Sea transport required shipbuilding materials; urban development depended on all manner of construction materials and supplies; and the aristocratic court – relocated from Moscow – created demand for luxury products, both local and foreign.

The nineteenth century to World War I (1800–1913)

Urban development and industrialization progressed rapidly in this period, reliant on imported capital equipment and consumer goods from the West, paid for by exports of grain and timber from Russia's countryside (Rutland, 1985, 68). Urban and rural populations were growing. Rural peasants depended on subsistence-level agriculture which required arable land that was in short supply. Most villages had 'an active sector of small traders and craftsmen', and some peasants found work in town for years at a time (Rutland, 1985, 67).

The urban marketing landscape

Retail businesses in cities and towns included small shops, street vending and open-air and covered markets (Hilton, 2012, 16–19). Significant retail centres were constructed as early as the eighteenth century and some are still in use. For example, Gostiny Dvor, an indoor mall in St Petersburg, opened in 1785; the fashionable Passazh opened nearby in 1848. The new premises of the Upper Trading Rows (later named GUM) on Red Square in Moscow were completed in 1893. Merchants could get advice from such handbooks as *Practical Advice from Trade Experience*, published in Odessa (Galperin, 1912). Full of creative, modern ideas, the book's headings include 'Store windows as advertising', 'Advertising to women', 'Poster advertising', 'How to advertise your business in restaurants' and 'Using humour in advertising'.

The rapidly growing nineteenth-century merchant class consisted of traditional merchant families and lesser nobility, as well as peasants who were able to move up. Former peasants 'lent a less refined aspect' to the merchant class and probably exacerbated the intelligentsia's disdain for merchants as a category (Ransel, 2009, p. xxiv). Literature amplified these negative attitudes. For example, Alexander Ostrovky's popular plays reinforced stereotypes of Russian merchants, portraying 'habitually dishonest traders, tyrannical merchant fathers, and dowerless merchant daughters sold to the highest bidder … [which] left an indelible mark on Russian consciousness' (Ransel, 2009, p. xxv). These images haunted the New Economic Policy (NEP) period in the 1920s, and shaped Soviet and even post-Soviet attitudes towards commerce and marketing.

Ubiquitous advertising in urban areas included posters, store signs, trade cards, hand bills, advertising in print media and business directories. From its inception in 1860 the mass-circulation newspapers and magazines solicited commercial advertising, mainly small announcements, and depended on this advertising revenue (West, 2011, 33). Advertising agencies functioned as placement services, not creating copy but simply soliciting ads and payment from enterprises and then delivering the ads and money, minus a commission, to newspapers and magazines (West, 2011, 34–7). The agencies also promoted the importance of advertising to reluctant business owners, some of whom 'adhered to the common belief that advertising was only necessary for shoddy goods and was used by swindlers' (West, 2011, 48).

Western enterprises, including American firms Singer and International Harvester, established manufacturing and sales operations in Russia. The Singer Sewing Machine Company had intended to sell its older products to the Russian market, but found a region eager for its latest technology (Carstensen, 2012, 87–8). Singer eventually created its own Russian sales organization, extended credit to individual purchasers, built a factory near Moscow, and in 1904 opened its Art Nouveau headquarters in St Petersburg. International Harvester built its own retail locations and purchased factory premises. Despite challenges the company continued to operate in the Soviet Union into the 1930s (Carstensen, 2012, 149, 226–7; Clawson, 1976; Sibley, 1996).

Russia as a developed country

In the second half of the nineteenth century, Russia was second only to the United States in total railroad mileage (Lyons, 1967, 76), and industrial, financial, and retail activity was vibrant. On the eve of World War I Russia was poised to become the economic peer to the major powers of Europe and the United States. Economic reports, government statistics, photographs and publications of the time demonstrate a high level of development: 'By 1913 [the Russian Empire] ranked fifth in the world league table of industrial powers, with an engineering industry larger than that of France' (Rutland, 1985, 68).

A visitor to Moscow or St Petersburg in the late nineteenth century would see avenues lined with shops with huge signs, offering a full range of imported and Russian-manufactured goods (Mineeva and Piotrovsky, 2003). Late-nineteenth-century business directories list hundreds of foreign-born entrepreneurs in St Petersburg. Russians of means in major cities had access to a variety of high-quality household furnishings, clothing and other goods, many of them made in the Russian Empire. Such was the material, commercial landscape in St Petersburg, the capital of the Russian Empire, and in Moscow at the turn of the twentieth century, soon to be swept away.

War, revolution and the New Economic Policy (1914–1928)

The Russian Empire entered World War I in August 1914 with the largest army in the world. By the end of 1917 the Bolsheviks had seized power, the Tsar was a captive in exile, 2.5 million Russians had died, nearly 4 million soldiers were in German hands, and the economy was in tatters. In 1918 the Soviet Union exited the war with Germany. The war debt and the cost of reconstruction were immense.

Despite the war's consequences, Lyons (1967, 79) described the Russian Empire in 1917 as 'a young but vigorous economy, with experienced manpower, technological literacy, an industrious population, an educated class of high intellectual caliber – in a gigantic country well-endowed with natural resources'. William Beable travelled throughout most of the Russian Empire in 1916 as the organizer of the Anglo-Russian Trade Commission 'for the purpose of investigating on the spot the possibilities for British manufacturers in Russia' and reported that there were opportunities everywhere (Beable, 1918, 1, 47).

The impact of the Bolshevik takeover

In October 1917 the Bolsheviks seized power. They acted quickly to bring the economy under state control. The Bolsheviks declared 'war on the market' and 'expropriation of the bourgeoisie', followed by steps to put retailers out of business through heavy taxes and eviction from commercial premises (Hessler, 2004, 24–5). The aim was to nationalize all commerce and production – foreign and domestic – and all distribution and retailing. Foreign trade was placed under the central government. They put in place an austerity programme under the rubric of 'War Communism'. Rationing was introduced for most food commodities. Private property was appropriated by the state.

The upheaval of the October Revolution and War Communism brought hunger and starvation, even in major cities, among all social classes (Sorokin, 1950, 229, 281–91;

Patenaude, 2002, 17–18). In 1918 department stores and other retail outlets were nationalized (Hilton, 2012, 21); by 1919 only 133 of Moscow's 3,409 closed retail stores had reopened (Hilton, 2004, 943). Small merchants moved outdoors to makeshift bazaars. 'Bagging' – individual traders carrying food, fuel and other goods between city and countryside – played a significant role in the survival of urban households (Hessler, 2004, 35). Large-scale industry production fell to less than 20 per cent of 1913 levels. International commerce was throttled by the breakdown of longstanding financial and trade ties. The cancellation of Tsarist-era loans caused bank failures and currency became worthless.

Introduction of the New Economic Policy and private enterprise

The New Economic Policy (NEP) was introduced by Vladimir Lenin in 1921 as an urgent response to impending catastrophe, to foster greater production and take the pressure off the inadequate network of official stores (Rutland, 1985, 72). The NEP authorized would-be shopkeepers, artisans and peasants to engage in private production and trade. The policy was politically controversial, a 'retreat to capitalism' that violated the Communist claim that private property and private enterprise should be swept away (Hoover, 1931, 227; Tolstikova, 2007, 46). Many Communists feared that private traders would enrich themselves at the expense of the goals of the revolution (Cox, 2006, 129), but the NEP temporarily returned near-normalcy to everyday life (Harvard Project, 1950–3).

While state enterprises and state stores were becoming more important in the 1920s, 'the private market, far from vanishing, represented the most important source of supply for the Russian people' and was essential to assist in the post-war recovery (Ball, 1987, 6). By 1927 there were 551,600 retail establishments, of which nearly 75 per cent were privately owned (Osokina et al., 2001, 5). Many 'Nepmen' had been businesspeople before the Revolution and readily took up their former occupations and found eager customers. They were able to charge much higher prices than state stores because they had better quality merchandise and actually had products to sell when state stores had empty shelves.

State retailing

The official state structures of production and retailing continued to evolve during and after the NEP. Many kinds of state retail stores operated, including shops tied to specific state industries or location-specific trusts, such as Moscow's Mosselprom Trust with its own network of shops, kiosks, restaurants and individual sellers carrying its diversified production of candies, tobacco, toys, beer and other items (Hoover, 1931, 131).

Some large Soviet retail stores were established in premises of 'the most capacious, elegant, well-appointed, and renowned commercial venues' of the previous era (Hilton, 2004, 946). The aim was 'to install in the Soviet Union a commercial aesthetic of elegance, quality, selection, value, cleanliness, attentive customer service, and cultured leisure and educational activities, similar to that being elaborated in Western Europe and the United States' (Hilton, 2004, 946). Official state stores included rural, urban and transport workers consumer co-operative shops which obtained their goods from wholesale centres that purchased from state enterprises and workshops. The workshops, some quite small, produced 'an astonishing variety of products' and some were highly successful, 'aided by a goods famine in a country that is straining every nerve to increase its industrial production' (Hoover, 1931, 237).

In the 1920s Soviet leaders condemned materialism as 'bourgeois and hedonistic', and praised production over consumption (Randall, 2008, 8). Few people had the means to pursue shopping as pleasure. Most official stores were dismal and bare, and required queuing to make basic purchases. Yet most consumers joined one of the three types of co-operative stores at the cost of a month's wages in order to purchase restricted (in short supply) commodities at co-op prices, which might be a third or a quarter cheaper than the prices in private shops (Hoover, 1931, 229). Membership in a consumer co-operative was restricted to employees in state enterprises, workshops or farms. Nepmen and dispossessed *kulaks* ('rich' peasants) were excluded (Hoover, 1931, 240). Communist Party members, especially in the upper echelons, had access to special stores with better assortments and higher quality goods, perquisites they lost if they were expelled for violating party discipline (Fitzpatrick, 1999, 19).

Advertising during the NEP

During the NEP advertising appeared in government publications, including *Pravda* and *Izvestia*. Some criticized such advertising for encouraging bourgeois consumerism, but Lenin pragmatically supported it because paid advertising underwrote publications (Cox, 2006, 124). A network of state and semi-state advertising agencies emerged, and by 1925 more than 50 Moscow agencies, employing more than 700 people, were selling advertising to state and even to private enterprises (Cox, 2006, 124–5). Most state enterprises considered their ad purchases as an obligation with no commercial value, because the ads appeared in publications of no interest to their intended consumers (Cox, 2006, 126).

Advertisers began to discuss how socialist advertising should differ from capitalist advertising (Cox 2006, 126). Socialist advertising was propaganda to shape the socialist identities of individual citizens and civilize them by promoting their improvement through purchase of such modern products as watches, light bulbs and insurance (Cox, 2006, 130, 138). By 1925 state enterprise directors concluded that such advertising was not productive and stopped advertising that solely supported publications (Cox, 2006, 143–4). Ad agency managers sought more effective advertising, and some argued for advertising campaigns integrating all forms of communication – newspapers, magazines, posters, flyers, billboards, public transit and even radio and film (Cox, 2006, 145). They observed that ads in Germany and the United States focused on pleasure and personal happiness, not on political imagery and duty, and they even proposed learning from these foreign advertising experts (Cox, 2006, 132–3).

The trade journal *Zhurnalist* in 1928 stated that Soviet ads should 'lead the consumer … showing the fastest way to the goods they need'; 'to direct the masses and to educate them in the problems of the industry'; and 'to be a branch of real art' (Tolstikova, 2007, 48). Revolutionary iconography dominated advertising in this period, presenting images of workers and peasants, Soviet symbols, and appeals to build a utopian society (Cox, 2006, 122). Advertising was hostile toward Nepmen, depicting them as evil outsiders and dishonest speculators, and visually representing them as overfed and conspicuously wealthy (Cox, 2006, 139)

The fate of Nepmen and the end of the NEP

Nepmen at first received grudging accommodation from the state as a necessary evil, but from the mid-1920s they were subjected to administrative harassment and excluded from buying supplies and raw materials from state-owned enterprises (Rutland, 1985, 89). Some highly successful Nepmen publicly flaunted their wealth, rousing negative public sentiment. Citizens were exhorted to patronize state stores as a patriotic duty; posters urged them 'Don't

Buy in Private Shops'. By 1928 the property of Nepmen was being confiscated. They were expelled from state housing and denied ration cards, and their children were unable to enter university (Ball, 1987, 76–7). They lost the right of employment and were left to fend for themselves as 'enemies of the people' (Fitzpatrick, 1986, 201–2). In Moscow house searches sought out clandestine private shops: 'In the near future, all these private entrepreneurs will be brought to court, many of them have been arrested, and the case[s] will be heard in a special judicial chamber. *Of course, many will be sent to distant parts of the USSR*' [1930s document cited in Fitzpatrick, 1986, 203). Some died. By the early 1930s all traces of the NEP were eliminated.

Some Nepmen and their families moved away and tried to hide their backgrounds in order to find employment. Some returned to villages where they worked as artisans or craftsmen or in agriculture. Others managed to move into the rapidly growing state trade sector: in the 1930s as many as a third of trade employees in state enterprises had backgrounds in private trade (Fitzpatrick, 1986, 208). Ball (1987) called the Nepmen 'Russia's last capitalists', until Gorbachev's *perestroika* starting in 1985 again legalized private enterprise.

The Stalin era (1928–1953)

The NEP came to an end because Stalin wanted to eliminate peasants and private enterprise as independent forces that might oppose the regime's drive for massive industrialization (Rutland, 1985, 76). Socialist solutions were to replace all vestiges of capitalism (Hoover, 1931, 2). But Marx and Lenin had left Stalin no blueprint for the structure of a socialist economy, or concrete guidance on how it would function in practice (Gregory, 2001, 11; Randall, 2008, 2). Socialist orthodoxy held that marketing was unnecessary because central planning would determine the right mix and quantity of products to produce and the correct prices to charge for them. Stores operating under state direction and control through central planning would provide more efficient distribution than going through what Lenin condemned as 'an abyss of small middlemen who also are ignorant to market conditions [which] creates both superfluous shipping and excessive buying' (Lenin, 1947, 36, cited by Felker, 1966, 23).

The 'socialist experiment'

The centrepiece of the socialist solution was to be a detailed programme carried out by government agencies in Moscow, in a series of 'five-year plans' (Hirsch, 1961). Calvin B. Hoover described the First Five-Year Plan as 'a grandiose program for the industrialization of the country, for the establishment of a solid point of support for the World Revolution' and a plan that 'shall be accomplished without regard to the suffering and privation which the enormous capital investment provided for in the Plan entails' (Hoover, 1931, 306).

The First Five-Year Plan focused on rapid industrialization, which in turn depended on feeding the influx of urban workers. Peasant landholdings were seized and peasants who resisted were exiled or shot. Expropriation of seeds, animals and farm equipment left peasants without inputs for the next planting. Thus the 1930s was 'a decade of enormous privation and hardship for the Soviet people, much worse than the 1920s', with harvest failures leading to breadlines, movement from rural areas to cities contributing to overcrowding, and rationing creating a struggle for the necessities of life (Fitzpatrick, 1999, 41). The persistent gap between plan and production almost always left shortages that resulted in queuing, rationing and a flourishing black market (Hilton, 2012, 4).

Fulfilling the First Five-Year Plan required hard currency to purchase heavy equipment in the international market. The Soviet Union sold gold bullion from its treasury; commandeered gold from private citizens; set up *Torgsin* shops where scarce food items and goods were sold at inflated prices in exchange for gold, silver, diamonds and hard currency; and sent people to forced labour camps to mine for gold (Tzouliadis, 2008, 164, 167; Osokina, 2006). Stalin sold thousands of treasures from Russia's museums (Smorodinskaya *et al.*, 2007, 38). In the 1930s Stalin's agents also imported skilled American machinists from the Ford Motor Car factory, as well as other specialists to support the industrialization effort (Robinson with Slevin, 1988; Clawson, 1976, 204, n. 1).

Central planners gave scant attention to product selection, quality and quantity, yet the regime's grandiose claim was that consumer-goods production should have a higher purpose: to disseminate socialist values (Randall, 2008, 11). Certain products were emphasized as signs of modernity and *kul'turnost'*, cultured living, uplifting the tastes of workers and peasants and enhancing their self-concept and identity as Soviet citizens. One such category was cosmetics, including soaps, creams and makeup (Kravets and Sandikci, 2013). Skilful marketing – through product formulation and differentiation, packaging and media advertising – was employed to emphasize the attractiveness and value of the products, and differential pricing attracted diverse consumers. For example, affordable quality soap encouraged peasant workers to adopt better hygiene habits.

Soviet retailing

In the 1930s, as the regime reasserted its control of virtually all assets and production, the state became responsible for meeting all of the everyday needs of Soviet citizens. Surprisingly, this time the state aspired not only to meet citizens' basic needs, but also 'to create a Soviet commercial culture that would rival Western standards' (Gorsuch, 2011, 136).

The Soviet retail network in the 1930s was small compared with advanced industrial countries and movement from the countryside to the cities required retail expansion (Randall, 2008, 4). Outlets included state stores and co-operative stores, as well as hard-currency-only *Torgsin* stores (1931–6), and *kolkhoz* (collective farm) markets where their products were sold at higher prices than at state stores (Davies, 1997, 141). Commission stores sold used goods, charging sellers a commission; *Lombard* – pawn shops – also operated. Rationed consumer goods were mainly available through 'closed distribution', in stores and cafeterias linked to one's workplace (Fitzpatrick, 1999, 56).

Even as product shortages and dismal store conditions persisted, Soviet retailing aspired to create 'a modern, rational, and hygienic retail environment where employees provided customers with attentive and friendly service, new retail amenities and services, creative displays, and a wide variety of goods' (Randall, 2008, 39). Stores were to have better equipment, well-organized stock, attractive displays and such innovations as selling items by the piece rather than by weight, and even offering self-service so that consumers could inspect items more easily and pay the salesperson directly (Randall, 2008, 54–8).

Gaps in available product assortment created lucrative black market opportunities. A 32-year-old engineer stated, 'I have known many people with a high university education, who could work as a good specialist in the economy, but in place of that they get some job in the Soviet trade system, because there is always the chance of black marketing', siphoning off goods for private sale and supplementary income (Harvard Project, 1950–2, Subject 25).

One retail practice that persisted into the 2000s was the *kassa* (for cashier or cash box) system. This required consumers to select an item, viewed from the other side of a counter or presented by the salesperson, then get a slip of paper with the price, queue to pay a cashier and retrieve a receipt, and finally return to the original counter to present the receipt and receive the purchase (Randall, 2008, 58). The *kassa* system was intended to reduce theft and graft, and to improve efficiency by having trained cashiers (Randall, 2008, 58).

It is important to keep in mind that these developments in marketing and retailing took place in the highly unsettled atmosphere of Stalin's intensifying political repression. The Great Terror – 1936–8 – began with a vast purge of Stalin's political opponents and extended to an irrational bloodbath of 'enemies of the people', including thousands of priests, Soviet military officers, noted cultural figures, kulaks, criminals and random individuals of all social classes – even children – killed to meet quotas (Kishkovksy, 2007).

Conditions after World War II

World War II's fierce battles on Soviet territory traumatized the population and required massive reconstruction. Rationing ended in 1947 (Dixon and Polyakov, 1998, 173). The late 1940s also saw a rapid rise in per capita personal consumption and increased consumer goods production – improvements which brought the Soviet standard of living approximately to 1914 levels (Skurski, 1983, 4). Some commercial advertising returned, even receiving the official imprimatur of Minister of Trade Anastas Mikoyan in 1953: 'Sophisticated trade calls for well organized advertising' to give consumers information about what is available; to create new demands, new tastes and needs; to promote new goods and explain their use (Szeplaki, 1974, 14).

The Soviet Union after Stalin (1954–1985)

Stalin's death in 1953 brought the end of terror and most political repression. Soviet consumers who had persevered through revolution, civil war, famine and World War II expected to achieve a semblance of stability and normalcy, and were looking for products to purchase with their earnings from state employment and pensions (Goldman, 1963, 87). In this period 'the production of consumer goods was raised to record levels, the variety of products was expanded and many consumer durables common in the West made their first appearance in the USSR' (Skurski, 1983, 4).

Comparing Soviet and Western marketing

Supervised group travel abroad gave some Soviet citizens access to foreign goods, giving the lie to propaganda claims that Soviet products were the best in the world (Gorsuch, 2011, 155–6). The Soviet Union opened its borders to receive more foreign visitors and their hard currency, and to create positive impressions of the Soviet way of life. Visitors included marketers interested in seeing Soviet products, advertising, promotional tools and channels of distribution, and in comparing Soviet and Western marketing.

Western economists and marketing experts, mostly academics, produced a flurry of books and articles starting in the 1960s of which the work of Marshall Goldman stands out for its depth and coverage for over a half century. In 'The marketing structure in the Soviet Union' Goldman presented changes in the overall structure of internal trade from the 1917 Revolution until late 1958, and the structure of internal trade from the city level up to the Ministry of Trade for each individual republic (Goldman, 1961). A table of 'Organization of the Ministry of Trade of the RSFSR, January, 1959' listed government offices responsible for pricing, warehousing, retailing, trade fairs and advertising, and Goldman stated that '[t]here are other marketing activities and functions over which the Ministry of Trade has ultimate administrative authority' (Goldman, 1963, 23–4, citing *Sovietskaia Torgovlia*). In the absence of official Soviet use of marketing terminology, Western authors aimed to identify marketing-like activities and to apply capitalist terms wherever appropriate.

Some Western authors speculated that marketing in the Soviet Union and marketing in the United States were moving in the same direction. Barksdale *et al.* (1979, 258) aimed to show 'recent developments that suggest a gradual convergence of thought in the two countries'. The 1970s consumer movement in the United States had revealed marketing abuses, which in turn led to passage of consumer protection legislation, which the authors termed 'a significant increase in government control of marketing' (Barksdale *et al.*, 1979, 261). Hanson (1974) perceived signs that the Soviet Union was moving towards the Western model of advertising. Goldman remarked that some aspects of US marketing during the 1973 oil shortage, including rationing, were handled in ways that reminded him of the Soviet Union (Goldman, 1975, 42), however he was quite aware of stark differences in the outcomes of the two systems (Goldman, 1960).

In contrast, Greer believed that 'the current hypotheses of convergence between the Soviet Union and the United States [are not] particularly convincing' (Greer, 1973, 184–5). Felker (1966) contrasted the evolution of the marketing concept in post-World War II Europe and the United States with what he observed in the Soviet Union. For him the Soviet Union reflected the rise of the '*anti*-marketing concept': the market economy had been replaced with 'a highly centralized, authoritative, and planned system of economics that substituted almost complete planners' sovereignty for that of the consumer' (Felker, 1966, 3).

Pricing

Hirsch (1961) and Goldman (1963) addressed the Soviet pricing system, which bore little resemblance to demand- or cost-based pricing in capitalist countries. (There was no competition.) Wholesale prices were composed of 'planned costs', namely operating cost, turnover tax and planned profit (or planned subsidies). Land cost (or imputed rent) and interest were not considered. Turnover tax and planned profit were in fact both payments that went to the state. The turnover tax was much higher for consumer goods than for producer goods, and bore no relationship to costs (Hirsch, 1961, 168). In fact, one of the difficulties in central planning was to determine cost data as a basis for pricing at various channel levels.

Goldman observed that retail prices were generally twice the wholesale price, with about 20 per cent allocated to distribution costs, some for planned profit, and the remainder as turnover tax (Goldman, 1963, 84). The turnover tax provided half the state's revenue and was varied to regulate demand (Goldman, 1963, 86–7). In a closed economic system Soviet planners had good measures of total disposable income and also predicted the available output based on formal plans. Thus final retail prices could be set to 'absorb as much of the [consumer's] excess purchasing power as possible and create a balance between supply and demand' (Goldman, 1963, 87). The turnover tax rate also was varied to encourage or discourage purchase of certain goods: e.g. low for books and children's items, high for jewellery and other luxury goods (Goldman, 1963, 89–91). These prices also could differ from one locality to another.

Advertising through the 1960s

An advertising bureau was opened in Moscow in 1957 and others were established throughout the Soviet Union; in 1960 they were integrated under one authority (Markham, 1964, 34). *Vechernyaya Moskva – Evening Moscow –* was one of few newspapers with advertising; ads appeared on the last page of the four-page issue. During the 1960s advertising caught on and was used to a greater extent by retailers, but messages remained formulaic and lacked 'vigor and emphasis': for example 'the quality of this herring is in no way inferior to other brands of herring' (Markham, 1964, 34), not much better than ad messages of the 1950s such as 'Buy canned goods', 'Buy cakes, sweet and plentiful', and 'Save money in savings banks' (Levine, 1959, 188).

Product assortment and availability

In the late 1960s the Soviet economy entered a downturn. Essential goods were in short supply at a time when consumers had growing expectations and greater purchasing power. Despite increased production, factories were not able to keep up with official production plans and consumer demand. For example, between 1966 and 1970 only 26 per cent of the cars, 50 per cent of foodstuffs and cheese, and 40 per cent of trams planned were actually produced, with significant shortfalls in many other product categories (Harvey, 2004, 198). From the 1950s through the 1980s queuing for hours, even overnight, was common to purchase a refrigerator or even a sought-after book (Kanevsky, 2015).

Product assortment was paltry; for example, a store might offer two shades of lipstick; a food shop might offer stacks of canned fish but lack basic staples. In response, the 'second economy' – black-marketing and all the other non-state, illegal ways of obtaining and selling goods at higher prices – continued to flourish (Dixon and Polyakov, 1998, 178–9). Since most essential and highly desired products were scarce or impossible to find, buying in this way became an accepted if resented way of life.

New product development

Independently some Soviet manufacturers created 'new products' by reverse-engineering successful Western products. 'The whole process was shockingly haphazard', often depending on some consumer product brought back from overseas by 'one Communist functionary or another', which was then copied and produced by a Soviet factory: 'Those who could draw were put in charge of logos, packaging, and other frivolities' (Idov, 2011, 8).

Soviet-made products attractive to the world market could bring hard currency. In April 1973 a new reform campaign was launched to enable Soviet enterprises to trade more competitively in international markets. Deputy Minister of Foreign Trade Nikolai Smelyakov enthusiastically moved ahead, signing a contract between Raymond Loewy, a world-recognized industrial designer, and the All-Union Research Institute of Industrial Design 'that puts the Loewy talent to work designing Russian cars, motorcycles, cameras, watches, refrigerators, tractors, large-capacity hydrofoil vessels and sports-type hydrofoils for two to three persons' that would appeal to consumers beyond the Soviet Union (Farnsworth, 1973, 67, 78). The failure of Loewy's firm ended this collaboration (Loewy Archives, 1903–82).

Soviet factory managers generally resisted new product development that could risk fulfilment of the formal plans on which their bonuses depended (Richman, 1963). A factory manager who fulfilled 98 per cent of the plan received no bonus at all, and the factory's workers likewise received no bonuses, which typically equalled an additional month's pay (Rutland, 1985, 120).

Product issues in the 1970s

Greer (1973) reviewed the conditions of marketing in the early 1970s and addressed product, price, promotion and distribution, including retailing. A key issue was the shortage of complementary goods – there might be plenty of cameras, but a shortage of photographic paper – and of assortments, such as a variety of sizes and colours of socks and stockings (Greer, 1973, 4, 25). Mail order retailing was small but growing, and instalment credit was available for large purchases (Greer, 1973, 57–9).

Lazer (1986) employed a marketing framework to identify and analyse all the marketing-related stories published in the official Communist Party newspaper *Pravda* for five calendar years, 1977–81. The largest category – comprising 22 per cent of the 737 items – was 'the inability of producers to provide consumers with products and services of the desired quality', with one *Pravda* report estimating that 30 per cent of all consumer products were rejected as unsaleable (Lazer, 1986, 124). Efforts to predict demand fell short because advising a factory to manufacture a specific product did not preclude other factories from doing the same, thus flooding the market (Lazer, 1986, 123).

Advertising in the 1970s and 1980s

Advertising in the Soviet Union in 1970–1 included shop window displays, outdoor neon signage, catalogues, cinema and TV advertising, and press (Hanson, 1974, 32–5, 59). Furthermore, 'the consumer can often choose between alternative branded versions of the same kinds of goods in a given shop or a given shopping area' (Hanson, 1974, 57).

From the late 1950s to 1991 Eesti Reklaamfilmi – Estonia Commercial Film Company (ERF) – set the pace as the first major Soviet producer of video commercials. The company won national and international awards and had accounts throughout the Soviet Union, providing product placement (a Soviet cosmonaut using a tube of marmalade in space), and ads with beautiful women. Despite severe product shortages, the firm was hired to create video ads for products so scarce and desirable that no promotion was needed, for excess and unwanted products, for products that did not yet exist (and thus could not be shown on screen), and even for some products so futuristic they never could be produced (*The Gold Spinners*, 2014).

Marketing for foreign trade

Through the 1970s state foreign trade organizations were the sole users of marketing as a coordinated system of business activities, a recognized necessity for selling abroad. Foreign trade specialists read Western marketing articles translated into Russian. A Russian-language glossary of marketing terminology was produced for their use (Kostyukin, 1974). In 1975, after the Soviet Union became a signatory of the Helsinki Accords (including marketing), Smelyakov invited nine other interested professionals to join with him to launch the Marketing Section of the USSR Chamber of Commerce. He urged the translation and publication of Philip Kotler's best-seller *Marketing Management,* positioned as a handbook 'for specialists working in planning organizations and for top-level managers in manufacturing and trade companies' (Fox *et al.,* 2005; Abramishvilli in Kotler, 1980, inside back cover). All 12,000 copies were quickly sold.

From Soviet perestroika to transforming Russia (1985–2005)

The contours of Soviet life began to change in the mid-1980s under General Secretary Mikhail Gorbachev's policies of *perestroika* – restructuring of the economic and political system – and *glasnost*, transparency. *Perestroika* was his response to the fact that the Soviet Union, although militarily strong, was falling behind economically and was unable to achieve the level of consumer well-being of modern capitalist countries. *Glasnost* was intended to increase the flow of information that would reveal problems and help to solve them, thus improving accountability, efficiency and productivity (Ries, 1997, 165).

Perestroika was intended to update, not replace, socialism. In 1987 state subsidies to state enterprises were eliminated, and enterprises were free to base their production on consumer demand and, after meeting state orders, sell their remaining output as they saw fit. Private businesses in services, manufacturing and foreign trade were permitted. Enterprises could conduct foreign trade directly, no longer going through the Ministry of Foreign Trade. *Perestroika* ended central planning. The intricate official networks of suppliers, manufacturers, wholesalers and retailers rapidly fell apart and there were no substitutes. Some well-placed people were able to seize advantages from the chaos and become very wealthy by appropriating assets as the underlying enterprises collapsed, leaving employees without jobs and purchasing power (Åslund, 2007, 58–9).

Glasnost gave Soviet citizens greater access to broader sources of information which revealed the benefits people enjoyed in other countries (Shane, 1994). Boris Yeltsin, on an unofficial trip to the United States in 1989, visited a Houston-area supermarket:

> When I saw those shelves crammed with hundreds, thousands of cans, cartons and goods of every possible sort, for the first time I felt quite frankly sick with despair for the Soviet people. That such a potentially super-rich country as ours has been brought to a state of such poverty!
>
> *(Yeltsin, 1990, 255)*

The formal declaration ending the Soviet Union in December 1991 precipitated economic collapse and widespread suffering. Shuttered state enterprises brought the end of near-assured employment, and salaries evaporated along with 'second incomes' attached to state employment. Poorly made Soviet goods were replaced by inexpensive imported products, including clothing, cosmetics, computers and facsimile machines. Those still employed and getting paid saw their purchasing power erode, and most savings evaporated in the devaluation that followed. State and collective farms struggled to get foodstuffs to market and many such farms closed down. Peasant households strove to increase the commercial yields of their private plots and get their production to market (O'Brien *et al.,* 2000, 1).

Although *perestroika* had already legalized small business, engaging in private business held special attraction for those who saw opportunities to bend or break the law. Overlapping tax laws made profitability elusive, and many businesses kept 'two sets of books' – one authentic, and one for the tax authorities. This precarious situation encouraged the rise of security services and criminal protection rackets to shelter these activities.

Many Soviet citizens rejected work in new private enterprises as risky and not respectable, but others began selling items on sidewalks or outside markets – paper cups of sunflower seeds or berries, sprigs of herbs or home-grown flowers, cigarettes or items of clothing – often out of desperation. Some became full-time street vendors of sought-after goods such as electronics. Such vendors were condemned by some because 'they do not have to do anything or produce anything' and 'they do not have to work with their hands or their head': 'You buy, you sell, and you get money. It used to be illegal, now it's allowed. It is a mixture of hackwork and freeloading sanctioned by the government' (Dutkina, 1996, 143). This Soviet-era mentality denigrated the vendors' contribution of product selection and the creation of time and place utility, and tarnished the image of private business.

Advertising

Young & Rubicam opened the first Western advertising agency in the Soviet Union in late 1988 as a joint venture with a Soviet state agency to create advertising for American and foreign companies entering the Soviet marketplace. Burandt and Giges (1992) reported struggles with Soviet bureaucracy, their Soviet colleagues' rigidity and lack of advertising expertise, and a general Soviet mindset that failed to understand the importance of focusing on the customer. In contrast, Wells (1994, 83) reported that interviews with Soviet advertising people in the late 1980s revealed their confidence in their knowledge and understanding of advertising and their rejection of the idea that 'the only "correct" advertising system was one based on a free-market Western model'. Despite gaps in advertising expertise, Wells concluded that Soviet/Russian advertising people had important insights and valuable cultural knowledge to contribute.

In the early 2000s poster advertising by international tobacco and liquor companies exploded on streets and in metro stations. Television advertising was relatively inexpensive, and foreign advertisers could dominate TV advertising for a time, such as TV spots for *Blendamed* (*Crest* in the United States). In general the Soviet public found Western advertising novel and amusing, but they also presumed – based on Soviet experience – that heavily advertised products were either in oversupply or of poor quality, and in many instances imported products were simply unaffordable.

In the 1990s and 2000s consumer nostalgia for products and images of the Soviet period was incorporated into branding and advertising (Holak *et al.*, 2005). For example, Домик в деревне (Little House in the Village) became a leading brand of Russian dairy products firm Wimm-Bill-Dann, which is majority owned by PepsiCo since 2010. In 2003 the state airline Aeroflot engaged a British consulting firm to modernize its visual image, including colours, uniforms and logo, but balked at eliminating the hammer and sickle – the ultimate Communist symbol – from its logo, describing it as 'the most cherished part of its 70-year-old heritage' (Aeroflot, 2003).

Professional marketers

The first generation of professionally trained marketers in post-Soviet Russia emerged only in the late 1990s. The first academic department of marketing in Russia was established at Plekhanov Russian University of Economics in 1990. Most Russian professors of marketing and advertising had no formal education or firsthand experience in marketing. During the Soviet period they often had been applied economists, linguists (who could teach from Western textbooks) and instructors of required courses in Marxism-Leninism (Fox *et al.*, 2001). The Guild of Marketers (*necommerceskoe partnerstvo Gildia Marketologov*), was founded in 2000 to bring together marketing professionals. Professional marketing journals and magazines include the prestigious and widely read *Marketing i Marketingovye Issledovania v Rossii* (Marketing and Marketing Research in Russia).

Russia in an international context (2000–2015)

A foreigner shopping in major Russian cities would be impressed by the plethora of familiar international brands and retailers, gargantuan supermarkets with dozens of check-out lanes in new high-rise residential areas, and even vending machines supplying prescription daily-wear contact lenses. Hypermarkets include Ashan (French) and IKEA (Swedish), and Russian retailers Magnit, X5 Retail Group, Lenta, Sedmoy Kontinent, and Dixi, among others.

Russians who amassed tremendous wealth during and after *perestroika* fuelled the growth of luxury-product marketing and the creation of higher-education specialties in luxury-brand management. Specialty glossy magazines advertised premium products and services. 'Luxury goods', variously defined, appealed to Russian consumers of all income levels (Kaufmann *et al.*, 2012). Yet the average monthly salary in 2015 was about $500, with many professionals earning considerably less (Spinella, 2015b).

Retailing innovations have changed the purchasing experience for the mass market as well. Medium-sized grocery stores now have at least partial self-service. Small neighbourhood shops still display most products behind the counter or in glass cases, so products must be requested from the shop assistant. The *kassa* payment system has largely disappeared. Large warehouses in Moscow and St Petersburg have improved the flow of goods through the channel. Internet sales have increased, even in areas away from major cities. Buying clothing from international e-retailers has become popular (Skorobogatykh, 2015). Catalogue sales have been largely superseded by online buying. The expansion of retailing, product selection and availability since 2000 fuelled enhancements in nearly every aspect of consumers' daily lives, including home renovations and furnishings, clothing, diet, entertainment and travel.

International companies have faced politically motivated difficulties in Russia, including inspections, audits, closures and permit delays. In 2014, in response to Russia's annexation of Crimea and involvement in eastern Ukraine, a number of Western countries imposed travel bans and financial sanctions on a few elite Russians. Despite Russia's reliance on imported food, the Russian government suspended imports of meat, fish, vegetables and milk products from the United States, the 28-member European Union, Norway, Canada and Australia, and encouraged protests against fast food chains perceived to be foreign.

The 2014 drop in the world price of oil, Russia's major export, along with external financial sanctions and the Russian counter-ban of much imported food, contributed to a steep drop in the value of the ruble and price inflation at home. Decreased buying power and increased prices of imported goods brought cutbacks in everyday purchases, as well as travel and dining out. At least a quarter of Moscow restaurants were expected to close in 2015 (Spinella, 2015a). Tourism to Russia dropped, and many Russians replaced international travel with travel inside Russia.

The turn of the millennium presaged Russia's arrival as a modern country, entwined in the world economy and sharing products, stores, marketing techniques and consumer aspirations with other advanced economies. As of 2015 this progress appears to have stalled. The government's focus has turned to import substitution for banned foreign products, with speculation about bans on additional foreign goods. Proposed budgets emphasize expanded military spending over social spending. Traditional trading partners are being sidelined while Russia turns to Asia and Latin America for potential trade. Russia's leadership aims to differentiate Russia from the West, embracing the Russian

Orthodox Church, advocating 'traditional values' and nationalism, and rejecting Western influences.

The Russian government now controls major sectors of the economy, replacing or discouraging market-based private investment, including foreign investment, in some sectors. While modern marketing has improved Russian consumers' lives in recent decades, the present question is whether state ideology will again alter the marketing landscape and stand in the way of Russians' achievement of the comfort and security to which they aspire.

References

Aeroflot (2003) 'Aeroflot sticks by hammer and sickle', press release, 16 Apr., available online: http://www.aeroflot.com/cms/en/press_release/6243 (accessed Apr. 2015).

Åslund, A. (2007) *Russia's Capitalist Revolution: Why Market Reform Succeeded and Democracy Failed,* Peterson Institute for International Economics, Washington, DC.

Ball, A.M. (1987) *Russia's Last Capitalists: The Nepmen, 1921–1929,* University of California Press, Berkeley, CA.

Barksdale, H.C., Kelly, W.J., and MacFarlane, I. (1979) 'The marketing concept in the U.S. and the U.S.S.R.: An historical analysis', *Journal of the Academy of Marketing Science,* 6, 258–77.

Beable, W.H. (1918) *Commercial Russia,* Constable, London.

Burandt, G., and Giges, N. (1992) *Moscow Meets Madison Avenue: The Adventures of the First American Adman in the U.S.S.R.,* HarperBusiness, New York.

Carstensen, F.V. (2012) *American Enterprise in Foreign Markets: Studies of Singer and International Harvester in Imperial Russia,* University of North Carolina Press, Chapel Hill, NC.

Chulkov, M.D. (1788) *Istoria kratkaya rossiiskoi torgovli,* Ponomareva, Moscow.

Clawson, R.W. (ed.) (1976) 'An American businessman in the Soviet Union: The Reimer report', *Business History Review,* 50, 203–18.

Cox, R. (2006) 'NEP without Nepmen! Soviet advertising and the transition to socialism in the 1920s', in C. Kiaer and E. Naiman (eds), *Everyday Life in Early Soviet Russia: Taking the Revolution Inside,* Indiana University Press, Bloomington, IN.

Davies, S. (1997) *Popular Opinion in Stalin's Russia: Terror, Propaganda, and Dissent, 1934–1941,* Cambridge University Press, Cambridge.

Dixon, D.F., and Polyakov, E.V. (1998) 'Business as an anathema to government: The path to private business in the USSR', *Business and Economic History,* 27, 173–84.

Dutkina, G. (1996) *Moscow Days: Life and Hard Times in the New Russia,* Kodansha International, New York.

Dyadkin, I.D. (1983) *Unnatural Deaths in the USSR, 1928–1954,* Transaction Books, New Brunswick, NJ.

Farnsworth, C.H. (1973) 'Loewy got a "da" for many consumer designs but "nyet" on vodka', *New York Times* (5 Dec.), 67.

Felker, J. L. (1966) *Soviet Economic Controversies; The Emerging Marketing Concept and Changes in Planning, 1960–1965,* MIT Press, Cambridge, MA.

Fitzpatrick, S. (1986) 'After NEP: The fate of NEP entrepreneurs, small traders, and artisans in the "socialist Russia" of the 1930s', *Russian History/Histoire Russe,* 13/2–3, 187–234.

Fitzpatrick, S. (1999) *Everyday Stalinism: Ordinary Life in Extraordinary Times. Soviet Russia in the 1930s,* Oxford University Press, New York.

Fitzpatrick, S. (2007) 'The Soviet Union in the twenty-first century', *Journal of European Studies,* 3/7, 51–71.

Florinsky, M.T. (1964). *Russia: A Short History,* Macmillan, New York.

Fox, K.F.A., Saginova, O.V., and Skorobogatykh, I.I. (2001) 'Stanovleniye Marketinga v Rossii: Kto Prepodyaet Marketing v Rossiskikh Vuzakh?' [The evolution of marketing in Russia: Who teaches marketing in Russian universities?], *Marketing i Marketingovie Issledovaniya v Rossii.* 5/35, 4–9.

Fox, K.F.A., Skorobogatykh, I.I., and Saginova, O.V. (2005) 'The Soviet evolution of marketing thought, 1961–1991: From Marx to marketing', *Marketing Theory*, 5, 283–307.

Fox, K.F.A., Skorobogatykh, I.I., and Saginova, O.V. (2008) 'Philip Kotler's influence in the Soviet Union and Russia', *European Business Review*, 20, 152–76.

Galperin, Z.S. (1912) *Prakticheskiye Sovyet iz Torgovoi Praktiki,* Torgovoye Delo, Odessa.

Goldman, M.I. (1960) 'The Soviet standard of living, and ours', *Foreign Affairs*, 38, 625–37.

Goldman, M.I. (1961) 'The marketing structure in the Soviet Union', *Journal of Marketing*, 25, 7–14.

Goldman, M.I. (1963) *Soviet Marketing: Distribution in a Controlled Economy,* Free Press of Glencoe, New York.

Goldman, M.I. (1975) 'Book review: Advertising and socialism. The nature and extent of consumer advertising in the Soviet Union', *Soviet Studies*, 27, 482–4.

Gorsuch, A.E. (2011) *All This is Your World,* Oxford University Press, Oxford.

Greer, T.V. (1973) *Marketing in the Soviet Union,* Praeger, New York.

Gregory, P.R. (2001) *Behind the Façade of Stalin's Command Economy: Evidence from the Soviet State and Party Archives,* Hoover Institution Press, Stanford, CA.

Halliday, S. (2009) 'The first common market? The Hanseatic League', *History Today*, 59, 31–7.

Hanson, P. (1974) *Advertising and Socialism: The Nature and Extent of Consumer Advertising in the Soviet Union, Poland, Hungary, and Yugoslavia,* International Arts and Sciences Press, White Plains, NY.

Harvard Project (1950–3) *The Harvard Project on the Soviet Social System online,* Harvard College Library, available online: http://hcl.harvard.edu/collections/hpsss/index.html (accessed Apr. 2015).

Harvey, R. (2004) *A Short History of Communism,* Thomas Dunne Books, New York.

Hellie, R. (1999) *The Economy and Material Culture of Russia, 1600–1725*, University of Chicago Press, Chicago, IL.

Hessler, J. (2004) *A Social History of Soviet Trade: Trade Policy, Retail Practices, and Consumption, 1917–1953,* Princeton University Press, Princeton, NJ.

Hilton, M.L. (2004) 'Retailing the revolution: The State Department Store (GUM) and Soviet society in the 1920s', *Journal of Social History*, 37, 939–64.

Hilton, M. L. (2012) *Selling to the Masses: Retailing in Russia, 1880–1930,* University of Pittsburgh Press, Pittsburgh, PA.

Hirsch, H. (1961) *Quantity Planning and Price Planning in the Soviet Union,* University of Pennsylvania Press, Philadelphia.

Hodges, R. (1988) *Primitive and Peasant Markets,* Blackwell, Oxford.

Holak, S., Matveev, A., and Havlena, W. (2007) 'Nostalgia in post-socialist Russia: Exploring applications to advertising strategy', *Journal of Business Research*, 60, 649–55.

Hoover, C.B. (1931) *The Economic Life of Soviet Russia,* Macmillan, New York.

Idov, M. (2011). *Made in Russia: Unsung Icons of Soviet Design,* Rizzoli, New York.

Kanevsky, S. (2015) Personal communications, 30 Mar.

Kaufmann, H. R., Vrontis, D., and Manakova, Y. (2012) 'Perception of luxury: Idiosyncratic Russian consumer culture and identity', *European Journal of Cross-Cultural Competence and Management,* 2, 209.

Kielberger, J. (1820) *Brief Accounts of Russian Trade as it was done in the whole of Russia in 1674* [translated title], in the Rare Book Storage of the Russian National Library, St Petersburg.

Kishkovksy, S. (2007) 'Former killing ground becomes shrine to Stalin's victims', *New York Times* (8 June), available online: www.nytimes.com/2007/06/08/world/europe/08butovo.html?_r=0 (accessed June 2015).

Kostyukin, D. (ed.) (1974) *Marketing* [collection of articles translated from English to Russian], Progress, Moscow.

Kotler, P. (1980). *Upravlenie Marketingom* [abridged Russian translation of 1976 edn, with a preface by G. Abramashvili], Moscow, Economika.

Kravets, O., and Sandikci, O. (2013) 'Marketing for socialism: Soviet cosmetics in the 1930s', *Business History Review*, 87, 461–87.

Lazer, W. (1986) 'Soviet marketing issues: A content analysis of *Pravda*', *Journal of Business Research*, 14, 117–31.

Levine, I.R. (1959) *Main Street, U.S.S.R.*. Doubleday. Garden City, NY.

Loewy Archives (1903–82) Hagley Museum and Archives, Wilmington, DE.

Lyons, E. (1967) *Workers' Paradise Lost: Fifty Years of Soviet Communism, a Balance Sheet*, Twin Circle, New York.

Markham, J.W. (1964) 'Is advertising important in the Soviet economy?', *Journal of Marketing*, 28, 31–7.

Magocsi, P.R. (2010) *A History of Ukraine: The Land and Its Peoples*, University of Toronto Press, Toronto.

Mineeva, A.V., and Piotrovsky, M.B. (2003) *Sankt-Peterburg v Svetopisi 1840–1920-kh Godov: Katalog Vystavki*, Slaviya, St Petersburg.

Moss, W. (2005) *A History of Russia*, McGraw-Hill, New York.

Naimark, N.M. (2010) *Stalin's Genocides,* Princeton University Press, Princeton, NJ.

O'Brien, D.J., Dershem, L.D., and Patsiorkovski, V.V. (2000) *Household Capital and the Agrarian Problem in Russia*, Ashgate, Aldershot.

Osokina, E. (2006) 'Torgsin: Gold for industrialization', *Cahiers du Monde Russe*, 47, 715.

Osokina, E.A., Transchel, K., and Bucher, G. (2001) *Our Daily Bread: Socialist Distribution and the Art of Survival in Stalin's Russia, 1927–1941,* M.E. Sharpe, Armonk, NY.

Paretskaya, A. (2013) 'A middle class without capitalism? Socialist ideology and post-collectivist discourse in the late-Soviet era', in N. Klumbyte and G. Sharafutdinova (eds), *Soviet Society in the Era of Late Socialism, 1964–1985,* Lexington Books, Lanham, MD.

Patenaude, B.M. (2002) *The Big Show in Bololand: The American Relief Expedition to Soviet Russia in the Famine of 1921,* Stanford University Press, Stanford, CA.

Randall, A.E. (2008) *The Soviet Dream World of Retail Trade and Consumption in the 1930s,* Palgrave Macmillan, Basingstoke.

Ransel, D.L. (2009) *A Russian Merchant's Tale: The Life and Adventures of Ivan Alekseevich Tolchënov, Based on his Diary,* Indiana University Press, Bloomington, IN.

Richman, B.M. (1963) 'Managerial opposition to product-innovation in Soviet Union industry', *California Management Review*, 6, 11–26.

Rieber, A.J. (1982) *Merchants and Entrepreneurs in Imperial Russia,* University of North Carolina Press, Chapel Hill, NC.

Ries, N. (1997) *Russian Talk: Culture and Conversation during Perestroika,* Cornell University Press, Ithaca, NY.

Robinson, R. with Slevin, J. (1988) *Black on Red: My 44 Years Inside the Soviet Union: An Autobiography,* Acropolis Books, Washington, DC.

Rutland, P. (1985) *The Myth of the Plan: Lessons of Soviet Planning Experience,* Open Court, La Salle, IL.

Shane, S. (1994) *Dismantling Utopia: How Information Ended the Soviet Union*, Ivan R. Dee, Chicago, IL.

Sibley, K.A.S. (1996) *Loans and Legitimacy: The Evolution of Soviet–American Relations, 1919–1933,* University Press of Kentucky, Lexington, KY.

Skorobogatykh, I. (2015) Email correspondence with author, Feb. 15.

Skurski, R. (1983) *Soviet Marketing and Economic Development,* St Martin's Press, New York.

Smorodinskaya, T., Evarts-Romaine, K. and Goscilo, H. (2007) *Encyclopaedia of Contemporary Russian Culture,* Routledge, London.

Sorokin, P.A. (1950) *Leaves from a Russian Diary, and Thirty Years After,* Beacon Press, Boston, MA.

Spinella, P. (2015a) 'Quarter of Moscow restaurants expected to close amid economic crisis', *Moscow Times* (15 Feb.).

Spinella, P. (2015b) 'Russians' average monthly salary falls to $500 as food prices skyrocket', *Moscow Times* (3 Mar.).

Szeplaki, L. (1974) 'Advertising in the Soviet bloc', *Journal of Advertising Research,* 14, 3, 13–17.

Taskovsky, Andrei (2014) *The Gold Spinners* (documentary film), Taskovski Films, Tallinn, Estonia.

Tolstikova, N. (2007) 'Early Soviet advertising: "We have to extract all the stinking bourgeois elements"', *Journalism History*, 33, 42.

Tzouliadis, T. (2008) *The Forsaken: An American Tragedy in Stalin's Russia*, Penguin, New York.

US Bureau of the Census (1991) *USA/USSR Facts and Figures & SShA/SSSR Fakty i Tsifry*, US Department of Commerce, Economic and Statistics Administration, Bureau of the Census, Washington, DC.

Wells, L.G. (1994) 'Western concepts, Russian perspectives: Meanings of advertising in the former Soviet Union', *Journal of Advertising*, 23, 83–95.

West, S. (2011) *I Shop in Moscow: Advertising and the Creation of Consumer Culture in Late Tsarist Russia*, Northern Illinois University Press, DeKalb, IL.

Yeltsin, B.N. (1990) *Against the Grain: An Autobiography*, Summit Books, New York.

Index

Italic page numbers indicate tables; bold indicate figures.